Janson's History of Art

THE WESTERN TRADITION

Reissued Eighth Edition

Volume I

PENELOPE J. E. DAVIES

WALTER B. DENNY

FRIMA FOX HOFRICHTER

JOSEPH JACOBS

ANN M. ROBERTS

DAVID L. SIMON

PEARSON

Boston   Columbus   Indianapolis   New York   San Francisco
Amsterdam   Cape Town   Dubai   London   Madrid   Milan   Munich   Paris   Montréal   Toronto
Delhi   Mexico City   São Paulo   Sydney   Hong Kong   Seoul   Singapore   Taipei   Tokyo

Editor-in-Chief: Sarah Touborg
Senior Sponsoring Editor: Helen Ronan
Editorial Assistant: Victoria Engros
Senior Digital Media Editor: David Alick
Senior Media Project Manager: Rich Barnes
Project Management Team Lead: Melissa Feimer
Project Manager: Marlene Gassler
Program Manager: Barbara Cappuccio
Senior Operations Specialist: Diane Peirano
Digital Imaging Specialist: Corin Skidds
Senior Art Director / Cover Designer: Kathryn Foot
Cover Printer: LSC Communications/Kendallville
Printer/Binder: LSC Communications/Kendallville

This book was produced by
Laurence King Publishing Ltd, London.
www.laurenceking.com

Editorial Manager: Kara Hattersley-Smith
Senior Editors: Susie May and Sophie Wise
Copy Editor: Robert Shore
Proofreader: Lisa Cutmore
Picture Researchers: Katharina Gruber and Julia Ruxton
Designers: Nick Newton, Randell Harris and Ian Hunt
Production Manager: Simon Walsh

Cover image: Bust of Queen Nefertiti from Amarna, Thutmosis's workshop. c. 1350 BCE. Egypt, eighteenth dynasty. Photo Scala, Florence / BPK, Bildagentur fuer Kunst, Kultur und Geschichte, Berlin.

Credits and acknowledgements borrowed from other sources and reproduced, with permission, in this textbook appear on the appropriate page within text or on the credit pages in the back of this book.

Library of Congress Cataloging-in-Publication Data

Janson's History of art : the Western tradition / Penelope J.E. Davies, Walter B. Denny, Frima Fox Hofrichter, Joseph Jacobs, Ann M. Roberts, David L. Simon. -- Eighth edition reissued.
    pages cm
  Includes bibliographical references and index.
  ISBN 978-0-13-387829-5 (alk. paper) -- ISBN 0-13-387829-5 (alk. paper) -- ISBN 978-0-13-388488-3 (alk. paper) -- ISBN 0-13-388488-0 (alk. paper)
1. Art--History. I. Davies, Penelope J. E.
  N5300.J3 2016
  709--dc23
                          2014026383

4   16

ISBN 10: 0-13-391011-3
ISBN 13: 978-0-13-391011-7

Contents

Preface

WELCOME TO THE EIGHTH EDITION OF JANSON'S CLASSIC TEXTBOOK, reissued to offer exciting new choices for students, in the form of REVEL, a highly interactive content-delivery system, and a wealth of custom options. For many of us who teach introductory courses in the history of art, the name Janson is synonymous with the subject matter we present

When Pearson/Prentice Hall first published the *History of Art* in 1962, John F. Kennedy occupied the White House, and Andy Warhol was an emerging artist. Janson offered his readers a strong focus on Western art, an important consideration of technique and style, and a clear point of view. The *History of Art*, said Janson, was not just a stringing together of historically significant objects, but the writing of a story about their interconnections—a history of styles and of stylistic change. Janson's text focused on the visual and technical characteristics of the objects he discussed, often in extraordinarily eloquent language. Janson's *History of Art* helped to establish the canon of art history for many generations of scholars.

Although revised to remain current with new discoveries and scholarship, the eighth edition continues to follow Janson's lead in important ways: It is limited to the Western tradition, with a chapter on Islamic art and its relationship to Western art. It keeps the focus of the discussion on the object, its manufacture, and its visual character. It considers the contribution of the artist as an important part of the analysis. This edition maintains an organization along the lines established by Janson, with separate chapters on the Northern European Renaissance, the Italian Renaissance, the High Renaissance, and Baroque art, with stylistic divisions for key periods of the modern era. Also embedded in this edition is the narrative of how art has changed over time in the cultures that Europe has claimed as its patrimony.

WHAT'S NEW IN JANSON'S HISTORY OF ART?

"The history of art is too vast a field for anyone to encompass all of it with equal competence."

H. W. JANSON, from the Preface to the first edition of *History of Art*

Janson's History of Art in its reissued eighth edition is once again the product of careful revision by a team of scholars with different specialties, bringing a readily recognized knowledge and depth to the discussions of works of art. We incorporate new interpretations such as the reidentification of the "Porticus Aemilia" as Rome's Navalia, or ship-shed (p. 186); new documentary evidence, such as that pertaining to Uccello's *Battle of San Romano* (p. 538); and new interpretive approaches, such as the importance of nationalism in the development of Romanticism (Chapter 24).

Organization and Contextual Emphasis

Most chapters integrate the media into chronological discussions instead of discussing them in isolation from one another, which reflected the more formalistic approach used in earlier editions. Even though we draw connections among works of art, as Janson did, we emphasize the patronage and function of works of art and the historical circumstances in which they were created. We explore how works of art have been used to shore up political or social power.

Interpreting Cultures

Western art history encompasses a great many distinct chronological and cultural periods, which we wish to treat as distinct entities. So we present Etruscan art as evidence for Etruscan culture, not as a precursor of Roman or a follower of Greek art. Recognizing the limits of our knowledge about certain periods of history, we examine how art historians draw conclusions from works of art. The boxes called *The Art Historian's Lens* allow students to see how the discipline works. They give students a better understanding of the methods art historians use to develop art-historical arguments. *Primary Sources*, a distinguishing feature of Janson for many editions, have been incorporated throughout the chapters to support the analysis provided and to further inform students about the cultures discussed, and additional documents can be found in the online resource, MyArtsLab (See p. xix for more detail.)

Women in the History of Art

Women continue to be given greater visibility as artists, as patrons, and as an audience for works of art. Inspired by contemporary approaches to art history, we also address the representation of women as expressions of specific cultural notions of femininity or as symbols.

Objects, Media, and Techniques

Many new objects have been incorporated into this edition to reflect the continuous changes in the discipline. The mediums we discuss are broad in scope and include not only modern art forms such as installations and earth art, but also the so-called minor arts of earlier periods—such as tapestries, metalwork, and porcelain. Discussions in the *Materials and Techniques* boxes illuminate this dimension of art history.

The Images

Along with the new objects that have been introduced, every reproduction in the book has been reexamined for excellence in quality, and when not meeting our standards has been replaced. Whenever possible we obtain our photography directly from the holding institutions to ensure that we have the most accurate and authoritative illustrations. Every image that could be obtained in color has been acquired. To further assist both students and teachers, we have sought permission for electronic educational use so that instructors who adopt *Janson's History of Art* will have access to an extraordinary archive of high-quality digital images for classroom use.

New Maps and Timelines

A new map program has been created to both orient students to the locations mentioned in each chapter and to better tell the story of the chapter narrative. Readers now can see the extent of the Eastern and Western Roman Empires, as well as the range of the Justinian's rule (p. 236). They can trace the migration routes of tribes during early medieval times (p. 314) and the Dutch trade routes of the seventeenth century (p. 702). This enriching new feature provides an avenue for greater understanding of the impact of politics, society, and geography on the art of each period. End of chapter timelines recap in summary fashion the art and events of the chapter, as well as showing key contemporaneous works from previous chapters (for example, pp. 345 and 759).

Chapter by Chapter Revisions

The following list includes the major highlights of this new edition:

CHAPTER 1: PREHISTORIC ART

Expands upon the methods scholars (both art historians and anthropologists) use to understand artwork, including, for instance, feminist interpretations. Includes new monuments such as Skara Brae and Mezhirich. A new box explains dating techniques.

CHAPTER 2: ANCIENT NEAR EASTERN ART

This chapter is expanded to include a discussion of Jerusalem.

CHAPTER 3: EGYPTIAN ART

Now includes a tomb painting from the pre-Dynastic age, and a discussion of jewelry. A new box names the major Egyptian gods.

CHAPTER 4: AEGEAN ART

Improved images and a reconstruction of Mycenae enhance the discussion of Aegean art.

CHAPTER 5: GREEK ART

This chapter is tightened to allow space for longer discussion of Greek sanctuaries, and the inclusion of Hellenistic works outside of the Greek mainland, such as the Pharos at Alexandria. The issue of homosexuality in fifth-century Athens is addressed, as well as women's roles in life and art. A new box deals with the issue of repatriation of works of art such as the Elgin marbles.

CHAPTER 6: ETRUSCAN ART

The range of artworks is increased to include, for instance, terracotta revetments and terra-cotta portraits.

CHAPTER 7: ROMAN ART

This chapter includes new interpretations such as the reidentification of the "Porticus Aemilia" as Rome's Navalia or ship-shed. It also has been tightened to allow space for more Republican works (such as the terra cotta pediment from Via di San Gregorio and the Praeneste mosaic) and a wider discussion of life in Pompeii. There is some rearrangement of art works to improve the chronological flow.

CHAPTER 8: EARLY CHRISTIAN AND BYZANTINE ART

A new section on early Jewish art is added, including three images of early synagogue wall paintings and mosaics (Dura Europos and Hammath Tiberias). Coverage of Late Byzantine art is increased, as is discussion of liturgical and social history.

CHAPTER 9: ISLAMIC ART

The relationship of Islamic art to early Jewish and Christian medieval art is accentuated.

CHAPTER 10: EARLY MEDIEVAL ART

Includes an expanded discussion and reorganization of Viking art, which is now placed later in the chapter.

CHAPTER 11: ROMANESQUE ART

Coverage of secular architecture is broadened to include the bridge at Puente la Reina on the pilgrimage route to Santiago de Compostela and a new section on the crusades and castle architecture.

CHAPTER 12: GOTHIC ART

This chapter is tightened to allow space for added focus on secular objects and buildings with the inclusion of a Guillaume de Machaut manuscript illumination and Westminster Hall from the royal palace in London. There is also expanded discussion of courtly art and royal iconography in later Gothic monuments.

CHAPTER 13: ART IN THIRTEENTH- AND FOURTEENTH-CENTURY ITALY

Organization now places less emphasis on religious architecture. Siena's Palazzo Pubblico is added. There is a more focused discussion of Tuscany, and a briefer treatment of Northern Italy and Venice. Images of key works of art, including Nicola and Giovanni Pisano and the Arena chapel are improved. Two maps in the chapter outline Italian trade routes and the spread of the plague in the 1340s.

CHAPTER 14: ARTISTIC INNOVATIONS IN FIFTEENTH-CENTURY NORTHERN EUROPE

Discussion of the *Très Riches Heures du Duc de Berry* is enlarged, and reproductions contrasting aristocratic "labors" and the images of peasants are added. Treatment of works by Van Eyck, Van der Weyden and Bosch is revised and sharpened. A new map of centers of production and trade routes in Northern Europe illustrates the variety of media produced in the region.

CHAPTER 15: THE EARLY RENAISSANCE IN FIFTEENTH-CENTURY ITALY

Reorganized for better flow and student comprehension, this chapter now begins with the Baptistery competition illustrating reliefs by both Ghiberti and Brunelleschi. It then looks at architectural projects by Brunelleschi and Alberti in Florence as a group, considering their patronage and function as well as their form. New art illustrates Brunelleschi's innovations at the Duomo, while his work at San Lorenzo is expanded to include the

Old Sacristy. Section on domestic life has been revised, but it still offers a contextualized discussion of works such as Donatello's *David*, Uccello's *Battle of San Romano* and Botticelli's *Birth of Venus*. This section now includes the Strozzi cassone at Metropolitan Museum of Art in New York and Verrocchio's *Lady with a Bunch of Flowers*. The discussion of Renaissance style throughout Italy is revised for greater clarity.

CHAPTER 16: THE HIGH RENAISSANCE IN ITALY, 1495–1520

A discussion of the portrait of Ginevra de' Benci is now included, permitting a revised discussion of the *Mona Lisa*. The section on the Stanza della Segnatura is revamped to focus on *The School of Athens*. Treatment of Giorgione and Titian is reorganized and revised to reflect current discussions of attribution and collaboration. A new Titian portrait, *Man with a Blue Sleeve*, is included.

CHAPTER 17: THE LATE RENAISSANCE AND MANNERISM IN SIXTEENTH-CENTURY ITALY

Florence in the sixteenth century is reorganized and refreshed with new images, including a view of the architectural context for Pontormo's *Pietà*. Michelangelo's New Sacristy is treated in terms of architecture as well as sculpture. Ducal Palaces of the Uffizi and the Pitti and of the Boboli Gardens receives a new focus. Cellini's Saltceller of Francis I is discussed in its Florentine context. Treatment of Il Gesù is revamped. New images enliven the Northern Italian art section and Sofonisba Anguissola's *Self Portrait* is compared to Parmigianino's. There is a revised consideration of Palladio, and a new Titian, *The Rape of Europa*, exemplifies the artist's work for elite patrons.

CHAPTER 18: RENAISSANCE AND REFORMATION IN SIXTEENTH-CENTURY NORTHERN EUROPE

Discussion of France, as well as Spain, is revised and images are improved. Includes new images and discussions of Cranach and Baldung: Cranach's *Judgment of Paris* in New York replaces another version of this theme, while Baldung is represented by his woodcut of *The Bewitched Groom* of 1544. The discussion of Holbein is enlivened by consideration of his *Jean de Dinteville and Georges de Selve* ("The Ambassadors"), allowing examination of him as an allegorist as well as a portraitist. Gossaert is now represented by the *Neptune and Amphitrite* of 1516, while a new Patinir, the triptych of *The Penitence of Saint Jerome*, represents the landscape specialty of that region.

CHAPTER 19: THE BAROQUE IN ITALY AND SPAIN

Chapter content benefits from insights gained through recent exhibitions and from the inclusion of new architectural image components. New illustrations better expand understanding of the Roman Baroque and the role of the Virgin in Spanish art including a view of the Piazza Navonna that shows Bernini's Four Rivers Fountain and as well as Borromini's church of S. Agnese, a cut-away of Borromini's complex star-hexagon shaped church,

S. Ivo, and one of Murillo's many depictions of the *Immaculate Conception* (St. Petersburg).

CHAPTER 20: THE BAROQUE IN THE NETHERLANDS

The importance of trade, trade routes and interest in the exotic is explored in this chapter. Gender issues—and the relationship between men and women—and local, folk traditions (religious and secular) play a role here in the exploration of the visual culture and social history. New images include: Peter Paul Rubens' *The Raising of the Cross*—the entire open altarpiece; Peter Paul Rubens' *Four Studies of the Head of a Negro*; Jacob Jordaens' *The King Drinks*; Judith Leyster's *The Proposition*; Rembrandt van Rijn's *Bathsheba with King David's Letter*, and Vermeer's *Officer and Laughing Girl*.

CHAPTER 21: THE BAROQUE IN FRANCE AND ENGLAND

New scholarship from the *Poussin and Nature: Arcadian Visions* exhibition in 2008 informs a more developed discussion of this artist's work. A fuller discussion of the role of the 1668 Fire of London and the re-building of St. Paul's Cathedral, in addition to a three-dimensional reconstruction of St. Paul's and a modern reconstruction of Sir Christopher Wren's plan of the city of London drawn just days after the fire, expands the coverage of this architect.

CHAPTER 22: THE ROCOCO

Expresses in greater depth the concept of the Rococo, the role of Madame da Pompadour and the expansion of the Rococo style in Germany. New images include Francois Boucher's *Portrait of Madame de Pompadour* (Munich); Jean-Simeon Chardin's *The Brioche (the Dessert)* and Egid Quirin Asam's interior and altar of the Benedictine Church at Rohr. Sections of this chapter are reorganized to accommodate the removal of Marie-Louise Élisabeth Vigée-Lebrun, Sir Thomas Gainsborough and Sir Joshua Reynolds to Chapter 23.

CHAPTER 23: ART IN THE AGE OF THE ENLIGHTENMENT, 1750–1789

Slightly restructured, the chapter keeps Neoclassicism and early Romanticism separated, thus making them more clearly defined. Joshua Reynolds, Thomas Gainsborough, and Vigée-Lebrun are placed here and into the context of Neoclassicism and Romanticism. Antonio Canova also is moved to this chapter to emphasize his importance in the development of Neoclassicism. Image changes include Joseph Wright's more clearly Romantic *The Old Man and Death*; Ledoux's Custom House with the entrance to the Saltworks at Arc-et-Senans; as well as the addition of Canova's tomb of Archduchess Maria Christina.

CHAPTER 24: ART IN THE AGE OF ROMANTICISM, 1789–1848

This chapter is tightened and has several new images. William Blake is now represented by *Elohim Creating Adam* and Corot by *Souvenir de Montrefontaine (Oise)*. Frederick Church's *Twilight in the Wilderness* is added. The discussion of architecture is changed by placing the Empire style at the very end, thus keeping the Neoclassical revival together.

CHAPTER 25: THE AGE OF POSITIVISM: REALISM, IMPRESSIONISM, AND THE PRE-RAPHAELITES, 1848–1885

Includes a number of image changes to better focus discussions. These include: Monet's *Gare St. Lazare*; Rossetti's *Proserpine*; Nadar's portrait *Édouard Manet*; and Le Gray's *Brig on the Water*.

CHAPTER 26: PROGRESS AND ITS DISCONTENTS: POST-IMPRESSIONISM, SYMBOLISM, AND ART NOUVEAU, 1880–1905

Now incorporates discussions of vernacular, or amateur, photography, represented by Henri Lartigue's *Avenue du Bois de Bologne; Woman with Furs*, and the advent of film, represented by Thomas Edison's *New Brooklyn to New York via Brooklyn Bridge*.

CHAPTER 27: TOWARD ABSTRACTION: THE MODERNIST REVOLUTION, 1904–1914

Discussion of the formal and stylistic developments between 1904 and 1914 that culminated in abstractionism is tightened and the number of images reduced. Discussion of the work of Karl Schmidt-Rotluff is now included.

CHAPTER 28: ART BETWEEN THE WARS

More compact discussion structured around the impact of World War I and the need to create utopias and uncover higher realities, especially as seen in Surrealism.

CHAPTER 29: POSTWAR TO POSTMODERN, 1945–1980

Polke is placed here from Chapter 30, thus putting him within the context of an artist influenced by Pop Art. David Hammons is moved to Chapter 30. Senga Nengudi's *Insides/Out* adds a woman to the discussion of African-American artists.

CHAPTER 30: THE POSTMODERN ERA: ART SINCE 1980

Architecture is reduced, and fine art is expanded. Neo-Expressionism benefits from the addition of Julian Schnabel's *The Exile*. The multi-culturalism of the period receives greater emphasis, especially feminism. Barbara Kruger is placed in a more feminist context with inclusion of a new image, *Untitled (We Won't Play Nature to Your Culture)*. The discussion of African-American identity is broadened by the placement of David Hammons here, and by the addition of Kara Walker's *Insurrection (Our Tools Were Rudimentary, Yet We Pressed On)*. Fred Wilson's *Mining the Museum* is also included. The discussion of González-Torres now stresses his involvement with the AIDS crisis. The importance of large-scale photography for the period is reinforced by the addition of Andreas Gursky's *Shanghai*. The truly global nature of contemporary art is strengthened by the addition of El Antsui's *Dzesi II*.

Acknowledgments

We are grateful to the following academic reviewers for their numerous insights and suggestions on improving Janson:

Amy Adams, College of Staten Island
Susan Benforado Baker, University of Texas Arlington
Jennifer Ball, Brooklyn College
Dixon Bennett, San Jacinto College – South
Diane Boze, Northeastern State University
Betty Ann Brown, California State University – Northridge
Barbara Bushey, Hillsdale College
Mary Hogan Camp, Whatcom Community College
Susan P. Casteras, University of Washington
Cat Crotchett, Western Michigan University
Tim Cruise, Central Texas College
Julia K. Dabbs, University of Minnesota – Morris
Adrienne DeAngelis, University of Miami
Sarah Diebel, University of Wisconsin-Stout
Douglas N. Dow, Kansas State University
Kim Dramer, Fordham University
Brian Fencl, West Liberty State College
Monica Fullerton, Kenyon College
Laura D. Gelfand, The University of Akron
Alyson A. Gill, Arkansas State University
Maria de Jesus Gonzalez, University of Central Florida

Bobette Guillory, Carl Albert State College
Bertha Steinhardt Gutman, Delaware County Community College
Marianne Hogue, University of North Carolina – Wilmington
Stephanie Jacobson, St. John's University
Ruth Keitz, University of Texas – Brownsville
Joanne Kuebler, Manhattan College
Adele H. Lewis, Arizona State University
Lisa Livingston, Modesto Junior College
Diane Chin Lui, American River College
B. Susan Maxwell, University of Wisconsin-Oshkosh
Paul Miklowski, Cuyahoga Community College
Charles R. Morscheck Jr., Drexel University
Elaine O'Brien, California State University – Sacramento
Matthew Palczynski, Temple University
Jason Rosenfeld, Marymount Manhattan College
Phyllis Saretta, The Metropolitan Museum of Art
Onoyom Ukpong, Southern University and A & M College
Kristen Van Ausdall, Kenyon College
Marjorie S. Venit, University of Maryland
Linda Woodward, Montgomery College
Ted M. Wygant, Dayton Beach Community College

The contributors would like to thank John Beldon Scott, Whitney Lynn, and Nicole Veilleux for their advice and assistance in developing this edition. We also would like to thank the editors and staff at Pearson Education including Sarah Touborg, Helen Ronan, Barbara Cappuccio, Marlene Gassler, and Cory Skidds who supported us in our work. At Laurence King Publishing, Sophie Wise, Kara Hattersley-Smith, Julia Ruxton, and Simon Walsh oversaw the production of this reissued edition.

Give Your Students Choices for Learning with *Janson's History of Art*

PEARSON arts titles are available in the following formats to give your students more choices—and more ways to save.

EXPLORE REVEL—DYNAMIC CONTENT MATCHED TO THE WAY TODAY'S STUDENTS READ, THINK, AND LEARN.

Ideal for Janson's approach to art history, REVEL includes
- spoken audio read by the authors
- pan/zoom and scale markers for nearly every image,
- 360-degree architectural panoramas and simulations of major monuments
- media interactives and videos, including "students on site" videos shot and narrated by proficient student learners, and
- quizzing that allows students to check their understanding at regular intervals

Fully mobile, REVEL enables students to interact with course material on the devices they use, anywhere and anytime.

REVEL's assignability and tracking tools help educators
- ensure that students are completing their reading and understanding core concepts
- establish a clear, detailed schedule that helps students stay on task
- monitor both class assignment completion and individual student achievement

SUPPORT STUDENTS WITH MYARTSLAB—A ROBUST COMPANION STUDY ENVIRONMENT.

For those customers who prefer companion study resources, MyArtsLab offers
- Writing Space, providing a single place to create and evaluate graded writing assignments, featuring tools for developing and assessing concept mastery and critical thinking
- media assignments such as Closer Look tours, panoromas, videos, and simulations
- study resources such as flashcards
- links to book specific test banks for quizzes

BUILD YOUR OWN PEARSON CUSTOM COURSE MATERIAL.

For enrollments of at least 25, the Pearson Custom Library allows you to create your own textbook by
- combining chapters from best-selling Pearson textbooks in the sequence you want
- adding your own content, such as a guide to a local art museum, a map of monuments in your area, your syllabus, or a study guide you've created

A Pearson Custom Library book is priced according to the number of chapters and may even save your students money. To begin building your custom text, visit www.pearsoncustomlibrary.com or contact your Pearson representative.

To request an examination copy or for additional information, please visit us at www.pearsonhighered.com/art.

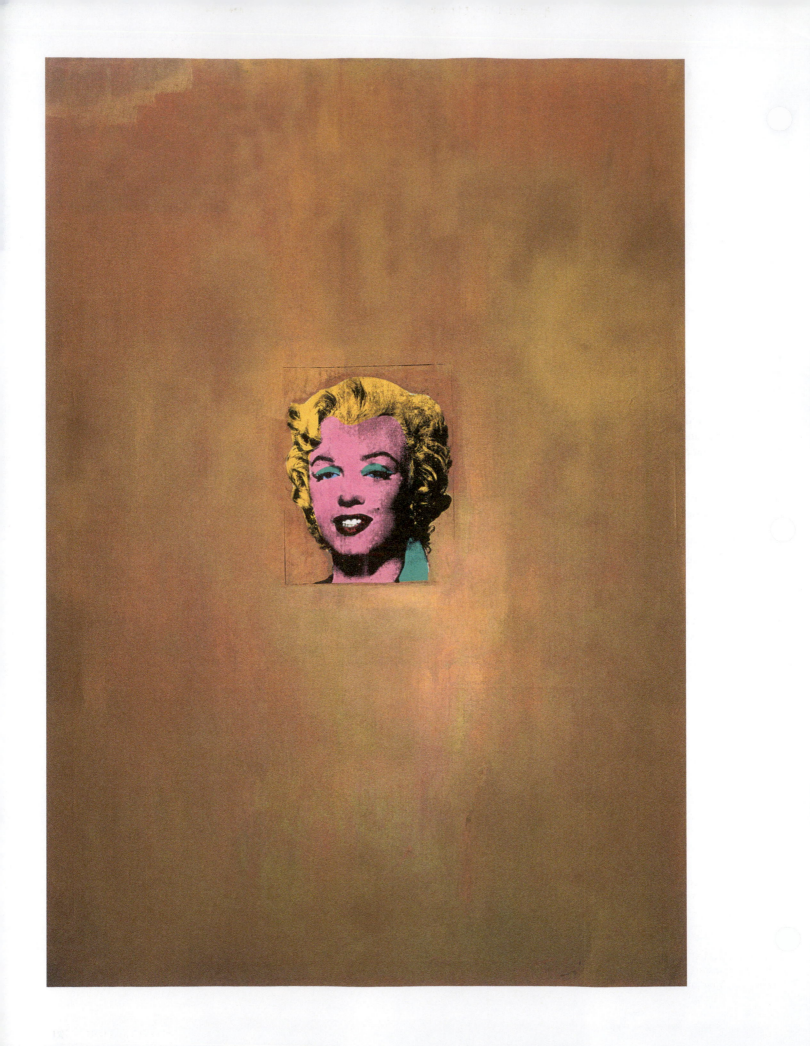

Introduction

WHY IN 1962 DID ANDY WARHOL MAKE A PAINTING ENTITLED *Gold Marilyn Monroe* (fig. **I.1**)? This almost 7-foot-high canvas was produced shortly after the death of the Hollywood screen star and sex symbol. It was not commissioned and obviously Monroe never "sat" for it, an activity that we generally associate with portraiture. Instead, Warhol

worked from a press photograph, a still from the 1953 movie *Niagara*, which he cropped to his liking and then transferred onto canvas using **silkscreen**. This process involves mechanically transferring the photograph onto a mesh screen, or in this case several screens, one for each color, and pressing printing ink through them onto canvas. Warhol then surrounded Marilyn's head with a field of broadly brushed gold paint.

Warhol's painting is not a conventional portrait of Monroe but rather a pastiche of the public image of the film star as propagated by the mass media. Warhol imitates the sloppy, gritty look and feel of color newspaper reproductions of the period, when the colors were often misregistered, aligning imperfectly with the image, and the colors themselves were "off," meaning not quite right. The Marilyn we are looking at is the impersonal celebrity of the media, the commodity being pushed by the film industry. She is supposedly glamorous, with her lush red lipstick and bright blond hair, but instead she appears pathetically tacky because of the grimy black ink and the garish color of her blond hair as it becomes bright yellow and her flesh tone turns pink. Her personality is impenetrable, reduced to a sad, lifeless public smile. Prompted by Monroe's suicide, *Gold Marilyn Monroe* presents the real Marilyn—a depressed, often miserable person, who, in

this textureless, detailless, unnaturalistic image, is becoming a blur fading into memory. Warhol has brilliantly expressed the indifference of the mass media, whose objective is to promote celebrities by saturating a thirsty public with their likenesses but which tells us nothing meaningful about them and shows no concern for them. Monroe's image is used simply to sell a product, much as the alluring and often jazzy packaging of Brillo soap pads or Campbell's soup cans is designed to make a product alluring without telling us anything about the product itself. The packaging is just camouflage. As a sentimental touch, Warhol floats Marilyn's head in a sea of gold paint, embedding her in an eternal realm previously reserved for use in icons of Christ and the Virgin Mary, which immerse these religious figures in a spiritual aura of golden, heavenly light (see fig. 13.22). But Warhol's revered Marilyn is sadly dwarfed by her celestial gold surrounding, adding to the tragic sense of this powerful portrait, which trenchantly comments on the enormous gulf existing between public image and private reality.

If we turn the clock back some 200 years and look at a portrait by the Boston painter John Singleton Copley, we again see an image of a woman (fig. **I.2**). But, made as it was in a different time and context, the story surrounding the painting is entirely different. The sitter is Freelove Olney Scott, and she is presented as a refined-looking woman, born, we would guess, into an aristocratic family, used to servants and power. As a matter of fact, we have come to accept Copley's portraits of colonial Bostonians, such as Mrs. Joseph Scott, as accurate depictions of their subjects

I.1 Andy Warhol, *Gold Marilyn Monroe*. 1962. Synthetic polymer paint, silk-screened, and oil on canvas, 6'11¼" × 4'7½" (2.11 × 1.44 m). Museum of Modern Art, New York. Gift of Philip Johnson 316.1962

I.2 John Singleton Copley, *Mrs. Joseph Scott*. Oil on canvas, 69½ × 39½" (176.5 × 100 cm). The Newark Museum, Newark, New Jersey. 48.508

and lifestyles. But many, like Mrs. Scott, were not what they appear to be. So, who was Mrs. Scott? Let's take a closer look at the context in which the painting was made.

Copley is recognized as the first great American painter. Working in Boston from about 1754 to 1774, he became the most sought-after portraitist of the period. Copley easily outstripped the meager competition, most of whom actually earned their living painting signs and coaches. After all, no successful British artist had any reason to come to America. The economically struggling colonies were not a strong market for art. Only occasionally was a portrait commissioned, and typically, artists were treated like craftsmen rather than intellectuals. Like most colonial portraitists, Copley was largely self-taught, learning his trade by looking at black-and-white prints of paintings by the European masters.

As we can see in *Mrs. Joseph Scott*, Copley was a master of painting textures, which is all the more astonishing when we remember that he had no one to teach him the tricks of the painter's trade. His pictorial illusions are so convincing, we think we are looking at real silk, ribbons, lace, pearls, skin, hair, and marble, quite the opposite of Warhol's artificial Marilyn. Copley's contemporaries also marveled at his sleight of hand. No other colonial painter attained such a level of realism.

But is Copley just a "face painter," as portraitists were derogatorily called at the time, offering mere resemblances of his sitters and their expensive accoutrements? Is this painting just a means to replicate the likeness of an individual in an era before the advent of photography? The answer to both questions is a resounding

"no." Copley's job was not just to make a faithful image of M Scott, but to portray her as a woman of impeccable character, limitless wealth, and aristocratic status. The flowers she holds are a symbol of fertility, faithfulness, and feminine grace, indicating that she is a good mother and wife, and a charming woman. Her expensive dress was imported from London, as was her necklace. Copley undoubtedly copied her pose from one of the prints he had of portraits of British or French royalty.

Not only is Mrs. Scott's pose borrowed, but most likely her clothing is as well, for her necklace appears on three other women in Copley portraits. In other words, it was a studio prop, as the dress may have been too. In fact, except for Mrs. Scott's face, the entire painting is a fiction designed to aggrandize the wife of a newly wealthy Boston merchant who had made his fortune selling provisions to the occupying British army. The Scotts were *nouveau-riche* commoners, not titled aristocrats. By the middle of the eighteenth century, rich Bostonians wanted to distinguish themselves from the multitude, and so, after a century of trying to escape their British roots, from which many had fled to secure religious freedom, they now sought to imitate the British aristocracy, even to the point of taking tea in the afternoon and owning English Spaniels, a breed that in England only aristocrats were permitted to own.

Joseph Scott commissioned this painting of his wife, as well as a portrait of himself, not just to record their features, but to sho off the family's wealth. The pictures were extremely expensi and therefore status symbols, much as a Rolls-Royce or a Tiffany diamond ring are today. The portraits were displayed in the public spaces of their house so that they could be readily seen by visitors. Most likely they hung on either side of the mantel in the living room, or in the entrance hall. They were not intended as mate affectionate resemblances destined for the bedroom. If patrons wanted cherished images of their loved ones, they would commission miniature portraits, which captured the likeness of the sitter in amazing detail and were often so small they could be encased in a locket that a woman would wear on a chain around her neck, or a gentleman would place in the inner breastpocket of his coat, close to the heart.

Warhol and Copley worked in very different times, a fact that has tremendous effect on the look and meaning of their portraits. Their paintings were made to serve very different purposes, and consequently they tell very different stories. And because art always serves a purpose, it is impossible for an artist to make a work that does not represent a point of view and tell a story, sometimes many stories. As we will see, great artists tell great and powerful stories. We shall find that an important key to unraveling these stories is understanding the context in which the work was made.

THE POWER OF ART AND THE IMPACT OF CONTEXT

In a sense, art is a form of propaganda, for it represents an individual's or group's point of view, and this view is often presented as truth or fact. For centuries, art was used by church and state propagate their importance, superiority, and greatness. *The Alba Madonna* (fig. I.3), for example, was designed to proclaim the idealized, perfect state of existence attainable through Catholicism in sixteenth-century Italy, while the Arch of Titus (fig. I.4) was erected to reinforce in the public's mind the military prowess of the first-century Roman emperor. Even landscape

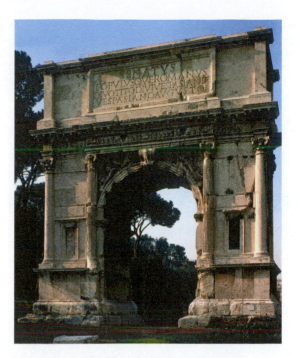

I.4 Arch of Titus, Forum Romanum, Rome. ca. 81 CE (restored)

paintings and still lifes of fruit, dead game, and flowers made in the seventeenth century are loaded with moral messages, and are far from simple attempts to capture the splendor and many moods of nature or show off the painter's finesse at creating a convincing illusionistic image.

Epitomizing the power of art is its ability to evoke entire historical periods. The words "ancient Egypt" will conjure up in most people's minds images of the pyramids, the Sphinx, and flat stiff figures lined up sideways across the face of stone (fig. I.5). Or look at the power of Grant Wood's famous 1930 painting

Raphael, *The Alba Madonna*. ca. 1510. Oil on panel transferred to canvas, diameter 37¼" (94 cm). Image courtesy of the Board of Trustees, National Gallery of Art, Washington, D.C., Andrew W. Mellon Collection, 1937.1.24. (24)

I.5 Palette of King Narmer, from Hierakonpolis. ca. 3150–3125 BCE. Slate, height 25" (63.5 cm). Egyptian Museum, Cairo

I.6 Grant Wood, *American Gothic*. 1930. Oil on beaverboard, 30¹¹/₁₆" × 25¹¹/₁₆" (78 × 65.3 cm). Unframed. Friends of American Art Collection. 1930.934. The Art Institute of Chicago

Many art historians, critics, and other viewers found the picture remarkably beautiful—glittering and shimmering with a delicate, ephemeral otherworldy aura. Many, especially Catholics, however, were repulsed by Ofili's homage to the Virgin and w[ ]infuriated. Instead of viewing the work through Ofili's eyes, they placed the painting within the context of their own experience and beliefs. Consequently, they interpreted the dung and graphic imagery—and perhaps even the black Virgin, although this was never mentioned—as sacrilegious. Within days of the opening of the exhibition, the painting had to be placed behind a large Plexiglas barrier. One artist hurled horse manure at the façade of the Brooklyn Museum, claiming, "I was expressing myself creatively," a defense often offered for Ofili. Another museum visitor sneaked behind the Plexiglas barrier and smeared the Virgin with white paint in order to cover her up. The biggest attack came from New York's mayor, Rudolph Giuliani, a Catholic, who was so outraged that he tried, unsuccessfully, to stop city funding for the museum. The public outrage at Ofili's work is just part of a long tradition that probably goes back to the beginning of image making. Art has consistently provoked anger, just as it has inspired pride, admiration, love, and respect, and the reason is simple: Art is never an empty container but rather a vessel loaded with meaning, subject to multiple interpretations, and always representing someone's point of view.

American Gothic (fig. I.6), which has led us to believe that humorless, austere, hardworking farmers dominated the American hinterlands at the time. The painting has virtually become an emblem of rural America for the period.

American Gothic has also become a source of much sarcastic humor for later generations, which have adapted the famous pitchfork-bearing farmer and his sour-faced daughter for all kinds of agendas unrelated to the artist's original message. Works of art are often later appropriated to serve purposes quite different from those initially intended, with context heavily influencing the meaning of a work. The reaction of some New Yorkers to *The Holy Virgin Mary* (fig. I.7) by Chris Ofili reflects the power of art to provoke and spark debate, even outrage. The work appeared in an exhibition titled *Sensation: Young British Artists from the Saatchi Collection*, presented at the Brooklyn Museum in late 1999. Ofili, who is a Briton of African descent, made an enormous picture of a black Virgin Mary using tiny dots of paint, glitter, map pins, and collaged images of genitalia from popular magazines. Instead of hanging on the wall, this enormous painting rested on two large wads of elephant dung, which had been a signature feature of the artist's large canvases since 1991. Elephant dung is held sacred in some African cultures, and for Ofili, a devout Catholic who periodically attends Mass, the picture was a modernization of the traditional presentation of the elemental sacredness of the Virgin, with the so-called pornographic images intended to suggest both procreation and hovering naked angels. While intentionally provocative, the picture was not conceived as an attack on the Catholic religion.

I.7 Chris Ofili, *The Holy Virgin Mary*. 1996. Paper, collage, oil paint, glitter, polyester resin, map pins, and elephant dung on linen, 7'11" × 5'11⁵/₁₆" (2.44 × 1.83 m). Victoria Miro Gallery, London

Because the context for looking at art constantly changes, our interpretations and insights into art and entire periods evolve as well. For example, when the first edition of this book is published in 1962, women artists were not included, which was typical for textbooks at the time. America, like most of the world, was male-dominated and history was male-centric. Historically, women were expected to be wives and mothers, and to stay in the home and not have careers. They were not supposed to become artists, and the few known exceptions were not taken seriously by historians, who were mostly male. The feminist movement, beginning in the mid-1960s, overturned this restrictive perception of women. As a result, in the last 40 years, art historians—many of them female—have "rediscovered" countless women artists who had attained a degree of success in their day. Many of them were outstanding artists, held in high esteem during their lifetimes, despite the enormous struggle to overcome powerful social and even family resistance against women becoming professional artists.

One of these "lost" women artists is the seventeenth-century Dutch painter Judith Leyster, a follower, if not a student, of the famed Frans Hals. Over the subsequent centuries, Leyster's paintings were either attributed to other artists, including Hals and Gerrit van Honthorst, or they were labeled "artist unknown." At the end of the nineteenth century, however, Leyster was rediscovered in her own right through an analysis of her signature, documents, and style, and her paintings were gradually restored to her name. It was only with the feminist movement that she was elevated from a minor figure to one of the more accomplished painters of her generation, one important enough to be included in basic histories of art. The feminist movement provided a new context for evaluating art, one that had an interest in rather than a denial of women's achievements and a study of issues relating to gender and how they appear in the arts.

A work like Leyster's *Self-Portrait* (fig. **I.8**) is especially fascinating from this point of view. Its size and date (ca. 1633) suggest that this may have been the painting the artist submitted as her presentation piece for admission into the local painters' guild, the Guild of St. Luke of Haarlem. Women were not generally encouraged to join the guild, which was a male preserve that reinforced the professional status of men. Nor did women artists generally take on students. Leyster bucked both traditions, however, as she carved out a career for herself in a man's world. In her self-portrait, she presents herself as an artist armed with many brushes, suggesting her deft control of the medium—an idea that the presentation picture itself was meant to demonstrate. On the casel is a segment of a genre scene of which several variations are known. We must remember that at this time artists rarely showed themselves working at their easels, toiling with their hands: They wanted to separate themselves from mere artisans and laborers, presenting themselves as intellectuals belonging to a higher class. As a woman defying male expectations, however, Leyster needed to declare clearly that she was indeed an artist. But she cleverly elevates her status by not dressing as an artist would when painting. Instead, she appears as her patrons do in their portraits,

I.8 Judith Leyster, *Self-Portrait*. ca. 1633. Oil on canvas, 29⅜ × 25⅝" (72.3 × 65.3 cm). National Gallery of Art, Washington, D.C. Gift of Mr. and Mrs. Robert Woods Bliss

well-dressed and well-off. Her mouth is open, in what is called a "speaking likeness" portrait, giving her a casual but self-assured animated quality, as she appears to converse on equal terms with a visitor, or with us. Leyster, along with Artemisia Gentileschi and Marie-Louise-Élisabeth Vigée-Lebrun, who also appear in this book, was included in a major 1976 exhibition titled *Women Artists 1550–1950*, which was shown in Los Angeles and Brooklyn, and played a major role in establishing the importance of women artists.

WHAT IS ART?

Ask most people "What is art?," and they will respond with the words "an oil painting" or "a marble or bronze sculpture." Their principal criterion is that the object be beautiful—whatever that may be—although generally they will probably define this as the degree to which a painting or sculpture is real looking or adheres to their notion of naturalism. Technical finesse or craft is viewed as the highest attribute of art making, capable of inspiring awe and reverence. Epitomizing these values is Greek and Roman sculpture, such as the fourth-century BCE sculpture the *Apoxyomenos (Scraper)* (fig. **I.9**), which for centuries was considered the high point of fine art. To debunk the myth that art is only about technique and begin to get at what it is really about, we return to Warhol's *Gold Marilyn Monroe*. The painting is rich with stories, one of which is how it poses questions about the meaning of art, how it functions, and how it takes on value, both financial and aesthetic. Warhol even begs the question of the significance of technical finesse in art making, an issue raised by the fact that he wants to give us the impression that he may not have even touched this painting himself. We have already seen how he appropriated someone else's photograph of Monroe, not even taking his own. Warhol then instructed his assistants to make the screens for the printing process. They may also have prepared the canvas, screened the image with the colors Warhol selected, and even painted the gold to Warhol's specifications.

By using assistants to make his work, Warhol is telling us that art is not necessarily about the artist's technical finesse, but about communicating an idea using visual language. The measuring stick for quality in art is the quality of the statement being made, or its philosophy, as well as the quality of the technical means for making this statement, even if not executed by the artist. Looking at *Gold Marilyn Monroe* in the flesh at New York's Museum of Modern Art is a powerful, even unforgettable experience. Standing in front of this large canvas, we cannot help but feel the

empty glory of America's most famous symbol of female sexuality and stardom. Because the artist's vision, and not his touch, is the relevant issue for the production of this particular work, it is of no consequence that Warhol makes it seem as though he never laid a hand on the canvas except to sign the back. We shall see shortly, however, that the artist's touch is indeed often critical to the success of a work of art, which is especially true for art made before 1900.

Warhol openly declared that his art was not about his technical ability when he named his midtown Manhattan studio "The Factory." By doing so, he told us that art was a commodity, and that he was manufacturing a product, even a mass-produced one. The factory churned out over a thousand paintings and prints of Marilyn based on the same publicity still. All Warhol appeared to do for the most part was sign them, his signature reinforcing the importance people placed on the idea of the artist's signature itself being an essential part of the work. Ironically, most Old Master paintings, dating from the fourteenth through the eighteenth centuries, are not signed; and despite giving the public the impression that he had little involvement in his work, Warhol was a workaholic and very hands-on in the production of his art.

Moreover, artists have been using assistants to help make their pictures for centuries. Peter Paul Rubens, an Antwerp painter working in the first half of the seventeenth century and one of the most famous artists of his day, had an enormous workshop that cranked out many of his paintings, especially the larger works. His assistants often specialized in particular elements such as flowers, animals, or clothing, for example, and many went on to become successful artists in their own right. Rubens would design the painting, and then assistants, trained in his style, would execute individual parts. Rubens would then come in at the end and pull the painting together as needed. The price the client was willing to pay often determined how much Rubens himself participated in the actual painting of the picture: Many of his works were indeed made entirely by him, and therefore commanded the highest prices. Rubens's brilliant flashy brushwork was in many respects critical to the making of the picture. Not only was his handling of paint considered superior to that of his assistants, the very identity of his paintings—their very life, so to speak—was linked to his unique genius in applying paint to canvas, almost as much as it was to the dynamism of his dramatic compositions. His brushwork complemented his subject matter. The two went hand in hand.

Warhol was not the first artist to make art that intentionally raised the issue of what art is and how it functions. This distinction belongs to the humorous and brilliant Parisian Marcel Duchamp, one of the most influential artists of the twentieth century. In 1919, Duchamp took a postcard reproduction of Leonardo da Vinci's *Mona Lisa*, which hangs in the Louvre Museum in Paris, and drew a moustache on the sitter's face (fig. **I.10**). Below he wrote the letters, "L.H.O.O.Q.," which when pronounced in French is *elle a chaud au cul*, or "She's got the hots." Duchamp was poking fun at the public's fascination with the mysterious smile on the Mona Lisa, which had intrigued

I.9 *Apoxyomenos (Scraper)*. Roman marble copy, probably after a bronze original of ca. 330 BCE by Lysippos. Height 6'9" (2.1 m). Musei Vaticani, Rome

I.10 Marcel Duchamp, *Mona Lisa (L.H.O.O.Q.)*. 1919. Rectified readymade; pencil on a postcard reproduction, 7 × 4⅞" (17.8 × 12 cm). Private collection

viewers for centuries and eluded suitable explanation. Duchamp irreverently provided one: She is sexually aroused. With the childish gesture of affixing a moustache to the image, Duchamp also attacked bourgeois reverence for Old Master painting, as well as the age-old ideal of oil painting representing the pinnacle of art.

Art, Duchamp is saying, can be made by merely drawing on a mass-produced reproduction. Artists can use any imaginable medium in any way in order to express themselves: not just oil on canvas or cast bronze or chiseled marble sculpture He is announcing that art is about ideas that are made visually, and not necessarily about craft. In this deceptively whimsical work, which is actually rich in ideas, Duchamp is telling us that art is anything someone wants to call art—which is not the same as saying it is good art. Furthermore, he is proclaiming that art can be small, since *Mona Lisa (L.H.O.O.Q.)* is a fraction of the size of its source, the *Mona Lisa*. By appropriating Leonardo's famous picture and interpreting it very differently from traditional readings (see pages 564–66), Duchamp suggests that the meaning of art is not fixed forever by the artist, that it can change and be reassigned by viewers, writers, collectors, and museum curators, who may use it for their own purposes. Lastly, and this is certainly one of Duchamp's many wonderful contributions to art, he is telling us that art can be fun, that it can defy conventional notions of beauty, and while intellectually engaging us in a most serious manner, it can also provide us with a smile, if not a good belly laugh. Many historians today consider *Mona Lisa (L.H.O.O.Q.)* as important as Leonardo's *Mona Lisa*, and put the two artists on the same plane of importance.

ART AND AESTHETICS: THE ISSUE OF BEAUTY

Mona Lisa (L.H.O.O.Q.) also raised the issue of aesthetics, which is the study of theories surrounding art, including the definition of beauty and the meaning and purpose of art. Duchamp selected the *Mona Lisa* for appropriation for many reasons, one of them no doubt being that many people considered it the greatest and therefore the most beautiful painting ever made. Certainly, it was one of the most famous paintings in the world, if not the most famous. In 1919, most of those who held such a view had probably never seen it and only knew if from reproductions, probably no better than the one Duchamp used in *Mona Lisa (L.H.O.O.Q.)*. And yet, they would describe the original painting as beautiful, but not Duchamp's comical version.

Duchamp called altered found objects such as *Mona Lisa (L.H.O.O.Q.)* "readymades" (for other examples, see *Bicycle Wheel*, fig. 27.29, and *Fountain*, fig. 28.2), and he was adamant that these works had no aesthetic value whatsoever. They were not to be considered beautiful; they were aesthetically neutral. What interested Duchamp were the ideas that these objects embodied once they were declared art.

Despite his claim, Duchamp's readymades can be perceived as beautiful, in ways, of course that are quite different from Leonardo's *Mona Lisa*, but beautiful all the same. *Mona Lisa (L.H.O.O.Q.)* has an aura about it, an aura of wit and ideas that are specific to Duchamp. As a result, this slightly altered cheap color postcard is a compelling work of art. The qualities that attract us to it, which we can describe as its beauty, could not be further from those of Leonardo's *Mona Lisa*, which have more to do with composition, color, and paint handling. Ultimately, beauty, in many respects, can be equated with quality, which to a large degree hinges on the power of the statement, not some pre-conceived notion of visual beauty.

Beauty is not just a pretty colorful picture or a perfectly formed, harmonious nude marble figure such as the *Apoxymenos*. Beauty resides as well in content and how successfully this content is made visual. This book is intended to suggest the many complex ways that quality, and thus beauty, manifests itself in art. Some of the greatest paintings are grotesque, depicting horrific scenes that many people do not find acceptable, but they are nonetheless beautiful—scenes such as beheadings, crucifixions (fig. I.11), death and despair, emotional distress, and the brutal massacre of innocent women and children. Like Duchamp's *Mona Lisa (L.H.O.O.Q.)*, these works possess an aura that makes them riveting, despite the repulsiveness of their subject matter. They have quality, and to those who recognize and feel this quality,

I.11 Matthias Grünewald, *The Crucifixion* (center panel). ca. 1509/10–15. Oil on panel, 9'9½" × 10'9" (2.97 × 3.28 m). Musée d'Unterlinden, Colmar, France

this makes them beautiful. Others will continue to be repulsed and offended by them, or at best fail to find them interesting.

ILLUSIONISM AND MEANING IN ART

The Roman historian Pliny tells the story about the competition between the Greek painters Zeuxis and Parrhasius to see who could make the most realistic work. Zeuxis painted grapes so real that birds tried to eat them. But it was Parrhasius who won the competition when he made a painting of a curtain covering a painting. So realistic was the work that Zeuxis asked him to pull back the curtain covering his painting only to discover that he was already looking at the painting.

Pliny's story is interesting, because despite a recurring emphasis on illusionism in art, the ability to create illusionistic effects and "fool the eye" is generally not what determines quality in art, and if it were, thousands of relatively unknown artists today would be considered geniuses. As we just discussed, quality in art comes from ideas *and* execution. Just being clever and fooling the eye is not enough.

A look at the sculpture of twentieth-century artist Duane Hanson shows us how illusionism can be put in the service of meaning to create a powerful work of art. Hanson's 1995 sculpture *Man on a Mower* (fig. **I.12**) is a work that is too often appreciated only for its illusionistic qualities, while the real content goes unnoticed. Yet, it is the content, not the illusionism itself, that makes this sculpture so powerful. Hanson began making his sculptures in the late 1960s, casting his figures in polyester resin, and then meticulously painting them. He then dressed them in real clothing, used real accessories (including wigs and artificial

eyeballs), and placed them with real bits of furniture. Most viewers are startled to discover his sculptures are not real people, and many have tried to interact with his characters, which include museum guards, tourists, shoppers, house painters, and sunbathers.

But Hanson's art is about more than just a visual sleight of hand. He is also a realist and a moralist, and his art is filled with tragic social commentary. By "realist," we mean that his sculpture is not limited to attractive, beautiful, and ennobling people, objects, and situations, but instead focuses on the base, crude, and unseemly. In *Man on a Mower*, which, with the exception of the lawnmower and aluminum can, is painted cast bronze, we see an overweight man clutching a diet soda. He dwarfs the riding mower he sits on. His T-shirt, baseball hat, pants, and sneakers are soiled. He is ordinary, and the entire sculpture is remarkably prosaic.

Man on a Mower is a tragic work. We see disillusionment in the man's eyes as he blankly stares off into space. The diet soda he holds suggests that he is trying to lose weight but is losing the battle. Cutting grass is another metaphor for a losing battle, since the grass is going to grow back. This work also represents the banality of human existence. What is life about? The monotony of cutting grass. In this last work, made when he knew he was dying of cancer, Hanson captured what he perceived to be the emptiness of human existence and contemporary life in the modern world. The illusionism of the sculpture makes this aura of alienation and lack of spirituality all the more palpable. This man is us, and this is our life, too. He embodies no poetry, nobility, or heroism. Our twentieth-century *Man on a Mower* has no fine causes or beliefs run to as he confronts the down-to-earth reality of life and death.

I.12 Duane Hanson, *Man on a Mower*. 1995. Bronze, polychromed in oil, with mower. Life-size. Courtesy Van de Weghe Fine Art, New York

CAN A MECHANICAL PROCESS BE ART? PHOTOGRAPHY

The first edition of this book did not include photography, reflecting on attitude dating back to the introduction of photography in 1839 that the medium, because it was largely a mechanical process, was not an art form, or certainly not one that had the same merit as painting and sculpture. Within the last 25 years, however, photography has been vindicated. Along with video and film, it has been elevated to the status of one of the most important artistic mediums, perhaps even outstripping painting. Pictures from the nineteenth and twentieth centuries that had interested only a handful of photography insiders suddenly became intensely sought-after, with many museums rushing to establish photography departments and amass significant collections. In other words, it took well over 125 years for people to understand photography and develop an eye for the special qualities and beauties of the medium, which are so radically different from those of the traditional twin peaks of the visual arts, painting and sculpture.

We need only look at a 1972 photograph titled *Albuquerque* (fig. **I.13**) by Lee Friedlander to see how photography operates as an artistic medium. In his black-and-white print, called a gelatin silver print since the pre-exposed paper surface consists of silver in a gelatin solution, Friedlander portrays a modern America which, he suggests, has been rendered vacuous and lifeless by modernity and twentieth-century technology. How does he make such a statement? The picture obviously has a haunting emptiness, for it contains no people and is instead filled with strange vacant spaces of walkway and street that appear between the numerous objects, such as a fire hydrant, street signs, and traffic light, that pop up everywhere. A hard, eerie geometry prevails, as seen in the strong verticals of poles, buildings, and wall. Cylinders, rectangles, and circles can be found throughout the composition, even in the background apartment building and the brick driveway in the foreground.

Despite the stillness and sense of absence, the picture is busy and restless. The vertical elements create a vibrant staccato rhythm, which is reinforced by the asymmetrical composition lacking a focus or center, and by the powerful intersecting diagonals of the street and foreground wall. Friedlander crafted his composition so carefully he gets the shadow of the hydrant to parallel the street. Disturbing features appear everywhere. There is a lopsided telephone pole, suggesting collapse. And there is the pole for a street sign, the top of which has been cropped, that visually cuts a dog in two while casting a mysterious shadow on a nearby wall. The fire hydrant appears to be mounted incorrectly, sticking too far out of the ground. The car on the right has been brutally cropped and appears to have a light pole sprouting from its hood. The entire picture is dominated by technology and synthetic, industrial, or mass-produced objects. Nature has been cemented over, reduced to a few straggly trees in the middle ground and distance and the thriving weeds surrounding the

I.13   Lee Friedlander, *Albuquerque*. 1972. Gelatin silver print, 11 x 14" (27.9 x 35.6 cm)

hydrant. In this brilliant print, Friedlander powerfully suggests that technology, mass-produced products, and a fast fragmented lifestyle are spawning alienation and a disconnection with nature. Friedlander also suggests that modernization is also making America homogeneous—if it were not for the title, we would have no idea that this photograph was taken in Albuquerque, New Mexico.

Friedlander did not just find this composition. He very carefully made it. He not only wanted a certainly quality of light for his picture, but probably even waited for the sun to cast shadows that aligned perfectly with the street. When framing the composition, he meticulously incorporated a fragment of the utility cover in the lower left foreground, while axing a portion of the car on the right. Nor did the geometry of the picture just happen. He made it happen. Instead of a soft focus that would create an atmospheric blurry picture, he used a deep focus that produces a sharp crisp image filled with detail, allowing, for example, the individual rectangular bricks in the pavement to be clearly seen. The strong white tones of the vertical rectangles of the apartment building, the foreground wall, and the utility box blocking the car on the left edge of the picture were most likely carefully worked up in the darkroom, as was the rectangular columned doorway on the house. Friedlander has exposed the ugliness of modern America in this hard, cold, dry image, and because of the power of its message has made an extraordinarily beautiful work of art, the kind of image that has elevated photography into the pantheon of art.

HOW ARCHITECTURE TELLS STORIES

An art form that is basically abstract and functional might be seen as a poor candidate for telling stories, conveying messages, and disseminating propaganda. And yet it can. We see Gianlorenzo Bernini doing it in 1657 when he was asked by Pope Alexander XVII to design a large open space, or piazza, in front of St. Peter's

Cathedral in Rome. Bernini's solution was to create a plaza that was defined by a colonnade, or row of columns, resembling arms that appear to embrace visitors maternally, welcoming them into the bosom of the church (fig. I.14). He thus anthropomorphized the building by emphasizing the identification of the church with the Virgin Mary. At the same time, the French architect Claude Perrault was commissioned to design the façade of Louis XIV's palace, the Louvre in Paris (fig. I.15). To proclaim the king's grandeur, he made the ground floor, where the day-to-day business of the court was carried out, a squat podium. In contrast, the second floor, where the royal quarters were located and Louis would have held court, was much higher and grander and served as the main floor, clearly supported by the worker-bee floor. Perrault articulated this elevated second story with a design that recalled Roman temples, thus associating Louis XIV with imperial Rome and worldly power. The severe geometry and symmetry of the building reflect the regimented order and tight control of Louis XIV's reign.

At first glance, it seems hard to project any story onto Frank Lloyd Wright's Solomon R. Guggenheim Museum (fig. I.16), a museum that, when it was built between 1956 and 1959, was largely dedicated to abstract art. Located on upper Fifth Avenue in New York and overlooking Central Park, the building resembled for many a flying saucer; it was certainly radically different from the surrounding residential apartment buildings, and for that matter, almost anything built anywhere up to that time. But if we had to guess, we would probably first divine that the building might be a museum, for the exterior resembles a work of art—a giant nonobjective sculpture. Made of reinforced concrete, the building even seems as though it were made from an enormous mold that formed its continuous upward spiral, which from any one side appears to consist of enormous, weighty, massive horizontal bands. There is no mistaking this structure for an apartment complex or office building.

Wright conceived the Guggenheim in 1945–46, when he received the commission, and his personal goal was to create an organic structure that deviated from the conventional static rectangular box filled with conventional rectangular rooms. The building is designed around a spiral ramp (fig. I.17), which is meant to evoke a spiral shell, and this ramp is what defines the design of the exterior. Wright also thought of the interior as a ceramic vase, for it is closed at the bottom, widens as it rises, and is "open" at the top since it is capped by a spectacular light-filled, cone-shaped glass roof. Essentially, the museum is a single ramp-lined space, although there are a handful of galleries off the ramp and separate spaces for offices, auditorium, and bookstore, for example. Wright expected visitors to take an elevator to the top of the ramp, and then slowly amble down its 3 percent gradient, gently pulled along by gravity. Because the ramp was relatively narrow, viewers could not stand too far back from the art, which seemed to float on the curved walls, enhancing the fluid effect of Wright's curved, organic design. As a result, visitors were forced into a more intimate relationship with the art. At the same time, however, they could look back across the open space of the room

to see where they had gone, comparing the work in front of them to a segment of the exhibition presented on a sweeping distant arc, Or they could look ahead as well, to get a preview of where they were going.

Not only do visitors see the art, they also see other visitors, sometimes just as distant specks, winding their way down the ramp. The building has a sense of continuity and mobility that Wright viewed as an organic experience, analogous to traveling along the continuous winding paths of the adjacent Central Park, which was designed in the nineteenth century to capture and preserve nature in the encroaching urban environment. Wright's enormous "room" reflects nature not only in its spiral shell design, but also in the organic concave and convex forms that can be seen from the top of ramp and that reflect the subtle eternal movement of nature. Wright even placed a lozenge-shaped pool on the ground floor, directly opposite the light entering from the skylight above, the two architectural touches reinforcing a sense of nature. Art historians have also likened the sense of constant

I.14   St. Peter's, Rome. Nave and façade by Carlo Maderno, 1607–15; colonnade by Gianlorenzo Bernini, designed 1657

I.15   Claude Perrault. East front of the Louvre, Paris. 1667–70

1.16 Frank Lloyd Wright. The Solomon R. Guggenheim Museum, New York. 1956–59

I.17 Frank Lloyd Wright. Interior of the Solomon R. Guggenheim Museum, New York. 1956–59

movement in Wright's seemingly endless ramp—which most people now ascend rather than descend because exhibitions begin at the foot of the ramp—to the American frontier, the ramp embodying "the expansive, directionless response of the frontiersman to limitless space," as expressed by James Fenimore Cooper's Natty Bumppo, Herman Melville's whaling chase, Mark Twain's Mississippi, and Walt Whitman's Open Road. Far-fetched as this may sound, we must remember that Wright was born in the Midwest in the nineteenth century, when it was still rural, and beginning with his earliest mature buildings, his designs, such as the Robie House (see fig. 26.39), were meant to capture the vast spread of the plains and were carefully integrated into the land.

If Wright's austere, abstract sculptural design for both the exterior and interior undermines his attempt to evoke nature, the building still retains a sense of open space and continuous

movement. Unlike any other museum, the Guggenheim has a sense of communal spirit, for here everyone is united in one large room and traveling the same path.

EXPERIENCING ART

You will be astonished when you see first-hand much of the art in this book. No matter how accurate the reproductions here, or in any other text, they are no more than stand-ins for the actual objects. We hope you will visit some of the museums where the originals are displayed. But keep in mind that looking at art, absorbing its full impact, takes time and repeated visits. In many respects, looking at art is no different than reading a book or watching a film—it requires extensive, detailed looking, a careful reading of the image or object, perhaps even a questioning of why every motif, mark, or color is used. Ideally, the museum will help you understand the art. Often, there are introductory text panels that tell you why the art has been presented as it is and what it is about, and ideally there will be labels for individual works that provide further information. Major temporary exhibitions generally have a catalog, which adds further information and sometimes another layer of interpretation. But text panels, labels, and catalogues generally reflect one person's reading of the art: Keep in mind there are usually many other ways to approach or think about it.

Art museums are relatively new. Before the nineteenth century art was not made to be viewed in museums, so when you are looking at work in a museum, you are often viewing it out of the original context in which it was meant to be seen. Much work can still be seen in its original context—churches, cathedrals, chateaux, public piazzas, and archaeological sites. Ultimately, however, art can be found everywhere—in commercial galleries, corporate lobbies and offices, places of worship, and private homes. It is displayed in public spaces, from subway stations and bus stops to public plazas and civic buildings such as libraries, performing arts centers, and city halls. University and college buildings are often filled with art, and the buildings themselves are art. The chair you are sitting in and the house or building you are reading this book in are also works of art—maybe not great art, but art all the same, as Duchamp explained. Even the clothing you are wearing is in a sense art, and for you it is a way to make a personal statement. Everywhere you find art, it is telling you something, and supporting a point of view.

Art is not a luxury, as many people would have us believe, but an integral part of daily life. It has a major impact on us, even when we are not aware of it, for we feel better about ourselves when we are in environments that are visually enriching and exciting. Most important, art stimulates us to think. Even when it provokes and outrages us, it broadens our experience by making us question our values, attitudes, and worldview. This book is an introduction to this fascinating field that is so intertwined with our lives. After reading it, you will find that the world will no longer look the same.

CHAPTER 1

Prehistoric Art

WHEN MODERN HUMANS FIRST ENCOUNTERED PREHISTORIC cave paintings in the 1870s, they literally could not believe their eyes. Although the evidence indicated that the site at Altamira in Spain dated to around 13,000 BCE, the paintings had been executed with such skill and sensitivity that historians initially considered them forgeries

(see fig 1.1). Since then, some 200 similar sites have been discovered all over the world. As recently as 1994, the discovery of a cave in southeastern France (see fig. 1.2) brought hundreds more paintings to light and pushed back the date of prehistoric painting even further, to approximately 30,000 BCE. Carved objects have been discovered that are equally old.

These earliest forms of art raise more questions than they answer: Why did prehistoric humans spend their time and energy making art? What functions did these visual representations serve? What do the images mean? Art historians often use contemporaneous written texts to supplement their understandings of art; prehistoric art, however, dates to a time before writing, for which works of art are among our only evidence. Art historians therefore deploy scientific and anthropological methods in their attempts to interpret them. Archaeologists report new finds with regularity, so the study of prehistoric art continues to develop and refine its interpretations and conclusions.

Fully modern humans have lived on the earth for over 100,000 years. At first they crafted tools out of stone and fragments of bone. About 40,000 years ago, they also began to make detailed representations of forms found in nature. What inspired this change? Some scholars suppose that image making and symbolic

language are the result of the new structure of the brain associated with *homo sapiens sapiens*. Art emerges at about the time that fully modern humans moved out of Africa and into Europe, Asia, and Australia, encountering—and eventually displacing—the earlier Neanderthals (*homo neanderthalensis*) of western Eurasia. On each of these continents, there is evidence of representational artwork or of body decoration contemporary with *homo sapiens sapiens*. Tens of thousands of works survive from this time before history, the bulk of which have been discovered in Europe. Many are breathtakingly accomplished.

The skill with which the earliest datable objects are executed may have been the product of a lengthy and lost period of experimentation in the techniques of carving and painting, so the practice of art making may be much older than the surviving objects. All the same, some scholars argue that a neurological mutation related to the structure of the brain opened up the capacity for abstract thought, and that symbolic language and representational art were a sudden development in human evolution. Whatever led to the ability to create art, whether a gradual evolutionary process, or a sudden mutation, it had an enormous impact on the emergence of human culture, including the making of naturalistic images. Such works force us to reevaluate many of our assumptions about art and the creative process, and raise fundamental questions, not least of which is why human beings make art at all.

Detail of figure 1.8, *Hall of the Bulls*, Lascaux Cave, Dordogne, France

Map 1.1   Prehistoric Europe and the Near East

PALEOLITHIC ART

Upper Paleolithic painting, drawing, and sculpture appeared over a wide swath of Eurasia, Africa, and Australia at roughly the same time, between 10,000 and 40,000 years ago (map **1.1** and *Informing Art*, page 9). This time span falls in the Pleistocene era, more commonly known as the Ice Age, when glaciers (the extended polar ice caps) covered much of the northern hemisphere. The Lower and Middle Paleolithic periods extend back as far as 2 million years ago, when earlier species of the *homo genera* lived. These cultures crafted stone tools, which they sometimes decorated with abstract patterns. The end of the most recent Ice Age corresponded with the movement of fully modern humans out of Africa and into Europe, newly habitable as the warming climate caused the glaciers to recede.

Prehistoric paintings first came to light in 1878 in a cave named Altamira, in the village of Santillana del Mar in northern Spain. As Count Don Marcelino Sanz de Sautuola scoured the ground for flints and animal bones, his 12-year-old daughter, Maria, spied bison, painted in bold black outline and filled with bright earth colors (fig. **1.1**), on the ceiling of the cave. There, and in other more recently discovered caves, painted and engraved images predominantly depict animals. The greatest variety known is in the vast cave complex of Chauvet, near Vallon-Pont-d'Arc in southeastern France, named after one of the spelunkers who discovered it in 1994. Here, the 427 animal representations found to date depict 17 species, including lions, bears, and aurochs (prehistoric oxen), in black or red outlines (fig. **1.2**), and are sometimes polychromatic (containing several colors). Abstract shapes may accompany the animals, or appear alone, such as those depicted

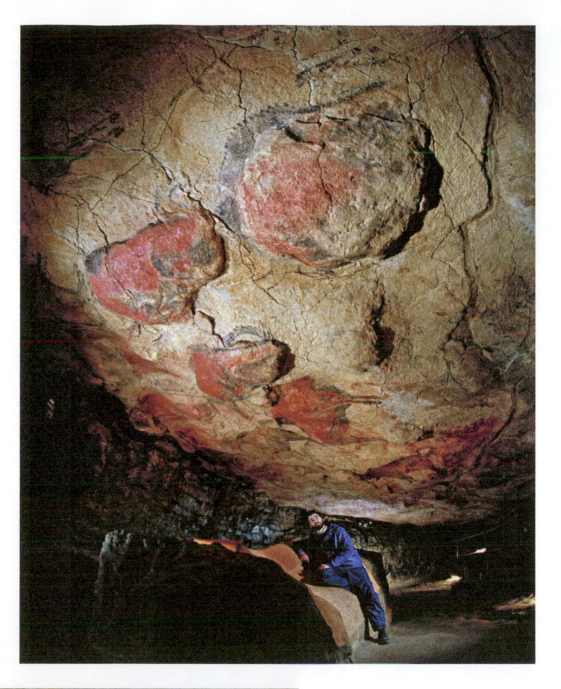

1.1 *Wounded Bison*, Altamira, Spain. ca. 15,000–10,000 BCE

1.2 *Bear*, Recess of the Bears, Chauvet Cave, Vallon-Pont-d'Arc, Ardèche Gorge, France. ca. 30,000–28,000 BCE

1.3 *Chinese Horse*, Lascaux Cave, Dordogne, France. ca. 15,000–13,000 BCE

next to the *Chinese Horse* at Lascaux in the Dordogne region of France (fig. **1.3**). Scholars have interpreted these as weapons, traps, and even insects. Human hands occasionally feature on the cave walls, stamped in paint or, more usually, in negative

silhouette (see *Materials and Techniques*, page 5). In rare instances, images depict human or partly human forms. At Chauvet, for instance, archaeologists identified the lower half of a woman painted on a projection of rock. At Les Trois Frères, a site in t[...] French Pyrenees, a human body depicted with its interior musc[...] and anatomy supports an animal head with antlers. At Lascaux, a male stick figure with a birdlike head lies between a woolly rhinoceros and a disemboweled bison, with a bird-headed stick or staff nearby (fig. **1.4**).

On first assessing the Altamira paintings toward the end of the nineteenth century, experts declared them too advanced to be authentic and dismissed them as a hoax. Indeed, though cave art may represent the dawn of art as we know it, it is often highly sophisticated. Like their counterparts at Chauvet and elsewhere, the bison of Altamira were painted from memory, yet their forms demonstrate the painters' acute powers of observation and skill in translating memory into image. Standing at rest, or bellowing or rolling on the ground, the bison behave in these paintings as they do in the wild. The painters' careful execution enhances the appearance of nature: Subtle shading (modeling) expresses the volume of a bison's belly or a lioness's head, and the forward contour of an animal's far leg is often rendered with a lighter hue to suggest distance.

Initially, scholars assigned relative dates to cave paintings by using stylistic analysis, dating them according to their degree of **naturalism**, that is, how closely the image resembled the subject

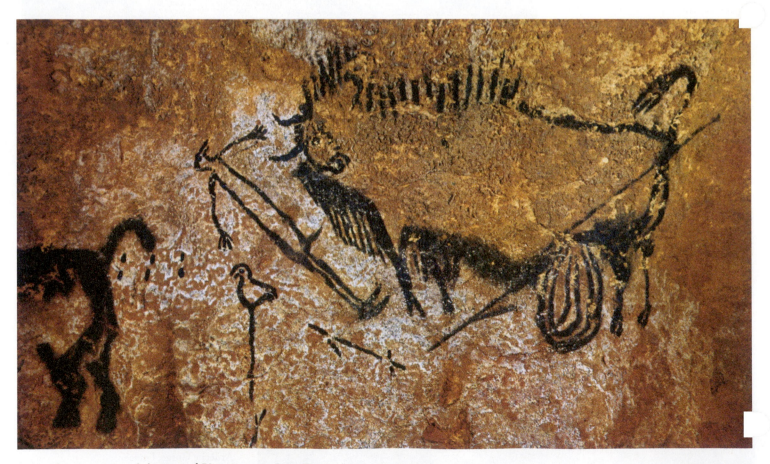

1.4 *Rhinoceros, Wounded Man, and Bison*, Lascaux Cave, Dordogne, France. ca. 15,000–13,000 BCE

Cave Painting

Paleolithic cave artists used a wide variety of techniques to achieve the images that have survived. Often working far from cave entrances, they illuminated the darkness using lamps carved out of stone and filled with fat or marrow. Archaeologists have found several of these lamps at Lascaux and elsewhere. Sometimes, when the area of rock to be painted was high above ground level, they may have built scaffolds of wood, which they stabilized against the wall by driving the poles into the limestone surface.

They prepared the surface by scraping the limestone with stone tools, bringing out its chalky whiteness as a background. They then engraved some images onto the wall, with a finger if the limestone was soft enough, or with a sharp flint. Sometimes they combined this technique with the application of color. They created black using vegetal charcoal and perhaps charred bones. Ocher, a natural iron ore, provided a range of vivid reds, browns, and yellows. For drawing—outlines of animals, for instance—they deployed charcoal and ocher in chunks, like a crayon; to generate paint, they ground the minerals into powder on a large flat stone. By heating them to extremely high temperatures, they could also vary the shades of red and yellow. They could then blow these mineral powders through tubes of animal bone or reed against a hand held up with fingers splayed to the rock surface to make hand silhouettes.

To fill in animal or human outlines with paint, they mixed the powders with blenders, which consisted of cave water, saliva, egg white, vegetal or animal fat, or blood; they then applied the colors the limestone surface, using pads of moss or fur, and brushes made of fur, feather, or chewed stick. Some scholars understand, by experimentation, that pigment was often chewed up in the mouth and then blown or spat directly onto the walls to form images. In some cases, like the *Spotted Horse* of Pech-Merle or at Chauvet, artists applied paint in dots, leading to what some scholars describe as a "pointilliste" effect. They achieved this by covering the palm with

Hand dots in the Brunel Chamber at Chauvet. Large dots were made by covering the palm with paint and applying it to the wall. In places, fingers are just visible.

ocher before pressing it against the limestone. Analysis of these marks has yielded rich results: Not only can archaeologists identify individual artists by their handprint, but they have even been able to determine that women and adolescents were at work as well as men.

in nature. As art historians at that time considered naturalism the most advanced form of representation, the more naturalistic the image, the more evolved and, therefore, the more recent it was considered to be. Radiocarbon dating has since exposed the flaws in this approach, however (see *Informing Art*, page 17). Judged to be more recent in the overall sequence on account of their remarkable naturalism, some of the paintings at Chauvet in fact proved to be among the earliest on record, dating to about 32,000 years ago. It is thus a mistake to assume that naturalism was a Paleolithic artist's—or any artist's—inevitable or only goal. A consistent use of conventions in depicting individual species (bulls at Lascaux shown in profile but with frontal horns, for instance) defies nature; these are not **optical images**, showing an animal as one would actually see it, but **composite** ones, offering any of the details that go toward making up the animal portrayed, though not necessarily in anatomically accurate positions. As the "stick man" at Lascaux may illustrate, artists may have judged their success by standards quite removed from naturalism.

Interpreting Prehistoric Painting

As majestic as these paintings can be, they are also profoundly enigmatic: What purpose did they serve? The simplest view, that they were merely decorative—"art for art's sake"—is highly unlikely. Most of the existing paintings and engravings are readily accessible, while many more that once embellished caves that open directly to the outside have probably perished. But some, at Lascaux and elsewhere, lie deep inside extended cave systems, remote from habitation areas and difficult to reach (fig. 1.5). In these cases, the power of the image may have resided in its making, rather than in its viewing: the act of painting or incising the image may have served some ritual or religious purpose.

After the images' initial discovery, scholars turned to approaches developed by ethnographers (anthropologists who study cultural behavior) to interpret cave paintings and engravings. Most often, they have attributed the inspiration for these works to magico-religious motives. Thus, early humans may have perceived an image as equivalent to the animal it represented; to

1.5   Schematic plan of Lascaux Cave system (based on a diagram by the Service de l'Architecture, Paris)

create or possess the image was to exert power over its subject, which might improve the success of a hunt. Gouge marks on cave walls indicate that in some cases spears were cast at the images (fig. **1.6**). Similarly, artists may have hoped to stimulate fertility in the wild—ensuring a continuous food supply—by depicting pregnant animals. A magico-religious interpretation might explain the choice to make animals appear lifelike, and to control them by fixing them within outlines; conversely, human fear of falling victim to the same magic may account for the decidedly unnaturalistic, abstract quality of the "stick figure" at Lascaux.

More recent theories concerning shamanism—a belief in a parallel spirit world accessed through alternative states of consciousness—build upon the earlier ethnographic interpretations, arguing that an animal's "spirit" was evident where a bulge in the wall or ceiling suggested its shape, as with the *Spotted Horses* (see fig. 1.6) at Pech-Merle in southwestern France. The artist's or shaman's power brought that spirit to the surface. Some scholars have cast the paintings in a central role in early religion, as images for worship. Others focus on a painting's physical context—this means examining relationships between figures to determine, the absence of an artificial frame, a ground-line or a landscape, whether multiple animal images indicate individual specimens or a herd, and whether these images represent a mythical past for early communities. Do Lascaux's *Rhinoceros, Wounded Man, and Bison* (see fig. 1.4) constitute separate images or the earliest known narrative—the gory tale of a hunt, perhaps, or a shaman's encounter with his spirit creature? Multiple animal engravings, one on top of another, as at Les Trois Frères (fig. **1.7**), may have recorded animal migrations throughout the passing seasons.

Assessing physical context also means recognizing that a cave 15 feet deep is a very different kind of space from another over a mile deep, and was possibly used for different purposes. Paintings in the spacious Hall of the Bulls at Lascaux and the stick man at the same site, located at the bottom of a 16-foot well shaft, may have functioned differently. It means factoring in the experiential aspects of caves: In order to reach these images, a prehistoric viewer had to contend with a precarious path, eerie flickering lights, echoing sounds, and the musty smells that permeate subterranean spaces, all of which added texture to the viewing process (fig. **1.8**). Most important, recent interpretations acknowledge that one explanation may not suffice for all times and places. For instance, even if sympathetic magic makes sense of the *Chinese Horse* from Lascaux with its distended belly (see f[...] 1.3), it hardly explains the art at Chauvet, where fully 72 perce[...] of the animals represented were not hunted, judging by organic remains found in the cave.

1.6   *Spotted Horses and Human Hands*, Pech-Merle Cave, Dordogne, France. Horses ca. 16,000 BCE; hands ca. 15,000 BCE. Limestone, approximate length 11′2″ (3.4 m)

Paleolithic Carving

Prehistoric artists also carved and modeled sculptures in a variety of materials. At just under a foot high, a carved figure from Hohlenstein-Stadel in Germany (fig. **1.9**) represents a standing creature, half human and half feline, crafted out of mammoth ivory. Although it is now in a poor state of preservation, the creation of this figure, with rudimentary stone tools, was clearly an arduous business. It involved splitting the dried mammoth tusk, scraping it into shape, and using a sharp flint blade to incise such features as the striations on the arm and the muzzle. Strenuous polishing followed, using powdered hematite (an iron ore) as an abrasive. Exactly what the figure represents is unclear. Like the hybrid figures painted on cave walls (see fig. 1.4), it may represent a human dressed as an animal, possibly for hunting purposes. Some prehistorians have named these composite creatures shamans or "sorcerers," who could contact the spirit world through ritualistic behavior.

As in cave paintings, animals were frequent subjects for sculpture. A miniature horse from a cave in Vogelherd along the Danube River in Germany, and a pair of interlocked ibexes, date

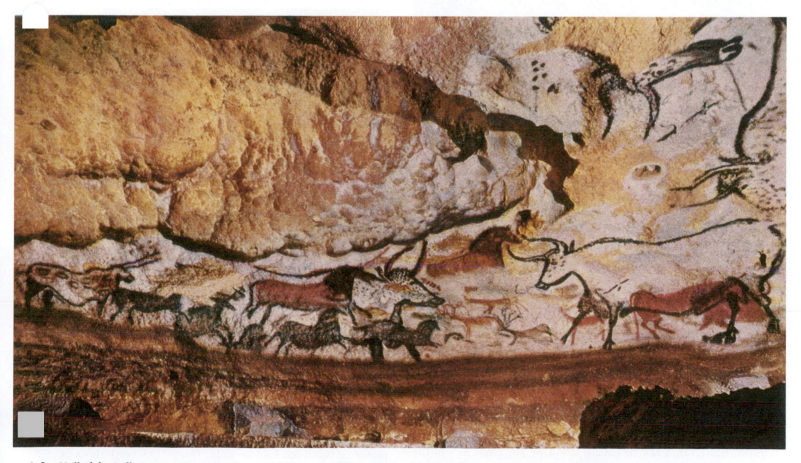

1.8   *Hall of the Bulls,* Lascaux Cave, Dordogne, France. ca. 15,000–13,000 BCE. Largest bull approximate length 11'6" (3.5 m)

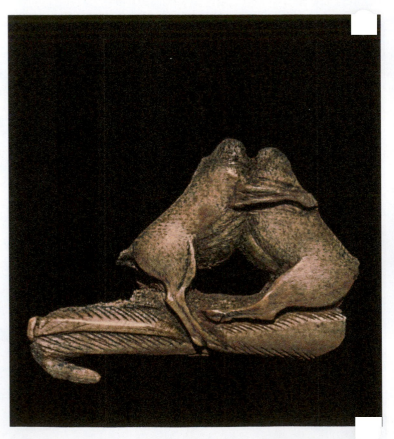

1.10 *Horse*, from Vogelherd Cave, Germany. ca. 28,000 BCE. Mammoth ivory, height 2″ (5 cm). Institut für Urgeschichte, Universität Tübingen

1.9 Hybrid figure with a human body and feline head, from Hohlenstein-Stadel cave, Asselfingen (Baden-Württemberg), Germany. ca. 40,000–35,000 BCE. Mammoth ivory, height 12¼″ (31.1 cm). Ulmer Museum, Ulm, Germany

to the beginning and end of the Upper Paleolithic era (figs. **1.10** and **1.11**). The horse is one of many portable carvings in woolly mammoth ivory created around 28,000 BCE. A small hole between its front legs suggests that it was a pendant. The ibexes, carved from reindeer ANTLER around 13,000 BCE, functioned as a spear-thrower. Once attached to a spear by the hook at the end of its shaft, it allowed a hunter to propel the weapon more effectively. The sculptor had an eye for strong outlines and finished the surface with painstaking care, marking the ibexes' coats with nicks from a stone tool and working up a high polish.

Just as cave artists sometimes transformed bulges in rock walls into painted animals, so, deep within a cave at Le Tuc d'Audoubert in the French Pyrenees, around 13,000 BCE, a sculptor used clay to build up a natural outcropping of rock into two bison (fig. **1.12**); a calf originally stood by the front legs of the right-hand figure. Each sculpture is about 2 feet long; their forms

1.11 *Spear Thrower with Interlocking Ibexes*, Grotte d'Enlène, Ariège, France. ca. 16,000 BCE. Reindeer antler, 3½ × 2¾″ (9 × 7 cm). Musée de l'Homme, Paris

Telling Time: Labels and Periods

While geologists have developed methods for dividing time based on the age of the Earth, historians have used the activity of toolmaking as the defining feature when measuring human time. For the era before the written word (prehistory), patterns apparent in stone tools serve as the basis for distinguishing different cultures. The Stone Age stretches from about 2 million years ago to about 2000 BCE.

Prehistorians divide this broad span of time into the Paleolithic or Old Stone Age (from the Greek *palaio-*, meaning "ancient," and *lithos*, meaning "stone"), the Mesolithic or Middle (*meso-*) Stone Age, and the Neolithic or New (*neo-*) Stone Age. The Paleolithic era reaches from 2 million years ago to about 10,000 BCE and the Mesolithic from about 10,000 to 8000 BCE. The Neolithic era spans from about 8000 to about 2000 BCE. At some time during the third millennium BCE, humans in some parts of the world replaced stone tools with tools made of metal, ushering in the Bronze Age in Europe and Asia.

Specific human cultures reached these phases at different times: The beginning of the Neolithic era appears to start earlier in western Asia than in Europe, for example. Yet the broad span of the Paleolithic era requires further refinement, and excavations of Paleolithic sites provide another framework for dividing time. The oldest material is at the bottom of an excavation, so scholars call the oldest Paleolithic era the Lower Paleolithic (ending about 100,000 years ago). The middle layers of Paleolithic excavations—thus the Middle Paleolithic era—date from 100,000 to about 40,000 years ago. The most recent layers in such excavations are called the Upper Paleolithic, and date from about 40,000 to around 8000 BCE.

Archaeologists have used many sites and different types of tools and tool-making technologies to identify specific culture groups within the Upper Paleolithic period. For example, they name the Aurignacian culture for Aurignac, a site in western France. The objects from this culture date from about 34,000 to 23,000 BCE. The Gravettian culture is named for La Gravette, a site in southwestern France, and dates from about 28,000 to 22,000 BCE. The most recent of these cultures is the Magdalenian, named for a site in southwestern France called La Magdaleine, with dates ranging from around 18,000 to 10,000 BCE. Many of these terms were coined in the nineteenth century, when the study of prehistoric culture first took root.

The Paleolithic Age

Lower Paleolithic	**2,000,000–100,000** BCE
Middle Paleolithic	**100,000–40,000** BCE
Upper Paleolithic	**40,000–10,000** BCE
Aurignacian	34,000–23,000 BCE
Gravettian	28,000–22,000 BCE
Solutrean	22,000–18,000 BCE
Magdalenian	18,000–10,000 BCE
Mesolithic	**10,000–8000** BCE
Neolithic	**8000–2000** BCE

1.12 *Two Bison*, Le Tuc d'Audoubert Cave, Ariège, France. ca. 13,000 BCE. Clay, length 23⅝″ (60 cm)

swell and taper to approximate the mass of a real bison. Despite the three-dimensional character of the representations (notice the fullness of the haunch and shoulder and the shaggy manes), the sculptures share conventions with cave paintings: The artist rendered them in fairly strict profile, so that they are viewable from one side only, but once again the function of the object is unclear to us. Among the human footprints found near this group are those of a two-year-old child. Along with the baby's handprint in a cave at Bedeilhac in France, and the women's handprints at Chauvet, these caution us against simply reconstructing Paleolithic works of art as the ritual centerpieces of a male-dominated hunting society.

Women were frequent subjects in prehistoric sculpture, especially in the Gravettian period (see *Informing Art*, page 9). In fact, so far do female images outnumber male images at that time that they may be evidence of a matrilineal social structure. In the late nineteenth century, a group of 12 ivory figurines were found together in the Grotte du Pape at Brassempouy in southern France. Among them was the *Woman from Brassempouy* (fig. **1.13**) of about 22,000 BCE. The sculpture is almost complete, depicting a head and long elegant neck. At a mere 1½ inches long, it rests comfortably in the hand, where it may have been most commonly viewed. Also hand-sized is the limestone carving of the nude *Woman of Willendorf* of Austria, from about 28,000 to 25,000 BCE (fig. **1.14**). Discovered in 1908, her figure still bears traces of ocher rubbed onto the carved surface. Both figurines are highly abstract. Instead of rendering the female form with the naturalism found in the representations of animals, the artist reduced it basic shapes. In the case of the *Woman from Brassempouy*, the artist rendered the hair schematically with deep vertical gouges and shallow horizontal cross-lines. There is no mouth and only the suggestion of a nose; hollowed-out, overhanging eye sockets and holes cut on either side of the bridge of the nose evoke eyes. The quiet power and energy of the figure reside in the dramatic way its meticulously polished surface responds to shifting light, suggesting movement and life.

The abstract quality of the *Woman of Willendorf* appears to stress a potent fertility. This kind of abstraction appears in many other figurines as well; indeed, some incomplete figurines depict only female genitalia. Facial features are not a priority: schematically rendered hair covers the entire head. Emphasis rests on the figure's reproductive qualities: Diminutive arms sit on pendulous breasts, whose rounded forms are echoed in the extended belly and copious buttocks. Genitalia are shown between large thighs.

The terminology applied to figures like the *Woman from Brassempouy* and the *Woman of Willendorf* in the past has complicated our interpretations of them. At the time of the first discovery of such female figurines in the mid-nineteenth century, scholars named them "Venus" figures: Venus is the Roman goddess of love (Aphrodite in the Greek world), whom ancient sculptors portrayed as a nude female; nineteenth-century archaeologists believed the prehistoric figures to be similar to the Roman goddess, in function if not in form. Today, we tend to avoid such anachronisms in terminology. We do not know whether the

1.13 *Woman from Brassempouy*, Grotte du Pape, Brassempouy, France. ca. 22,000 BCE. Ivory, height 1½″ (3.6 cm). Musée des Antiquités Nationales, Saint-Germain-en-Laye

1.14 *Woman of Willendorf*. ca. 28,000–25,000 BCE. Limestone, height 4⅜″ (11.1 cm). Naturhistorisches Museum, Vienna

1.15 House at Mezhirich, Ukraine. 16,000–10,000 BCE. Mammoth bone

discovered a series of oval dwellings with central hearths, dating to between 16,000 and 10,000 BCE (fig. **1.15**). The distinctive feature of these huts was that they were constructed out of mammoth bones: interlocked pelvis bones, jawbones and shoulder blades provided a framework, and tusks were set across the top. The inhabitants probably covered the frame with animal hides. Archaeological evidence shows that inside these huts they prepared foods, manufactured tools, and processed skins. Since these are cold-weather occupations, archaeologists conclude that the structures were seasonal residences for mobile groups, who returned to them for months at a time over the course of several years.

NEOLITHIC ART

Around 10,000 BCE, the climate began to warm, and the ice that had covered almost a third of the globe started to recede, leaving Europe with more or less the geography it has today. New vegetation and changing animal populations caused human habits to mutate, especially in relation to their environment. In the Neolithic period, or New Stone Age, they began to build more substantial structures, choosing fixed settlement places on the basis of favorable qualities such as a water supply, rather than moving seasonally. Instead of hunting and gathering what nature supplied, they domesticated animals and plants. This gradual change occurred at different moments across the world; in some places, hunting and gathering are still the way of life today.

Settled Societies and Neolithic Art

The earliest evidence of these adjustments to environmental shifts appears in the fertile regions of the eastern Mediterranean and Mesopotamia, between the Euphrates and Tigris rivers. A small settlement developed in the ninth millennium BCE by the Jordan River at the site of Jericho, of biblical fame, in the present West Bank territory. Over time its inhabitants built houses of

Woman of Willendorf represents a specific woman, or a generic or ideal woman. Indeed, she may not represent the idea of woman at all, but rather the notion of reproduction or, as some have argued, the fertile natural world itself. The emphasis on the reproductive features has suggested to many that she may have been a fertility object; the intention may have been to ensure a successful birth outcome rather than an increase in the number of pregnancies. According to one feminist view, the apparently distorted forms of figures like this specifically reflect a woman's view of her own body as she looked down at it. If so, some of the figures may have served as obstetric aids, documenting different stages of pregnancy to educate women toward healthy births. Moreover, this may indicate that at least some of the artists were women.

Paleolithic Houses

the Paleolithic period, people generally built small huts and used caves for shelter and ritual purposes. In rare cases, traces of dwellings survive. At Mezhirich, in the Ukraine, a local farmer

1.16 Neolithic plastered skull, from Jericho, Jordan. ca. 7000 BCE. Life-size. Archaeological Museum, Amman

sun-baked mud brick on stone foundations. They plastered the floors and crafted roofs of branches and earth. Skeletal remains indicate that they buried the bodies of their dead beneath the floors; they displayed the skulls separately above ground, reconstructing them with tinted plaster to resemble flesh, and crafting eyes of seashell fragments (fig. **1.16**). The subtlety of their modeling, and the close observation of the interplay between flesh and bone, make these works remarkably lifelike, each as individual as the skulls they encased. Perhaps these funerary practices reflect a concept of an afterlife; at the very least, they suggest a respect for the dead or even ancestor worship. Around 7500 BCE, the people of Jericho, now numbering over 2,000, dug a wide ditch and raised a solid stone wall around their town, which by this time had expanded to cover some 10 acres. Built with only the simplest stone tools, the wall was 5 feet thick and over 13 feet high. Into it they set a massive circular tower, perhaps one of several, 28 feet tall and 33 feet in diameter at the base, with a staircase inside providing access to the summit (fig. **1.17**). The wall may have functioned as a fortification system against neighboring settlements, or as a barrier against rising floodwaters. With its construction, monumental architecture was born.

1.17 Jericho, Jordan (aerial view)

At Ain Ghazal, near Amman in Jordan, over 30 fragmentary plaster figures, dating to the mid-seventh millennium BCE, represent a starkly different sculptural tradition from the Jericho heads (fig. 1.18). Some are only bust-size, but the tallest statues, when restored, are 3 feet in height, and constitute the first known large-scale sculptures. Conservators have studied the construction technique of these figures, and conclude that large size was the motivating force behind their design, directly resulting in their flat, shallow appearance. These investigations have shown that artists applied plaster to bundles of fresh reeds, bound with cordage, which they kept horizontal during the assembly process. They added the legs separately, then applied paint and added cowrie shells for eyes, darkened with bitumen (a black, tarlike substance) for pupils. Once the plaster was dry, they stood the fragile figures upright and probably added wigs and clothing. Like the Jericho heads, the figures may have represented ancestors. Alternatively, as some of the bodies are two-headed, they may have had a mythical function.

1.19   Reconstruction of Çatal Hüyük, Turkey

ÇATAL HÜYÜK   In Anatolia (modern Turkey), excavations since 1961 have revealed a Neolithic town at Çatal Hüyük, dating from about 7500 BCE, a thousand years later than Jericho (see map 1.1). Flourishing through trade in ores—principally obsidian, a highly valued glasslike volcanic stone, used to make strong, sharp blades—the town developed rapidly through at least 12 successive building phases between 6500 and 5700 BCE. Its most distinctive feature is that it lacked streets, and the mud-brick and timber houses had no doors at ground level: Each house stood side by side with the next, accessed by ladder through a hole in the roof that doubled as a smoke vent (fig. 1.19). The advantages of this design were structural—each house buttressing the next—and defensive, since any attacker would have to scale the outer walls before facing resistance on the rooftops. The design also made economic use of available building stone and provided thick-walled insulation. The rooms inside accommodated activities ranging from working and cooking to sleeping, on platforms lining the walls. As at Jericho, burials were beneath the floor.

In most of the rooms at Çatal Hüyük, plaster covered the walls; often it was painted. Many of the paintings depict animal hunts, with small human figures running around disproportionately large bulls or stags. The images have a static quality, quite unlike the earlier cave paintings that seem to embody motion. One unusual painting in an early room appears to depict rows of irregular blocklike houses, and probably represents Çatal Hüyük itself (fig. 1.20). Above the town, a bright red feature spotted with black and topped with black lines and dots may represent Hasan Dag, a twin-peaked volcano in view of the town. If archaeologists have properly identified this site, the image is the first known landscape painting. It may indicate a sense of community

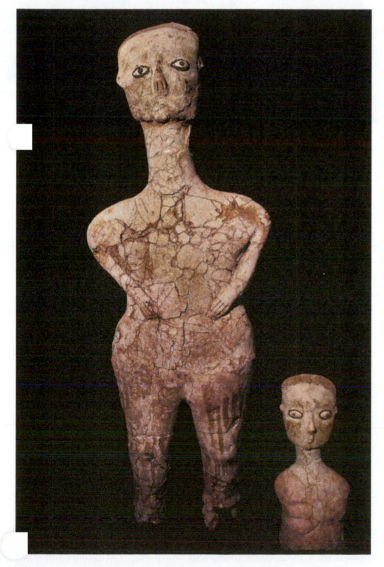

1.18   Human figures, from Ain Ghazal, Jordan. ca. 6750–6250 BCE. Height of larger figure 33″ (84 cm). Department of Antiquities, Amman

1.20   *View of Town and Volcano*, Shrine VII.14, Çatal Hüyük. ca. 6000 BCE. Wall painting

in this early settlement, with inhabitants specifically identifying themselves with place. Some archaeologists speculate that the more ornate rooms at Çatal Hüyük functioned as shrines; in some of them, bulls' horns and plaster breasts may have signified fertility (fig. **1.21**).

1.21   *Animal Hunt.* Restoration of Main Room, Shrine A.III.1, Çatal Hüyük. ca. 6000 BCE (after Mellaart)

OVEN-FIRED POTTERY   A number of new technologies that developed during the Neolithic period collectively suggest the beginnings of specialization. As the community could count on a regular food supply, some of its members were able to devote time to acquiring special skills. These included pottery, weaving, and the smelting of copper and lead. Oven-fired pottery is extremely durable, and often survives in the form of discarded shards. Though absent from early Jericho, a great variety of clay vessels painted with abstract forms survive in regions stretching from Mesopotamia, where pottery may have originated in the sixth millennium BCE, to Egypt and Anatolia, where it was discovered at Çatal Hüyük (see map 1.1) and other settlements. Archaeologists have found pottery from this period in the Balkans, and by about 3500 BCE the technology of pottery making appeared in western Europe.

In Europe, artists also used clay to fashion figurines, such as a woman and man from Cernavoda in Romania, of about 3500 BCE (fig. **1.22**). Like the *Woman of Willendorf* and the Ain Ghazal figurines, they are highly abstract, yet their forms are more linear than rounded: The woman's face is a flattened ov poised on a long, thick neck, and sharp edges articulate her co poreality—across her breasts, for instance, and at the fold of her pelvis. Elbowless arms meet where her hands rest on her raised

1.22 Female and male figures, from Cernavoda, Romania. ca. 3500 BCE. Ceramic, height 4½″ (11.5 cm). National Museum of Antiquities, Bucharest

knee, delineating a triangle and enclosing space within the sculptural form. This emphasizes the figurine's three-dimensionality, encouraging a viewer to look at it from several angles, moving around it or shifting it in the hand. The abstraction highlights the pose; yet, tempting as it may be to interpret this, perhaps as coquettishness, we should be cautious about reading meaning into it, since gestures can have dramatically different meanings from one culture to another. Found in a tomb, the couple may represent the deceased, or mourners; perhaps they were gifts that had a separate purpose before burial.

Architecture in Europe: Tombs and Rituals

Neolithic people of western and northern Europe framed their dwellings mostly in wood, with walls of wattle (branches woven into a frame) and daub (mud or earth dried around the wattle) and roofs of thatch, which rarely survive. At Skara Brae, on the island of Orkney just off the northern tip of Scotland, is a group of ten houses built of stone, dating to between 3100 and 2600 BCE. The builders sunk them into mounds for protection against the harsh weather, and connected them by covered passages. A typical house had a square room, with walls of flat unmortared stones (fig. **1.23**). Driftwood and whalebone supported a roof of turf thatch. At the center of the room was a hearth for cooking, and the inhabitants built furniture—such as beds and shelving—out of large flat stones.

It was a concern for ceremonial burial and ritual, rather than for protection, that inspired Neolithic people of western and northern Europe to create monumental architecture. They defined spaces for tombs and rituals with huge blocks of stone known as **megaliths**. Often they mounted the blocks in a **trilithic** (three-stone) **post-and-lintel** arrangement (with two upright stones supporting a third horizontal capstone) (see fig. 1.25) to construct tombs for the dead with one or more chambers. Termed

1.23 House at Skara Brae, Orkney, Scotland. ca. 3100–2600 BCE

dolmen tombs, they were both impressive and durable. At some sites, upright megaliths known as **menhirs** marked out horizontal space in distinct ways, and perhaps served as ritual centers. Between 4250 and 3750 BCE at Ménec, in the Carnac region on the south coast of Brittany (see map 1.1), over 3,000 megaliths set upright at regular intervals in long, straight rows stretch out over 2 miles (3 km). Typically, the smaller stones of about 3 feet in height stand at the eastern end, and, gradually, the height of the stones increases, reaching over 13 feet at the western end (fig. **1.24**). Scholars argue that the lines, with their east–west orientation, gauged the sun's position in the sky at different times of the year, functioning as a calendar for an agrarian people whose sustenance depended on the sun's cycle. Quarrying, shaping, transporting, and erecting these blocks was an extraordinary feat. Quite apart from remarkable engineering expertise, it required a highly efficient organization of manpower. The resulting monument, with its simple repeated forms identical in shape yet diverse in size, static yet cast into motion by the sun's slow and constant passage, has a calm grandeur and majesty that imposes quiet order on the open landscape.

Often, megaliths appear in circles, known as cromlechs. This is the prevalent arrangement in Britain, where the best-known megalithic structure is Stonehenge, on the Salisbury Plain (figs. 1.25 and 1.26). What now appears as a unified design is in fact the result of at least four construction phases, beginning with a huge ditch defining a circle some 330 feet in diameter in the white chalk ground, and an embankment of over 6 feet running around the inside. A wide stone-lined avenue led from the circle to a pointed gray sandstone (sarsen) megalith, known today as the Heel Stone. By about 2100 BCE, Stonehenge had grown into a horseshoe-shaped arrangement of five sarsen triliths, encircled by a ring of upright blocks capped with a lintel; between the rings was a circle of smaller bluestone blocks. Recent excavations exposed remains of a similar monument built of wood 2 miles (3 km) away, as well as remnants of a village. Archaeologists believe the structures are related.

Exactly what Stonehenge—and its nearby counterpart—signified to those who constructed them is a tantalizing mystery. Many prehistorians believe that Stonehenge, like Ménec, marked the passing of time. Given its monumentality, most also concur that it had a ritual function, perhaps associated with burial; its careful circular arrangement supports this conjecture, as circles are central to rituals in many societies. Indeed, these two qualities led medieval observers to believe that King Arthur's magician, Merlin, created Stonehenge, and it continues to draw crowds on summer solstices. What is certain is that, like Ménec,

Dating Techniques

One of the chief concerns of archaeologists and art historians, regardless of the period in which they conduct research, is to be able to place works of art in a historical context. This means that dating an object is of paramount importance. Scholars assign two types of date: relative dates and absolutes dates. A relative date indicates that one object is older or more recent than another. To determine these dates, archaeologists tend to use stratigraphy: An object found at a lower layer or *stratum* of an excavation is normally older than an object found above it. The relative chronology of one site can be transferred to another site if objects of a similar kind appear at both. Pottery is a useful indicator of relative date for most ancient cultures because it is so durable that it exists in great profusion, often in an uninterrupted sequence.

Absolute dating assigns a calendar date to an object. In historical cultures (those with written documents), written records might preserve a date. For instance, building inscriptions indicate that the Athenians constructed the Parthenon between 447 and 432 BCE. Researchers have developed numerous other methods for establishing absolute dates. These include radiometric dating, which works well for dating organic materials up to approximately 40,000 years old. Living organisms contain radioactive isotopes (such as carbon-14) that decay at a known rate after its death. By measuring the level of isotopes in organic material, archaeologists can gauge when it lived. Though effective, this method requires destroying part of the object, and can only establish when an organism died, not when an artist turned it into an artifact.

Some other techniques measure radiation levels. For instance, thermoluminescence is an effective dating technique for objects containing crystalline materials that have been exposed to high temperatures—such as pottery, which has been fired. Heat releases electrons trapped in the object's crystalline lattice, resulting in a "zeroing" radiation moment. Thereafter, electrons accumulate again. By measuring the luminescence (light, which is proportional to the number of electrons released) of the object during a second heating, archaeologists can determine the length of time since the zeroing event.

1.24   Menhir alignments at Ménec, Carnac, France. ca. 4250–3750 BCE

1.25   Stonehenge (aerial view), Salisbury Plain, Wiltshire, England. ca. 2100 BCE. Diameter of circle 97′ (29.6 m)

Stonehenge represents tremendous organization of labor and engineering skill. The largest trilith, at the center of the horseshoe, soars 24 feet, supporting a lintel 15 feet long and 3 feet thick. The sarsen blocks weigh up to 50 tons apiece, and traveled 23 miles (37 km) from the Marlborough Downs; the bluestones originated 200 miles (320 km) away, in the Welsh Preseli mountains. The blocks reveal evidence of meticulous stone working. Holes hollowed out of the capstones fit snugly over projections on the uprights (forming a mortise-and-tenon joint), to make a stable structure. Moreover, upright megaliths taper upward, with a central bulge, visually implying the weight they bear, and capturing an energy that gives life to the stones. The lintels are worked in two directions, their faces inclining outward by about 6 inches to appear vertical from the ground, while at the same time they curve around on the horizontal plane to make a smooth circle. Art historians usually associate this kind of refinement with the Parthenon of Classical Athens (see fig. 5.40).

Prehistoric art raises many questions. While we know humans began to express themselves visually during the prehistoric age, there are no written records to explain their intentions. Even so, by the end of the era, people had established techniques of painting, sculpting, and pottery making, and begun to construct monumental works of architecture. They developed a strong sense of the power of images and spaces: They recognized how to produce naturalistic and abstract figures, and how to alter space in sophisticated ways.

1.26   Diagram of original arrangement of stones at Stonehenge

Prehistoric Art

ca. 28,000–25,000 BCE
Woman of Willendorf

16,000–10,000 BCE Mammoth bone houses at Mezhirich

ca. 13,000 BCE Clay sculpture of two bison crafted on a rock outcropping

ca. 7500 BCE Jericho's fortification system; beginning of monumental architecture

ca. 3100–2600 BCE
Stone houses at
Skara Brae

ca. 2100 BCE Final phase of construction at Stonehenge

40,000 BCE

30,000 BCE

20,000 BCE

10,000 BCE

5000 BCE

4000 BCE

3000 BCE

2000 BCE

◄ ca. 38,000 BCE Humans produce the earliest objects classed as "art"

◄ ca. 32,000 BCE Oldest-known cave paintings, at Chauvet

◄ ca. 10,000 BCE Earth's climate gradually begins to warm

◄ Sixth millennium BCE Pottery may have originated in Mesopotamia

◄ ca. 3500 BCE Pottery manufacturing appears in Western Europe

CHAPTER 2

Ancient Near Eastern Art

GROWING AND STORING CROPS AND RAISING ANIMALS FOR FOOD, the signature accomplishments of Neolithic peoples, would gradually change the course of civilization. Not long before they ceased to follow wild animal herds and gather food to survive, people began to form permanent settlements. By the end of the Neolithic era, these settlements grew

beyond the bounds of the village into urban centers. In the fourth millennium BCE, large-scale urban communities of as many as 40,000 people began to emerge in Mesopotamia, the land between the Tigris and Euphrates rivers. The development of cities had tremendous ramifications for the development of human life and for works of art.

Although today the region of Mesopotamia is largely an arid plain, written, archaeological, and artistic evidence indicates that at the dawn of civilization lush vegetation covered it. By mastering irrigation techniques, populations there exploited the rivers and their tributaries to enrich the fertile soil even further. New technologies and inventions, including the wheel and the plow, and the casting of tools in copper and bronze, increased food production and facilitated trade. As communities flourished, they grew into city-states with distinct patterns of social organization to address the problems of urban life. Specialization of labor and trade, mechanisms for the resolution of disputes, and construction of defensible walls all required a central authority and government.

It was probably the efficient administration that developed in response to these needs that generated what may have been the earliest writing system, beginning around 3400–3200 BCE, consisting of pictograms pressed into clay with a stylus to create inventories. By around 2900 BCE, the Mesopotamians had refined the pictograms into a series of wedge-shaped signs known as **cuneiform** (from *cuneus*, Latin for "wedge"). They used this system for administrative accounts and the Sumerian *Epic of Gilgamesh* in the late third millennium BCE. Cuneiform writing continued through much of the ancient era in the Near East and formed a cultural link between diverse groups who established power in the region. With the invention of writing, we enter the realm of history.

The geography of Mesopotamia had other profound effects on developing civilizations. Unlike the narrow, fertile strip of the Nile Valley in Egypt, protected by deserts on either side, where urban communities now also began to thrive, Mesopotamia is a wide, shallow trough, crisscrossed by the two rivers and their tributaries and with few natural defenses. People wanting to exploit its fertile soil constantly traversed the region, entering easily from any direction. Indeed, the history of the ancient Near East is a multicultural one; city-states were constantly at war with one another and only sometimes united under a single ruler. Still, Mesopotamian visual culture retains a surprisingly constant character. Two dominant themes emerge: Art enabled and reflected political power; and Mesopotamians used visual narrative, exploring strategies for telling stories through art.

Detail of figure 2.33, *Peroz I (457–483) or Kavad I hunting rams.*

Map 2.1   The Ancient Near East

2.1   Babylonian deed of sale. ca. 1750 BCE. This deed graphically shows the impressions made by the stylus in the soft clay. Department of Western Asiatic Antiques, No. 33236. The British Museum, London

SUMERIAN ART

The first major civilization in Mesopotamia was in the southern region of Sumer, near the junction of the Tigris and Euphrates rivers, where several city-states flourished from before 4(BCE (map 2.1) until about 2340 BCE. Who the Sumerians were is not clear; often scholars can establish linkages between peoples through common linguistic traditions, but Sumerian is not related to any other known tongue. Archaeological excavations since the middle of the nineteenth century have unearthed many clay tablets with cuneiform writing including inventories and lists of kings, as well as poetry (fig. 2.1). Many of the earliest excavations concentrated on Sumerian cities mentioned in the Bible, such as Ur (the birthplace of Abraham) and Uruk (the biblical Erech). Along with architecture and writing, works of art in the form of sculpture, **relief**, and pottery inform us about Sumerian society.

For Sumerians, life itself depended on appeasing the gods, who controlled natural forces and phenomena such as weather and water, the fertility of the land, and the movement of heavenly bodies. Each city had a patron deity, to whom residents owed both devotion and sustenance. The god's earthly steward was the city's ruler, who directed an extensive administrative staff based in the temple. As the produce of the city's land belonged to the god, the temple staff took charge of supplying farmers with seed, work animals, and tools. They built irrigation systems, and stored and distributed the harvest. Centralized food production meant that much of the population could specialize in other trades. In turn, they donated a portion of the fruits of their labor to t temple. This system is known as theocratic socialism.

Mud Brick

Mud brick was made primarily from local clay. Raw clay absorbs water, and then cracks after drying. As a binding agent and to provide elasticity and prevent cracking, Sumerian builders would add vegetable matter, such as straw, to the clay. By forcing the mud mixture into wooden frames, the brick makers obtained uniformly rectangular bricks. They then knocked the molded bricks out of the frames and placed them in the sun to bake. To erect walls, they joined the bricks together with wet clay. One disadvantage of mud brick is that it is not durable. The Sumerians would therefore seal important exterior walls with bitumen, a tarlike substance, or they would use glazed bricks. Sometimes they covered interior walls with plaster.

Mud brick is not a material that readily excites the imagination today (in the way that, for instance, marble does), and because it is so highly perishable, it has rarely survived from ancient times to indicate how Sumerian temples might once have looked. However, more recent examples of mud-brick architecture like the kasbahs (citadels) south of Morocco's Atlas mountains, at Aït Ben Haddou and elsewhere, reveal the extraordinary potential of the material. There, the easy pliability of mud brick allows for a dramatic decorative effect that is at once man-made and in total harmony with the natural colors of the earth. Notice, too, the geometric designs echoed in the woodwork of doorways and windows.

t constructed in the sixteenth century CE, these buildings ergo constant maintenance (recently funded by UNESCO) to undo the weather's frequent damage. Naturally, Sumerian temples may have looked quite different, but the kasbahs serve as a useful reminder that mud-brick construction can produce magnificent results.

Mud-brick kasbahs at Aït Ben Haddou, Morocco

Mud bricks at Aït Ben Haddou, Morocco

Temple Architecture: Linking Heaven and Earth

The temple was the city's architectural focus. Good stone being scarce, Sumerians built predominantly with mud brick covered with plaster. (See *Materials and Techniques*, above).

Scholars distinguish two different types of Sumerian temple. "Low" temples sat at ground level. Usually their four corners were oriented to the cardinal points of the compass. The temple was tripartite: Rooms serving as offices, priests' quarters, and storage areas lined a rectangular main room, or **cella**, on its two long sides. The essential characteristics of "high" temples were similar, except that a platform raised the building above ground level; these platforms were gradually transformed into squat, stepped pyramids known as **ziggurats**. The names of ne ziggurats—such as Etemenanki at Babylon ("House temple, nd between heaven and earth")—suggest that they may have been links or portals to the heavens, where priest and god could commune.

At approximately 40 to 50 feet high (at Warka and Ur), ziggurats functioned analogously as mountains, which held a sacred status for Sumerians. A source of water flowing to the valleys, mountains were also a place of refuge during floods, and symbolized the Earth's generative power. Indeed, Sumerians knew their mother goddess as the Lady of the Mountain. Significantly, raised platforms made temples more visible. Mesopotamian texts indicate that the act of seeing was paramount: In seeing an object and finding it pleasing, a god might act favorably toward those who made it. The desired response of a human audience, in turn, was wonder. Finally, there was probably a political dimension to the high platform: It emphasized and maintained the priests' status by visually expressing their separation from the rest of the community.

Around 3500 BCE, the city of Uruk (present-day Warka and the biblical Erech) emerged as a center of Sumerian culture, flourishing from trade in its agricultural surplus. One of its temples, the White Temple, named for its whitewashed brick surfaces, probably honored the sky-god Anu, chief of the Sumerian gods (fig. **2.2**). It sits on a 40-foot mound constructed by filling in the ruins of older temples with brickwork, which suggests that the site itself was sacred (fig. **2.3**). Recessed brickwork articulated its sloped sides. A system of stairs and ramps led counterclockwise around the mound, culminating at an entrance in the temple's long north side. This indirect approach is characteristic of Mesopotamian temple architecture (in contrast to the direct axial approach favored in Egypt), and the winding ascent mirrored a visitor's metaphorical ascent into a divine realm. From three sides, members of the community could also witness the ceremonial ascent of priests and leaders who had exclusive access to the temple. Enough survives of the superstructure to indicate that thick buttressed walls surrounded a central, rectangular hall (cella) housing a stepped **altar**. Along the long sides of the cella were smaller rooms, creating an overall tripartite layout typical of the earliest temples.

Uruk was the home of the legendary king Gilgamesh, hero of an epic poem that describes his adventures. Gilgamesh purportedly carved his tale on a stone marker—which suggests the importance of narrative in Sumerian culture. The epic credits Gilgamesh with building the city walls of Uruk and the Eanna, a temple of Inanna (goddess of love and war) or Ishtar. The poem describes the temple's gleaming walls, built with "kiln-fired brick." In the Eanna precinct, archaeologists found several temples whose walls were decorated with colored stone or painted clay cones set into plaster to form mosaic patterns. (See *Primary Source*, page 25.)

2.2   Plan of the White Temple on its ziggurat (after H. Frankfort)

2.3   Remains of the White Temple on its ziggurat. ca. 3500–3000 BCE. Uruk (Warka), Iraq. Photographed during excavations in 1935–36

The Gilgamesh Epic

.. of the earliest written epics, the Gilgamesh epic survives on
.eiform tablets. Although the earliest texts to survive come from
Akkadian tablets written after 2150 BCE, the text itself dates to the
Sumerian era, about 2800 BCE. The surviving parts of the epic recount
the tale of Gilgamesh, the king of Uruk, who first battles, then befriends
the wild man Enkidu. When his friend dies, Gilgamesh goes in search
of a way to defeat death, but eventually returns to Uruk, accepting his
own mortality. This excerpt from the beginning of the poem describes
(with gaps from the sources) Gilgamesh's accomplishments as king.

Anu granted him the totality of knowledge of all.
He saw the Secret, discovered the Hidden,
he brought information of (the time) before the Flood.
He went on a distant journey, pushing himself to exhaustion,
but then was brought to peace.
He carved on a stone stela all of his toils,
and built the wall of Uruk-Haven,
the wall of the sacred Eanna Temple, the holy sanctuary.

Look at its wall which gleams like copper(?),
inspect its inner wall, the likes of which no one can equal!
Take hold of the threshold stone—it dates from ancient times!
Go close to the Eanna Temple, the residence of Ishtar,
such as no later king or man ever equaled!
Go up on the wall of Uruk and walk around,
examine its foundation, inspect its brickwork thoroughly.
Is not (even the core of) the brick structure made of kiln-fired
  brick,
and did not the Seven Sages themselves lay out its plans?
One square mile is devoted to city, one to palm gardens, one to
  lowlands, the open area(?) of the Ishtar Temple,
three leagues and the open area(?) of Uruk it (the wall) encloses.
Find the copper tablet box,
open the ... of its lock of bronze,
undo the fastening of its secret opening.
Take out and read the lapis lazuli tablet
how Gilgamesh went through every hardship.

Source: *The Epic of Gilgamesh*, tr. Maureen Gallery Kovacs (Stanford, CA:
Stanford Univ. Press, 1989)

Sculpture and Inlay

The cella of Uruk's White Temple would once have contained a
cult statue, which is now lost. Yet a female head dating to about
3100 BCE, found in the Eanna sanctuary of Inanna at Uruk, may
..icate what a cult statue looked like (fig. **2.4**). The sculptor
carved the face of white limestone, and added details in precious

materials: a wig, perhaps of gold or copper, secured by the ridge
running down the center of the head, and eyes and eyebrows
of colored materials. Despite the absence of these features, the
sculpture has not lost its power to impress: The abstraction of its
large eyes and dramatic brow contrasts forcefully with the delicate modeling of the cheeks. Flat on the back, the head was once
attached to a body, presumably made of wood, and the full figure
must have stood near life-size.

TELL ASMAR A group of sculptures excavated in the 1930s at a
temple at Tell Asmar illustrates a type of limestone, alabaster, and
gypsum figures that artists began to make about 500 years after
the carving of the Uruk head (fig. **2.5**). Ranging in height from
several inches to 2½ feet, these figures probably originally stood
in the temple's cella. They were purposely buried near the altar
along with other objects, perhaps when the temple was rebuilt
or redecorated. All but one of the figures in this group stand in a
static pose, with hands clasped between chest and waist level. The
style is decidedly abstract: On most of the standing male figures,
horizontal or zigzag ridges define long hair and a full beard; the
arms hang from wide shoulders; hands are clasped around a cup;
narrow chests widen to broad waists; and the legs are cylindrical. The male figures wear fringed skirts hanging from a belt in a
stiff cone shape, while the women have full-length drapery. Most
scholars identify the two larger figures as cult statues of Abu, god
of vegetation, and his consort. The others figures probably represent priests, since the fringed skirt is the dress of the priesthood.
Some statues of this kind from elsewhere are inscribed with the
name of the god and of the worshiper who dedicated the statue.

The poses and the costumes represent conventions of Sumerian
art that later Mesopotamians adopted. Most distinctive are the
faces, dominated by wide, almost round eyes. Dark inlays of lapis

2.4   *Female Head*, from Uruk (Warka), Iraq. ca. 3200–3000 BCE.
Limestone, height 8″ (20.3 cm). Iraq Museum, Baghdad

2.5   Statues from the Abu Temple, Tell Asmar, Iraq. ca. 2700–2500 BCE. Limestone, alabaster, and gypsum, height of tallest figure approx. 30″ (76.3 cm). Iraq Museum, Baghdad, and The Oriental Institute Museum of the University of Chicago

lazuli and shells set in bitumen accentuate the eyes, as do powerful eyebrows that meet over the bridge of the nose. As noted above, seeing was a major channel of communication with gods, and the sculptures may have been responding to the god's awe-inspiring nature with eyes wide open in admiration. Enlarged eyes were also a conventional means of warding off evil in Mesopotamia, known today as an **apotropaic device**. Several of these statues were in the Iraq Museum, and were looted during recent unrest in Baghdad (see *The Art Historian's Lens*, page 29).

THE ROYAL CEMETERY AT UR The Sumerian city of Ur in southern Mesopotamia first attracted archaeologists because of its biblical associations. Its extensive cemetery was well preserved under the walls of King Nebuchadnezzar II's later city, and Leonard Woolley discovered a wide variety of Sumerian objects in excavations there during the 1920s. The cemetery contained some 1,840 burials dating between 2600 and 2000 BCE. Some were humble, but others were substantial subterranean structures and contained magnificent offerings, earning them the designation

2.6   *Goat in Thicket (Ram and Tree)*, one of the pair from the Great Death Pit in the Royal Cemetery of Ur, Muqaiyir, Iraq. ca. 2600 BCE. Wood, gold, lapis lazuli, height 20″ (50.8 cm). University Museum, University of Pennsylvania, Philadelphia

2.7 *Royal Standard of Ur*, front and back sides. ca. 2600 BCE. Wood inlaid with shell, limestone, and lapis lazuli, height 8″ (20.3 cm). The British Museum, London

of "royal graves," even though it remains uncertain whether the deceased were royalty, priests, or members of another elite. So-called Death Pits accompanied the wealthiest burials. Foremost among them was the Great Death Pit, in which 74 soldiers, attendants, and musicians were interred, apparently drugged before lying down in the grave as human sacrifices. Even in death, the elite maintained the visible trappings of power and required the services of their retainers. These finds suggest that Sumerians may have believed in an afterlife.

Among the many kinds of grave goods Woolley found in the Royal Cemetery were weapons, jewelry, and vessels. Many of the objects display the great skill of Sumerian artists in representing nature. A pair of wild goats rearing up on their hind legs against a flowering tree probably functioned as stands for offerings to a deity. Gold leaf is the dominant material, used for the goat's head, legs, and genitals, as well as for the tree and a cylindrical support strut rising from the goat's back in the one shown here (fig. **2.6**). Lapis lazuli on the horns and neck fleece complements the shell

fragments decorating the body fleece and the ears of copper. The base is an intricately crafted pattern of red limestone, shell, and lapis lazuli. Images on cylinder seals show that a bowl or saucer would have been balanced on the horns and the support cylinder. The combination of the goat (sacred to the god Tammuz) and the carefully arranged flowers (rosettes sacred to Inanna) suggests that the sculpture reflects Sumerian concerns about fertility, both of plants and animals.

Visual Narratives

Two objects from the Royal Cemetery at Ur offer glimpses of the development of visual narrative in Mesopotamia. The *Royal Standard of Ur*, of about 2600 BCE, consists of four panels of red limestone, shell, and lapis lazuli inlay set in bitumen, originally attached to a wooden framework (fig. **2.7**). The damaged side panels depicted animal scenes, while the two larger sections show a military victory and a celebration or ritual feast, each unfolding

2.8 *Bull Lyre*, from the tomb of Queen Pu-abi, Ur (Muqaiyir), Iraq. ca. 2600 BCE. Wood with gold, lapis lazuli, bitumen, and shell, reassembled in modern wood support. University Museum, University of Pennsylvania, Philadelphia

2.9 Inlay panel from the soundbox of lyre, from Ur (Muqaiyir), Iraq. ca. 2600 BCE. Shell and bitumen, 12¼ × 4½″ (31.1 × 11.3 cm). University Museum, University of Pennsylvania, Philadelphia

in three superposed **registers**, or horizontal bands. Reading from the bottom, the "war" panel shows charioteers advancing from the left, pulled by onagers (wild asses), and riding over enemy bodies. In the middle register, infantry soldiers do battle and escort prisoners of war, stripped of armor and clothing. At the top, soldiers present the prisoners to a central figure, whose importance the artist signals through his position and through his larger size, a device known as **hieratic scale**; his head even breaks through the register's frame to emphasize his importance. In the "banquet" panel, figures burdened with booty accompany onagers and animals for a feast. Their dress identifies them as travelers from northern Sumer and probably Kish, the region later known as Akkad. In the top register, the banquet is already under-way. Seated figures raise their cups to the sound of music from a nearby harpist and singer; a larger figure toward the left of the scene is presumably a leader or king, perhaps the same figure as on the "war" side. Together, the panels represent the dual aspects of kingship: the king as warrior, and the king as priest and mediator with the gods. Despite the action in the scenes, the images have a static quality, which the figures' isolation emphasizes (a staccato treatment): Their descriptive forms (half frontal, half profile)

rarely overlap. This, and the contrasting colored materials, give the narrative an easy legibility, even from a distance.

On excavating the *Royal Standard of Ur*, Woolley envisioned it held aloft on a pole as a military standard, and named it accordingly. In fact, it is unclear how the Sumerians used the object. It may have been the sounding-box for a stringed instrument, an object that was commonly deposited in burials. In one of the cemetery's most lavish graves, the grave of "Queen" Pu-abi, Woolley discovered a lyre decorated with a bull's head of gold gilt and lapis lazuli, dating to ca. 2600 BCE (fig. **2.8**), comparable to the lyre on the *Standard*. On its sounding-box, a panel of shell inlaid in bitumen depicts a male figure in a heraldic composition, embracing two human-faced bulls and facing a viewer with a frontal glare (fig. **2.9**). In the lower registers, animals perform human tasks such as carrying foodstuffs and playing music. These scenes may have evoked a myth or fable that contemporary viewers knew either in written or in oral form, and that was perhaps associated with a funerary context. In so cultures, fantastic hybrid creatures, such as the bulls or the m with a braided, snakelike body in the bottom scene, served an apotropaic function.

Losses Through Looting

The archaeologist's greatest nemesis is the looter, who pillages ancient sites to supply the world's second largest illicit business: the illegal trade in antiquities. The problem is worldwide, but recent publicity has focused on Iraq, where thousands of archaeological sites still await proper excavation. Looters are often local people, living in impoverished conditions but supported and organized by more powerful agents; just as frequently, looters work in organized teams, arriving on site with jackhammers and bulldozers, wielding weapons to overcome whatever meager security there might be. Often employing the most sophisticated tools, such as remote-sensing and satellite photography, they move quickly and unscrupulously through a site, careless of what they destroy in their search for treasure. Loot changes hands quickly as it crosses national borders, fetching vast sums on the market. Little or none of this fortune returns to local hands.

Even more is at stake in these transactions than the loss of a nation's heritage. Only a fraction of the value of an archaeological find resides in the object itself. Much more significant is what its findspot—the place where it was found—can tell archaeologists, who use the information to construct a history of the past. An object's location within a city or building reveals how it was used. A figurine, for instance, could be a fertility object, doll, or cult image, depending on its physical context. The exact level, or stratum, at which archaeologists find an object discloses when it was in use.

On some sites, stratigraphy (reading levels/strata) yields very precise dates. If an object comes to light far from its place of manufacture, its findspot can even document interactions between cultures.

A 1970 UNESCO Convention requires member states to prohibit the importation of stolen antiquities from other member states, and offers help in protecting cultural property that is in jeopardy of pillage. To date, 115 countries are party to the convention.

Looters at the archaeological site of Isin, southern Iraq, January 2004

Cylinder Seals

The Mesopotamians also produced vast numbers of cylinder seals, which the administration used to seal jars and secure storerooms. The seals were cylindrical objects usually made of stone, with a hole running through the center from end to end. A sculptor carved a design into the curved surface of the seal, so that when the owner impressed it in soft clay, a raised, reverse image would unfold, repeated as the cylinder rolled along. Great quantities of seals and sealings (seal impressions) have survived. Many are of modest quality, reflecting their primarily administrative purpose, but the finest examples display a wealth of detail and a high level of sculptural expertise. With subjects ranging from divine and royal scenes to monumental architecture, animals, and daily activities, the seals provide critical information about Mesopotamian existence and values. The sealing illustrated here appears to show the feeding of the temple herd, which provided a significant portion of the temple's wealth (fig. 2.10). The human figure's distinctive costume and hat may identify him as a priest-king; some have seen the large vessels as a reference to sacred offerings, and excavators found one such vase, measuring nearly 3 feet in height, in the Eanna precinct at Uruk, dating to ca. 3200 BCE.

2.10 *Priest-King Feeding Sacred Sheep*, from vicinity of Uruk (Warka), Iraq. ca. 3300 BCE. Cylinder sealing, height 2⅛" (5.4 cm), diameter 1¾" (4.5 cm). Staatliche Museen zu Berlin, Preussischer Kulturbesitz, Vorderasiatisches Museum

ART OF AKKAD

Around 2350 BCE, Sumerian city-states began to fight over access to water and fertile land. Gradually, their social organization was transformed as local "stewards of the god" positioned themselves as ruling kings. The more ambitious tried to enlarge their domains through conquest. Semitic-speaking people (those who used languages in the same family as Hebrew and Arabic) from the northern region gradually assumed positions of power in the south. Although they adopted many features of Sumerian civilization, they were less bound to the tradition of the city-state. Sargon (meaning "true king") conquered Sumer, as well as northern Syria and Elam (to the northeast of Sumer) in about 2334 BCE (see map 2.1), basing himself in the city of Akkad (a site unknown today, but probably to the northwest of Sumer, near present-day Baghdad). Akkadian then became the language of authority in Mesopotamia. Sargon's ambitions were both imperial

and dynastic. He combined Sumerian and Akkadian deities in a new pantheon, hoping to break down the traditional link between city-states and their local gods, and thereby to unite the region in loyalty to his absolute rule. Under his grandson, Naram-S who ruled from 2254 to 2218 BCE, the Akkadian Empire stretched from Sumer in the south to Elam in the east, and then to Syria in the west and Nineveh in the north.

Sculpture: Power and Narrative

Akkadian rulers increasingly exploited the visual arts to establish and reflect their power. A magnificent copper portrait head found in a rubbish heap at Nineveh, dated to between 2250 and 2200 BCE and sometimes identified as Naram-Sin himself (fig. 2.11), derives its extraordinary power from a number of factors: The intended view of the portrait was from the front, and this **frontality** makes it appear unchanging and eternal. The abstract treatment of beard and hair (which is arranged like a Sumerian king's) contrasts with the smooth flesh to give the head a memorable simplicity and strong symmetry, which denote control and order. The intricate, precise patterning of hair and beard testifies to the metalworker's expertise in hollow casting (see *Materials and Techniques*, page 128). Furthermore, at a time before many people understood the science of metallurgy, the use of cast metal for a portrait demonstrated the patron's control of a technology that most associated primarily with weaponry. In its original form, the portrait probably had eyes inlaid with precious and semiprecious materials as other surviving figures do. The damage to the portrait w probably incurred during the Medes' invasion of Nineveh in 612 BCE. The enemy gouged out its eyes and hacked off its ears, nose, and lower beard, as if attacking the person represented. Many cultures, even today, practice such acts of ritualized vandalism as symbolic acts of violence or protest.

The themes of power and narrative combine in a 6½-foot **stele** (upright marker stone) erected in the Akkadian city of Sippar during the rule of Naram-Sin (fig. 2.12). The stele commemorates Naram-Sin's victory over the Lullubi, people of the Zagros mountains in eastern Mesopotamia, in relief. This time the story does not unfold in registers; instead, ranks of soldiers, in composite view, climb the wavy contours of a wooded mountain. Their ordered march contrasts with the enemy's chaotic rout: As the victorious soldiers trample the fallen foe underfoot, the defeated beg for mercy or lie contorted in death. Above them, the king's large scale and central position make his identity clear. He stands isolated against the background, next to a mountain peak that suggests his proximity to the divine. His horned crown, formerly an exclusive accoutrement of the gods, marks him as the first Mesopotamian king to deify himself (an act that his people did not unanimously welcome). The bold musculature of his limbs and his powerful stance cast him as a heroic figure. Solar deities shine auspiciously overhead, as if witnessing his victory.

The stele of Naram-Sin still communicated its message of power over a thousand years later. In 1157 BCE, the Elamites of southwestern Iran invaded Mesopotamia and seized it as war

2.11   *Head of an Akkadian Ruler*, from Nineveh (Kuyunjik), Iraq. ca. 2250–2200 BCE. Copper, height 12″ (30.7 cm). Iraq Museum, Baghdad

2.12 Stele of Naram-Sin.
r. 2254–2218 BCE. Height 6′6″ (2 m).
Musée du Louvre, Paris

2.13 Great Ziggurat of King Urnammu, Ur, Muqaiyir, Iraq. ca. 2100 BCE

booty. An inscription on the stele records that they then installed it in the city of Susa (see map 2.1). By capturing the defeated city's victory monument, they symbolically stole Naram-Sin's former glory and doubly defeated their foe.

NEO-SUMERIAN REVIVAL

The rule of the Akkadian kings came to an end when a mountain people, the Guti, gained control of the Mesopotamian Plain in about 2230 BCE. The cities of Sumer rose up in retaliation and drove them out in 2112 BCE, under the leadership of King Urnammu of Ur (the present-day city of Muqaiyir, Iraq, and the birthplace of the biblical Abraham), who united a realm that was to last 100 years. As part of his renewal project, he returned to building on a magnificent scale.

Architecture: The Ziggurat of Ur

Part of Urnammu's legacy is the Great Ziggurat at Ur of about 2100 BCE, dedicated to the moon god, Nanna (Sin in Akkadian) (fig. **2.13**). Its 190-by-130-foot base soared to a height of 50 feet in three stepped stages. The base consisted of solid mud brick faced with baked bricks set in bitumen, a tarry material used here as mortar. Although not structurally functional, thick **buttresses** (vertical supporting elements) articulate the walls, giving an impression of strength. Moreover, a multitude of upward lines adds a dynamic energy to the monument's appearance. Three staircases, now reconstructed, converged high up at the fortified gateway. Each consisting of 100 steps, one stood perpendicular to the temple, the other two parallel to the base wall. From the gateway, a fourth staircase, which does not survive, once rose to the temple proper. The stairways may have provided an imposing setting for ceremonial processions.

Sculpture: Figures of Gudea

Contemporary with Urnammu's rule in Ur, Gudea became ruler of neighboring Lagash (in present-day Iraq), a small Sumerian city-state that had retained independence after the collapse of Akkad. Reserving the title of king for Lagash's city-god, Ningirsu, Gudea promoted the god's cult through an ambitious reconstruction of his temple. According to inscriptions, Ningirsu appeared to Gudea in a dream after the Tigris River had failed to rise and instructed him to build the temple.

2.14 Head of Gudea, from Lagash (Telloh), Iraq. ca. 2100 BCE. Diorite, height 9⅛″ (23.2 cm). Museum of Fine Arts, Boston. Francis Bartlett Donation of 1912. 26.289

Texts on Gudea Figures from Lagash and Surrounding Areas, c. 2100

Gudea, the ruler of Lagash, commissioned numerous temples and many figures of himself to be placed in the temples. Many of these figures (compare figs. 2.14 and 2.15) are inscribed with cuneiform texts that provide insight into the function of each image.

In this excerpt, the god Ningirsu speaks to Gudea, encouraging him to rebuild his temple:

When, O faithful shepherd Gudea,
Thou shalt have started work for me on Eninnu, my royal abode,

I will call up in heaven a humid wind.
It shall bring thee abundance from on high
And the country shall spread its hands upon riches in thy
   time.
Prosperity shall accompany the laying of the foundations of my
   house.
All the great fields will bear for thee;
Dykes and canals will swell for thee;
Where the water is not wont to rise
To high ground it will rise for thee.
Oil will be poured abundantly in Sumer in thy time,
Good weight of wool will be given in thy time.

Source: H. Frankfort, *The Art and Architecture of the Ancient Orient*, 4th ed.
(New Haven: Yale University Press, 1970, p. 98).

Of the building itself, nothing now remains. Yet some 20 examples of distinctive statues representing Gudea survive. He had dedicated (or given as an offering) the images at the temple and in other shrines of Lagash and vicinity (figs. **2.14** and **2.15**), and they served as a mark of his piety, at the same time as they also extended the Akkadian tradition of exalting the ruler's person. Carved of diorite, a dark stone that was as rare and expensive as it was hard to work, they testify to Gudea's great wealth. Whether standing or seated in pose, the statues are remarkably consistent in appearance: Often wearing a thick woolen cap, Gudea has a long garment draped over one shoulder, and clasps his hands across his front in a pose similar to statues from Tell Asmar of 500 years earlier. Like those figures, Gudea's eyes are wide open, in awe. The highly polished surface and precise modeling allow light to play upon the features, showcasing the sculptors' skills. Rounded forms emphasize the figures' compactness, giving them an impressive monumentality.

In the life-size seated example shown in figure 2.15, Gudea holds the ground plan of Ningirsu's temple on his lap. Inscriptions carved on the statue reveal that the king had to follow the god's instructions meticulously to ensure the temple's sanctity. The inscriptions also provide Gudea's motivation for building the temple, and his personal commitment to the project: By obeying the god, he would bring fortune to his city. (See *Primary Source*, above.) Following Ningirsu's instruction, Gudea purified the city and swept away the soil on the temple's site to expose bedrock. He then laid out the temple according to the design that Ningirsu had revealed to him, and helped manufacture and carry mud bricks.

2.15   Seated statue of Gudea holding temple plan, from Girsu (Telloh), Iraq. ca. 2100 BCE. Diorite, height approx. 29″ (73.7 cm). Musée du Louvre, Paris

BABYLONIAN ART

The late third and early second millennia BCE were a time of turmoil and warfare in Mesopotamia. The region was then unified for over 300 years under a Babylonian dynasty. During the reign of its most famous ruler, Hammurabi (r. 1792–1750 BCE), the city of Babylon assumed the dominant role formerly played by Akkad and Ur. Combining military prowess with respect for Sumerian tradition, Hammurabi cast himself as "the favorite shepherd" of the sun-god Shamash, stating his mission "to cause justice to prevail in the land and to destroy the wicked and evil, so that the strong might not oppress the weak nor the weak the strong." Babylon retained its role as cultural center of Sumer for more than 1,000 years after its political power had waned.

The Code of Hammurabi

Posterity remembers Hammurabi best for his law code. It survives as one of the earliest written bodies of law, engraved on a black basalt stele reaching to over 7 feet in height (fig. **2.16**). The text consists of 3,500 lines of Akkadian cuneiform, and begins with an account of the temples Hammurabi restored. The largest portion concerns commercial and property law, rulings on domestic issues, and questions of physical assault, detailing penalties for noncompliers (including the renowned Hebrew Bible principle of "an eye for an eye"). (See *Primary Source*, page 35.) The text concludes with a paean to Hammurabi as peacemaker.

At the top of the stele, Hammurabi appears in relief, standing with his arm raised in greeting before the enthroned sun-god Shamash. The god's shoulders emanate sun rays, and he extends his hand, holding the rope ring and the measuring rod of kingship; this single gesture unifies both the scene's composition and the implied purpose of the two protagonists. The image is a variant on the "introduction scene" found on cylinder seals, where a goddess leads a human individual with his hand raised in salute before a seated godlike figure, who bestows his blessing. Hammurabi appears without the benefit—or need—of a divine intercessor, implying an especially close relationship with the sun-god. Still, the smaller scale of Hammurabi compared to the seated god expresses his status as "shepherd" rather than god himself. The symmetrical composition and smooth surfaces result in a legible image of divinely ordained power that is fully in line with Mesopotamian traditions. Like the stele of Naram-Sin, Hammurabi's stele later became war booty, when the Elamites carried it off to Susa.

ASSYRIAN ART

Babylon fell around 1595 BCE to the Hittites, who had established themselves in Anatolia (present-day Turkey). When they departed, they left a weakened Babylonian state vulnerable to other invaders: the Kassites from the northwest and the Elamites from the east. Although a second Babylonian dynasty rose to great heights under Nebuchadnezzar I of Isin (r. 1125–1104 BCE), the Assyrians more or less controlled southern Mesopotamia by the end of the millennium. Their home was the city-state of Assur, sited on the upper course of the Tigris and named for the god Ashur.

2.16 Upper part of stele inscribed with the Law Code of Hammurabi. ca. 1760 BCE. Diorite, height of stele approx. 7′ (2.1 m); height of relief 28″ (71 cm). Musée du Louvre, Paris

Art of Empire: Expressing Royal Power

Under a series of able rulers, beginning with Ashur-uballit (r. 1363–1328? BCE), the Assyrian realm expanded. At its height, in the seventh century BCE, the empire stretched from the Sinai peninsula to Armenia; the Assyrians even invaded Egypt successfully in about 670 BCE (see map 2.1). They drew heavily on the artistic achievements of the Sumerians and Babylonians, but adapted them to their own purpose. The Assyrians' was clearly an art of empire: propagandistic and public, designed to proclaim and sustain the supremacy of Assyrian civilization, particularly through representations of military power. The Assyrians continued to build temples and ziggurats based on Sumerian models, but their architectural focus shifted to constructing royal palaces. These grew to unprecedented size and magnificence, blatantly expressing royal presence and domination.

The proclamation of Assyrian royal power began well outside the palace, as is clear in the plan for the city of Dur Sharrukin

The Code of Hammurabi

PRIMARY SOURCE

...scribed on the stele of Hammurabi in figure 2.16, the Code of ...ws compiled by King Hammurabi offers a glimpse of the lives and values of Babylonians in the second millennium BCE.

Prologue

When Anu the Sublime, King of the Anunaki, and Bel, the lord of Heaven and earth, who decreed the fate of the land, assigned to Marduk, the over-ruling son of Ea, God of righteousness, dominion over earthly man, and made him great among the Igigi, they called Babylon by his illustrious name, made it great on earth, and founded an everlasting kingdom in it, whose foundations are laid so solidly as those of heaven and earth; then Anu and Bel called by name me, Hammurabi, the exalted prince, who feared God, to bring about the rule of righteousness in the land, to destroy the wicked and the evil-doers; so that the strong should not harm the weak; so that I should rule over the black-headed people like Shamash, and enlighten the land, to further the well-being of mankind. …

The Code of Laws [excerpts]

If any one bring an accusation against a man, and the accused go to the river and leap into the river, if he sink in the river his accuser shall take possession of his house. But if the river prove that the accused is not guilty, and he escape unhurt, then he who had brought the accusation shall be put to death, while he who ...ped into the river shall take possession of the house that had ...onged to his accuser. …

If any one bring an accusation of any crime before the elders, and does not prove what he has charged, he shall, if it be a capital offense charged, be put to death. …

If any one steal the property of a temple or of the court, he shall be put to death, and also the one who receives the stolen thing from him shall be put to death. …

If any one steal cattle or sheep, or an ass, or a pig or a goat, if it belong to a god or to the court, the thief shall pay thirtyfold; if they belonged to a freed man of the king he shall pay tenfold; if the thief has nothing with which to pay he shall be put to death …

If any one break a hole into a house (break in to steal), he shall be put to death before that hole and be buried …

If any one be too lazy to keep his dam in proper condition, and does not so keep it; if then the dam break and all the fields be flooded, then shall he in whose dam the break occurred be sold for money, and the money shall replace the corn which he has caused to be ruined. …

If any one be on a journey and entrust silver, gold, precious stones, or any movable property to another, and wish to recover it from him; if the latter do not bring all of the property to the appointed place, but appropriate it to his own use, then shall this man, who did not bring the property to hand it over, be convicted, and he shall pay fivefold for all that had been entrusted to him. …

If a man wish to separate from a woman who has borne him children, or from his wife who has borne him children: then he shall give that wife her dowry, and a part of the usufruct of field, garden, and property, so that she can rear her children. When she has brought up her children, a portion of all that is given to the children, equal as that of one son, shall be given to her. She may then marry the man of her heart. …

If a son strike his father, his hands shall be hewn off.

If a man put out the eye of another man, his eye shall be put out.

If he break another man's bone, his bone shall be broken.

If a builder build a house for some one, and does not construct it properly, and the house which he built fall in and kill its owner, then that builder shall be put to death.

If it kill the son of the owner, the son of that builder shall be put to death.

If it kill a slave of the owner, then he shall pay slave for slave to the owner of the house. …

Source: *World Civilizations Online Classroom* "The Code of Hammurabi" tr. L. W. King (1910). Edited by Richard Hooker www.wsu.edu:8080/2dee. © 1996.
Note: The Epilogue of *The Code of Hammurabi* appears at www.myartslab.com.

(present-day Khorsabad, Iraq), where Sargon II (r. 721–705 BCE) had his royal residence (fig. **2.17**). Though much of the city remains unexcavated, archaeologists estimate that it covered an area of nearly a square mile, enclosed within an imposing mud-brick fortification wall. To reach the palace, a visitor had to cross the city, traversing open plazas and climbing broad ramps. On the northwest side, a walled and turreted citadel closed the zig-gurat and the palace off from the rest of the town and empha-sized their dominant presence. Enclosing temple and palace, the citadel revealed the privileged relationship between the king ...d the gods. Both structures stood atop a mound 50 feet high,

2.17 Reconstruction drawing of the citadel of Sargon II, Dur Sharrukin (Khorsabad), Iraq. ca. 721–705 BCE (after Charles Altman)

2.18   Gate of the citadel of Sargon II, Dur Sharrukin (Khorsabad), Iraq (photo taken during excavation). 742–706 BCE

which raised them above the flood plain and expressed the king's elevated status above the rest of society. The ziggurat had at least four stages, each about 18 feet high and of a different color, and a spiral ramp wound around it to the top.

The palace complex comprised about 30 courtyards and 200 rooms, and monumental imagery complemented this impressive scale. At the gateways stood huge, awe-inspiring guardian figures known as **lamassu**, in the shape of winged, human-headed bulls (fig. **2.18**). The illustration here shows the lamassu of Khorsabad during excavation in the 1840s; masons subsequently sawed up one of the pair for transportation to the Louvre in Paris. The massive creatures are almost in the round (fully three-dimensional and separate from the background). Carved out of the limestone of the palace wall, they are one with the building. Yet the addition of a fifth leg, visible from the side, reveals that the sculptor conceived of them as deep relief sculptures on two sides of the stone block, so that the figures are legible both frontally and profile. From the front, the lamassu appear stationary, yet the additional leg sets them in motion when seen from the side. With their tall, horned headdresses and deep-set eyes, and the powerful muscularity of their legs and bodies, all set off by delicate patterning of the beard and feathers, they towered over any approaching visitor, embodying the king's fearful authority. The Assyrians may have believed the hybrid creatures had the power to ward

2.19   *Fugitives Crossing River*, from the Northwest Palace of Ashurnasirpal II, Nimrud (Calah), Iraq. ca. 883–859 BCE. Alabaster, height approx. 39" (98 cm). The British Museum, London

off evil spirits. Contemporary texts indicate that sculptors also cast lamassu in bronze, but because these images were later melted down, none now survives.

Once inside a royal palace, a visitor would confront another distinctive feature of Assyrian architecture: upright gypsum slabs called **orthostats**, with which builders lined the lower walls. Structurally, the slabs protected the mud brick from moisture and wear, but they served a communicative purpose as well. On their surfaces, narrative images in low relief, painted in places for emphasis, glorified the king with detailed depictions of lion hunts and military conquests (with inscriptions giving supplementary information). In these reliefs, the Assyrian forces march indefatigably onward, meeting the enemy at the empire's frontiers, destroying his strongholds, and carrying away booty and prisoners of war. Actions take place in a continuous band, propelling a viewer from scene to scene, and repetition of key images creates the impression of an inevitable Assyrian triumph. This detail (fig. 2.19), from the Northwest Palace of Ashurnasirpal II (r. 883–859 BCE) at Nimrud (ancient Kalah, biblical Calah, Iraq), shows the enemy fleeing an advance party by swimming across a river on inflatable animal skins. From their fortified city, an archer—possibly the king—and two women look on with hands raised. The artist intersperses landscape elements with humans, yet shows no concern to capture relative scale, or to depict all elements from a single viewpoint. This suggests that the primary purpose of the scenes was to recount specific enemy conquests in descriptive detail; depicting them in a naturalistic way was not critical.

As in Egypt (discussed in Chapter 3), royal lion hunts were staged events that took place in palace grounds. Royal attendants released animals from cages into a square formed by troops with shields. Earlier Mesopotamian rulers hunted lions to protect their subjects, but by the time of the Assyrians, the activity had become more symbolic, ritually showcasing the king's strength and serving as a metaphor for military prowess. On a section of Assyrian relief from the North Palace of Ashurbanipal (r. 668–627 BCE) at Nineveh, dating to roughly 645 BCE (fig. 2.20), the king races forward in his chariot with bow drawn, leaving wounded and dead lions in his wake. A wounded lion leaps at the chariot as attendants plunge spears into its chest. Its body is hurled flat out in a clean diagonal line, its claws spread and mouth open in what appears to be pain combined with desperate ferocity. To ennoble the victims of the hunt, the sculptor contrasted the limp, contorted bodies of the slain animals with the taut leaping lion and the powerful energy of the king's party. Yet we should not conclude that the artist necessarily hoped to evoke sympathy for the creatures, or to comment on the cruelty of a staged hunt; it is more likely that by ennobling the lions the sculptor intended to glorify their vanquisher, the king, even more intensely.

LATE BABYLONIAN ART

Perpetually under threat, the Assyrian Empire came to an end in 612 BCE, when Nineveh fell to the Medes (an Indo-European-speaking people from western Iran) and the resurgent Babylonians. Under the Chaldean dynasty, the ancient city of Babylon had a final brief flowering between 612 and 539 BCE, before the Persians conquered it. The best known of these Late Babylonian rulers was Nebuchadnezzar II (r. 604–ca. 562 BCE), builder of the biblical Tower of Babel, which soared 270 feet high and came to symbolize overweening pride. He was also responsible for the famous Hanging Gardens of Babylon, numbered among the seven wonders of the ancient world compiled by Greek historians by the second century BCE.

The Royal Palace

The royal palace at Babylon was on almost the same scale as Assyrian palaces, with numerous reception suites framing five huge courtyards. Instead of facing their buildings with carved stone, the Late Babylonians adopted baked and **glazed brick**, which they molded into individual shapes. Glazing brick involved putting a film of glass over the brick's surface. Late Babylonians used it both for surface ornament and for reliefs on a grand scale. Its vivid coloristic effect appears on the courtyard façade of the Throne Room and the Processional Way leading to the Ishtar Gate and the gate itself, now reassembled in Berlin (fig. **2.21**). A framework of brightly colored ornamental bands contains a procession of bulls, dragons, and other animals, set off in molded brick against a deep blue background. The animals portrayed were sacred: White and yellow snake-necked dragons to Marduk, the chief Babylonian god; yellow bulls with blue hair to Adad, god of storms; and white and yellow lions to Ishtar herself, goddess of love and war. Unlike the massive muscularity of the lamassu,

their forms are light and agile-looking, arrested in a processional stride that slowly accompanies ceremonial processions leading to the archway of the gate.

REGIONAL NEAR EASTERN ART

Alongside the successive cultures of Mesopotamia, a variety of other cultures developed in areas beyond the Tigris and Euphrates. Some of them invaded or conquered contemporaneous city-states in Mesopotamia, as did the Hittites in the north and the Iranians in the east. Others, such as the seagoing Phoenicians on the Mediterranean coast to the west, traded with the people of Mesopotamia and in so doing spread Mesopotamian visual forms to Africa and Europe.

The Hittites

The Hittites were responsible for Babylon's overthrow in 1595 BCE. An Indo-European-speaking people, they had probably entered Anatolia from southern Russia in the late third millennium BCE and settled on its rocky plateau as one of several cultures that developed independently of Mesopotamia. As they came into contact with Mesopotamian traditions, the Hittites adopted cuneiform writing for their language, and preserved details of their history on clay tablets. Emerging as a power around 1800 BCE, they rapidly expanded their territory 150 years later under Hattusilis I. Their empire extended over most of present-d Turkey and Syria, which brought them into conflict with the imperial ambitions of Egypt. The Hittite Empire reached its apogee between 1400 and 1200 BCE. Its capital was Hattusa, near the present-day Turkish village of Bogazköy. Fortification walls protected the city, constructed of huge, irregularly shaped stones that were widely available in the region. At the city gates, massive limestone lions and other guardian figures protruded from the blocks that formed the **jambs** (fig. 2.22). The Lion Gate is 7 feet high, and though badly weathered, the figures still impress visitors with their ferocity and stark frontality. These powerful guardians probably inspired the later Assyrian lamassu (see fig. 2.18).

The Phoenicians

The Phoenicians, too, contributed a distinctive body of work to Near Eastern art. Living on the eastern coast of the Mediterranean in the first millennium BCE in what is now Lebanon, they developed formidable seafaring skills, which led them to found settlements farther west in the Mediterranean (most notably on the North African coast and in Spain). They became a linchpin in the rapidly growing trade in objects—and ideas—between East and West. The Phoenicians were especially adept in working metal and ivory, and in making colored glass. They readily incorporated motifs from Egypt and the eastern Mediterranean coa as seen in the open-work ivory plaque illustrated here (fig. **2.23**), on which is poised an Egyptian winged sphinx. The plaque dates

2.21 Ishtar Gate (restored), from Babylon, Iraq. ca. 575 BCE. Glazed brick originally 40′ high (12.2 m). Staatliche Museen zu Berlin, Preussischer Kulturbesitz, Vorderasiatisches Museum

2.22 The Lion Gate, Bogazköy, Anatolia (Turkey). ca. 1400 BCE

2.23 Phoenician ivory plaque depicting a winged sphinx, found at Fort Shalmaneser, Nimrud (ancient Kalhu), northern Iraq. ca. 8th century BCE. The British Museum, London

2.24   Temple of Solomon (reconstruction), Jerusalem. ca. 457–450 BCE

to the eighth century BCE, and came to light in Fort Shalmaneser at Nimrud, the Assyrian capital where the conquering Assyrian kings had probably taken it as booty. Though the details are Egyptian—its wig and apron, the stylized plants—the carver has reduced its double crown to fit neatly within the panel, suggesting that what mattered was a general quality of "Egyptianness" rather than an accurate portrayal of Egyptian motifs. The rounded forms and profile presentation translate the Egyptian motif into a visual form more familiar to Mesopotamian eyes.

The Hebrews

According to later tradition, the Akkadians expelled the Hebrews from Mesopotamia in about 2000 BCE. The latter settled in Canaan, on the eastern Mediterranean, before moving to Egypt in around 1600 BCE. There, they were bound into slavery. Moses led their flight from Egypt into the Sinai desert, where they established the principles of their religion. Unlike other Near Eastern peoples, the Hebrews were monotheistic. Their worship centered on Yahweh, who provided Moses with the Ten Commandments, a set of ethical and moral rules. After 40 years, they returned to Canaan, which they named Israel. King David, who ruled until

961 BCE, seized the city of Jerusalem from the Canaanites, and began to construct buildings there worthy of a political and religious capital for Israel, including a royal palace. His son, Solomon, completed a vast temple for worship, now known as the First Temple (fig. 2.24). The temple stood within a sacred precinct on Mount Moriah (the present-day Temple Mount), where, according to the scriptures, the patriarch Abraham had prepared to sacrifice his son, Isaac. Archaeological evidence for the massive building is controversial, and literary descriptions are incomplete. According to the Hebrew Bible, Solomon covered the entire temple and the altar inside with gold. For the inner sanctuary, which held the Ark of the Covenant (a chest containing the Commandments), sculptors created two monumental cherubim (angels depicted as winged children) out of gilded olive wood. They also covered the walls with carvings of cherubim, palm trees, and flowers. Brass pillars stood at the front of the temple, with pomegranate-shaped **capitals**. King Hiram of Tyre (Phoenicia) is credited with providing resources for the construction of the temple, such as materials and artisans, which is furth evidence of the close connections between Near Eastern cultur

Babylonian forces under King Nebuchadnezzar II destroyed the temple in 587/86 BCE, forcing the Israelites into exile. Upon their return in 538, they built the temple anew, and under Herod the Great, king of Judea from 37 BCE to 4 CE, the Second Temple was raised up and substantially enlarged. Roman soldiers razed ⟨it⟩ rebuilding in the reign of the emperor Vespasian, in the first century CE. The only vestige of the vast complex Herod commissioned is the western wall, known today as the Wailing Wall.

IRANIAN ART

Located to the east of Mesopotamia, Iran was a flourishing agricultural center in Neolithic times, starting in about 7000 BCE. During that period, Iran became a gateway for migrating tribes

2.25 Painted beaker, from Susa. ca. 4000 BCE. Height 11¼″ (28.3 cm). Musée du Louvre, Paris

from the Asiatic steppes to the north as well as from India to the east. While it is distinctive, the art of ancient Iran still reflects its intersections with the cultures of Mesopotamia.

Early Iranian Art

The early nomadic tribes left no permanent structures or records, but the items they buried with their dead reveal that they ranged over a vast area—from Siberia to central Europe, from Iran to Scandinavia. They fashioned objects of wood, bone, or metal, and these diverse works share a common decorative vocabulary, including animal motifs used in abstract and ornamental ways. They belong to a distinct kind of portable art known as **nomad's gear**, including weapons, bridles, buckles, **fibulae** (large clasps or brooches), and other articles of adornment, as well as various kinds of vessels.

The handleless beaker in figure **2.25**, dating to about 4000 BCE, originates from a pottery-producing center at Susa on the Shaur River. On the surface of its thin shell of pale yellow clay, a brown **glaze** defines an ibex (mountain goat), whose forms the painter has reduced to a few dramatic sweeping curves. The circles of its horns reflect in two dimensions the cup's three-dimensional roundness. Racing hounds above the ibex stretch out to become horizontal streaks, and vertical lines below the vessel's rim are the elongated necks of a multitude of birds. This early example of Iranian art demonstrates the skill of the potter in both the construction of the cup and its sensitive painted design. It prefigures a later love of animal forms in the nomadic arts of Iran and Central Asia.

The Persian Empire: Cosmopolitan Heirs to the Mesopotamian Tradition

During the mid-sixth century BCE, the small kingdom of Parsa to the east of lower Mesopotamia came to dominate the entire Near East. Under Cyrus the Great (r. 559–530/29 BCE), ruler of the Achaemenid dynasty, the people of Parsa—the Persians—overthrew the king of the Medes, then conquered major parts of Asia Minor in ca. 547 or 546 BCE, and Babylon in 538 BCE. Cyrus assumed the title "king of Babylon," along with the broader ambitions of Mesopotamian rulers. The empire he founded continued to expand under his successors. Egypt fell in 525 BCE, while Greece only narrowly escaped Persian domination in the early fifth century BCE. At its height, under Darius I (r. 521–486 BCE) and his son Xerxes (r. 485–465 BCE), the territorial reach of the Persian Empire far outstripped the Egyptian and Assyrian empires combined. It endured for two centuries, during which it developed an efficient administration and monumental art forms.

Persian religious beliefs related to the prophecies of Zoroaster (Zarathustra) and took as their basis the dualism of good and evil, embodied in Ahuramazda (Light) and Ahriman (Darkness). The cult of Ahuramazda focused its rituals on fire altars in the open air; consequently, Persian kings did not construct

2.26   Palace of Darius and Xerxes, Persepolis. 518–460 BCE

monumental religious architecture. Instead they concentrated their attention and resources on royal palaces, which were at once vast and impressive.

PERSEPOLIS   Darius I began construction on the most ambitious of the palaces, on a plateau in the Zagros highlands at Parsa or Persepolis, in 518 BCE. Subsequent rulers enlarged it (fig. **2.26**). Fortified and raised on a platform, it consisted of a great number of rooms, halls, and courts laid out in a grid plan. The palace is a synthesis of materials and design traditions from all parts of the far-flung empire; brought together, they result in a clear statement of internationalism. Darius boasts in his inscriptions that the palace timber came from Lebanon (cedar), Gandhara and Carmania (yaka wood), and its bricks from Babylon. Items for palace use (such as the golden **rhyton**, or ritual cup, in fig. **2.27**), were of Sardian and Bactrian gold, Egyptian silver, and ebony, and Sagdianan lapis lazuli and carnelian. To work these materials, the Achaemenids brought in craftsmen from all over the empire, who

2.27   Achaemenid rhyton. 5th–3rd centuries BCE. Gold. Archaeological Museum, Tehran, Iran

2.28   Audience Hall of Darius and Xerxes, Persepolis, Iran. ca. 500 BCE

then took this international style away with them on returning to their respective homes. The gold-worker responsible for the rhyton shaped it as a senmurv, a mythical creature with the body of a lion sprouting griffin's wings and a peacock's tail. It belongs firmly to the tradition of Mesopotamian hybrid creatures.

Visitors to the palace were constantly reminded of the theme of empire, beginning at the entrance. There, at the massive "Gate of All the Lands," stood colossal winged, human-headed bulls, like the Assyrian lamassu (see fig. 2.18). Inside the palace, architects employed columns on a magnificent scale. Entering the 217-foot-square Audience Hall, or *apadana*, of Darius and Xerxes, a visitor would stand amid 36 columns, which soared 40 feet up to support a wooden ceiling. A few still stand today (fig. **2.28**). The concept of massing columns in this way may come from Egypt; certainly Egyptian elements are present in the vegetal (plantlike) detail of their bases and capitals. The form of the shaft, however, echoes the slender, fluted column shafts of Ionian Greece (see fig. 5.8). Crowning the column capitals are "cradles" for ceiling beams composed of the front parts of two bulls or similar creatures (fig. **2.29**). The animals recall Assyrian sculptures, yet their truncated, back-to-back arrangement evokes animal motifs of Iranian art, as seen in the form of the rhyton.

2.29   Bull capital, from Persepolis. ca. 500 BCE. Musée du Louvre, Paris

2.30 *Darius and Xerxes Giving Audience.* ca. 490 BCE. Limestone, height 8′4″ (2.5 m). Archaeological Museum, Tehran, Iran

In marked contrast to the military narratives of the Assyrians, reliefs embellishing the platform of the Audience Hall and its double stairway proclaim a theme of harmony and integration across the multicultural empire (fig. **2.30**). Long rows of marching figures, sometimes superposed in registers, represent the empire's 23 subject nations, as well as royal guards and Persian dignitaries. Each of the nations' representatives wears indigenous dress and brings a regional gift—precious vessels, textiles—as tribute to the Persian king. Colored stone and metals applied to the relief added richness to a wealth of carved detail. The relief is remarkably shallow, yet by reserving the figures' roundness for the edge of their bodies (so that they cast a shadow), and by cutting the background away to a level field, the sculptors created an impression of greater depth. Where earlier Mesopotamian reliefs depict figures in mixed profile and frontal views, most of these figures are in full profile, even though some figures turn their heads back

2.31 *Shapur I Triumphing over the Roman Emperors Philip the Arab and Valerian,* Naksh-i-Rustam (near Persepolis), Iran. 260–272 CE

to address those who follow. Through repetition of the walking human form, the artists generated a powerful dynamic quality that guides a visitor's path through the enormous space. The repetition also lends the reliefs an eternal quality, as if preserving the action in perpetual time. If, as some believe, the relief represents the recurring celebration of the New Year Festival, this timeless quality would be especially apt.

The Achaemenid synthesis of traditions at Persepolis demonstrates the longevity and flexibility of the Near Eastern language of rulership. The palace provides a dramatic and powerful setting for imperial court ritual on a grand scale.

Mesopotamia Between Persian and Islamic Dominion

Rebuffed in its attempts to conquer Greece, the Persian Empire eventually came under Greek and then Roman domination, but like many parts of the Greek and Roman empires, it retained numerous aspects of its own culture. The process began in 331 BCE with Alexander the Great's (356–323 BCE) victory over the Persians, when his troops burnt the palace at Persepolis in an act of symbolic defiance. After his death eight years later, his generals divided his realm among themselves, and Seleukas (r. 305–281 BCE) inherited much of the Near East. The Parthians, who were Iranian nomads, gained control over the region in 238 BCE. Despite fairly constant conflict, they fended off Roman advances until a brief Roman success under Trajan in the early second century CE, after which Parthian power declined. The last Parthian king was overthrown by one of his governors, Ardashir or Artaxerxes, in 224 CE. This Ardashir (d. 240 CE) founded the Sasanian dynasty, named for a mythical ancestor, Sasan, who claimed to be a direct descendent of the Achaemenids, and this dynasty controlled the area until the Arab conquest in the mid-seventh century CE.

Ardashir's son, Shapur I (r. 240–272 CE), proved to be Darius' equal in ambition, and he linked himself directly to the Persian king. He expanded the empire greatly, and even succeeded in defeating three Roman emperors in the middle of the third century CE. Two of these victories Shapur commemorated in numerous reliefs, including an immense panel carved into rock at Naksh-i-Rustam, near Persepolis, where Darius I and his successors had previously located their rock-cut tombs (fig. 2.31). The victor, on horseback, raises his hand in a gesture of mercy to the defeated "barbarian," who kneels before him in submission. This was a stock Roman scene, recognizable to Roman viewers, and this quotation gives the relief an ironic dimension, for the victorious Shapur here expropriates his enemy's own **iconography** of triumph. Elements of style are typical of late or provincial Roman sculpture, such as the linear folds of the emperor's billowing cloak. However, Shapur's elaborate headdress and clothing, his heavily caparisoned horse, and his composite pose are all distinctly Near Eastern.

Roman and Near Eastern elements are combined again in Shapur I's palace (242–272 CE) at Ctesiphon, near Baghdad, with its magnificent brick, barrel-vaulted audience hall, or **iwan** (fig. 2.32). It was a Roman practice to exploit the **arch** to span huge spaces (see fig. 7.61), and the architect used it here to enclose a space 90 feet high, typical of the Near Eastern tradition of large-scale royal building. The registers of arched blank windows or **blind arcades** may derive from Roman façades, such as those in the stage buildings of theaters or ornamental fountains (see fig. 7.7). Yet the shallowness of the arcades creates

2.32 Palace of Shapur I, Ctesiphon, Iraq. 242–272 CE

a distinctly eastern surface pattern, in turn subordinated to an awe-inspiring entryway.

Metalwork continued to flourish in the Sasanian period, using a wide variety of techniques. Hunting scenes were a popular subject, as seen in figure **2.33**, a late fifth-century CE silver bowl that probably represents King Peroz I hunting gazelles. A metalworker turned the bowl on a lathe, and hammered out the king and his prey from behind (a technique known as **repoussé**), before applying gilt and inlaying details such as the horns of the animals and the pattern on the quiver, with **niello**, a compound of sulphur. The hunting subject continues a tradition known to Assyrians, as well as to Egyptians and Romans. Sasanians exported many of their wares to Constantinople (see map 1) and to the Christian West, where they had a strong impact on the art of the Middle Ages. Artists would manufacture similar vessels again after the Sasanian realm fell to the Arabs in the mid-seventh century CE, and these served as a source of design motifs for Islamic art as well (see Chapter 9).

2.33 *Peroz I (457–483) or Kavad I hunting rams*. 5th–6th century CE. Silver, mercury gilding, niello inlay, diameter 8⅝″ (21.9 cm), height 1⅞″ (4.6 cm). Metropolitan Museum of Art, New York, Fletcher Fund, 1934 (34.33)

ca. 4000 BCE
Handleless beaker
from Susa

ca. 2600 BCE The *Royal Standard of Ur*

ca. 2100 BCE King Urnammu commissions the Great Ziggurat at Ur

ca. 957 BCE Solomon's Temple is completed
in Jerusalem

ca. 668–627 BCE Assyrians
construct the North Palace
of Ashurbanipal

ca. 518 BCE Construction of the Persian palace
at Persepolis begins

242–272 CE Shapur I's palace at Ctesiphon built

4000 BCE

3500 BCE

3000 BCE

2500 BCE

2000 BCE

1500 BCE

1000 BCE

500 BCE

0

500 CE

◄ ca. 3500 BCE Sumerian city of Uruk emerges
ca. 3500 BCE Pottery manufacturing appears
in western Europe

ca. 3100–2600 BCE Neolithic stone houses at
Skara Brae

◄ ca. 2900 BCE Mesopotamians begin using
cuneiform writing

◄ ca. 2350 BCE Conflict begins among Sumerian
city-states over access to water and fertile land
◄ after 2150 BCE Earliest surviving Akkadian tablets
of the *Epic of Gilgamesh*
ca. 2100 BCE Final phase of construction at
Stonehenge

◄ ca. 1792–1750 BCE Hammurabi rules Babylon

◄ ca. 1595 BCE The Hittites conquer Babylon

◄ 1400–1200 BCE Apogee of the Hittite Empire

◄ 612 BCE Nineveh falls to the Medes and resurgent
Babylonians; end of the Assyrian Empire
ca. 604–562 BCE Reign of the Late Babylonian
ruler Nebuchadnezzar II
ca. 559–530/29 BCE Rule of Cyrus the Great, who
leads Persians to overthrow the Medes

◄ 331 BCE Alexander the Great defeats the Persians

◄ 224 CE Ardashir founds the Sasanian dynasty

CHAPTER 3

Egyptian Art

EGYPT HAS LONG FASCINATED THE WEST. THE ANCIENT GREEKS AND the Romans knew and admired Egypt, and Renaissance collectors and scholars took up their esteem. Napoleon's incursions into Egypt in the late eighteenth century brought artifacts and knowledge back to France and stimulated interest throughout Europe. European-sponsored excavations have been

going on in Egypt since the nineteenth century, sometimes, as in the case of the discovery in 1922 of the tomb of King Tutankhamun, with spectacular results.

One reason that ancient Egypt enthralls us is the exceptional technique and monumental character of its works of art. Most surviving objects come from tombs, which Egyptians built to assure an afterlife for the deceased. They intended the paintings, sculptures, and other objects they placed in the tombs to accompany the deceased into eternity. Thus, Egyptian art is an art of permanence. In fact, the fourth-century BCE Greek philosopher Plato claimed that Egyptian art had not changed in 10,000 years. The reality is more complex, but it is fair to say that most Egyptian artists did not strive for innovation or originality, but adhered instead to traditional formulations that expressed specific ideas. Continuity of form and subject is a characteristic of ancient Egyptian art.

Egyptian artists executed works of art mainly for the elite patrons of a society that was extremely hierarchical. Contemporary with the Egyptian development of writing around 3000 BCE there emerged a political and religious system that placed a god-king (called a pharaoh from the New Kingdom on) in charge of the physical and spiritual well-being of the land and its people. Many of the best-known works of Egyptian art

exalted these powerful rulers, and express the multifaceted ways that Egyptians envisioned their king: as a human manifestation of the gods, as a god in his own right, as a beneficent ruler, and as an emblem of life itself. Royal projects for the afterlife dominated the landscape and provided the model for elite burials. These two categories of art—royal commissions and funerary objects—constitute a large proportion of surviving Egyptian art. Religion accounts for the predominance of both types of art.

Egyptian geography also played a formative role in the development of art. The land was established on the course of the Nile River in North Africa, exploiting the natural protection of the surrounding desert, or "red land." The river floods annually, inundating the land on either side. As it recedes, the water leaves a dark strip of soil fertilized by silt. The Egyptians called this rich soil the "black land." They irrigated and farmed it, and regularly produced surplus food. This allowed them to diversify and develop a complex culture. Egypt's agrarian society depended on the annual flooding of the Nile to survive. The king had to assure continuity of life through intercession with the gods, who often represented natural forces. (See *Informing Art*, page 52.) The chief deity was the sun, whom they worshiped as Ra-Horakhty. In matters concerning the afterlife, the deities Osiris, Isis, and Horus played key roles. Osiris was the mythical founder of Egypt, and Isis was his consort. Osiris's brother Seth (god of chaos) murdered him, and having dismembered him, scattered his remains far and wide. Isis eventually recovered them, and reassembled them

Detail of figure 3.41, The Weighing of the Heart and Judgment by Osiris

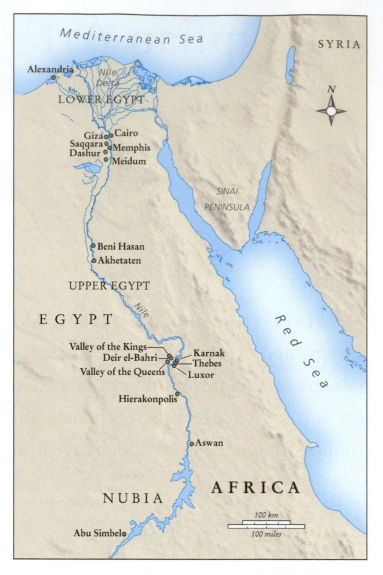

Map 3.1 Ancient Egypt

between present-day Aswan and the point where the river fans out into the Delta, near present-day Cairo. Lower Egypt, in the north, consists mainly of the vast Delta, from ancient Memphis to the Mediterranean. In Upper Egypt, independent cities sh[...] a rich culture that archaeologists know as Naqada II/III (from the location where they first discovered it). One of those cities was Hierakonpolis, where a number of well-constructed tombs contained valuable furnishings. In one, known as Tomb 100 and probably built for a ruler, paintings embellished the walls (fig. **3.1**). Human figures with rectangular torsoes, stick limbs, and simple round heads ride in boats, and engage in battle with one another. Unlike later Egyptian tomb paintings, the design is not arranged in registers (rows). A group of animals at the top sit on a ground-line, but the painter dispersed most of the figures freely against the background. In the lower left corner, a figure raises a stick against three smaller figures, who may be prisoners. This scheme will reappear in later Egyptian art (see fig. **3.2**).

With time, the culture of Upper Egypt spread northward, ultimately dominating the centers of Lower Egypt. Tradition maintained that the first king of the first dynasty founded the city of Memphis, at the mouth of the Nile Delta, uniting Upper and Lower Egypt (map **3.1**). The traditional division of Egypt into two distinct regions arises from the Egyptian worldview, which saw the world as a set of dualities in opposition: Upper and Lower Egypt; the red land of the desert and the black land of cultivation; the god of the earth (Geb) balanced by the sky (Nut); Osiris (god of civilization) opposed to Seth (god of chaos). The king had to balance the forces of chaos and order, and bring m[...] (harmony or order) to the world. Recognizing this worldview has led some scholars to question the traditional explanation that Upper and Lower Egypt were independent regions unified by King Narmer. Instead, they argue that this division was an imaginative reconstruction of the past.

to create the first mummy (an embalmed and wrapped body). From it she conceived her son, Horus, who avenged his father's death by besting Seth in a series of contests. Gods took many forms: Ra might appear as a falcon-headed man; Osiris as a mummy. Egyptians called the king himself the son of Ra and saw him as the human embodiment of Horus. As an equal to the gods, he controlled the land, the future, and the afterlife. A large priesthood, an administrative bureaucracy, and a strong military assisted him.

PRE DYNASTIC AND EARLY DYNASTIC ART

The origins of Egyptian culture stretch back into the Neolithic period. By at least 5000 BCE, humans were growing crops and domesticating animals in the Nile Valley. Settlements there gradually transformed into urban centers.

According to tradition, Egypt initially consisted of two regions. Upper Egypt, in the south, includes the Nile Valley

The Palette of King Narmer

The *Palette of King Narmer* (fig. **3.2**), dated to around 3000 BCE, visually expressed the concept of the king as unifier. A **palette** is a stone tablet with a central depression for grinding the protective paint that Egyptians applied around their eyes to protect them from ailments and the sun's glare. Its size—more than 2 feet high—suggests that it was not for ordinary use, but was probably reserved for a ceremony to ornament a cult statue. This ritual function may explain its findspot (where it was found) in the temple of Hierakonpolis, where it had been buried along with other offerings to the god Horus.

Shallow relief carvings in registers decorate both sides of the *Palette*. At the top of each side, in the center, **hieroglyphs** spell out Narmer's name, within an abstract rendering of the king's palace. The Egyptians developed hieroglyphs as a writing system at about the same time as the Mesopotamians were inventi[...] cuneiform, and used them in both religious and administrati[...] contexts. They called them "god's words"; the Greeks later saw them as sacred carvings, and their name for them, derived from

3.1 *People, boats, and animals.* First example of an Egyptian decorated tomb chamber showing people, boats and animals in the late predynastic Tomb 100 at Hierakonpolis. ca. 3000 BCE. Height 43.3″ (110 cm). Egyptian Museum, Cairo

3.2 *Palette of King Narmer* (both sides), from Hierakonpolis. ca. 3150–3125 BCE. Slate, height 25″ (63.5 cm). Egyptian Museum, Cairo

Egyptian Gods and Goddesses

Religion permeated every aspect of Egyptian life. According to Egyptian belief, the gods not only created the world, but remained involved in its existence. From artistic and textual evidence, we know the names of over 1,500 deities, some of whom are named below. The Egyptians conceived of their gods in myriad human, animal, and hybrid forms, and assigned numerous functions to them, which evolved over the course of time.

AMUN: One of Egypt's most important gods, associated with the sun, creation, and fertility. When combined with Ra as Amun-Ra in the Middle and New Kingdoms, he became the supreme Egyptian god. Usually represented as a man with a double plumed crown, a ram, or a human with a ram's head.

ANUBIS: God of the dead and embalming. Usually depicted as a jackal or another canine, or as a man with a jackal's head.

ATEN: A manifestation of the sun-god, supreme and only god under Akhenaten. Represented by the disk of the sun, emanating rays ending in hands.

HAPY: God of the inundation of the Nile, associated with life-giving and creation. Usually represented as a man with a swollen belly.

HATHOR: One of Egypt's most important goddesses. Mother or wife of Horus, wife or daughter and "Eye" of Ra, mother or wife of the king. Goddess of the sky, of women, female sexuality, and motherhood, of foreign lands, of the afterlife, and of joy, music, and happiness, and cow-goddess. Shown as a woman in a long wig or in a vulture cap with cow horns and a sun-disk, or as a cow.

HORUS: God of the sky, of the sun, and of kingship, with whom the living king was associated. Son of Isis and Osiris. Represented as a falcon or hawk, or as a man with a falcon's head.

ISIS: Egypt's most important goddess. Sister and wife of Osiris, mother and protector of Horus, and mother of the king. Cosmic goddess, goddess of magic, and protector of the dead. Usually represented as a woman crowned with the hieroglyphic throne sign, or with horns and a sun-disk.

MA'AT: Personification of truth, justice, and order. Represented as a woman with a tall feather headdress, or as a feather.

NEPHTHYS: Sister of Isis, funerary goddess. Represented as a woman.

NUT: Personification of the heavens, associated with thunder, rain, and stars, and with resurrection. Mother of Isis, Osiris, Nephthys, and Seth. Usually shown as a woman, often with limbs or body extended across the sky.

OSIRIS: One of Egypt's chief deities. Ruler of the underworld, god of death, resurrection, and fertility, and associated with the king. Murdered and dismembered by his brother, Seth, he was reassembled by his consort Isis and sister Nephthys, and brought back to life. Represented as a white or black mummy, often wearing the white crown of Upper Egypt.

RA: The most important Egyptian deity. Creator, king and father of the king. Combined with Ra-Horakhty as the morning sun. Often shown as a sun-disk surrounded by a cobra, or as a man with a hawk's head and headdress with a sun-disk.

SETH: Brother of Osiris and Isis, who murdered Osiris; brother and husband of Nephthys. Desert deity, associated chiefly with chaos, violence, and destruction. Represented as an animal with a curved head, or as a man with a curved animal head.

THOTH: Moon-god, associated with writing and knowledge. Represented as an ibis, a baboon, or an ibis-headed man with a writing palette.

the Greek words *hieros* (sacred) and *gluphein* (to carve), has endured. Flanking the hieroglyphs, heads of cows represent the sky goddess, locating the king in the sky. On one side of the *Palette* (shown on the left), King Narmer holds a fallen enemy by the hair, as he raises his mace—an emblem of kingship—with the other hand. The king appears in the composite view that will be the hallmark of Egyptian two-dimensional art: with a frontal view of eye, shoulders, and arms, but a profile of head and legs. He wears the white crown of Upper Egypt and from the belt of his kilt hangs the tail of a bull, a symbol of power that Egyptian kings would wear as part of their ceremonial dress for 3,000 years. The large scale of his figure compared with others immediately establishes his authority. For his part, the enemy, like those in the bottom register, is stripped of clothing as an act of humiliation. Behind the king, and standing on his own ground-line, an attendant carries the king's sandals. Hieroglyphs identify both the sandal-carrier and the enemy. To the right of Narmer appears a falcon resting on a papyrus stand, which grows from a human-headed strip of land; the falcon holds a rope tethered to the face.

On the other side of the *Palette* (on the right in fig. 3.2), Narmer appears in the highest register, now wearing the red crown of Lower Egypt. Flanked by the sandal-carrier and a long-haired figure, he follows four standard-bearers to inspect the decapitated bodies of prisoners, arranged with their heads between their legs. In the larger central register are two animals, each roped in by a male figure. They twist their long necks to frame a circle in the composition. The symmetrical, balanced motif may represent *ma'at*. Similar beasts occur on contemporary Mesopotamian cylinder seals, and may have influenced this design. In the lowest register, a bull representing the king attacks a city and tramples down the enemy.

The *Palette* communicates its message by combining several different types of signs on one object. Some of these signs—the king, attendants, and prisoners—are literal representations. Others are symbolic, such as the depiction of the king as a bull denoting his strength. **Pictographs**, small symbols based on abstract representations of concepts, encode further information: In the falcon and papyrus group, the falcon represents Horus, whom the Egyptians believed the king incarnated, while the human-headed papyrus stand represents Lower Egypt, where papyrus grew abundantly. A possible interpretation is that this [pic]tograph expresses Narmer's control of that region. Finally, the artist included identifying texts in the form of hieroglyphs. Together, the different signs on the *Palette of King Narmer* drive home important messages about the nature of Egyptian kingship: The king embodied the unified Upper and Lower Egypt, and though human, he occupied a divine office, as shown by the placement of his name in the sky, the realm of Horus.

As Horus's manifestation on earth, the king provided a physical body for the royal life force (*ka*) that passed from monarch to succeeding monarch. Positioned at the pinnacle of a highly stratified human hierarchy (indicated by his scale), the king was between mortals and gods, a kind of lesser god. His role was to enforce order over its opposing force, chaos, which he does on the *Palette* by overcoming foreign foes and establishing visible authority over them.

THE OLD KINGDOM: A GOLDEN AGE

The *Palette of King Narmer* offers an image of kingship that transcends earthly power, representing the king as a divinity as well as a ruler. The kings of the Old Kingdom (Dynasty Three to Dynasty Six, ca. 2649–2150 BCE) found more monumental ways to express this notion. Other dynasties would emulate their [w]orks of art for the following two millennia. (See *Informing Art*, page 54.)

Old Kingdom Funerary Complexes

During the Old Kingdom, Egyptians fashioned buildings to house the day-to-day activities of the living mainly out of perishable materials, with the result that little now survives. The bulk of archaeological evidence comes instead from tombs. The great majority of the population probably buried their dead in shallow desert graves, but the elite had the resources to build elaborate funerary monuments with luxury provisions for the afterlife. The survival of these tombs is no accident; they were purposely constructed to endure.

These structures had several important functions. As in many cultures, tombs gave the deceased a permanent marker on the landscape. They expressed the status of the dead and perpetuated their memory. Generally a rectangular mud-brick or stone edifice marked an early elite or royal burial (fig. **3.3**), known today as a **mastaba**, from the Arabic word for "bench." Plaster covered its exterior sloping walls, which were painted to evoke a niched palace façade. Often this superstructure was solid mud brick or filled with rubble, but sometimes it housed a funerary [ch]apel or storerooms for equipment needed in funerary rituals. [T]hese monuments also served a critical function in ensuring the preservation of a deceased individual's life force, or *ka*. Egyptians considered the *ka* to live on in the grave, and in order to do so, it

3.3   Group of mastabas, 4th Dynasty (after A. Badawy)

required a place to reside for eternity. This need led embalmers to go to great lengths to preserve the body through mummification (a process that they only perfected in the Eleventh and Twelfth Dynasties). The mummified body was usually placed within a **sarcophagus** (a stone coffin) and buried in a chamber at some depth below the mastaba, surrounded by subsidiary chambers for funerary apparatus. Egyptians believed that a statue could serve as a surrogate home for the *ka* in the event that the embalmers' efforts failed and the body decayed, so they set a sculpture within the burial chamber. They also equipped their tombs with objects of daily life for the *ka*'s enjoyment.

THE FUNERARY COMPLEX OF KING DJOSER   Out of this tradition emerges the first known major funerary complex, that of the Third Dynasty King Djoser (Netjerikhet), at Saqqara (figs. **3.4**, **3.5**, and **3.6**), who ruled between 2630 and 2611 BCE. On the west side of the Nile, Saqqara was the **necropolis** (cemetery or city of the dead) of the capital city of Memphis in Lower Egypt. Encircling the entire complex is a rectangular stone wall stretching over a mile in length and 33 feet high. The dominant feature of the complex is a stepped pyramid, oriented to the

3.4   Imhotep. Step pyramid and funerary complex of King Djoser, Saqqara. 3rd Dynasty. ca. 2681–2662 BCE

Major Periods in Ancient Egypt

In Egyptian society, a king's life was the measure of time. To organize the millennia of Egyptian culture, scholars use a chronology devised in the third century BCE by the priest-historian Manetho, who wrote a history of Egypt in Greek for Ptolemy I, based on Egyptian sources. He divided the list of Egyptian kings into 31 dynasties, beginning with the First Dynasty shortly after 3000 BCE. Modern scholars have organized the dynasties into kingdoms, beginning with the Old Kingdom, which covers from ca. 2649 BCE to 2150 BCE. The period before this, between prehistory and the First Dynasty, is known as the Predynastic period. Further subdivisions include the Middle Kingdom (ca. 2040–1640 BCE) and the New Kingdom

(ca. 1550–1070 BCE). Scholars still debate the actual dates for these broad periods and even for the reigns of kings, as Manetho's offered only a relative chronology (that is, the order in which kings succeeded one another) rather than absolute dates.

Major Periods in Ancient Egypt

ca. 5450–2960 BCE—Predynastic

ca. 2960–2649 BCE—Early Dynastic (Dynasties 1, 2)

ca. 2649–2150 BCE—Old Kingdom (Dynasties 3–6)

ca. 2040–1640 BCE—Middle Kingdom (Dynasties 11–13)

ca. 1550–1070 BCE—New Kingdom (Dynasties 18–20)

---

cardinal points of the compass (figs. 3.4 and 3.5). It began as a 26-foot-high mastaba, which the enclosure wall would originally have concealed. Over the course of years it rose to its towering 204-foot height as builders added progressively diminishing layers of masonry to its form. These layers resulted in the emergence of a kind of a staircase, perhaps the means by which the king could ascend to the gods after death. The treads of the "steps" incline downwards and the uprights outwards, giving the structure an impressively stable appearance. A chamber cut into the rock about 90 feet beneath the pyramid and lined with Aswan granite contained the burial, and additional chambers held funerary provisions. North of the pyramid was a labyrinthine funerary temple, where the living performed offering rituals for the dead king.

The buildings in the burial complex reproduce the palace architecture inhabited by the king while alive. The niched enclosure wall evokes a palace façade. In the palace, large courts accommodated rituals of kingship; similarly, a large court to the south of the pyramid may have housed rituals for receiving tribute or asserting royal dominion. Shrines of Upper and Lower Egypt flanked a smaller oblong court to the east, which may have been the site of the sed-festival, a ceremony that celebrated the king's 30-year jubilee and rejuvenated his power. Unlike palace structures, however, many of the buildings in the funerary complex are nonfunctional: Of 14 gateways indicated in the enclosure wall, only one (on the southeast corner) allows entrance, while the rest are false doors. Likewise, chapels dedicated to local gods were simply façades with false doors, behind which was a fill of rubble, sand, or gravel. Furthermore, while architects chose perishable materials for palaces—primarily mud brick—they constructed the funerary complex entirely in limestone: It was built to last.

court with *serdab*

funerary temple

step pyramid

stone platform with steps

crescent-shaped markers

sed-festival court between two rows of the shrines of Upper and Lower Egypt

open court

platform for dual *sed*-festival kiosk

enclosure wall

roofed entrance colonnade

0   100   200 meters

0   300   600 feet

3.5 Plan of the funerary district of King Djoser, Saqqara (Claire Thorne, after Lloyd and Müller)

3.6 Papyrus-shaped half-columns, North Palace, funerary complex of King Djoser, Saqqara

3.7 The pyramids of Menkaure, ca. 2533–2515 BCE, Khafra, ca. 2570–2544 BCE, and Khufu, ca. 2601–2528 BCE, Giza

All the same, masons treated the durable limestone to mimick the perishable fabrics of the palace: They dressed the limestone blocks of the enclosure wall to resemble the niched façades of mud-brick architecture. Additionally, the now reconstructed façade of a shrine echoes the form of an Upper Egyptian tent building, with tall poles supporting a mat roof that billows in the wind. Engaged columns imitate the papyrus stems or bundled reeds that Egyptian builders used to support mud-brick walls, with capitals shaped to resemble blossoms (fig. 3.6). Paint over the stone lintels disguised them as wood, and inside the tomb chamber, blue and green tiles covered false doors to imitate rolled-up reed matting.

Many elements of the complex served as permanent settings for the dead king to perpetually enact rituals of kingship—rituals that maintained order among the living. The installation of a life-sized seated statue of the king in a **serdab** (an enclosed room without an entrance) to the east of the funerary temple assured his presence in the complex. Two holes in the serdab's front wall enabled his *ka*, residing in the statue, to observe rituals in his honor and draw sustenance from offerings of food and incense. The entire complex was oriented north–south, and the king's statue looked out toward the circumpolar stars in the northern sky. With these provisions, his *ka* would remain eternally alive and vigilant.

Inscriptions on statue fragments found within the complex preserve the name of the mastermind behind its construction,

a high official at Djoser's court and high priest of Ra named Imhotep. Egyptians in Imhotep's own time and beyond credited him with advancing Egyptian culture through his wisdom and knowledge of astronomy, architecture, and medicine; they regarded him so highly that they deified him. This complex, the first large-scale building constructed entirely in stone, preserves at least one of his legacies. Scholars often identify him as the first named architect in history.

The Pyramids at Giza: Reflecting a New Royal Role

Other kings followed Djoser's lead, but during the Fourth Dynasty, ca. 2575–2465 BCE, funerary architecture changed dramatically. To the modern eye, the most obvious change is the shift from a step pyramid to a smooth-sided one. A pyramid at Meidum attributed to Sneferu, the founder of the Fourth Dynasty, underlines the deliberateness of the transformation. It was originally built as a step pyramid, but its steps were later filled in to produce smooth sides.

The best-known pyramids are the three Great Pyramids at Giza (fig. 3.7), commemorating Sneferu's son, Khufu (the first and largest pyramid), Khafra (r. 2520–2494) (a somewhat smaller one), and Menkaure (r. 2490–2472) (the smallest pyramid). (See *Materials and Techniques*, page 56.) Throughout the ages since

Building the Pyramids

In spite of much research, many aspects of pyramid design remain a mystery to Egyptologists. Elevations of other types of building—palaces and pylons, for instance—are preserved on the walls of New Kingdom tombs and temples, and a few plans survive. Pyramid architects may have worked from similar guidelines. Orienting the pyramids to the cardinal points of the compass appears to have been critical, and the architects probably achieved this by observing the stars. The greatest deviation is a meager 3 degrees east of north, in the pyramid of Djoser.

During the Old and Middle Kingdoms, builders constructed a pyramid's core out of local limestone. Quarries are still visible around the Great Pyramids and the Great Sphinx (fig. a and see fig. 3.9). For the casing (the outer surface), they must have brought Tura limestone and Aswan granite from quarries some distance away, as these are not local materials. Using copper tools, levers, and rope, workers cut channels in the rock and pried out blocks averaging 1½ to 5′ in length but sometimes much larger. Somehow they hauled these blocks overland, on hard-packed causeways built for that purpose. Some scholars believe teams of men or oxen pulled them on sleds, basing this view primarily upon a tomb painting showing 172 men dragging a huge statue of the Twelfth Dynasty king Djehutihopte on a sled. When documentary filmmakers tried to replicate the process using blocks of stone, it proved extraordinarily slow and cumbersome. Yet estimates of 2.3 million stone blocks in the pyramid of Khufu, constructed within 23 years, suggest that quarries must have moved stone at tremendous rates: approximately 1,500 men had to produce at least 300 blocks a day. In Hatshepsut's mortuary temple, late nineteenth century archaeologist William Flinders Petrie discovered models of wooden cradles in the shape of a quarter-circle. If four cradles were fitted to the four sides of a block of stone, these frames would have allowed a small team of men to roll a block relatively quickly.

Archaeological remains of pyramids indicate that methods of construction evolved over time. In early pyramids, builders used a buttressing technique, with inclined layers around a central core, diminishing in height from inside out (fig. b). They then set a smooth outer casing of cut stones at an angle to the ground. When this technique proved unstable at the beginning of the Fourth Dynasty, architects turned to courses of stone, built up layer by layer. They designed outer casing blocks as right-angled trapezoids and set them level to the ground as the pyramid rose (fig. c). Scholars believe that workers constructed ramps to raise blocks into place as the monument grew, but still debate the ramps' design; since builders dismantled them after use, they have left little trace in the archaeological record. The simplest solution would be a linear ramp leading up to one face of the pyramid, made out of debris left over from building. As the pyramid grew, however, the slope would have become so steep that workers would have needed steps to haul the blocks up. At this point, they could only have maneuvered the blocks with levers. A spiraling ramp, which worked its way around the pyramid at a shallower incline, would have concealed the base corners of the pyramid, making calculations difficult for surveyors, and it would have been hard to construct at the highest levels. Another alternative is a ramp zigzagging up one side of the monument. One scholar proposes that workers used sand and rubble ramps for roughly the lowest sixth of the Great Pyramid, followed by stone ramps at the higher levels, resting on the untrimmed outer steps. As they removed the ramps, the builders would have smoothed out the outer casing blocks to form a slope.

(a) Limestone quarry to the north of the Pyramid of Khafra

Buttressing Technique
Third Dynasty

(b) Buttressing technique

core
casing

Layering Technique
Fourth Dynasty?

(c) Layering technique

their construction, the pyramids have continued to fascinate and impress (see *The Art Historian's Lens*, page 75.) Their lasting grandeur derives both from their sheer monumentality (Khafra's covers 13 acres at the base, and still rises to a height of about 450 feet) and from their extraordinary simplicity. On a square plan, ir four surfaces, shaped as equilateral triangles, taper up from the desert sand toward the sky. At any time of day, one side will hold the sun's full glare, while another is cast into shadow. Before Islamic builders plundered their stone, each pyramid was dressed with white limestone, preserved now only on the pinnacle of the pyramid of Khafra; at the tip of each, moreover, was a thin layer of gold. On Khafra's pyramid, a course of red granite set off the limestone's whiteness at ground level. The entrance to each pyramid was on its north face, and somewhere within the solid stone mass, rather than below ground, the architect concealed a burial chamber in the hopes of foiling tomb robbers (see fig. 3.3). Encircling each pyramid was an enclosure wall, and clustered all around were smaller pyramids and mastabas for members of the royal family and high officials.

Like Djoser's complex at Saqqara and most subsequent royal burials, Fourth Dynasty burials took place on the Nile's west bank, the side of the setting sun, across from living habitations on the east bank (fig. **3.8**). Yet in contrast to Djoser's complex, where the compact arrangement was laid out on a north–south axis, the architects at Giza set out the monuments on an extended east–west axis. At the start of the funeral ceremony, attendants transported the body westward across the Nile. Once beyond the land under cultivation, the procession reached the valley ple, connected to the Nile by a canal. In the valley temple of afra is a central T-shaped hallway, where floors of white calcite set off walls and pillars of costly red Aswan granite. Light cascaded in through slits in the upper walls and the red granite roof.

Beyond the valley temple, a raised and covered causeway led westward into the desert for about a third of a mile (0.2 km) to the funerary temple, adjoined to the pyramid's east face. Here an embalmer preserved the dead king's body, and the living perpetuated the cult for his *ka*. Again, a rich variety of hard stone made for a vivid coloristic effect; relief sculptures probably added to the funerary temple's decoration, but most have perished over time. Next to the valley temple of Khafra stands the Great Sphinx, carved from an outcropping of rock left after quarrying stone (fig. **3.9**). (Like pyramid, sphinx is originally a Greek term.) Uncomfortable with human representation in art, later Islamic residents of Giza damaged the massive sculpture, obscuring details of its face, and the top of the head is also missing. Still, scholars believe that the sculptors combined a portrait of Khafra (or possibly Khufu) with the crouching body (and thus strength) of a lion. Its vast scale also proclaims the king's power.

The change in funerary architecture suggests a shift in the way Egyptians perceived their ruler. The smooth-sided pyramid was the shape of the *ben-ben*, a sacred stone relic in Heliopolis, center of the sun cult. These monumental tombs may therefore have emphasized the solar aspect of the king's person; indeed, the change in building practice coincides more or less with the king's adoption of the title "son of Ra." The change in orientation for the complexes also meant that the king's funerary temple did not face the northern stars, as before, but the rising sun in the east, which signified eternity through its daily rising and setting. In contrast to the funerary complex for Djoser (see figs. 3.4 and 3.5), the Giza complex contains no buildings for reenacting rituals of kingship. This suggests that the perpetual performance of these rituals was no longer the dead king's task. Now, his role was to rise to the sun-god on the sun's rays, perhaps symbolized by the pyramid's sloping sides, and to accompany him on his

Excerpt from the Pyramid Text of Unis (r. 2341–2311 BCE)

King Unis of the Fifth Dynasty built a pyramid at Saqqara on the walls of which were inscribed a series of incantations and prayers for the afterlife of the pharaoh. So-called Pyramid Texts such as these were placed in tombs throughout Egyptian history for both royal and nonroyal burials. Some of their formulas were adapted for different versions of the Book of the Dead. Though the earliest text to survive dates from about 2320 BCE, the prayers may have been composed much earlier.

The Resurrection of King Unis

A pale sky darken, stars hide away,
Nations of heavenly bowmen are shaken,
Bones of the earth gods tremble—
All cease motion, are still, for they have looked upon Unis,
    the King,
Whose soul rises in glory, transfigured, a god,
Alive among his fathers of old time, nourished by ancient
    mothers.

The King, this is he! Lord of the twisty ways of wisdom
(whose very mother knew not his name),
His magnificence lights the black sky,
His power flames in the Land of the Risen—
Like Atum his father, who bore him;
And once having born him, strong was the Son more than
    the Father!

The *Kas* of the King hover about him;
Feminine spirits steady his feet;
Familiar gods hang over him;
Uraei (cobras) rear from his brow;
And his guiding Serpent precedes:
"Watch over the Soul! Be helpful, O Fiery One!"
All the mighty companions are guarding the King!

Source: *Ancient Egyptian Literature: An Anthology*, tr. John I. Foster (Austin, TX: University of Texas Press, 2001)

---

endless cycle of regeneration. Texts in the form of chants or prayers inscribed on the interior walls of some later Old Kingdom pyramids express this conception of the role of the king vividly. The *Primary Source* text reproduced above, from the pyramid of Unis in Saqqara, dates to about 2320 BCE and describes the king's resurrection and ascension.

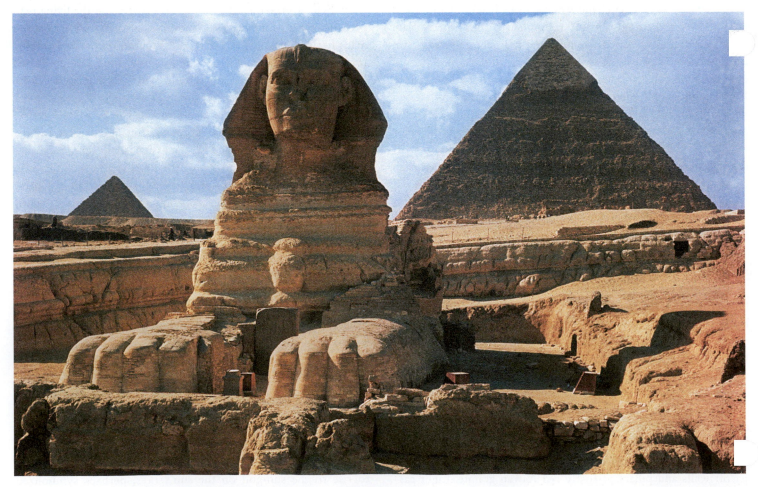

3.9   The Great Sphinx, Giza. ca. 2570–2544 BCE. Sandstone, height 65′ (19.8 m)

Representing the Human Figure

In the hall in the valley temple of Khafra, a series of indentations in the paving show that 23 seated statues of the king once lined the walls. Archaeologists discovered one of these almost intact and six in poorer condition, interred in the temple floor. The best-preserved statue represents the seated king in a rigidly upright and frontal pose (fig. **3.10**). This pose allowed him to watch—and thus take part in—rituals enacted in his honor; frontality gave him presence. Behind him, the falcon Horus spreads his wings protectively around his head. Like the *Palette of King Narmer*, this sculpture neatly expresses qualities of kingship. Horus declares the king his earthly manifestation and protégé, and the king's muscular form indicates his power. The smooth agelessness of the latter's face bespeaks his eternal nature, while the sculpture's compact form gives it a solidity that suggests permanence. The intertwined plants —papyrus and perhaps sedge—carved between the legs of his chair

3.11   Menkaure and His Wife, Queen Khamerernebty II, from Giza. ca. 2515 BCE. Slate, height 56″ (142.2 cm). Museum of Fine Arts, Boston. Harvard University—Boston Museum of Fine Arts Expedition

3.10   *Khafra*, from Giza. ca. 2500 BCE. Diorite, height 66″ (167.7 cm). Egyptian Museum, Cairo

are indigenous to both Lower and Upper Egypt, indicating the territorial reach of royal authority and the unity of the land. Even the stone used for his image expresses the king's control of distant lands: Diorite came from the deserts of Nubia. A hard stone, it lends itself to fine detail and a high polish, and the strong Egyptian light pouring in through the temple's louvered ceiling and reflected off the white calcite pavement must have made the figure glisten.

A slightly later, three-quarter-life-size group in schist represents King Menkaure and his chief wife Khamerernebty II (fig. **3.11**). It shares important features with the statue of Khafra. Carved in one piece with an upright back slab, it exhibits a similar rigid frontality. One reason for this may have been the sculpture's intended location and function. This group, too, may have come from the king's valley temple.

The artist depicted Menkaure and his queen with several characteristics in common. Of almost identical height, both are frozen in a motionless stride with the left foot forward. Though the king is more muscular than Khamerernebty, and though she is draped in a thin dress hemmed at her ankles while he is half nude, smooth surfaces and a high polish characterize both bodies. Menkaure's headdress even echoes the form of Khamerernebty's hair. These common qualities establish an appearance of unity, and the queen's embrace further unifies the pair.

In some cases, traces of paint show that sculptors added details to their work in color, though whether they always painted statues carved in high-quality hard stone is hard to assess. A pair of Fourth Dynasty sculptures from a mastaba tomb at Meidum are carved from limestone, which is softer than diorite and does not yield such fine surface detail (fig. **3.12**). Here, the artist painted skin tones, hair, garments, and jewelry, using the standard convention of a darker tone for a male, a lighter tone for a female. Rock-crystal pupils so animate the eyes that, in later years, fearful robbers gouged the eyes out of similar figures before looting tombs they occupied. Inscriptions identify this pair as Rahotep and his wife Nofret, and describe their social status: He is a government official and she is a "dependent of the king." Like the royal portraits, these figures are represented with ritualized gestures and in full frontality.

This rigid frontality is the norm for royal and elite sculptures in the round. In relief and painting, there is also a remarkable consistency in stance among royal and elite subjects. The standard pose, as illustrated on the *Palette of King Narmer* (see fig. 3.2) and on a wooden stele found in the mastaba of a court official of Djoser, Hesy-ra, at Saqqara (fig. 3.13), is altogether nonnaturalistic. In the case of the latter, frontal shoulders and arms and a frontal kilt combine with a profile head (with a frontal eye) and legs; the figure has two left feet, with high arches and a single toe.

3.12 Prince Rahotep and His Wife, Nofret. ca. 2580 BCE. Painted limestone, height 47¼" (120 cm). Egyptian Museum, Cairo

3.13 *Relief Panel of Hesy-ra*, from Saqqara. ca. 2660 BCE. Wood, height 45" (114.3 cm). Egyptian Museum, Cairo

3.14 Grid showing proportional guidelines for relief panel of Hesy-ra.

The representation is conceptual or intellectual rather than visual: The artist depicts what the mind knows, not what the eye sees. This artificial stance contributes to the legibility of the image, but so makes the figure static.

THE CANON Body proportions are also consistent enough in royal and elite sculpture in the round and in relief and painting to suggest that artists relied on guidelines for designing the human image. In fact, traces of such guidelines are still visible on reliefs and paintings. This **canon** (set of rules) began in the Fifth Dynasty with a grid superimposed over the human image: One vertical line ran through the body at the point of the ear, and as many as seven horizontal lines divided the body according to a standard module. Over time, the guidelines changed, but the principle of the canon remained: Although body-part measurements might vary from person to person, the relationship between parts remained constant. With that relationship established, an artist could make a human portrait at any scale, taking the proportions of body parts from copybooks. Unlike later systems of perspective, where a figure's size suggests its distance from a viewer, in the Egyptian canon size signaled social status.

For elite male officials, there were two kinds of ideal image, each representing a different life stage. One is a youthful, physically fit image, like that of Hesy-ra (see fig. 3.13). In the other, a paunch, rolls of fat, or slack muscles, and signs of age on the face indicate maturity. A painted limestone figure of a scribe, perhaps

3.16   *Ti Watching a Hippopotamus Hunt*, Tomb of Ti, Saqqara. ca. 2510–2460 BCE. Painted limestone relief, height approx. 45″ (114.3 cm)

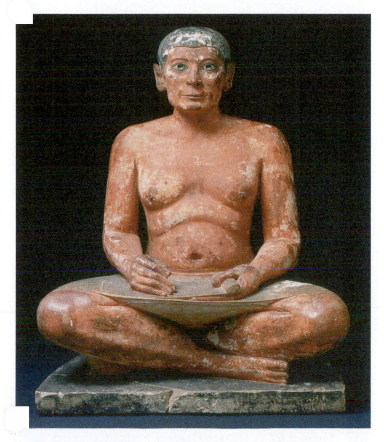

3.15   *Seated Scribe*, from Saqqara. ca. 2400 BCE. Limestone, height 21″ (53.3 cm). Musée du Louvre, Paris

named Kay, from his mastaba at Saqqara, is an example of the second type (fig. **3.15**). He is depicted rigidly upright and frontal but, unlike Hesy-ra, his body shows signs of slackening, in the sallow cheeks, sagging jaw, and loose stomach. Since Egyptian society was mostly illiterate, a scribe had high status; indeed, the artist depicted the figure seated on the floor in the act of writing, the very skill in which his status resided. The image reinforces his social status: It shows an official who has succeeded in his career, eats well, and relies on subordinates to do physical work on his behalf.

These conventions of pose, proportion, and appearance applied only to the highest echelons of society—royalty and courtiers. By contrast, the lower the status of the subject, the more relaxed and naturalistic their pose. Once the conventions were established, ignoring them could even result in a change of meaning for a figure, especially a change of status, from king or official to servant or captive. Fine low-relief paintings in the tomb chapel of Ti, a high official during the Fifth Dynasty, at Saqqara encapsulate the correlation between rank and degree of naturalism neatly (fig. **3.16**). In one section, Ti stands on a boat in a thicket of papyrus, observing a hippopotamus hunt. He stands rigidly in the traditional composite view, legs and head in profile, torso and eye frontal, while hunters, shown on a smaller scale, attack their prey from a second boat in a variety of active poses that more closely resemble nature. Zigzagging blue lines beneath the boats denote the river, where hippopotami and fish—on the lowest rung of the natural world—swim about in naturalistic poses. Similarly, nesting birds and predatory foxes freely inhabit the papyrus blossoms overhead.

PAINTINGS AND RELIEFS Like statues in tombs, paintings and reliefs played a role in the Egyptian belief system. Images such as *Ti Watching a Hippopotamus Hunt* (see fig. 3.16) allowed the deceased to continue activities he or she had enjoyed while alive. They also functioned on metaphorical levels. The conquest of nature, for instance, served as a metaphor for triumph over death. Death was the realm of Osiris, as god of the underworld, and so were the life-giving waters of the Nile, because of his regeneration after Seth had murdered him. Osiris was the god of fertility and resurrection, to whom Egyptians could liken the deceased. And, because Isis hid Horus in a papyrus thicket to protect him from Seth, they saw a papyrus stand as a place of rebirth, much like the tomb itself. Traditionally, too, a boat was the vehicle that carried the *ka* through its eternal journey in the afterlife. By contrast, Egyptians viewed the crop-destroying hippopotamus as an animal of evil and chaos, and so as the embodiment of the destructive Seth, lord of the deserts. Thus, meanings specific to its funerary context may have encoded the entire painting. Other Old Kingdom tomb paintings depict family members buried alongside the principal tomb owner, or as company for the *ka* in the afterlife. Some scenes depict rituals of the cult of the dead (that is, rituals in honor of the dead), or portray offerings and agricultural activities designed to provide the *ka* with an eternal food supply. In these scenes, the deceased typically looks on, but does not participate.

THE MIDDLE KINGDOM: REASSERTING TRADITION THROUGH THE ARTS

The central government of the Old Kingdom disintegrated with the death of the Sixth Dynasty king Pepy II in around 2152 BCE. This led to the turbulent First Intermediate Period, which lasted over a century and when local or regional overlords fostered antagonisms between Upper and Lower Egypt. The two regions reunited in the Eleventh Dynasty, as King Nebhepetra Mentuhotep or Mentuhotep II (ca. 2061–2010 BCE) gradually reasserted regal authority over all of Egypt. The late Eleventh, Twelfth and Thirteenth Dynasties make up the Middle Kingdom (ca. 2040–1640 BCE), when much of the art deliberately echoed Old Kingdom forms, especially in the funerary realm. The art asserted continuity with the golden days of the past. Sculptures of some members of the royal family, however, also show breaks with tradition.

Royal Portraiture: Changing Expressions and Proportions

A fragmentary quartzite sculpture of Senwosret III (r. 1878–1 BCE) indicates a rupture with convention in the representation of royalty (fig. 3.17). Rather than sculpting a smooth-skinned, idealized face, untouched by time—as had been done for over 1,000 years—the artist depicted a man scarred by signs of age. His brow creases, his eyelids droop, and lines score the flesh beneath his eyes. Scholars have described the image as "introspective," and reading it against the background of Senwosret III's troubled campaign of military expansion in Nubia to the south, they see the portrait's physical imperfections as reflections of the king's stress. Facial expressions or signs of age, however, can signify different things to different societies, and it is equally likely that the tight-lipped expression reflects a new face of regal authority, projecting firm resolve. Sculptors of this time tended to combine the aged face with a body that was still youthful and powerful.

As facial expressions became more naturalistic in royal images of this time, so the canon of proportions changed too. This is clear if we compare the Old Kingdom sculpture of Queen Khamerernebty (see fig. 3.11) with a sculpture of Lady Sennuwy (fig. 3.18), the wife of a provincial governor, found at Kerma in Upper Nubia. Depictions of women during the Middle Kingdom

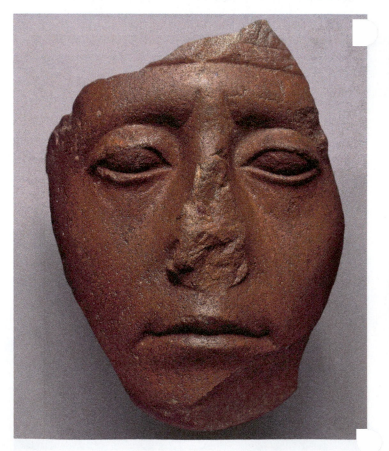

3.17 *Senwosret III*. ca. 1850 BCE. Quartzite, height 6½" (16.5 cm). Metropolitan Museum of Art, New York. Purchase, Edward S. Harkness Gift, 1926 (26.7.1394)

have increasingly narrower shoulders and waists, and slimmer limbs. Males have proportionally smaller heads, and lack the tight musculature of their Old Kingdom counterparts. Though subtle, these changes distinguish representations of the human body from period to period.

3.19 Rock-cut tombs, Beni Hasan, B-H 3-5, 11th and 12th Dynasties. ca. 1950–1900 BCE

Funerary Architecture

Burial patterns among court officials and other members of the elite stayed relatively constant during the Middle Kingdom, with most choosing interment in sunken tombs and mastabas. Already known in the Old Kingdom, rock-cut tombs were especially popular at this time. Fine examples still exist at Beni Hasan, the burial place of a powerful ruling family of Middle Egypt in the Eleventh and Twelfth Dynasties (fig. 3.19). The tombs were hollowed out of a terrace of rock on the east bank of the Nile and offered stunning views across the river. Inside, a vestibule led to a columned hall and burial chamber, where a niche framed a statue of the deceased (fig. 3.20). As in Old Kingdom tombs, paintings and painted relief decorated the walls. The section illustrated in figure 3.21, from the restored tomb of Khnum-hotep, shows workers restraining and feeding oryxes (a type of antelope trapped in the desert and raised in captivity as a pet).

As in the Old Kingdom, tomb owners believed the paintings provided nourishment, company, and pastimes for the dead. The living placed a wide variety of objects in tombs along with the dead, including objects made of **faience**, a glass paste fired to a shiny opaque finish. The figurine shown in figure 3.22 came from a tomb in Thebes, and represents a schematized woman. Her legs stop at the knees, possibly to restrict her mobility, or because legs were not essential to her function. The artist delineated her breasts and pubic area, and painted a cowrie-shell girdle to emphasize her belly and hips. Her function may have been as a fertility object, to enhance family continuity among the living and regeneration of the dead into a new life in the beyond. Egyptians associated the blue-green color of the faience with fertility, regeneration, and the goddess Hathor.

3.18 *Lady Sennuwy*. ca. 1920 BCE. Granite, height 67¾" (172 cm), depth 45⅞" (116.5 cm). Museum of Fine Arts, Boston. Harvard University—Boston Museum of Fine Arts Expedition. 14.720

3.21 *Feeding the Oryxes.* Tomb of Khnum-hotep, Beni Hasan. ca. 1928–1895 BCE. Wall painting (detail)

Often, the living buried jewelry with the deceased. Egyptians used jewelry widely, for daily personal adornment, for formal occasions such as court audiences, to bedeck cult statues, and to protect mummies. Many of the surviving pieces show extraordinary technological skill on the part of the jewelers. In the pyramid complex at Dahshur, the tomb of Mereret, a royal woman at the court of Senwosret III, contained two valuable pectorals, or large pendants. One is designed as a shrine with lotus-capital columns, within which two sphinxes trample enemies underfoot. With one raised forepaw, they support a cartouche of the king's name (fig. **3.23**). A vulture spreads its wings overhead. In wearing the pectoral, Mereret broadcast Senwosret's power to overcome foes and assert order. At the same time, the pectoral expressed royal wealth: The jeweler fashioned it in **cloisonné** (a metalworking technique often used for enamel), using a gold framework for valuable stones brought from afar: carnelian from the easte desert, turquoise from Sinai, and lapis lazuli from present-d Afghanistan. As a mummy ornament, the pectoral may have offered protection against malevolent forces.

5.22 *Female Figurine*, from Thebes. 12th–13th Dynasties.
Faience, height 3⅓″ (8.5 cm). The British Museum, London.
Courtesy of the Trustees

5.23 Pectoral of Mereret, from tomb in pyramid complex of
Senwosret III at Dahshur. 12th Dynasty. Gold, carnelian, lapis lazuli,
and turquoise, height 2⅖″ (6.1 cm). Egyptian Museum, Cairo

The stability of the Middle Kingdom was not to last. As
central authority weakened after about 1785 BCE, local governors usurped power. During the Twelfth Dynasty, immigrants
from Palestine known as the Hyksos (a Greek rendering of the
Egyptian for "rulers of foreign lands") moved into the Nile
Delta, gaining control of the area and forcing the king south-
ward to Thebes. The era of their control is known as the Second
Intermediate Period.

THE NEW KINGDOM: RESTORED GLORY

The first king of the Eighteenth Dynasty, Ahmose (r. 1550–1525
BCE), finally expelled the Hyksos from Egypt. The 500 years
after their expulsion—covering the Eighteenth, Nineteenth, and
Twentieth Dynasties—are designated the New Kingdom. They
constitute a time of renewed territorial expansion and tremendous prosperity for Egypt, and a time when the arts flourished.
Tremendous architectural projects were accomplished along the
full length of the Nile, centering on the region of Thebes (present-
day Luxor). Of these projects, many of the secular buildings,
including palaces and forts, were made of mud brick and have
perished. Stone tombs and temples, however, retain a measure of
their former glory.

Royal Burials in the Valley of the Kings

Changes in burial practices expose a major difference between the
Old Kingdom and the New. Having witnessed the loss of order
that allowed plundering of royal burials, Eighteenth Dynasty
kings abandoned the practice of marking their tombs with pyramids. Instead, they excavated tombs out of the rock face in the
Valley of the Kings west of Thebes, and their entrances were
concealed after burial. Excavations have revealed that in these
tombs a corridor led deep into the rock to a burial chamber
flanked by storage rooms. Decorating the burial chamber were
paintings of the king with Osiris, Anubis, and Hathor, funerary deities who assured his passage from this world to the next.
Rituals of the funerary cult took place away from the tomb, over
a rocky outcropping to the east, at a temple on the edge of the
land under cultivation.

HATSHEPSUT'S TEMPLE   The best-preserved example of
a New Kingdom funerary temple is that of the female king
Hatshepsut (ca. 1478–1458 BCE) (fig. **3.24**). Hatshepsut was the
chief wife—and half-sister—of Thutmose II. On his death in 1479
BCE, power passed to Thutmose III, his young son by a minor
wife. Designated regent for the young king, Hatshepsut ruled
with him as female king until her death in 1458 BCE. She justified
her unusual rule by claiming that her father, Thutmose I, had
intended her to be his successor.

Nestled in the cliffside at Deir el-Bahri, Hatshepsut's
temple sat beside the spectacular Eleventh Dynasty temple of

3.24 Temple of Hatshepsut, Deir el-Bahri. ca. 1478–1458 BCE

Mentuhotep II (fig. **3.25**), who had reunited Egypt over 500 years earlier during the Middle Kingdom. Senenmut, the architect who designed Hatshepsut's temple, may have modeled some of its features after this earlier temple, with its crowning pyramid or mastaba and terraces extending into the cliff face. Hatshepsut's temple is a striking response to its physical setting. Its ascending white limestone courts, linked by wide ramps on a central axis, echo the desert's strong horizontal ground-line and the clifftop above. Meanwhile, the bright light and shadows of the colonnades create a multitude of vertical lines that harmonize with the fissures of the cliff. With its clean contours, the royal structure imposes order on the less regularized forms of nature, just as the king's role was to impose order on chaos. At the time of its construction, a causeway led from a valley temple by the Nile to the funerary temple. Trees lined the entrance way, and paired sphinxes faced each other. Cut into the rock at the farthest reach of the temple was the principal sanctuary, dedicated to Amun-Ra, god of the evening sun. Smaller chapels honored Anubis, god of embalming, and Hathor, goddess of the west. An altar dedicated to Ra-Horakhty stood on the upper terrace.

Throughout the complex, painted relief sculptures brought the walls to life, describing battles, a royal expedition to the land of Punt in search of myrrh trees for the terraces, and scenes of

3.25 Reconstruction of Temples, Deir el-Bahri, with temples of Mentuhotep II, Thutmose III, and Hatshepsut (after a drawing by Andrea Mazzei, Archivio White Star, Vercelli, Italy)

3.26 *Kneeling Figure of King Hatshepsut*, from Deir el-Bahri. ca. 1473–1458 BCE. Red granite, height approx. 8′6″ (2.59 m). Metropolitan Museum of Art, New York. Rogers Fund, 1929 (29.3.1)

Thutmose I legitimizing his daughter's rule. Sculptures of the king and deities abounded. One of eight colossal red-granite statues from the third court (fig. **3.26**) depicts Hatshepsut kneeling as she makes an offering of two spherical jars. An inscription on the base records that the king is presenting *ma'at* (order) to Amun. Since kingship was a male office, she wears the regalia of a male king: a kilt, a false beard, and the **nemes headdress**, the striped cloth worn by kings. Although she is visibly female in some images, in this and many others she is depicted without breasts.

Sometime after Hatshepsut's demise, Thutmose III (r. 1479–25) constructed his own temple between his mother's and ....entuhotep's, with the purpose of eclipsing Hatshepsut's. He designated his own temple as the destination of the divine boat carrying the statue of Amun in the Festival of the Wadi, held at

Deir el-Bahri. At some point after Hatshepsut's death, the uraeus cobras were meticulously removed from the granite sphinxes and seated statues at her mortuary complex. Perhaps the intention was to repudiate her royal descent. By the forty-second year of Thutmose III's reign, a more systematic elimination of her images and removal of her name from inscriptions was underway. Workmen smashed her statues and buried the fragments in two pits in front of the temple complex. Still, Hatshepshut's temple remains a monument to her memory. Archaeologists have recently identified an obese mummified body in an unmarked tomb in the Valley of the Kings as her mortal remains.

Temples to the Gods

Besides building their own funerary temples, Eighteenth Dynasty kings expended considerable resources on temples to the gods, such as the Theban divine triad: Amun, his consort Mut, and their son Khons. At Karnak and nearby Luxor, successive kings built two vast temple complexes to honor this triad, and on special festivals divine boats conveyed the gods' images along waterways between the temples.

THE TEMPLE OF AMUN-RA At the Temple of Amun-Ra (a manifestation of the god Amun) at Karnak, a vast wall encircled the temple buildings (fig. **3.27**). Entering the complex, a visitor walked through massive **pylons**, or gateways built as monuments to individual kings (and sometimes dismantled as building proceeded over the years). As a ceremonial procession moved within the buildings, these pylons marked its progress deeper and deeper into sacred space. Within the complex, a vast **hypostyle** hall (room with many columns) was the farthest point of access for all but priests and royalty (fig. **3.28**). Here, a forest of columns would awe the mind, their sheer mass rendering the human form almost insignificant. The architect placed the columns close to one another to support a ceiling of stone lintels which had to be shorter than wooden lintels to prevent them from breaking under their own weight. Nevertheless, the columns are far heavier than they needed to be, with the effect that a viewer senses the overwhelming presence of stone all around—heavy, solid, and permanent. Beyond the hall, a sacred lake allowed the king and priests to purify themselves before entering the temple proper. They proceeded through smaller halls, sun-drenched courts, and processional ways decorated with **obelisks**, tall stone markers topped by pyramid-shaped points, and chapels where they would pause to enact ceremonies. Every day the priests would cleanse and robe the images of the gods, and offer sacred meals to nourish them. The king and the priests conducted these rituals away from the public eye, with the result that they gained power for being shrouded in mystery.

Essential to the temple's ritual functioning was its metaphorical value: It symbolized the world at its inception. The columns of the hypostyle hall represented marsh plants in stylized form: Their capitals emulated the shape of papyrus flowers and buds—so that the building evoked the watery swamp of chaos out of

3.27 Reconstruction drawing of Temple of Amun-Ra, Karnak, Thebes

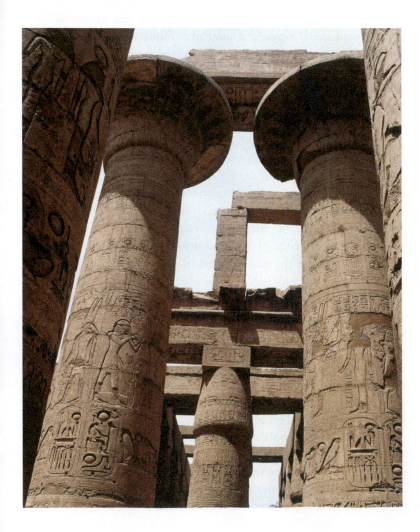

which the mound of creation emerged. The temple was thus the king's exhortation in stone to the gods to maintain cosmic order

Throughout the complex, a distinctively Egyptian form of decoration covered the pylons and hall and enclosure walls: **sunken relief**. In this technique, the sculptor cut sharp outlines into the stone's face, and modeled the figures within the outlines, below the level of the background, rather than carving away the surface around figures to allow them to emerge from the stone. Light shining onto the stone's surface then cast shadows into the outlines, animating the figures without compromising the solid planar appearance of the wall. This type of relief was especially popular for decorating hard stone, since it required less carving away.

The subject of the reliefs at Karnak was the king's relationship with the gods. In one section, from the north exterior wall of the hypostyle hall, an upper register shows Seti I sacking the Hittite city of Kadesh on the Orontes River, and, in a lower register, his Libyan campaign (fig. **3.29**). Following convention, the king and his horse-drawn chariot are frozen against a background filled with hieroglyphs and soldiers, whose smaller scale glorifies the king's presence. The figures of the king and his horse are also cut more deeply than surrounding figures, resulting in a bolder outline. The king's might and the ruthless efficiency of his forces seem to assure victory, although neither battle was, in fact, decisive. Through his conquest of foreign forces, the king established order, *ma'at*.

3.28 Hypostyle hall of Temple of Amun-Ra, Karnak, Thebes. ca. 1290–1224 BCE

ABU SIMBEL Seti I's son, Ramesses II, ruled for 67 years during the Nineteenth Dynasty (ca. 1290–1224 BCE). He commissioned more architectural projects than any other Egyptian king, including a monumental temple dedicated to himself and Amun, Ra-Horakhty, and Ptah, carved into the sandstone at Abu Simbel on the west bank of the Nile (fig. **3.30**). Location alone made an eloquent statement: With the temple, the king marked his claim to the land of Kush in Lower Nubia, which was the origin of precious resources of gold, ivory, and animal pelts. A massive rock façade substitutes for a pylon, where four huge seated statues of the king almost 70 feet high flank the doorway, dwarfing any approaching visitor. Between the statues' legs, small figures represent members of the royal family. A niche above the entrance holds an image of Amun, who is shown as a falcon-headed figure crowned by a sun disk. Flanking this deeply carved sculpture are sunk-relief depictions of Ramesses holding out a statue of

3.30 Temple of Ramesses II, Abu Simbel. 19th Dynasty. ca. 1279–1213 BCE

3.31 Interior of Temple of Ramesses II, Abu Simbel. 19th Dynasty. ca. 1279–1213 BCE

ground with knees drawn up to the chest and wrapped in a cloak, to a cubic abstraction. Above the block is a portrait head, and feet protrude at the bottom; sometimes arms are folded across the knees. Like the more conventional full-body sculptures, these images functioned as seats for the *ka* in tombs. When they first appear in the Sixth Dynasty, the figures are found in model funerary boats, transporting the dead to the cult center of Osiris at Abydos. They may, therefore, represent the deceased as a being sanctified by this journey in the afterlife. The example illustrated in figure **3.32** may come from the temple at Karnak. It presents two portraits. Above is the head of Senenmut, a high official at the court of Hatshepsut and Thutmose III and master of works for the temple at Deir el-Bahri. Below Senenmut's head is a very small head, portraying Nefrua, daughter of Hatshepsut and Thutmose II. Featuring the sidelock of hair that identifies her as a child, her head emerges from the block in front of Senenmut's face, as if held in an embrace, perhaps reflecting his protective role as her tutor. Omitting anatomical features in favor of the block form left an ample surface for a hieroglyphic text of prayers or dedications.

the goddess of order, Ma'at, to the god. The image thus demonstrates the king's role as keeper of terrestrial order at the gods' request. On the interior of the temple are more colossal figures of Ramesses, shaped from the same rock as the columns behind them. Their size (32 feet high) and frontality presented an awe-inspiring sight to priests who conducted rituals inside (fig. **3.31**).

Ramesses commissioned a second, complementary temple about 500 feet away from his own, in honor of his wife, Nefertari, and Hathor. Here, too, sculptors cut figures into the rock as a façade for the temple, which, though colossal in scale, was significantly smaller than Ramesses' temple. The topographical relationship between the two temples may be significant. Their central axes, when extended forward, intersected in the Nile's life-giving waters, so their locations may express the generative force embodied in the royal couple. This relationship has hardly been visible since the 1960s, when engineers moved the temple of Ramesses upward nearly 700 feet to raise it above flood levels resulting from the construction of the Aswan Dam.

Block Statues

In the New Kingdom, a type of sculpture known since the late Old Kingdom experienced fresh popularity. This was the block statue, where the artist reduced the body, shown seated on the

3.32 *Senenmut with Nefrua,* from Thebes. ca. 1470–1460 BCE. Granite, height approx. 3'3⅜" (1 m). Ägyptisches Museum, Berlin

Images in New Kingdom Tombs

New Kingdom artists continued to paint tomb chapels with scenes similar to those in Old and Middle Kingdom tombs. In the New Kingdom, however, additional images showed the deceased worshiping deities whose interventions could ease their transition to the next world—most typically, Osiris and Anubis. In the tomb chapel that featured in the annual festival of the Wadi at Thebes, when the living crossed to the west bank of the Nile and feasted with the dead, artists also painted banquet scenes. Music, dance, and wine were sacred to Hathor, who could lead the dead through the dangerous liminal phase between death and the afterlife. A fragment of painting from the Tomb of Nebamun at Thebes (ca. 1350 BCE) shows that painters still employed hierarchical conventions established in the Old Kingdom 1,000 years previously (fig. **3.33**). While elite diners sit in rigid composite view (half profile, half frontal) in an upper register, musicians and dancers below move freely in pursuit of their crafts. A flute player and a clapper have fully frontal faces, and they even turn the soles of their feet to face a viewer—an extreme relaxation of elite behavior. The nude dancers twist and turn, and the loosened, separated strands of the entertainers' long hair further animate their painted images. The freedom of movement inherent in these figures has suggested to some that works from contemporary Crete may have been available for these painters to study. Art historians have gone so far as actually to attribute paintings elsewhere to artists from this Aegean island culture.

New Kingdom artists and patrons also followed Middle and Old Kingdom precedents in designing sculpted tomb images. Some reliefs executed for an unfinished tomb in Thebes belonging to Ramose, vizier for Amenhotep III (ca. 1375 BCE), depict Ramose's brother, Mai, and his wife, Urel (fig. **3.34**). The relief is shallow, but the carving distinguishes different textures with great mastery. The composite postures and the gestures of the wife embracing her husband reflect conventions going back at least to the Old Kingdom; all the same, the canon of proportions differs from earlier representations, and some of the naturalism seen in other New Kingdom works informs the profiles of this couple. The united front that husband and wife present through eternity may be compared to a New Kingdom love song that extols the joy of spending "unhurried days" in the presence of one's beloved. (See www.myartslab.com.)

3.33 *Musicians and Dancers*, from the Tomb of Nebamun, Thebes. ca. 1350 BCE. Wall painting, painted plaster, height 24″ (61 cm). The British Museum, London

AKHENATEN AND THE AMARNA STYLE

Amenhotep III, whom Ramose served as vizier, raised the level of devotion to the sun-god during his reign (1391–1353 BCE). In temple complexes at Karnak and elsewhere, the king established wide open-air courtyards where Egyptians could worship the sun in its manifestation as a disk (or Aten) in the sky. Aten worship increased dramatically under his son, Amenhotep IV, who stressed the sun's life-giving force and began to visualize the god not in the traditional guise of a falcon-headed figure, but as a disk that radiated beams terminating in hands. Enraged by the young king's monotheistic vision of Aten, a powerful conservative priesthood thwarted his attempts to introduce this new cult to traditional religious centers such as Thebes. In response, Amenhotep IV established a new city devoted entirely to Aten on the Nile's east bank in central Egypt. He named his new city Akhetaten (now known as Amarna), meaning "horizon of Aten," and changed his own name to Akhenaten, "beneficial to Aten." Akhenaten's belief in Aten as the source of life found expression in the "Hymn to Aten" which is sometimes attributed to the king. This text (see www.myartslab.com) expresses joy in the daily rising of the sun by describing the world coming back to life at its appearance. Akhenaten's new cult and fledgling city lasted only as long as its founder; after his death, his opponents razed the city to the ground. Still, archaeological remains suggest that Akhenaten built temples in the contemporary style, using massive pylons and obelisks, as at Karnak, but with an emphasis on open-air courts directly exposed to the sun's glare.

The Amarna Style

Sculptures of Akhenaten and his family break dramatically with long-established conventions for depicting royal subjects. In numerous depictions, the figure of Akhenaten exhibits radically different proportions from those of previous kings. A colossal figure of Akhenaten installed at the temple of Amun-Ra in Karnak between 1353 and 1335 represents the king with narrow shoulders lacking in musculature, and with a marked pot belly, wide hips, and generous thighs (fig. **3.35**). His large lips, distinctive nose and chin, and narrow eyes make his face readily recognizable. The Amarna style, which was not reserved for the king's image but influenced representations of court officials and others as well, specifically emphasized naturalism in the body. Still, these unusual portraits of Akhenaten have puzzled scholars. Some dismiss them as caricatures, yet such expensive and prominent images must have had the king's approval. There have also been attempts to diagnose a medical condition from these representations, by reading the king's features as symptoms of Frolich's Syndrome, a hormonal deficiency that produces androgynous (both male and female) characteristics. Possibly he simply intended his "feminized" appearance to capture the androgynous fertile character of Aten as life-giver.

Group representations of Akhenaten with his family—his consort Nefertiti and three oldest daughters—are equally remarkable for the apparent intimacy among the figures. This is clear on a sunk-relief scene on an altar stele, of the kind that Egyptians would erect in small shrines in their homes and gardens (fig. **3.36**). Beneath the disk of the sun, its life-giving beams radiate downward with hands at their terminals. Attenuated reed columns

3.35 *Akhenaten*, from Karnak, Thebes. 1353–1335 BCE. Sandstone, height approx. 13′ (3.96 m). Egyptian Museum, Cairo

3.36 *Akhenaten and His Family*. ca. 1355 BCE. Limestone, 12¾ × 15¼″ (32.5 × 39 cm). Staatliche Museen zu Berlin, Preussischer Kulturbesitz, Ägyptisches Museum

suggest that the scene takes place within a garden pavilion, which is stocked with wine jars. The king and his consort sit facing each other on stools. They hold three lively daughters, who clamber on their laps and in their arms, uniting the composition with animated gestures that reach across the relief in marked contrast to the static quality of scenes of other times. The deliberate emphasis on the daughters' childishness marks a change: In the past, artists had represented children with a hieroglyphic pictograph of an adult in miniature, sucking a finger. The emphasis on children epitomizes the regeneration that the royal couple represent, and especially the king as manifestation of Aten.

QUEEN TIY The surprising transience implicit in the children's youthfulness and animated gestures on the altar also characterizes a one-third-life-size portrait of Akhenaten's mother Queen Tiy, chief wife of Amenhotep III (fig. **3.37**). Using the dark wood of the yew tree, with precious metals and semiprecious stones for details, the artist achieved a delicate balance between idealized features and signs of age. Smooth planes form the cheeks and abstract contours mark the eyebrows, which arch over striking eyes inlaid with ebony and alabaster. Yet the downturned mouth and the modeled lines running from the sides of the nose to the mouth offer careful hints of the queen's advancing years.

The sculpture went through two stages of design: Initially, the queen wore gold jewelry and a silver headdress ornamented with golden cobras, which identified her with the funerary goddesses Isis and Nephthys. A wig embellished with glass beads and topped with a plumed crown (the attachment for which is still extant) later concealed this headdress. Although excavators discovered the sculpture with funerary paraphernalia for her husband, Amenhotep III, these changes indicate that it was adapted to suit the beliefs of Akhenaten's new monotheistic religion.

PORTRAITS OF NEFERTITI As with Akhenaten's images, early depictions of Nefertiti emphasize her reproductive capacity by contrasting a slender waist with large thighs and buttocks. Sculptures from the second half of Akhenaten's reign, however, are less extreme. At Amarna, archaeologists discovered the studio of the king's chief sculptor, Tuthmosis, whom court records call "the king's favorite and master of the works." This yielded sculptures at every stage of production: heads and limbs of quartzite and jasper, and torsos of royal statues to which they could be affixed. Plaster casts were found, modeled from clay or wax studies taken from life. The most famous of these sculptures is a bust of Nefertiti, plastered over a limestone core and painted—a master portrait, perhaps, from which artists could copy other images (fig. **3.38**). The sculpture's left eye lacks the inlay of the right, showing that the bust remained unfinished, but an extraordinary

3.37 *Queen Tiy*, from Kom Medinet el-Ghurab. ca. 1352 BCE. Yew, ebony, glass, silver, gold, lapis lazuli, cloth, clay, and wax, height 3¾″ (9.4 cm). Staatliche Museen zu Berlin, Preussischer Kulturbesitz, Ägyptisches Museum

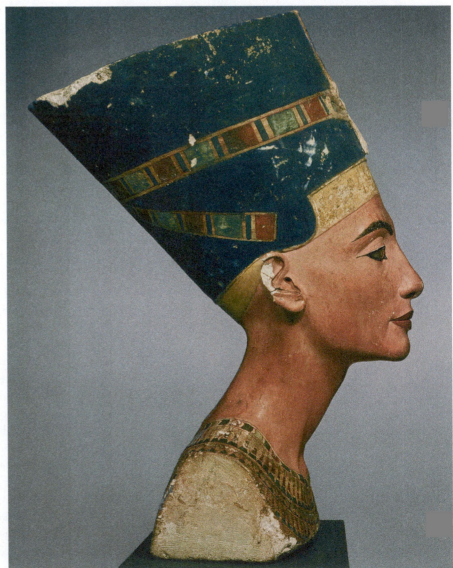

3.38 *Queen Nefertiti*. ca. 1348–1336/35 BCE. Limestone, height 19½″ (50 cm). Staatliche Museen zu Berlin, Preussischer Kulturbesitz, Ägyptisches Museum

Interpreting Ancient Travel Writers

A great many Greeks went to Egypt; some, as might be expected, or business, some to serve in the army, but also some just to see the country itself.

—Herodotus

One of the primary sources available to art historians is the writing of ancient travelers. Despite the dangers of travel in antiquity, from shipwrecks to thievery, Egypt became a prime destination for curiosity-seekers, beginning around 1500 BCE, and peaking during the first and second centuries CE. Locals did what they could to entice travelers. In Roman times, men from Busiris, near Giza, would climb the pyramids' slippery slopes as a tourist attraction. Some early travelers painted or scratched their names on works of art, among them Hadrian's wife, Sabina. Others made a crucial—if complex—contribution to our knowledge of ancient monuments by writing about their journeys. Born in the early fifth century BCE in Halicarnassos (present-day Bodrum, Turkey), Herodotus spent the best part of his adulthood traveling throughout the Mediterranean and the Near East. His account of his Egyptian travels still survives. In the late first century BCE, the Greek geographer Strabo also wrote a valuable description of his experiences in Egypt and elsewhere.

These authors saw the "great wonders" at first hand, at a time when much more survived of them than is the case today. Often, their accounts supply vital information for reconstructions, or other details, such as the names of artists, architects, or patrons; but it is a mistake to accept the writers' words uncritically. These ancient travelers had different priorities from the modern art historian, and this fact would certainly have affected the accuracy of their accounts. Herodotus, for instance, was much more interested in religion than in works of art or architecture. This results in him giving considerably less detailed or precise information about artistic monuments than we might desire. It is also all too easy to forget that even ancient travelers visited Egypt at least a millennium after the pyramids and other monuments had been built. Furthermore, they relied on traditions handed down by guides and other locals, who, research shows, were often misinformed. Herodotus insists that the blocks of Khufu's pyramid were all at least 30 feet long, when 3 feet would have been more accurate. He also attributes the work to slaves, thus denigrating Khufu as a tyrant. Local priests may have broadcast this view in the fifth century BCE to please their Persian rulers. A long tradition among scholars of giving greater credence to classical texts than other types of evidence has led, in many instances, to an undue acceptance of ancient authors' words as "truth," even when archaeological evidence paints a different picture.

---

gance still derives from the sculptor's command of geometry, which is at once precise—the face is completely symmetrical—and subtle. The sculptor abandoned this piece and another similar head in the workshop when he moved from Amarna to Memphis after Akhenaten's death in 1335 BCE and the subsequent razing of his city.

Tutankhamun and the Aftermath of Amarna

Shortly after Akhenaten's death, a young king ascended the throne. Married to Akhenaten's daughter, even perhaps himself one of Akhenaten's sons, Tutankhaten was only nine or ten when he became king. Possibly under the influence of the priests of Amun, he restored the royal residence to Memphis and resurrected the orthodox religion of Egypt that Akhenaten had rejected. He changed his name to Tutankhamun to reflect the monarchy's renewed alliance with Amun, before dying unexpectedly at the age of 19. His sudden death has inspired numerous murder and conspiracy theories, but recent scientific studies of his mummy point to natural causes.

Tutankhamun's greatest fame results not from his life, but from his death and the discovery of his tomb in 1922 by the British archaeologist Howard Carter. Although robbers had entered the tomb twice, much of it remained untouched when Carter found it (fig. **3.39**). With a stairway, corridor, and four chambers, the tomb is uncharacteristically small for a royal burial, leading scholars to suppose that a nonroyal tomb might have been hastily coopted

for the king at the time of his unanticipated death. All the same, offerings buried with him lacked nothing in volume or quality. Indeed, the immense value of the objects makes it easy to understand why grave robbers have been active in Egypt ever since the Old Kingdom. The tomb contained funerary equipment, such as

3.39 Tomb of Tutankhamun. 18th Dynasty

The Book of the Dead

This text is an incantation from Plate III of the Papyrus of Ani in British Museum, from the latter half of the Eighteenth Dynasty. It accompanies the weighing of the soul illustrated in the closely related The Book of the Dead of Hunefer (see fig. 3.40).

Saith Thoth the righteous judge of the cycle of the gods great who are in the presence of Osiris: Hear ye decision this. In very truth is weighed the heart of Osiris, is his soul standing as a witness for him; his sentence is right upon the scales great. Not hath been found wickedness [in] him any; not hath he wasted food offering in the temples; not hath he done harm in deed; not hath he let go with his mouth evil things while he was upon earth.

Saith the cycle of the gods great to Thoth [dwelling] in Hermopolis [the god's cult-center along the Nile in Upper Egypt]: Decreed is it that which cometh forth from thy mouth. Truth [and] righteous [is] Osiris, the scribe Ani triumphant. Not hath he sinned, not hath he done evil in respect of us. Let not be allowed to prevail Amemet [Ammut, the devourer of souls] over him. Let there be given to him cakes, and a coming forth in the presence of Osiris, and a field abiding in Sekhet-hetepu [Field of Peace] like the followers of Horus.

---

coffins, statues, and masks, as well as items used during the king's lifetime, such as furniture, clothing, and chariots. Many of the objects feature images of Tutankhamun battling and overcoming foreign enemies, as part of his kingly duty to maintain order amid chaos. Three coffins preserved the king's mummified corpse, the innermost of which is gold and weighs over 250 pounds. Most impressive is the exquisite workmanship of its cover, with its rich play of colored inlays against polished gold surfaces (fig. **3.40**). The number and splendor of the objects in the burial of a minor king like Tutankhamun make the loss of the burial finery of powerful and long-lived kings all the more lamentable.

Tutankhamun's short-lived successor, the aged Ay, continued the process of restoring the old religion. He married Tutankhamun's widow, perhaps to preserve, rather than usurp, succession to the throne. Head of the army under Tutankhamun and last king of the Eighteenth Dynasty, Horemheb completed the restoration process: He set out to erase all traces of the Amarna revolution, repairing shattered images of the traditional gods and rebuilding their temples; but the effects of Akhenaten's rule lived on in Egyptian art for some time to come.

PAPYRUS SCROLLS: *THE BOOK OF THE DEAD*

Inscriptions on walls and furnishings accompanied royal burials like Tutankhamun's. Yet in the Middle Kingdom, the desire to include the prayers and incantations that accompanied kings to the afterlife spread to other classes of patrons. By the New Kingdom, these patrons commissioned scribes to make illustrated funerary texts such as *The Book of the Dead* which first appeared in the Eighteenth Dynasty. This is a collection of over 200 incantations or spells that ultimately derived from the Coffin Texts of the Middle Kingdom, which scribes copied onto scrolls made of papyrus reeds. The popularity of *The Book of the Dead* in the

New Kingdom signals a change in Egyptian beliefs about the afterlife: Any member of the elite could enjoy an afterlife, as long as the deceased had lived in accordance with *ma'at* and could pass tests imposed by the gods of the underworld. In order to ensure that the deceased had the knowledge required to do this and progress to the hereafter, relatives generally placed a version of *The Book of the Dead* inside the coffin or wrapped within the mummy bandaging itself. Among the scenes illustrating the book are the funeral procession, the weighing of the heart, and the provision of nourishment for the dead.

One of the finest surviving examples is *The Book of the Dead of Hunefer*, dating from about 1285 BCE. The scene representing the weighing of the heart and Osiris' judgment of the dead in Chapter 125 (see *Primary Source*, above) conforms to a well-defined type that many workshops shared (fig. **3.41**). Derived from traditional tomb painting, its imagery has been adapted to the format of the scroll to be a continuous narrative, repeating protagonists in one scene after another without a dividing framework. At the left, Anubis, the jackal-faced guardian of the underworld, leads Hunefer into the Hall of the Two Truths. Anubis then weighs Hunefer's heart, contained in a miniature vase, against the ostrich feather of Ma'at, who symbolized divine order and governed ethical behavior. Ma'at's head appears on the top of the scales. Thoth, the ibis-headed scribe, records the outcome. Looking on with keen interest is Ammut. Made up of the parts of various ferocious beasts—the head of a crocodile, the body and forelegs of a lion, and the hindquarters of a hippopotamus—she was the devourer of those whose unjust life left them unworthy of an afterlife.

The deceased had to swear to each of the deities seen overhead that he or she had lived according to *ma'at*. When he had been declared "true of voice," Horus presented him to his father, Osiris, shown with emblems of kingship, wrapped in a white mummy-like shroud, and seated in a pavilion floating above a lake of natron, a salt used for preserving the body. With him are Isis and her sister Nephthys, mother of Anubis and protector of the dead. In front of the throne, the four sons of Horus stand on a white lotus blossom, symbol of rebirth. Also considered the gods of the cardinal points, they protected the internal organs that were removed as part of the embalming process and placed in containers known

3.40 Cover of the coffin of Tutankhamun. 18th Dynasty. Gold, height 72″ (182.9 cm). Egyptian Museum, Cairo

3.41 *The Weighing of the Heart and Judgment by Osiris*, from *The Book of the Dead of Hunefer*. 1285 BCE. Painted papyrus, height 15⅝″ (39.5 cm). The British Museum, London

as canopic jars. Above, Horus, identified by the eye he lost in his struggle with Seth, called the udjat eye, bears an ostrich feather, representing the favorable judgment of Ma'at. In the afterlife, as on earth, the desire for order was paramount.

LATE EGYPT

Tutankhamun's revival of the cult of Amun and the ancient sources of *The Book of the Dead* demonstrate that New Kingdom Egyptians deeply venerated the traditions of the past. Even as Ramesses II extended the borders of his realm to the south and the east, the cult centers at Luxor and Karnak absorbed great wealth and developed great influence. About 1076 BCE, barely 70 years after the end of the reign of Ramesses III, priests began to exert more and more power, until during the Twenty-first Dynasty the cult of Amun dominated Egypt. Thereafter, successive groups of foreigners controlled the area, including Nubians, Persians, and Macedonians, and the era known as the New Kingdom comes to an end.

The final phase of ancient Egypt belongs to the history of Greece and Rome. Alexander the Great conquered Egypt and founded the city of Alexandria before his death in 323 BCE. His general, Ptolemy (d. 284 BCE), became king of the region, and established a dynasty that lasted nearly 300 years, until the death of Ptolemy XIV or Caesarion, Cleopatra's son by the Roman dictator Julius Caesar. In 30 BCE, the Roman general Octavian, soon to be the emperor Augustus, claimed Egypt as a Roman province. Despite its lack of autonomy, Egypt flourished economi-

cally under the Greeks and Romans. In the Ptolemaic period, Alexandria became one of the most vibrant centers of culture and learning in the Hellenistic world, and its port ensured a live trade that reached as far as China and India. In Roman times, the Nile's life-giving waters made Egypt the chief source of grain in the empire, earning it the title of Rome's granary. But in addition to this commercial function, Egypt provided Rome and its successors with inspiring models of kingly power and imagery that lasted through the ages.

For some 3,000 years, from the era of the pyramids down to the time of the Ptolemies, Egyptian kings built magnificent structures that expressed their wealth and their control over the land and its resources. All aspects of royal patronage demonstrated the intimate link between the king and the gods. Building in stone and on a grand scale, Egyptian kings sought to impress a viewer with the necessity and inevitability of their rule. The formulas for representing the power of the king are as old as Egypt itself.

Egyptian kings and other elite patrons built structures for both the living and the dead. The objects and images placed in their tombs for the afterlife offer a modern viewer a glimpse of the material goods that they enjoyed in their lifetimes. The tombs provided a safe haven for the body and the soul (*ka*) of the deceased. They were built to endure, and they were equipped with numerous representations of the dead. These representations were also designed to last by virtue of being made of the most permanent of materials. Permanence was also sought through the consistent use of conventions for representing the patron. The longevity of Egyptian art forms testifies to the longevity of Egyptian social structures, political organization, and beliefs.

ca. 3500–3200 BCE Predynastic painting at Hierakonpolis

ca. 3150–3125 BCE The *Palette of King Narmer*

2630–2611 BCE Rule of King Djoser, and construction of his mortuary complex at Saqqara

ca. 2575–2465 BCE The Fourth Dynasty, and construction of the three Great Pyramids at Giza

ca. 1870s–1840s BCE Naturalistic sculpture of King Senwosret III

ca. 1458 BCE King Hatshepsut dies; her mortuary temple was designed by Senenmut

ca. 1348–1336/35 BCE Plaster and limestone portrait bust of Akhenaten's wife, Nefertiti

ca. 1290–1224 BCE Rule of King Ramesses II, who commissioned a monumental temple at Abu Simbel

Egyptian Art

5000 BCE	◄ ca. 5000 BCE Human settlements along the Nile Valley
4500 BCE	
	ca. 4250–3750 BCE Neolithic menhirs at Ménec
4000 BCE	
3500 BCE	ca. 3500 BCE Pottery manufacturing appears in western Europe
3000 BCE	◄ ca. 2900 BCE Mesopotamians begin using cuneiform writing
2500 BCE	
	ca. 2100 BCE Final phase of construction at Stonehenge
2000 BCE	◄ ca. 2040 BCE Beginning of the Middle Kingdom
	◄ 1792–1750 BCE Hammurabi rules Babylon after 1785 BCE The Hyksos gain control of the Nile Delta
1500 BCE	◄ ca. 1595 BCE The Hittites conquer Babylon ca. 1550–1525 BCE Rule of King Ahmose; expulsion of the Hyksos from Egypt
	◄ ca. 1400–1200 BCE Apogee of the Hittite Empire
	◄ ca. 1353–1335 BCE Rule of King Akhenaten; new religious center at Amarna
1000 BCE	ca. 957 BCE Solomon's Temple is completed in Jerusalem
500 BCE	
	◄ 323 BCE Alexander the Great dies, leading to Ptolemy's kingdom of Egypt
0	◄ 30 BCE Roman general Octavian proclaims Egypt a Roman province

CHAPTER 4

Aegean Art

THE MEDITERRANEAN WAS ONE OF THE PRIMARY HIGHWAYS THAT connected the cultures of antiquity. With North Africa on the south, Asia on the east, and Europe on the west and north, this body of water brought disparate cultures into contact for both trade and conflict. The Greeks named one branch of the Mediterranean, between Greece and Turkey,

the Aegean Sea, and on islands and peninsulas there several closely related but distinct cultures developed in the third and second millennia BCE. The Cycladic culture emerged on the islands forming an irregular circle between the Greek mainland and the island of Crete. The British archaeologist Sir Arthur Evans named the culture on the island of Crete Minoan, because the later Greeks associated Crete with the legendary King Minos, son of the Greek god Zeus, and a mortal princess, Europa. The culture on the mainland is called Helladic, from the Greek *Hellas*. Together, these separate cultures formed a civilization we know today as Aegean, after the sea that both separates and unites them.

Until the second half of the nineteenth century, Aegean civilization was known principally from *The Iliad* and *The Odyssey*, epic tales of gods, kings, and heroes attributed to the eighth-century BCE Greek poet (or group of poets) known as Homer. His story of the siege of Troy and its aftermath still excites the modern imagination. Prompted by these stories, and curious to determine whether they had a factual basis, German archaeologist Heinrich Schliemann excavated sites in Asia Minor and Greece during the 1870s. Following his lead, Arthur Evans began exca-vations in Crete in 1900. Since then, a great deal of archaeologi-cal evidence has come to light, some consistent with, but much contradicting, Homer's tales. Although writing has been found

in Minoan and Mycenaean contexts, it is not bountiful and schol-ars are still working on its decipherment. (Note the absence of *Primary Source* boxes in this chapter.) Consequently, we under-stand less about Aegean civilization than we do about the cultures of Egypt or the ancient Near East.

There is evidence of human habitation throughout the Aegean as early as the Paleolithic period, though settlements spread and grew mainly in the Neolithic and Early Bronze ages. Scholars divide the Aegean Bronze Age into three phases: Early, Middle, and Late, each of which is further subdivided into three phases, I, II, and III. Archaeologists often prefer these relative dates to abso-lute dates, because the chronology of the Aegean Bronze Age is so open to debate. The Early phase (ca. 3000–2000 BCE) corresponds roughly to the Predynastic and Old Kingdom period of Egypt, and Sumerian and Akkadian culture in Mesopotamia. The Middle phase (ca. 2000–1600 BCE) is contemporaneous with the Middle Kingdom in Egypt and the rise of Babylon in Mesopotamia. And the Late phase (ca. 1600–1100 BCE) is contemporaneous with the Second Intermediate Period and the New Kingdom in Egypt, the Hittite overthrow of Babylon, and the rise of the Assyrians in Mesopotamia. A mass destruction of Aegean sites, from a cause still unknown to us, led to significant depopulation in about 1200 BCE, and, despite a slight resurgence, by 1100 BCE the Aegean Bronze Age had come to an end.

The different cultures of the Aegean produced distinct art forms. Stylized marble representations of the human figure and

Detail of figure 4.20, Corbeled casemate at Tiryns, Greece

Map 4.1 The Bronze Age Aegean

frescoes are paramount in the Cyclades. Large palaces with elaborate adornments on their walls dominate on Crete. Citadels and grave goods remain from the Greek mainland. In the absence of extensive writing, these works of art provide valuable insights into Aegean practices and ideals. The fact that the tales of Homer and Greek myths look back to these cultures testifies to their importance in the development of later Greek culture.

EARLY CYCLADIC ART

Information about the culture of the Cyclades comes entirely from the archaeological record, which indicates that wealth accumulated there early in the Bronze Age as trade developed, especially in obsidian, a dark volcanic stone. Funerary practice reflects this prosperity. At the beginning of the Early Bronze Age, around 2800 BCE, the islanders started to bury their dead in stone-lined pits sealed with stone slabs, known today as cist graves. Although they lacked large-scale markers, some of these graves contained offerings, such as weapons, jewelry, and pottery. Potters crafted their wares by hand in the Early Cycladic period, and in addition to drinking and eating vessels, they produced flat round objects with handles, decorated with incised or stamped spirals and circles, and sometimes with abstract renderings of ships (fig. 4.1).

Archaeologists nickname them "frying pans" because of their shape, but they may in fact have been **palettes** for mixing cosmetics, or, once polished, served as an early kind of mirror.

Some Cycladic burials included striking figures, usually female, carved from the local white marble. The Early Cycladic II example illustrated here represents the prevalent type (fig. 4.2). The figure is nude, with arms folded across the waist, and toes extended. The flat body has a straight back, and a long, thick neck supports a shield-shaped face at a slight angle. The artist used abrasives, probably emery from the island of Naxos, to distinguish details on the figure, such as a ridgelike nose, small pointed breasts, a triangular pubic area, and eight toes. Traces of pigments on a few figures indicate that the artist painted on other details, including eyes, hair, jewelry, and body markings similar to tattoos.

Female figures of this type are always standing (or reclining). They come in many sizes (the largest reaching 5 feet long and the smallest only a few inches), but their form is consistent enough to indicate a governing canon of proportions, as with Egyptian sculptures (see Chapter 3). All the same, a number of figures clearly stand outside this canon. For instance, some appear be pregnant. There are also some male figures. These are usua seated and play a musical instrument, such as a flute or a harp, like the player illustrated in figure 4.3.

"Frying pan," from Chalandriani, Syros. Early Cycladic II. 2500–2200 BCE. Terra cotta, diameter 11″ (28 cm), depth 2⅜″ (6 cm). National Archaeological Museum, Athens

4.2 Figure, from the Cyclades. ca. 2500 BCE. Marble. Height 15¾″ (40 cm). Nicholas P. Goulandris Foundation. Museum of Cycladic Arts, Athens. N.P. Goulandris Collection, No. 206

For many years, archaeologists called these figures Cycladic "idols," and pictured them playing a central role in a religion focusing on a mother goddess. More recently scholars have offered two other plausible explanations for their functions. Perhaps sculptors crafted them purely for funerary purposes, to represent servants or surrogates for human sacrifices, or even for the body of the deceased. Alternatively, they may have served a different function before burial, possibly within household shrines. Although most have come to light in a reclining position, they may once have been propped upright. Some examples show signs of repair with wire, which is a strong indication that people used—and valued—them before depositing them in graves.

Most likely, no single explanation applies to all of them. The greatest obstacle to determining their function is our general ignorance about their **provenance**, that is, where and how they were found and their subsequent history. The simplicity and clear geometry of the figures appeals to a twentieth- and twenty-first-century aesthetic that favors understated and clean geometric forms. Those qualities and the luscious white marble used to form the figures have led to their widespread appearance on the t market, often without any record of archaeological context.

4.3 *Harpist*, from Amorgos, Cyclades. Latter part of the 3rd millennium BCE. Marble. Height 8½″ (21.5 cm). Museum of Cycladic Art, Athens

In order to better interpret these figures, archaeologists need to know their exact findspots, whether in a burial context or in living quarters.

The carved figures of women and musicians that survive from these Aegean islands seem to look back to Paleolithic and Neolithic figures, such as the *Woman of Willendorf* (see fig. 1.14). Yet the characteristic pattern of these figures—the canon that they followed—is distinct to these islands (and to Crete, where some examples have surfaced). The tradition of making figural imagery in the marble native to these islands would become a dominant feature of later Greek art.

MINOAN ART

Archaeologists have found a wider range of objects and structures on the island of Crete than on the Cyclades. This large island, south of the Cyclades, and about 400 miles (640 km) northwest of Egypt, stretches over 124 miles (200 km) from east to west, divided by mountain ranges, and with few extensive areas of flat, arable land (map **4.1**). This geography, along with continuous migration throughout the Bronze Age, encouraged diversity and independence among the population: Minoan communities tended to be small and scattered. All the same, as a result of inhabiting an island that is centrally placed in the Mediterranean, Minoans became skilled seafarers and developed a powerful fleet of ships.

The major flowering of Minoan art occurred about 2000 BCE, when Crete's urban civilizations constructed great "palaces" at Knossos, Phaistos, and Mallia. At this time, the first Aegean script, known as Linear A, appeared. This is known as the First Palace period, comprising Middle Minoan I and II. Little evidence of this sudden spurt of large-scale building remains, as all three early centers suffered heavy damage, probably from an earthquake, in about 1700 BCE. A short time later, the Minoans built new and even larger structures on the same sites. This phase constitutes the Second Palace period, which includes Middle Minoan III and Late Minoan IA and IB. An earthquake demolished these centers, too, in about 1450 BCE. After that, the Minoans abandoned the palaces at Phaistos and Mallia, but the Mycenaeans, who gained control of the island almost immediately, occupied Knossos.

The "Palace" at Knossos

The buildings of the Second Palace period are our chief source of information for Minoan architecture. The largest is the structure at Knossos, which its excavator, Arthur Evans, dubbed the Palace of Minos (figs. **4.4** and **4.5**). In fact, the city of Knossos may have been the most powerful Cretan center of the Middle and Late Bronze Age, with its most impressive structures dating from between 1700 and 1400 BCE. These included courts, halls, shrines, workshops, storerooms (housing vast clay jars for oil and other provisions), and perhaps residential quarters, linked by corridors,

staircases, and porticoes. Frequent **light wells** (open spaces reaching down through several floors) illuminated and ventilated interior spaces (as seen in fig. **4.6**). Other amenities in the buildings included a system of clay pipes for drainage. Conspicuously lacking are exterior fortifications to protect the complex. Given their strength at sea, the Minoans may have had little fear of invasion.

As well-preserved as it appears, the present complex is a little deceptive: Evans reconceived and reconstructed much of it in concrete when he worked there between 1900 and 1932 (see *The Art Historian's Lens*, page 87). The original builders at Knossos framed the walls with timbers and constructed them out of rubble masonry or mud brick. Some they built of **ashlar masonry** (cut and dressed stone), which gave them a more ornamental appearance. Columns, often made of wood with a stone base, supported the porticoes. Their form was unusual: A smooth shaft tapered downward from a generous cushionlike capital. Often the shaft was oval in cross section rather than round. Wall paintings suggest that capitals were painted black and the shaft red or white. The origin of this type of column remains a mystery.

At first glance, the plan of the complex (see fig. **4.4**) may appear confusing and haphazard. This probably explains why later Greek legend referred to it as the labyrinth, home of the Minotaur, a half-human, half-bull creature who devoured the youths the Athenians offered him in tribute, and whom the hero Theseus killed after penetrating the maze. Coupled with the natural defenses of the island's geography, this mazelike arrangement of rooms, and a general lack of emphasis on entrances, may have been part of a moderate internal defensive strategy. The small si of the rooms and the careful control of the sun's penetration into living spaces through light wells may also have been deliberate decisions to keep the buildings cool in hot weather.

Moreover, the design does have an underlying logic. At its core is a large central court, onto which important rooms opened. The court divides the plan on an approximately north–south axis. On the west, a corridor running north–south separates long, narrow storerooms from rooms of less uniform shapes close to the court; the latter rooms may have performed a ceremonial role. An east–west corridor divides the east wing into (perhaps) a workshop area on the north side, and grander halls on the south. The complex appears to grow outward from the court, and using flat (rather than pitched) roofs would have greatly facilitated the building of additional structures. Compared to Assyrian and Persian palaces, such as the citadel of Sargon II at Dur Sharrukin (fig. **2.17**) or the palace of Darius and Xerxes at Persepolis (fig. **2.26**), the overall effect at Knossos is modest; individual units are relatively small and the ceilings low. Still, the rich decoration of some of the interior walls made for a set of elegant spaces. We should also remember that much of what remains belongs to subterranean or ground-floor levels, and archaeologists have long believed that grander rooms existed on a lost upper level.

Exactly how the grand structures of Crete functioned, ar who lived in them, is still a subject of debate. As noted abov Arthur Evans described the complex at Knossos as a "palace" when he first excavated it (assigning royal names to various

4.4 Plan of the "palace" complex, Knossos, Crete. ca. 1500 BCE

theatral area

North entrance

East entrance

corridor access to magazines

temple repositories

throne room

staircase

lapidary's workshop

West entrance

main shrine

pillar crypt

altars

grand staircase

Corridor of the Procession

Hall of the Double Axes

bathroom

storeroom

South entrance

staircase

lavatory

Queen's Hall

0   10   20   30   meters
0   20 40 60 80 100 feet

4.5 Reconstruction of the "palace" complex, Knossos, Crete

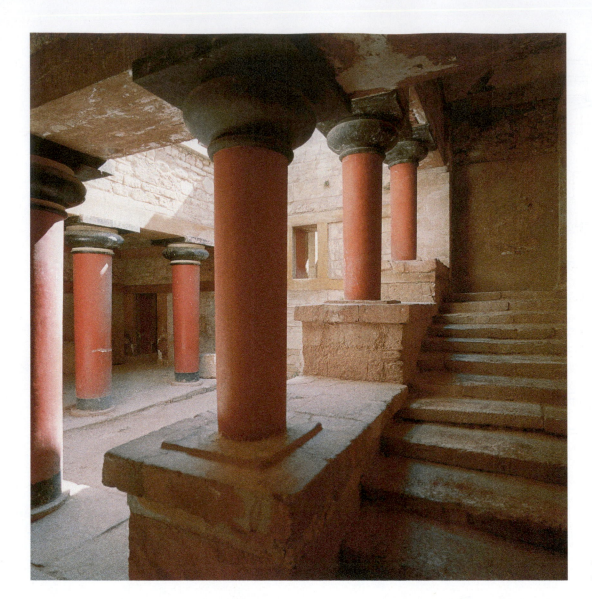

4.6 Staircase, east wing, "palace" complex, Knossos, Crete

rooms), and the term stuck, regardless of its accuracy. Evans conceived of the complex as a palace or an elite residence for several reasons. He was reacting partly to recent discoveries on the Mycenaean mainland, described below, and partly to the presence of a grand room with a throne. But the social and political realities of Evans's own homeland may have been even more influential in his thinking: He would have been familiar with the large palaces that the extended royal family occupied in late Victorian England. In fact, excavation of the complex at Knossos suggests that a variety of activities went on there. Extensive storage areas support a hypothesis that the palace was a center of manufacturing, administration, and commerce. Additionally, some spaces that seem ceremonial, such as the great court with its triangular raised causeway, and small shrine-like rooms with apparently religious paraphernalia, suggest that political and sacred activities occurred there too. There is no reason to believe that the Minoans segregated these activities as neatly as we often do today. Moreover, there is no evidence to suggest that the functions of the various complexes, at Knossos and elsewhere, were identical, or that they remained constant over time.

Wall Paintings: Representing Rituals and Nature

Grand rooms within the complexes at Knossos and elsewhere were decorated with paintings. Archaeologists found most of them in extremely fragmentary condition, so that what we see today is the result of extensive restoration, which may not always be entirely reliable. Vibrant mineral colors characterize the frescoes, applied to wet or dry plaster in broad washes without shading, in a technique known as **buon fresco**; wide bands of geometric patterns serve as elaborate frames. The prevalent subjects of paintings at Knossos go a long way toward supporting a hypothesis of ritual activity there. For instance, a miniature Second Palace period painting, dating to around 1500 BCE, depicts a crowd of spectators attending an event—a ritual or a game perhaps (fig. **4.7**). Art historians know it as the *Grandstand Fresco*. A tripartite building features at the center, which scholars identi as a shrine because of the stylized bulls' horns on its roof a in front of its façade. On either side sit two groups of animated women, bare-breasted and dressed in flounced skirts. Above

Two Excavators, Legend, and Archaeology

In the mid-nineteenth century, most scholars believed that Homer's epic tales of the Trojan War and its aftermath, *The Iliad* and *The Odyssey*, were merely the stuff of legend. But just a few decades later, that view had radically changed. Two extraordinary men were key figures in bringing about that change. One of them was Heinrich Schliemann (1822–1890). The German-born son of a minister, Schliemann became wealthy through a succession of business ventures and retired at the age of 41. From a young age, he had been fascinated by Homer's world of gods and heroes, vowing to learn ancient Greek (one of about 15 languages he would eventually master). He became convinced that a historical framework supported Homer's poetry, and during his extensive travels, he learned that a handful of archaeologists believed the Turkish site of Hissarlik to be the site of Homer's Troy. After gaining permission from the Turkish government to excavate there, he began working officially in 1871. Among the spectacular finds he described in print was "Priam's Treasure," a hoard of vessels, jewelry, and weapons made of precious metals, which he named after Homer's king of Troy. Then, turning his attention to Mycenae, Schliemann discovered the shaft graves of Circle A, some of which contained magnificent objects, such as the gold mask in figure 4.27.

Schliemann was also intrigued by the site of Knossos on Crete, but he was unable to purchase the land. The opportunity fell instead to Arthur Evans (1851–1941), the son of a renowned British naturalist, and himself Keeper of the Ashmolean Museum in Oxford. By 1900, he had begun excavating the so-called Palace of Minos at Knossos with extraordinary results. In 1911, In recognition of his contribution to the field of archaeology, Evans received a knighthood.

Until recently, scholars judged these two early archaeologists very differently. They deemed Schliemann's excavation technique destructive and considered Schliemann himself little more than a treasure hunter. Some scholars questioned whether he actually discovered "Priam's Treasure" as a hoard, or whether he assembled sporadic finds to make more of a news splash. Tales of his excavations have been embellished into myth in their own right. By some accounts, Schliemann had his Greek wife, Sofia, model ancient jewelry. Of late, scholars have recognized the unfairness of assessing Schliemann by modern scientific standards, and they have acknowledged his critical role in igniting scholarly and popular interest in the pre-Hellenic world.

Evans's reputation has fared better than Schliemann's, largely because of his close attention to stratigraphy, that is, using layers of deposit in excavations to gauge relative time. Geologists had developed this technique in the seventeenth and eighteenth centuries and archaeologists still use it today in a refined form. Evans employed it to assess the relative positions of walls and other features, and it led him to establish a relative chronology for the entire site. His designations of Early, Middle, and Late Minoan periods defined an essential historical framework for the Aegean world as a whole in the Bronze Age. Evans's work at Knossos included a considerable amount of reconstruction. His interventions help to make the site comprehensible to laypeople, but can also mislead an unknowing viewer. In fact, it was Evans, not the Minoans, who built much of what a visitor now sees at Knossos. One significant consequence of Evans's restorations at Knossos is that they have kindled debate among conservators about how much to restore and how to differentiate visually between ancient ruin and modern reconstruction.

4.7 *Grandstand Fresco*, from Knossos, Crete. ca. 1500 BCE. Archaeological Museum, Iráklion, Crete

4.8   The "Queen's Megaron," from Knossos, Crete. ca. 1700–1300 BCE. Archaeological Museum, Iráklion, Crete

4.9   *Spring Fresco*, from Akrotiri, Thera. ca. 1600–1500 BCE. National Archaeological Museum, Athens

and below, the painter used countless disembodied heads as a shorthand technique to denote the crowd, rendered with simple, impressionistic black strokes, on a swath of brown for males and te for females. The crowd figures are smaller in scale than the central women, suggesting that they are of lesser importance. The fresco may represent an event that took place in the palace's central court, as archaeologists have unearthed remains of a tripartite room on the west side of the court.

In many other Minoan paintings, nature is the primary subject. A painting found in fragments in a light well has been restored to a wall in the room Evans called the "Queen's Megaron" in Knossos' east wing (fig. **4.8**), though some have contended that it actually belongs on the floor. Blue and yellow dolphins swim against a blue-streaked cream background, cavorting with small fish. Within the upper and lower frames, multilobed green forms represent plants and rocks. Sinuous outlines suggest the creatures' forms, while the curving, organic elements throughout the composition animate the painting. Such lively representations of nature occur frequently in Minoan art in a variety of mediums, and the many images of sea creatures probably reflect the Minoans' keen awareness of and respect for the sea. The casual quality of Minoan images contrasts forcefully with the rigidity and timelessness of many Egyptian representations, even though there is good evidence for contact between Minoan artists and Egypt.

PAINTED LANDSCAPES IN A SEASIDE TOWN In the mid-second millennium BCE, a volcano erupted on the Cycladic island Thera (present-day Santorini), about 60 miles (96 km) north of Crete. The eruption covered the town of Akrotiri in a deep layer of volcanic ash and pumice. Beginning in 1967, excavations directed by Spyridon Marinatos and then Christos Doumas uncovered houses dating from the Middle Minoan III phase (approximately 1670–1620 BCE) preserved up to a height of two stories. On their walls was an extraordinary series of paintings.

Landscapes dominate. In a small ground-floor room, a rocky landscape known as the *Spring Fresco* occupies almost the entire wall surface (fig. **4.9**). The craggy terrain undulates dramatically, its dark outline filled with rich washes of red, blue, and ocher—colors that were probably present in the island's volcanic soils—with swirling black lines to add texture within. Sprouting from its surface, lilies flower in vivid red trios, while swallows dart between them, painted in a few graceful black lines.

In other rooms at Akrotiri, painters inserted humans into the landscape. Often they are life-size, but sometimes smaller, as in a painting on the upper section of at least three walls in a large second-floor room (fig. **4.10**). The scene reflects the town's role as a harbor: A fleet of ships ferries passengers between islands, set within a sea full of leaping dolphins. The ships vary, some being under sail and some rowed by oarsmen, but the painter's brush describes them all carefully. The same is true of the islands, each of which features a port city with detailed stone architecture. Crowds of people watch the spectacle from streets, rooftops, and windows. The painting may represent an actual event—a memorable expedition to a foreign land, perhaps, or an annual festival.

Minoan Pottery

Like the wall paintings, Minoan painted pottery was inspired by the natural world of the Aegean. Minoan potters painted their vessels sensitively with lively organic forms that enhance the curving shapes of the vases. By the Middle and Late Minoan periods, they manufactured pottery on the wheel, allowing for a variety of rounded forms and many sizes. Minoans used large and rough vessels for storage, while inhabitants of the "palaces" used the finest wares, which were often very thin-walled. Minoans also exported these "eggshell" ceramics in great quantities to markets all around the Mediterranean, creating one of the first major international industries.

4.10 *Flotilla Fresco*, from Akrotiri, Thera. ca. 1600–1500 BCE. National Archaeological Museum, Athens

KAMARES WARE The shape of a vase from Phaistos in southern Crete, dating to the Middle Minoan II period (about 1800 BCE), illustrates the organic approach of many Minoan potters to their wares (fig. **4.11**). Its neck curves upward into a beak shape, which the vase painter has emphasized by giving it an eye. Bold curvilinear forms in white, red, orange, and yellow stand out against a black background to form abstracted sea horses, which endow the vessel with life and movement. This style, known today as Kamares ware, first appears at the beginning of the Middle Minoan phase and took its name from the cave on Mount Ida where it originally came to light.

MARINE MOTIFS Marine motifs gained prevalence in the pottery of the slightly more recent Late Minoan IB phase. A stirrup jar, with two round handles flanking its narrow spout, makes a vivid example of this "marine style." A wide-eyed black octopus swirls its tentacles around the body, contrasting with the light eggshell-colored clay (fig. **4.12**). Clumps of algae float between the tentacles. As with Minoan wall paintings, an extraordinarily dynamic and naturalistic quality energizes the painting. Moreover, the painting's forms express the shape of the vessel they decorate: The sea creature's rounded contours emphasize the jar's swollen belly, while the curves of its tentacles echo the curved handles. Exactly beneath the spout, the end of a tentacle curls to define a circle of the same size as the jar's opening.

4.12 *Octopus Vase*, from Palaikastro, Crete. ca. 1500 BCE. Height 11″ (28 cm). Archaeological Museum, Iráklion, Crete

Carved Minoan Stone Vessels

From an early date, Minoan artists also crafted vessels of soft stone, either from black steatite (soapstone), which was locally available, or from stones imported from other Aegean islands. They carved it with tools of a harder stone, hollowing out the interior with a bow-driven drill before finishing surfaces with an abrasive, probably emery. Traces of gold on some pieces reveal that the stone was often gilded. Fragments of such works were discovered at Hagia Triada on the southern side of Crete, including a black steatite vessel known as the *Harvester Vase*, with a large hole at the top and a smaller hole at the base (fig. **4.13**). This type of vessel was used for pouring liquid offerings or drinking. Later Greeks called it a rhyton (plural rhyta), and archaeologists suppose that, like many stone vessels, it had a ceremonial use.

Only the upper part of the rhyton survives. Twenty-seven slim, muscular men, mostly nude to the waist and clad in flat caps and pants, seem to move around the vessel in a lively rhythm and with raucous energy. Their dynamic movement is a counterpart to the animated imagery on Minoan pots and wall paintings. Hoisting long-handled tools over their shoulders, fo bare-headed singers bellow with all their might. Their leade chest is so distended that his ribs press through his skin. A single long-haired male in a scaly cloak, holding a staff, seems to head

4.11 Beaked jug (Kamares ware), from Phaistos. ca. 1800 BCE. Height 10⅝″ (27 cm). Archaeological Museum, Iráklion, Crete

Excavators have discovered similar vessels elsewhere in Crete, for instance at the palace at Zakros, on the east coast of Crete, and contemporaneous Egyptian tomb paintings depict Cretans carrying bull-headed rhyta, suggesting that the civilizations with which Minoans traded identified them with these distinctive vessels. The prevalence of the bull motif, coupled with evidence of altars decorated with horns, suggest that bulls played a part in Minoan religious ritual. Rhyta are often found smashed to pieces. Although later vandalism or earthquakes might account for the damage, their smashed state suggests that ceremonial vessels were ritually destroyed after use.

Religious life on Minoan Crete centered on shrines and on natural places deemed sacred, such as caves, mountain peaks, or groves. No temples or large cult statues have been discovered. Archaeologists did find two small-scale faience statuettes from

4.13 *Harvester Vase*, from Hagia Triada. ca. 1500–1450 BCE. Steatite (soapstone), width 4½″ (11.3 cm). Archaeological Museum, Iráklion, Crete

the procession. The leader of the singers holds a sistrum, a rattle that originated in Egypt. This detail and the composite depiction of the men's bodies provide evidence of contact between Crete and Egypt.

Interpretations of the scene depend partly on identifying the tools carried by the crowd and the objects suspended from their belts. If they are hoes and bags of seed corn, then the subject may be a sowing festival; if, instead, they are winnowing forks and whetstones, it is more likely a harvest festival. Alternatively, some see the scene as a warriors' triumph, while still others see a representation of forced labor. In the absence of further evidence, either archaeological or written, debate about the meaning of the image will certainly continue.

Another magnificent rhyton in the shape of a bull's head comes from Knossos, and dates to the Second Palace period (about 1500–1450 BCE) (fig. **4.14**). Like the *Harvester Vase*, it is carved from steatite, with white shell inlaid around the muzzle. For the eyes, the artist inserted a piece of rock crystal, painted on the underside with a red pupil, black iris, and white cornea, so that it has a startlingly lifelike appearance. The horns, now restored, were once of gilded wood. Light incisions in the steatite, dusted with white powder, evoke a shaggy texture and variegated color in the animal's fur. The vessel was filled through a hole in the neck, and a second hole below the mouth served as a spout.

4.14 Rhyton in the shape of a bull's head, from Knossos, Crete. ca. 1500–1450 BCE. Serpentine, steatite, crystal, and shell inlay (horns restored), height 8⅛″ (20.6 cm). Archaeological Museum, Iráklion, Crete the Middle Minoan III phase (about 1650 BCE) at Knossos. One shows a female figure raising a snake in each hand and wearing a headdress topped by a feline creature (fig. **4.15**). She is clad in a flounced skirt similar to those worn by women in the *Grandst Fresco* (see fig. 4.7), and bares her breasts. Her tiny waist is another consistent feature of Minoan representations of humans, like the men on the *Harvester Vase* (see fig. 4.13). These statuettes came to light along with remnants of furniture in pits sunk in the floor of a room on the west side of the central court. Because some ancient religions associated snakes with earth deities and male fertility, and because of this statuette's bared breasts, some scholars have associated them with a mother goddess or ritual attendants, and identified the room as a shrine.

Late Minoan Art

It is unclear what brought Minoan civilization to an end. In the past, scholars argued that the eruption of the volcano on the island of Thera may have hastened its decline. Recent discoveries and dating of the volcanic ash from the eruption, however, indicate that the civilization on Crete survived this natural disaster, though perhaps in a weakened state. About 1450 BCE (Late Minoan II), invaders from the Greek mainland, whom archaeologists call Mycenaeans, took over the complexes on Crete. They established themselves in the center at Knossos until around 1375 BCE, when Knossos was destroyed and the Mycenaeans abandoned most of the island's sites. During the period of Mycenaean control, however, artists at Knossos worked in Minoan styles

The fragmentary *Toreador Fresco* dates from the Mycenaean occupation of Knossos (Late Minoan II–IIIA), and appears to

4.15 *Snake Goddess*, from the palace complex, Knossos, Crete. ca. 1650 BCE. Faience, height 11⅝" (29.5 cm). Archaeological Museum, Iráklion, Crete

4.16 *Toreador Fresco*, from the palace complex, Knossos, Crete. ca. 1550–1450 BCE (restored). Fresco. Height including upper border approx. 24½" (62.3 cm). Archaeological Museum, Iráklion, Crete

have been one of a series that decorated an upper room in the northeast part of the palace (fig. **4.16**). Against a deep-blue background, a white-skinned figure clad in a kilt clasps the horns huge curvaceous bull, painted at a full gallop. Behind the a similar white-skinned figure stands on tiptoe with arms outstretched, while above the bull's back, a dark-skinned figure performs a backward somersault. The figures have long limbs and small waists, and they are painted in profile. The strong washes of color, and animated though somewhat stylized poses, demonstrate the continuity of Minoan practice into the Late period.

Scholars continue to debate the meaning of this scene. Although most agree that such bull-leaping performances had a ritual function, the purpose of the activity and the identity of the participants remain unclear. Following the widespread Mediterranean convention for distinguishing gender by skin tone, Arthur Evans identified the light-skinned figures as female and the darker one as male. In this case, the presence of women in such a prominent role in Minoan imagery may serve as evidence of their importance in ritual activities. Others have seen the three figures as sequential representations of the same person, taking part in a coming-of-age initiation ceremony in which boys cast off their earlier "feminine" guise and emerge as fully masculine.

MYCENAEAN ART

By the time the Mycenaeans conquered Crete in about 1450 BCE, y had been building cities of their own on the Greek mainland since the start of the Late Helladic period, ca. 1600 BCE. They probably made early contact with Minoan Crete, which exerted important influences on their own culture. From the dating of Mycenaean sites and the objects discovered in them, archaeologists place the height of the culture between about 1500 and 1200 BCE (Late Helladic III). The most imposing remains are the citadels at sites that Homer named: Mycenae, Pylos, and Tiryns. The culture takes its name from the first of these, the legendary home of King Agamemnon, who led the Greek forces in Homer's account of the Trojan War.

Architecture: Citadels

At the beginning of the Second Palace period on Crete, growing settlements throughout the Greek mainland, including at Mycenae itself (figs. **4.17** and **4.18**), centered around large structures known as citadels (when fortified) or palaces. In some of them, most particularly Pylos on the southern coast of the Peloponnesian region (see map 4.1), archaeologists found clay

4.17   Aerial view of Mycenae, Greece. ca. 1600–1200 BCE

4.18   Reconstruction of Mycenae, Greece

lower
citadel

megaron

gates

propylea

courtyard

N

0   50   meters

0   200 feet

vaulted galleries

4.19   Plan of palace and citadel at Tiryns, Greece. ca. 1400–1200 BCE

the Mycenaeans as quite different from the Minoans, with a culture focused primarily on warfare. The contrast is often stated in terms that imply an essential character difference between nature-loving Minoans and warmongering Mycenaeans. Hom~~ ~~ characterizations of the kings of this era and, in fact, his en~~ ~~ narrative of the Trojan War, only reinforce modern ideas about the Mycenaeans as warlike. The poet describes the city of Tiryns, set on a rocky outcropping in the plain of Argos in the northeastern Peloponnesus, as "Tiryns of the Great Walls." We should note, however, that Mycenaean fortifications date to after the destruction of Minoan centers, so the Mycenaeans may have been responding to a new set of political and social circumstances.

The inhabitants at Tiryns fortified their citadel in several stages around 1365 BCE (fig. **4.19**). Like the slightly later walls at Mycenae, those at Tiryns consist of massive blocks of limestone, weighing as much as 5 tons. For most of the wall, the blocks were irregularly shaped (or polygonal), wedged together with smaller stones and fragments of pottery. At entrances or other highly visible places, the stones might be saw-cut and dressed, or smoothed with a hammer. In its final form, the outer wall at Tiryns was a full 20 feet thick, and a second inner wall was just as impressive. Centuries later, the massiveness of these walls so awed the Greeks that they declared them the work of the Cyclopes, a mythical race of one-eyed giants. Even today, archaeologists term such walls "Cyclopean."

Builders designed the fortifications at Tiryns carefully to manipulate any visitor's approach to the residents' military advantage, just as the slightly earlier Hittite fortifications did (fig. 2.22). A narrow fortified ramp circled the walls, so that an aggressor approaching in a clockwise direction would have his nonshield-bearing side vulnerable to attack by defenders on the walls. If an aggressor reached the entrance, two sets of fortified **propylons** (gateways) presented further obstacles: Inhabitants could trap the aggressor between the propylons and attack from above. Within the walls, rooms and passages known as **casemates** provided storage for weapons (fig. **4.20**). They also offered safety for townspeople or soldiers during an assault. The gallery passage was built using a **corbel** technique: Each course of masonry projects slightly beyond the course below it, until the walls meet in an irregular arch to cover the span (fig. **4.21**). When a corbel roofs an entire space, as it does here, it is called a **corbel vault**.

A corbel arch served effectively to create the Lioness Gate at Mycenae of about 1250 BCE. When the inhabitants enlarged the city walls to improve its defenses, they built this gate as a principal entrance into the citadel (fig. **4.22**). Two massive stone posts support a huge lintel to form the opening. Above the lintel, a corbel arch directs the weight of the heavy wall to the strong posts below it. The corbel thus relieves the weight resting on the vast stone lintel, which itself weighs 25 tons; this form of construction is known as a **relieving triangle**. To seal the resulting gap, the builders inserted a triangular gray limestone slab above the lint~~ ~~ carved with a huge pair of animals, probably lionesses. Th~~ ~~ stand in a **heraldic pose** (as mirror images of each other), with their front paws on a pair of altars of a Minoan type, and flanking

tablets inscribed with a second early writing system, which they dubbed Linear B because of its linear character and because it derived, in part, from earlier Minoan Linear A. Architect and classical scholar Michael Ventris decoded the system in 1952. The tablets proved to have been inventories and archival documents, and the language of Linear B was an early form of Greek. The inhabitants of these Late Bronze Age sites, therefore, were the precursors of the Greeks of more recent times.

The Linear B tablets refer to a *wanax* ("lord" or "king"), suggesting something of a Mycenaean social order, so it is reasonable to suppose that Mycenaean citadels and palaces may have incorporated royal residences. The inhabitants of many of these sites gradually enclosed them with imposing exterior walls. They exploited the sites' topography for defense purposes, and often expanded and improved their walls in several building phases. They constructed these fortifications of large stone blocks laid on top of each other, creating walls that were at times 20 feet thick. These walls, and tunnels leading from them to wells that would provide water during a siege, have led scholars to regard

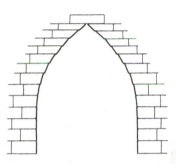

4.20 Corbeled casemate at Tiryns, Greece. ca. 1400–1200 BCE

4.21 Drawing: corbel arch

4.22 The Lioness Gate, Mycenae, Greece. ca. 1250 BCE

a tapering Minoan-style column, which may have supported another element of some kind. Dowel holes in their necks suggest that their heads were added separately, in wood or a different stone. At almost 10 feet high, this relief is the first large-scale sculpture known on the Greek mainland. The lionesses function as guardians, and their tense, muscular bodies and symmetrical design suggest an influence from the Near East. Mycenaeans ventured all over the Mediterranean, including Egypt and Anatolia, and Hittite records suggest contact with a people who may have been Mycenaean. Similar structures such as the Hittite Lion Gate at Bogazköy in Anatolia (fig. 2.22) may have suggested the concept of animal guardians at the gate of a palace.

The fortifications of Mycenaean citadels protected a variety of buildings (see figs. 4.17 and 4.18). These interior structures were built of rubble in a timber framework, as in Minoan palaces, sometimes faced with limestone. The dominant building was a **megaron**, a large rectangular audience hall. At Tiryns (see fig. 4.19) the megaron lay adjacent to an open courtyard. Two columns defined a deep porch that led into a vestibule and then into the hall. The hall contained a throne and a large central hearth of stuccoed clay, surrounded by four columns supporting the roof beams. Above the hearth, the ceiling may have been left open to the sky or covered by a raised roof, allowing smoke to escape and light to enter.

The design of a megaron is essentially an enlarged version of simple houses of earlier generations; its ancestry goes back at least to Troy in 3000 BCE. A particularly well-preserved example survives at the southern Peloponnesian palace of Pylos of about 1300 BCE. There, the hearth is set into a plastered floor decorated to resemble flagstones of varied ornamental stone (fig. **4.23**). A rich decorative scheme of wall paintings and ornamental carvings enhanced the megaron's appearance. The throne stands against the northeast wall, and painted griffins flank it on either side, similar

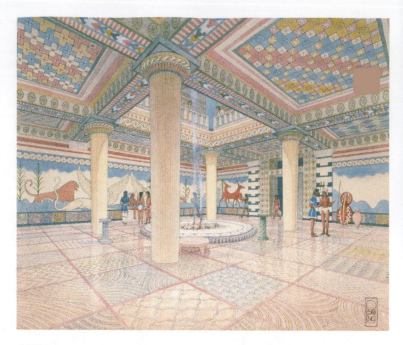

4.23   Reconstruction of megaron at Pylos. ca. 1300–1200 BCE

to those decorating the throne room at Knossos, elaborated under Mycenaean rule. Other elements of the decoration, such as the shape of the columns and the ornament around the doorways, reveal further Minoan influence at Pylos.

Mycenaean Tombs and Their Contents

At the end of the Middle Helladic period at Mycenae, ca. 1600 BCE, the ruling elite began to bury their dead in deep rectangular shafts, marking them at ground level with stones shaped like stelai. The burials were distributed in two groups (known as

4.24   "Treasury of Atreus," Mycenae, Greece. ca. 1300–1250 BCE

4.25   Reconstruction of "Treasury of Atreus," Mycenae, Greece

Grave Circles A and B), which later generations eventually set off and monumentalized with a low circular wall. As time passed, the elite built more dramatic tombs, in a round form known as a **tholos**. Over 100 tholoi are known on the mainland, nine of them near Mycenae.

One of the best-preserved and largest of these tombs is at Mycenae. Dubbed the "Treasury of Atreus" after the head of the clan that Homer placed at Mycenae, it dates to about 1250 BCE (Late Helladic III B). A great pathway, or **dromos**, lined with carefully cut and fitted ashlar masonry, led to a spectacular entrance (figs. **4.24** and **4.25**). The door slopes inward, in a style associated with Egyptian construction. Flanking the opening were columns of Egyptian green marble, carved with spirals and zigzags. Above the doorway, small columns framed decorative marble bands that concealed a relieving triangle.

The tomb itself consisted of a large circular chamber dug into sloping ground and then built up from ground level with a corbel vault: Courses of ashlar blocks protruded inward beyond one another up to a capstone (fig. **4.26**). When built in rings rather than parallel walls (as at Tiryns, see fig. 4.20), the corbel vault

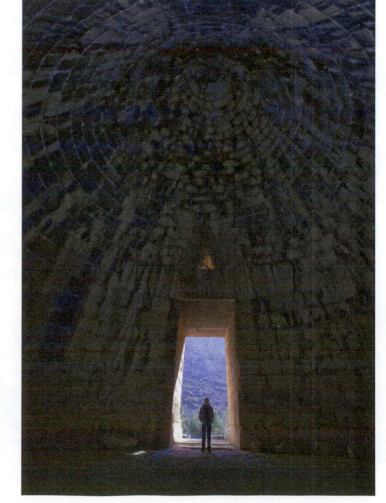

4.26   Interior of "Treasury of Atreus," Mycenae, Greece

4.27   *Mask of Agamemnon*, from shaft grave, Grave Circle A, Mycenae, Greece. ca. 1600–1500 BCE. Gold, height 12″ (35 cm). National Archaeological Museum, Athens

4.28 Inlaid dagger blade, from shaft grave IV, Grave Circle A, Mycenae, Greece. ca. 1600–1550 BCE. Length 9⅜″ (23.8 cm). National Archaeological Museum, Athens

results in a beehive profile for the roof. Gilded rosettes may once have decorated the ashlar blocks of the vault to resemble a starry sky. The vault rose 43 feet over a space 48 feet in diameter. Architects would not dare such a large unsupported span again until the Pantheon of Roman times (see Chapter 7). To one side of the main room, a small rectangular chamber contained subsidiary burials. Earth covered the entire structure, helping to stabilize the layers of stone and creating a small hill, which was encircled with stones.

METALWORK   Like the Great Pyramids of Egypt, these monumental *tholos* tombs exalted the dead by drawing attention to themselves. As a result, they also attracted robbers throughout the ages, and the grave goods that once filled them have long been dispersed. Many of the earlier shaft graves also contained lavish burial goods, ranging from luxurious clothing and furniture to fine weaponry. On excavating Grave Circle A, Heinrich Schliemann discovered five extraordinary death masks of hammered gold, covering the faces of dead males. Although far from naturalistic, each mask displays a distinct treatment of physi-ognomy: Some faces are bearded while others are clean-shaven. This suggests that the goldsmiths individualized the masks somewhat to correspond to the deceased's appearance. On finding one of them in 1876 (fig. 4.27), Schliemann telegraphed a Greek news-paper, "I have gazed on the face of Agamemnon." Since modern archaeology places the mask between 1600 and 1500 BCE, and the Trojan War—if it happened—would date to about 1300–1200 BCE, this could not in fact be a mask of Agamemnon, despite its title. But it may represent a Mycenaean king of some stature, given the expense of the materials and the other objects found near it. Among the weapons in the graves were finely made ornamental bronze dagger blades, some of them inlaid with spirals or figural scenes in gold, silver, and niello (a sulfur alloy that bonds with silver when heated to produce a shiny black metallic finish). The example in figure 4.28 depicts a lion preying on gazelles; the dagger's owner claims the lion's predatory strength.

THE *VAPHIO CUPS*   While the burial method used in the shaft graves is distinctively Mycenaean, the treasures found within them raise an interesting question about the interactions between Minoans and Mycenaeans. Many objects show Minoan influence, while others appear so Minoan that they must have come from Crete or been created by Cretan craftsmen. Two gold cups from a Mycenaean tomb at Vaphio near Sparta, in the southern Peloponnesus, are particularly intriguing (fig. 4.29). Probably crafted between 1500 and 1450 BCE, they are made of two skins of gold: The outer layer was embossed with scenes of bull-catching—a theme with Minoan roots—while the inner lining is smooth. A cylindrical handle was riveted to one side. On one cup, bull-trappers try to capture the animal with nets, while on the other, a cow is set out to pasture to entice a bull into captivity. The subject matter of the cups suggests that they refer to one another, yet they are not, strictly speaking, a pair. One cup has an upper border framing the scene, but the other does not, and stylistic analyses suggest that different artists crafted them. Where the cups or the artists originated is a matter for debate. For some, the "finer" cup (with the pasture scene) must be Minoan on account of its peaceful quality, and the other a more violent Mycenaean complement made by a Mycenaean—or a Minoan—artist. What the cups underline is how little we understand about the interplay between, and the movements of, Minoan and Mycenaean artists, and, indeed, how arbitrary and subjective our attempts to distinguish between them may be.

Sculpture

Mycenaean religious architecture apparently consisted of modest structures set apart from the palaces. At these small shrines, Mycenaeans worshiped a wide variety of gods. Names recorded on Linear B tablets indicate that some of them, such as Poseidon, are the predecessors of the later Olympian gods of Greece. The Greek Poseidon was the god of the sea, and was probably of some importance to the seafaring Mycenaeans.

4.29 *Vaphio Cups.* ca. 1500–1450 BCE. Gold, height 3½″ (3.9 cm). National Archaeological Museum, Athens

4.30 *Three Deities*, from Mycenae, Greece. 14th–13th century BCE. Ivory, height 3″ (7.5 cm). National Archaeological Museum, Athens. Ministry of Culture Archaeological Receipts Fund. 7711

Free-standing sculptures are rare, but one small, finely carved ivory group depicting two kneeling women with a young child came to light in a shrine next to the palace at Mycenae in 1939 (fig. **4.30**). The women wear flounced skirts similar to the one worn the Minoan *Snake Goddess* (see fig. 4.15), suggesting that the work came from Crete or was carved by an artist from Crete working on the Greek mainland for Mycenaean patrons. Yet the material is ivory, and probably originated in Syria or Egypt, documenting Mycenaean trade links. The figures' intertwined limbs and the child's unsettled pose describe a transient moment. For some scholars, the close physical interaction among the figures suggests that this small object is a rendering of a family group, including grandmother, mother, and child. Others argue that it represents three separate divinities, one of whom takes the form of a child.

Along with the "Treasury of Atreus," with its echoes of Egypt, and the Lioness Gate, which is a blend of Minoan and Near Eastern influences, this sculpture and others that survive from Bronze Age Greece reveal a culture with contacts throughout the Mediterranean. Whether those contacts came as a result of war or trade, the culture of Mycenaean Greece was receptive to the ideas and forms of other regions. Despite its warlike and dynamic character, Mycenaean civilization collapsed around 1200 or 1100 BCE, probably in the chaos caused by the arrival of new peoples on the Greek mainland. Whether or not the inhabitants of these powerful citadels actually took part in a legendary ten-year-long siege of Troy in Asia Minor, their descendants believed they did. For the Greeks, the Mycenaean Age was an age of heroes.

ca. 2500 BCE White marble
Cycladic figurines

ca. 1700–1300 BCE Minoans construct the
Second "Palace" at Knossos

ca. 1600–1500 BCE *Spring Fresco* at
Akrotiri, Thera

ca. 1650 BCE *Snake
Goddess* from Knossos

ca. 1500 BCE
Octopus Vase, an
example of Minoan
"marine style" pottery

ca. 1600–1500 BCE Mycenaean death
masks of hammered gold

ca. 1250 BCE Construction of the Lioness
Gate at Mycenae

Aegean Art

3000 BCE

2750 BCE

◄ ca. 2800 BCE Cycladic Islanders start to bury their
dead in stone-lined pits

2500 BCE

·········· ca. 2575–2465 BCE Egypt's 4th Dynasty;
construction of the three Great Pyramids
at Giza

2250 BCE

·········· ca. 2100 BCE King Urnammu commissions the
Great Ziggurat at Ur
·········· ca. 2100 BCE Final phase of construction at
Stonehenge

2000 BCE

◄ ca. 2000 BCE Minoans build the first "palaces"
on Crete, and develop Linear A

1750 BCE

◄ ca. 1792–1750 BCE Hammurabi rules Babylon

1500 BCE

◄ ca. 1500 BCE Volcano erupts on Thera
ca. 1500–1200 BCE Height of Mycenaean culture
◄ ca. 1450 BCE Earthquake demolishes Knossos and
other Minoan centers; Mycenaeans invade Crete

1250 BCE

·········· ca. 1290–1224 BCE King Ramesses II rules
Egypt, and commissions a monumental temple
at Abu Simbel
◄ ca. 1200 BCE Depopulation of Aegean sites

1000 BCE

◄ 8th century BCE *The Iliad* and *The Odyssey*,
attributed to Homer

CHAPTER 5

Greek Art

G REEK ARCHITECTURE, SCULPTURE, AND PAINTING ARE immediately recognizable as ancestors of Western civilization. A Greek temple recalls countless government buildings, banks, and college campuses, and a Greek statue evokes countless statues of our own day. This is neither coincidental nor inevitable: Western civilization has carefully

constructed itself in the image of the Greek and Roman worlds. Through the centuries, these worlds have represented a height of cultural achievement for Western civilization, which looked to them for artistic ideals as well as for philosophical models such as democracy.

The great flowering of ancient Greek art was just one manifestation of a wide-ranging exploration of humanistic and religious issues. Artists, writers, and philosophers struggled with common questions, preserved in a huge body of works. Their inquiries cut to the very core of human existence, and form the backbone of much of Western philosophy. For the most part, they accepted a pantheon of gods, whom they worshiped in human form. (See *Informing Art*, page 105.) Yet they debated the nature of those gods, and the relationship between divinities and humankind. Did fate control human actions, or was there free will? What was the nature of virtue? Greek thinkers conceived of many aspects of life in dualistic terms. Order (*cosmos* in Greek) was opposed to disorder (*chaos*), and both poles permeated existence. Civilization—which was, by definition, Greek—stood in opposition to an uncivilized world beyond Greek borders; non-Greeks were "barbarians," named for the nonsensical sound of their languages to Greek ears ("bar-bar-bar-bar").

Reason, too, had its opposite: the irrational, mirrored in light and darkness, in man and woman. In their art as in their literature, the ancient Greeks addressed the tension between these polar opposites.

Trying to understand the visual culture of the worlds on which Western civilization so deliberately modeled itself presents a special challenge for the art historian: It is tempting to believe that something familiar on the surface holds the same significance for us today as it did for Greeks or Romans. Yet scholars have discovered time and time again that this is a dangerous fallacy.

A further complication in studying Greek art is that there are three separate, and sometimes conflicting, sources of information on the subject. First, there are the works themselves—reliable, but only a fraction of what once existed. Secondly, there are Roman copies of Greek originals, especially sculptures. These works tell us something about important pieces that would otherwise be lost to us, but pose their own problems. Without the original, we cannot determine how faithful a copy is, and sometimes multiple copies present several different versions of a single original. This is explained by the fact that a Roman copyist's notion of a copy was quite different from ours: It was not necessarily a strict imitation, but allowed for interpreting or adapting the work according to the copyist's taste or skill or the patron's wishes. Moreover, the quality of some Greek sculpture owed much to surface finish, which, in a copy, is entirely up to the copyist. If the original

Detail of figure 5.6, Griffin-head protome from a bronze tripod-cauldron, from Kameiros, Rhodes

Map 5.1   Greece in the Archaic and Classical periods

was bronze and the copy marble, not only would the finish differ dramatically, but the copyist might alter the very composition to accommodate the different strengths of stone and bronze. In rare cases, works that appear to be copies because of their general style or subject matter are of such high quality that we cannot be sure that they really are copies. Lastly, Roman copies tend to come to light in Roman contexts, which allows archaeologists to glean information about Roman collectors but not about the contexts in which Greeks displayed the originals.

The third source of information about Greek works is literature. The Greeks were the first Western people to write at length about their artists. Roman writers incorporated Greek accounts into their own; many of these survive, although often in fragmentary condition. These written sources offer a glimpse of what the Greeks considered their significant achievements in architecture, sculpture, and painting. They name celebrated artists and monuments, but often deal with lost works and fail to mention surviving Greek works that we number among the greatest masterpieces of their time. Weaving these strands of information into a coherent picture of Greek art has been the difficult task of archaeologists and art historians for several centuries.

THE EMERGENCE OF GREEK ART: THE GEOMETRIC STYLE

The first Greek-speaking groups came to Greece about 2000 BCE, bringing a culture that soon encompassed most of mainland Greece, the Aegean Islands, and Crete. By the first millennium BCE, they had colonized the west coast of Asia Minor and Cyprus. In this period we distinguish three main subgroups: the Dorians, centered in the Peloponnese; the Ionians, inhabiting Attica, Euboea, the Cyclades, and the central coast of Asia Minor; and the Aeolians, who ended up in the northeast Aegean (map 5.1). Despite cultural differences, Greeks of different regions had a strong sense of kinship, based on language and common beliefs. From the mid-eighth through the mid-sixth centuries BCE, Greeks spread across the Mediterranean and as far as the Black Sea in a wave of colonization. At this time, they founded settlements in Sicily and southern Italy, collectively known as Magna Graecia, and in North Africa.

After the collapse of Mycenaean civilization described in t last chapter, art became largely nonfigural for several centuries. In the ninth century BCE, the oldest surviving style of Greek art

Greek Gods and Goddesses

All early civilizations and preliterate cultures had creation myths to explain the origin of the universe and humanity's place in it. Over time, these myths evolved into complex cycles that represent a comprehensive attempt to understand the world. Greek gods and goddesses, though immortal, behaved in human ways. They quarreled, and had offspring with one another's spouses and often with mortals as well. Their own children sometimes threatened and even overthrew them. The principal Greek gods and goddesses, with their Roman counterparts in parentheses, are given below.

ZEUS (Jupiter): son of Kronos and Rhea; god of sky and weather, and chief Olympian deity. After killing Kronos, Zeus married his sister HERA (Juno) and divided the universe by lot with his brothers: POSEIDON (Neptune) was allotted the sea, and HADES (Pluto) received the underworld, which he ruled with his queen, PERSEPHONE (Proserpina).

Zeus and Hera had several children:
ARES (Mars), the god of war
HEBE, the goddess of youth
HEPHAISTOS (Vulcan), the lame god of metalwork and the forge

Zeus also had numerous children through his love affairs with other goddesses and with mortal women, including:
ATHENA (Minerva), goddess of crafts, war, intelligence, and wisdom. A protector of heroes, she became the patron goddess of Athens, an honor she won in a contest with Poseidon. Her gift to the city was an olive tree, which she caused to sprout on the Akropolis.

APHRODITE (Venus), the goddess of love, beauty, and female fertility. She married Hephaistos, but had many other liaisons. Her children were HARMONIA, EROS, and ANTEROS (with Ares); HERMAPHRODITOS (with Hermes); PRIAPOS (with Dionysos); and AENEAS (with the Trojan prince Anchises).

APOLLO (Apollo), god of the stringed lyre and bow, who therefore both presided over the civilized pursuits of music and poetry, and shot down transgressors; a paragon of male beauty, he was also the god of prophecy and medicine.

ARTEMIS (Diana), twin sister of APOLLO, virgin goddess of the hunt and the protector of young girls. She was also sometimes considered a moon-goddess with SELENE.

DIONYSOS (Bacchus), the god of altered states, particularly that induced by wine. Opposite in temperament to Apollo, Dionysos was raised on Mount Nysa, where he invented winemaking; he married the princess Ariadne after the hero Theseus abandoned her on Naxos. His followers, the goatish satyrs and their female companions, the nymphs and humans who were known as maenads (bacchantes), were given to orgiastic excess. Yet there was another, more temperate side to Dionysos' character. As the god of fertility, he was also a god of vegetation, as well as of peace, hospitality, and the theater.

HERMES (Mercury), the messenger of the gods, conductor of souls to Hades, and the god of travelers and commerce.

---

developed, known today as the Geometric Style because of the predominance of linear designs. Artists created works of painted pottery and small-scale clay and bronze sculpture in this style. The forms are closely related: the types of figures found in sculpture often adorned the pottery.

Geometric Style Pottery

As quickly as pottery became an art form, Greek potters began to develop an extensive, but fairly standardized, repertoire of vessel shapes (fig. **5.1**), and adapted each type to its function. Making and decorating vases were complex processes, usually performed

amphora

pelike

volute krater

krater

hydria

lekythos

amphora

kylix

skyphos

kantharos

aryballos

5.1 Some common Greek vessel forms

the lasting epic poems *The Iliad* and *The Odyssey*, tales of the Trojan War and the return home of one of its heroes, Odysseus, to Ithaka.

The vase shown here, from a cemetery near the later Dipy[lon] gate in northwestern Athens, dates to around 750 BCE (fig. 5.2, see fig. 5.37). Known as the Dipylon Vase, it was one of a group of large vessels Athenians used as funerary markers over burials. Holes in its base allowed mourners to pour liquid offerings (libations) during funerary rituals; the libations filtered down to the dead buried below. In earlier centuries, Athenians had placed the ashes of their dead inside vases, choosing the vase's shape according to the sex of the deceased: They placed a woman's remains in a belly-handled amphora, a type of vase they used more commonly for storing wine or oil; a man's ashes were stored in a neck-amphora (a wine jar with a long neck). Since the early first millennium, Athenians had also used **kraters** as burial markers, large bowl-like vessels in which they normally mixed wine with water (see fig. 5.1). The shape of the vase illustrated here shows that the person buried beneath was a woman; its monumentality indicates that she was a woman of considerable means.

The amphora is a masterpiece of the potter's craft. At over 5 feet tall, it was too large to be thrown in one piece. Instead, the potter built it up in sections, joined with a clay slip (clay mixed with water or another liquid). A careful proportional scheme governed the vessel's form: Its width measures half of its height and the neck measures half the height of the body. The potter placed the handles so as to emphasize the widest point of the body. Most of the decoration is given over to geometric patterns dominated by a **meander** pattern, also known as a maze or Greek key pattern (fig. 5.3), a band of rectangular scrolls, punctuated with bands of lustrous black paint at the neck, shoulder, and base. The geometric design reflects the proportional system of the vase's shape. Single meander patterns run in bands toward the top and

5.2 Dipylon Vase. Late Geometric belly-handled amphora, from the Dipylon Cemetery, Athens. ca. 750 BCE. Height 5'1" (1.55 m). National Archaeological Museum, Athens

by different artisans. Each pottery shape presented its own challenges to the painter, and some became specialists at decorating certain types of vases. Large pots often attracted the most ambitious craftsmen because they provided a generous field on which to work. At first painters decorated their wares with abstract designs, such as triangles, "checkerboards," and concentric circles. Toward 800 BCE, human and animal figures began to appear within the geometric framework, and in elaborate examples these figures interact in narrative scenes. This development occurred at about the time the alphabet was introduced (under strong Near Eastern influence), and contemporaneous, too, with the compositions of the poet (or group of poets) known as Homer, who wrote

guilloche

acanthus

palmette

meander

rosette

egg-and-dart

5.3 Common Greek ornamental motifs

bottom of the neck; the triple meander encircling the neck at the center emphasizes its length. The double and single meanders on the amphora's body appear stocky by contrast, complementing body's rounder form. On the neck, deer graze, one after the other, in an identical pattern circling the vase. At the base of the neck, they recline, with their heads turned back over their bodies, like an animate version of the meander pattern itself, which moves forward while turning back upon itself. These animal **friezes** prefigure the widespread use of the motif in the seventh century BCE.

In the center of the amphora, framed between its handles, is a narrative scene. The deceased lies on a bier, beneath a checkered shroud. Standing figures flank her with their arms raised above their heads in a gesture of lamentation; four additional figures kneel or sit beneath the bier. Rather than striving for naturalism, the painter used solid black geometric forms to construct human bodies. A triangle represents the torso, and the raised arms extend the triangle beyond the shoulders. The scene represents the *prothesis*, part of the Athenian funerary ritual, when the dead person lay in state and public mourning took place. For the living, a lavish funeral was an occasion to display wealth and status, and crowds of mourners were so desirable that families would hire professionals for the event. Thus the depiction of a funeral on the vase is not simply journalistic reportage but a visual record of the deceased person's high standing in society.

Archaeologists have found Geometric pottery in Italy and the Near East as well as in Greece. This wide distribution reflects the important role of not only the Greeks but also the Phoenicians, rth Syrians, and other Near Eastern peoples as agents of diffusion around the Mediterranean. What is more, from the second half of the eighth century onward, inscriptions on these vases show that the Greeks had already adapted the Phoenician alphabet to their own use.

5.4 *Man and Centaur*, perhaps from Olympia. ca. 750 BCE. Bronze, height 4⅜″ (11.1 cm). Metropolitan Museum of Art, New York. Gift of J. Pierpont Morgan, 1917. 17.190.2072

Geometric Style Sculpture

A small, bronze sculptural group representing a man and a centaur dates to about the same time as the funerary amphora, and there are similarities in the way the artist depicted living forms in both works of art (fig. **5.4**). Thin arms and flat, triangular chests contrast with rounded buttocks and legs. The heads are spherical shapes, with beards and noses added. The metalworker cast the sculptural group in one piece, uniting the figures with a common base and through their entwined pose. Indeed, the figures obviously interact, revealing the artist's interest in narrative, a theme that persists throughout the history of Greek art. The figures' helmets suggest that their encounter is martial, and the larger scale of the man may indicate that he will prevail in the struggle. It is hard to say whether the artist was referring to a story known to the audience. Many scholars believe the male figure represents the hero Herakles, son of Zeus and a mortal woman, who fought ntaurs many times in the course of his mythical travails. The _up probably came to light in the great Panhellenic (all-Greek) sanctuary at Olympia, home of the Olympic games. This sanctuary, like the Panhellenic sanctuary at Delphi, home of the

Panhellenic games (see fig. 5.19), was not specific to one city-state: People from cities all over the Greek world routinely visited it for festivals and to make dedications to the gods, which accounts for its gradual monumentalization. There was a distinct rise in dedications there and at Delphi in the eighth century BCE, especially of small metal objects. Judging by the figurative quality of the sculptural group, by the costliness of the material, and the complexity of the technique, it was probably a sumptuous votive offering.

THE ORIENTALIZING STYLE: HORIZONS EXPAND

Between about 725 and 650 BCE, a new style of art emerged in Greece that reflects strong influences from the Near East and Egypt. Scholars call this the Orientalizing period, when Greek art and culture rapidly absorbed Eastern motifs and ideas, including hybrid creatures such as griffins and sphinxes. This movement led to a vital period of experimentation, as artists strove to master new forms.

Miniature Vessels

The Orientalizing style replaced the Geometric in many Greek city-states, including Athens. One of the foremost centers of its production, though, was Corinth, at the northeastern gateway to the Peloponnese. During this period, Corinth came to dominate colonizing ventures to the west, as well as the trade in pottery exports. Its workshops had a long history of pottery production, and at this time vase painters learned to refine a black gloss slip, which they used to create silhouette or outline images. By incising the slip, they could add fine detail and vivacity to their work. They particularly specialized in crafting miniature vessels like the vase shown here, which is a Proto-Corinthian **aryballos** or perfume jar, dating to about 680 BCE (fig. **5.5**). Despite its small size, intricate decoration covers the vase's surface. Around the shoulder stalks a frieze of animals, reminiscent of Near Eastern motifs and of the frieze on the Dipylon Vase (see figs. 2.21 and 5.2). Bands of real and imaginary animals are a hallmark of Corinthian and other Orientalizing wares: They cover later vases from top to bottom. A **guilloche pattern** ornaments the handle, and meander patterns enliven the edge of the mouth and the handle (see fig. 5.3). The principal figural frieze offers another early example of pictorial narrative, but the daily-life scenes that are characteristic of Geometric pottery yield here to the fantastic world of myth.

5.6 Griffin-head protome from a bronze tripod cauldron, from Kameiros, Rhodes. ca. 650 BCE. Cast bronze, height 9³⁄₁₆″ (23.4 cm), width (central plate) 1¹⁄₁₆″ (2.7 cm). The British Museum, London

5.5 The Ajax Painter. Aryballos (perfume jar). Middle Proto-Corinthian I A, 690–675 BCE. Ceramic, height 2⅞″ (7.3 cm), diameter 1¾″ (4.4 cm). Museum of Fine Arts, Boston. Catharine Page Perkins Fund. 95.12

On one side, a stocky nude male wielding a sword runs toward a vase on a stand. On the side shown here, a bearded male struggles to wrest a scepter or staff from a centaur. According to one theory, the frieze represents a moment in Herakles' conflict with a band of centaurs on Mount Pholoë. In Greek mythology centaurs were notoriously susceptible to alcohol, and the mixing bowl for wine represented on the other side may indicate the reason for their rowdiness. Others interpret the "Herakles" figure as Zeus, brandishing his thunderbolt or lightning. No matter how one reads this scene, it was clearly meant to evoke a myth. Greeks buried vessels like this aryballos in tombs as offerings the dead, and dedicated them in sanctuaries throughout the Greek world.

BRONZE TRIPODS Among the costliest dedications in Greek sanctuaries during the Geometric and Orientalizing periods were bronze tripod cauldrons, large vessels mounted on three legs. Some of them reached truly monumental proportions, and the dedication was not only an act of piety, but also a way to display status through wealth. From the early seventh century BCE, bronze-workers producing these vessels in the Orientalizing style attached **protomes** around the edge of the bowl—images of sirens (winged female creatures) and griffins, which were fantasy creatures known in the Near East. The cast protome shown here, from the island of Rhodes, is a magnificently ominous creature, standing watch over the dedication (fig. **5.6**). The boldly upright ears and the vertical knob on top of the head contrast starkly with the strong curves of the neck, head, eyes, and mouth, while its menacing tongue is silhouetted in countercurve against the beak. The straight lines appear to animate the curves, so that the dangerous hybrid seems about to spring.

ARCHAIC ART: ART OF THE CITY-STATE

During the course of the seventh and sixth centuries BCE, the Greeks refined their notion of a **polis**, or city-state. Once merely a citadel, a place of refuge in times of trouble, the city came to represent a community and an identity. They governed these city-states in various ways, including monarchy (from *monarches*, "sole ruler"), aristocracy (from *aristoi* and *kratia*, "rule of the best"), tyranny (from *tyrannos*, "king"), and oligarchy (from *oligoi*, "the few," a small ruling elite). The citizens of Athens ruled their city-state by democracy (from *demos*, "the people"). The path to democracy was a slow one, starting with the reforms of Solon, a statesman of the late sixth century. Even after Perikles' radical democratic reforms of 462 BCE, women played no direct role in civic life, and slavery was an accepted practice, as it was throughout the Greek world. With the changing ideal of the city-state came transformations in its physical appearance. Scholars know the artistic style of this time as Archaic (from *archaios*, Greek for "old"). Architects began to design monumental buildings in canonical styles, while artists started to explore human movement and emotion.

The Rise of Monumental Temple Architecture

Early Greeks worshiped their gods in open-air sanctuaries. The indispensable installation for cult (religious practice) rituals was an altar, where priests performed sacrifices standing before the worshiping community of the Greek polis. Increasingly, though,

Greeks built temples to accompany these altars. Usually the entrance of the temple faced east, toward the rising sun, and the altar stood to the east of the temple. The chief function of a temple was not so much to house rituals, most of which occurred outside the building, but to provide safe shelter for the cult image of the god to whom the temple was dedicated, and to store valuable dedications. At some point in the seventh century BCE, they began to design temples in stone rather than wood. Corinthian architects were probably the first to make the change, designing in a style known as Doric, named for the region where it originated. From there, the concept spread across the isthmus of Corinth to the mainland and up to Delphi and the island of Corfu, then rapidly throughout the Hellenic world. A second style, the Ionic, soon developed on the Aegean Islands and the coast of Asia Minor. The style known as Corinthian did not develop until the late fifth century BCE (see page 142).

Greeks recognized the importance of this architectural revolution even as it happened: Architects wrote treatises on their buildings—the first we know of—and the fame they achieved through their work has lasted to this day. Writing in the first century BCE, the Roman architect Vitruvius described the Greek styles of architecture, and his work has been central to our understanding of Greek building. However, our readings of his text have been mediated through early modern commentators and illustrators, who wrote of Doric and Ionic "orders" rather than "types," which is a better translation of Vitruvius' "*genera*." The distinction is important: "Order" suggests an immutable quality, a rigid building code, when in fact there is a subtle but rich variation in surviving Greek architecture.

The essential, functioning elements of Doric and Ionic temples are very similar, though they vary according to the building's size or regional preferences (fig. **5.7**). The nucleus of the building—its very reason for existing—is its main chamber, its cella or **naos**. This chamber housed the god's image. Often, interior columns lined the cella walls and helped to support the roof, as well as visually framing the cult statue. Approaching the cella is a porch or **pronaos**, and in some cases architects added a second porch behind the cella, making the design symmetrical and providing

5.7 Ground plan of a typical Greek peripteral temple (after Grinnell)

5.8 Doric and Ionic styles in elevation

Doric Style

Ionic Style

space for apparatus used in rituals and religious dedications. In large temples, a colonnade or **peristyle** surrounds the cella and porches; Vitruvius called this type a **peripteral temple**. The peristyle commonly consists of 6 to 8 columns at front and back, and usually 12 to 17 along the sides, counting the corner columns twice; the largest temples of Ionian Greece had a double colonnade. The peristyle added more than grandeur: It offered worshipers shelter from the elements. Being neither entirely exterior nor entirely interior space, it also functioned as a transitional zone, between the profane world outside and the sanctity of the cella. Some temples stood in sacred groves, and the strong vertical form of the columns integrated the building with the environment of trees. Echoed again by columns inside the cella, the peristyle also unified the exterior and interior of the building.

Differences between the Doric and Ionic styles are apparent in a head-on view, or elevation. Many terms that Greeks used to describe the parts of their buildings, shown in figure **5.8**, are still in common usage. The building proper rests on an elevated level (the **stylobate**), normally approached by three steps, known as the **stereobate**. A **Doric column** consists of a shaft, usually

marked by shallow vertical grooves, known as **flutes**, and a capital, made up of a flaring, cushionlike **echinus** and a square tablet called the **abacus**. The **entablature** includes all the horizontal elements that rest on the columns: the **architrave** (a row of stone blocks directly supported by the columns); the **frieze**, made up of alternating triple-grooved **triglyphs** and smooth or sculpted **metopes**; and a projecting horizontal cornice, or **geison**. The architrave in turn supports the triangular **pediment** and the roof elements.

An **Ionic column** differs from a Doric column in having an ornate base, perhaps designed initially to protect the bottom from rain. Its shaft is more slender, less tapered, and the capital has a double scroll or **volute** below the abacus. Masons left a sharp angle where the flutes met, instead of flattening it as on Doric columns. The Ionic column lacks the muscular quality of its mainland cousin. Instead, it evokes a growing plant, like a formalized palm tree, a characteristic it shares with its Egyptian predecessor, though it may not have come directly from Egypt. Above the architrave, the frieze is continuous, not broken up visually into triglyphs and metopes.

Greek builders created temples, whether Doric or Ionic, out of stone blocks fitted together without mortar. This required them to shape the blocks precisely to achieve smooth joints. Where necessary, metal dowels or clamps fastened the blocks together. With rare exceptions, they constructed columns out of sections called **drums**, and stonemasons fluted the entire shaft once it was in position. They used wooden beams for the ceiling, and terra-cotta tiles over wooden rafters for the roof. Fire was a constant threat.

Why and how either style came to emerge in Greece, and why they came together into succinct systems so quickly, are questions that still puzzle scholars. Remains of the oldest surviving temples show that the main features of the Doric style were already established soon after 600 BCE. It is possible that the temple's central unit, the cella and porch, derived from the plan of the Mycenaean megaron (see fig. 4.23), either through continuous tradition or by way of revival. If this is true, this relationship may reflect the revered place of Mycenaean culture in later Greek mythology. Still, a Doric column shaft tapers upward, not downward like the Minoan-Mycenaean column. This recalls fluted half-columns in the funerary precinct of Djoser at Saqqara of over 2,000 years earlier (see fig. 3.6). In fact, the very notion that temples should be built of stone and have large numbers of columns was an Egyptian one, even if Egyptian architects designed temples for greater internal traffic. Scholars believe that the rise of monumental stone architecture and sculpture must have been based on careful, on-the-spot study of Egyptian works and the techniques used to produce them. The opportunity for just such a study was available to Greek merchants living in trading camps in the western Nile Delta, by permission of the Egyptian king Psammetichus I (r. 664–610 BCE).

Some scholars see Doric architecture as a petrification (or turning to stone) of existing wooden forms, so that stone form follows wooden function. Accordingly, triglyphs once masked the ends of wooden beams, and the droplike shapes below, called **guttae**, mimic the wooden pegs that held them in place. Metopes evolved from boards that filled gaps between triglyphs to guard against moisture. Some derivations are more convincing than others, however. The vertical subdivisions of triglyphs hardly seem to reflect the forms of three half-round logs, as some have suggested, and column flutings need not have developed out of tool marks on a tree trunk, since Egyptian builders also fluted their columns and yet rarely used timber for supporting members. The question of how well function explains stylistic features faces the architectural historian repeatedly.

DORIC TEMPLES AT PAESTUM Whatever the reason for the emergence of the Doric and Ionic styles, architects continued to refine them throughout Greek times. The early evolution of Doric temples is evident in two unusually well-preserved examples located in the southern Italian polis of Paestum (ancient Poseidonia), where a Greek colony flourished during the Archaic period. The residents dedicated both temples to the goddess Hera, wife of Zeus; however, they built the Temple of Hera II almost a century after the Temple of Hera I (fig. **5.9**). The differences in their proportions are striking. The Temple of Hera I (on the left

5.9   The Temple of Hera I ("Basilica"), ca. 550 BCE, and the Temple of Hera II ("Temple of Poseidon"), Paestum. ca. 460 BCE

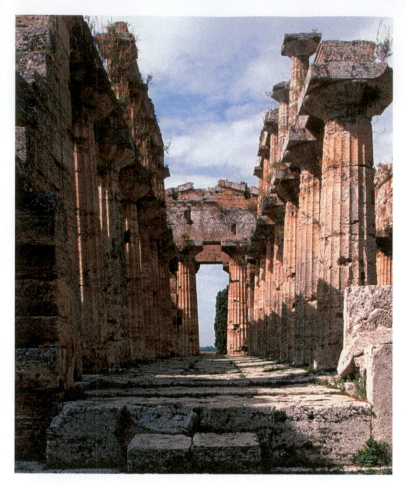

5.10 Interior of Temple of Hera II. ca. 500 BCE

of fig. 5.9) appears low and sprawling—and not just because so much of the entablature is missing—whereas the Temple of Hera II looks tall and compact. One reason is that the Temple of Hera I is **enneastyle** (with nine columns across the front and rear), w the later temple is only **hexastyle** (six columns). Yet the differe in appearance is also the result of changes to the outline of the columns. On neither temple are the column shafts straight from bottom to top. About a third of the way up, they bulge outward slightly, receding again at about two-thirds of their height. This swelling effect, known as **entasis**, is much stronger on the earlier Temple of Hera I. It gives the impression that the columns bulge with the strain of supporting the superstructure and that the slender tops, although aided by the widely flaring capitals, can barely withstand the crushing weight. The device, seen also in the monoliths at Stonehenge, adds an extraordinary vitality to the building—a sense of compressed energy awaiting release.

Being so well preserved, the Temple of Hera II shows how the architect supported the ceiling in a large Doric temple (fig. **5.10**). Inside the cella, the two rows of columns each support a smaller set of columns scaled in such a way that the tapering seems continuous despite the intervening architrave. Such a two-story interior is first found at the Temple of Aphaia at Aegina around the beginning of the fifth century BCE. A reconstruction drawing of that temple (fig. **5.11**) illustrates the structural system in detail.

EARLY IONIC TEMPLES The Ionic style first appeared about a half-century after the Doric. With its vegetal decoration, it seems to have been strongly inspired by Near Eastern for The closest known parallel to the Ionic capital is the **Aeolic** capital, found in the region of Old Smyrna, in eastern Greece, and in the northeast Aegean, itself apparently derived from North Syrian and Phoenician designs. Leading cities of Ionian Greece commissioned the earliest Ionic temples in open rivalry with one another. Little survives of these vast, ornate buildings. One of them, the Temple of Artemis at Ephesos, gained tremendous

5.11 Sectional view (restored) of Temple of Aphaia, Aegina. ca. 500–480 BCE

pronaos   dipteral colonnade   cella/naos

5.12 Restored plan of Temple of Artemis at Ephesos, Turkey. ca. 560 BCE fame in antiquity, and earned a place among the seven wonders of the ancient world. The Ephesians hired Theodoros of Samos to work on its foundations in about 560 BCE, shortly after he and another architect, Rhoikos, had designed a vast temple to Hera on the island of Samos. The temple's subsequent architects, Chersiphron of Knossos and his son Metagenes, wrote a treatise on it. The temple was **dipteral** (with two rows of columns surrounding it) (fig. **5.12**), and this feature emphasized the forestlike quality of the building, as did its vegetal capitals. In this much, it resembled the temple on Samos. Yet in other respects the Temple of Artemis clearly outshone Hera's: It was larger, and it was the first monumental building constructed mostly of marble. These Ionic colossi had blatant symbolic value: They represented their respective city's bid for regional leadership.

5.13 *Kore (Maiden).*
. 630 BCE. Limestone,
height 24½″ (62.3 cm).
Musée du Louvre, Paris.
Fletcher Fund, 1932. (32.11.1)

STONE SCULPTURE

According to literary sources, in the eighth century BCE Greeks erected simple wooden sculptures of their gods for worship in sanctuaries; but since wood deteriorates, none of them now survives. In about 650 BCE, sculptors, like architects, made the transition to working in stone, and so began one of the great traditions of Greek art.

KORE AND KOUROS Early Greek statues clearly show affinities with the techniques and proportional systems used by Egyptian sculptors, whose work Greek artists could observe first hand in the Nile Delta. Two are illustrated here: one a small female figure of about 630 BCE, probably from Crete (fig. **5.13**); the other a life-size nude male youth of about 600 BCE (fig. **5.14**), known as the *New York Kouros* because it is displayed in the Metropolitan Museum of Art. Like their Egyptian forerunners (see figs. 3.10 and 3.11), the statues are rigidly frontal, and conceived as four distinct sides, reflecting the form of the block from which the sculptor carved them. Like Menkaure, the Greek male youth is slim and broad-shouldered; he stands with his left leg forward, and his arms by his sides, terminating in clenched fists. His shoulders, hips, and knees are all level. Both figures have stylized, wiglike hair like their Egyptian counterparts, and like some Near Eastern sculptures (see fig. 2.11). All the same, there are significant differences. First, the Greek sculptures are truly freestanding, without the back slab that supports Egyptian stone figures. In fact, they are the earliest large stone images of the human figure that can stand on their own. Moreover, Greek sculptures incorporated empty space (between the legs, for instance, or between arms and torso), whereas Egyptian figures remained embedded in stone, with the spaces between forms partly filled. Early Greek sculptures are also more stylized than their Egyptian forebears. This is most evident in the large staring eyes, emphasized by bold arching eyebrows, and in the linear treatment of the anatomy: The sculptor appears almost to have etched the male youth's pectoral muscles and rib-cage onto the surface of the stone, whereas the Egyptian sculptor modeled Menkaure's musculature. Unlike Menkaure, the male youth is nude. Earlier cultures, like the Egyptians, forced nudity on slaves, whereas ancient Greeks considered public nudity acceptable for males, but not for females. Accordingly, like most early Greek female sculptures, this one is draped, in a close-fitting garment that reveals her breasts but conceals her hips and legs.

Dozens of Archaic sculptures of this kind survive throughout the Greek world. Some have come to light in sanctuaries and cemeteries, but most were found in reused contexts, which complicates any attempt to understand their function. Scholars describe them by the Greek terms for maiden (**kore**, plural korai) and youth (**kouros**, plural kouroi), terms that gloss over

5.14 *New York Kouros (Youth).* ca. 600–590 BCE.
Marble, height 6′1½″ (1.88 m). Metropolitan Museum of Art,
New York

the difficulty of identifying their function. Some bear inscriptions, such as the names of artists ("'So-and-so' made me") or dedications to various deities, chiefly Apollo. The latter, then, were votive offerings. But in most cases we do not know whether the sculptures represent the donor, a deity, or a person deemed divinely favored, such as a victor in the athletic games that were so central to ancient Greek life. Those placed on graves probably represent the person buried beneath.

Sculptors made no clear effort to give the statues portrait features, so the images can represent an individual only in a general way. It might make sense to think of them as ideals of physical perfection and vitality shared by mortals and immortals and given meaning by their physical context. What is clear is that only the wealthy could afford them, since many were well over life-size and carved from high-quality marble. Indeed, the very stylistic cohesion of the sculptures may reveal their social function: By

5.16   *Kore*, from Chios (?). ca. 520 BCE. Marble, height 21⅞" (55.3 cm). Akropolis Museum, Athens

5.15   *Kroisos (Kouros from Anavysos)*. ca. 540–525 BCE. Marble, height 6'4" (1.9 m). National Museum, Athens erecting a sculpture of this kind, a wealthy patron declared his or her status and claimed membership in ruling elite circles.

TING AND NATURALISM The Archaic period stretches from the mid-seventh century to about 480 BCE. Within this time frame, there are few secure dates for free-standing sculptures. Scholars have therefore established a dating system based upon the level of naturalism in a given sculpture. According to this system, the more stylized the figure, the earlier it must be. Comparing figures 5.14 and **5.15** illustrates how this model works. An inscription on the base of the latter identifies it as the funerary statue of Kroisos, who died a hero's death in battle. Like all such figures, it was painted, and traces of color are still discernible in the hair and the pupils of the eyes. Instead of the sharp planes and linear treatment of the *New York Kouros* (see fig. 5.14), the sculptor of the kouros from Anavysos modeled its anatomy with swelling curves; a viewer can imagine flesh and sinew and bones in the carved stone. A greater plasticity gives the impression that the body could actually function. The proportions of the facial features are more naturalistic as well. The face has a less masklike quality than the *New York Kouros*, though the lips are drawn up in an artificial smile, known as the **Archaic smile,** that is not reflected in the eyes. Based on these differences, scholars judge the *Kroisos* more "advanced" than the *New York Kouros,* and date it some 75 years later. Given the later trajectory of Greek sculpture, there is every reason to believe that this way of dating Archaic sculpture is more or less accurate (accounting regional differences and the like). All the same, it is worth emphasizing that it is based on an assumption—that sculptors, or their patrons, were striving toward naturalism—rather than on factual data.

There is more variation in types of kore than in types of kouros. This is partly because a kore is a clothed figure and therefore presents the problem of how to relate body and drapery. It is also likely to reflect changing habits or local styles of dress. The kore in figure **5.16**, from about 520 BCE, was a dedication on the Akropolis of Athens, though she probably came from Chios, an island of Ionian Greece. She has none of the severity of the earlier kore from Crete. She wears the light Ionian **chiton** (a rectangle of fabric draped and fastened at the shoulder by pins) under the heavier diagonally shaped himation, which replaced the earlier peplos (plain woolen garment) in fashion. The layers of the garment still loop around the body in soft curves, but the play of richly differentiated folds, pleats, and textures has almost become an end in itself. Color played an important role in such works, and is unusually well preserved in this example.

Architectural Sculpture: The Building Comes Alive

on after the Greeks began to dedicate stone temples, they also arted to use architectural sculpture to articulate their buildings and bring them to life. Indeed, early Greek architects such as Theodoros of Samos were often sculptors as well. Traces of pigment show that these sculptures were normally vividly painted. (See *Materials and Techniques,* page 223.)

The Egyptians had been covering walls and columns with reliefs since the Old Kingdom. Their carvings were so shallow (see fig. 3.28) that they did not break the continuity of the surface and had no volume of their own. Thus, like the reliefs on Assyrian, Babylonian, and Persian buildings, they related to their architectural setting in the same way as wall paintings (see figs. 2.19 and 2.20). Another kind of architectural sculpture in the Near East, however, seems to have begun with the Hittites: the lamassu protruding from stone blocks that framed the gateways of fortresses or palaces (see fig. 2.22). Directly or indirectly, this tradition may have inspired the carving over the Lioness Gate at Mycenae (see fig. 4.22).

THE TEMPLE OF ARTEMIS, CORFU The façade of the early Archaic Temple of Artemis on the island of Corfu, built soon after 600 BCE, suggests that the Lioness Gate relief, which was still visible in the sixth century, is a conceptual ancestor of later Greek architectural sculpture (figs. **5.17** and **5.18**). Sculpture on the temple is confined to the pediment, a triangle between the ceiling and the roof that serves as a screen to protect the wooden rafters behind it from moisture. Technically, the pedimental sculptures are in high relief, like the guardian lionesses at Mycenae. However, the sculptor undercut the figures so strongly that they are nearly detached from the background, and appear to be almost independent of their architectural setting. Indeed, the head of the central figure actually overlaps the frame; she seems to emerge out of the pediment toward a viewer. This choice on the sculptor's part heightens the impact of the figure and strengthens her function.

Although the Greeks of Corfu dedicated their temple to Artemis, the figure represents the snake-haired Medusa, one of the Gorgon sisters of Greek mythology. Medusa's appearance was so monstrous, the story went, that anyone who beheld her

5.17 Central portion of west pediment of Temple of Artemis, Corfu, Greece. ca. 600–580 BCE. Limestone, height 9′2″ (2.8 m). Archaeological Museum, Corfu

5.18 Reconstruction drawing of west front of Temple of Artemis, Corfu (after Rodenwaldt)

would turn to stone. With the aid of the gods, the hero Perseus managed to behead her using her reflection in his shield to guide his sword. Traditionally, art historians have interpreted the figure of Medusa as a protective device, used to ward evil spirits away from the temple. However, scholars now argue that she served as a visual commentary on the power of the divinity: As a mistress of animals, she exemplifies the goddess' power and dominance over Nature. To emphasize this, two large feline creatures flank Medusa, in a heraldic arrangement known from the Lioness Gate and from earlier Near Eastern examples.

To strengthen the sculptures' message, the designer included narrative elements in the pediment as well. In the spaces between and behind the main group, the sculptor inserted subsidiary figures. On either side of Medusa are her children, the winged horse Pegasus, and Chrysaor, who will be born from drops of the blood she sheds when Perseus decapitates her. Pegasus was a symbol of Corinth. Since Corfu was Corinth's colony, the winged horse reminded residents of Corinth's control. Logically speaking, Pegasus and Chrysaor cannot yet exist, since Medusa's head is still on her shoulders; and yet their presence in the heraldic arrangment alludes to the future, when Perseus will have claimed the Gorgon's power as his own—just as the sculptor has here, in the service of Artemis. To bring the story to life, the sculptor fused two separate moments from a single story, in what is known as a **synoptic narrative.** Two additional groups filled the pediment's corners. They may depict Zeus and Poseidon battling the giants (a gigantomachy), a mortal race who tried to overthrow the gods. If so, they strike a cautionary note for a viewer, warning mortals not to aim higher than their natural place in the order of things, since the gods destroyed the giants for their overreaching ambitions.

With their reclining pose, the felines fit the shape of the pediment comfortably. Yet in order to fit Pegasus and Chrysaor between Medusa and the felines, and the groups into the corners, the sculptor carved them at a significantly smaller scale than the dominant figures. Later solutions to the pediment's awkward shape suggest that this one, which lacks unity of scale, was not wholly satisfactory.

Aside from filling the pediment with sculpture, Greeks often affixed free-standing figures, known as **acroteria**, above the corners and center of the pediment, to soften the severity of its outline (see fig. 5.20). In Ionic buildings, female statues or **caryatids** might substitute for columns to support the roof of a porch (see figs. 5.20 and 5.51). Sculptors also decorated the frieze. In Doric temples, they would often embellish the metopes with figural scenes. In Ionic temples, they treated the frieze with a continuous band of painted or sculpted decoration. For the frieze as for the pediment, the designer frequently selected mythological subjects with a topical relevance.

THE SIPHNIAN TREASURY, DELPHI These Ionic features came together in a building constructed at Delphi shortly before 525 BCE by the people of the Ionian island of Siphnos. Delphi was the site of an important Panhellenic sanctuary to Apollo, to which people traveled from all over Greece to consult its oracle (fig. **5.19**). The sanctuary gradually came to incorporate a theater and a stadium as well as several temples. Individuals and cities made dedications there, such as statues and spoils of war, and many cities built treasuries on the course of the principal thoroughfare, the Processional Way, to store their votive offerings. Treasuries resembled miniature temples, and typically had an ornate quality. Although the Treasury of the Siphnians no longer stands, archaeologists can reconstruct its appearance from surviving blocks (figs. **5.20** and **5.21**). Two caryatids supported the architrave of the porch. Above the architrave was a magnificent sculptural frieze (see fig. 5.21), part of which depicts the mythical battle of the gods against the giants, possibly also seen at Corf At the far left, the two lions pull the chariot of Themis, and te apart an anguished giant. In front of them, Apollo and Artemis advance together, shooting arrows, originally added in metal,

5.19 Plan of Sanctuary of Apollo in ancient times, Delphi

into a phalanx of giants. Stripped of his armor, a dead giant lies at their feet. Though the subject is mythical, its depiction provides historians with a wealth of detail on contemporary weaponry and military tactics.

Astonishingly, the relief is only a few inches deep from front to back. Within that shallow space, the sculptors (scholars discern more than one hand) created several planes. They carved the arms and legs of those nearest a viewer in the round. In the second and third layers, the forms become shallower, yet even those farthest from a viewer do not merge into the background. The resulting relationships between figures give a dramatic sense of the turmoil of battle and an intensity of action not seen before in narrative reliefs. As at Corfu, the protagonists fill the sculptural field from top to bottom, and this compositional choice enhances the frieze's power. It is a dominant characteristic of Archaic and Classical Greek art, and in time sculptors sought ways to fill the triangular field of the pediment, too, while retaining a unity of scale. Taking their cue, perhaps, from friezes such as that found on the Siphnian

5.20 Reconstruction drawing of Treasury of the Siphnians, Sanctuary of Apollo, Delphi. ca. 525 BCE

5.21 *Battle of the Gods and Giants*, from the north frieze of the Treasury of the Siphnians, Delphi. ca. 530 BCE. Marble, height 26″ (66 cm). Archaeological Museum, Delphi

Treasury, they introduced a variety of poses for figures, and made great strides in depicting the human body in naturalistic motion. The pediments of the Temple of Aphaia at Aegina illustrate this well (see fig. 5.11).

PEDIMENTS OF THE TEMPLE OF APHAIA AT AEGINA

In ca. 480 BCE, the Aeginetans replaced the sculptures in the east pediment of their Temple of Aphaia. Scholars hypothesize that the Persian invasion of Greece may have caused damage to the earlier sculptures. The new pediment (fig. **5.22**) depicts the first sack of Troy, by Herakles and Telamon, king of Salamis. The west pediment, which was not replaced at the time and dates from about 500–490 BCE, shows the second siege of Troy (recounted in *The Iliad*) by the Greek king Agamemnon, who was related to Herakles. The pairing of subjects commemorates the important role the heroes of Aegina played in both legendary battles—and, by extension, at Salamis, where their navy helped to overcome the Persians in 480. The use of **allegory** to elevate historical events to a universal plane is a frequent strategy in Greek art.

The figures of both pediments are fully in the round, independent of the stone background. For centuries, those of the east pediment lay in pieces on the ground, and scholars now debate their exact arrangement. All the same, they can determine the relative position of each figure within the pediment with reasonable accuracy, since the designer introduced a range of action poses for the figures, so their height, *but not their scale*, varies to suit the

gently sloping sides of the pedimental field. In the center stands the goddess Athena, presiding over the battle between Greeks and Trojans that rages on either side of her. Kneeling archers shoot across the pediment to unite its action. The symmetrical arrangement of poses on the two halves of the pediment creates a balanced design, so that while each figure has a clear autonomy, it also exists within a governing ornamental pattern.

A comparison of a fallen warrior from the west pediment (fig. **5.23**) with its counterpart from the later east pediment (fig. **5.24**) exposes the extraordinary advances sculptors made toward naturalism during the decades that separate them. As they sink to the ground in death, both figures present a clever solution to filling the difficult corner space. Yet while the earlier figure props himself up on one arm, only a precariously balanced shield supports the later warrior, whose full weight seems to pull him irresistibly to the ground. Both sculptors contorted their subjects' bodies in agonies of death: The earlier sculptor crosses the warrior's legs in an awkward pose, while the later sculptor twists the body from the waist, so that the left shoulder moves into a new plane. Although the later warrior's anatomy still does not fully respond to his pose (note, for instance, how little the pectorals stretch to accommodate the strenuous motion of the right arm, and the misplaced navel), his body is more modeled and organic than the earlier warrior's. He also breaks from the head-on stare of his predecessor, turning his gaze to the ground that confronts him. The effect suggests introspection: The inscrutable smiling mask of the earlier warrior yields to the suffering and emotion of a warrior in his final moments of life. Depictions of suffering, and how humans respond to it, are among the most dramatic developments of late Archaic art.

Vase Painting: Art of the Symposium

A similar experimentation with figural poses and emotion occurred in Archaic vase painting, which replaced the Orientalizing style as workshops in Athens and other centers began to produce extremely fine wares, painted with scenes from mythology, legend, and everyday life. The difference between Orientalizing and Archaic vase painting is largely one of technique. On the aryballos from Corinth (see fig. 5.5), the figures appear partly as solid silhouettes, partly in outline, or as a combination of the two. Toward the end of the seventh century BCE, influenced by Corinthian products, Attic vase painters began to work in the **black-figured** technique: They painted the entire design in black silhouette against the reddish clay, and then incised internal details into the design with a needle. Next, they painted white and purple over the black to make chosen areas

5.22 Reconstruction of the east pediment of the Temple of Aphaia, Aegina. Greek, ca. 500–480 BCE. Glyptothek, Staatliche Antikensammlungen, Munich, Germany

5.23 *Dying Warrior*, from west pediment of the Temple of Aphaia. ca. 500–490 BCE. Marble, length 5′2½″ (1.59 m). Staatliche Antikensammlungen und Glyptothek, Munich

5.24 *Dying Warrior*, from east pediment of the Temple of Aphaia. ca. 480 BCE. Marble, length 6′ (1.83 m). Staatliche Antikensammlungen und Glyptothek, Munich

stand out. The technique lent itself to a two-dimensional and highly decorative effect. This development marks the beginning of an aggressive export industry, the main consumers of which were the Etruscans. Vast numbers of black-figured vases were found in Etruscan tombs. Thus, although in terms of conception these vases (and later red-figured vessels) represent a major chapter in Greek (and specifically Athenian) art, with regard to their actual use, painted vases are a major component of Etruscan culture, both visual and funerary.

Greeks used the vases illustrated in these pages to hold wine. For everyday use, they generally poured wine from plainer, unadorned vases. They reserved decorated vases for special occasions, like the **symposium** (*symposion*), an exclusive drinking party that was a central feature of Greek life. Symposia were exclusively for men and courtesans; wives and other respectable citizen women did not attend. Participants reclined on couches around the edges of a room, and a master of ceremonies filled their cups from a large painted mixing bowl (a krater) at the center. Music, poetry, storytelling, and word games accompanied the festivities. Often the event ended in lovemaking, which is frequently depicted on drinking cups. Sometimes this was homosexual in orientation, since it was not unusual in the fifth century BCE for a mature Greek man to have a younger male lover, for whom he acted as a social and political mentor. There was also a serious side to symposia, as described by Plato and Xenophon, which centered on debates about politics, ethics, and morality. The great issues that Greeks pondered in their philosophy, literature, and theater—the nature of virtue, the value of an individual man's life, or mortal relations with the gods, to name a few—were mirrored in, and prompted by, the images with which they surrounded themselves.

After the middle of the sixth century BCE, many of the finest vessels bear the signatures of the artists who made them, indicating the pride that potters and painters alike took in their work. In many cases, vase painters had such distinctive styles that scholars can recognize their work even without a signature, and use modern names to identify them. Dozens of vases (in one instance, over 200) might survive by the same hand, allowing scholars to trace a single painter's development over many years.

A fine example of the black-figured technique is an Athenian amphora signed by Exekias as both potter and painter, dating to the third quarter of the sixth century BCE (fig. 5.25). The painting shows the Homeric heroes Achilles and Ajax playing dice. The episode does not exist in surviving literary sources, and its appearance here hints at a wide field of lost traditions that may have inspired Exekias. The two figures lean on their spears; their shields are stacked behind them against the inside of a campaign tent. The black silhouettes create a rhythmical composition, symmetrical around the table in the center. Within the black paint, Exekias incised a wealth of detail, focusing especially upon the warriors' cloaks; their intricately woven texture contrasts with the lustrous blackness of their weapons.

The extraordinary power of this scene derives from the tension within it. The warriors have stolen a moment of relaxation during a fierce war; even so, poised on the edge of their stools, one heel raised as if to spring into action, their poses are edgy. An inscription on the right reads "three," as if Ajax is calling out his throw. Achilles, who in his helmet slightly dominates the scene, answers with "four," making him the winner. Yet many Greek viewers would have understood the irony of the scene, for when they return to battle, Achilles will die, and Ajax will be left to bear his friend's lifeless body back to the Greek camp, before falling on his own sword in despair. Indeed, Exekias himself would paint representations of the heroes' tragic deaths. This amphora is the first known representation of the gaming scene, which subsequently became popular, suggesting that vase paintings did not exist in artistic isolation; painters responded to one another's work in a close and often clever dialogue.

Athenian vase painters seem to have intended most of the scenes on their vessels for a male audience. There are cases, however, when vases reflect female life and appear to be intended for a female audience. A black-figured **hydria** (water jar) by the Priam Painter is one such vase (fig. 5.26). The belly of the water jug shows a scene in a columned fountain house, where three women collect water into hydriai from animal-headed spigots, and a fourth supports a hydria on her head. Their poses, with knees and arms raised, allow the painter to experiment with figural movement. The animated gesture of a fifth woman reflects the fact that, for Athenian women, the daily outing to the public fountain house was the only opportunity to leave the confines of the home; the fountain house represented a rare chance to socialize outside the immediate family.

Despite its decorative potential, the silhouettelike black-figured technique limited artists to incision for detail, leading them to develop the reverse procedure of leaving the figures red and filling in the background. This **red-figured** technique gradually replaced the older method between 520 and 500 BCE. The effects of the change would become increasingly evident in the decades to come, but they are already discernible on an amphora of about

5.25 Exekias. *Achilles and Ajax Playing Dice*. Black-figured amphora. ca. 540–530 BCE. Height 2′ (61 cm). Vatican Museums

5.26 Priam Painter. *Women at a fountain house.* 520–510 BCE. Black-figured hydria. Ceramic. Height 20⅞″ (53 cm). Museum of Fine Arts, Boston, William Francis Warden Fund, 1961. 61.195

5.27 Euthymides. *Dancing Revelers.* Red-figured amphora. ca. 510–500 BCE. Height 2′ (60 cm). Museum Antiker Kleinkunst, Munich

510–500 BCE, signed by Euthymides (fig. **5.27**). No longer is the scene so dependent on profiles. The painter's new freedom with the brush translates into a freedom of movement in the dancing revelers he represents. They cavort in a range of poses, twisting their bodies and showing off Euthymides' confidence in rendering human anatomy. The shoulder blades of the central figure, for instance, one higher than the other, reflect the motion of his raised arm. The turning poses allow Euthymides to tackle **foreshortening**, as he portrays the different planes of the body (the turning shoulders, for instance) on a single surface. This was an age of intensive and self-conscious experimentation; indeed, so pleased was Euthymides with his painting that he inscribed a taunting challenge to a fellow painter: "As never Euphronios."

On a slightly later **kylix** (wine cup) by Douris, dating to 490–480 BCE, Eos, the goddess of dawn, tenderly lifts the limp body of her dead son, Memnon, whom Achilles killed after their mothers sought the intervention of Zeus (fig. **5.28**). Douris traces the contours of limbs beneath the drapery, and balances vigorous outlines with more delicate secondary strokes, such as those indicating the anatomical details of Memnon's body. The dead weight of Memnon's body contrasts with the lift of Eos' wings, an ironic commentary, perhaps, on how Zeus decided between the two warriors by weighing their souls on a scale that

5.28 Douris. *Eos and Memnon.* Interior of an Attic red-figured kylix. ca. 490–480 BCE. Ceramic. Diameter 10½″ (26.7 cm). Musée du Louvre, Paris

tipped against Memnon. After killing him, Achilles stripped off Memnon's armor as an act of humiliation, and where the figures overlap in the image, the gentle folds of Eos' flowing chiton set ......Memnon's nudity. His vulnerability in turn underlines his ......her's desperate grief at being unable to help her son.

At the core of the image is raw emotion. Douris tenderly exposes the suffering caused by intransigent fate, and the callousness of the gods who intervene in mortal lives. In this mythological scene, Athenians may have seen a reflection of themselves during the horrors of the Persian Wars of 490–479 BCE. Indeed, an inscription brings the vase into the realm of everyday life, with the signatures of both painter and potter, as well as a dedication typical of Greek vases: "Hermogenes is beautiful."

THE CLASSICAL AGE

The beginning of the fifth century BCE brought crisis. A number of Ionian cities rebelled against their Persian overlords, and after Athens came to their support, the Persians invaded the Greek mainland, under the leadership of Darius I. At the Battle of Marathon in 490 BCE, a contingent of about 10,000 Athenians, with a battalion from nearby Plataea, repulsed a force of about 90,000 Persians. Ten years later, an even larger force of Persians returned under Darius' son, Xerxes I. Defeating a Spartan force at Thermopylae, they took control of Athens, burning and pillaging temples and statues. The Greeks fought them again at Salamis and ......taea in 480–479 BCE, and finally defeated them. These battles were defining moments for the Greeks, who first faced destruction in their cities, and then emerged triumphant and confident after the horrors of invasion. At least in Athens, Persian destruction of public monuments and space is visible in the archaeological record, and, for archaeologists and art historians, signals the end of the Archaic period. The period stretching from the end of the Persian Wars to the death of Alexander the Great in the late fourth century BCE is known as the Classical Age. During this time, architects and sculptors alike sought visual harmony in proportional systems, and artists achieved a heightened naturalism in depicting the human form.

The struggle against the Persians tested the recently established Athenian democracy. Athens emerged from the war as the leader of the Delian League, a defensive alliance against the Persians, which quickly evolved into a political and economic empire that facilitated many architectural and artistic projects. The Classical era was when the playwrights whose names are still so familiar—Aristophanes, Aeschylus, Sophocles, and Euripides—were penning comedies and tragedies for performance at religious festivals, and thinkers like Socrates and Plato, and then Aristotle, engaged in their philosophical quests. Perhaps the most influential political leader of the day was Perikles, who ......ne to the forefront of Athenian public life in the mid-fifth ......ntury BCE, and played a critical role in the city's history until his death in 429 BCE. An avid patron of the arts, he focused much of his attention on beautifying the city's highest point or Akropolis.

Classical Sculpture

The Persian sack of 480 BCE left the Athenian Akropolis in ruins. Among many statues that were once dedications there and were later excavated from the debris, one kouros stands apart (fig. 5.29). Archaeologists sometimes attribute it to the Athenian sculptor Kritios, and know it as the *Kritios Boy*. On account of its

5.29 *Kritios Boy.* ca. 480 BCE. Marble, height 46″ (116.7 cm). Akropolis Museum, Athens

and rigid. The *Kritios Boy* has one leg forward like earlier kouroi, yet an important change has occurred. The sculptor has shifted the youth's weight, creating a calculated asymmetry in the two sides of his body. The knee of the forward leg is lower than other, the right hip is thrust down and in, and the left hip up and out. The axis of the body is not a straight vertical line, but a reversed S-curve. Taken together, these small departures from symmetry indicate that the youth's weight rests mainly on the left leg, while the right leg acts as a prop to help balance the body.

The *Kritios Boy* not only stands; he stands at ease. The artist masterfully observed the balanced asymmetry of this relaxed natural stance, which is known to ancient art historians as a **chiastic pose** (from "χ," the Greek letter *chi*), and to Renaissance art historians as **contrapposto** (Italian for "counterpoise"). The leg that carries the main weight is called the engaged leg, the other, the free leg. This simple observation led to radical results, for with it came a recognition that if one part of the body is engaged in a task, other parts respond. Bending the free knee results in a slight swiveling of the pelvis, a compensating curvature of the spine, and an adjusting tilt of the shoulders. This unified approach to the body led artists to represent movement with a new naturalism. Indeed, even though the *Kritios Boy* is at rest, his muscles suggest motion, and the sculpture has life; he seems capable of action. At the same time, the artist recognized that strict adherence to nature would not always yield the desired result. So, as in the later Parthenon (see pages 131–37), refinements are at work. The sculptor exaggerated the line of muscles over the pelvis to create a greater unity between thighs and torso, and a m fluid transition from front to back. This emphasized the sculpture's three-dimensionality, and encouraged a viewer to move around it.

The innovative movement in the musculature gives a viewer the sense, for the first time, that muscles lie beneath the surface of the marble skin, and that a skeleton articulates the whole as a real organism. A new treatment of the flesh and the marble's surface adds to this impression: The flesh has a soft sensuousness that is quite alien to earlier kouroi, and the sculptor has worked the surface of the marble to a gentle polish. Gone, also, is the Archaic smile. The face has a soft fleshiness to it, especially marked around the chin, which is characteristic of sculpture in the early Classical period. The head is turned slightly away from the front, removing the direct gaze of earlier kouroi and casting the figure into his own world of thought.

A sculpture discovered in the Graeco-Punic settlement of Motya in western Sicily exhibits a similar sensuousness (see map 5.1 and fig. **5.30**). Like the *Kritios Boy*, it represents a youth standing in a sinuous chiastic pose, his head turned from a frontal axis. The sculptor has used the fine fabric of a charioteer's tunic to "mask" the full curves of the body, revealing the flesh while simultaneously concealing it. Athletic contests were a prominent component of male life in Greece and its colonies. Greeks view physical prowess as a virtue, and victors in games won a meas of fame. Sculptures like this one, set up in public places, commemorated their success.

5.30 *Charioteer from Motya*, Sicily. ca. 450–440 BCE. Marble, height 6′3″ (1.9 m). Museo Giuseppe Whitaker, Motya

findspot, they date it to shortly before the Persian attack. It differs significantly from earlier, Archaic kouroi (see figs. 5.14 and 5.15), not least because it is the first surviving statue that stands in the full sense of the word. Although the earlier figures are in an upright position—instead of reclining, sitting, kneeling, or running—their stance is really an arrested walk, with the body's weight resting evenly on both legs. This pose is nonnaturalistic

5.31 *Zeus*. ca. 460–450 BCE. Bronze, height 6′10″ (1.9 m). National Archaeological Museum, Athens. Ministry of Culture Archaeological Receipts Fund. 15161

The *Kritios Boy* marks a critical point in Greek art. One of the changes it engendered was a wholehearted exploration of the representation of movement, another hallmark of early Classical sculpture. A magnificent nude bronze dating to about 460–450 ᴇ recovered from the sea near the Greek coast (fig. **5.31**) was obably in the cargo of a Roman vessel that sank on its voyage to Italy. At almost 7 feet tall, it depicts a spread-eagled male figure in the act of throwing—probably Zeus casting a thunderbolt, or Poseidon throwing his trident. In a single figure, the sculptor captures and contrasts vigorous action and firm stability. The result is a work of outright grandeur, expressing the god's awe-inspiring power. The piece shows off not only the artist's understanding of bodies in motion, but also an expert knowledge of the strengths of bronze, which allowed the god's arms to stretch out without support. (See *Materials and Techniques*, page 128.) Some ten years later, in about 450 BCE, a sculptor named Myron created a bronze

5.32 *Diskobolos* (*Discus Thrower*). Roman copy after a bronze original of ca. 450 BCE by Myron. Marble, life-size. Museo delle Terme, Rome

statue of another athlete, a discus thrower, the *Diskobolos,* which earned great renown in its own time. Like most Greek sculptures in bronze, it is known to us only from Roman copies (fig. **5.32**). (See www.myartslab.com.) If the bronze Zeus suggested impending motion by portraying the moment before it occurred, Myron condensed a sequence of movements into a single pose, achieved through a violent twist of the torso that brings the arms into the same plane as the legs. The pose conveys the essence of the action by presenting the coiled figure in perfect balance.

THE *DORYPHOROS*: IDEALS OF PROPORTION AND HARMONY Within half a century of the innovations witnessed in the *Kritios Boy,* sculptors were avidly exploring the body's articulation. One of those sculptors was Polykleitos of Argos, whose most famous work, the *Doryphoros* (*Spear Bearer*) (fig. **5.33**),

5.33 *Doryphoros* (*Spear Bearer*). Roman copy after an original of ca. 450–440 BCE by Polykleitos. Marble, height 6′6″ (2 m). Museo Archaeologico Nazionale, Naples

is known to us through numerous Roman copies. In this sculpture, the chiastic pose is much more emphatic than in the *Kritios Boy*, the turn of the head more pronounced. Polykleitos seems to delight in the possibilities the pose offers, examining how the anatomy on the two sides of the body responds to it. The "working" left arm balances the engaged right leg in the forward position, and the relaxed right arm balances the free left leg. Yet, in this sculpture, Polykleitos did more than study anatomy. He explored principles of commensurability, *symmetria*, where part related to part, and all the parts to the whole: He proposed an ideal system of proportions, not just for individual elements of the body but for their relation to one another and to the body as a whole. He also addressed *rhythmos* (composition and movement). According to one ancient writer, Greeks knew this work as his *kanon* (canon, meaning "rule" or "measure"). (See www.myartslab.com.) Egyptian artists had earlier aimed to establish guidelines for depiction based on proportion. Yet for Polykleitos, the search for an ideal system of proportions was more than an artist's aid: It was rooted in a philosophical quest for illumination, and in a belief that harmony (*harmonia*)—in the universe, as in music and in all things—could be expressed in mathematical terms. Only slightly later than this sculpture, Plato would root his doctrine of ideal forms in numbers, and acknowledge that beauty was commonly based on proportion. Philosophers even referred to works of art to illustrate their theories. Moreover, beauty was more than an idle conceit for Classical Athenians; it also had a moral dimension. Pose and expression reflected character and feeling, which revealed the inner person and, with it, *arete* (excellence or virtue). Thus contemplation of harmonious proportions could be equated with the contemplation of virtue. (See *Primary Source*, page 133.)

Much of the *Doryphoros'* original appearance may have been lost in the copy-making process: Bronze and marble differ greatly in both texture and presence. Surviving Greek bronzes are extremely rare, and when a pair of over-life-size figures was found in the sea near Riace, Italy, in 1972, they created a sensation (fig. **5.34**). Their state of preservation is outstanding, and shows off to advantage the extraordinarily fine workmanship. Greek sculptors used a refined version of the lost-wax technique familiar to Near Eastern artists. The process differs radically from cutting away stone, since the technique is additive (the artist builds the clay model in the first phase of the process). Further, where marble absorbs light, a bronze surface reflects it, and this led sculptors to explore a variety of surface textures—for hair and skin, for instance. They could add different materials for details: These statues have ivory and glass-paste eyes, bronze eyelashes, and copper lips and nipples. Statue A (or *Riace Warrior A*), shown here, has silver teeth. Who these figures represented is still unknown: a pair of heroes, perhaps, or warriors. They may have formed part of a single monument. Though they strike similar poses, the men have differing body types, which has led some scholars to date them apart and attribute them to two separate sculptors. They could equally be the work of a single artist exploring the representation of character and age.

5.34 *Riace Warrior A*, found in the sea off Riace, Italy. ca. 450 BCE. Bronze, height 6′8″ (2.03 m). Museo Archaeologico, Reggio Calabria, Italy

THE SCULPTURES OF THE TEMPLE OF ZEUS, OLYMPIA

The Riace bronzes may once have stood in a sanctuary, where Greeks customarily celebrated great men. There, they were in the presence of the gods, whose temples featured additional sculpture

The Indirect Lost-Wax Process

Zeus (see fig. 5.31) is one of the earliest surviving Greek statues that was made by the indirect lost-wax process. This technique enables sculptors to create spatially freer forms than they can in stone. They make projecting limbs separately and solder them onto the torso, and no longer need to support them using unsightly struts. Compare, for example, the freely outstretched arms of the *Zeus* with the strut extending from hip to drapery on the *Aphrodite of Knidos* (see fig. 5.56).

The Egyptians, Minoans, and early Greeks had often made statuettes of solid bronze using the *direct* lost-wax process. The technique was simple. The sculptor modeled his figure in wax; covered it with clay to form a mold; heated out the wax; melted copper and tin in the ratio of nine parts to one in a crucible; and poured this alloy into the space left by the "lost wax" in the clay mold. Yet, because figures made in this way were solid, the method had severe limitations. A solid-cast life-size statue would have been prohibitively expensive, incredibly heavy, and prone to developing bubbles and cracks as the alloy cooled. So from the eighth through the sixth centuries BCE, the Greeks developed the *indirect* lost-wax method, which allowed them to cast statues hollow and at any scale.

First, the sculptor shaped a core of clay into the basic form of the intended metal statue, before covering this core with a layer of wax to the thickness of the final metal casting, and carving the details of the statue carefully in the wax. The figure was then sectioned into its component parts—head, torso, limbs, and so on. For each part, the artist applied a heavy outer layer of clay over the wax and secured it to the inner core with metal pegs. The package was then heated to melt the wax, which ran out. Molten metal—usually bronze, but sometimes silver or gold—was then poured into the space left by this "lost wax." When the molten metal cooled, the outer and inner molds were broken away, leaving a metal casting—the statue's head, torso, or arm—and these individual sections were then soldered together to create the statue. The sculptor completed the work by polishing the surface, chiseling details such as strands of hair and skin folds, and inlaying features such as eyes, teeth, lips, nipples, and dress patterns in ivory, stone, glass, copper, or precious metal.

The indirect lost-wax process

5.35 Photographic reconstruction (partial) of *Battle of the Lapiths and Centaurs*, from west pediment of Temple of Zeus at Olympia. ca. 460 BCE. Marble, slightly over-life-size. Archaeological Museum, Olympia as ornamentation. The chief temple in the sanctuary at Olympia honored Zeus. Spoils from a victory of Elis over its neighbor Pisa in 470 BCE provided funds for the temple's construction, to a design by the architect Libon from Elis. Its fragmentary pediments, perhaps the work of Ageladas from nearby Argos in about 460 BCE, are highpoints of the early Classical style, and are reassembled in the Archaeological Museum at Olympia. In the east pediment, mythology provides an analogy for the recent victory, as at Aegina. The subject is the triumph of Pelops over Oinomaos, king of Pisa, in a chariot race, for which the prize was the hand of the king's daughter, Hippodameia. Pelops (for whom the Peloponnesos is named) was an important figure for Greeks, for they credited him with founding the athletic games at Olympia. Yet he prevailed in the race by trickery, with the result that he and his descendants, including Agamemnon, king of Mycenae, lived under a curse. Thus, the myth was topical in a second way: Pelops' example served as a warning against foul play to Olympic contestants as they paraded past the temple.

The west pediment represents the struggle of the Lapiths, a tribe from Thessaly, with the centaurs (a centauromachy) (fig. 5.35). Centaurs were the offspring of Ixion, king of the Lapiths, and Hera, whom he tried to seduce while in Olympos (with the result that Ixion was chained forever to a fiery wheel in Tartarus). As half-brothers of the Lapiths, the centaurs were guests at the wedding of the Lapith king Peirithoös and Deidameia. Unable to tolerate alcohol, they got into a drunken brawl with the Lapiths, who subdued them with the aid of Peirithoös' friend Theseus.

At the center of the composition stands the commanding figure of Apollo. His outstretched right arm, the strong turn of his head, and his powerful gaze show his engagement in the drama, as he wills the Lapiths to victory. At the same time, his calm, static pose removes him from the action unfolding around him; he does not help physically. To the left of Apollo, the centaur king, Eurytion, has seized Hippodameia. Both figures are massive and simple in form, with soft contours and undulating surfaces. The artist entangled them in a compact interlocking group, which is quite different from the individual conflicts of the Aegina figures. Moreover, the artist expressed their struggle in more than action and gesture: The centaur's face mirrors his anguish, and his pain and desperate effort contrast vividly with the calm on the young bride's face. In setting the centaurs' evident suffering against the emotionlessness of the Lapiths, the pediment draws a moral distinction between the bestial centaurs and the civilized humans, who share in Apollo's remote nobility. Apollo, god of music and poetry but also of light and reason, epitomizes rational behavior in the face of adversity. By partaking in divine reason, humans triumph over animal nature. This conflict between the rational and the irrational, order and chaos, lay at the heart of Greek art, both in its subject matter and in its very forms. It exposes the Greeks' sense of themselves, representing civilization in the face of barbarianism—always neatly encapsulated in the Persians.

Like the west pediment, the east pediment may have had a local relevance, encouraging fair play among Olympic competitors. The metopes were certainly topical: They depict the labors of Herakles, Pelops' great-grandson, who according to legend laid out the stadium at Olympia. Narrative scenes had been a feature of metopes since the early sixth century BCE, but at Olympia the designer exploited the pictorial and dramatic possibilities fully for the first time. The metope illustrated here, which was inserted prominently over the entrance on the temple's east side, shows Atlas returning to Herakles with the apples of the Hesperides (fig. 5.36). Atlas was one of the Titans, the race of gods before the Olympians, and it was his charge to support the Earth on his shoulders. Herakles agreed to hold the world for him, and thus persuaded Atlas to go to the gardens of the Hesperides to fetch the apples in fulfillment of his final labor. On returning, Atlas refused to accept his burden back, until Herakles cheated him into doing so. In the metope, Herakles supports a cushion (which held the globe) on his shoulders, with the seemingly effortless assistance of a young Athena. He eyes the apples as he tries to conceive of a way to trick Atlas into giving them up. This is not the grim combat so characteristic of Archaic Greek art (see figs. 5.23 and 5.24); the burly Herakles has assumed the thoughtful air that is central to the Classical spirit. The figures have all the characteristics of early Classical sculpture: fleshy faces (often described as "doughy"), an economy of pose and expression, and simple, solemn drapery.

5.36 *Atlas Bringing Herakles the Apples of the Hesperides.* ca. 460 BCE. Marble, height 63″ (160 cm). Archaeological Museum, Olympia

5.37 Plan of the agora at Athens

to Dipylon Gate

altar

Painted Stoa

Eridamos River

N

Stoa of Zeus

Royal Stoa

shops

Temple of Hephaistos

Altar of the Twelve Gods

courtroom

drainage system

racetrack

Panathenaic Way

shops and private houses

new bouleuterion

old bouleuterion

tholos

courthouse of the heliaia

military headquarters

shrine, possibly to the Eponymous Heroes

Enneakrounos ("nine-jets") Fountain House

mint

to Piraeus Harbor

house

0   200ft

50 m

south stoa

to Acropolis

5.38 Akropolis (view from west), Athens. Propylaia, 437–432 BCE; with Temple of Athena Nike, 427–424 BCE

- N
- statue of Athena Promachus
- Erechtheum
- old Temple of Athena
- Propylaea
- precinct or terrace walls
- sanctuary of Artemis Brauronia
- Nike Temple
- Mycenaean fortification
- Chalcotheca
- Parthenon

0   40   80 meters

0   60   300 feet

Architecture and Sculpture on the Athenian Akropolis

As in many Greek cities, the principal centers of Athenian public life were the agora and the Akropolis. The agora (fig. 5.37) was primarily a marketplace, but as time passed Athenians dedicated temples and civic buildings such as stoas (colonnaded porticoes) there, and the space took on a monumental character. The Akropolis had been a fortified site since Mycenaean times, around 1250 BCE (figs. 5.38 and 5.39). During the Archaic period, it was home to at least one sizeable temple dedicated to the city's patron goddess, Athena, as well as several smaller temples or treasuries, and votive statues. For over 30 years after the Persian sack of 480 BCE, the Athenians left the sacred monuments on the Akropolis in ruins, as a solemn reminder of the enemy's ruthlessness. This changed in the mid-fifth century BCE, with the emergence of Perikles into political life. Perikles' ambitions for Athens included transforming the city—with its population of about 150,000—into the envy of the Mediterranean world. His projects, which the democratic assembly approved, began on the Akropolis. Individually and collectively, the structures there expressed the ideals of the Athenian city-state, and have come to exemplify Classical Greek art at its height. (See www.myartslab.com.)

THE PARTHENON The dominant temple on the Akropolis is the Parthenon (fig. 5.40). Perikles conceived it to play a focal role in the cult of Athena, though there is no evidence that Athenians used it directly for cult practices; there is no altar to the east, and the chief center of cult practice remained on the site of the Erechtheion, north of the Parthenon (see fig. 5.51). Built of gleaming white marble from nearby Mount Pentelikon, the Parthenon occupies a prominent site on the southern flank of the Akropolis. From there it dominates the city and the surrounding countryside, a brilliant landmark against the backdrop of mountains to the north, east, and west. Contemporary building records, and a biography of Perikles written by the Greek historian Plutarch, indicate that two architects named Iktinos and Kallikrates oversaw its construction between 447 and 432 BCE. To meet the expense of building the largest and most lavish temple of its time on the Greek mainland, Perikles resorted in part to funds collected from the Delian League, its allies against the Persians. Perhaps the Persian danger no longer seemed real; still, the use of these funds weakened Athens' position in relation to its allies. Centuries later, Plutarch still remembered accusations against Perikles for adorning the city "like a harlot with precious stones, statues, and temples costing a thousand talents."

5.40   Iktinos and Kallikrates. The Parthenon (view from the west). Akropolis, Athens. 447–432 BCE

When read against the architectural vocabulary of Classical Greece, the Parthenon emerges as an extraordinarily sophisticated building. Its parts integrate fully with one another, so that its spaces do not seem to be separate, but to melt into one another. Likewise, architecture and sculpture are so intertwined that discussion of the two cannot be disentangled. The temple stood near the culminating point of a grand procession that wound its way through the agora and onto the Akropolis during the Panathenaic festival in Athena's honor; as magnificent as it was to observe from a distance, it was also a building to experience from within. Imitating the grandiose temples of Archaic Ionia, the Parthenon featured an **octastyle** (eight-column) arrangement of its narrow ends. This was unusually wide, offering a generous embrace and enough space for an arrangement of a U-shaped colonnade in the cella and an enormous statue of Athena by the famed sculptor Pheidias. She stood with one hand supporting a personification of Victory, and a shield resting against her side. Pheidias fashioned the figure out of ivory and gold (a combination known as **chrys-elephantine**), supported on a wooden armature (fig. **5.41**). It was extraordinarily valuable, and the building's forms drew visitors in to view it. Like all peripteral temples, the encircling colonnade gave the impression that a visitor could approach the temple from all sides. In fact, a prostyle porch of six columns (where the columns stand in front of the side walls, rather than between them) mediated entry to the cella at the east end, and

to an **opisthonaos** (rear room), on the west, containing four tall, slender Ionic columns. The porches are unusually shallow. This allowed light into the cella, which otherwise came in through two large windows on either side of the cella's main entrance. In its combination of a well-lit interior and the rational articulation of the interior space with a colonnade, the Parthenon initiated a new interest in the embellishment of interior space.

Compared with the Temple of Hera II at Paestum (see fig. 5.9, right), the Parthenon appears far less massive, despite its greater size. One of the reasons for this is a lightening and an adjusting of proportions since the Archaic period. The columns are more slender, their tapering and entasis less pronounced, and the capitals are smaller and less flaring. Practical necessity partly determined the diameter of the columns: For convenience and economy, the architects reused many drums from the earlier Parthenon, still unfinished at the time of the Persian sack. Yet how these columns would relate to the rest of the building was a matter for new design. Their spacing, for instance, is wider than in earlier buildings. The entablature is lower in relation to their height and to the temple's width, and the **cornice** (protruding horizontal element) projects less. The load the columns carry seems to have decreased, and as a result the supports appear ab' to fulfill their task with a new ease.

Like Polykleitos, Iktinos and Kallikrates grappled with issues of commensurability. The governing principle behind their design

Aristotle (384–322) BCE

The Politics, from Book VIII

The Politics is a counterpart to Plato's Republic, *a treatment of the constitution of the state. Books VII and VIII discuss the education prescribed for good citizens. Drawing is included as a liberal art—that is, a skill not only useful but also conducive to higher activities. Yet painting and sculpture are said to have only limited power to move the soul.*

There is a sort of education in which parents should train their sons, not as being useful or necessary, but because it is liberal or noble. ... Further, it is clear that children should be instructed in some useful things—for example, in reading and writing—not only for their usefulness, but also because many other sorts of knowledge are acquired through them. With a like view they may be taught drawing, not to prevent their making mistakes in their own purchases, or in order that they may not be imposed upon in the buying or selling of articles [works of art], but perhaps rather because it makes them judges of the beauty of the human form. To be always seeking after the useful does not become free and exalted souls. ...

The habit of feeling pleasure or pain at mere representations is not far removed from the same feeling about realities; for example, if any one delights in the sight of a statue for its beauty only, it necessarily follows that the sight of the original will be pleasant to him. The objects of no other sense, such as taste or touch, have any resemblance to moral qualities; in visible objects there is only a little, for there are figures which are of a moral character, but only to a slight extent, and all do not participate in the feeling about them. Again, figures and colors are not imitations, but signs, of character, indications which the body gives of states of feeling. The connexion of them with morals is slight, but in so far as there is any, young men should be taught to look ... at [the works] of Polygnotus, or any other painter or sculptor who expresses character.

Source: Aristotle, *The Politics*, ed. Stephen Everson (NY: Cambridge University Press, 1988)

was a ratio of 9:4 or $2x + 1:x$. Thus, for instance, the 8 (x) columns across the façades answer seventeen ($2x + 1$) columns along the sides. Additionally, the ratio of the spacing between two columns (the **intercolumniation**) to the diameter at the lowest point of the column was 9:4. It was not just a matter of design convenience, but an attempt to produce harmony through numerical relation-

5.41 Model of *Athena Parthenos* by Pheidias. ca. 438 BCE. Royal Ontario Museum, Toronto

ships. Libon of Elis first used this proportional scheme in the Temple of Zeus at Olympia. Iktinos and Kallikrates employed it pervasively in the Parthenon, though never dogmatically. In fact, despite the relative precision the formula dictated, they built intentional departures from the design's strict geometric regularity into the Parthenon (as architects did in other temples). For instance, the columns are not vertical, but lean in toward the cella (the corner columns in two directions), and the space between the corner column and its neighbors is smaller than the standard intercolumniation of the colonnade as a whole. Moreover, the stepped platform on which the temple rests is not fully horizontal, but bows upward, so that the center of the long sides is about 4 inches higher than the corners. This curvature reflects up through the temple's entablature, and every column capital is slightly distorted to fit the bowed architrave. That these irregularities were intentional is beyond doubt, as masons tailormade individual blocks to accommodate them. Why they were desirable is less clear.

When architects first introduced irregularities into temple architecture, some 100 years earlier, they may have intended to solve drainage problems. Yet in the Parthenon, they are so exaggerated that scholars consider them to be corrections of optical illusions. For instance, when viewed from a distance, straight horizontals appear to sag, but if the horizontals curve upward, they look straight. When seen close up, a long straight line seems to curve like the horizon; by exaggerating the curve, the architects could make the temple appear even larger than it was. These two apparently contradictory theories could work in tandem, since different optical distortions would prevail depending on a viewer's vantage point. What is certain is that these refinements give

Repatriation of Cultural Heritage

In 2008, a new Acropolis Museum in Athens opened for preliminary viewing. Swiss-French architect Bernard Tschumi designed the museum to hold finds from the Akropolis; but it also incorporates a hall to house the Elgin Marbles from the Parthenon, a move designed to put pressure on the British Museum in London to send them home. Ever since 1978, when UNESCO established a department entitled the Intergovernmental Committee for Promoting the Return of Cultural Property to its Countries of Origin or its Restitution in Case of Illicit Appropriation, the Elgin Marbles have stood at the center of a heated debate on the repatriation of antiquities: Should museums around the world be required to return objects of cultural value to their countries of origin? And should museums purchase works of art that have been illegally trafficked? Recently, the Italian government made headlines by publicly requesting the return of objects illegally looted from Italy and purchased (generally in good faith) by museums in the United States. And to celebrate the successful outcome of negotiations with museums such as the Metropolitan Museum of Art in New York, the Boston Museum of Fine Arts, and the Getty, it mounted a free exhibition of works of art that had "come home," in the Italian president's Quirinal Palace.

The issues might seem straightforward, but repatriation and museum acquisition of illegally trafficked objects are actually complex questions. It is understandable that a country should want to retain its cultural heritage. Moreover, for archaeologists, objects removed by looting lose much of their value (see *The Art Historian's Lens*, page 29). Yet the grand-scale return of works of art to their home countries would cut the heart out of many established museums with valuable educational functions. Should all objects be returned, or just the more out-standing works of art—in which case, who should make such qualitative judgment? If repatriation were to apply only to re[cent] acquisitions, how long must an object's pedigree be to make it legal? If looting is inevitable, is it better that a museum purchase illegal objects and display them publicly, or that they should disappear into private collections? Is it better for a work of art to decay in its home country if conditions there prevent adequate preservation, or to be maintained elsewhere? And what if an individual or museum purchased antiquities legally from an invading force (such as the Ottoman authorities, who controlled Greece in Lord Elgin's day)? Such issues are not easily resolved.

North frieze of the Parthenon

---

the temple a dynamic quality that it might otherwise lack. Rather than sitting quietly on its platform, the building derives energy from its swelling forms as if it were about to burst out of its own skin; through the refinements, the temple comes alive.

THE PARTHENON SCULPTURES The largest group of surviving Classical sculptures comes from the Parthenon, which had a more extensive decorative program than any previous temple. The sculptures have a vivid and often unfortunate history.

Christians converted the temple into a church, probably in the sixth century CE, and much of the decoration on the east side was destroyed or vandalized. In 1687, Venetian cannon fire ignited ammunition that the Turkish forces were storing in the temple. The west pediment figures survived the explosion, but not the war's aftermath. They shattered when a crane dropped them while removing them so that the Venetian commander could take them to Venice. Over 100 years later, Lord Elgin, British ambassador to Constantinople, purchased what he could of the

5.42 Jacques Carrey. Drawings of east pediment of the Parthenon. 1674 CE. Bibliothèque Nationale, Paris

5.43   Three goddesses, from east pediment of the Parthenon. ca. 438–432 BCE. Marble, over-life-size. The British Museum, London

temple's decoration from the Turks and shipped it to England. In 1816, needing money, he sold it to the British Museum. Today, the Elgin Marbles, as they are known, stand at the center of a heated debate on the repatriation of national treasures. (See *The Art Historian's Lens*, page 134.)

Thirteen years before the explosion in the Parthenon, an art-named Jacques Carrey was traveling in Athens as part of the retinue of the French ambassador to the Ottoman court. He executed a series of drawings of surviving Parthenon sculptures, which, along with literary sources, have become invaluable resources for understanding the decorative program as a whole (fig. **5.42**). Like the sculptures on the Temple of Zeus at Olympia, the Parthenon sculptures had topical relevance. The west pediment portrayed the struggle between Athena and Poseidon to be Athens' patron deity. The east pediment represented the birth of Athena from the head of Zeus, in the presence of other gods. All but the central figures survive, and Carrey's drawing allows for a confident reconstruction of their arrangement. Bursting from the left corner is the upper body of Helios, the sun-god, whose rearing horses draw him into view. Balancing him in the right corner, Selene, the moon-goddess, or Nyx, the night, sinks away with her horses. These celestial gods define the day's passing, and place the scene in an eternal cosmic realm. To the right of Helios, a nude male figure in a semireclining position is probably Dionysos. On the other side of the pediment, a closely knit group of three female deities was long identified as Hestia, Dione, and Aphrodite. A recent analysis of the group sees them instead as Leto, Artemis, and Aphrodite (fig. **5.43**).

As a group, the pediment figures are strikingly impressive. Like the building in which they are embedded, their forms are long and solid, yet their implied power contrasts with their languid poses and gains strength from the contrast. The female group is a masterpiece of swirling drapery, which disguises the sheer bulk of the marble. The garments cling to the bodies beneath as if wet, both concealing and revealing flesh. Yet the drapery does not follow the lines of the body, as it does on the *Charioteer of Motya* (see fig. 5.30), so much as struggle with them, twisting around the legs in massive folds. The effect is extraordinary: Although a viewer can only see the deities from a frontal vantage point, as if the figures were two-dimensional, the curves of the deeply cut folds echo their forms in **section** (i.e., along a plane made by an imaginary vertical slice from front to back), and thereby broadcast their three-dimensionality. The effect goes against nature; yet the sculptor, possibly Pheidias himself, could better express nature through the *appearance* of truth than through truth itself. This optical device is a sculptural equivalent of the deliberate distortions in the temple's architecture.

Running the whole way around the building (rather than just at the ends, as at Olympia) was a full program of metopes, numbering 92 in all, depicting scenes of violent action. On the west side, sculptors described the battle of the Greeks against the Amazons (an Amazonomachy), a mythical race ruled by their warrior women. Metopes on the north side portrayed the Sack of Troy (the *Ilioupersis*), the conclusion of the Trojan War, when Greek forces fought the Trojans over Paris' abduction of Helen, wife of Menelaus, brother of King Agamemnon. On the east side, the gods fought the giants. The metopes of the south side mostly depict the Battle of the Lapiths and the Centaurs, already seen at Olympia. The four cycles come together to form a thematic whole: All depict the tension between the civilized and uncivilized worlds, between order and chaos; and all are therefore allegories for the Athenian victory over the Persians. Historical events are cloaked again in the guise of myth; myth elevates life so that the triumph of order over chaos has a preordained inevitability. Little survives of the metope cycles except for those on the south side, which are relatively well preserved.

Plutarch (ca. 46–after 119 CE)

Parallel Lives of Greeks and Romans, from the lives of Perikles and Fabius Maximus

A Greek author of the Roman period, Plutarch wrote Parallel Lives *to show that ancient Greece matched or exceeded Rome in its great leaders. Comparing Perikles (d. 429 BCE) with Fabius Maximus (d. 203 BCE), he concludes that Perikles' buildings surpass all the architecture of the Romans. Plutarch is the only ancient source to say that Pheidias was the overseer of Perikles' works.*

But that which brought most delightful adornment to Athens, and the greatest amazement to the rest of mankind; that which alone now testifies for Hellas that her ancient power and splendour, of which so much is told, was no idle fiction—I mean his construction of sacred edifices. ... For this reason are the works of Perikles all the more to be wondered at; they were created in a short time for all time. Each one of them, in its beauty, was even then and at once antique; but in the freshness of its vigour it is, even to the present day, recent and newly wrought. Such is the bloom of perpetual newness, as it were, upon these works of his, which make them ever to look untouched by time, as though the unfaltering breath of an ageless spirit had been infused into them.

His general manager and general overseer was Pheidias, although the several works had great architects and artists besides. Of the Parthenon, for instance, with its cella of a hundred feet in length, Kallicrates and Iktinus were the architects. ...

By the side of the great public works, the temples, and the stately edifices, with which Perikles adorned Athens, all Rome's attempts at splendour down to the times of the Caesars, taken together, are not worthy to be considered, nay, the one had a towering preeminence above the other, both in grandeur of design, and grandeur of execution, which precludes comparison.

Source: *Plutarch's Lives*, vol. 3, tr. Bernadotte Perrin (Cambridge: Harvard University Press, 1916)

Their quality varies dramatically: Not all of them are as successful as the balletlike choreography of figure **5.44**, which reminds us that a vast crew of workers must have been engaged in completing the Parthenon in such a short period: They executed two pediments and the frieze in under ten years (ca. 440–432 BCE).

5.44 *Lapith and Centaur*, metope from south side of the Parthenon. ca. 440 BCE. Marble, height 56″ (142.2 cm). The British Museum, London

The Parthenon is often viewed as the perfect embodiment of the Classical Doric style. Although this may be the impression from the outside, it is far from accurate. At architrave level within the peristyle, a continuous sculpted frieze runs around all sides of the building, in a variation of the Ionic style (see fig. 5.8). In a continuous sculpted band, some 525 feet long (fig. **5.45**), the frieze depicts a procession, moving from west to east, propelling the viewer around the temple, drawn close to the building to read the images. Horsemen jostle with musicians, water-carriers, and sacrificial beasts. Figures overlap to create the illusion of a crowd, even though the relief is only inches deep. Frenzied animals underline the calm demeanor of the human figures (see *The Art Historian's Lens*, page 134), who have the ideal proportions of the *Doryphoros*.

According to the traditional view, the procession depicted in the frieze is the Panathenaic procession, part of a festival held annually to honor Athena in the presence of the other Olympian gods, and on a grander scale every four years. The figures and their groupings are typical of the participants in these processions, and the frieze represents an idealized event, rather than a specific moment. If this view is correct, the frieze is remarkable in that for the first time it exalts mortal Greeks by depicting them in a space usually reserved for divine and mythological scenes. The most problematic aspect of the relief is the detail in figure **5.46**, from the center of the east end of the temple, where there are five unidentified figures, three of them young. Two of the young figures carry stools on their heads, while the third, in a group with one of the adults, handles a piece of cloth. According to the traditional view, the cloth is a new robe for Athena, woven by Athenian girls and women and depicting Athena's triumph against the giants in the gigantomachy. An alternative and controversial theory, however, places the entire frieze in the realm of myth, interpreting this scene as the three daughters of Erechtheus, a legendary king of Athens. According to Athenian myth, the oracle at

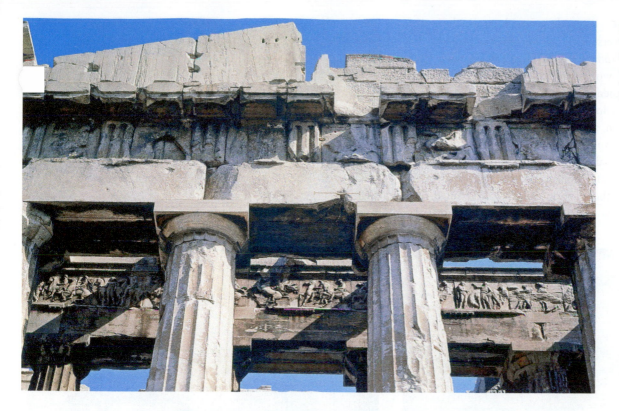

Delphi demanded the death of one of Erechtheus' daughters if Athens was to be saved from its enemies. Here, one of the daughters calmly receives the garment in which she will be sacrificed.

: myth had obvious resonance for Athens after its victory over the Persians, and the playwright Euripides made it the subject of a tragedy.

Whatever the meaning of the frieze, its iconography integrated Athenians and divine space, time, and ritual practice in a unity that reflected the Athenians' sense of superiority and self-confidence. The problem of the frieze is exacerbated by the discovery, during the building's recent preservation and reconstruction, that the pronaos featured another frieze in its upper well. Nothing survives of this frieze, but if it was thematically connected with the frieze around the cella, we lack a crucial piece of evidence for a secure identification and interpretation of the iconography.

5.46 East frieze of the Parthenon. ca. 440 BCE. Marble, height 43″ (109.3 cm). The British Museum, London

THE PHEIDIAN STYLE According to Plutarch, the sculptor Pheidias was chief overseer of all the artistic projects that Perikles sponsored. (See *Primary Source*, page 136.) Ancient literary sources attribute few works directly to his hand: His huge sculpture of Athena Parthenos, and a second chryselephantine colossus of a seated Zeus in the Temple of Zeus at Olympia, aroused extreme admiration, not only due to their religious roles, but also because of their vast size and the sheer value of the materials employed. An equally large bronze sculpture of Athena that stood on the Akropolis facing the Propylaia was also by the master sculptor. None of these works survives, and small-scale copies made in later times convey little of their original majesty.

5.48 *Grave Stele of Hegeso*. ca. 410–400 BCE. Marble, height 59″ (150 cm). National Archaeological Museum, Athens

He may have worked personally on the Parthenon's architectural sculpture, which undoubtedly involved a large number of masters, but equally he may have simply been a very able supervisor. We can therefore know little for certain about his artistic style. Nevertheless, Pheidias has come to be associated with the Parthenon style, which is often synonymous with the "Pheidian style." The term conveys an ideal that was not merely artistic but also philosophical: The idealized faces and proportions of the Athenians elevate them above the uncivilized world in which they operate. They share the calmness of the gods, who are aware of, yet aloof from, human affairs as they fulfill their cosmic roles.

Given the prominence of the Parthenon, it is hardly surprising that the Pheidian style should have dominated Athenian sculpture until the end of the fifth century BCE and beyond, even though large-scale sculptural enterprises gradually dwindled with the onset of the Peloponnesian War. The style is clear in one of the

5.47 *Nike*, from balustrade of Temple of Athena Nike. ca. 410–407 BCE. Marble, height 42″ (106.7 cm). Akropolis Museum, Athens

last of these projects, a balustrade built around the small Temple of Athena Nike on the Akropolis in about 410–407 BCE (see fig. 5.50). Like the Parthenon frieze, it shows a festive procession, but participants are not Athenians but winged personifications of victory (**Nike**, plural **Nikai**). One Nike is taking off her sandals, indicating that she is about to step on holy ground (fig. 5.47). Her wings keep her stable, so that she performs this normally awkward act with elegance and ease. The Pheidian style is most evident in the deeply cut folds of her "wet look" garments, which cling to her body and fall in deep swags between her legs.

On the *Grave Stele of Hegeso* (fig. 5.48), also from the last years of the fifth century BCE, the Pheidian style is again recognizable in the drapery, but also in the smooth planes of the idealized faces, and the quiet mood of the scene. The artist represented the deceased woman seated on an elegant chair, in a simple domestic scene that became standard for funerary markers for young women, whose realm was almost exclusively within the home. She has picked a piece of jewelry from a box held by a girl servant and seems to contemplate it. The delicacy of the carving is especially clear in the forms farthest away from a viewer, such as the servant's left arm, or the veil behind Hegeso's right shoulder. Here, the relief merges with the background, strengthening the illusion that the background is empty space rather than a solid surface. This stele is a fine example of a type of memorial that Athenian sculptors produced in large numbers from about 425 BCE onward, perhaps following a relaxation of earlier sumptuary laws that had curbed expenditure on funerary commemoration.

Their export must have helped to spread the Pheidian style throughout the Greek world.

THE PROPYLAIA In the year of the Parthenon's dedication, 437 BCE, Perikles commissioned another costly project: the monumental gate at the western end of the Akropolis, called the Propylaia (see fig. 5.38). Mnesikles was the architect in charge, and he completed the main section in five years; the remainder was abandoned with the onset of the Peloponnesian War in 431 BCE. He designed the entire structure in marble, and incorporated refinements similar to those in the Parthenon. In fact, Mnesikles cleverly adapted elements of traditional temple design to a totally different task, and to a site that rose steeply and irregularly. Conceived on two levels, the design transforms a rough passage among rocks into a magnificent entrance to the sacred precinct. Only the eastern porch (or façade) is in fair condition today. It resembles a Classical Doric temple façade, except for the wide opening between the third and fourth columns, which allowed traffic to pass onto the Akropolis; this feature is common in Ionian architecture. Placed along this central passageway through the Propylaia were two rows of slender Ionic columns, echoing the Ionic columns in the Parthenon. Flanking the western porch (fig. 5.49) were two wings, of unequal size because of constraints imposed by the terrain (figs. 5.38 and 5.39). The larger one to the north contained a picture gallery (**pinakotheke**), the first known instance of a public room specially designed for the display of paintings. The southern wing may have held a library.

5.49 Mnesikles. The Propylaia, 437–432 BCE (view from west). Akropolis, Athens

THE TEMPLE OF ATHENA NIKE The architects who designed the Parthenon and the Propylaia incorporated Ionic elements into essentially Doric buildings for a reason that may have had as much to do with politics as with design. In pre-Classical times, the only Ionic structures on the Greek mainland were small treasuries, like the Siphnian Treasury (fig. 5.20), which eastern Greek

states erected at Delphi in their regional styles. When Athenian architects used the Ionic style, Perikles may have been making a deliberate symbolic gesture, uniting the disparate regions of Greece in an international style. The Akropolis, in fact, houses finest surviving examples of Ionic architecture. One is the small Temple of Athena Nike, to the south of the Propylaia (fig. **5.50**). Kallikrates may have designed it 20 years earlier to celebrate the Athenian victory over the Persians, but building probably only occurred between 427 and 424 BCE. The decorative quality of the Ionic style, with finer proportions than those found in the Doric style, made it a natural choice for the jewel-like building. Standing on a projecting bastion, it was the first structure to greet a visitor to the Akropolis.

THE ERECHTHEION A second, larger Ionic temple stood alongside the Parthenon. The Erechtheion was built between 421 and 405 BCE, and was probably another of Mnesikles' projects (fig. **5.51** and plan in fig. 5.39). As with the Propylaia, the architect had to deal with difficult terrain: Not only did the site slope, but it already accommodated various shrines associated with the mythical founding of Athens that could not be moved. Beneath it, for instance, was the spot where, so Athenians believed, Poseidon and Athena competed for custody of Athens. In addition to the olive tree that Athena gave the city in the contest, the temple enclosed a saltwater pool that supposedly sprang up where Poseidon threw his trident. The architect therefore designed the Erechtheion to serve several religious functions simultaneously. Its highly irregular plan included four rooms well as a basement on the western side. The main, eastern room was dedicated to Athena Polias (Athena as the City Goddess) and contained the old cult image, an amorphous piece of olive wood that was the most sacred cult object in Athens; the western room was sacred to Poseidon. Another room held a cult of King Erechtheus, who promoted the worship of Athena and for whom the building is named.

5.50 Temple of Athena Nike. 427–424 BCE (view from east). Akropolis, Athens

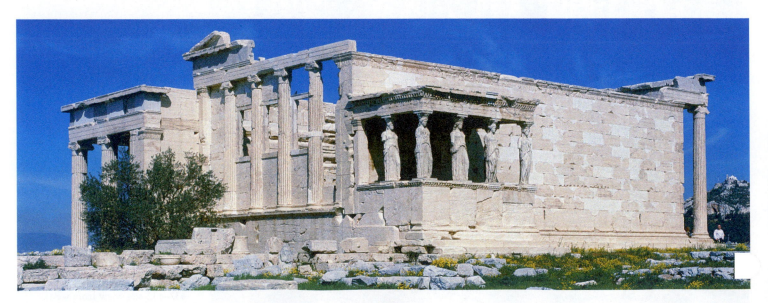

5.51 The Erechtheion. 421–405 BCE (view from the southeast). Akropolis, Athens

Instead of a west façade, the Erechtheion has two porches attached to its flanks. A very large one dedicated to Poseidon faces north and served as the main entrance, while a smaller one out toward the Parthenon. The latter is the famous Porch of the Maidens (see fig. 5.51), so named because six caryatids, instead of columns, support its roof on a high parapet. The Roman architect Vitruvius wrote that these figural columns represented the women of Caryae, a city-state in the Peloponnese that formed an alliance with the Persians in the Persian Wars. When the war was over, the triumphant Greeks killed the men of Caryae, and took the women as slaves, forcing them nonetheless to retain their fine clothing and other marks of their former status as visible reminders of their shame. Thus, Vitruvius continues, architects designed images of these women to bear the burden of their state's dishonor in perpetuity. Vitruvius' explanation for the origin of caryatids is inconsistent with the fact that they appear on the Siphnian Treasury well before the Persian Wars (see fig. 5.20); but it may reveal the special significance of caryatids for Athenians after the war. Even beyond the caryatids, the Erechtheion was a highly decorative temple. Its pediments remained bare, perhaps for lack of funds at the end of the Peloponnesian War, and little survives of the sculptural frieze. However, the carving on the bases and capitals of the columns, and on the frames of doorways and windows, is extraordinarily delicate and rich. Indeed, according to stone inscriptions detailing construction expenses for the building, it cost more than the temple's figural sculpture.

Although the Akropolis buildings arose over the course of several decades, Perikles clearly intended them as a programmatic unit. The solid, stately forms of the Doric Parthenon and Propylaia complemented the lighter, more decorative style of the Temple of Athena Nike and Erechtheion, and together they honored Athens' protective goddess, and expressed the ideals and grandeur of the city-state and its place in the wider Greek world.

THE LATE CLASSICAL PERIOD

By the end of the fifth century BCE, Athens' supremacy was on the wane. Conflict between Athens and the Peloponnesian cities of Corinth and Sparta, which had been smoldering since about 460 BCE, gradually escalated into the great Peloponnesian War in 431. By the time this ended in 404, Athens had lost. During the following century, the Greek city-states were constantly at odds with one another. In 338 BCE, Philip II, who had acceded to power in the kingdom of Macedon, to the north, exploited their disunity by invading Greece, and decisively defeated the Athenians and Thebans at the Battle of Chaironeia. The change in Greece's fortune finds its reflection in the art and architecture of the time, as artists and architects start to move away from traditional forms and subjects.

Late Classical Architecture: Civic and Sacred

Two notable changes occurred in monumental architecture in the late fifth and fourth centuries BCE. One was a shift in emphasis: As well as constructing temples, architects explored a range of other building types. Many of these—stoas, meeting houses for the governing council, and the like—had long existed, but now took on grander form. The other was the development of a new style: the Corinthian.

THE MAUSOLEUM AT HALIKARNASSOS In Halikarnassos (present-day Bodrum, in southwest Turkey; see map 5.1), the tendency toward monumentalization resulted in a vast tomb for Mausolos, who ruled Caria from 377 to 353 BCE as satrap for the Persians. His wife and sister, Artemisia, commissioned Pytheos of Priene to design the sepulcher to commemorate Mausolos as hero-founder of Halikarnassos. Such was its renown in antiquity that the ancients counted it among the seven wonders of the ancient world and by Roman imperial times its title, the Mausoleum, was used to describe any monumental tomb. It stood reasonably intact until the thirteenth century CE, when an earthquake brought down the upper sections. Then, in the late fifteenth and early sixteenth centuries, the Knights of St. John used the site as a source of squared stone to refortify their castle. In 1857, the British archaeologist Charles Newton removed many sculptural fragments to the British Museum. Danish excavations continue to yield information at the site. When coupled with literary evidence, archaeological data permits reconstructions, though none has met with universal approval (see www.myartslab.com). One hypothesis appears in figure **5.52**.

5.52 Reconstruction drawing of the Mausoleum at Halikarnassos. ca. 359–351 BCE (from H. Colvin)

The tomb was rectangular in plan, and soared 140 feet high in at least three sections, covered with sculpture: A high podium, an Ionic colonnade, and a pyramidal roof, where steps climbed to a platform supporting a statue of Mausolos or one of his ancestors in a chariot.

The Mausoleum combined the monumental tomb-building tradition of the region, Lycia, with a Greek peristyle and sculpture, and an Egyptian pyramid. The grouping of these elements in a single monument is evidence of a growing diversity in architecture. It may also have had a propagandistic function: It may have expressed Carian supremacy in the region and the symbiosis of Greek and non-Greek civilizations that might be achieved through founding a Carian empire headed by Halikarnassos.

5.54 Polykleitos the Younger. Corinthian capital, from tholos at Epidauros. ca. 350 BCE. Museum, Epidauros, Greece

CORINTHIAN CAPITAL The other major change in architecture that took place in the late fifth century BCE was the development of the **Corinthian capital** (fig. **5.53**) as an elaborate substitute for the Ionic. Its shape is an inverted bell covered with the curly shoots and leaves of an acanthus plant, which seem to sprout from the top of the column shaft. Writing about four centuries later in Italy, Vitruvius ascribed its invention to the metalworker Kallimachos. At first, Greek builders only used Corinthian capitals in temple interiors, perhaps because of the conservative nature of Greek architecture, or because of the perceived sanctity of its vegetal forms. It was not until the second century BCE that Corinthian columns appeared on the exteriors of buildings. The capital in figure **5.54** belongs to a circular shrine, or tholos at Epidauros designed by Polykleitos the Younger. The circular form of the shrine is further evidence of the preoccupation with new types of building, and its elaborate interior continues the tradition, begun with the Parthenon, of stressing the articulation of interior space.

Late Classical Sculpture

The Pheidian style, with its apparent confidence in the transcendence of the Athenian city-state, did not survive Athens' devastating defeat in the Peloponnesian War. At the end of the fifth century, a shift in mood is perceptible in sculpture, which seems to reflect a different—and less optimistic—view of man's place in the universe.

Scholars attempt to match surviving sculptures with fourth-century BCE sculptors named in literary sources. Among these is Skopas of Paros. According to the Roman writer Pliny the Elder, he was one of four masters chosen to work on the Mausoleum Halikarnassos, and art historians recognize his dynamic style in some parts of a frieze from the tomb depicting the battle of the Greeks and the Amazons. His greatest fame, though, derives from

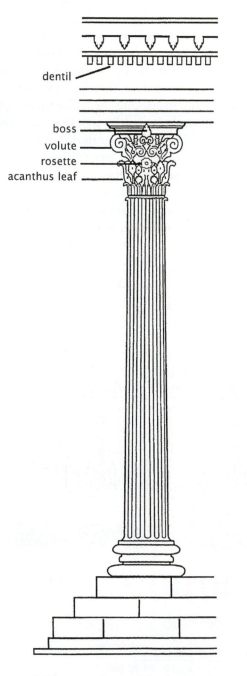

dentil

boss
volute
rosette
acanthus leaf

5.53 Corinthian style in elevation

5.55   Head of Herakles or Telephos, from west pediment of Temple
of Athena Alea, Tegea. ca. 340 BCE. Marble, height 12½" (31.75 cm).
Stolen from the Archaeological Museum, Tegea

the way he infused emotion into the faces he sculpted. A fragmentary head from a pediment of the Temple of Athena Alea at Tegea
of about 340 BCE is either by Skopas, or an artist deeply influenced
by his work (fig. **5.55**). A lion skin covering the head identifies it as
either Herakles or his son Telephos. The smooth planes and fleshy
treatment of the face are characteristic of Classical art, as seen on
the Parthenon. What is new, however, is how the sculptor cut the
marble away sharply over the eyes toward the bridge of the nose
to create a dark shadow. At the outer edge, the eyelid bulges to
overhang the eye. This simple change charges the face with a depth
of emotion not seen before. The slightly parted lips and the sharp
turn of the head enhance the effect.

PRAXITELES   If the Greeks were less confident of their place in
the world in the Late Classical period, they were also less certain
of their relationship to fate and the gods. This is reflected in the
work of Praxiteles, who was at work at roughly the same time
as Skopas. Choosing to work in marble rather than bronze, he
executed several statues of divinities. Where fifth-century BCE artists had stressed the gods' majesty, Praxiteles gave them a youthful sensuousness that suggests their willful capriciousness toward
humans. His most famous work is a sculpture of Aphrodite,
dating to about 340–330 BCE (fig. **5.56**). Pliny records that the
people of Kos commissioned a cult statue of Aphrodite from

5.56   *Aphrodite of Knidos*. Roman copy after an original of
ca. 340–330 BCE by Praxiteles. Marble, height 6'8" (2 m).
Musei Vaticani, Rome

Praxiteles, but rejected the nude statue he offered them in favor of a draped version. But the inhabitants of Knidos purchased the nude statue, and profited from the risk: Her fame spread fast, and visitors came to the island from far and wide to see her. (See www.myartslab.com.) Perhaps it was her nudity that drew so much attention: She was the first nude monumental statue of a goddess in the Greek world. Yet even if artists had previously reserved female nudity principally for representations of slaves or courtesans, the clinging drapery of the fifth century BCE had exposed almost as much of the female anatomy as it concea Her appeal may have resided just as much in the blatant eroticism of the image. A viewer catches Aphrodite either as she is about to bathe or as she is rising from her bath. With her right hand, she covers her nudity in a gesture of modesty, while grasping for a robe with her left. Her head is slightly turned, so she does not engage a viewer's gaze directly, but a viewer is made complicit with the sculpture, willingly or not, by having inappropriately witnessed her in her nudity. Perhaps, in her capriciousness, Aphrodite intended to be surprised as she bathed; the uncertainty for a viewer augments the erotic quality of the image. By some accounts, the Knidians displayed Praxiteles' sculpture in a circular shrine with entrances at front and back, so visitors could view the cult statue from all sides. A viewer's role is more complex here than in the Classical period: The sculpture invites physical and emotional engagement, not merely respect.

Praxiteles' Aphrodite is known to us only through Roman copies. In this respect, a group representing Hermes holding the infant Dionysos poses complicated questions (fig. 5.57). The Roman writer Pausanias mentions seeing such a statue by Praxiteles in the Temple of Hera at Olympia, where this marble was found in 1877. It is of such high quality that art historians have long regarded it as a late work by Praxiteles himself. Now, however, most scholars believe it to be a fine copy of the first century BCE because of the strut support and unfinished ba analysis of the tool marks on the surface of the marble support this date, as do the sandals, which are distinctly Roman in style. Still, the group has all the characteristics of Praxitelean sculpture. Hermes is more slender in proportion than Polykleitos' *Doryphoros* (see fig. 5.33), and the chiastic pose is so exaggerated as to have become a fully relaxed and languid curve of the torso. The anatomy, so clearly defined on the *Doryphoros*, blurs to suggest a youthful sensuousness rather than athletic prowess. The surface treatment of the marble is masterful, contrasting highly polished skin with rough, almost expressionistic hair. The group has a humorous quality typical of Praxiteles' work as well: The messenger god originally dangled a bunch of grapes in front of Dionysos, whose attempts to reach for them foreshadow his eventual role as the god of wine. Yet, depending upon a viewer's mood (or worldview), Hermes' distant gaze may also hold a callous disregard for the child's efforts.

LYSIPPOS A third great name in fourth-century BCE sculpture is Lysippos, who had an extremely long career. He may have begun sculpting as early as about 370 BCE and continued almost to the end of the century. Known from Roman copies, his *Apoxyomenos* (a youth scraping oil from his skin with a strigil) dates to about 330 BCE (fig. 5.58) and is in dialogue with Polykleitos' *Doryphor* (see fig. 5.33). Lysippos preferred more slender proportions f his athlete, calculating the length of the head as one-eighth of the body's length, rather than one-seventh as Polykleitos had.

5.57 *Hermes*. Roman copy after an original of ca. 320–310 BCE by Praxiteles. Marble, height 7′1″ (2.16 m). Archaeological Museum, Olympia

(See www.myartslab.com.) The *Apoxyomenos* leans further back into his chiastic pose, too—a sign of Praxiteles' influence—and the diagonal line of the free leg suggests freedom of movement. Most innovative, however, is the positioning of the athlete's arms. The outstretched arm reaches forward into a viewer's space. Since a frontal view foreshortens the arm, it entices a viewer to move around the sculpture to understand the full range of the action;

like Praxiteles, Lysippos breaks the primacy of the frontal view for a standing figure. The athlete's left arm bends around to meet the right at chest height, so the sculpture deliberately contains space within its composition. Lysippos challenges the stark opposition between sculpture and its environment; the two begin to merge. This device is symptomatic of a new interest in illusionism in the Late Classical and Hellenistic ages.

5.58 *Apoxyomenos* (*Scraper*). Roman marble copy, probably after a bronze original of ca. 330 BCE by Lysippos. Height 6'9" (2.1 m). Musei Vaticani, Rome

Painting in the Late Classical Age

Written sources name some of the famous painters of the Classical age, and reveal a good deal about how painting evolved, but they rarely include details of what it actually looked like. The great age of Greek painting began early in the Classical period with Polygnotos of Thasos and his collaborator, Mikon of Athens, who both worked as sculptors as well. Polygnotos was known for paintings depicting the aftermath of the Trojan War in Delphi, and mythological paintings coupled with a depiction of the Battle of Marathon decorating the Stoa Poikile (Painted Stoa) in the Athenian agora (see fig. 5.37). He introduced several innovations in painting, including the depiction of emotion and character, which became as central to Classical painting as they were to sculpture. He was also first to depict women in transparent drapery, and to forgo the notion of a single ground-line, placing figures instead at varying levels in a landscape setting.

The placement of figures at different levels of terrain seems to have influenced a contemporary vase painter, known today as the Niobid Painter. His name vase (the vase for which scholars name him) is a calyx krater (a wine-mixing bowl), which shows the outcome of Niobe's foolish boast that she had more—and more beautiful—children than Leto, mother of Apollo and Artemis: The sibling gods of hunting shoot down Niobe's sons and daughters (fig. **5.59**). Each of the figures has his or her own ground-line, which undulates to suggest a rocky landscape. Artemis and Apollo stand above two of their victims, who are sprawled over boulders, but we should probably understand the terrain to recede into the distance.

5.60   Reed Painter. White-ground lekythos. ca. 425–400 BCE. Height 18⅞" (48 cm), diameter 5⅛" (13 cm). National Archaeological Museum, Athens

5.59   Niobid Painter. Red-figured calyx krater, from Orvieto. ca. 460–450 BCE. Height 21¼" (54 cm), diameter 22⅟₁₆" (56 cm). Musée du Louvre, Paris

Significant technical differences separated wall painting from red-figured vase painting. Much closer to wall painting was a technique reserved almost exclusively for the vases Greeks deposited with burials: **white-ground** vase painting. Artists working in this technique painted a range of colors onto a wh— slip background, and favored a type of oil flask used in funera—y rituals, known as a **lekythos**. On a lekythos from the last quarter of the fifth century BCE, attributed to the Reed Painter (fig. **5.60**), a disconsolate young man sits on the steps of a tomb. A woman on the right holds his helmet, while a second man stands to the left with one arm raised in a gesture of farewell. Black outlines [...]ne the scene, filled with washes of vivid color. Some blue still survives on parts of the tomb and the seated man's cloak, and brown in the figures' hair, but most of the colors have long vanished, since fugitive paints sufficed for a vessel that did not have to withstand prolonged or repeated use. The freedom of the technique allowed the painter to explore foreshortening and depth, and to achieve a remarkably expressionistic effect with a few fluid lines. The deceased man's deep-set brooding eyes give some indication of the emotion painters could capture. Despite the artistic advantages of the white-ground technique, from the mid-fifth century BCE on monumental painting gradually eclipsed vase painting, though in some cases vase painters tried to reproduce large-scale compositions.

THE AGE OF ALEXANDER AND THE HELLENISTIC PERIOD

In 336 BCE, Philip II of Macedon died, and his kingdom passed to his son Alexander. Alexander the Great is one of the romantic figures of history, renowned for his military genius and personal charm. He embarked upon a great campaign of conquest, overcoming Egypt and the Persians, then continuing on to Mesopotamia and present-day Afghanistan. In 323 BCE, having founded over 70 cities, he died at the age of 33. His conquests changed the face of the Greek world dramatically, expanding it into unknown spheres, creating new political alignments, and breaking down cultural boundaries (see map 5.2).

The years following Alexander's death were fraught with struggles between members of his family and his generals, as each tried to establish himself as his sole successor; none succeeded. By about 275 BCE, Alexander's lands had coalesced into three main kingdoms, which would dominate the Mediterranean until the Romans gradually assumed control. Ptolemy founded a dynasty in Egypt that reigned until Octavian (later the Roman emperor Augustus) defeated Cleopatra VII in 31 BCE. In the east, the Seleucid family captured Babylon in 312 BCE. From Syria they ruled a kingdom which, at its largest, extended from present-day western Turkey to Afghanistan. They lost control of a small pocket of territory around Pergamon to the Attalids, who bequeathed their city to the Romans in 133 BCE. In 64 BCE, the Seleucid kingdom came under Roman control. Most coveted was Alexander's ancestral Macedon, which the Antigonids controlled until the Roman conquest in 168 BCE. Within these kingdoms, powerful cities grew—among them, Alexandria, Antioch, and

Map 5.2 Hellenistic Greece

Pergamon—with teeming populations drawn from all over the new Greek world. They vied for cultural preeminence, and art played a large part in the rivalry. Scholars call the period from the death of Alexander until Roman rule the Hellenistic period, and Hellenistic culture was radically different from that of Classical times. The expansion of Greek dominance meant that Greek cultural institutions prevailed over a vast territory; those institutions commingled with the strong cultural traditions of the indigenous peoples. The result was a rich and diverse society, in which an individual's identity was more complex than before: the kings of Pergamon, for instance, were not Greek but strove for Greekness and identified themselves as Greek. All the same, over a wide region, people were united by a common cultural vocabulary, known as a *koine* (Greek for "common thing"). The art of the time reflects this richness: diverse styles coexisted, and artists drew inspiration from indigenous forms as well as the Greek heritage.

Architecture: The Scholarly Tradition and Theatricality

Within the cultural centers of the Hellenistic world, academies emerged, which fostered avid debate among scholars in a range of fields. They engaged, among other things, in a close analysis of the arts, and developed canons by which they could judge works of literature, art, and architecture. In architecture, this led, predictably, to a heightened interest in systems of proportions, recorded in architectural treatises by practitioners of the day. Vitruvius asserts that the leading protagonist in this movement was Pytheos of Priene, one of the architects of the Mausoleum at Halikarnassos (see fig. 5.52). Like most, his treatise does not survive, but Vitruvius notes that he was dismissive of the Doric style because problems with the spacing of corner triglyphs made it impossible to impose the style without compromise. Pytheos worked instead in the Ionic style (in which the volutes of corner capitals could be angled), as seen in his temple to Athena at Priene, dedicated in 334 BCE (fig. 5.61).

5.61 Plan of Pytheos. Temple of Athena, Priene. 334 BCE

The temple's colonnade had 6 columns by 11, and a grid of squares, each 6 by 6 Attic feet (the Attic foot is slightly longer than the English foot), that dictated the proportions of all of its elements. Proportions controlled the elevation as well: For instance, the columns were 43 feet high and the entablature was 7 feet high —a total of 50 feet, half the external length of the cella. Unlike the Parthenon and other Classical temples, there were no deviations from the rule, and no refinements. The temple is a work of the intellect, the product of a didactic tradition, rather than a compromise between theory and practice. In fact, Vitruvius faults Pytheos precisely for his inability to differentiate between the two.

While this scholarly tradition flourished, the relaxation of architectural guidelines and the combination of architectural types that had occurred in the Late Classical period heralded another development. This was a penchant for dramatic siting, impressive vistas, and surprise revelations. Scholars have termed this movement "theatricality," and it balanced and complemented the scholarly tradition. As the glory of Athens declined, the Athenians and other Greeks came to think of themselves less as members of a city-state and more as individuals; architecture, in turn, began to cater more and more to personal experience, often manipulating visitors toward a meaningful revelation.

THE TEMPLE OF APOLLO, DIDYMA Begun in about 300 BCE and still unfinished by the end of the Roman period, the Temple of Apollo at Didyma is a good example of architectural theatricality (figs. **5.62** and **5.63**). Its ground plan and design appear to have been established by the renowned architects Paionios of Ephesos and Daphnis of Miletos, on the site and at the scale of an Archaic temple destroyed by the Persians in 494 BCE.

From the outside, the temple appeared similar to other large-scale dipteral Ionic buildings of the area. A visitor would naturally expect the interior to repeat the format of canonical Greek temples such as the Parthenon; but, in fact, the architects constantly defied these expectations, leading visitors instead to dramatic vistas, perhaps intending to heighten their religious experience. Although the temple appeared to be accessible from all sides, its seven massive steps were on a divine, not a mortal scale, and far too high to climb comfortably. Instead, visitors climbed a set of shallower steps at the front, and entered the porch between its vast columns, set to mimic the grove of sacred trees around the building. As expected, an opening led to the cella—but this cella stood approximately 5 feet off the ground, so access was impossible. From this raised threshold, scholars believe, the oracular priestess may have uttered her prophecies to those standing below in the porch. The path further into the building led to the right or left of the threshold, where dark barrel-vaulted tunnels led downward. For a Greek visitor, a barrel-vaulted tunnel evoked a dark interior such as a cave. Yet these passages did not lead to a covered cella, but a vast open courtyard drenched with bright sunshine: A revelation, it must have seemed.

At the end of the courtyard was the shrine itself, a small Ionic building dedicated to Apollo. Near the shrine were sacred laurel bushes and a spring of holy water. Turning back from the shrine, a visitor faced another astonishing sight: A wide, steep staircase dwarfed the tunnels through which he or she had entered the courtyard, and led up to a pair of towering **engaged** Corinthian columns (joined to the wall). These may have signaled that the room that lay beyond them was the priestess' innermost sanctuary. We know little of the goings-on inside Greek temples, yet the processional quality of this staircase and the large scale of the courtyard suggest that large crowds of worshipers could have gathered there to witness ritual ceremonies. Also unknown is the function of small staircases leading off from the sanctuary and up to the roof over the colonnades. Building inscriptions describe them as "labyrinths," and the ceiling above them is

5.62   Paionios of Ephesos and Daphnis of Miletos. Temple of Apollo, Didyma, Turkey. Begun 313 BCE

5.63   Plan of Temple of Apollo, Didyma, Turkey

carved with a brightly painted meander pattern (see fig. 5.3), the Egyptian hieroglyphic sign for a maze. They may have provided maintenance workers with access to the roof, but they may equally have accommodated revelatory dramas in honor of Apollo.

As a whole, the temple's design manipulated visitors along unexpected paths, and offered constant surprises. Yet the temple is remarkable for another reason besides. Inside the courtyard, archaeologists unexpectedly discovered diagrams incised (so lightly that they are visible only under a strong raking light) upon its walls. These etchings are scale drawings for aspects of the building's design, ranging from capital decoration to column entasis. They provide a rare insight into the design process in Greek building. They suggest that architects drew a building's design onto its surfaces as it rose, and workers then polished them off as they finished those surfaces. This temple's incompletion preserved the design drawings in place.

City Planning

Early Greek cities such as Athens grew organically, transforming gradually from small settlements into larger urban develop-

ments. Streets were typically winding, and building blocks were irregular. From the seventh century BCE onward, colonization offered Greeks an opportunity to conceive cities as a whole, and to assess different types of city planning, while from the I Classical period, philosophers debated the structure of ideal cities. Hippodamos of Miletos was the first to write a treatise on city design, advocating grid planning—that is, laying out city streets in intersecting horizontals and verticals. In the mid-fifth century BCE, he designed the Piraeus, near Athens, as a grid, and the pattern is still used in many Western cities today. The design offered many advantages: For an architect, it provided regularity; for colonists, it simplified the distribution of allotments; and for inhabitants, it meant a new ease of orientation. When the inhabitants of Priene relocated their city to avoid flooding, in approximately 350 BCE, they opted for the efficiency of a grid plan (fig. **5.64**). As the model demonstrates, the city planners applied the grid to the sloping terrain uncompromisingly. On some longitudinal axes, they inserted staircases to climb straight, steep inclines. Useful for pedestrians, the stairs must have been impassable by wheeled vehicles. Though perhaps a misjudgment, this may equally have been a form of traffic control.

5.64   Model of the city of Priene. 4th century BCE and later. Staatliche Museen, Berlin

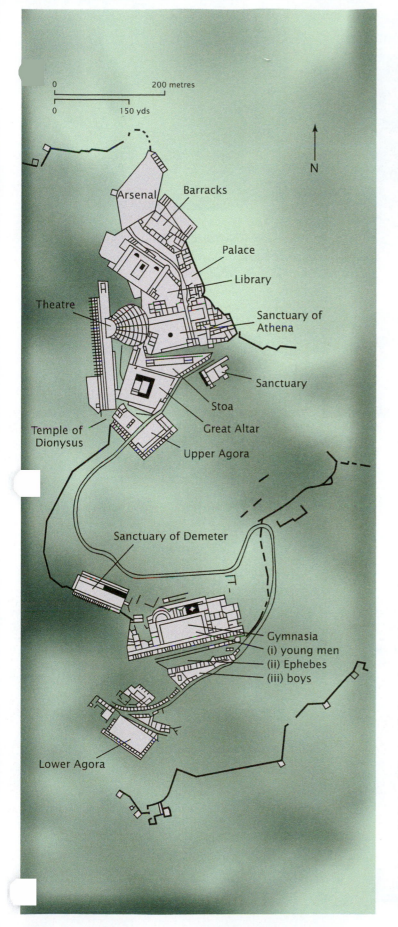

Theatre

Arsenal

Barracks

Palace

Library

Sanctuary of
Athena

Sanctuary

Stoa

Temple of
Dionysus

Great Altar

Upper Agora

Sanctuary of Demeter

Gymnasia
(i) young men
(ii) Ephebes
(iii) boys

Lower Agora

0   200 metres

0   150 yds

N

5.65   Plan of Pergamon, Turkey. ca. 2nd century BCE

PERGAMON: A THEATRICAL PLAN A visitor to the city of Pergamon would have had a dramatically different experience. There, in the early second century BCE, King Eumenes II and his architects eschewed a grid as they planned an expansion of the city (fig. **5.65**). Residential areas lay mainly on the plain of the Kaikos River; nearby was the towering Akropolis. The new design exploited the dramatic rise in terrain from one to the other, apparently assigning symbolic meaning to the ascent as well. On the lower levels were amenities of everyday life, such as the agora. As the road climbed the southern slope of the Akropolis, it passed through vaulted entrance tunnels to emerge at three *gymnasia* (schools); the first was for boys, the second for ephebes (adolescents aged 15–17), and the third and highest for young men. Farther up the road were sanctuaries to Hera and Demeter.

The road followed the terrain, snaking past an earlier agora, now chiefly used for legal and political purposes, to the Akropolis proper, where Eumenes II, or perhaps his successor Attalos II, dedicated a magnificent altar court to Zeus (see fig. 5.72). Further up and to the east was a shrine for the hero cult, a **heroön**. A long portico temporarily obscured any view of the journey's great crescendo; passing through it, a visitor entered the sanctuary of Athena, patron goddess of Pergamon, where the city's oldest temple stood, alongside Eumenes' celebrated library, with an over-life-size marble version of Pheidias' *Athena Parthenos* (see fig. 5.41). This sanctuary marked the privileged place of learning in Pergamene culture. On its own, the temple was not remarkable. Yet it acquired meaning from the symbolic journey required to reach it. From the sanctuary, a visitor could look out over the steep **cavea** (or seating area) of the Theater of Dionysos across the plain's breathtaking panorama. Beyond the sanctuary, to the northeast, were the royal residence and barracks for the guard. Like the sanctuary, the residence offered magnificent views of the river and the receding countryside, and cool breezes blowing through the valley and up to the Akropolis must have provided relief from the fierce summer heat. At every turn, the city's designer considered a visitor's experience. The impressive vistas and sudden surprises are hallmarks of Hellenistic theatricality.

THE THEATER AT EPIDAUROS Within these cities, architects continued the Late Classical trend toward formalizing a variety of types of architecture. Given the propensity for theatricality, it is no surprise that they paid close attention to theater buildings. Theaters had long been part of the religious landscape of Greek cities, since Greeks gathered in their communities for the choral performances and plays that were central to festivals of Dionysos. The basic prerequisites for a theater were a hillside, on which an audience could sit (the cavea), and a level area for the performance (the **orchestra**). In the Late Classical and Hellenistic periods, however, theaters became more formalized as their essential components took on architectural form.

In the sanctuary of the healing god Asklepios at Epidauros on the Peloponnese, a magnificent stone theater was constructed

5.66 Theater, Epidauros. Early 3rd to 2nd centuries BCE

5.67 Plan of the theater, Epidauros (after Picard-Cambridge)

in the early third century BCE; its upper tier was completed in the second century BCE (figs. **5.66** and **5.67**). Row upon row of stone seats lined the sloping hillside, covering slightly more than ̇ ̇nicircle. To facilitate the audience's circulation, the architect grouped the seats in wedgelike sections (**cunei**), separated by staircases; a wide horizontal corridor divides the upper and lower sections. Actors performed in the level circle at the center, with a stage building (**skene**) behind as a backdrop, containing utility rooms for storage and dressing. Because it was open to the sky, no roof supports obstructed the audience's view of the performance, and many of the seats offered spectacular vistas across the landscape as well. Yet perhaps the most astonishing feature of the theater is its acoustics, which visitors can still experience: Its funnel shape carries the slightest whisper up to the highest points of the auditorium. This form is familiar to theatergoers today, a testament to its success.

THE PHAROS AT ALEXANDRIA In Alexandria, on the northwest coast of the Nile Delta, a vast and innovative lighthouse was a testament to the city's cosmopolitan nature and the vitality of shipping and commerce throughout the Hellenistic Mediterranean (fig. **5.68**). Alexander the Great founded the city to a grid design by Dinocrites of Rhodes, but the famed lighthouse, or Pharos, was not begun until the reign of Ptolemy I, in ca. 279 BCE, and was completed under his son, Ptolemy II Philadelphos. Some sources attribute it to an architect named Sostratus. The building has long collapsed, but a French team has recently recovered some of its blocks in underwater excavations. Together with mosaic depictions and medieval descriptions, archaeological evidence suggests a building with a square, slightly tapering base, an octagonal central drum, and a tholos-like element, crowned by a huge bronze statue at the dizzying height of about 400 feet. Ancient sources describe a fire at the summit, and an annular corridor circled up through

5.68   Alexandria (Egypt), Pharos (lighthouse) completed under Ptolemy II Philadelphos 280–79 BCE, height over 394 ft (120 m); one of the Seven Wonders of the World

the tower, wide enough for mules to climb to the top with fuel—a type of petroleum called naphtha, perhaps, that is found in ponds. Yet archaeologists are uncertain how to reconcile a fire with a stone tholos, which would have cracked if exposed to intense heat. The building became an icon for the city. Its monumentality earned it a place among the seven wonders of the ancient world, and it was widely imitated by other cities.

Hellenistic Sculpture: Expression and Movement

Hellenistic sculptors also responded to the cultural changes of the Hellenistc world. Fourth-century BCE sculptors had explored the portrayal of emotion and three-dimensional movement, and their Hellenistic successors made further radical strides in these directions. Both resulted in heightened drama and viewer involvement. That said, one can make only broad generalizations about Hellenistic sculpture, as it is notoriously difficult to date and to attribute to a firm place of origin. Often it is style alone that leads scholars to ascribe a sculpture to this period, and even that is not always straightforward: Although there is good evidence of a dia-

logue between sculptors, they were working throughout a vast territory where numerous local influences were at play, making the body of material much less homogeneous than Classical sculpture.

PORTRAITURE A chief development in sculpture in this perio was portraiture. If Archaic artists depicted individuals at all, they represented them with the all-purpose figures of kouroi and korai. Individual likenesses were unknown in art of the Classical period, which sought a timeless ideal. A copy of a famous sculpture of Perikles dating from about 425 BCE, for instance, differs from the idealized youths of the Parthenon frieze only in that the Perikles wears a beard and a helmet. Later, in the mid-fourth century BCE, portraiture became a major branch of Greek sculpture, and it continued to flourish in Hellenistic times. One of the catalysts for this change was Alexander the Great himself. Recognizing the power of a consistent visual image, he retained Lysippos as the exclusive creator of his sculpted portraits. No surviving original preserves Lysippos' touch, but scholars consider the so-called "Azara Herm" to be relatively faithful to its model (fig. **5.69**). To be sure, the face has an idealized quality: Its planes are smooth, especially around the brow. Yet individuality emerges in the unruly hair, raised at the front in Alexander the Great's characteristic cowlick (or *anastole*), and in the twist of

5.69 Lysippos. Portrait of Alexander the Great, the "Azara Herm." Roman copy after an original of the late 4th century BCE. Marble, height 27″ (68 cm). Musée du Louvre, Paris

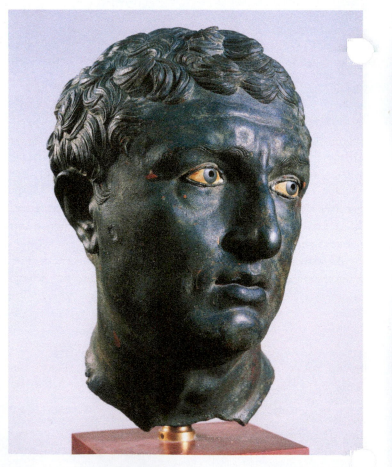

5.70 *Portrait Head*, from Delos. ca. 80 BCE. Bronze, height 12¾″ (32.4 cm). National Archaeological Museum, Athens. Ministry of Culture Archaeological Receipts Fund. 14612

5.71 Epigonos of Pergamon (?). *Dying Trumpeter*. Perhaps a Roman copy after a bronze original of ca. 230–220 BCE, from Pergamon, Turkey. Marble, life-size. Museo Capitolino, Rome

the head, which removes the portrait from a timeless realm and animates it with action. Moreover, Alexander does not engage with a viewer, but has a distant gaze. These characteristics would become emblematic of Alexander, and Hellenistic and Roman generals would adopt them as attributes in their own portraiture. With this image, the individual came to inhabit the sculpture, and portraiture began to flourish as a genre.

As with so many Greek sculptures, original Hellenistic portraits are extremely rare. One is an early first-century BCE bronze head from Delos (fig. **5.70**), which may portray a trader: The island of Delos was a lively trading port, and many merchants there became extremely wealthy. Unlike the Romans, the Greeks did not isolate an individual's personality in portrait busts, but considered it to animate the full body. Thus this head is just a fragment of a full-length statue. The artist fused the heroic qualities of Alexander's likeness—the whimsical turn of the head, for instance, and the full head of hair—with modeled surfaces. The fleshy features, the uncertain mouth, and the furrowed brows cap-[tur]e an individual likeness. If they also suggest character traits, it [is] hard to read them with any precision at such a cultural distance.

Like architects, Hellenistic sculptors engaged their audience in the experience of their work, and favored dramatic subjects infused with emotion. The *Dying Trumpeter*, preserved in a Roman copy (fig. **5.71**), probably belonged on one of two statue bases found in the Sanctuary of Athena on the Akropolis of Pergamon, and commemorated Attalos I's defeat of the Gauls in about 233 BCE. Gone is the Classical tradition of referring to the enemy through mythological analogy (see figs. 5.35 and 5.44). Instead, the sculptor specifically identifies the enemy as a Gaul through his bushy hair and moustache, and by the torque, or braided gold band, that he wears around his neck. Gone, too, is any suggestion of the inferiority of the vanquished. The Gaul dies nobly, sinking quietly to the ground or struggling to prop himself up, as blood pours from a wound in his chest. His body is powerful, his strength palpable. He faces his agonies alone, mindless of any viewer. A viewer, in turn, is drawn in by the privateness of the moment, and drawn around the sculpture by the pyramidal composition and the foreshortening witnessed from every angle. The *Dying Trumpeter* was probably one sculpture in a group, but the victor, always present in Classical battle scenes, was absent. The monument celebrates the conqueror's valor by exalting the enemy he overcame; the greater the enemy, the greater the victory. Pliny records a famous sculpture by Epigonos of a trumpet player, and this Roman copy may reflect that work.

5.72 West front of Great Altar of Zeus at Pergamon (restored). Staatliche Museen zu Berlin, Preussischer Kulturbesitz, Antikensammlung

DRAMATIC VICTORY MONUMENTS Sculptures decorating the Great Altar of Zeus at Pergamon exemplify the highly emotional, dramatic style at its height (figs. **5.72** and **5.73**). The monument dates to the second quarter of the second century BCE, when Eumenes II, or Attalos II, built it to commemorate territorial victories over Pontos and Bithynia and the establishment of a grand victory festival, the *Nikephoria*. The altar stood high on a podium within a large rectangular enclosure defined by an Ionic colonnade. A wide staircase at the front provided access. The altar and its enclosure, which both go by the name of the Great Altar, stood on a terrace on the Pergamene Akropolis. A German team excavated the monument from 1878 to 1886, and its entire west front, with the great flight of stairs leading to its entrance, has been reconstructed in Berlin (see fig. 5.72). The vast enclosure belongs to a long Ionian tradition of massive altars, but this is by far the most elaborate extant example. Its boldest feature is a frieze encircling the base, which extends over 400 feet in length and over 7 feet in height. Its subject, the Battle of the Gods and Giants, was a familiar theme in architectural sculpture. Here, as before, it worked allegorically, symbolizing Eumenes' victories. Never before, however, had artists treated the subject so extensively or so dramatically. About 84 figures crowd the composition, interspersed with numerous animals. This was no mean feat: The designer must have relied upon research by scholars

5.73 *Athena and Alkyoneus*, from east side of Great Frieze of the Great Altar of Zeus at Pergamon, second quarter of the 2nd century BCE. Marble, height 7′6″ (2.29 m). Staatliche Museen zu Berlin, Preussischer Kulturbesitz, Antikensammlung

working in the Pergamene library (such as Krates of Mall a renowned Stoic theoretician and literary critic) to identify protagonists for this great battle. The scholars may also have

J. J. Winckelmann and the Apollo Belvedere

Despite the best efforts of contemporary art historians, many assessments of art today are deeply informed by a notion of beauty rooted in Greek **Classicism**. This bias has been present through the ages since antiquity; but its abiding power is also the legacy of a pioneering German antiquarian, Johann Joachim Winckelmann, who is often called the father of art history. Born in Stendal in Prussia in 1717, Winckelmann studied in Halle and Jena before becoming librarian for Count Heinrich von Bünau near Dresden. It was in von Bünau's library that he gained an education in the visual arts, which led to his first publication, *Reflections on the Imitation of Greek Works of Art in Painting and Sculpture*, in 1755. In that same year he moved to Rome, and was soon appointed librarian and advisor to Cardinal Alessandro Albani. In 1764, after the publication of his seminal *History of Art of Antiquity*, he became papal antiquary and director of antiquities in Rome. *Unpublished Antiquities*, of 1767, was his last work before his rather ignominious death a year later at the hands of a petty criminal.

The impact of his published works has been enormous. He was first, for instance, to determine that most Greek sculptures (which he often conflated with their Roman copies) represented not historical figures but mythological characters. Even more significant was his contention that Greek art captured an ideal beauty that transcended nature. He established a model for the development of art that divided art history into periods that coincided with political events. The Older Style was the precursor to the High or Sublime Style. Next came the Beautiful Style, and finally the Style of the Imitators. ... ancient art, these correspond to the Archaic, fifth-century BCE Classical, Late Classical, and Hellenistic and Roman periods. This progression from rise to eventual decline still lies at the heart of most studies of art history, regardless of the era. When it came to assigning works of art to these phases, Winckelmann was, in a sense, trapped by his own scheme. Reluctant to allot works he admired to the "decline" phase of Hellenistic and Roman art, he often dated sculptures much too early; such was the case with the *Laocoön* (see *The Art Historian's Lens*, page 183), which he placed in the fourth century BCE, and the *Apollo Belvedere*, which he considered a Greek original.

The *Apollo Belvedere* first came to light again in the fifteenth century CE, and quickly made its way into the collection of Pope Julius II. It represents the god in an open pose, with his left arm outstretched, perhaps to hold a bow. Winckelmann was one of many antiquarians to be profoundly moved by the statue. Combined in its form he perceived both power and desirability, and he penned a rhapsodic description of it that is tinged with eroticizing overtones. "I forget all else at the sight of this miracle of art," he wrote. "My breast seems to enlarge and swell with reverence." Few scholars share his enthusiasm for the piece today. Its significance for art historians resides more in its modern reception—the role it played for admiring Renaissance artists, for instance—than in its place in ancient culture. As for its date, most scholars now identify it as a second-century CE copy or interpretation of a Greek original; the latter is sometimes attributed to Leochares, who worked at the end of the fourth century BCE.

Apollo Belvedere. Roman marble copy, probably of a Greek original of the late 4th century BCE. Height 7′4″ (2.3 m). Musei Vaticani, Rome

5.74   Pythokritos of Rhodes (?). *Nike of Samothrace*. ca. 190 BCE. Marble, height 8' (2.44 m). Musée du Louvre, Paris assisted with creating a balanced and resonant composition, for despite the chaotic appearance of the mêlée, guiding principles lurk behind it. Modern scholars still struggle to understand these nciples fully, even with the help of inscriptions naming some of the gods on the molding in the entablature and giants on the base molding. On the eastern frieze, facing the sanctuary's great propylon and the rising sun, were the Olympian gods. The most prominent position belonged to Athena. On the south, drenched in sun, were heavenly lights such as Helios; on the shadowy north were divinities of the night. Deities of the earth and sea were on the west. Compositional parallels unified the four sides. The frieze is direct evidence of the Hellenistic scholarly tradition at work.

On the other hand, it is also deeply imbued with Hellenistic theatricality. Sculptors carved the figures so deeply, and undercut them in places so forcefully, that they are almost in the round. The high relief creates a vivid interplay of light and dark, and on the staircase, the figures seem to spill out onto the steps and climb alongside an ascending visitor. Muscular bodies rush at each other, overlapping and entwining (see fig. 5.73). The giants' snaky extremities twist and curl, echoed in their deeply drilled tendrils of ropelike hair. Wings beat and garments blow furiously in the wind or twist around those they robe, not to reveal the anatomy beneath but to create motion; they have a life of their own and their texture contrasts with the smoothness of the giants' flesh. The giants' emotion is palpable: They agonize in the torment of their defeat, their brows creased in pain, their eyes deep-set in exaggerated style reminiscent of Skopas. A writhing motion pervades the entire design, and links the figures in a single continuous rhythm. This rhythm, and the quiet Classicism of the gods' faces, so starkly opposed to the giants' faces, create a unity that keeps the violence of the struggle from exploding its architectural frame—but only just. For the first time in the long tradition of its depiction, a viewer has a visceral sense of what a terrible cosmic crisis this battle would be.

The weight and solidity of the great gigantomachy make it a fitting frieze for its place on the building's platform. A second, lighter frieze encircled the inside of the colonnade, and may be slightly later. This frieze portrays the life of Telephos, son of Herakles and legendary founder of Mysia, the region of Pergamon.

Though an altar first and foremost, the Great Altar of Zeus also commemorates Eumenes' victory. Its magnificence underscores the precariousness of the Hellenistic world, and the importance of conquest to a ruler's image. Dramatic location and style combine in another victory monument of the early second century BCE, the *Nike of Samothrace* (fig. **5.74**). The sculpture probably celebrates the naval victories—*nike* means "victory"—of Eudamos, an admiral in command of the fleet at Rhodes, over Antiochos the Great and the Seleucid forces in 190 BCE. he Rhodian marble of the sculpture's base, and evidence from inscriptions, suggest that the sculpture comes from Rhodes, and may be the work of the renowned artist Pythokritos from that island. The victory goddess seems to be landing on the prow of a ship, as if to bestow a crown of victory upon Eudamos. Alternatively, she could be about to take flight. Her massive wings soar out behind her, stretching the limits of the marble's tensile strength. The lift of the wings makes the whole statue appear weightless, despite the great mass of stone: In a new variant of the chiastic stance, neither leg holds the body's full weight. The wings and the drapery give the sculpture its energy. The drapery swirls around the goddess's body, exposing her anatomy and stressing the sensuous curves of her form. Yet it has its own function as well: Its swirling motion suggests the headwind she struggles against, which, in turn, balances the rushing forward thrust of her arrival. The drapery creates the environment around the figure.

This sculpture is a rare instance of a monument coming to light, in 1863, in its original location—in the Sanctuary of the Great Gods at Samothrace, where it must have been a dedication. The stone prow stood high on a terrace overlooking the theater and the sea, within a pool of water that must have reflected the Nike's white marble forms. The pool was raised above a second water basin filled with rocks, to evoke a coastline.

PLAYFULNESS IN SCULPTURE Scholars use the term **baroque** to describe the extreme emotions, extravagant gestures, and theatrical locations that characterize the Great Altar of Zeus and the *Nike of Samothrace*. Art historians first used the word to describe seventeenth-century CE art, but the scholars of Hellenistic art borrowed it on recognizing similarities between the two styles. With its dramatic qualities, the Hellenistic baroque style has tended to eclipse the many other contemporary movements in sculpture. One of these is a penchant for works of a light-hearted and sometimes faintly erotic quality. These appear to be a reaction to the weightiness of the baroque style, and sometimes they have an element of parody to them, suggesting that the sculptor hoped to reduce the grand themes of the classical and baroque styles to a comical level. Scholars describe these works somewhat inadequately by the term **Rococo**, which they also borrow from scholarship on later European art. Some of them represent amorous interactions between divine or semidivine and human figures. In the example shown here, dating to about 100 BCE, Aphrodite wields a slipper to fend off the advances of a lecherous Pan, the half-man, half-goat god of the forests (fig. **5.75**). Eros hovers mischievously between them. With her sensuous roundness and her modest hand gesture, the goddess recalls Praxiteles' bathing *Aphrodite of Knidos* (see fig. 5.56). Here, the erotic possibilities that Praxiteles dangled provocatively in the air are unambiguously answered, and by a humorously undesirable partner. Rather than grasping for her drapery to preserve her dignity, the majestic Aphrodite is reduced to grabbing a slipper in self-defense. This sculpture is another rare example of a Greek original found in the location in which it was used in antiquity. Archaeologists unearthed it in the clubhouse of a group of merchants from Berytus (Beirut) on Delos. Still, it is unclear whether the sculptural group was a cult image or a decorative piece.

5.75 *Aphrodite, Pan, and Eros.* ca. 100 BCE. Marble, height 51″ (132 cm). National Archaeological Museum, Athens

HELLENISTIC REALISM Scholars sometimes group these light-hearted sculptures together with a series of works depicting unidealized and realistic everyday life. Their genre is known as Hellenistic realism, and a sculpture of a drunken old woman illustrates it well (fig. **5.76**). Known from Roman copies, this piece has at times been ascribed to Myron of Thebes, who may have worked at Pergamon. The evidence is slim, and the figure may fit better with the cultural context of Alexandria, where realism seems to have been particularly prevalent. The woman crouches on the ground, clasping a wine bottle, her head flung far back.

Wrinkles cover her face, and the skin on her exposed shoulder and chest sags with age. She wears a buckled tunic, which identifies her as a member of an affluent social class. Other sculptures of this kind focus on the ravaging effects of a rustic life on poor—an old shepherdess, for instance; yet in this sculpture, the artist explores drunkenness and old age. With her wine jar and her garment slipping from her shoulder, she may even be in ironic dialogue with figures of Aphrodite with her water vessel (see fig. 5.56). Without further insights into the cultural context for the image, it is hard to know if the sculptor intended to offer a sympathetic view of his subject, exalting her nobility, or to engage in hard social commentary.

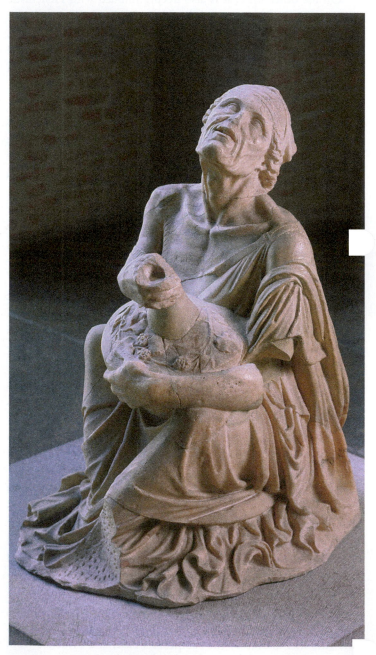

5.76 *Drunken Old Woman.* Roman copy of an original of the late 3rd or late 2nd century BCE. Marble, height 36″ (92 cm). Staatliche Antikensammlungen und Glyptothek, Munich

Hellenistic Painting

It was in the fourth century BCE that Greek wall painting came into its own. Pliny names a number of leading painters, but ⸺ surviving work can be attributed to them to give proof of ⸺ words. (See www.myartslab.com.) All the same, paintings are preserved in Macedonian tombs, several of which have recently come—and keep coming—to light in northern Greece (in the region of Macedonia). These tombs are of great importance because they contain the only surviving relatively complete Greek wall paintings, and offer a tantalizing glimpse of what painters

could accomplish. The section shown here (fig. **5.77**) comes from a small tomb at Vergina, dating to about 340–330 BCE. The subject, the abduction of Persephone, is appropriate to the funereal setting. Pluto, ruler of the underworld, carries away Persephone to be his queen. Thanks to Zeus' intervention, Persephone would be allowed to return to the world of the living for six months of every year. Here, the artist has chosen the moment when Pluto seizes Persephone into his speeding chariot, her handmaiden rearing back in fright and horror. This is the most harrowing moment, before Persephone knows that Zeus will find a compromise, when

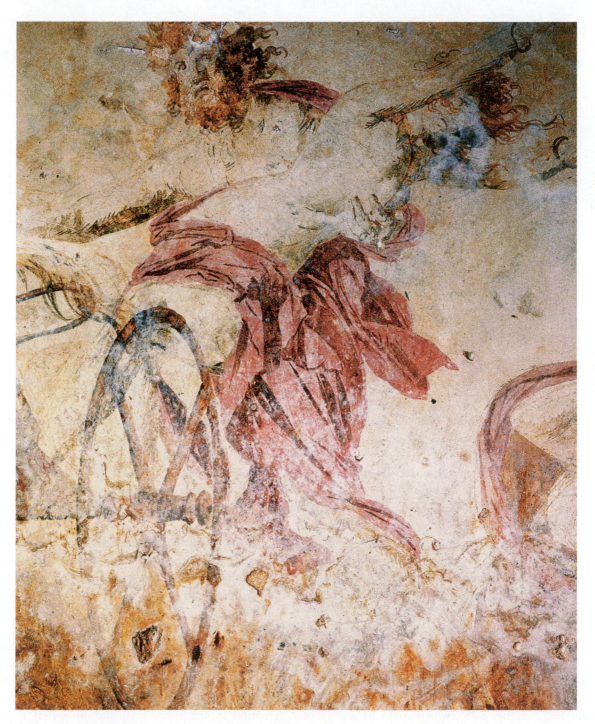

5.77 *The Abduction of Persephone*, Tomb I, Vergina, Macedonia (detail). ca. 340–330 BCE

5.78 *The Battle of Issos* or *Battle of Alexander and the Persians*. Mosaic copy from Pompeii of a Hellenistic painting of ca. 315 BCE. ca. 100 BCE. 8'11" × 16'9½" (2.7 × 5.1 m). Museo Archaeologico Nazionale, Naples

her futile struggle seems the only possible escape from the underworld. The painting captures all of the myth's drama. Persephone flings her body backward, while the chariot rushes onward with her captor; their bodies cross as a sign of conflict. The chariot plunges toward a viewer, its wheel sharply foreshortened. Masterful brushwork animates the scene. With swift flourishes, the artist sends hair and drapery flying, and lends plasticity to the garments. Hatchwork rounds out the bodies' flesh, as on the arms and shoulders. The colors are brilliant washes, with shading for texture. Literary sources attribute the discovery of **shading** (the modulation of volume by means of contrasting light and shade), known as skiagraphia, to a painter named Apollodorus, who used the technique perhaps as early as the fifth century BCE. They also associate **spatial perspective** (rendering recession of space) with Agatharchos and the art of stage scenery during the heyday of Athenian drama. The exploration and perfection of both devices during the course of the fourth century BCE illustrate the fascination with illusionism at this time.

Roman copies and imitations may also provide a general impression of Greek wall painting. According to Pliny, at the end of the fourth century BCE, Philoxenos of Eretria painted Alexander the Great's victory over Darius III at Issos. This is the subject of a large and masterful floor mosaic from a Pompeian house of about 100 BCE (fig. **5.78**), which could be a copy of Philoxenos' painting. Yet a female painter named Helen, from

Alexandria, also painted the subject, and most scholars believe the mosaic copies her work. It depicts Darius and the fleeing Persians on the right and, in the badly damaged left-hand portion, the figure of Alexander. The mosaic follows a four-color scheme (yellow, red, black, and white) that is known to have been widely used in the late fourth century BCE. (See www.myartslab.com.) The crowding, the air of frantic excitement, the powerfully modeled and foreshortened forms, and the precise shadows also place the scene in the fourth century BCE, as does the minimal treatment of landscape, suggested by a single barren tree to the left of center.

The abundance of surviving Greek art from a period of over seven centuries is a testimony to great intellectual fervor and political change. Devastating wars with their own and neighboring peoples continually shaped Greek culture and art. In the course of those centuries, Greek art changed almost unrecognizably. From the abstract forms of the Geometric period, it transformed itself into the myriad styles of the Hellenistic period. To be sure, the quest for naturalism in sculpture and painting was a driving force in this change. Yet that quest in art was merely part of a more pervasive philosophical outlook, which led to a fascination with proportions and with scholarly analysis of the arts. If the Persian and Peloponnesian Wars, and the Macedonian conquests took their toll, they also fueled the urge to express emotion in the visual arts, and to appeal to an individual's personal experience of the world.

ca. 750 BCE *Dipylon Vase*

600 BCE Temple of Artemis, Corfu

ca. 525 BCE Siphnian Treasury at Delphi

ca. 480 BCE *Kritios Boy*

ca. 447 BCE Perikles orders the construction of the Parthenon

340–330 BCE *The Abduction of Persephone* at Vergina

ca. 279 BCE Ptolemy I commissions the Pharos at Alexandria

ca. 100 BCE *Aphrodite, Pan, and Eros*

Greek Art

800 BCE

◄ ca. 8th century BCE Homer writes *The Iliad* and *The Odyssey*

◄ 776 BCE First Olympic Games

700 BCE

◄ mid-7th century BCE Black-figured vase-painting technique develops

◄ ca. 650 BCE Greeks establish trading posts in Egypt

◄ 7th century BCE Doric and Ionic styles develop

600 BCE

ca. 518 BCE Construction of the Persian palace at Persepolis begins

500 BCE

◄ ca. 500 BCE Red-figured vase-painting technique becomes prevalent in Athens
490 BCE Greeks defeat the Persians at the Battle of Marathon
478 BCE Greek city-states found the Delian League against the Persians
458 BCE Aeschylus writes the *Oresteia* trilogy

◄ 431–404 BCE Peloponnesian War

400 BCE

◄ 387 BCE Plato founds the Academy in Athens

◄ 338 BCE Philip II of Macedon invades Greece
336–323 BCE Reign of Alexander the Great

300 BCE

200 BCE

◄ 168 BCE Romans conquer Macedon

100 BCE

CHAPTER 6

Etruscan Art

EARLY ETRUSCAN CULTURE, KNOWN AS VILLANOVAN, APPEARED ON the Italian peninsula in the tenth century BCE. Who the Etruscans were remains a mystery; even in antiquity, writers disputed their origins. The Greek historian Herodotus believed that they had left their homeland of Lydia in Asia Minor in about 1200 BCE, and settled in what are now the Italian

regions of Tuscany, Umbria, and Lazio (map **6.1**). Recent DNA sampling may support his view. Others claimed they were indigenous. Wherever they came from, the Etruscans had strong cultural links with Asia Minor and the ancient Near East. In fact, their visual culture is a rich blend of distinctly Etruscan traits with influences from the East and from Greece. Since Greek city-states had established colonies in Italy from the eighth century BCE, contact between the two cultures was inevitable. The close relationship between Etruscan and Greek art forms has led scholars to define the stylistic periods of Etruscan art with terms that are similar to those used for Greece. Toward the end of the eighth century BCE the Etruscans began to use the Greek alphabet, and this makes it possible to read their inscriptions, which survive in the thousands; but since their language is unrelated to any other, we cannot always understand their meaning.

The Etruscans reached the height of their power in the seventh and sixth centuries BCE, coinciding with the Archaic period in Greece. They amassed great wealth from mining metals, and their cities rivaled those of the Greeks; their fleet dominated the western Mediterranean and protected a vast commercial network that competed with the Greeks and Phoenicians; and their territory extended from the lower Po Valley in the north to Naples the south. But, like the Greeks, the Etruscans never formed a

unified nation. They remained a loose federation of individual city-states, united by a common language and religion, but given to conflict and slow to unite against a common enemy. This may have been one cause of their gradual downfall. In 474 BCE, the Etruscans' archrival, Syracuse, defeated the Etruscan fleet. And during the later fifth and fourth centuries BCE, one Etruscan city after another fell to the Romans. By 270 BCE, all the Etruscan city-states had lost their independence to Rome, although if we are to judge by the splendor of their tombs during this period of political struggle, many still prospered.

The bulk of our knowledge about Etruscan culture comes from art, and especially from their monumental tombs. These structures provide information about Etruscan building practices, and artists often painted them with scenes that reveal a glimpse of Etruscan life. Objects found within them attest to the Etruscans' reputation as fine sculptors and metalworkers. Large numbers of painted vases from Athens have also come to light in tombs, demonstrating the Etruscans' close trade ties with Greece.

FUNERARY ART

As with burials elsewhere in prehistoric Europe, early burials on the Italian peninsula were modest. The living either buried the deceased in shallow graves or cremated them, and placed the ashes, in a pottery vessel or cinerary urn, in a simple pit.

Detail of figure 6.6, Charun from the Tomb of the Anina Family

Map 6.1 Italian Peninsula in Etruscan times

Sometimes they buried offerings with the dead—weapons for men, and jewelry and weaving implements for women. Early in the seventh century BCE, as Etruscans began to bury their dead in family groups, funerary customs for men and women became more elaborate, and the tombs of the wealthy gradually transformed into monumental structures.

Tombs and Their Contents

Named for the amateur archaeologists who excavated it, the Regolini-Galassi Tomb at Cerveteri is an early example of this more elaborate burial practice, dating to the so-called Orientalizing phase of the mid-seventh century BCE, when Etruscan arts show a marked influence from Eastern motifs. Etruscans formed tombs in the shape of mounds called **tumuli**, which were grouped together outside the living spaces of Etruscan towns to create a city of the dead, or necropolis. In this example, builders roofed the long dromos (plural, dromoi) or pathway leading into the tomb with corbeled vaults built of horizontal, overlapping courses of stone blocks, similar to the casemates at Tiryns (see fig. 4.20). Among the grave goods was a spectacular fibula (fig. **6.1**). A fibula resembled a brooch or a

6.1 Fibula, from Regolini-Galassi Tomb, Cerveteri. ca. 670–650 BCE. Gold, length 11½″ (29.2cm). Musei Vaticani, Museo Gregoriano Etrusco, Città del Vaticano, Rome

6.2   Aerial view of part of Banditaccia Cemetery, Cerveteri. 7th–2nd centuries BCE

6.3   Plan of Tomb of the Shields and Chairs, Cerveteri. ca. 550–500 BCE

decorative safety pin, and often served to hold a garment together at the neck. At 11½ inches in length, this magnificent example is a *tour de force* of the goldsmith's art (see *Materials and Techniques*, page 169), and justifies the fame Etruscan goldsmiths enjoyed in antiquity. Covering the lower leaflike portion are 55 gold ducks in the round. On the upper portion, shaped like a three-quarter-moon, repoussé work defines pacing lions, whose profile pose and erect stance may derive from Phoenician precedents. Indeed, though the workmanship is probably Etruscan, the animal motifs suggest familiarity with the artworks of Near Eastern cultures (see fig. 2.10). Also buried in tombs of this time were precious objects imported from the ancient Near East, such as ivories.

The Regolini-Galassi Tomb is but one of many tumulus tombs built at necropoleis near Cerveteri over the course of several centuries until about 100 BCE (fig. 6.2). The local stone is a soft volcanic rock known as *tuff*, which is easy to cut and hardens after prolonged exposure to the air. Those who created the tumuli excavated into bedrock, cutting away a path and burial chambers. They used excavated stone to build a circular retaining wall around the chambers, and piled up soil above it. Often several dromoi led to independent networks of chambers within a single mound. The layout of the burial chambers varies (fig. 6.3), and scholars have supposed that these dwellings of the dead mimicked contemporary houses, often complete with chairs or beds carved

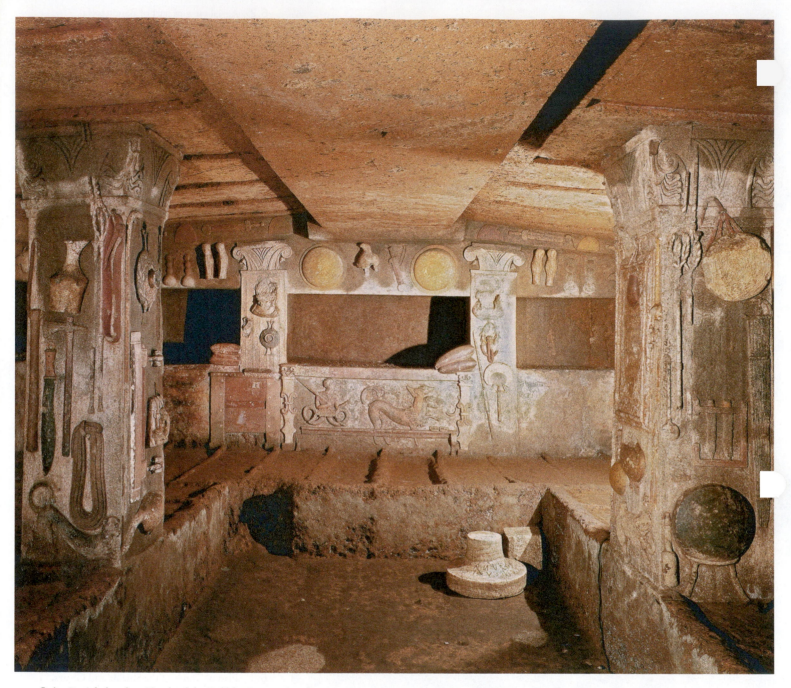

6.4   Burial chamber, Tomb of the Reliefs, Cerveteri. 3rd century BCE

out of the rock as furnishing. This may be true, but it is hard to confirm given the scant evidence for Etruscan residences. In a late example, the Tomb of the Reliefs at Cerveteri, an artist applied everything the dead might want in the afterlife onto the walls in stucco (fig. 6.4). Reproductions of weapons, armor, household implements, and domestic animals cover the piers and the walls between the niches. Two damaged busts may have represented the dead or underworld deities. The concept of burying items that would be of service in the afterlife is reminiscent of Egyptian funerary practice, though replicas of actual items differ markedly between the two cultures.

Farther north, at Tarquinia, tombs consist of chambers sunk into the earth with a steep underground dromos. Vibrant paintings cover the walls, executed while the plaster was wet. At one end of the low chamber in the Tomb of Hunting and Fishing is a marine panorama, dating to about 530–520 BCE (fig. 6.5) during the Archaic period. In the vast expanse of water and sky, fishermen cast lines from a boat, as brightly colored dolphins leap through the waves. A figure on a rocky promontory aims h slingshot at large birds in bright red, blue, and yellow that swo through the sky. Unlike Greek landscape scenes, where humans dominate their surroundings, here the figures are just one part of

Etruscan Gold-Working

Early in their history, the Etruscans became talented metalworkers, with special proficiency in gold-working. The goldsmith responsible for the fibula in figure 6.1 was a master of two complex techniques: filigree and granulation.

Filigree is the art of soldering fine gold wires—singly or twisted together into a rope—onto a gold background. The goldsmith used this process to outline the ornamental decoration and two-dimensional animals on the fibula's surface. Etruscan artists were so expert that they could even create openwork designs independent of a backplate.

Granulation describes the process of soldering tiny gold balls or grains onto a background. Skilled Etruscan artists worked with grains as small as 1/250", using them to decorate large areas, or to define linear or geometric patterns. Alternatively, they might employ them in conjunction with embossed designs, or in a mass to create a silhouette against the background. Finally, they might cover the background with grains, leaving a design in silhouette.

Mastery of granulation was lost in early medieval Europe, as tastes changed and different gold-working techniques came to be preferred. Goldsmiths use various methods today, but scholars do not know how Etruscan artists prepared the grains. They may have placed fragments of gold in a crucible, separating them with charcoal. When heated, the gold would melt into separate balls. Goldsmiths would then remove the charcoal that kept the balls apart. Alternatively, they may have poured molten gold into water from a height, to ensure that tiny grains would form into small balls. When the liquid metal reached the water, it would cool into solid form.

Pendant representing the head of Acheloos, decorated with granulation. 6th century BCE. Musée du Louvre, Paris

For all but the simplest designs (which were applied straight to the background), the artist probably arranged the grains in a design engraved on a stone or metal plate, and lowered a piece of adhesive-covered papyrus or leather, fixed to the end of a tube, over the design, to pick up the grains. They could then be treated with solder and transferred to the gold backplate.

6.5 Tomb of Hunting and Fishing, Tarquinia. ca. 530–520 BCE

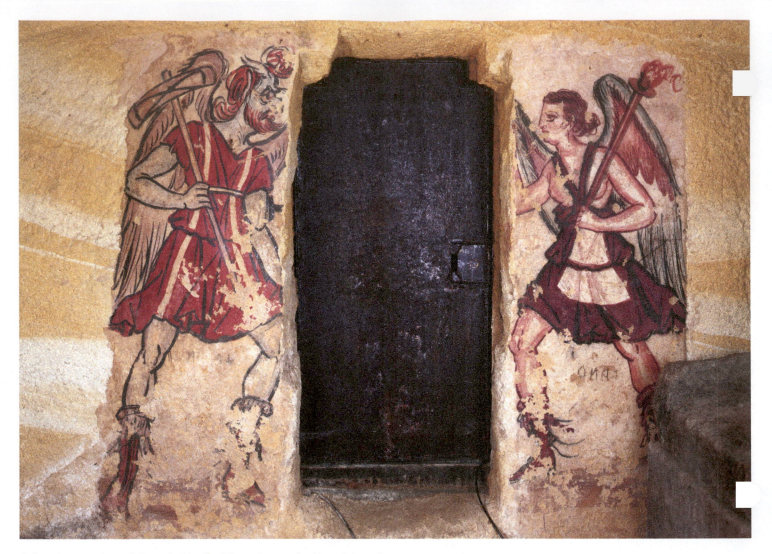

6.6   Charun and Vanth from the Tomb of the Anina Family, Tarquinia. 3rd century BCE

a larger scheme. The exuberance of the colors and gestures, too, is characteristically Etruscan. All the same, here as in most tombs, the treatment of drapery and anatomy reveals that developing Greek painting influenced Etruscan tomb painters.

The artist seems to have conceived of the scene as a view from a tent or hut, defined by wide bands of color at cornice level and roofed with a light tapestry. Hanging from the cornice are festive garlands of the kind probably used during funerary rituals. In many tombs, images of animals fill the **gable**—leopards, sometimes, or fantastic hybrids—perhaps used as guardian figures to ward off evil. Above the fishing scene, a man and woman recline together at a banquet, where musicians entertain them and servants attend to their needs. One draws wine from a large mixing bowl, or krater, while another makes wreaths. In contrast to Greek drinking parties (symposia), which were reserved for men and courtesans, Etruscan banquet scenes include respectable women reclining alongside men. Banquet paintings appear frequently in Etruscan tombs; athletic games were another common subject, as were scenes that focused on musicians and dancers.

The purpose of these paintings is hard to determine. They may record and perpetuate activities the deceased once enjoyed,

or depict rituals observed at the funeral (the games, in fact, are probably the forerunners of Roman gladiatorial contests). Or, like Egyptian tomb paintings, they may have served as provisions for the afterlife of the deceased. At the heart of the problem of interpretation lies our general ignorance about Etruscan beliefs concerning death and the afterlife. Roman writers describe them as a highly religious people, and their priests are known to have read meaning into the flight of birds in different sectors of the sky; beyond that, as enigmatic as they are, these paintings actually constitute a large part of our evidence for understanding Etruscan beliefs. In a few tombs, paintings seem to reflect Greek myths, but these images merely compound the problem, since we cannot be sure that the Etruscans intended the same meaning as Greek artists.

However we interpret these Archaic and Classical images, it is clear that a distinct change in the content of tomb paintings begins in the Late Classical period during the fourth century BCE. An overwhelming sense of sadness replaces the energetic mood of the foregoing periods. The exuberant **palette** of the earlier phases, with its bright reds and yellows, gives way to a somber range of darker colors. At this time, funerary images often depict processions taking the deceased to a world of the dead, or they are set in a shadowy underworld. In the Tomb of the Anina Family at Tarquinia, dating to about the end of the fourth century BCE, two winged demons flank a door to another world (fig. 6.6). A hook-nosed male demon Charun, on the left, is the soul's guide to the underworld. He holds the hammer with which he will open the door, while Vanth, a female demon on the right, bears a torch to light the darkness. It is possible that the gloomy subjects reflected difficult times, as they coincide with the Roman conquest and subordination of Etruscan cities.

Containers used for the remains of the dead manifest similar changes. In the Orientalizing period, the pottery urns traditionally used for ashes gradually took on human characteristics (fig. **6.7**). The lid became a head, perhaps intended to represent the deceased, and body markings appeared on the vessel itself. Hair and jewelry may have been attached where holes appear in the terra-cotta surface. Sometimes the urn was placed on a sort of throne in the tomb, which may have indicated a high status for the deceased.

In Cerveteri, two monumental sarcophagi of the Archaic period have come to light, molded in terra cotta in two separate halves. One of them, dating to about 520 BCE, is shown here (fig. **6.8**). The artist shaped the lid to resemble a couch, and reclining side by side on top are full-length sculptures of a man and woman, presumably a married couple. A wineskin (a soft canteen made from an animal skin) cushions the woman's left elbow, and the man has his arm around her shoulders. Both figures once held

6.7 Human-headed cinerary urn. ca. 675–650 BCE. Terra cotta, height 25½″ (64.7 cm). Museo Etrusco, Chiusi, Italy

6.8 Sarcophagus, from Cerveteri. ca. 520 BCE. Terra cotta, length 6′7″ (2 m). Museo Nazionale di Villa Giulia, Rome

6.9 *Youth and Female Demon*. Cinerary container. Early 4th century BCE. Stone (*pietra fetida*), length 47" (119.4 cm). Museo Archaeologico Nazionale, Florence.

out objects in their hands—a cup or an **alabastron** (a perfume container), perhaps, or an egg, symbol of eternity. Despite the abstract forms and rigid poses of the Archaic style, the soft material allows the sculptor to model rounded forms and capture an extraordinary directness and vivacity. The artist painted the entire work in bright colors, which conservators have revealed more clearly in a recent cleaning.

The change in mood, from optimistic to somber, that characterizes tomb paintings between the fifth and fourth centuries BCE also becomes apparent if we compare the sarcophagus in figure 6.8 with a cinerary container made of soft stone soon after 400 BCE (fig. **6.9**). At one end reclines a young man wearing his mantle pulled down around his waist, in the Etruscan style. As in the paintings of this period, a woman sits at the foot of the couch. Yet she is not his wife. Her wings identify her as a demon from the world of the dead, and the scroll in her left hand may record his fate. The two figures set at either end of the couch create a balanced composition, but their separation marks a new mood

6.10 Funerary urns in the Inghirami Tomb, Volterra. Hellenistic period, ca. 2nd century BCE

6.11 Sarcophagus lid of Larth Tetnies and Thanchvil Tarnai.
ca. 350–300 BCE. Marble, length 7' (2.13 m). Museum of Fine Arts,
Boston. Gift of Mrs. Gardner Brewer, 86.145 a-b

of melancholy associated with death, which each individual must
face alone. Still, wealthy Etruscans continued to bury their dead
together in family tombs, and the familial context for cinerary
urns like this one must have gone some way toward mitigating
the isolation of death (fig. **6.10**). Moreover, while cinerary urns of
this kind were typical, usually with a single figure reclining on the
lid, a few grand sarcophagi survive. On the lid of one are carved a
man and woman in a tender embrace, lying under a sheet as if
their marital bed (fig. **6.11**). The coiffures and beard reflect
Greek fashion, and the sides of the chest feature battle scenes
influenced by Greek iconography, yet the finished product is
definitively Etruscan.

ARCHITECTURE

According to Roman writers, the Etruscans were masters of
engineering, town planning, and surveying. Almost certainly,
the Romans learned from them, especially in water management (drainage systems and aqueducts) and bridge building.
Exactly *what* they learned is hard to determine, however. Since
it was built predominantly of wood or mud brick, relatively little
Etruscan and early Roman architecture survives. Additionally,
many Etruscan towns lie beneath existing Italian towns, and any
permanent materials employed in their construction have often
been reused.

Etruscan cities generally sat on hilltops close to a navigable
river or the sea. From the seventh century BCE on, in some places
the inhabitants added massive defensive walls. A late example of
civic architecture survives in the city of Perugia, where sections
of a fortification wall and some of its gates still stand. The best-
known of these is the Porta Marzia (Gate of Mars) of the second
century BCE, the upper portion of which the Renaissance architect
Antonio da Sangallo encased in a later wall (fig. **6.12**). The gate is
an early example of a voussoir arch, built out of a series of truncated wedge-shaped stones called **voussoirs** set in a semicircle
against a wooden framework, which was removed after construction. Once the voussoirs were in place, they were remarkably
strong; any downward thrust from above (the weight of the wall
over the void, for instance) merely strengthened their bond by
pressing them more tightly against one another. Above the arch,
and separated from one another by engaged pilasters, sculpted figures of Tinia (the Etruscan equivalent of Zeus or Jupiter) and his
sons (equivalent to Castor and Pollux) with their horses look out
over a balustrade. The arch is visual evidence of the confluence

6.12 Porta Marzia, Perugia. 2nd century BCE

of cultures so prevalent in the Mediterranean in the last centuries before the Common Era.

City Planning

The hilltops of Etruria did not lend themselves to grid planning, yet there is good evidence at sites like Marzabotto that when the Etruscans colonized the flatlands of the Po Valley in northern Italy, from the sixth century BCE on, they laid out newly founded cities as a network of streets. These centered on the intersection of two main thoroughfares, one running north–south (known in Latin as the *cardo*) and one running east–west (the *decumanus*). The resulting four quarters could be further subdivided or expanded, according to need. This system seems consistent with religious beliefs that led the Etruscans to divide the sky into regions according to the points of the compass. The Romans also adopted it for the new colonies they founded throughout Italy, Western Europe, and North Africa, and for military camps.

Little survives of the houses that composed Etruscan towns. Unlike tombs, they were built with a packed-earth technique (**pisé**) similar to wattle and daub or adobe, with only the base made of stone. Even these stone footprints are hard to discern, since the hilltops favored by the Etruscans have been inhabited more or less continually since their days. In a few places, however, archaeologists have unearthed the remains of monumental building complexes that may have been palaces or large villas. An especially fine example existed at Poggio Civitate (present-day Murlo) in the sixth century BCE, where numerous rooms framed a large central courtyard (fig. **6.13**). This kind of architecture is conceptually linked to typically Roman **atrium** houses (see fig. 7.50). In order to protect the wooden fabric of their monumental buildings, Etruscans nailed terra-cotta revetment plaques over exposed parts of beams. A mid-sixth-century BCE monumental residential building at Acquarossa yielded a fine set of molded

6.13   Plan of residential complex, Murlo (Poggio Civitate). 6th century BCE

and painted revetments. One of them shows a banquet scene, with diners on couches amid musicians (fig. 6.14), and others depicted Herakles accomplishing his labors. With their bright colors, the revetments enlivened the building, but they may also have aligned the elite property owners with the Greek hero.

Etruscans built their temples of mud brick and wood, so once again only the stone foundations survive. Early temples consisted of little more than modest rectangular cellas (rooms for holding cult figures). Later temples seem to have fallen heavily under the influence of the innovative design of the massive Temple of Jupiter Optimus Maximus on the Capitoline Hill in Rome (see fig. 7.1). As a result, they are characterized by a tall base, or podium, with steps only on the front (fig. **6.15**). The steps lead to a deep porch with rows of columns, and to the cella beyond,

6.14   Revetment plaque, from Acquarossa. ca. 575–550 BCE. Painted terra cotta, height 8.3″ (21 cm). Museo Archeologico Nazionale, Viterbo

6.15 Reconstruction of an Etruscan temple, as described by Vitruvius. Museo delle Antichità Etrusche e Italiche, Università di Roma "La Sapienza"

which was often subdivided into three compartments. The terra-cotta tile roof hung well over the walls in wide eaves, to protect the mud bricks from rain, and terra-cotta revetments sheathed the beams.

SCULPTURE

As with their Greek counterparts, Etruscan temples were highly ornate, but where Greeks used marble to adorn their temples, Etruscans had little access to this material. The decoration on Etruscan temples usually consisted of the brightly painted terra-cotta revetments that protected the architrave and the edges of the roof. After about 400 BCE, Etruscan artists sometimes designed large-scale terra-cotta groups to fill the pediment above the porch. The most dramatic use of sculpture, however, was on the ridgepole—the horizontal beam at the crest of a gabled roof. Terra-cotta figures at this height depicted not only single figures but narratives.

Dynamism in Terra Cotta and Bronze

One of the most famous surviving temple sculptures comes from Veii, a site some 14 miles (22 km) north of Rome. Both Roman texts and archaeological evidence indicate that Veii was an important sculptural center by the end of the sixth century BCE.

The late sixth-century BCE temple at Veii was probably devoted to the Etruscan gods Menrva, Aritimi, and Turan. Four life-size terra-cotta statues crowned the ridge of the roof. (Similar examples appear in the reconstruction model, see fig. 6.15.) They formed a dynamic and interactive group representing the contest of Hercle (equivalent to Hercules) and Aplu (Apollo) for the sacred hind (female deer) in the presence of other deities. The best-preserved of the figures is Aplu (fig. 6.16). He wears a mantle with curved hem later known to Romans as a toga. The drapery falls across his form in ornamental patterns and exposes his

6.16 Vulca of Veii (?). *Aplu (Apollo)*, from Veii. ca. 510 BCE. Terra cotta, height 5′9″ (1.75 m). Museo Nazionale di Villa Giulia, Rome

6.17 *She-Wolf*. ca. 500 BCE. Bronze, height 33½" (85 cm). Museo Capitolino, Rome

massive body, with its sinewy, muscular legs. The stylistic similarity to contemporary Greek kouroi and korai signals the influence Greek sculpture must have had on the Etruscans. Yet this god moves in a hurried, purposeful stride that has no equivalent in free-standing Greek statues of the same date. Rendered in terra cotta, which allowed the sculptor greater freedom than stone to experiment with poses, this is a purely Etruscan energy. These sculptures have been attributed to a famous Etruscan sculptor, Vulca of Veii, celebrated in Latin literary sources.

Etruscan sculptors also demonstrated extraordinary skill as bronze-casters. One of the most renowned works of Etruscan sculpture is the bronze *She-Wolf* now housed in the Capitoline Museums in Rome (fig. **6.17**). Its most likely date is the fifth century BCE, and, judging by its workmanship, it is probably by the hand of an Etruscan artist. The stylized, patterned treatment of the wolf's mane and hackles sets off the bold but smoothly modeled muscularity of her body, tensed for attack. Simple lines augment her power: The straight back and neck contrast with the sharp turn of the head toward a viewer, highlighting her feroci So polished is the metal's surface that it almost seems wet; I fangs seem to glisten. The early history and subject matter of this statue is unknown. However, evidence suggests that it was highly valued in later antiquity, particularly by the Romans. According to Roman legend, the twin brothers Romulus and Remus, descendants of refugees from Troy in Asia Minor, founded Rome 753/52 BCE. Abandoned as babies, they were nourished by a she-wolf in the wild. Romans may have seen in this Etruscan bronze a representation of their legendary mother wolf. In fact, the early fourth-century CE emperor Maxentius built a grand palace in Rome, where, in a large **exedra** (alcove) framed by a walkway, archaeologists found a statue base with fittings that exactly match the footprints of the she-wolf. A later sculptor—probably Antonio Polaiuolo—added the twins Romulus and Remus beneath her between 1471 and 1473, to resemble Roman coin images of the lactating she-wolf with the babies.

The Etruscan concern with images of the dead might lead us to expect an early interest in portraiture. Yet the features of funerary images such as those in figures 6.8 and 6.9 are stylized rather than individualized. Not until a century later, toward 300 BCE, did individual likenesses begin to appear in Etruscan sculpture. Greek portraiture may have influenced the change, but terra cotta, the material of so much Etruscan sculpture, lent itself to easy modeling of distinctive facial features and a sensitive treatment of flesh, and must have facilitated the development of the genre. The artist individualized an example from Cerveteri by giving it protruding

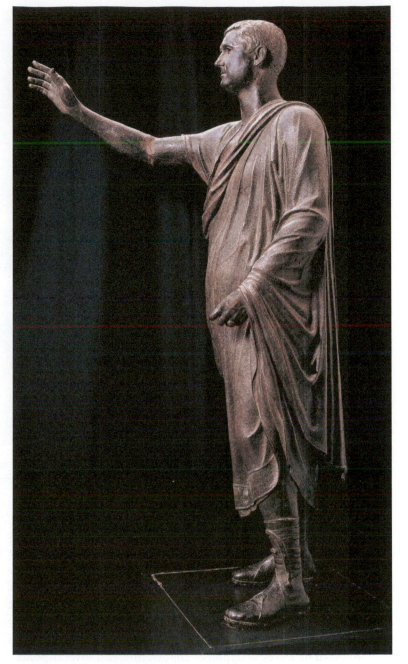

6.19 *L'Arringatore (the Orator)*. Early 1st century BCE. Bronze, height 5′11″ (2.80 m). Museo Archaeologico Nazionale, Florence

ears, a crooked nose, and blond hair. Many Etruscan portraits, like this one, come from votive deposits, where Etruscans left them as offerings to the gods (fig. **6.18**).

Etruscan artists also produced fine portraits in bronze. A life-size sculpture of an orator known today as *L'Arringatore (the Orator)* shows how impressive their full-length sculptures were (fig. **6.19**). Most scholars place this sculpture in the early years of the first century BCE. It comes from Lake Trasimene, in the central Etruscan territory, and bears an Etruscan inscription that includes the name Aule Meteli (*Aulus Metellus* in Latin), presumably the name of the person it represents. The inscription shows that the workmanship is Etruscan, yet the high boots mark the subject

6.18 *Portrait of a Man*, from Manganello. 1st century BCE. Terra cotta, height 12″ (30.5 cm). Museo Nazionale di Villa Giulia, Rome

6.20 Engraved back of a mirror. ca. 400 BCE. Bronze, diameter 6″ (15.3 cm). Musei Vaticani, Museo Gregoriano Etrusco, Città del Vaticano, Rome

as Roman, or at least an official appointed by the Romans. The raised arm, a gesture that denotes both address and salutation, is common to hundreds of Roman statues. The sculpture raises questions about the roles of artist and patron in the conquered Etruscan territories. The high quality of the casting and finishing of Etruscan bronze works bears out their fame as metalworkers. Their skill is hardly surprising in a land whose wealth was founded on the exploitation of copper, iron, and silver deposits.

From the sixth century BCE on, Etruscans produced large numbers of bronze statuettes, mirrors, and other objects for domestic use and for export. They often engraved the backs of mirrors with scenes from Etruscan versions of Greek myths devoted to the loves of the gods. Such amorous subjects were appropriate for objects used for self-admiration. The design on the back of a mirror created soon after 400 BCE (fig. 6.20) is of a different genre, and shows how the Etruscans adapted Greek traditions to their own ends. Within an undulating wreath of vines stands a winged old man, one foot raised upon a rock. An inscription identifies him as the seer Chalchas, an Etruscan version of the Greek figure known from Homer's *Iliad*. Yet this is the full extent of the borrowing, for the wings make the figure entirely Etruscan, and he is engaged in haruspicy, a pursuit that was central to Etruscan ritual: He is gazing intently at the liver of a sacrificial animal, searching for omens or portents. The Etruscans believed that

signs in the natural world, such as thunderstorms or, as we have seen, the flight of birds, or even the entrails of sacrificed animals, expressed the will of the gods. In fact, they viewed the liver as a sort of microcosm, divided into sections that corresponded to the 16 regions of the sky. By reading natural signs, those priests who were skilled in the arts of augury, as this practice was also called, could determine whether the gods approved or disapproved of their acts. These priests enjoyed great prestige and power, and they continued to thrive long after the Romans had subordinated Etruscan culture. The Romans themselves consulted them before any major public or private event. As the Roman philosopher and statesman Seneca wrote: "This is the difference between us and the Etruscans…Since they attribute everything to divine agency, they are of the opinion that things do not reveal the future because they have occurred, but that they occur because they are meant to reveal the future." Mirrors, too, were valued for their ability to reveal the future, which is probably why the artist represented this scene here.

Etruscan artists and architects show immense skill and versatility when working in many different mediums. Their work is a true product of the Mediterranean crossroads. Their Greek counterparts exerted some influence on them, and they exchanged inspiration with the Romans. Still, Etruscan works stand distinctly apart.

6th century BCE Monumental building complex at Murlo

ca. 670–650 BCE Regolini-Galassi gold fibula

ca. 520 BCE Etruscan terra-cotta sarcophagus from Cerveteri

ca. 500 BCE The Capitoline *She-Wolf*

end of 4th century BCE Tomb of the Anina Family at Tarquinia

ca. 400 BCE *Aplu (Apollo)* of Veii

2nd century BCE The Porta Marzia in Perugia

ca. 100 BCE *L'Arringatore* (the Orator)

1000 BCE

◄ ca. 1000 BCE Etruscan culture appears on the Italian peninsula

900 BCE

800 BCE

ca. 750 BCE Greek sculptural group, *Man and Centaur*, possibly from Olympia

700 BCE

mid-7th century BCE Black-figured vase-painting technique develops in Athens
ca. 668–627 BCE Assyrian construction of the North Palace of Ashurbanipal

600 BCE

◄ ca. 600s–500s BCE The height of Etruscan power

ca. 575 BCE Babylonians construct the Ishtar Gate

500 BCE

◄ 500s BCE Etruscans begin colonizing the flatlands south of Rome

◄ ca. 480–336 BCE Classical period in Greece
447–432 BCE Construction of the Parthenon in Athens

400 BCE

◄ ca. 396 BCE The Romans besiege and conquer Veii

ca. 380–330 BCE The Mausoleum at Halikarnassos

◄ 331 BCE Alexander the Great defeats the Persians

300 BCE

ca. 300 BCE Construction begins on the Temple of Apollo at Didyma

◄ 270 BCE All Etruscan city-states had lost their independence to Rome

200 BCE

ca. 175 BCE Great Altar of Zeus at Pergamon

100 BCE

ca. 80 BCE Greek portrait head from Delos

PINOKEPVE

Roman Art

OF ALL THE CIVILIZATIONS OF THE ANCIENT WORLD, THE MOST accessible to modern scholars is that of ancient Rome. Romans built countless monuments throughout their empire, many of which are extraordinarily well preserved. A vast literary legacy, ranging from poetry and histories to inscriptions that recorded everyday events, also reveals

a great deal about Roman culture. Yet few questions are more difficult to address than "What is Roman art?"

Rome was a significant power in the Mediterranean from the fifth century BCE until the fourth century CE. At the Empire's height, its borders stretched from present-day Morocco to Iran, and from Egypt to Scotland (map 7.1). Greece was a relatively early addition to Roman territory, and much of Roman public art draws heavily on Greek styles, both Classical and Hellenistic. In the nineteenth and early twentieth centuries, influenced by early art historians like Winckelmann (see *The Art Historian's Lens*, page 157), art connoisseurs exalted Greek Classicism as the height of stylistic achievement, and considered Roman art derivative, the last chapter, so to speak, of Greek art history. This view changed radically in the ensuing years, especially as pure connoisseurship (an assessment of quality and authenticity) began to yield to other branches of art history. Scholars now focus, for instance, on the roles of a work of art in its social and political contexts. Yet regardless of how one assesses Roman artists for drawing on Greek styles, these were by no means the only styles at play in the Roman world. Works of art created in the provinces or for the nonelite have their own style, as do those of late antiquity. There were also phases of distinct "Egyptianizing" in Rome.

Detail of figure 7.15, *Nile Mosaic*, from Sanctuary of Fortuna Primigenia

Roman art was the art of both Republic and Empire, the art of a small city that became a vast empire. It was created by Roman artists, but not exclusively; the greatest architect of Trajan's time may have been from Damascus. Perhaps the most useful way to think of Roman art is to see it as an art of **syncretism**—an art that brings diverse elements together to produce something entirely new, with a powerful message-bearing potential. Syncretism was a profoundly Roman attitude, and was probably the secret to Rome's extraordinarily successful expansion. From the very start, Roman society was unusually tolerant of non-Roman traditions, as long as they did not undermine the state. Romans did not, on the whole, subordinate the populations of newly conquered regions, eventually according many the rights of citizenship and receiving non-Roman gods hospitably in the capital. This Roman propensity for integrating other cultures led to a remarkably diverse world.

EARLY ROME AND THE REPUBLIC

According to Roman legend, Romulus founded the city of Rome in 753/52 BCE, in the region known as Latium, on a site near the Tiber River. The sons of Mars and Rhea Silvia, who later became a Vestal Virgin, Romulus and his twin, Remus, were abandoned at birth, and raised by a she-wolf (see fig. 6.17). Yet archaeological

Map 7.1　Roman Empire in the early 2nd century CE

evidence shows that people had actually lived on the site since about 1000 BCE. From the eighth to the sixth centuries BCE, a series of kings built the first defensive wall around the settlement, drained and filled the swampy plain of the Forum, and built a vast temple on the Capitoline Hill, making an urban center out of what had been little more than a group of villages. The kings established many of Rome's lasting institutions, such as priesthoods and techniques of warfare. In about 509 BCE, the Roman elite expelled the last king, and gradually established a republic, with an unwritten constitution.

Under the Republic, a group of elected magistrates managed the affairs of the growing state. Two consuls headed them, and a Senate served as an advisory council. Popular uprisings led to greater rights and representation for the nonelite over the next 200 years. Rome gained most of its territorial empire during the course of the republic. First Rome and its allies, the Latin League,

destroyed the southern Etruscan city of Veii in 396 BCE. The Gauls, from the north, sacked Rome in 390 BCE, but this seems only to have spurred Rome on to greater conquest. By 275 BCE, Rome controlled all of Italy, including the Greek colonies of the south. Three Punic (from the Latin for "Phoenician") Wars against the North African city of Carthage ended with the decisive razing of Carthage in 146 BCE, and during the second century BCE all of Greece and Asia Minor also came under Roman control. Yet despite its successes, from about 133 BCE to 31 BCE, the Late Republic was in turmoil. Factional politics, mob violence, assassination, and competition among aristocratic families led to the breakdown of the constitution and to civil war. Julius Caesar became perpetual dictator in 46 BCE, a position that other senat[...] were unable to tolerate. Two years later, they assassinated him[...]

During the course of the Republic, magistrates commissioned works of architecture and sculpture to embellish the city as well as

Recognizing Copies: The Case of the Laocoön

In one of the most powerful passages of *The Aeneid*, Vergil describes the punishment of Laocoön, who, according to legend, was a priest at the time of the Trojan War. He warned the Trojans against accepting the wooden horse, the famous gift that hid invading Greeks within. The goddess Minerva, on the side of the Greeks, punished Laocoön by sending two giant serpents to devour him and his sons. Vergil describes the twin snakes gliding out of the sea to the altar where Laocoön was conducting a sacrifice, strangling him in their terrible coils, turning sacrificer into sacrificed. (See www.myartslab.com.)

In January 1506, a sculptural group depicting Laocoön and his sons writhing in the coils of snakes was unearthed on the Esquiline Hill in Rome. Renaissance humanists immediately hailed the group as an original Greek sculpture describing this brutal scene. It was, they thought, a sculpture that Pliny the Elder praised in his *Natural History* (completed in 77 CE). Pliny believed the Laocoön group that stood in Titus' palace to be the work of three sculptors from Rhodes: Hagesandros, Polydorus, and Athenodorus. Within a year of its rediscovery, the group had become the property of Pope Julius II, who installed it in his sculpture gallery, the Belvedere Courtyard in the Vatican. The sculpture quickly became a focus for contemporary artists, who both used it as a model and struggled to restore Laocoön's missing right arm (now bent behind him in what art historians consider the correct position). Its instant fame derived in part from the tidy convergence of the rediscovered sculpture with ancient literary sources: The masterpiece represented a dramatic moment in Rome's greatest epic and was described by a reputable Roman author.

The Laocoön group caught the rapt attention of the eighteenth-century art historian J. J. Winckelmann (see *The Art Historian's Lens*, page 157). He recognized a powerful tension between the subjects' agonizing death throes and a viewer's pleasure at the work's extraordinary quality. Such was his admiration that he could only see the piece as a Classical work, and dated it to the fourth century BCE; any later and it would be Hellenistic, a period that he characterized as a time of artistic decline. So began a wide debate on not only the date of the sculpture, but also its originality. For many scholars, the writhing agony of the Trojan priest and his sons bears all the hallmarks of the Hellenistic baroque style, as seen in the gigantomachy (the war between gods and giants) of the Great Altar of Zeus at Pergamon (see figs. 5.72 and 5.73). A masterpiece of the Hellenistic style, it should accordingly date to the third or second century BCE. On the other hand, evidence from inscriptions links the three artists named by Pliny to sculptors at work in the mid-first century BCE, making the sculpture considerably later and removing it from the apogee of the Hellenistic age. Yet there are cases of artists' names being passed down through several generations, and it is not at all clear that the group is in fact the sculpture Pliny admired.

Pliny specified that Laocoön was sculpted from a single piece of marble, and this sculpture is not; even more telling is the fact that a slab of Carrara marble—which was not exploited until the reign of Augustus (r. 27 BCE–14 CE)—is incorporated into the altar at the back. Is the sculpture then an early imperial work? Or is this much-lauded masterpiece a Roman copy of a Hellenistic work? If so, does that reduce its status? As if this were not debate enough, one contention takes Laocoön out of the realm of antiquity altogether, and identifies it instead as a Renaissance work by none other than Michelangelo. Evidence cited includes a pen study by the artist depicting a male torso resembling Laocoön's, dating to 1501. At this point, all that can be said with certainty about Laocoön is that the tidy picture imagined by sixteenth-century admirers has become considerably murkier.

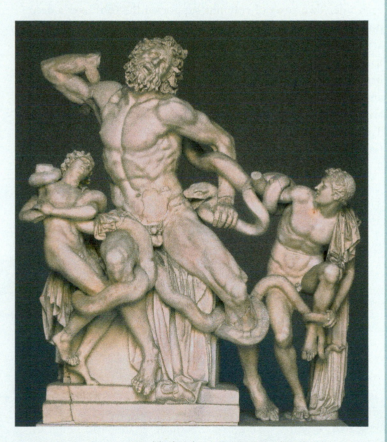

Laocoön, 1st century CE. Marble, height 7′ (2.1 m). Musei Vaticani, Museo Pio Clementino, Cortile Ottagono, Città del Vaticano, Rome

to enhance their own careers. Roman conquests abroad brought new artistic forms to the city, especially from Greece, which merged with Italic (i.e., typical of people of the Italian peninsula) forms to create a Roman artistic vocabulary, and the development of new building technologies such as concrete strongly influenced architectural designs.

NEW DIRECTIONS IN ARCHITECTURE

Roman architecture has had a more lasting impact on Western building through the ages than any other ancient tradition. It is an architecture of power, mediated through the solidity of its forms, and through the experience of those forms. Roman builders were indebted to Greek traditions, especially in their use of the Doric, Ionic, and Corinthian styles, yet these traditions inspired buildings that were decidedly Roman.

THE DEVELOPMENT OF FORMS The Temple of Jupiter Optimus Maximus on the Capitoline Hill was the first truly monumental building of Rome (fig. **7.1**). Romans worshiped a wide range of gods, some of them indigenous, but many others adopted from other cultures; in fact, their pantheon of state gods was roughly equivalent to the Greek pantheon. The Capitoline temple honored the chief god, Jupiter, roughly equivalent to the Greek Zeus. Its construction began under two sixth-century BCE kings, Tarquinius the Ancient and Tarquinius the Proud, but it was one of Rome's first consuls who actually dedicated the finished temple. Its scale was unprecedented on the Italian peninsula, evoking the massive Ionic temples of eastern Greece (see fig. 5.12). It stood on a high masonry platform, with steps leading up to the façade. Six wooden columns marked the front, and six columns flanked each side. Two rows of columns supported the roof over a deep porch. An Etruscan artist, Vulca of Veii, crafted a vast terra-cotta acroterion for the peak of the pediment, representing Jupiter in a four-horse chariot. A triple cella with walls of wood-framed mud brick accommodated cult statues of Jupiter, Juno, and Minerva, and recent excavations suggest that two additional rooms were arranged across the rear, accessed from the lateral colonnades. The rectilinear forms, the use of columns, and a gabled roof echo Greek design; yet the high podium and the emphatic frontal

7.1 Restored plan of Temple of Jupiter Optimus Maximus, Capitoline Hill, Rome. Dedicated ca. 509 BCE

7.2 Temple of Portunus, Rome. ca. 80–70 BCE

access set it apart. Scholars call these features Etrusco-Italic, and they characterize most Roman temples in centuries to come.

Although the practice of borrowing Greek forms began early ... the Republic, it was particularly marked during the period of Rome's conquest of Greece, when architects used Greek building materials as well as essential building forms. After celebrating a triumph over Macedonia in 146 BCE, the general Metellus commissioned Rome's first all-marble temple and hired a Greek architect, Hermodorus, for the job. It no longer survives, but was probably close in form to the remarkably well-preserved temple to the harbor-god Portunus near the Tiber (fig. 7.2). Dating from 80 to 70 BCE, the temple is in the Italic style: It stands on a podium, and engaged lateral columns (instead of a true peristyle)

emphasize the frontal approach. All the same, the Ionic columns have the slender proportions of Classical Greek temples, and a white marble stucco covering their travertine and tufa shafts, bases, and capitals deliberately evoked the translucent marbles of Greek architecture.

Roman architects quickly combined the rectilinear designs of Greek architecture with the curved form of the arch (fig. 7.3). An arch could be a free-standing monument in its own right, or be applied to a building, often to frame an entrance. To construct arches, builders assembled wedge-shaped voussoirs, as seen in the Etruscan Porta Marzia at Perugia (see fig. 6.12). These arches are extremely strong, in contrast to corbeled arches (see fig. 4.21). Voussoir arches were not a Roman or an Etruscan invention:

round arch

barrel vault

groin vault

7.3 Arch, barrel vault, and groin vault

Near Eastern architects used them in ziggurat foundations and in city gates, and Egyptian builders employed them, as well as their extension, the **barrel vault**, as early as about 1250 BCE, mainly in underground tombs and utilitarian buildings, rather than for monumental public buildings; Greeks architects constructed underground structures or simple gateways with arches. The Romans, however, put them to widespread use in public architecture, making them one of the hallmarks of Roman building.

THE CONCRETE REVOLUTION It was the development of concrete, however, that was a catalyst for the most dramatic changes in Roman architecture. Concrete is a mixture of mortar and pieces of aggregate such as tufa, limestone, or brick. At first, Roman architects used it as fill, between walls or in podiums. Yet on adding *pozzolana* sand to the mortar, they discovered a material of remarkable durability—which would even cure (or set) under water—and they used it with growing confidence from the second century BCE onward. Despite its strength, it was not attractive to the eye, and builders concealed it with cosmetic facings of stone, brick, and plaster, which changed with the passing years and therefore provide archaeologists with an invaluable tool for dating Roman buildings. The advantages of concrete were quickly evident: It was strong and inexpensive, and could be worked by relatively unskilled laborers. It was also extraordinarily adaptable. By constructing wooden frameworks into which they poured the concrete, builders could mold it to shapes that would have been impossible or prohibitively time-consuming to make using cut stone, wood, or mud brick. In terms of design, the history of Roman architecture is a dialogue between the traditional rectilinear forms of Greek and early Italic post-and-lintel traditions (construction using vertical posts to support vertical elements) on the one hand, and the freedoms afforded by this malleable material on the other.

Two quite different Republican structures demonstrate concrete's advantages. A building of the second century BCE, long identified as the Porticus Aemilia, but almost certainly the Navalia, or ship shed for the Roman fleet, is the earliest known building in Rome constructed entirely of concrete. Its dimensions were simply staggering: It stretched 1,600 Roman feet (a little shorter than modern feet) along the Tiber and was 300 feet deep. As the partial reconstruction in figure **7.4** illustrates, the architects took advantage of the new material to create a remarkably open interior space. Soaring barrel vaults roofed 50 transverse corridors, built in four rising sections to accommodate the sloping terrain. Arches pierced the walls supporting the vaults, so that air could circulate freely. Roman sailors could pull the ships into these spaces for easy maintenance in the winter months.

East of Rome, in the Apennine foothills, the town of Palestrina (ancient Praeneste) is home to another masterpiece of concrete construction (figs. **7.5** and **7.6**). The spectacular sanctuary to the goddess Fortuna Primigenia, dated to the late second century BCE, was an oracular center where priests interpreted divine will by drawing lots. Architects used concrete to mold structures over the entire surface of the hillside and to craft spaces that controlled

7.4   Navalia, Rome. First half of the 2nd century BCE. Partial reconstruction drawing

and heightened a visitor's experience. The sanctuary ascended in seven levels. At the bottom stood an early temple, a **basilica** (see page 225), and a senate house. The upper terraces rose in a grand crescendo around a central axis, established by a series of statue niches and staircases. A visitor climbed lateral staircases to the third terrace, where steep ramps, roofed with sloping barrel vaults, led upward. A bright shaft of daylight beckoned from t end of the ramp, where an open landing provided the first of several stunning views across the countryside.

On the fourth level, colonnaded exedrae (semicircular recesses) framed the altars. Barrel vaults roofed the colonnades, inscribing a half-circle both horizontally and vertically (**annular** barrel vaults). Their curved forms animate the straight lines, since columns set in a semicircle shift their relationship to the environment with every step a visitor takes. A wide central staircase leads upward to the next level. After the confinement of the ramps, its steps were exposed, engendering a sense of vulnerability in the visitor. On this level, shops probably sold souvenirs and votive objects. Standing on this terrace, a visitor was directly above the voids of the barrel vaults below, evidence of the architects' confidence in the structure. The next terrace was a huge open court, with double colonnades on three sides. The visitor climbed to a small theater topped by a double annular colonnade. Here religious performances took place against the magnificent backdrop of the countryside beyond, and in full sight of Fortuna, the goddess whose circular temple crowned the complex. Its diminutive size drew grandeur from the vast scale of the whole—all accomplished with concrete. The hugely versatile material plays easily with the landscape, transforming nature to heighten a visitor's religious experience.

The first century BCE was a turning point in the use of architecture for political purposes. One of the most magnificent buildings of this time was the vast theater complex of Pompey, which would remain Rome's most important theater throughout antiquity. Like

7.5 Sanctuary of Fortuna Primigenia, Praeneste (Palestrina). Late 2nd century BCE

7.6 Reconstruction of Sanctuary of Fortuna Primigenia, Praeneste

Julius Caesar after him, Pompey (active in Roman politics in the 70s and 60s BCE) maneuvered his way into a position of sole authority in Rome and used architecture to express and justify his aconstitutional power. To commemorate his conquests, he conceived of a theater on the Field of Mars, just outside the northern city boundary, dedicated to his patron goddess Venus Victrix (the Conqueror) (fig. 7.7). Later buildings on the site incorporate traces of its superstructure, and the street plan still reflects its curved form. Moreover, its ground plan is inscribed on an ancient marble map of the city, carved in the early third century CE, and new excavations may uncover more of its vaulted substructure. The reconstruction in figure 7.7 is therefore provisional, a com-·· ¹ation of archaeological evidence and conjecture; it is likely   change as new evidence emerges. In some respects, Pompey's theater resembled its Greek forebears, with sloping banks of seats in a semicircular arrangement, a ground-level **orchestra** area, and

a raised stage for scenery. In other ways, however, it was radically different. It was not, for instance, nestled into a preexisting hillside. Instead, the architect created an artificial slope out of concrete, rising on radially disposed barrel vaults, which buttressed one another for a strong structure. Concrete, in other words, gave the designer freedom to build independent of the landscape. The curved cavea (seating area), moreover, was a true half-circle, rather than the extended half-circle of Greek theaters. At the summit of the cavea were three shrines and a temple dedicated to Venus. The curved façade held statues personifying the nations Pompey had subdued. Beyond the theater, and adjoining it behind the stage building, porticoes defined a vast garden, where Romans could admire valuable works of art, such as sculptures, paintings, and tapestries, many of which had been brought from Greece. These public gardens were Pompey's gift to the people of Rome—an implicit way of winning political favor.

7.7 Theater complex of Pompey, Rome. Dedicated in 55 BCE. Provisional reconstruction by James E. Packer and John Burge

Pompey's theater complex dwarfed the smaller, scattered buildings that individual magistrates had commissioned up to that point. It was also Rome's first permanent theater. As in Greece, plays were an essential component of religious ceremonies, and Romans had always constructed the buildings that accommodated them out of wood, assembling them for the occasion and then dismantling them. In fact, some elite Romans spoke out against the construction of permanent theaters—ostensibly on moral grounds, but also because they were places for the nonelite to meet. Pompey circumvented such objections by describing his theater as a mere appendage to the temple of Venus at its summit, and in building the complex he set the precedent for the great forum project of Julius Caesar, and the imperial fora that would follow (see page 196).

Sculpture

FREE-STANDING SCULPTURE In early Rome, as elsewhere in Italy, sculptors worked primarily in terra cotta and in bronze. Countless terra-cotta votive objects survive from sanctuaries, where visitors dedicated them in hope of divine favor. The gradual conquest of Greece in the second century BCE had led to a fascination with Greek works of art, which flooded into Rome as booty. So intense was the fascination, in fact, that in the late first century BCE, the poet Horace commented ironically, "Greece, having been conquered, conquered her wild conqueror, and brought the arts into rustic Latium." Paraded through the

streets of Rome as part of the triumphal procession, the work[ ] art ended their journey by decorating public spaces, such as the theater complex of Pompey (see fig. 7.7).

These glistening bronze and marble works provoked reaction. For most, it seems, they were a welcome sign of Rome's cultural advance, more visually pleasing than indigenous sculptures in terra cotta. Elite Romans assembled magnificent collections of Greek art in their homes; through their display they could give visual expression to their erudition. The Villa of the Papyri in Herculaneum, a city built on the slopes of Vesuvius in southwest Italy, preserved an extensive collection *in situ* when the volcano erupted. The villa and its collection are partially reconstructed in the Getty Museum in Malibu, California. When Greek originals were not available, copyists provided alternatives in the styles of known Greek artists. (See *Materials and Techniques*, page 193, and *The Art Historian's Lens*, page 183.) A series of letters from Cicero, a lawyer and writer of the mid-first century BCE, to his friend Atticus in Athens shows the process at work: he asks Atticus to send him sculptures to decorate the various parts of his villa. (See *Primary Source*, page 192.) The stylistic borrowings also had a bold political dimension, showing that Rome had bested the great cultures of Greece.

RELIEF SCULPTURE A few strident voices spoke out agai[ ] the invasion of Greek art. Most vociferous was Cato ("[ ] Moralist"), for whom traditional Roman art forms symbolized the staunch moral and religious values that had led to, and justified,

Rome's political ascent. A set of magnificent terra-cotta pediment sculptures discovered on Via di San Gregorio in Rome during sewer repairs in 1878 gives an impression of the art form he was intent on defending (figs. **7.8** and **7.9**). The subject of the pediment appears to be a *suovetaurilia*, a sacrifice of a pig, a sheep, and a bull. The larger-scale figures probably represent divinities—perhaps Mars in the center, with breastplate and spear, and two flanking goddesses. Smaller figures include a male in a toga, 'haps the presiding magistrate; a male in tunic and mantle; and several *victimarii* (attendants to the sacrificial animals). The artists sculpted the figures in such high relief that they are almost fully in the round, and applied them to a smooth background, painted black; they protrude emphatically toward the top, in order to be legible from below. As in Egypt, color conventions distinguish the female figures, with their cream skin tones, from the deeper red males.

The pediment may have belonged to a temple to Mars on the Caelian Hill. Scholars date it to the third quarter of the second century BCE, which places it at the height of Greek influence in Rome. This is clearly evident in Mars' Hellenistic breastplate, the **classicizing** treatment of the drapery and faces, and the musculature. All the same, the material and technique are distinctly Italic, and the refined modeling and high polish demonstrate how striking terra-cotta works could be.

Sometimes Roman sculpture commemorated specific events, as it did in the ancient Near East (see figs. 2.12 and 2.19). Classical Greek sculptors disguised historical events in mythical clothing— a combat of Lapiths and Centaurs, for instance, or Greeks and Amazons (see figs. 5.35, and 5.44)—and this convention broke down only slightly in the Classical period. The Romans, by contrast, represented actual events, developing a form of sculpture own as historical relief—although many were not historically

7.9 Victimarius from the Via di San Gregorio pediment. Painted terra cotta, height 41½" (106 cm). Museo Capitolino, Rome

7.10 Sculptural reliefs from statue base, showing sea thiasos and census, from the so-called Altar of Domitius Ahenobarbus or Base of Marcus Antonius. Late 2nd to early 1st century BCE. Marble. Musée du Louvre, Paris, and Glyptothek, Staatliche Antiken-sammlungen, Munich

accurate. The reliefs shown in figure **7.10**, sometimes called the Base of Marcus Antonius, probably decorated a base for a statuary group, which scholars place near the route used for triumphal processions through Rome. One long section shows a census, a ceremony during which individuals recorded their property holdings with the state to qualify for military service (which was a prerequisite for public office). On the left side, soldiers and civilians line up to be entered into the census. Two large figures flanking an altar represent a statue of Mars, god of war, and the officiating censor, who probably commissioned the monument. Attendants escort a bull, a sheep, and a pig for sacrifice at an altar, marking the closing ceremony of the census.

On the same monument, the remaining reliefs depict a marine thiasos (procession) for the marriage of the sea-god Neptune and a sea-nymph, Amphitrite. But these reliefs are in an entirely different style. The swirling motion of the marriage procession and its Hellenistic forms contrast dramatically with the static composition of the census relief and the stocky proportions of its figures. Moreover, the panels are carved from different types of marble. Scholars suppose that the sea-thiasos sections were not original to

this context, but that a triumphant general brought them back as spoils from Greece to grace a triumphal monument—proof, as it were, of his conquest. By contrast, artists carved the census relief in Rome to complement the thiasos. Together, the reliefs may represent the patron's military and political achievements.

PORTRAIT SCULPTURE Literary sources reveal that the Senate and People (the governing bodies of the Republic) of Rome honored political or military figures by putting their statues on public display, often in the Roman Forum, the civic heart of the city (see page 196). The custom began in the early Republic and continued until the end of the Empire. Many of the early portraits were bronze and were melted down in later years for coinage or weaponry. A magnificent bronze male head dating to the late first century BCE, a mere fragment of a full-length figure, gives a tantalizing sense of how these statues once looked (fig. **7.11**). Sixteenth-century antiquarians dubbed it "Brutus," after the founder and first consul of the Republic. Strong features characterize the over-life-size portrait: a solid neck, a square jaw accentuated by a short beard, high cheekbones, and a firm brow.

7.11 *"Brutus."* Late 1st-century BCE head, modern bust. Bronze, slightly over-life-size. Museo del Palazzo dei Conservatori, Rome

Cicero (106–43 BCE)

Letters to Atticus I. 9–10 (67 BCE, Rome)

Marcus Tullius Cicero was a leading politician and orator in Rome during the turbulent days of the late Republic. He is known through his extensive writings, which include orations, rhetorical and philosophical treatises, and letters. Like many other Roman statesmen, he filled his many houses and villas with works of Greek art, either original or copied. Atticus was his childhood friend, who maintained communication with Cicero after moving to Athens and served as his purchasing agent for works of art.

IX

Cicero to Atticus, Greeting

Your letters are much too few and far between, considering that it is much easier for you to find someone coming to Rome than for me to find anyone going to Athens. Besides, you can be surer that I am at Rome than I can be that you are in Athens. The shortness of this letter is due to my doubts as to your whereabouts. Not knowing for certain where you are, I don't want private correspondence to fall into a stranger's hands.

I am awaiting impatiently the statues of Megaric marble and th___ of Hermes, which you mentioned in your letter. Don't hesitate to send anything else of the same kind that you have, if it is fit for my Academy. My purse is long enough. This is my little weakness; and what I want especially are those that are fit for a Gymnasium. Lentulus promises his ships. Please bestir yourself about it. Thyillus asks you, or rather has got me to ask you, for some books on the ritual of the Eumolpidae.

Source: *Cicero, Letters to Atticus*, 3 vols., tr. E.O. Winstedt (1912–18)

The image derives its power not from classical idealization or the stylized qualities of, for instance, the portrait of an Akkadian ruler (see fig. 2.11), but from the creases and furrows that record a life of engagement. The slight downward turn of the head may indicate that it once belonged to an equestrian portrait, originally displayed raised above a viewer.

The majority of Republican portraits were stone and date to the end of the second century and the first century BCE. Most represent men at an advanced age (fig. **7.12**). Wrinkles cover their faces, etching deep crags into their cheeks and brows. Artists played up distinguishing marks—like warts, a hooked nose, or a receding hairline—rather than smoothing over them. In the example illustrated here, remnants of a veil suggest that the subject was represented as a priest. Although there is no way of knowing what the sitter looked like, the images appear realistic, so that scholars term the style **veristic**, from the Latin *verus*, meaning "true." Cultures construct different ideals, and to Romans, responsibility and experience came with seniority. Military service was a prerequisite for office, and most magistracies had minimum-age requirements. An image marked by age therefore conveyed the necessary qualities for winning votes for political office, and the veristic style became the hallmark of Late Republican portraiture.

Where the impetus to produce likenesses came from is a mystery that scholars have struggled to solve. For some, its roots lie in an Italic practice of storing ancestral masks in the home to provide a visual genealogy—in this society, a good pedigree was a reliable steppingstone to political success. Polybius, a Greek historian of the mid-second century BCE, recounts that before burying a family member, living relatives would wear these ancestral masks in a funerary procession, parading the family's history in front of bystanders. (See *Primary Source*, page 194.) Other scholars trace it to a Greek custom of placing votive statues of athletes and other important individuals in sacred precincts, and indeed some Roman portraits were executed in Greek styles.

7.12 Veristic male portrait. Early 1st century BCE. Marble, life-size. Musei Vaticani, Rome

Copying Greek Sculptures

In order to satisfy a growing demand for Greek sculptures, artists set up copying workshops in Athens and Rome, where they produced copies of famous "masterpieces." Some of these copies may have been relatively close replicas of the originals; others were adaptations, where the copyist's own creativity came freely into play. Given the paucity of surviving Greek originals, it is often difficult for scholars to determine the appearance of the original, and thus to distinguish replica from adaptation. One clue to recognizing a marble copy (whether a true replica or a free adaptation) of a bronze original is to look for the use of struts to strengthen the stone, since marble has a different tensile strength from bronze (see the tree trunk and the strut at the hip in fig. 5.33).

Scholars have long believed that Roman copyists used a pointing machine (a duplicating device that takes one to one measurements), similar to a kind that was used in the early nineteenth century, but evidence from unfinished sculptures now suggests a different technique using calipers, known as triangulation. By establishing three points on the model, and the same three points on a new block of stone, an artist can calculate and transfer any other point on the model sculpture to a new place on the copy. The sculptor takes measurements from each of the three points on the original to a fourth new point, and, using those measurements, makes arcs with the calipers from each of the three points on the new block of stone.

Where the arcs intersect is the fourth point (see fig. 4) on the copy. In order to alter the scale from original to copy, the artist simply multiplies or divides the measurements. Having taken a number of points in this way, the sculptor uses a chisel to cut away the stone between the points. The accuracy of the resultant copy depends upon how many points the sculptor takes.

The triangulation process

Aspiring politicians probably commissioned many of these Republican portraits, but scholars can rarely give a name to the individuals portrayed. Inscriptions identifying the subject are scarce, and the coin portraits that help to identify later public figures only appear from the mid-first century BCE on. By contrast, we can readily identify individuals represented in a related class of monument. In the Late Republican and Augustan periods, emancipated slaves commissioned group portraits in relief, which they mounted on roadside funerary monuments (fig. 7.13).

Usually, a long rectangular frame surrounds shoulder-length truncated busts of the subjects. The very fact that the ex-slaves are depicted visually reflects their freed status; other visual cues reinforce it, such as a ring, either painted or carved on a man's hand, or the joined right hands of a man and woman, symbolizing marriage, which was not legal among slaves. An inscription records their names and status. In this example, the freed slaves' one-time owner appears in the center of the relief.

7.13 Funerary relief of the Gessii. ca. 50 BCE. Marble, 25⁹/₁₆ × 80½ × 13⅜″ (65 × 204.5 × 34 cm). Museum of Fine Arts, Boston, Archibald Cary Coolidge Fund. 37.100

Polybius (ca. 200–ca. 118 BCE)

Histories, from Book VI

Polybius was a Greek historian active during the Roman conquest of his homeland. His Histories *recount the rise of Rome from the third century BCE to the destruction of Corinth in 146 BCE. In Book VI he considers cultural and other factors explaining Rome's success.*

Whenever any illustrious man dies … they place the image of the departed in the most conspicuous position in the house, enclosed in a wooden shrine. This image is a mask reproducing with remarkable fidelity both the features and complexion of the deceased. On the occasion of public sacrifices they display these images, and decorate them with much care, and when any distinguished member of the family dies they take them to the funeral, putting them on men who seem to them to bear the closest resemblance to the original in stature and carriage. These representatives wear togas, with a purple border if the deceased was a consul or praetor, whole purple if he was a censor, and embroidered with gold if he had celebrated a triumph or achieved anything similar. They all ride in chariots preceded by the fasces, axes, and other insignia … and when they arrive at the rostra they all seat themselves in a row on ivory chairs. There could not easily be a more ennobling spectacle for a young man who aspires to fame and virtue. For who would not be inspired by the sight of the images of men renowned for their excellence, all together and as if alive and breathing? … By this means, by this constant renewal of the good report of brave men, the celebrity of those who performed noble deeds is rendered immortal…. But the most important result is that young men are thus inspired to endure every suffering for the public welfare in the hope of winning the glory that attends on brave men.

Source: *Polybius: The Histories*, Vol. 3, tr. W.R. Paton (Cambridge, MA: Harvard University Press, 1923)

Painting and Mosaic

Lamentably few free-standing portraits come from known archaeological contexts. Romans appear to have displayed them in tombs as well as in homes and public places. Tombs were more than just lodging places for the dead. They were the focus of routine funerary rituals, and during the course of the Republic they became stages for displaying the feats of ancestors in order to elevate family status. Paintings, both inside and out, served this purpose well.

A tomb on the Esquiline Hill in Rome yielded a fragmentary painting of the late fourth or early third century BCE, depicting scenes from a conflict between the Romans and a neighboring tribe, the Samnites (fig. **7.14**). A label identifies a toga-clad figure on the upper right as Quintus Fabius, a renowned general who may have been the tomb's owner. He holds out a spear to a figure identified as Fannius on the left, who wears golden greaves and loincloth. Behind Fannius is a crenelated city wall, and in the lower registers are scenes of battle and parlay. The labels suggest that the images record specific events, relating the subject matter to the relief sculptures discussed previously. Literary sources state that Roman generals also made a practice of commissioning panel paintings of their military achievements, which they displayed in triumphal processions before installing them in a public building such as a temple.

As well as ornamenting walls with narrative paintings, Roman artists also decorated floors with mosaics. They fitted together minute colored stones called **tesserae** to create a pattern or a figured image. An extraordinary example survives from an apsidal room opening onto the forum at Praeneste (Palestrina) (fig. **7.15**; see figs. 7.5 and 7.6), probably dating to the end of the second century BCE. The mosaic is a large visual map of Egypt, perhaps inspired by an Alexandrian work. The Nile dominates. In the foreground is Alexandria, with its monumental buildings, lush vegetation, and cosmopolitan lifestyle. A vignette at the lower right may show a Roman general's visit to Egypt. The mosaicist

7.14 Esquiline tomb painting. Late 4th or early 3rd century BCE. Painted on plaster, 34½ × 17¾″ (87.6 × 45 cm). Museo Montemartini, Rome

depicted different buildings from different perspectives to accommodate a viewer's movement across the floor, and suggested recession by placing distant scenes at the top of the mosaic: the river winds away into the distance toward Ethiopia where hunt-

7.15 *Nile Mosaic*, from Sanctuary of Fortuna Primigenia, Praeneste (Palestrina). First century BCE. Height approx. 16′ (4.88 m), width approx. 20′ (6.10 m). Museo Archaeologico Nazionale, Palestrina

ers pursue wild animals—such as crocodiles and hippopotami—labeled with Greek names. Colors also become less vibrant in the faraway scenes, a device known as **atmospheric perspective**. Remarkable for its fine execution and the richness of its colors, the mosaic is a testament to a fascination with far-off lands during a phase of Rome's rapid expansion.

THE EARLY EMPIRE

The last century of the Republic witnessed a gradual breakdown of order in Rome, as ambitious men vied for sole authority in e city. Julius Caesar's assassination on the Ides of March of .. BCE was a last-ditch effort to safeguard the constitution. His heir, Octavian, took revenge on the principal assassins, Brutus and Cassius, and then eliminated his own rival for power, Mark

Antony, who had made an alliance with the Egyptian queen Cleopatra. In 27 BCE, the Senate named Octavian as Augustus Caesar, and he became *princeps*, or first citizen. History recognizes him as the first Roman emperor. The arts flourished in the Augustan age. Artists took a new interest in classicism, while Virgil penned *The Aeneid* as a Latin response to Homer's epics, and Horace and Ovid wrote poetry of lasting renown.

The birth of the Roman Empire brought a period of greater stability to the Mediterranean region than had previously been known. Roman domination continued to spread, and at its largest extent, in the time of Trajan (98–117 CE), the Empire stretched through most of Europe, as far north as northern England, through much of the Middle East including Armenia and Assyria, and throughout coastal North Africa. Romanization spread through these regions. Roman institutions—political, social, and religious—mingled with indigenous ones, leading to a degree of homogenization through much of the Roman world. Increasingly, the emperor and his family became the principal patrons of public art and architecture in Rome. Often, their public monuments stressed the legitimacy of the imperial family.

Architecture

THE IMPERIAL FORA During the Republic, the Roman Forum was the bustling center of civic life (figs. 7.16 and 7.17). It was there, in markets and basilicas, that people shopped and attended court cases and schools. The Senate deliberated in the Forum's Senate House, and temples to the state gods housed cult statues as well as the state treasury. Gladiators fought in the open space in the center of the Forum, where temporary wooden bleachers were erected for spectators. The Forum continued to accommodate many essential Roman functions during the Empire, but some moved to new imperial complexes. Pompey's theater complex was the first of a series of huge urban interventions through which Rome's autocrats curried favor with the populace. Julius Caesar and Augustus each commissioned a forum, separate from but close to the Roman Forum, establishing a tradition that Vespasian, Domitian, and Trajan followed. As the plan in figure 7.17 reveals, these fora were closely connected to each other topographically and drew significance from their proximity. A visitor entered the Forum of Augustus directly from that of his divinized ancestor Caesar, cementing the connection through physical experience. Augustus' Forum was a large open plaza

with porticoes lining the long sides. At the end of the plaza was a temple to Mars the Avenger, which Augustus had vowed to erect after Caesar's assassination. When compared with the free forms of the Sanctuary of Fortuna Primigenia at Praeneste, this comp is overwhelmingly rectilinear and Classically inspired, as was most Augustan architecture. This deliberate choice evoked the pinnacle of Greek achievement in fifth-century BCE Athens, and the pervasive use of marble, available from newly opened quarries at Carrara, underlined the effect. Sculpture filled the Forum. The porticoes housed full-length, labeled portraits of great men from Rome's legendary past and recent history, suggesting a link between the past and the Augustan present. In the attic (upper level) of the porticoes, engaged caryatids (supporting columns in the shape of draped female figures) flanked shields decorated with heads of Jupiter Ammon (god of the Sahara, sometimes described as Alexander the Great's father). The carved women replicated the figures on the south porch of the Erechtheion on the Athenian Akropolis (see fig. 5.51), where Augustus' architects were engaged in restoration work. Many of the rituals once accommodated by Rome's historic buildings such as the Temple of Capitoline Jupiter now moved to Augustus' Forum, and by diverting these state activities to an arena associated with his name, Augustus placed himself explicitly at the head of Roman public life.

The largest of all the imperial fora was Trajan's, financed with the spoils of his wars against the Dacians. Reconstructions of the complex give a sense of its former magnificence (fig. 7.18). Located alongside Augustus' Forum, it adapted many of that

7.16 View of the Forum in Rome

7.17 Plan of the Fora, Rome

Temple of Trajan

Basilica Ulpia

Temple of Capitoline Jupiter

Temple of Venus Genetrix

N

Forum of Trajan

Market of Trajan

Tabularium

Temple of Concord

Temple of Saturn

Temple of Mars Ultor

Senate Chamber

Forum of Augustus

Basilica Julia

Forum of Julius Caesar

Roman Forum

Temple of Minerva

Basilica Aemilia

Forum of Nerva

Temple of Castor

Forum of Vespasian

Arch of Augustus

Temple of Antoninus and Faustina

Temple of Julius Caesar

"Temple of Romulus"

House of the Vestal Virgins

Basilica of Maxentius and Constantine

Sacred Way

Temple of Vesta

7.18 Forum of Trajan, Rome. Restored view by Gilbert Gorski

cornice
frieze
architrave

entablature

volute
acanthus leaf

capital

shaft

column

base
cornice

dado

pedestal

plinth

Composite Style   **Tuscan Style**

7.19   Tuscan and composite styles

THE COLOSSEUM Tuscan columns frequently appear in a decorative capacity on entertainment buildings. Vespasian was the first to construct a permanent amphitheater for the gladiatorial games and mock sea battles that were so central to Roman entertainment and to Rome's penal system (figs. **7.20, 7.21,** and **7.22**). Putting on shows for the populace was a crucial form of favor-gaining benefaction, and the audience assembled for diversion but also to see their emperor and to receive the free handouts that he would make on these occasions. Vespasian died before completing the Colosseum, and his son Titus inaugurated it in 80 CE with over 100 days of games, at a cost of over 9,000 animal lives.

In terms of sheer mass, the Colosseum was one of the largest single buildings anywhere: It stood 159 feet high, 616 feet 9 inches long, and 511 feet 11 inches wide, and held well over 50,000 spectators. Concrete—faced with travertine—was the secret of its success. In plan, 80 radial barrel-vaulted wedges ringed an oval arena. Each barrel vault buttressed the next, making the ring remarkably stable (see fig. 7.22). The wedges sloped down from the outside to the ringside to support seating, as in Pompey's theater, and the architects accommodated countless stairways and corridors within the wedges to ensure the smooth flow of traffic between the entrances and the seating areas and the arena. During the performances, Romans took their seats strictly according to social rank, and the distinctive clothing of each order visually set off one group from another. On the hottest days, sailors stationed nearby

7.20   Exterior of Colosseum

forum's features to new effect. In place of the caryatids in the portico attics, for instance, were statues of captive Dacians carved from exotic marbles. Beyond a basilica at the far end, two libraries and a temple defined a small courtyard, where Trajan's Column stood (see figs. 7.39 and 7.40). The Forum's message is clear: The Dacian Wars brought Rome great financial benefit. As in many societies, the ruling elite hoped to dispel the starker realities of war through visual propaganda.

The change in patronage from magistrates to emperor is one of the major developments in architecture during the Empire. Another is the invention of the **composite capital**. To the building styles that they borrowed from Greece, Roman architects added two more (fig. **7.19**). One was the **Tuscan style**, which resembled the Doric style except that the shaft stood on a base. This style was in use throughout the Roman period. The composite capital was an imperial phenomenon: Architects used it as a substitute for the Ionic capital on secular buildings, especially from the reign of the first Flavian emperor, Vespasian (69–79 CE). It combined the volutes of an Ionic capital with the acanthus leaves of the Corinthian capital, to rich decorative effect.

7.22 Sectional view of Colosseum

rigged a *velarium*, huge canvas sheets, over the seating areas to provide shade. Dignified and monumental, the exterior reflects the structure's interior organization. Eighty arched entrances led into the building, framed with engaged Tuscan columns. On the second story, Ionic columns framed a second set of arches, and on the third are engaged Corinthian columns. Engaged Corinthian pilasters embellish the wall on the fourth.

THE PANTHEON But of all the masterpieces Roman architects accomplished with concrete, the Pantheon is perhaps the most remarkable (fig. **7.23**). Augustus' right-hand man, Agrippa, built the first Pantheon on the site. Its name suggests that he intended it as a temple to all the gods. This was a Hellenistic concept, and it included living and deceased members of the ruling family among the gods. When a fire destroyed this temple in 80 CE, Domitian built a reconstruction, which perished after a lightning strike. The Pantheon we see today, which has a substantially different design, is probably the work of Trajan's architect, perhaps Apollodorus. The temple was completed in Hadrian's reign, and as an act of piety, Hadrian left Agrippa's name in the inscription (see *The Art Historian's Lens*, page 202). It owes its status as one of the best-preserved temples of Rome to its transformation into a church in the early seventh century CE. All the same, its surroundings have changed sufficiently through the ages to alter a visitor's experience of it quite profoundly.

7.23 Pantheon, Rome. 117–25 CE

7.24 Schematic drawing of Pantheon

In Roman times, the Pantheon stood, raised on a podium, at the south end of a large rectangular court (fig. **7.24**). Porticoes framed the three remaining sides of the court and extended on south up to the sides of the temple's pedimented porch, hiding the temple's circular drum from view. A visitor approaching the temple's broad octastyle façade would have been struck by the forest of massive monolithic gray and pink granite columns soaring upward; but in most other respects, the temple's form would have been familiar, evoking an expectation of a rectangular cella beyond the huge bronze doors, and a large cult statue. Yet a surprise was in store. On stepping across the threshold (figs. **7.25** and **7.26**), a visitor faced a vast circular hall, with seven large niches at ground level at the cardinal points. Engaged pilasters and bronze grilles decorated an attic level, and high above soared an enormous **dome**, pierced with a 27-foot hole, or **oculus**, open to the sky. Through the oculus came a glowing shaft of light, slicing through the shadows from high overhead. Dome and drum are of equal height, and the total interior height, 143 feet, is also the dome's diameter (fig. **7.27**). For many ancient viewers, the resultant sphere would have symbolized eternity and perfection, and the dome's surface, once emblazoned with bronze rosettes in its **coffers** (recessed panels), must have evoked a starry night sky.

For a visitor entering the cella, there was no obvious cue to point out where to go, except toward the light at the center.

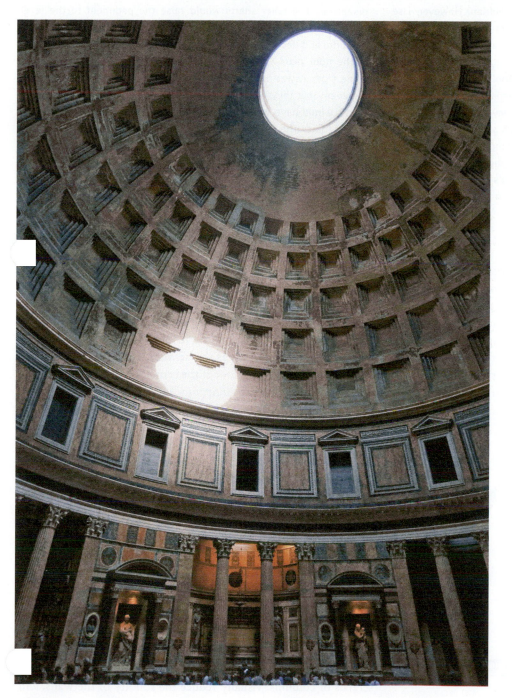

7.26 Plan of Pantheon

7.25 Interior of Pantheon

Two Pantheon Problems

Until the early twentieth century, most scholars believed that the existing Pantheon was an Augustan building, partially because its inscription attributes it to Agrippa, Augustus' right-hand man. In 1936–38, archaeologist Herbert Bloch produced a masterly analysis of Roman brick-stamps—stamps that manufacturers impressed on bricks while they were wet. Often, these incorporated the names of consuls, especially in the second century CE, which allows scholars to date bricks to a span of years, and sometimes even to a precise year. Bloch's assessment of bricks used in the Pantheon led him to confirm what archaeologists had begun to suspect on the basis of excavations: that the Pantheon was not Agrippa's temple but a later rebuilding of it. Bloch assigned it to the reign of Hadrian. However, Lise Hetland's new reading of the Pantheon brick-stamps stresses the presence of Trajanic bricks in early stages of the temple's construction. This suggests that building began in Trajan's reign, and ended under Hadrian. The Pantheon may be the work of Apollodorus, designer of Trajan's Forum, who also constructed an imperial bath building with similar design features. If true, as many believe, this redating will engender new interpretations of the building's significance and new assessments of the emperors' respective building programs.

Since the fifteenth century, architects studying the Pantheon have struggled with a paradox: Despite the building's profound impact on Western architecture from the moment of its construction, irregularities in its design suggest that it is seriously flawed. These irregularities include an inexplicable second pediment, above and be[l] the first; the fact that the exterior cornices are at different levels on circular drum and porch; and unaccountable misalignments in the floor plan. To explain these irregularities, scholars initially concluded that the present building is the result of several different building campaigns—a theory that Bloch's brick analysis roundly disproved.

In 1987, while doodling on a napkin over a beer at a pub, three British scholars, Paul Davies, David Hemsoll and Mark Wilson Jones, recognized that if the 40-foot column shafts of the Pantheon's porch were replaced with 50-foot shafts, the irregularities would disappear. The taller shafts would raise the pediment to the level of the "ghost" pediment; the cornices would align around the entire building; and because the shafts would be thicker, the imperfections in the floor plan would be resolved. Gray and pink granite shafts come from Aswan in Egypt. Fifty-foot shafts are relatively rare; in the event that they were—for instance—lost at sea, 40-foot replacements would have been more readily available to keep construction on schedule. The British scholars' contention—which is now widely accepted—is that an unforeseen circumstance forced the builders to deviate from the design mid-construction. One of the most admired buildings of antiquity, in other words, is probably a brilliant compromise between design and necessity.

In fact, the dome's coffers only make sense perspectivally from directly beneath the oculus. Once a visitor reached the center, molded space and applied decoration combined to provide a stunning effect. Beginning in the Renaissance, scholars have found fault with the Pantheon's architect for neglecting to align the ribs between the dome coffers with the pilasters in the attic zone and the ground-floor columns. The design is not without logic: a void or a row of coffers aligns exactly over each central intercolumniation (space between columns) on the ground floor. All the same,

the absence of a systemic network of continuous vertical lines between top and bottom means that, visually speaking, the dome is not anchored. The optical effect is that it hovers unfettered above the visitor—who feels, paradoxically, both sheltered and exposed. The dome seems to be in perpetual motion, spinning overhead in the same way as the heavens it imitates. An all-but-imperceptible rise in the floor at the center exaggerates this sensation, which can incite an unnerving feeling similar to vertigo. A visitor's instinct, in response, is to take refuge in the safety of the curved wall. The building is all experience, and photographs do it no justice. This is the place, so literary sources relate, where Hadrian preferred to hold court, greeting foreign embassies and adjudicating disputes here. The temple's form cast the emperor in an authoritative position as controller of his revolving universe. He must have appeared like a divine revelation before his guests, who were already awed and completely manipulated by the building that enclosed them.

The Pantheon is the extraordinary result of an increased confidence in the potential and strength of concrete. The architect calibrated the aggregate as the building rose, from travertine to tufa, then brick, and finally pumice, to reduce its weight. The dome's weight is concentrated on eight wide pillars between the interior alcoves, rather than resting uniformly on the drum (t[he] circular cella wall) (see fig. 7.26). The alcoves, in turn, with th[e] screens of columns, visually reduce the solidity of the walls, and colored marbles on the interior surfaces add energy to the whole.

7.27   Transverse section of Pantheon

As in Trajan's Forum, the marbles were symbolic. They underlined the vast reach of imperial authority, assuming trade with or control over Egypt (gray and rose-pink granite, porphyry), �557ygia (Phrygian purple and white stone), the island of Teos (�557cullan red and black stone), and Chemtou in Tunisia (Numidian yellow stone).

HADRIAN'S VILLA AT TIVOLI As well as commissioning public architecture, emperors also built magnificent residences for themselves. From the start of the Empire, the emperor's principal home was on the Palatine Hill in Rome (from which the term "palace" derives). Yet, like many members of the elite, he had several properties, many of which were outside of Rome. The most famous is the Villa of Hadrian at Tibur (present-day Tivoli). Built on the site of a Republican villa, this residence was a vast sprawling complex of buildings, some or all of which Hadrian may have designed himself. The villa's forms appear to follow the natural line of the landscape, but in fact massive earthworks rearranged the terrain to accommodate the architecture and to allow for impressive vistas, cool retreats, and surprise revelations. Water was a common feature, in pools and running channels, adding sound and motion, reflecting light, and offering coolness in the summer heat. Throughout the villa were mosaics, paintings, and sculptures. The emperor may have collected some of these works of art during his extensive travels, especially in Egypt and Greece. A desire to evoke the far-flung regions of the Empire may also have inspired some of the buildings: A fourth-century CE biographer claims that Hadrian "built up his villa at Tibur in an extraordinary way, applying to parts of it the renowned names of provinces and places, such as the Lyceum, the Academy, the *prytaneum*, the Canopus, the *Poecile*, and Tempe. And so as to omit nothing, he even fashioned 'infernal regions.'" This statement has led modern scholars to give fanciful names to many parts of the villa. Few of them are based on archaeological evidence, and they lead visitors to faulty conclusions about the buildings' functions. The canal shown in figure **7.28** has long been known as the Canopus, after a town in Egypt. Only recently have scholars proposed more neutral terms for the villa's components, in this case the "Scenic Canal."

Portrait Sculpture

By the time Augustus had effectively become emperor, he was no more than 36. With its stress on maturity, the veristic portrait style so characteristic of the Republic might have served to underline his unusual, not to say aconstitutional, status in Rome. Perhaps as a consequence, Augustus turned instead to a more Hellenizing style. Portraits made right up to his death in his late

7.28 Scenic Canal, Hadrian's Villa, Tivoli. ca. 130–38 CE

seventies depict him as an ageless youth, as seen in a statue discovered in the house of his wife Livia at Primaporta (fig. **7.29**). The emperor appears in battledress with his arm raised in a gesture of address. The portrait seems to combine a series of references to previous works of art and historical events in order to strengthen Augustus' claim to authority.

7.29 *Augustus of Primaporta.* Possibly Roman copy of a statue of ca. 20 CE. Marble, height 6′8″ (2.03 m). Musei Vaticani, Braccio Nuovo, Rome

7.30 *Portrait of Vespasian.* ca. 75 CE. Marble, life-size. Museo Nazionale Romano, Rome

The chiastic stance, and the smooth features of Augustus' face, are so reminiscent of Polykleitos' *Doryphoros* (see fig. 5.33) that scholars assume that Augustus turned deliberately to this w known image. There was good reason for this kind of imitation: The Classical Greek style evoked the apogee of Athenian culture, casting Augustan Rome as Greece's successor (and conqueror) in cultural supremacy. Even Augustus' hair is similar to that of the Doryphoros—except, that is, at the front, where the locks part slightly over the center of the brow, a subtle reference to Alexander the Great, another youthful general, whose cowlick was such a distinctive feature of his portraits (see fig. 5.69).

Next to Augustus' right ankle, a cupid playfully rides a dolphin, serving as a strut to strengthen the marble. Most Romans would have recognized that Cupid, or Eros, the son of Venus, symbolized Augustus' claim of descent from the goddess of love through his Trojan ancestor Aeneas. The dolphin evoked the sea, and specifically the site off the coast of Actium where Augustus had prevailed over Mark Antony and Cleopatra in a celebrated naval battle in 31 BCE. By associating Augustus with historical or divine figures, these references projected an image of earthly and divinely ordained power, thereby elevating the emperor above other politicians.

The iconography of Augustus' breastplate serves a similar purpose by calling attention to an important event in 20 BCE, when the Parthians returned standards that they had captured, to Roman shame, in 53 BCE. A figure usually identified as Tiberius, August eventual successor, or the god Mars, accepts the standards fr a Parthian soldier, possibly King Phraates IV. Celestial gods and terrestrial personifications frame the scene, giving the event a cosmic and eternal significance. This diplomatic victory took on momentous proportions in Augustan propaganda. The scene suggests that the portrait dates to about 19 BCE. The emperor is barefoot, which usually denotes divine status. Later in the Roman period, or in the Eastern Empire, emperors might be depicted as gods while still alive, but with Caesar's legacy still fresh in Roman minds, it is unlikely that Augustus would have been so presumptuous. Some scholars therefore conclude that the statue is a posthumous copy of a bronze original dating to about 20 BCE.

The *Primaporta Augustus* offers a good example of a tendency in Roman art to express a message through references to earlier works. Naturally, not all Romans would have understood all the references in any given work, but the frequency of visual "quotations" suggests that Romans, like many other ancient peoples, were extremely visually astute. In fact, the history of Roman portraiture, as with many other branches of Roman art, is one of constant association with, and negation of (or conscious turning away from), past images. In their portraits, Augustus' dynastic successors, for instance, look very much like the first emperor from whom they drew their authority, even though they were rarely (or at best distantly) related by blood. But then, with the emperor Vespasian, founder of the Flavian dynasty, there was a return to a more veristic style of portrait (fig. **7.30**). Scholars reason that this maneuver was part of a deliberate attempt to restore social order when he came into power in 69 CE, after a year of civil war. A soldier by background, Vespasian justified his authority through his military success, and appealed to the rank and file through this harshly matter-of-fact image. However,

7.32 *Portrait of Domitia Longina*. Late 1st century CE. Marble, height 24″ (60.8 cm). Courtesy of San Antonio Museum of Art, San Antonio, Texas. Gift of Gilbert M. Denman, Jr. 86.134.99

several years later, Hadrian's portraits revived the classicism associated with Augustus, taking the Greek style even further. Nicknamed "The Greekling" by the ancients for his admiration of Greek culture, he adopted the full beard that was characteristic of Greek philosophers (fig. **7.31**); ancient reports that he was trying to conceal scars from acne are unlikely to be true. It was in his reign that sculptors began to carve the pupils and irises of eyes, rather than painting them.

Imperial portraits survive in great multitudes. They fall into a number of types, suggesting that there was a master portrait, often executed for a specific occasion, which sculptors would copy for dissemination within and outside of Rome; other sculptors would copy these copies, in turn, leading to a ripple effect around the empire. Thousands of portraits of nonimperial subjects also survive. Scholars can rarely identify them, but date them on the basis of similarities with members of the imperial family. When dealing with female portraits, hairstyles are especially useful since they change relatively rapidly. Livia's simple coiffure, with a roll, or *nodus*, at the front is a far cry from the towering hairstyle of Domitia Longina, wife of Domitian, one of Vespasian's sons (fig. **7.32**). Built around a framework (often of wicker), her coiffure was a masterpiece in itself, and its representation in

7.31 *Portrait of Hadrian*. After 117 CE. Marble, height 16.7″ (42.5 cm). Museo Nazionale Romano, Rome

7.33 *Equestrian Statue of Marcus Aurelius.* 161–80 CE. Bronze, over-life-size. Museo del Palazzo dei Conservatori, Rome sculpture reflected her status, as well as affording the sculptor an opportunity to explore contrasts of texture between skin and hair, and to drill deep into the marble for a strong play of light ꞏ d shadow.

Beginning in the second half of the second century CE, Roman portraits gradually take on a more abstract quality. This is perceptible in a spectacular gilded bronze portrait of Marcus Aurelius, which was spared the melting pot in the medieval period because Christians misidentified the subject as Constantine the Great, champion of Christianity (fig. **7.33**). With one arm outstretched in a gesture of mercy, the emperor sits calmly astride a spirited horse, whose raised front leg once rested on a conquered barbarian. As in the portrait of Hadrian and the vast majority of second- and third-century CE male portraits, Marcus Aurelius is bearded. He was interested in philosophy, and his Stoic musings still survive as the "Meditations." Sculpture of the time reflects such abstract concerns. For example, his eyelids fall in languid fashion over his pupils, lending them a remote quality.

Relief Sculpture

The Republican practice of commissioning narrative reliefs to record specific events continued well into the Empire. The reliefs were mounted on public buildings and monuments, such as the *Ara Pacis Augustae*, or Altar of Augustan Peace, as well as commemorative columns and arches.

THE *ARA PACIS AUGUSTAE* ALTAR OF AUGUSTAN PEACE The Senate and People of Rome vowed the *Ara Pacis Augustae* (fig. **7.34**) in 13 BCE when Augustus returned safely from Spain and Gaul, and it was dedicated in 9 BCE. It stood inside a marble enclosure, which was open to the sky and richly sculpted over its entire surface. On east and west sides, flanking two entrances, relief panels represent allegorical figures, or personifications, and figures from Rome's legendary past. On the west end, a fragmentary panel shows a she-wolf suckling the infants Romulus and Remus, under the watchful eyes of the shepherd

7.34 West façade of *Ara Pacis Augustae*. 13–9 BCE. Marble, width of altar approx. 35′ (10.7 m). Museum of the Ara Pacis, Rome

7.35 Imperial Procession south frieze, *Ara Pacis Augustae*. 13–9 BCE. Marble, height 5′3″ (1.6 m). Rome

Faustulus, who discovered and adopted them. In a second relief, Aeneas (or perhaps, according to a recent interpretation, Numa, second king of Rome) makes a sacrifice at an altar of roughly hewn stones. At the east end, a relief depicting the goddess Roma seated on her weapons balances a panel with a female figure (the goddess Venus or Ceres, perhaps, or Peace, Italia, or Mother Earth) embodying the notion of peace. Together, the panels express the message of peace that Augustus was intent on promoting, in contrast with the bleakness of the preceding civil wars. The same message was implicit in the acanthus relief that encircles the enclosure in a lower register. Vegetation unfurls in rich abundance, populated with small creatures such as lizards and frogs.

On north and south sides, the upper register contains continuous procession friezes that portray members of the imperial family interspersed with the college of priests and senators (fig. **7.35**). The friezes record a particular event on the day of the altar's dedication. A large gap in the relief falls exactly on Augustus, whose action remains unidentified. Still, the friezes are significant for a number of reasons. In their superficial resemblance to the Greek Parthenon frieze (see figs. 5.45 and 5.46), they bear witness, once again, to a preference for Greek styles in the Augustan age. They also include a number of women from the imperial family, including Livia, and small children. Their inclusion probably denotes the importance of dynasty, as well as referring to moral legislation Augustus enacted to curb adultery and promote childbirth among the elite.

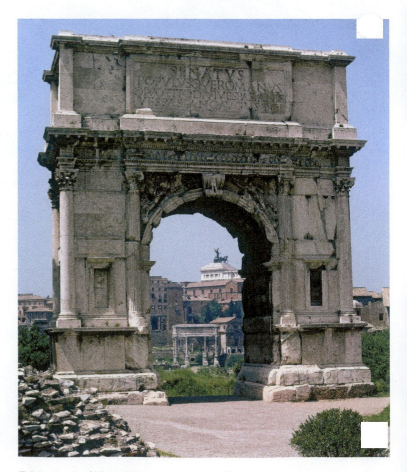

7.36 Arch of Titus, Rome. ca. 81 CE. Marble

37 Relief in bay of Arch of Titus, showing procession of spoils from the Temple in Jerusalem. ca. 81 CE. Marble, height 7'10" (2.39 m)

THE ARCH OF TITUS Reliefs also decorated free-standing arches. Members of the elite first erected arches during the Republic, though no early examples survive. During the Empire, many arches celebrated triumphs, but they also served as commemorative monuments for the dead. Their enduring impact on Western architecture is readily understandable: As with free-standing columns, their chief *raison d'être* was to express a visual message. Often they stood at or near an entrance to a public area, and framed the transition, or **liminal space** (from *limen*, Latin for "threshold"), between one place and another. Many societies consider liminal spaces unsettling and in need of protection; the lamassu of Mesopotamia, one might note, guarded doorways (see fig. 2.18). The Arch of Titus, son and successor of Vespasian, stands at the far eastern end of the Roman Forum. It is the earliest surviving free-standing arch in Rome, though much of it is the product of architect Giuseppe Valadier's restoration from 1822 to 1824 (fig. **7.36**). It may have been a triumphal monument, but given that its inscription and a small relief panel describe Titus as a god, it is more likely that it commemorates his apotheosis (or divinization) ter his death in 81 CE. Its principal sculptural relief panels are within the bay, and both refer to the triumph after the destruction of the Second Temple in Jerusalem in 70 CE. In one of them, soldiers carry booty through the streets, including a seven-branched menorah (a Jewish candelabra) and other sacred furniture looted from the Temple (fig. **7.37**). The panel marks an important move toward spatial illusionism. Two ranks of figures appear, carved in different levels of relief. The background figures are in such shallow relief that they seem to fade into the distance. The procession breaks away abruptly at the sides, so that it appears to continue beyond a viewer's line of sight. On the right, it disappears through a triumphal arch, placed at an angle to the background so that only the nearer half emerges in relief, giving the illusion of spatial depth. The panel even bulges out slightly at the center, so that it seems to turn right in front of a viewer standing inside the arch's bay, making the viewer a part of the action. In the other panel, Titus rides in a triumphal chariot, high above a teeming crowd, signified through differing levels of relief (fig. **7.38**). The horses appear in profile, but the chariot is frontal, giving the illusion that the procession is approaching a viewer before turning sharply. Behind the emperor, a personification of victory crowns him for his success. Additional personifications—Honor and Virtue, perhaps, or Roma—accompany the chariot. Their presence, and the absence of Vespasian, whom the Jewish historian Josephus places in the scene, sound a cautionary note for those who

Josephus (37/8–ca. 100 CE)

The Jewish War, from Book VII

The Jewish soldier and historian Josephus Flavius was born Joseph Ben Matthias in Jerusalem. He was named commander of Galilee during the uprising of 66–70 CE against the Romans in the reign of Nero. After surrendering, he won the favor of the general Titus Flavius Sabinus Vespasian and took the name Flavius as his own. Josephus moved to Rome, where he wrote an account of the war (75–79 CE) and Antiquities of the Jews *(93 CE). The following passage from his history of the rebellion describes the triumphal procession into Rome following the Sack of Jerusalem in 70 CE, which is depicted on the Arch of Titus (figs. 7.38 and 7.39).*

It is impossible to give a worthy description of the great number of splendid sights and of the magnificence which occurred in every conceivable form, be it works of art, varieties of wealth, or natural objects of great rarity. For almost all the wondrous and expensive objects which had ever been collected, piece by piece, from one land and another, by prosperous men—all this, being brought together for exhibition on a single day, gave a true indication of the greatness of the Roman Empire. For a vast amount of silver and gold and ivory, wrought into every sort of form, was to be seen, giving not so much the impression of being borne along in a procession as, one might say, of flowing by like a river. Woven tapestries were carried along, some

dyed purple and of great rarity, others having varied representations of living figures embroidered on them with great exactness, the handiwork of Babylonians. Transparent stones, some set into gold crowns, some displayed in other ways, were borne by in such g[reat] numbers that the conception which we had formed of their rarity seemed pointless. Images of the Roman gods, of wondrous size and made with no inconsiderable workmanship, were also exhibited, and of these there was not one which was not made of some expensive material. …

The rest of the spoils were borne along in random heaps. The most interesting of all were the spoils seized from the temple of Jerusalem: a gold table weighing many talents, and a lampstand, also made of gold, which was made in a form different from that which we usually employ. For there was a central shaft fastened to the base; then spandrels extended from this in an arrangement which rather resembled the shape of a trident, and on the end of each of these spandrels a lamp was forged. There were seven of these, emphasizing the honor accorded to the number seven among the Jews. The law of the Jews was borne along after these as the last of the spoils. In the next section a good many images of Victory were paraded by. The workmanship of all of these was in ivory and gold. Vespasian drove along behind these and Titus followed him; Domitian rode beside them, dressed in a dazzling fashion and riding a horse which was worth seeing.

Source: J.J. Pollitt, *The Art in Rome, c. 753 B.C.–A.D. 337: Sources and Documents* (NJ: Cambridge University Press, 1983)

7.38 Relief in bay of Arch of Titus, showing Titus riding in triumph

would read Roman visual narratives as accurate accounts of historical events. (See *Primary Source*, above.) Artists constructed these narratives to express a version of events that served the patron's ideology.

THE COLUMN OF TRAJAN The exploration of space and n[arrative] rative strategies comes into full bloom in the Column of Traj[an] (fig. **7.39**), erected between 106 and 113 CE in a small court to the west of Trajan's Forum (see figs. 7.17 and 7.18). Soaring about 150

7.40 Lower portion of Column of Trajan, Rome. 106–13 CE. Marble, height of relief band approx. 50″ (127 cm)

Roman feet high, this supported a gilded statue of the emperor, lost in medieval times. Winding through the interior of its shaft was a spiral staircase leading to a viewing platform, from which a visitor could look out over Trajan's extraordinary building complex. Free-standing columns had been used as commemorative monuments in Greece from Hellenistic times, but the sheer scale of Trajan's Column, usually credited as the work of Apollodorus, along with its role as **belvedere** (or viewing station), makes it nothing short of a world wonder. However, art historians have tended to focus not on the engineering feat the column represents, but on the 656-foot-long continuous narrative relief that winds around its shaft in a counterclockwise direction, celebrating the emperor's victorious campaigns against the people of Dacia (in present-day Romania).

The narrative begins with the Roman army's crossing of the Danube to reach Dacian territory (fig. **7.40**). The river appears as a large personification. To the left are riverboats loaded with supplies and a Roman town on a rocky bank. The second band shows Trajan speaking to his soldiers, and soldiers building fortifications. In the third, soldiers construct a garrison camp and bridge as the cavalry sets out on a reconnaissance mission; and

7.39 Column of Trajan, Rome. 106–13 CE. Marble, height 125′ (38 m)

in the fourth, foot soldiers cross a stream while, to the right, the emperor addresses his troops in front of a Dacian fortress. These scenes are a fair sampling of events shown on the column. Among the more than 150 episodes, combat occurs only rarely. The geographic, logistic, and political aspects of the campaign receive more attention, much as they do in Julius Caesar's literary account of his conquest of Gaul.

Individual scenes are not distinctly separate from one another. Sculptors placed trees and buildings in such a way as to suggest divisions, but the scenes still merge into a continuous whole, with important protagonists, such as Trajan, appearing multiple times. Thus, they preserved visual continuity without sacrificing the coherence of each scene. Although Assyrian and Egyptian artists created visual narratives of military conquests, this relief is by far the most ambitious composition so far in terms of the number of figures and the density of the narrative, and understanding it is a complicated matter. Continuous illustrated **rotuli** (scrolls) are a likely inspiration for the composition, if such things existed before the column's construction.

Also problematic is the fact that in order to follow the narrative sequence, a viewer has to keep turning around the column, head inclined upward. Above the fourth or fifth turn, details become hard to make out with the naked eye, even if the addition of paint made the sculpture more vivid. It might have been possible to view the upper spirals from balconies on surrounding buildings in antiquity, but the format would still have required an encircling motion. These problems have led scholars to propose viewing strategies. They have long noted that the relief is formulaic; that is, the sculptors repeated a fairly limited number stock scenes again and again. These include, for instance, sacrifice scenes, the emperor addressing his troops, or soldiers constructing forts and dismantling enemy cities. Though these are not identical, they are similar enough to be recognized at a distance, which helps make the upper spirals more legible. The designer may also have aligned important and representative scenes on the cardinal axes of the column, so that a viewer could grasp an abbreviated version of the whole from a single standpoint. Yet there is always the possibility that the designer intended viewers to have to turn around the column in order to read its narrative. The column's base would serve as a burial chamber for Trajan's ashes after his death in 117 CE, and an encircling motion would be entirely consistent with a widespread Roman funerary ritual known as the *decursio*, in which visitors to a tomb walked around it to protect the dead buried within, to keep harmful spirits in the grave, and to pay perpetual homage to the deceased.

THE COLUMN BASE OF ANTONINUS PIUS The point at which the classicizing phase of Roman sculpture, still so evident on the Column of Trajan, starts to yield to the more abstract style of late antiquity—with its less naturalistic, more linear treatment

7.41 Column base of Antoninus Pius and Faustina. "Apotheosis" and "*decursio*" reliefs. ca. 161 CE. Marble. Musei Vaticani, Rome

7.42 Funerary relief of a butcher and a woman. Mid-2nd century CE. Marble, 13½ × 26½″ (34.5 × 67.3 cm). Staatliche Kunstsammlungen, Dresden

from the side. Both of these factors find parallels in sculpture commissioned in the provinces and in nonelite circles. Figure **7.42** shows a nonelite style, in a funerary relief commemorating a butcher and a woman. The image has a flatness that is different from the illusionistic treatment of space on the panels of the Arch of Titus (see figs. 7.37 and 7.38) The figures are stocky, and the butcher's head is large in proportion to his body. The artist's priority was probably legibility: The patron would have mounted the panel on the façade of a tomb, so that viewers could see it from a distance. The linear treatment of the image and the boldness of the forms served this goal well. The introduction of these qualities into imperial commissions in Rome signals a change in the way state art expressed messages.

Art and Architecture in the Provinces

The spread of Rome's authority over a wide geographical reach had a profound impact on artistic and architectural production in those areas. As Rome's political and cultural institutions reached the provinces, so did the architectural and artistic forms that accommodated them. Sometimes provincial monuments are all but indistinguishable from those in the city of Rome; but more often the syncretism of Roman forms and indigenous styles and materials led to works that were at once recognizably Roman and yet distinctive to their locale.

The principal written sources on the provinces tend to be works by Romans. For this reason, it is hard to assess how provincial peoples reacted to Roman rule. But it certainly brought them some benefits. For instance, Roman engineers had mastered the art of moving water efficiently, and the new aqueducts that sprang up in urban centers around the Empire must have improved local standards of living immeasurably. A striking aqueduct still stands at Segovia in Spain, dating to the first or early second century CE (fig. **7.43**). It brought water from Riofrío,

of the body—is a matter of some debate. A critical shift may have taken place with the column base of Antoninus Pius and his wife, Faustina the Elder. Antoninus died in 161 CE. His successors, Marcus Aurelius and Lucius Verus, erected a 50-foot porphyry column in his honor, surmounted by his statue. Its white marble base is all that survives. One side bears an inscription. On another is an apotheosis scene, where a winged figure bears the emperor and his wife to the heavens, while personifications of the Field of Mars (where the cremation took place) and Rome look on (fig. **7.41**). The figures have lithe, Classical proportions, and idealized es, with smooth, even planes and ageless features. On the two remaining sides of the base, Roman cavalrymen ride in a counter-clockwise circle around a group of infantrymen, in nearly identical scenes that probably represent the *decursio* around the funeral pyre. The sculptural style of these scenes is unlike the apotheosis scene. The soldiers have stocky, squat proportions, and the action unfolds in a bird's-eye perspective, while the soldiers are viewed

7.43 Aqueduct, Segovia. 1st or early 2nd century CE

about 10½ miles (17 km) away, flowing for most of its length through an underground channel. Approaching the town, however, architects built a massive bridge stretching 2,666 feet long and up to 98 feet high to span a valley. One hundred and eighteen arches support the water channel, superimposed in two registers at the highest point. Like most provincial builders, the architects used a local stone, in this case granite, which they assembled without mortar and left unfinished to give it an air of strength. Despite the obvious practical advantages the aqueduct provided, the design also illustrates how Roman architecture could effect dominion. The arches—such a quintessentially Roman form—march relentlessly across the terrain, symbolically conquering it with their step. Even the act of moving water was a conquest of a kind, a conquest of Nature.

THE MAISON CARÉE, NÎMES Romans carried their way of life with them across the Empire, constructing theaters and amphitheaters in a Roman style, and temples to accommodate their rituals. A well-preserved temple (fig. **7.44**) known as the Maison Carrée (Square House) survives in the French town of Nîmes (ancient Nemausus). Typically Roman, it stands on a high podium, with a frontal staircase. Six Corinthian columns across the front lead into a deep porch and to the cella; engaged columns decorate the cella's exterior walls. Reconstructing an inscription in bronze letters on its architrave from the evidence of dowel holes, scholars long thought the temple to have been dedicated to Rome and Augustus during the Augustan age. Acanthus scrolls in the frieze appeared to be reminiscent of the *Ara Pacis*, the masonry style showed similarities to that of the Temple of Mars the Avenger in Augustus' Forum. Indeed, scholars once considered the temple evidence for traveling workshops. Recent research has cast doubt on this view, though, and illustrates the danger that historians may construct the very history they are looking for by interpreting evidence to fit preconceived theories. As it turns out, the dowel holes could support any number of different inscriptions; and the **module** (construction measure) employed throughout the building only came into use under Trajan. The building could be a temple dedicated to Trajan's wife, Plotina, as attested in literary sources.

EL KHASNEH, PETRA In some cases, the syncretism of indigenous building traditions with Roman styles resulted in powerful new effects. This appears to be the case with the extraordinary rock-cut façade known as El Khasneh, or the Treasury, at the site of Petra in present-day Jordan (fig. **7.45**). This façade is the first sight to greet a visitor who wanders through the long, twisting gorge known as the Siq, leading to the town center. The Nabataeans, a nomadic people who settled this area before

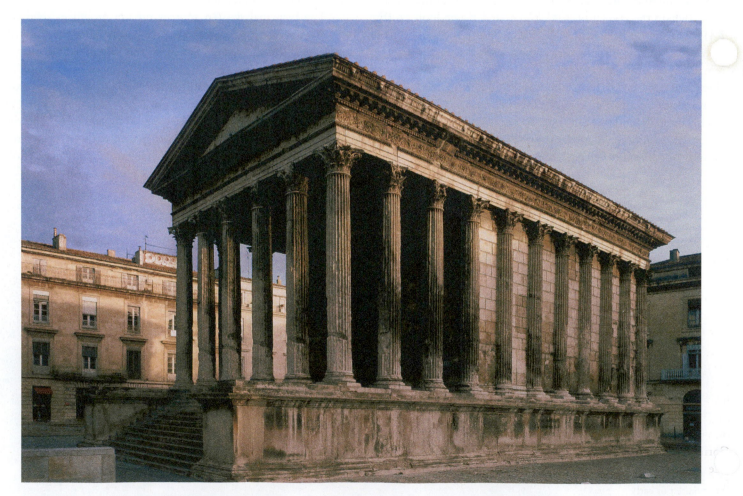

7.44 Maison Carrée, Nîmes. Early 2nd century CE (?)

This playful treatment of once-structural elements became popular in the provinces and in Rome in the second century CE, and scholars sometimes describe it as a "baroque" phase, for its similarities to Italian Baroque architecture. The monument's function may have changed for Roman usage as well: Relief sculptures between the columns seem to represent figures from the cult of Isis, suggesting that it was a temple. In some cases, inscriptions and other written documents indicate who commissioned monuments in the provinces; the patron might be local, a Roman official, or even the emperor himself. More often, as in this case, there is no such evidence, which makes it hard to determine meaning in a particular choice of design.

SCULPTURE AND PAINTING Sculpture in the Roman provinces also has a distinctive look—the result, generally, of a merging of different traditions. A limestone funerary relief from Palmyra in Syria from the second half of the second century CE (fig. **7.46**) once sealed the opening to a burial within a characteristically Palmyrene monument, a tower tomb. An Aramaic inscription identifies the subject as Tibnan, an elite woman, who holds a small child in one arm. The language bespeaks her origin, and the strict frontality, large staring eyes, and local dress and headband set her apart from elite women of Rome (see fig. 7.32). All the same, the portrait has distinctly Roman qualities: Tibnan

7.45   El Khasneh, Petra, Jordan. Probably early 2nd century CE

the Romans took control in 106 CE, buried their wealthy dead in tombs cut out of the pink sandstone cliffs, and some have seen El Khasneh as one of their monuments. Most now agree, however, that it belongs to the Trajanic or Hadrianic period. Carved from the living rock, the monument resembles a temple façade, with six columns beneath an architrave decorated with floral designs and a pediment. In a second story, lateral columns support the angles of a broken pediment. Between them is a tholos with a conical roof, surmounted by an ornamental finial. In modern times, locals imagined that pirates had stored their treasure in the finial, lending the monument its name; bullet holes show how they tried to knock it down. The façade is a striking amalgamation of a Nabataean concept with Roman decorative features—the Corinthian column capitals, for instance, and the vegetal designs. The architectural elements are not structural, and this allows for a freedom and quality of fantasy in the design, not unlike the fantasy vistas of Second Style wall paintings (see page 221).

7.46   Funerary relief of Tibnan, from Palmyra, Syria. ca. 150–200 CE. Painted limestone. Musée du Louvre, Paris raises her right hand, for instance, to hold her veil, in a Roman gesture that signified chastity (or *pudicitia*, defined as loyalty to one's husband) (see fig. 7.13). The portrait neatly encapsulates the dual identity of this provincial woman, who is both Palmyrene and Roman.

The largest body of painting to survive from the Roman world is wall painting (see page 218). Yet the sands of Fayum, in Lower Egypt, preserved a magnificent group of painted portraits, once attached over the faces of embalmed, mummified corpses (fig. 7.47). The earliest of them appear to date from the second cen-

tury CE. Artists painted them on wooden panels in the **encaustic** technique, which involves suspending pigments in hot wax. The mixture can be opaque and creamy, like oil paint, or thin and translucent. The medium is extremely durable, and the pai retain an extraordinary freshness; the wax also gives then a lustrous vitality. The quality of the portraits varies dramatically. At their best, they have a haunting immediacy, largely the result of the need to work quickly before the hot wax set. The woman pictured here wears a crimson tunic and a wealth of jewelry. Rows of black circles denote the ringlets of her hair, bound with a golden diadem. Her appearance is Roman, yet the portrait itself speaks of her local identity, since she was buried in the Egyptian, not the Roman, fashion. As a result, these portraits belong rightly in the history of both Roman art and Egyptian art.

Domestic Art and Architecture

The Romans are one of the few ancient peoples to have left abundant evidence of domestic architecture and its decoration. This is largely due to the catastrophic eruption of Vesuvius in 79 CE, which left the nearby cities of Pompeii and Herculaneum buried under a thick blanket of ash and lava. When excavations began in Pompeii in the eighteenth century, archaeologists discovered a city frozen in time. Utensils and remnants of furniture were still in place in houses, inns, and bath buildings, allowing historians to reconstruct the rituals of daily life in extraordinary detail.

POMPEII AND HERCULANEUM In its early days, the Osc inhabited Pompeii. Another early Italic tribe, the Samnites, took control in the late fifth century BCE, and the city's monumentalization began under their aegis, and under the influence of nearby Greek cities. After the Social War of 90–89 BCE, the Roman dictator Sulla refounded Pompeii as a Roman colony. Like other colonies, which took their design from Roman army camps, Pompeii had two main streets, the *cardo* and the *decumanus* (fig. 7.48). At their intersection stood the forum, the civic heart of the city, near which the Pompeiians built the principal temples and two theaters. Interspersed among surrounding streets were houses and the other buildings that accommodated everyday Roman life: baths for daily bathing and socializing, taverns and fast-food kitchens, launderers with their great vats of urine for washing clothes, and brothels. A state-of-the-art amphitheater on the outskirts of the city, which was a prototype for the Colosseum, provided gladiatorial entertainments, and outside the city gates the wealthy buried their dead in monumental tombs. In the Augustan period, an aqueduct brought fresh water to the public fountains that flowed continuously throughout the city. Water flushed the basalt-paved streets to keep them clean, and raised stepping-stones allowed pedestrians to cross from sidewalk to sidewalk without getting wet.

The unusually good state of preservation of the houses Pompeii and Herculaneum means that they dominate schola discussion, as they will here; yet such was the durability of Roman domestic construction that houses survive elsewhere as

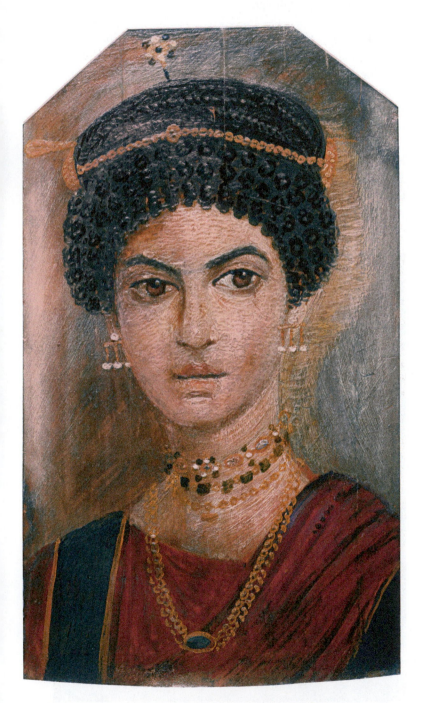

7.47 *Portrait of a Woman*, from Hawara in the Fayum, Lower Egypt. ca. 110–30 CE. Encaustic on wooden panel. Royal Museum of Scotland. © Trustees of the National Museum of Scotland

7.48   Aerial view of Pompeii

7.49   Reconstruction of Pompeiian house

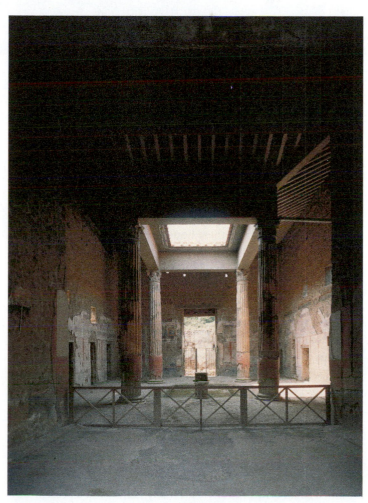

7.50   Atrium of the House of the Silver Wedding, Pompeii.
2nd century BCE–79 CE

well, as far afield as Morocco and Jordan, and although Roman houses have many common qualities, they also differ from one region to the next, to cater, for instance, to local climates. One should be cautious, therefore, about conceiving of a "typical" Roman house.

Scholars describe elite Roman houses by their Latin name, **domus**, known from Vitruvius and other ancient writing (fig. **7.49**). (See www.myartslab.com.) Its most distinctive feature is an atrium, a square or oblong central hall lit by an opening in the roof, answered by a shallow pool, or **impluvium**, in the ground to collect rainwater. The airy quality of the atrium confers an element of grandeur upon the house, visible here in the House of the Silver Wedding (fig. **7.50**), and by tradition it was where Romans kept portraits of ancestors. Other rooms, such as bedrooms

7.51 Model of apartment block

(**cubicula**), group around the atrium, which often leads to a *tablinum*, a reception room, where the family kept its archives. Beyond the tablinum, a colonnade (the *peristyle*) surrounds a garden, where the owner could display sculpture and take fresh air. There might be additional rooms at the back of the house. The chief light source was the atrium and the peristyle; walls facing the street did not typically have windows, but one should not be misled into believing that these houses were therefore particularly private. Romans routinely used rooms flanking the entryway as shops, and the front door often stood open. At the heart of Roman society was a client–patron relationship, and clients routinely visited their patrons in their homes, in a morning ritual known as the *salutatio*. The householder also conducted business in his home, even in the bedrooms. A visitor's access to the different parts of the house depended on his relationship with the owner, who would greet most visitors in the large central rooms.

In any given region of the Empire, there were huge discrepancies between the houses of the rich and the dwellings of the poor. Abandoned in the Middle Ages, Rome's port city, Ostia, preserves many examples of high-occupancy dwellings, known as **insulae** (literally "islands") (fig. **7.51**). An **insula** was generally a substantial concrete-and-brick building (or chain of buildings) around a small central court, with many features of a present-day apartment block. On the ground floor, shops and taverns opened to the street; above lived numerous families in cramped quarters.

Some insulae had as many as five stories, with balconies above the second floor. Wealthy property owners often made a handsome income from these buildings.

MAU'S FOUR STYLES OF PAINTING Compared with Greek painting, Roman domestic painting—mostly wall painting—survives in great abundance. It comes mainly from Pompeii and Herculaneum, and also from Rome and its environs, and it dates mostly to a span of less than 200 years, from the end of the second century BCE to the late first century CE. Given the public character of a domus, these paintings were more than mere decoration: They also testified to a family's wealth and status.

Basing his analysis partly on Vitruvius' discussion of painting, the late nineteenth-century German art historian August Mau distinguished four styles of Roman wall painting (fig. **7.52**), which are useful as general guidelines. (See www.myartslab.com.) In the First Style, dating to the late second century BCE, artists used paint and stucco to imitate expensive colored marble paneling. Starting about 100 BCE, Second Style painters sought to open up the flat expanse of the wall by including architectural features and figures. In a room in the Villa of the Mysteries just outside Pompeii, dating from about 60 to 50 BCE, the lower part of the wall (the **dado**) and the upper section above the cornice level are painted in rich mottled colors to resemble exotic stone (fig. **7.53**). Figures interact as if on a narrow ledge set against

August Mau (1840–1909 produced what remains the scheme that underpins all stylistic analysis of Pompeian decor: he divided the wall painting into four 'Styles,' each representing a phase in the chronology of Pompeian painting, from the second century BCE to the final eruption in 79 CE.

7.52 August Mau's Four Styles of Pompeiian wall painting

1. 'The First, or Incrustation, style': the wall is painted (and moulded in stucco) to imitate masonry blocks, no figured scenes. Second century BCE.

2. 'The Second, or Architectural, style': characteristically featuring illusionistic architectural vistas. c.100—15 BCE.

3. 'The Third, or Ornate, style': the vistas here give way to a delicate decorative scheme, concentrating on formal ornament. c.15 BCE.—50 CE.

4. 'The Fourth, or Intricate, style': a more extravagant painterly style, parading the whole range of decorative idioms. c.50 CE.

7.53 *Scenes of Dionysiac Mystery Cult*, from the Villa of the Mysteries, Pompeii. Second Style wall painting. ca. 60–50 BCE

7.54 Second Style wall painting, from the Villa of Publius Fannius Synistor at Boscoreale, near Pompeii. Mid-1st century BCE. Fresco on lime plaster, 8′8½″ × 19′7⅛″ × 10′11½″ (2.65 × 5.84 × 3.34 m). Metropolitan Museum of Art, New York, Rogers Fund, 1903 (03.14.13)

7.55 Second Style wall painting of garden, from the Villa of Livia at Primaporta. ca. 20 BCE. Museo delle Terme, Rome a deep red background, articulated by upright strips of black resembling stylized columns. They are engaged in rites associated with the Dionysiac mysteries, one of the so-called mystery religions originating in Greece. The scene may represent an initiation into womanhood or marriage, in the presence of Dionysos and Ariadne with a train of satyrs. The solidity of the near-life-size figures, the bold modeling of their bodies, and their calm but varied poses lend a quiet power and vivid drama to the room.

In some cases, Second Style artists employed architectural vistas to open the wall into a fantasy realm, suggesting another world beyond the room. This movement may reflect architectural backdrops in contemporaneous theaters. In an example from the Villa of Publius Fannius Synistor at Boscoreale, near Pompeii, now reconstructed in the Metropolitan Museum of Art in New York (fig. **7.54**), there is a foreground of architectural features: A painted parapet wall runs around the lower part of the surface, and resting on it are columns, which support a cornice. Receding away from the foreground, in a range of different perspectives, stoas and tholoi and scenic gazebos mingle with one another in a maze of architectural fantasy, flooded with light to convey a sense of open space. A viewer struggles to disentangle the structures from one other; their size and spatial relationships are hard to determine. The world of the painting is a world inaccessible to those who view it, hovering out of reach. In the Villa of Livia at Primaporta, the garden beyond the trellis fence and low wall is an idyll of nature, filled with flowers, fruit trees, and birds (fig. **7.55**). Although its lushness beckons, this fantasy garden is only for looking. Here the artist employed atmospheric perspective: Plants and animals become less distinct as they recede into the background.

The Third Style dominated wall decoration from about 20 BCE until at least the middle of the first century CE. In this phase, artists abandoned illusionism in favor of solid planes of intense colors like black and red, which they often articulated with attenuated architectural features and imitation panel paintings. The Fourth Style, which prevailed at the time of Vesuvius' eruption, was the most intricate of the four, uniting aspects of all three preceding styles to create an extravagant effect. The Ixion Room in the House of the Vettii (fig. **7.56**) combines imitation

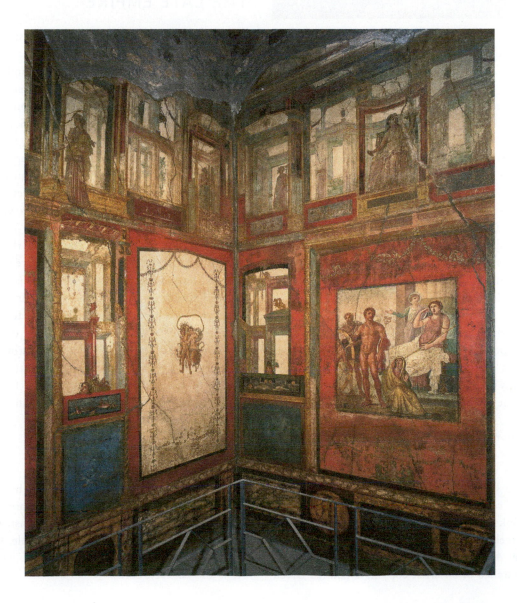

7.56 Fourth Style wall painting, Ixion Room, House of the Vettii, Pompeii. 63–79 CE

7.57 Still-life painting of peaches and water jar, from Herculaneum. ca. 50 CE. Museo Archaeologico Nazionale, Naples

marble paneling, framed mythological scenes resembling panel pictures set into the wall, and fantastic architectural vistas receding into space.

Within these Fourth Style designs, the artist might insert **still life** panels, which usually took the form of **trompe-l'oeil** (intended to trick the eye) niches or cupboards, with objects on shelves. A twenty-first-century viewer finds little unusual about this, yet these are the only visual studies of mundane, inanimate objects until the early modern period. The driving force in these paintings was not a narrative, as in many Roman paintings, but a close analysis of life. The example illustrated here depicts green peaches and a jar half-filled with water (fig. **7.57**). Touches of white paint capture the effect of light playing on the surface of the jar and the water within. Shadows fall in different directions around the peaches, suggesting that the artist was more interested in forging a spatial relationship between the peaches and their surroundings than in indicating a single light source. It is possible, too, that the painting reflects the shadow's movement as the artist worked.

As in the Ixion Room in the House of the Vettii (see fig. 7.56), many Roman paintings depicted Greek themes. The few painters' names on record show that at least some of them were of Greek origin. There are also sufficient cases of paintings (or elements of paintings) closely resembling one another to indicate that artists used copybooks; in some cases, they may have been working from a Greek original, adapting the image to their own purposes. The *Alexander Mosaic* in the House of the Faun is a possible instance of an artist copying a famous Greek

painting, albeit into a different medium (see fig. 5.78). Given the scarcity of Greek mural paintings, however, it is rarely possible to demonstrate a clear connection between Greek original and Roman copy. Given the evident innovation Roman painting, there is no reason to suppose that Roman artists were not capable of creating their own compositions and narratives when they chose. In recent years, scholarship has become less preoccupied with tracing Greek influences, and more focused on ways in which painting ensembles affected experience or dictated movement through a house, and expressed the owner's status. In fact, a genre of ancient literature known as *ekphrasis* is a learned exposition on a real or imagined painting. (See www.myartslab.com.) On the basis of these writings, scholars believe that homeowners sometimes conceived paintings as conversation pieces for their guests, who might discuss them as they dined. A painting program, then, takes on a new level of importance for what it might disclose about the patron's erudition, status, or aspirations.

THE LATE EMPIRE

During Marcus Aurelius' reign, incursions at the Empire's German and Danubian borders were a constant threat. His son Commodus succeeded him in 180 CE, and was assassinated in 192 CE. The imperial administration then hit an all-time low when, in 193 CE, the throne was auctioned off to the highest bidder. After a brief respite under the Severan dynasty, Ro entered a half-century of civil war, when a succession of emperors came to power and quickly fell through violence. Diocletian (r. 284–305 CE) finally restored imperial authority. His approach was to impose rigid order on all aspects of civil as well as military life. Recognizing the emperor's vulnerability, he also chose to divide authority among four rulers, known as the tetrarchs. Two were senior emperors, the Augusti; and two juniors, the Caesars. Terms of power were to be limited, and the Caesars were to succeed the Augusti. The tetrarchy dissolved in the early fourth century CE, and Constantine the Great, the first emperor to embrace Christianity, rose to power, overcoming his chief rival, Maxentius, at the Battle of the Milvian Bridge in Rome in 312 CE. Art forms are distinctly abstract in late antiquity, and scholars sometimes associate the change with the militaristic mood of the time. Sculptural forms are less naturalistic than before, and architects focus on simple but powerful geometric shapes.

Architecture

By the Late Empire, architects in Rome had more or less abandoned the straightforward use of post-and-lintel construction. Their interests appear to have focused instead on exploring the interior spaces that concrete made possible. Column, architrave, and pediment took on decorative roles, superimposed on vaulted brick-and-concrete cores.

Painted Stone in Greece and Rome

For many people, the prevailing image of Greek and Roman architecture and sculpture is white marble. There is good reason for this: As ancient works emerge from the ground, white is the dominant color. White columns still gleam majestically against the blues skies of lands once Greek or Roman, and white sculptures line the halls of European and American museums. Moreover, architects and sculptors such as Michelangelo drew their inspiration from these colorless pieces, and their pristine classicizing works have helped to perpetuate the impression.

Yet art historians have long noted traces of paint on Greek and Roman works of all kinds. As early as 1812, when German archaeologists unearthed the pedimental sculptures from the Temple of Aphaia at Aegina (see fig. 5.22), vestiges of paint fueled a lasting debate about color on ancient stone. Initially, attention focused on architecture, but with the discovery of the portrait of Augustus from Primaporta in 1863 (see fig. 7.29), scholars intensified their analysis of sculpture as well. Still, as the debate gained strength between the twentieth-century world wars, researchers discovered that their labors encountered ideological and aesthetic resistance.

In recent decades, researchers have profited from advances in technology to attempt convincing reconstructions of well-known ancient works as they might once have appeared, including two examples shown here: an archer from Aegina and a portrait of the Roman emperor Caligula. They use improved ultraviolet light techniques (first pioneered by P. de la Coste-Messelière to examine the frieze of the Treasury of the Siphnians at Delphi, see fig. 5.21), and analysis by raking light and microscope to find traces of paint that are invisible to the naked eye. Other techniques include X-ray diffractometry and infrared spectography, which identify specific organic and mineral compounds. From these analyses, and from literary evidence such as the writings of Pliny the Elder, Vinzenz Brinkmann and others conclude that ancient artists employed a rich array of pigments that sometimes originated far from their use. Among them were cinnabar for red (from Istria and Andalusia), widely available ocher for yellow, azurite for blue (from Sinai as well as Italy and Spain), green malachite (from Laurion, near Athens), and arsenic for a luminous yellow and orange (from Anatolia). To make black paint, they collected smoke from burning bones or green wood. Artists also added gold and silver leaf to their sculptures. Recent analyses indicate that ancient artists often used strong, vibrant colors, a far cry from the muted tones that archaeologists first envisioned.

Head of Caligula, color reconstruction

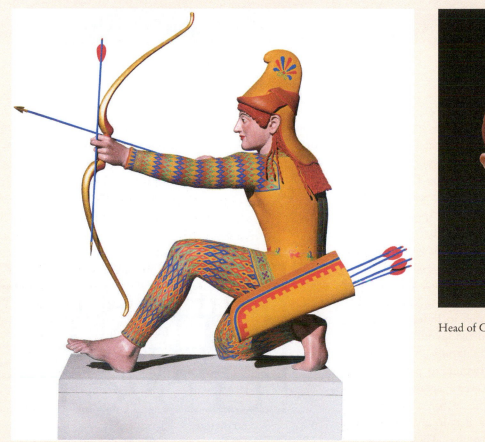

Trojan archer from the west pediment of the Temple of Aphaia on Aegina, color reconstruction

7.58 Baths of Caracalla, Rome. ca. 211–16 CE

THE BATHS OF CARACALLA Imperial bath buildings demonstrate the new Late Empire architectural interests very clearly. By the beginning of the third century CE, public baths were a long-established tradition in Roman life. Emperors had routinely embellished the city with baths as an act of benefaction. Romans who did not own private baths expected to bathe publicly most days, but the baths served other functions as well. They became a place of social interaction, where Romans conducted business and the wealthy flaunted troops of slaves. The Baths of Caracalla, built between 211 and 216 CE, were the most extensive and lavish of their kind (figs. **7.58** and **7.59**). Set within a rectangular perimeter wall, they included the essential bathing facilities, arranged in a standardized layout: a cold room (*frigidarium*), a circular hot room (*caldarium*), and a warm room (*tepidarium*), as well as a vast swimming pool (*natatio*), changing rooms (*apodyteria*), and exercise areas (*palaestrae*). Lecture halls, libraries, and temples made for a multifaceted experience within its walls. Engineers had long mastered the technology for heating the warm rooms: They raised the floors on brick piers, and directed hot air from a furnace into the open space below. This is known as a *hypocaust* system. The sheer scale of Caracalla's complex must have been astounding:

The principal block of buildings measured an immense 656 by 374 feet. Three vast groin vaults roofed the largest room, the frigidarium. Luscious marble panels revetted the walls, and sculptures animated the halls.

7.59 Plan of Baths of Caracalla

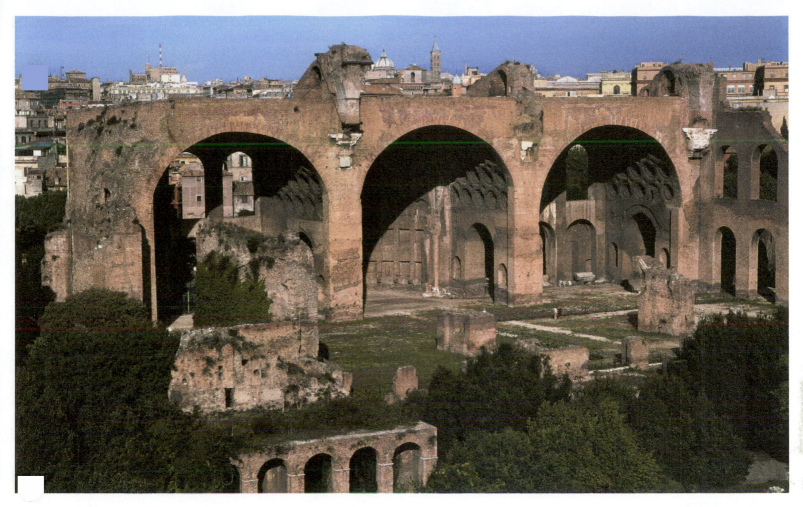

7.60 Basilica of Maxentius, renamed Basilica of Constantine, Rome. ca. 307 CE

THE BASILICA OF MAXENTIUS When Maxentius commissioned a vast basilica for the center of Rome, the architects looked to the massive uninterrupted spaces of bath buildings for inspiration. Basilicas (from the Greek *basileus*, meaning "king") had a long history in Rome. Since the Republic, they had served as civic halls, and they became a standard feature of Roman towns. One of their chief functions was to provide a dignified setting for the courts of law that dispensed justice in the name of the emperor. Vitruvius prescribed principles for their placement and proportions, but in practice they never conformed to a single type and varied from region to region. The Basilica of Maxentius (figs. **7.60** and **7.61**) was built on an even grander scale than the Baths of Caracalla and was probably the largest roofed interior in Rome. It had three **aisles**, of which only the north one still stands. Transverse barrel vaults covered the lateral aisles, and the wider, taller central aisle or nave was covered with three massive groin vaults. Since a groin vault concentrates its weight and thrust at the four corners (see fig. 7.3), the architect could pierce the nave's upper walls with large **clerestory** (window in the topmost wall zone). As a result, the interior of the basilica must have had a light and airy quality. The building had two entrances, each faced by an **apse**: through a transverse vestibule at the east end, and through a stepped door-

way on the south, leading from the Roman Forum. On overcoming Maxentius, Constantine expropriated the basilica. He gave it his own name, and placed his colossal portrait in the western apse (see fig. 7.68). Expropriations of this kind were not uncommon in Rome, and show how critical it was to have a physical presence in the city.

7.61 Basilica of Maxentius, renamed Basilica of Constantine. Reconstruction (after Huelsen)

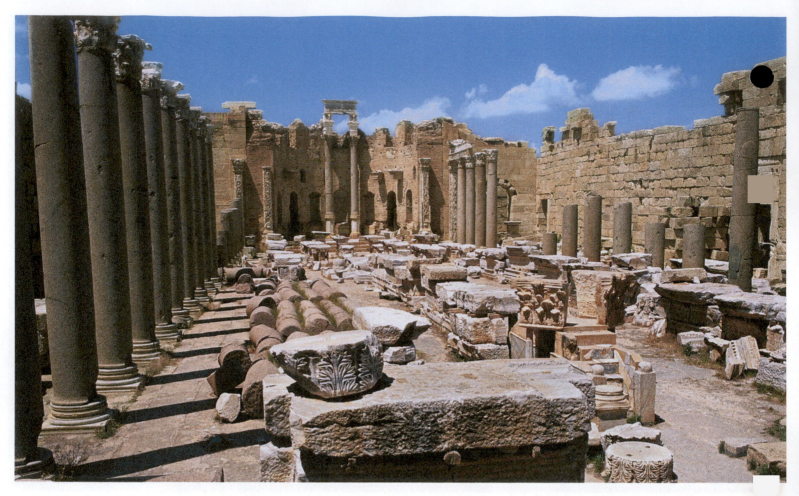

7.62   Basilica,
Lepcis Magna, Libya.
Early 3rd century CE

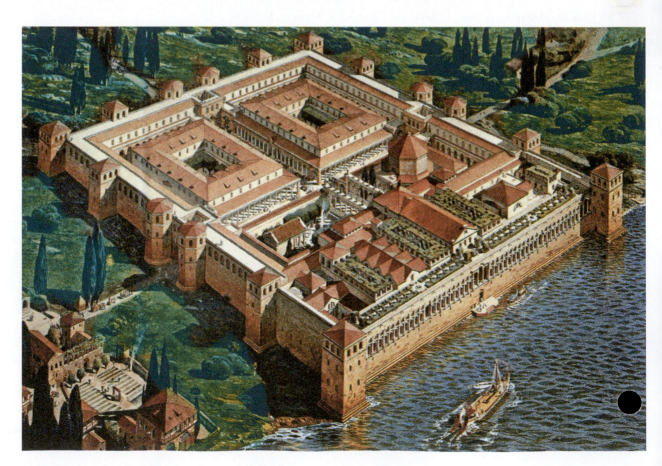

7.63   Palace of
Diocletian, Spalato
(Split), Croatia.
Restored view.
ca. 300 CE

7.64   Peristyle, Palace of Diocletian

Architecture in the Provinces

By the early second century CE, Roman emperors were no longer exclusively from Italy; Trajan came from Spain and Septimius Severus was from North Africa. Both emperors embellished their native cities with new construction. Severus' home, Lepcis Magna, in present-day Libya, remains remarkably well preserved. The emperor was responsible for a grand new forum there, and a magnificent basilica with a long central aisle closed by an apse at either end (fig. **7.62**). Colonnades in two stories provide access to the side aisles, which were lower than the nave to permit clerestory windows in the upper part of the wall. The wooden ceiling has long since perished.

DIOCLETIAN'S PALACE, SPLIT   Developments in Roman architecture after Diocletian came to power appear to go hand-in-hand with the profound changes he made to society. This is clear in his palace at Split (ancient Spalato, in Croatia) overlooking the Adriatic Sea, which he commissioned for his abdication in 305 CE (figs. **7.63** and **7.64**). Although intended as a residence,

it is essentially a military fort, with defensive walls, gates, and towers. As in a military camp, two intersecting colonnaded streets stretched between the gates and divided the rectangular space within the walls, measuring about 650 by 500 feet, into four blocks. The street from the main gate led to a sunken peristyle court. Columns on two sides support **arcuated** (arched) lintels, used only sporadically since the early Empire and popular in late antiquity. They direct a visitor's gaze to the far end of the court, where an arcuated lintel set between the two central columns within a pediment creates a frame. It was here that the former emperor made public appearances. Behind this grand entrance was a vestibule, opening onto the audience hall. To the left of the peristyle court stood a large octagonal mausoleum, now used as a cathedral. Loosely based upon the Pantheon (see figs. 7.23–7.27), this type of imperial mausoleum would be one of the prototypes for Christian **martyria**, burial places of martyred saints. To the right of the court Diocletian dedicated a small temple to Jupiter, his patron god. The topographical relationship between mausoleum and temple implied an equivalency between emperor and god.

7.65 Basilica of Constantius Chlorus, Trier, Germany.
Early 4th century CE

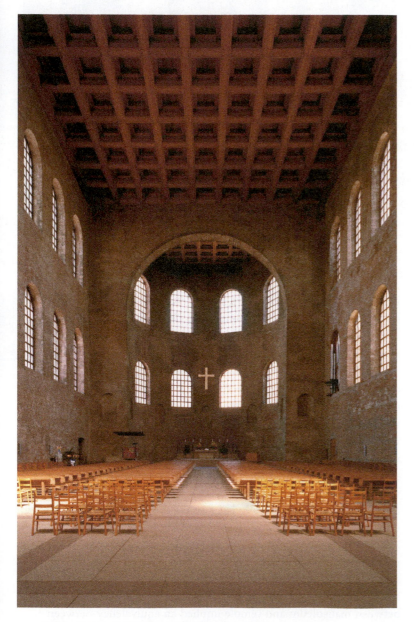

7.66 Interior of Basilica of Constantius Chlorus

THE BASILICA OF CONSTANTIUS, TRIER When Diocletian divided authority between the tetrarchs, each of them established a capital in a different region of the empire and embellished it with appropriate grandeur. Constantius Chlorus, father Constantine the Great, made his seat at Trier, in present-day Germany. There he constructed a basilica, which now functions as a church (figs. **7.65** and **7.66**). In its design, Classical forms have dissolved entirely, leaving vast abstract expanses of solid and void. Elongated arches break the great mass of its walls, and serve as visual buttresses to frame the windows, beneath which were balconies. As vast as the interior was, the architect aspired to achieving an illusion of even greater dimensions. The windows in the apse are significantly smaller than those in the side walls, and the apse ceiling is lower than the ceiling over the main hall. Both devices make it appear that the apse recedes farther into the distance than it does. Not only did this make the building appear grander, but the apse was where the emperor—or his image—would hold sway, and the altered dimensions would have made him appear significantly larger than life. The vocabulary of Roman building had changed, in other words, but it remained an architecture of power.

Portrait Sculpture

During the tetrarchy, portraiture took on a radically abstract quality. Two porphyry sculptural groups now immured in the Basilica of San Marco in Venice were probably originally mounted on columns (fig. **7.67**). Each group shows two tetrarc in elaborate military dress, with bird-headed sword hilts and flat Pannonian caps that probably represent the powerful Illyrian officer class from which they came. The figures are all but indistinguishable from one another (except that in each group, one is bearded, the other close-shaven). Their proportions are squat and nonnaturalistic, their facial features abstract rather than individualized. The portraits suggest that authority resides in the office of emperor, not in the individual who holds the office. The sameness of the portraits underlines the tetrarchs' equality, while their close embrace stresses unanimity and solidarity. The choice of material speaks volumes too: Porphyry, a hard Egyptian stone of deep purple color, had long been reserved for imperial use.

The severe abstraction abates only a little under Constantine, whose portraitist combined it with an Augustan classicism to create the colossal head of figure **7.68.** The head is one fragment of a vast seated portrait that once occupied an apse in the basilica Constantine expropriated from Maxentius (see figs. **7.60** and **7.61**). The head alone is 8 feet tall, and its dominant feature is the disproportionately large and deeply carved eyes. Combined with the stiff frontality of the face, they give the image an iconic quality. Some scholars associate changes like these with the spirituality of the later Empire, exemplified by Constantine's adherence to Christianity. Perhaps the eyes gaze at something beyond th world; perhaps they are a window to the soul. At the same tim a soft modeling to the cheeks and mouth renders the portrait more naturalistic than its tetrarchic predecessors. Moreover, the

7.67   Portrait group of the tetrarchs. ca. 305 CE. Porphyry, height 51″ (129.5 cm). Basilica of San Marco, Venice

7.68   *Portrait of Constantine the Great.* Early 4th century CE. Marble, height 8′ (2.4 m). Museo del Palazzo dei Conservatori, Rome

full cap of hair, and the absence of a beard, appear to be direct references to Trajan and Augustus, great emperors of the past whose achievements still gave the office its authority.

Relief Sculpture

The second century CE witnessed a shift in Roman funerary customs. Inhumation gradually took the place of cremation for all but the imperial family. This led to a demand for marble sarcophagi in place of cinerary urns, and sculptors decorated them with a profusion of designs, which they passed from shop to shop, probably in pattern books of some kind. Preferences changed over time. For example, under Marcus Aurelius, patrons favored battle sarcophagi. In the third century CE, biographical and historical scenes preserved aspects of the deceased's life. Most popular were scenes taken from Greek mythology. Their purpose may have been to glorify the deceased through analogy to the legendary heroes of the past; they may equally have expressed the owner's erudition. Figure **7.69** illustrates a moment from the myth of Meleager. In Homer's account, Meleager saved Calydon from a ferocious boar, which Artemis had sent to ravage his father's land; he then died in a battle over its pelt. For the Romans, Meleager

7.69   *Meleager Sarcophagus.* ca. 180 CE. Marble. Galleria Doria Pamphilj, Rome

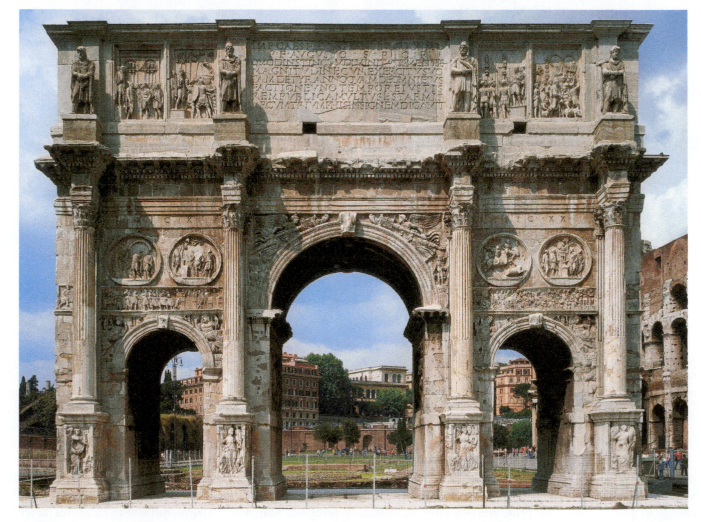

7.70   Arch of Constantine, Rome. 312–15 CE

was an example of noble *virtus*, or manly prowess. For his heroism and death in the service of his city, he earned immortality. The relief's style owes much to Greek sculpture, but crowding the [entir]e surface with figures (known as *horror vacui*) is an entirely [Rom]an practice.

THE ARCH OF CONSTANTINE In 315 CE, the Senate and People of Rome dedicated a triple-bayed arch to Constantine near the Colosseum to celebrate his ten-year anniversary and his conquest of Maxentius (fig. **7.70**). It is one of the largest imperial arches, but what makes it unusual is that so little of the sculptural relief on its surface was specifically designed for this monument (fig. **7.71**). The free-standing Dacian captives on the attic (upper portion) probably originated in Trajan's Forum, as did the Great Trajanic Frieze on the ends of the attic and inside the central bay. Eight hunting and sacrifice tondi above the lateral bays once belonged to a Hadrianic monument, and eight Aurelian panels on the attic may have decorated an arch to Marcus Aurelius. When the arch was constructed, sculptors recarved the heads of earlier emperors to resemble Constantine and his coemperor, Licinius. A modern restoration replaced some of them with heads of Trajan.

Scholars describe sculptural and architectural borrowings of this kind by the modern term **spolia**, from the Latin *spolium*, meaning "hide stripped from an animal," a term primarily used for spoils taken in war. No ancient testimony acknowledges or explains the practice, and the spolia raise all manner of questions—such as how Romans perceived the stripping of one monument in favor of another, and what became of the original monument if it was still standing. In a renowned assault on late antique sculpture in the 1950s, art historian Bernard Berenson condemned the use of spolia as evidence of a pervasive artistic decline in the period, which he attributed to a mass exodus of artists from a city on the brink of destruction. Other scholars, assuming that Romans recognized style differences, see the spolia as part of a legitimation ideology, expressing qualities of "emperorness." By leaning on "good" rulers of the past, Constantine may have hoped to harness the reputations that they had earned during their lifetimes, as well as the nostalgic idealization that

North

East

Trajanic source ▢ Aurelian source ▨
Hadrianic source ▨ Constantinian source ■

South

West

7.71   Schematic drawing of Arch of Constantine showing reused sculpture

7.72 Constantinian relief from Arch of Constantine

had accrued to those reputations through the intervening years. Constantine had reason to legitimize his authority: Maxentius had been a formidable opponent, with his efforts to reposition Rome at the Empire's center through a policy of revivalism. Moreover, as the first openly Christian emperor, Constantine risked alienating a pagan Senate. If this interpretation is correct, it is not dissimilar from readings of the Republican statue base, partly made up of Greek reliefs, as seen in figure 7.10.

To complement the borrowed pieces, Constantinian artists carved bases for the columns that flank the bays, a continuous relief to encircle the arch above the lateral bays, and roundels for the sides of the arch. One scene depicts Constantine addressing the Senate and people of Rome from the speaker's platform, or **rostrum**, in the Forum, after entering Rome in 312 CE (fig. **7.72**). Figures crowd the scene. Their heads are disproportionately large, their bodies stocky, and their poses unnaturally rigid. Lines carved on the flat surface render anatomical details in place of modeling. The artist eschewed devices used on the Arch of Titus panels to give an illusion of depth; a second row of heads arranged above the first indicates recession (see figs. 7.37 and 7.38). Berenson judged the Constantinian reliefs just as harshly as the act of spoliation. Yet their abstract quality makes them unusually

legible from a distance, which is how viewers would have seen them. A careful order governs the composition, with the frontal emperor occupying the center; other figures turn and focus attention on him. Buildings in the background are sufficiently distinct to make the setting recognizable even today as the Roman Forum. The artists privileged the reliefs' message-bearing potential over illusionism or naturalism.

During the course of about a millennium, Rome grew from a small city to the capital of a massive, culturally diverse empire. Those years witnessed huge developments in architecture, due as much to changes in technology as to political motivations. Post-and-lintel construction combined with free forms made possible by concrete, and then dissolved in favor of new abstract concepts of space. In the provinces, architecture brought some improvements in standards of living, but also helped to secure Roman control, exerting a constant Roman presence far from the center of administration. Sculpture and painting abounded within public and private buildings. Often sculpture carried a strong political message, its style chosen to best reinforce its content. As with architecture, an abstract style came to dominate sculpture in late antiquity, due perhaps to a change in concepts of rulership and an increased spirituality.

200–150 BCE Navalia in Rome, earliest known building constructed entirely of concrete

Roman Art

ca. 60–50 BCE Paintings from the Villa of the Mysteries, outside Pompeii

1st century CE rait of Domitia Longina

13–9 BCE Dedication of the *Ara Pacis Augustae*, the Altar of Augustan Peace

early 100s CE El Khasneh in Petra, Jordan

106–13 CE The Column of Trajan is erected in Rome

ca. 300 CE Diocletian builds his palace in Spalato, Croatia

315 CE Dedication of the Arch of Constantine in Rome

1000 BCE ◄ ca. 1000 BCE Earliest inhabitants of Rome

500 BCE ◄ ca. 509 BCE Elite Romans turn against the monarchy, expelling the last king

400 BCE ca. 447 BCE Perikles orders the construction of the Parthenon

340–330 BCE *The Abduction of Persephone* tomb painting at Vergina

300 BCE ca. 279 BCE Ptolemy I commissions the Pharos at Alexandria

◄ by 275 BCE Rome controls all of Italy

200 BCE

100 BCE ◄ 106 BCE Birth of the Roman orator and statesman Cicero

◄ 100s BCE Rome controls Greece and Asia Minor

◄ 46–44 BCE Julius Caesar becomes perpetual dictator of Rome and is assassinated

◄ 27 BCE The Roman Senate names Octavian Augustus Caesar

0 ◄ 19 BCE The poet Vergil dies, leaving *The Aeneid* unfinished

◄ 23/24–79 CE Pliny the Elder; wrote *Natural History*

◄ 79 CE Vesuvius erupts

100 CE 100s CE The earliest painted portraits from the Fayum, Lower Egypt

200 CE

242–72 CE Shapur I's Sassanian palace at Ctesiphon

300 CE ◄ ca. 284 CE Diocletian establishes the tetrarchy

400 CE

CHAPTER 8

Early Jewish, Early Christian, and Byzantine Art

THE LATE ROMAN EMPIRE WAS HOME TO A VAST MELTING POT OF creeds—including the ancient faith of Judaism, as well as Christianity, Mithraism, Manichaeism, and Gnosticism, to name a few. These competing faiths shared several features, including an emphasis on divine revelation through a chief prophet or messiah and the hope of salvation. Of

these religions, Christianity became the most widespread and influential. The art, principally Jewish and Christian, discussed in this chapter reflects the importance of these religions at a time when Roman authority waned. The unified political structure that Rome had created began to break apart by the fourth century ce, with the result that separate imperial centers were established for the Western Empire and its eastern counterpart, called the Byzantine Empire, each of which developed distinctive forms of art.

The Jews of the Late Roman Empire were a Semitic people descended from the ancient Hebrews. The Hebrew people—their tradition recounts—arrived in Canaan on the eastern shores of the Mediterranean from Egypt around the thirteenth century BCE, as a result of a long journey chronicled in the Hebrew Bible, the so-called Old Testament. They established themselves as a United Kingdom of Israel a generation or so before 1000 BCE, when Jerusalem was made the capital under King David, and it was shortly afterward that King Solomon built a Temple there. The area was subsequently ruled by a series of foreign occupiers, including Babylonians, Assyrians, Persians, Greeks (under Alexander the Great), and, most significantly for our studies, Romans, who under General Pompey conquered Israel in 63 BCE. The Romans referred to this land as Palestine.

Christianity was centered on the life and teaching of Jesus of Nazareth, who himself as well as many of his followers came from the ranks of the Jews. The religion spread from Palestine, first to Greek-speaking communities, notably to Alexandria, in Egypt, then reached the Latin-speaking world by the end of the second century CE. The Gospels of Matthew, Mark, Luke, and John, our principal source of information about Jesus' life, were probably written in the late first century CE, some decades after Jesus' death. The Gospels present him as a historical person and as the Son of God and Messiah, or the "Anointed One." The eloquence and significance of Christ's teachings, the miracles attributed to him, and his innate goodness were considered signs of his divinity. The Roman authorities, viewing Jesus' teaching as subversive, had him arrested, tried, and ultimately punished and executed by crucifixion. As the faith spread, the Romans believed Christians threatened the status quo, and intermittently persecuted them. Still, by 300 CE, nearly one-third of Rome was Christian, though the new faith had little standing until it gained the support of the Emperor Constantine the Great.

Constantine was battling his fellow tetrarch, Maxentius, for control of the Western Empire. According to his biographer, Bishop Eusebius of Caeserea, Constantine claimed to have seen a sign in the sky in the form of the monogram of Christ, formed by the Chi Rho, the first letters of Christ's name in Greek, and to have had a dream in which Christ himself assured him of his victory over Maxentius, which took place in 312 CE at the Milvian

Detail of figure 8.33, *The Archangel Michael.* Leaf of a diptych

Map 8.1 Eastern and Western Roman Empires

Bridge in Rome. This is the triumph commemorated by the Arch of Constantine (see fig. 7.70). After having consolidated imperial power, Constantine promoted Christianity throughout the Empire. He began building important religious structures and convening Church councils. He claimed that his political authority was granted by God, and placed himself at the head of the Church as well as of the state. His choice to accept and promote Christianity was a turning point in history, as it resulted in the union of Christianity with the legacy of the Roman Empire. The character of the Middle Ages—and thus of the rest of European history—depended directly on Constantine's decision.

Constantine also decided to build a new capital for the Roman Empire at the strategically located Greek town of Byzantium, which was renamed Constantinople (present-day Istanbul). Constantine certainly did not anticipate it, but within a century of this event, Rome had divided into two halves: an Eastern Empire, of which Constantinople was the capital, and a Western Empire centered at Rome (see map **8.1**). Imperial might and wealth were concentrated in Constantinople, enriching and protecting the Eastern Empire. In the West, imperial authority was less effective in the face of new challenges, as non-Roman groups first invaded

and then settled. The two empires grew apart, in their institutions and in the practice of their common faith.

Into the vacuum of power left by the decline of imperial institutions in the West stepped the Bishop of Rome. Deriving his authority from St. Peter, the Pope, as the Bishop of Rome became known, claimed to be the head of the universal Christian Church, although his Eastern counterpart, the patriarch of Constantinople, disputed this claim. Differences in doctrine and **liturgy** continued to develop until eventually the division of Christendom into a Western or Catholic Church and an Eastern or Orthodox Church became all but final. The Great Schism, or final break, between the two churches occurred in the eleventh century.

The religious separation of East and West profoundly affected the development of Christian art in the Late Roman Empire. "Early Christian" does not, strictly speaking, designate a style. It refers, rather, to any work of art produced by or for Christians during the time prior to the splitting off of the Eastern Chu_ _ from the Western Church: that is, roughly during the first f_ _ centuries after the birth of Jesus. "Byzantine," on the other hand, designates not only the art of the Eastern Roman Empire but also its specific culture and style, which was linked to the imperial court of Constantinople.

Both Early Christian and Byzantine, and to some extent early ish, art have their origins in Rome, and at various moments ﹍sical style is preserved or revived. But the art forms of Early Christian art differ from those of the Greek and Roman world. Whereas the ancients expressed the physical presence of their gods in naturalistic sculpture and paintings, Early Christian artists explored a different vision. In the service of their new faith, they concentrated on symbolic representation, using physical means to express a spiritual essence. Early Christian art refined the increasingly stylized and abstracted art forms of the Late Roman Empire into a visual language that could express both profoundly spiritual and unmistakably secular power.

This culture of Christianity—shaped by Rome, by migrations of northern European peoples, and by Christian faith and institutions—lasted a thousand years. Later historians, looking back from the Renaissance, when Roman forms were deliberately being revived, called this civilization medieval; they saw the Middle Ages as an epoch between themselves and the ancient world. (The term "medieval" is derived from the Latin *medium aevum*, and is thus a synonym for the Middle Ages.) The chronological limits of the Middle Ages are somewhat fluid, but for many historians, the victory of Constantine the Great in 312 marks the beginning of the Middle Ages, while the Renaissance in the 1400s marks its end.

ARLY JEWISH ART

The art of a variety of religions and by a range of peoples continued to be produced during the Late Roman Empire. Indeed, the relationships among these various religious arts make clear that none of them was produced in a vacuum and that each affected the others. Of particular interest is Jewish art, both as a subject worthy of study in its own right and because its development is acutely intertwined with that of Christian art, establishing connections nearly as profound as are the relationships between the two religions themselves. The artistic influences, perhaps better-termed "dependencies," between the two religions go both ways: Each seems to have been interested in and stimulated by the artistic production of the other. At the same time, both Jewish and Christian art developed within an environment where the dominant artistic force was clearly Roman.

DURA-EUROPOS SYNAGOGUE Discoveries in Palestine and other neighboring regions within the last century have forced scholars to revise their estimation of the quantity and quality of Jewish art produced in antiquity. Central to this reevaluation was the fortuitous and remarkable discovery of a synagogue in the Syrian town of Dura-Europos, a Roman outpost on the upper Euphrates. In 256 CE, in order to protect itself from imminent attack by Persians, the town strengthened its protective walls, which involved filling in some adjacent streets in order to form a defensive bunker. Buried as a result, and thus preserved, were a number of buildings, including a shrine to Mithras (worshiped in Zoroastrianism, the ancient religion of Persia), a Jewish synagogue, and a house that was used for Christian rituals. These buildings were excavated in the late 1920s and early 1930s.

The bench-lined sanctuary of the Dura-Europos synagogue (fig. **8.1**) would have seated about 120 people. It was decorated with painted ceiling tiles and with four registers of **tempera** paintings on its walls, more than half of which have survived. The mural paintings illustrate episodes from the Hebrew Bible, including scenes featuring Moses and other patriarchs and

8.1   West wall of sanctuary of synagogue, Dura-Europos, Syria. 245–46 CE. Tempera on plaster. Reconstructed in the National Museum, Damascus, Syria

prophets. The synagogue was rebuilt or refurbished in 245 and 246, just a decade before the defenses against Persian attack were raised; as such, it was virtually new when buried. A niche in the center of the Jerusalem-facing west wall housed a shrine for the Torah, the **parchment** scroll containing the first five books of the Hebrew Bible. The shrine is decorated with a representation of a temple and a menorah, the seven-branched candelabrum that was housed in the Second Temple in Jerusalem, the center of Jewish worship and ritual for centuries, which was destroyed by the Romans in 70 CE (see page 209 and fig. 7.37). The message—one confirmed by writings by rabbis, those Jewish religious leaders and teachers who became increasingly important after the first century CE—is that the synagogues in which Jews practice their religion are to be equated with the Temple in Jerusalem. Indeed, the synagogue was the place where many rituals, for example, the blowing of the ram's horn (the *shofar*), historically practiced in the Temple, came to be performed. Prayers offered in the synagogue substituted for sacrifices that originally took place in the Temple.

The Dura-Europos paintings were created in a space that served a ritual function, where the practice of the liturgy, a body of rites prescribed for public worship, was consistent and alive. To some extent, the decoration of this synagogue provides both a setting for, and a reflection of, ceremonial performance by the local community. In addition to wall murals, ritual objects, and other decorations, the sounds of prayer and the aroma of incense embellished the synagogue and accentuated the sense of a charged space created for the enactment of the liturgy.

Previous to the discovery of the Dura-Europos wall painting it had traditionally been assumed that Jews rarely produced art, a notion based on the biblical proscription against making graven images as described in the Second Commandment (Exodus 20:4–6; Deuteronomy 5:8–10: "You shall not make to you any graven image, or any likeness of any thing that is in heaven above, or that is in the earth beneath....You shall not bow down yourself to them, nor serve them"). While the Dura-Europos paintings are the most extensive figural body of early Jewish art to survive, early writings by rabbis specifically mention the existence of mural programs in third-century CE Palestine and, as we shall see, synagogue decorations survive there in some number. Representations of God do not appear in Jewish contexts, and it is here that we should understand the significance of the edict against the production of graven images. The Second Commandment was not an injunction against representation, but rather, more specifically against making idols.

Although the Dura-Europos wall paintings would not have been unique in their own time, the lack of surviving comparable material makes any attempt to see a systematic program of images far from secure, and some scholars claim that there was in fact none. One suggestion is that the scenes could have been used by

8.2 *Consecration of the Tabernacle and Its Priests*, detail of west wall of sanctuary of synagogue, Dura-Europos, Syria. Tempera on plaster, 4′8¼″ × 7′8¼″ (1.4 × 2.3 m)

preachers as illustrations for their sermons, turning from one to the other as appropriate. However, others have argued that the scenes selected for illustration emphasize the Lord's special covenant with the chosen people of Israel; still others have noted the concentration of scenes, for example those in which Moses and the prophets Elijah and Ezekiel figure, that offer the promise of revival in both a personal and a messianic sense. This message of redemption is reinforced by the identification of the synagogue with the Temple in Jerusalem.

The Dura-Europos west-wall panel of the *Consecration of the Tabernacle* (fig. **8.2**) illustrates details mentioned in the Hebrew Bible, in various chapters of Exodus and in Numbers 7:89–8:2, which chronicle the creation and consecration of a portable tent used during the Israelites' Exodus from Egypt and that housed the Ark of the Covenant, the chest in which Moses placed the tablets containing the Ten Commandments, the foundation of Jewish law that God delivered to him on the journey from Egypt. The Tabernacle, described in the Bible as tentlike and composed of poles and goat's-hair curtains, is here a Roman temple (see figs. 7.2 and 7.44) surrounded by a defensive wall pierced by three portals. It is not clear whether the permanent building represented here, rather than the portable tent described in the Bible, is a result of scriptural interpretation, or whether it perhaps reflects concern on the part of the population of a frontier town for security and defense; it might also replicate a pictorial source relied upon by the artist.

The golden menorah (described in Exodus 25:31–40) is placed front of the temple and below the Ark of the Covenant, which bears a strong resemblance to the Dura-Europos Torah-shrine niche. The attendant and the red heifer in the lower left-hand corner are derived from Roman scenes of animal sacrifice; hence, they show remnants of foreshortening that are not found among the other figures. Other echoes of Roman painting appear in the perspective view of the altar table next to the figure of Aaron, the first Jewish high priest, whose name, interestingly, is inscribed in Greek. Most of the rest of the scenes reveal little interest in either light or space in the Roman sense. The spatial sequence of objects and people is conveyed by other means. The menorah, the two incense burners on either side of it, the altar, and Aaron are to be seen as behind, rather than on top of, the wall in vertical perspective. Their size, however, is based on their importance, not on their position in space. Aaron, as the main figure, is not only larger than the attendants but also more abstract. Because of its ritual meaning, his costume is shown in detail, at the cost of the body underneath. The attendants, on the other hand, show some mobility and three-dimensional form. Their garments, surprisingly, are Persian, a sign of the mixture of civilizations and the melting-pot conditions in this border area. In terms of style, the synagogue paintings should be seen in the context of the developing abstraction of later Roman art (see figs. 67 and 7.72).

The west-wall mural, then, combines a variety of elements that suggest that the ritual being performed is timeless and recurring. The mural depicts an event of great religious importance: the consecration of the Tabernacle and its priests. We can read the details—animals, human beings, buildings, cult objects—without trouble, but their relationship to one another is not clear. There is no action, no story, only an assembly of forms and figures, which, however, the synagogue members would have been able to link together.

HAMMATH TIBERIAS SYNAGOGUE In addition to wall paintings and liturgical objects, a number of synagogues, particularly in Palestine, were decorated with floor mosaics. The fourth-century mosaic floor of a synagogue at Hammath Tiberias (fig. **8.3**) on the shore of the Sea of Galilee contains motifs that are typical of synagogue pavements, including a wheel with the signs of the zodiac between its spokes and in the center a representation of Helios, the Greek sun-god, bearing a staff and globe, with rays emanating from his head and riding a quadriga, a two-wheeled chariot drawn by four horses. Scholars have debated this reliance on the art of another culture for sources of imagery; some see it as a formal borrowing without overt concern for meaning, while

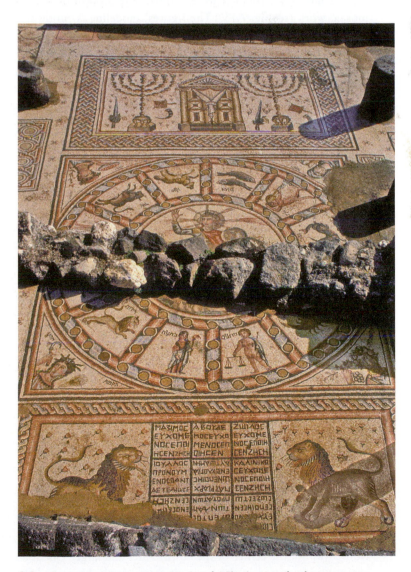

8.3 Floor mosaic, synagogue, Hammath Tiberias, Israel. 4th century CE

others recognize a desire to transfer the authority of traditional pagan images to a new context.

In the corners between the circle of the zodiac and the square frame that encloses it are representations of the seasons, while below the zodiac panel, two lions flank an inscription in Greek that praises the synagogue's builders and describes the donation of precious metals to the synagogue, referred to as a "holy place." A number of Palestinian synagogue mosaics took the zodiac as their central feature: This might be related to the Jews' sense of themselves as distinctive in part because of their use of a calendar different from those of other peoples. The zodiac undoubtedly refers as well to God's creation of the universe.

Represented above the zodiac is a Torah shrine, framed by menorahs and other ritual objects, including incense shovels and the *shofar*, as well as a tied bundle of palm, willow, and myrtle branches (the *lulav*) and citrons (*etrogs*), used in the harvest festival, all elements from the liturgy. The mosaic of the ark and menorah panel was placed facing Jerusalem, in front of the raised podium where the actual Torah shrine was located. The mosaic at Hammath Tiberias creates and unifies sacred time and sacred space.

The mosaic's style of representation is reminiscent of Roman mosaic work (see fig. 7.15). The figures' modeling is subtle and shadows suggest solid, if squat, bodies. Some scholars have cited the fact that the nude figures of Libra and Gemini are uncircumcised as evidence for the Jewish resistance to making images, suggesting that the artists responsible for these works were Gentiles. But at other sites inscriptions identify the mosaicists as Jewish, and it is more probable, given the long history of the representation of the zodiac, that this detail reflects pictorial sources rather than any comment, conscious or otherwise, by the makers of the mosaic.

The Hebrew and Greek used in the mosaic—and there are inscriptions in Aramaic (a Semitic language) as well—reflect the fact that multiple traditions are at work here. Indeed, although the images at Hammath Tiberias and at Dura-Europos have special relevance to Jewish history, beliefs, and rituals, many reflect Graeco-Roman content, even if it was Judaized in accordance with the special concerns and needs of the communities the images served. A similar pattern is also evident in the development of the earliest Christian art.

EARLY CHRISTIAN ART

Christian Art before Constantine

We do not know when or where the first Christian works of art were produced. None of the surviving paintings or sculptures can be dated to earlier than about 200 CE. In fact, we know little about Christian art before the reign of Constantine the Great. This is hardly accidental. It is in Rome that we have the greatest concentration of the earliest surviving works, yet before Constantine, Rome was not the center of the faith. Older and larger Christian communities existed in the great cities of North Africa and the Near East, such as Alexandria and Antioch, but we only have hints of what Christian places of worship there and in centers such as Syria and Palestine might have looked like.

THE ART OF THE CATACOMBS The painted decoration of the Roman **catacombs**, underground burial places, is the only sizable body of material we have from which to study the earliest Christian art. The burial rite and the safeguarding of the tomb were of vital concern to early Christians, whose faith rested on salvation, the hope of eternal life in paradise. As such, paintings in catacombs tell us a good deal about the spirit of the communities that commissioned them.

The ceiling of one of the more elaborate chambers in the catacomb of Santissimi Pietro e Marcellino in Rome (fig. **8.4**) is decorated in a style that is at once formal and uncomplicated. Fixed borders control the overall organization; a central medallion or circle contains the figure of a shepherd, who is flanked by sheep and carries a lamb across his shoulders. The circle is connected to four **lunettes** (semicircular spaces), and in the four corners are single figures with outstretched, raised arms. The style of painting reflects Roman murals, both in the landscape settings and in the use of linear devices to divide the scenes into compartments (see figs. 7.55 and 7.56). But the representations seem sketchier, less grounded in natural observation than their Roman relatives. The differences are partly due to the nature of the subterranean spaces, their use, and their meaning.

Catacombs would have been used only occasionally beyond the actual circumstance of burial, perhaps for a commemorative celebration. This is probably one reason why the wall paintings do not show much detail and care of execution. One imagines as well that artists of the first rank would have chosen more salubrious locations in which to work. Another reason for the sketchiness of these paintings is that their primary value is symbolic. Consistent with the biblical prohibition against image making, as specified in the Second Commandment, Christ is generally not represented in the catacombs, except by metaphor. The shepherd with a sheep on his shoulder is a potent allusion to Christ, since in a number of biblical accounts Christ refers to himself as the Good Shepherd, concerned for the well-being of his flock and willing to sacrifice himself in order to guarantee the salvation of those who follow him (Luke 15:4–6; John 10:1–18). This Good Shepherd metaphor also builds on references in the Hebrew Bible, as in Psalm 23:

The Lord is my shepherd; I shall not want.
He makes me to lie down in green pastures:
he leads me beside the still waters.
He restores my soul...
Surely goodness and mercy shall follow me
all the days of my life:
and I will dwell in the house of the Lord for ever.

This correlation between New Testament and Hebrew Bible reflects the fact that many of the converts to the new faith were Jewish.

The Life of Jesus

Events in the life of Jesus, from his birth through his ascension to *heaven, are traditionally grouped in cycles, each with numerous* *episodes. The scenes most frequently depicted in European art are* *presented here.*

Incarnation Cycle and The Childhood of Jesus

These episodes concern Jesus' conception, birth, infancy, and youth.

Annunciation The archangel Gabriel tells Mary that she will bear God's son. The Holy Spirit, shown usually as a dove, represents the Incarnation, the miraculous conception.

Visitation The pregnant Mary visits her older cousin Elizabeth, who is to bear John the Baptist and who is the first to recognize the divine nature of the baby Mary is carrying.

Nativity At the birth of Jesus, the Holy Family—Mary, his foster father, Joseph, and the Christ Child—is usually depicted in a stable or, in Byzantine representations, in a cave.

Annunciation to the Shepherds and Adoration of the Shepherds An angel announces the birth of Jesus to shepherds in the field at night. The shepherds then go to the birthplace to pay homage to the child.

Adoration of the Magi The Magi, wise men from the East (called the Three Kings in the Middle Ages), follow a bright star for 12 days until they find the Holy Family and present their gifts to Jesus.

Presentation in the Temple Mary and Joseph take the infant Jesus to the Temple in Jerusalem, where Simeon, a devout man, and Anna, a prophetess, foresee Jesus' messianic mission (his mission as Savior) and martyr's death.

Massacre of the Innocents and Flight into Egypt King Herod orders all male children under the age of two in and around Bethlehem to be killed in order to preclude his being murdered by a rival newborn king spoken of in a prophecy. The Holy Family flees to Egypt.

Public Ministry Cycle

These accounts of Jesus' public career include his gathering of disciples, his preaching, and the performance of miracles.

Baptism John the Baptist baptizes Jesus in the Jordan River, recognizing his incarnation as the Son of God. This marks the beginning of Jesus' ministry.

Calling of Matthew The tax collector Matthew becomes Jesus' first disciple (apostle) when Jesus calls to him, "Follow me."

Jesus Walking on the Water During a storm, Jesus walks on the water of the Sea of Galilee to reach his apostles in a boat.

Raising of Lazarus Jesus brings his friend Lazarus back to life four days after his death and burial.

Delivery of the Keys to Peter Jesus names the apostle Peter as his successor by giving him the "keys" to the Kingdom of Heaven.

Transfiguration As Jesus' closest disciples watch, God transforms Jesus into a dazzling vision and proclaims him to be his own son.

Cleansing the Temple Jesus clears the Temple in Jerusalem of money-changers and animal traders.

Passion Cycle

The Passion (from passio, Latin for "suffering") cycle relates Jesus' *death, resurrection from the dead, and ascension to heaven.*

Entry into Jerusalem Welcomed by crowds as the Messiah, Jesus triumphantly rides an ass into the city of Jerusalem.

Last Supper At the Passover seder, Jesus tells his disciples of his impending death and lays the foundation for the Christian rite of the Eucharist: the taking of bread and wine in remembrance of Christ. (Strictly speaking, Jesus is called Jesus until he leaves his earthly physical form, after which he is called Christ.)

Jesus Washing the Disciples' Feet Following the Last Supper, Jesus washes the feet of his disciples to demonstrate humility.

Agony in the Garden In Gethsemane, the disciples sleep while Jesus wrestles with his mortal dread of suffering and dying.

Betrayal (Arrest) The disciple Judas Iscariot takes money to identify Jesus to Roman soldiers. Jesus is arrested.

Denial of Peter As Jesus predicted, Peter, waiting outside the high priest's palace, denies knowing Jesus three times as Jesus is being questioned by the high priest Caiaphas.

Jesus before Pilate Jesus is questioned by the Roman governor Pontius Pilate regarding whether or not he calls himself King of the Jews. Jesus does not answer. Pilate reluctantly condemns him.

Flagellation (Scourging) Jesus is whipped by Roman soldiers.

Jesus Crowned with Thorns (The Mocking of Christ) Pilate's soldiers mock Jesus by dressing him in robes, crowning him with thorns, and calling him King of the Jews.

Carrying of the Cross (Road to Calvary) Jesus carries the wooden Cross on which he will be executed from Pilate's house to the hill of Golgotha, which means "the place of the skull."

Crucifixion Jesus is nailed to the Cross by his hands and feet, and dies after great physical suffering.

Descent from the Cross (Deposition) Jesus' followers lower his body from the Cross and wrap it for burial. Also present are the Virgin Mary, the apostle John, and, in some accounts, Mary Magdalen.

Lamentation (*Pietà* or *Vesperbild*) The grief-stricken followers gather around Jesus' body. In the *Pietà*, his body lies in the lap of the Virgin.

Entombment The Virgin Mary and others place the wrapped body in a sarcophagus, or rock tomb.

Descent into Limbo (Harrowing of Hell or Anastasis in the Orthodox Church) Christ descends to Hell, or Limbo, to free deserving souls who have not heard the Christian message—the prophets of the Hebrew Bible, the kings of Israel, and Adam and Eve.

Resurrection Christ rises from the dead on the third day after his entombment.

The Marys at the Tomb As terrified soldiers look on, Christ's female followers (the Virgin Mary, Mary Magdalen, and Mary, mother of the apostle James the Greater) discover the empty tomb.

Noli Me Tangere, Supper at Emmaus, and the Doubting of Thomas In three episodes during the 40 days between his resurrection and ascent into Heaven, Christ tells Mary Magdalen not to touch him (*Noli me tangere*), shares a supper with his disciples at Emmaus, and invites the apostle Thomas to touch the lance wound in his side.

Ascension As his disciples watch, Christ is taken into Heaven from the Mount of Olives.

8.4 Painted ceiling, Catacomb of Santissimi Pietro e Marcellino, Rome, Italy. 4th century CE

The four lunettes around the Good Shepherd form a cycle dedicated to the Hebrew prophet Jonah. (See *Informing Art*, page 273.) Here, too, the symbolic references to Christian beliefs about Christ are clear: Just as it is a principle of faith that Jonah spent three days within the belly of the whale, so Christ is supposed to have spent three days in the tomb, and just as Jonah was released with unharmed body, so Christ was resurrected from his tomb in physical wholeness. Indeed, in Matthew 12:40 Christ compares himself to Jonah. Recent converts would probably have felt comfortable knowing that didactic aspects of their old faith could find a sympathetic response in the new religion. Jonah's story is presented as a **prefiguration** (foreseeing) of events in Christ's life, thus assigning the Hebrew Bible story the role of prophecy and the Christian Bible one of its fulfillment. As Christian thinkers increasingly analyzed the prophetic relationship of the Hebrew Bible to the Christian one, they developed a virtual system of concordances, called **typology**, that was to have far-reaching significance.

The painted ceiling in the Santissimi Pietro e Marcellino catacomb also borrows imagery from classical sources. The Good Shepherd himself is a reminder of pagan symbols of charity in the form of ancient sculptures of men carrying sacrificial animals on their shoulders. The posture of Jonah, reclining under the gourd bush, benefiting from God's beneficence, derives from Roman pagan mythological representations of Endymion, a youth so beautiful that he was rewarded with eternal sleep. So, as with their Jewish counterparts, former practitioners of pagan religions who had converted to Christianity would also have been familiar with some of the images and ideas expressed in Early Christian art.

Both the Good Shepherd and Jonah are associated with messages of comfort, reminding us that Early Christian art developed during the turmoil of Rome's decline, a time of political, social, and economic instability. The allure of the new religion must have been profound indeed, suggesting that things of this world were of less significance than those of a future world, which offered the hope of eternal peace. The four standing figures between the lunettes are **orants** (worshipers), represented in what had long been the standard pose of prayer, signifying the virtues of faith and piety that make personal salvation possible.

One might question the extent to which the Christian use of pagan and Jewish subjects had a political agenda. After all, on some level, to borrow forms from other cultures and religions and to use them for new purposes are acts of appropriation. By adopting forms used by an older, more established culture, Christians expressed their ambition to dominate that culture—indeed, to supplant it. Such appropriation becomes more systematic as the new religion of Christianity becomes increasingly powerful.

SCULPTURE Sculpture seems to have played a secondary role in Early Christian art. The biblical prohibition on graven images was thought to apply with particular force to large cult statues, idols worshiped in pagan temples. In order to avoid the taint of idolatry, therefore, Christian sculpture had to shun life-size representations of the human figure. Sculpture thus developed in an antimonumental direction: away from the spatial depth, naturalism, and massive scale of Graeco-Roman sculpture and toward shallow, small-scale forms and lacelike surface decoration.

The earliest works of Christian sculpture are sarcophagi, stone coffins, which from the middle of the third century on were produced for the more important members of the Church. They evolved from the pagan examples that had replaced cinerary urns in Roman society around the time of Hadrian. Before Constantine, their decoration consisted mostly of a repertory of familiar themes from the catacombs. Examples of these can be seen on the marble sarcophagus of the mid-third century from Santa Maria Antiqua in Rome (fig. 8.5). On the left are scenes featuring Jonah: the ship, the sea monster, and the reclining prophet. Jonah's well-chiseled anatomy and the elegance of his pose remind us of the classical sources that must have served as a model for the artist. So, too, the Good Shepherd, though stylized, reminds of us of classical statuary in that he is able to

distribute weight well enough to manage with some comfort the burden of the sheep he carries. Again, the orant in the center, with hands upraised in prayer, is a subject we have seen in catacomb painting. The seated figure holding a scroll derives from antique representations of writers or philosophers and is another of the metaphoric references to Christ, in this case to his role as teacher. On the right is a scene of baptism. The figure being baptized may be Christ himself. If so, this might indicate an increased movement toward narrative, since baptism was an event in the life of Jesus (see *Informing Art*, page 241), and a willingness to represent him directly. On the other hand, the figure appears to be generic, nonindividualized, virtually childlike in its proportions. This generic representation could be a result of both a fear of making an idolatrous image and an interest in expressing the more essential nature of the scene, from which a portrait of the person of Christ would detract.

THE HOUSE CHURCH Although we have little archaeological evidence of the places where Early Christians gathered, literary accounts, including biblical references, suggest that Christians met regularly to celebrate their shared belief in Christ as the Son of God and Savior and to observe some type of Eucharist, or spiritual union, with him by the partaking of consecrated bread and wine (representing Christ's flesh and blood) in remembrance of the Last Supper, at which Jesus and his disciples enjoyed a final communal meal. Such gatherings of Christians probably originally took place in private homes, which were only later replaced by public spaces designed specifically for Christian worship. This situation is perhaps to be expected, both because

8.5 Sarcophagus, Santa Maria Antiqua, Rome, Italy. ca. 270 CE. Marble, 1'11¼" × 7'2" (0.85 × 2.2 m)

The Book of the Popes (Liber Pontificalis)

From the Life of Pope Sylvester I

This text is an official history of the Roman papacy from St. Peter (died ca. 64 CE) to the twelfth century. Its biographies of the early popes were compiled from archival documents. What follows, for example, is a list of gifts to Old St. Peter's by Emperor Constantine in the time of Pope Sylvester I (314–335 CE). Lavish imperial donations such as these set a standard that subsequent popes and other prelates continued to match.

Constantine Augustus built the basilica of blessed Peter, the apostle, and laid there the coffin with the body of the holy Peter; the coffin itself he enclosed on all sides with bronze. Above he set porphyry columns for adornment and other spiral columns which he brought from Greece. He made a vaulted apse in the basilica, gleaming with gold, and over the body of the blessed Pe above the bronze which enclosed it, he set a cross of purest gold. gave also 4 brass candlesticks, 10 feet in height, overlaid with silver, with figures in silver of the acts of the apostles, 3 golden chalices, 20 silver chalices, 2 golden pitchers, 5 silver pitchers, a golden paten with a turret of purest gold and a dove, a golden crown before the body, that is a chandelier, with 50 dolphins, 32 silver lamps in the basilica, with dolphins, for the right of the basilica 30 silver lamps, the altar itself of silver overlaid with gold, adorned on every side with gems, 400 in number, a censer of purest gold adorned on every side with jewels.

Source: Caecilia Davis-Weyer, *Early Medieval Art 300–1150* (Upper Saddle River, NJ: Prentice Hall, 1st ed., 1971)

Christianity was something of an underground religion and because other religions also seem to have used private houses as gathering places; for instance, the Villa of the Mysteries in Pompeii (see fig. 7.53).

The same defensive barrier that preserved the Dura-Europos synagogue (see page 237) also buried what must have been a traditional Christian meeting place. The house is in most ways a typical two-story Roman domus. A large room opened onto the atrium and would have served as a community assembly room, while another space, judging by a font that takes up an entire wall of the room (fig. 8.6), was apparently reserved for baptism, the rite whereby Christians are initiated into the religion by virtue of being sprinkled or immersed in water. The font is covered by a stone canopy, and frescoed scenes decorate the lunette on the end wall under the canopy and also the side walls. Some of the subjects represented are familiar: In the lunette is a Good Shepherd balancing a sheep on his shoulders with his flock before him, and, at the bottom left, now barely visible, are figures of Adam and Eve. Represented on the side wall are three women holding candles who proceed toward a stone sarcophagus. This scene represents the three Marys at the Tomb (see *Informing Art*, page 241), who, when approaching the tomb of Christ (as described Matthew 28:1–10), meet an angel who tells them that the tomb is empty because the entombed Christ has risen.

8.6 Model of the Baptistery, the Christian Meeting House (*domus ecclesiae*) at Dura-Europos, Syria. Before 256 CE. Yale University Art Gallery, New Haven, CT

The representations on the wall of the Dura-Europos house can be connected with those found in Early Christian catacombs and on sarcophagi through shared imagery, such as the depic-ns of the Good Shepherd and Adam and Eve. Such images ᴉndicate a general concern with issues of death and retribution, resurrection and salvation. The inclusion here of Adam and Eve reminds the viewer of the Original Sin, committed by Adam and passed from one generation to the next, from which humankind will be redeemed as a result of Christ's sacrificial death and his resurrection, which the scene of the Marys visiting his empty tomb emphasizes. The association of these funerary subjects with baptism was a logical pairing for Christians, who view baptism as a rebirth into the new faith, just as they see physical death as a rebirth into everlasting life. Even when artists were experiment-ing with how best to depict entirely new subject matter, those responsible for its creation, whether artists or patrons, applied an overwhelming conceptual consistency to Christian art during the first several centuries of the Christian era. This was perhaps a result of the new religion's need for didactic representations that could be readily understood.

Christians in other areas of the Empire also used the type of the *domus ecclesiae*, or **house church**, seen at Dura-Europus. In Rome itself we know of 25 private houses—and undoubt-edly there were more—reserved as places of Christian worship, although most of them were destroyed by the later building of churches on their sites.

ᴄhristian Art after Official Recognition of Christianity

The building of churches on the sites of what once were pri-vate houses used for Christian worship reflects a change in the status of Christianity during the fourth century from an alter-native religion to an official religion endorsed by the emperor Constantine. Almost overnight, an impressive architectural set-ting had to be created for the new official faith, so that the Church might be visible to all. Constantine himself devoted the full resources of his office to this task. Within a few years, an aston-ishing number of large, imperially sponsored churches arose, not only in Rome but also in Constantinople, in the Holy Land, and at other important sites.

THE CHRISTIAN BASILICA The most important Constantinian church structures were a type of basilica, and this form provided the basic model for the development of church architecture in Western Europe. The Early Christian basilica owes its essential features to imperial basilicas, such as the Basilica Ulpia (see fig. 7.17). As with the imperial basilicas, it is characterized by a long **nave** flanked by side aisles and lit by clerestory windows in the upper part of the wall, with an apse (though only at one ᴇnd) and a **trussed** wooden roof. The Roman basilica was a ᴤuitable model since it combined the spacious interior needed to accommodate a large number of people with (perhaps most important) imperial associations that proclaimed the privileged

status of Christianity. As the largely civil functions of the Roman basilica were quite different from its new uses as a house of worship, the Roman-style basilica had to be redesigned to acknowledge these changes. Therefore, the longitudinal plan of the basilica was given a new focus: the altar placed in front of the semicircular apse, normally at the eastern end of the nave. The significance of the altar's placement in the east, where the sun rises, reminds us that Christian art, like that of Judaism (see page 240), inherited many divine attributes from other religions. In this case, Christ shares an imagery with the Roman god Apollo, in his manifestation as sun-god.

The greatest Constantinian church was Old St. Peter's Basilica in Rome (figs. **8.7** and **8.8**). It was torn down and replaced by the

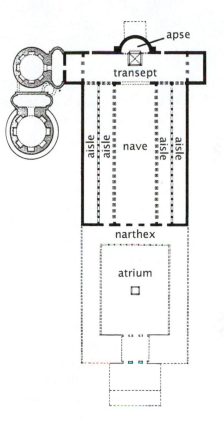

8.7 Plan of Old St. Peter's, Rome, Italy. ca. 324–400 CE (after Frazer)

8.8 Reconstruction of Old St. Peter's, Rome, Italy, as it appeared ca. 400 CE (after Krautheimer)

8.9 Jacopo Grimaldi, *Interior of Old St. Peter's, Rome*. Drawing, 1619. MS: Barbarini Lat. 2733, fols. 104v–105r. Vatican Library, Rome, Italy

present St. Peter's Basilica, in the Vatican, during the sixteenth and seventeenth centuries, but its appearance is preserved in a seventeenth-century album of copies of earlier drawings (fig. **8.9**), and there are literary descriptions as well. Together these sources give us a clear idea of the original plan for the church. Begun as early as 319 and finished by 329, Old St. Peter's was built on the Vatican Hill next to a pagan burial ground. It stood directly over the grave of St. Peter, which was marked by a shrine covered with a **baldacchino**, a canopy that designates a place of honor. As such, Old St. Peter's served as the apostle's martyrium, a building that housed sacred relics or the remains of a holy person. The location of St. Peter's burial spot was the focus of the church, and due to site restrictions, its apse was at the west end of the church, an unusual feature. Rituals were conducted from a portable altar placed before the shrine, using gold and silver implements donated by the emperor himself. (See *Primary Source*, page 244.)

To enter the church, the congregation first crossed a colonnaded court, the **atrium**, which was added toward the end of the fourth century; this feature derived from the Roman basilica. Congregants then passed through the **narthex**, an entrance hall, into the church itself. The steady rhythm of the nave colonnade would have pulled them toward the **triumphal arch** that separates the nave from the apse, which it also serves to frame. The shrine stood at the junction of the nave and the **transept**, a separate space placed perpendicular to the nave and aisles. Spaces at the end of the transept, marked off by columns, might have served to prepare items used during church rites and to hold offerings brought by the faithful.

The main focus of Christian liturgy was, and is, the Mass, which includes the sacrament of Communion, the symbolic

reenactment on the altar of Jesus' sacrifice. The Early Christian basilica encouraged attention to the altar, making it the focal point of the church by placing it opposite the entrance and at the end of a long nave. Even beyond this general emphasis on the altar, Old St. Peter's gave special prominence to the altar zone through its special, additional function as a martyrium.

Although today we think of the practice of religion as an open one, in the early Church only those who had proven themselves Christians could witness the complete performance of the liturgy. It was through baptism that catechumens, those receiving instruction in preparation for their initiation into the new religion, became full-fledged Christians. Before baptism, they could hear, but not see, parts of the Mass. Even today, Christians refer to this as the "mystery" of the Mass.

CENTRAL-PLAN STRUCTURES Buildings of round or polygonal shape capped by a dome entered the tradition of Christian architecture in Constantine's time. Roman emperors had built similar structures to serve as monumental tombs or mausoleums, such as the one Diocletian had built for himself at his palace at Spalato (see fig. 7.63). Not surprisingly, therefore, the Early Christian central-plan building was often associated with funerary functions, as was Santa Costanza, in Rome, the mausoleum of Constantine's daughter Constantia (figs. **8.10** and **8.11**). Built over a catacomb, it was originally attached to the now-ruined basilican church of Sant'Agnese fuori le mura (St. Agnes Outside the Walls). The focus of the building is the central space, illuminated by clerestory windows, over which rises a dome supported by twelve pairs of columns. Four of the arches of this colonnade stand slightly higher than the others

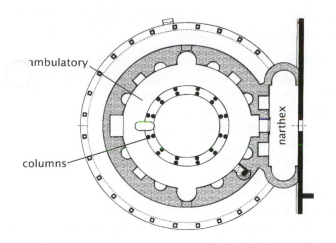

8.10   Plan of Santa Costanza, Rome, Italy. ca. 350 CE

8.11   Interior (view through ambulatory into rotunda) of Santa Costanza, Rome, Italy

the building, the central plan, as seen in Santa Costanza, spins the section on axis, accentuating the center. You can see this clearly by comparing figures 8.9 and 8.11.

MERGING THE BASILICAN AND CENTRAL PLANS Since Constantine continued to follow Roman imperial traditions even as he accepted the tenets of Christianity, it is not surprising that when he supported the construction of buildings in the Holy Land to mark places significant in the life of Jesus, he chose plans based on Roman imperial building types, thus accentuating his ambitions for his new religion. The basilican Church of the Holy Sepulcher (fig. **8.12**), in Jerusalem, marked the location where St. Helena, mother of Constantine, had found the True Cross (that is, the cross on which Jesus was crucified as opposed to those crosses on which the thieves who were sentenced to death along with Christ were crucified). Beyond the basilica was the Rotunda of the Anastasis (Greek for "resurrection"), built over the tomb where Christ's body is reputed to have lain for the three days before his resurrection. Although the Constantinian building was subsequently destroyed and later rebuilt in a somewhat different form, this aisled basilica included a **gallery**, a second story placed over the side aisles of a church, increasing the space available for the throngs of pilgrims who flocked to key sites. The apse was ringed with twelve columns, which Eusebius, Constantine's confidant and biographer, equated with Jesus' twelve apostles. (See *Informing Art*, page 273.) In the Anastasis rotunda, too, there would have been a gallery, but in all other ways this rotunda has the same silhouette as Santa Costanza. Both have ambulatories formed by columns arranged around a domed central space, although unlike Santa Costanza's masonry dome, the dome of the Anastasis rotunda was probably made of wood. The similarity of form is not surprising. Both were products of the benefaction of the imperial family and both served funereal functions. As such, their roots in imperial mausoleums are appropriate, even as their forms become conveyers of new meaning. The Church of the Holy Sepulcher complex shares with Old St. Peter's a desire to combine the congregational aspects of a Roman basilica with a martyrium in a monument that eulogizes the deceased whom it commemorates—Christ himself.

and suggest a cross inscribed within a circle. The significance of the cross in a funerary context results from its association with Christ, who, though martyred on a cross, rose victorious over death. The Cross was meaningful to all Christians but particularly to the family of Constantine, whose personal conversion was a result of his vision of the Cross, which had signaled his victory at the Battle of the Milvian Bridge in 312. The sarcophagus of Constantia was originally placed under the eastern, more-elevated arch. Encircling the building is an **ambulatory**, a ring-shaped aisle, covered by a barrel vault (see fig. 7.3).

Central-plan and basilican structures are not as different as they might first appear. In fact, a **section** of a central-plan building parallels a section of a basilican church in that both have a high central space with a **clerestory** flanked by a lower aisle. While the basilica plan stretches this form so that emphasis is on the end of

8.12   Reconstruction of Church of the Holy Sepulcher, Jerusalem, Israel, as it appeared ca. 350 CE (after Conant)

Mosaics

Mosaics—designs composed of small pieces of colored material set in plaster or mortar—had been used by the Sumerians as early as the third millennium BCE to decorate architectural surfaces. The Hellenistic Greeks used pebbles and the Romans, using small cubes of marble called tesserae, had refined the technique to the point that it could be used to copy paintings, as seen in The Battle of Alexander (see fig. 5.78). Although most Roman mosaics were for floors, the Romans also produced wall mosaics, but these were usually reserved for special purposes, for example in fountain rooms or outdoor spaces where fresco would be vulnerable to deterioration.

The extensive and complex wall mosaics of Early Christian art are essentially without precedent. The color scale of Roman mosaics, although rich in gradations, lacked brilliance, since it was limited to the kinds of colored marble found in nature. Early Christian mosaics, by contrast, consist of tesserae made of colored glass, which the Romans had known but never fully exploited. Glass tesserae offered colors, including gold, of far greater range and intensity than marble tesserae. Moreover, the shiny, somewhat irregular faces of glass tesserae, each set slightly askew from its neighbor, act as tiny reflectors, so that the overall effect is like a glittering, immaterial screen rather than a solid, continuous surface. All these qualities made glass mosaic the ideal material for the new architectural aesthetic of Early Christian basilicas.

Glass for tesserae was made by combining sand, soda or potash, and lime with metallic oxides, which determined the resultant hues. Hardened sheets of glass were marked off and cut into tesserae of approximately cubic shape. For gold mosaics, gold leaf was placed on a sheet of glass, then glass, still in liquid form, was applied over it and heat applied to bond the glass layers, effectively embedding the gold leaf within glass.

The mosaic process was labor-intensive, not only to create the design, but also to set the tesserae. Hundreds of thousands of tesserae were needed to cover a church interior, and setting them required skill and training. The process typically began by applying multiple layers of plaster (about 3 inches thick in all) to a wall. Recent investigations have shown that mosaics were generally prepared in situ. A drawing was done directly on the surface to be decorated, which was then painted in order to create a guide for the design. Red was used in areas that were to be covered with gold, since red added richness to the gold ground.

Tesserae were then laid into still-fresh plaster, which was sufficiently soft so that at least half the surface of the tesserae could be submerged; a secure attachment was thus guaranteed. The process required deliberate planning, since only the section of wall that could be finished in a day, roughly the time it would take for plaster to dry, would receive the final coat of plaster into which the tesserae were set.

Some medieval treatises distinguish between *pictores imaginarii* (mosaic painters) and *musearii* (mosaic workers), suggesting a hierarchy in the division of labor. Under any circumstances, mosaic production was a costly enterprise; it has been estimated that it was at least four times more expensive than wall painting. Clearly the aesthetic advantages of mosaics, as well as their durability, were thought sufficient to justify the expense.

Detail of *Good Shepherd*, figure 8.15

ARCHITECTURAL DECORATION: WALL MOSAICS The rapid growth of large-scale Christian architecture had a revolutionary effect on Early Christian pictorial art. All of a sudden, huge wall surfaces had to be covered with images worthy of their monumental framework. Out of this need emerged a new art form, the Early Christian wall mosaic, which to a large extent replaced the older and cheaper medium of mural painting. (See *Materials and Techniques*, above.) The challenge of inventing a body of Christian imagery produced an extraordinary creative outpouring. Large pictorial cycles of subjects selected from the Hebrew and Christian Bibles were spread over the nave walls, the triumphal arch, and the apse. These cycles must have drawn on sources that reflected the whole range of Graeco-Roman painting as well as artistic traditions that had developed in the Christian communities of North Africa and the Near East.

Decoration of fourth-century churches is largely fragmentary or known only from literary accounts; it is in fifth-century churches that we can see the full development of mosaic-decorated Christian structures. During the fifth century, the Late Empire was threatened at all its borders by migrating tribes. Even the capital of the Western Empire at Rome was vulnerable. So the emperor Honorius moved it north, first to Milan, and when that city was besieged in 402, to Ravenna on the Adriatic coast, thought to be more easily defensible than inland sites.

The Mausoleum of Galla Placidia (fig. 8.13) was named after Honorius' sister (who ruled the Empire as regent) because it was believed that she was buried there, though it is likely that it was begun as a chapel dedicated to the martyr St. Lawrence. Its central plan takes the form of a **Greek cross**, that is, a cross with arms equal length. The exterior brick walls of the building, although perhaps originally covered, were always much simpler than the rich

8.13 Mausoleum of Galla Placidia, Ravenna, Italy. 425–50 CE

interior (fig. **8.14**). Having left the everyday world behind, a visitor would encounter a shimmering realm of light and color where precious marble surfaces and glittering mosaics evoke the spiritual splendor of the Kingdom of God. To some extent, the building is analogous to the ideal Christian, simple in external body and glorious in inner spirit, an analogy certainly not missed by early Christians.

The barrel vaults and dome of the Mausoleum of Galla Placidia are covered with luxurious leaflike decoration and fields of stars. Above the vaults, apostles flank a pair of doves and fountains, symbolic of souls drinking from the waters of Paradise. In one lunette, St. Lawrence is shown beside the flame-racked grill on which he was martyred. A cabinet holding books, identified as the four Gospels, reminds us that Lawrence was martyred for refusing to surrender the riches of the Church, here represented as books, to the Roman authorities. That books would be equated with treasure is perhaps not surprising, for, as we shall see, they were luxurious objects that played a vital function within the Church. The books also remind us that Christians referred to themselves as people of the Book, a designation they shared with earlier Hebrew and later Muslim faiths.

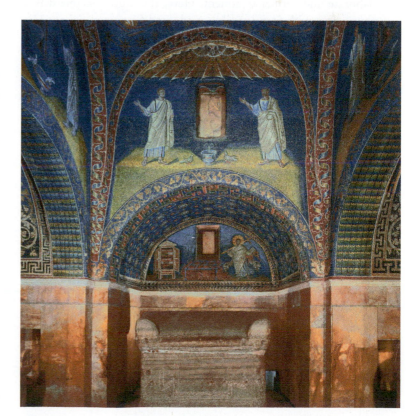

8.14 Interior of Mausoleum of Galla Placidia, Ravenna, Italy

8.15 *Good Shepherd*, Mausoleum of Galla Placidia, Ravenna, Italy. Mosaic

Another lunette contains a mosaic of the Good Shepherd seated in a fully realized landscape (fig. **8.15**), expanding the central subject of so many catacomb paintings with its more elaborate and formal treatment. Here, the Good Shepherd is a young man with many attributes adopted from imperial art. His halo comes from representations of the emperor as sun-king, and his gold robes and purple scarf are traditional signifiers of royal stature. These attributes are appropriate to a commission by the imperial family, but equally significant is the way formal features further the message, and perhaps here there is a paradox. While Christ, with realistically modeled face, flowing hair and garments, sits comfortably in a lush landscape with a sky-blue background, the prevalence of gold denies naturalism to the scene. The paradox is that Christ is at once human, imperial, and of this world, and yet also beyond it, existing within a glimmering ethereal realm of which he is a natural part. Roman mural painting used illusionistic devices to suggest a reality beyond the surface of the wall (see figs. 7.54 and 7.55), whereas Early Christian mosaics used the glitter of gold tesserae to create a luminous realm filled with celestial beings, symbols, or narrative action. Thus, Early Christian mosaics transform the illusionistic tradition of ancient painting with the new Christian message.

The basilica of Santa Maria Maggiore in Rome (fig. **8.16**), built between 432 and 440, was the first church dedicated to Mary, begun only a year after she was declared the *Theotokos* (Greek for "the bearer of god") by the Council of Ephesus. The apse is a later replacement, but the general outline of the original building and much of the mosaic decoration survive. These mosaics include triumphal arch decoration and more than half of the 42 mosaic panels that were placed above the classically inspired entablature of the nave colonnade. Pilasters and colonettes framed these panels. Sadly, much of this architectural decoration is now missing. An enthroned Virgin in the original apse was framed by the triumphal arch, which contains stories from Jesus' infancy—an appropriate introduction to Mary, because of her involvement in those episodes.

The panels above the nave colonnade illustrate scenes from the Hebrew Bible. They combine narration with a concern for structured symmetry. For instance, in the left half of *The Parting of Lot and Abraham* (fig. **8.17**), Abraham, his son Isaac, and the rest of his family depart for the land of Canaan. On the right, Lot and his clan, including his two small daughters, turn toward the city of Sodom. The artist who designed this scene from Genesis 13 faced the same task as the ancient Roman sculptors of the Column of Trajan (see fig. 7.39): He needed to condense complex actions into a form that could be read at a distance. In fact, he employed many of the same shorthand devices, such as the formulas for house, tree, and city, and the device of showing a crowd of people as a cluster of heads, rather like a bunch of grapes.

In the Trajanic reliefs, these devices were used only to the extent that they allowed the artist to portray actual historic events. The mosaics in Santa Maria Maggiore, by contrast, dep the history of human salvation, beginning with scenes from the Hebrew Bible along the nave and ending with the life of Jesus

8.16 Interior of Santa Maria Maggiore, Rome, Italy. ca. 432–40 CE

the Messiah on the triumphal arch. For those who read the Bible literally, the scheme is not only a historical cycle but also a symbolic program that presents a higher reality—the Word of God. Hence, the artist was not concerned with the details of historical narrative. Glances and gestures were more important than realistic movement or three-dimensional form. In *The Parting of Lot and Abraham*, the symmetrical composition, with its gap in the center, makes clear the significance of this parting: Abraham represents the way of righteousness, while Sodom, which was destroyed by the Lord, signifies the way of evil. Beneath *The Parting of Lot and Abraham* is a classically inspired but thoroughly transformed landscape, its shepherds placed on a green ground, while their sheep, as if on little islands, float in gold surroundings.

What were the visual sources of the mosaic compositions at Santa Maria Maggiore and other churches like it? These were certainly not the first depictions of scenes from the Bible. For certain subjects, such as the Last Supper, models could have been found among the catacomb murals, but others, such as the story of Joshua, may have come from illustrated manuscripts, to which, since they were portable, art historians have assigned an important role as models.

8.17 *The Parting of Lot and Abraham* and *Shepherds in a Landscape*, Santa Maria Maggiore, Rome, Italy. Mosaic

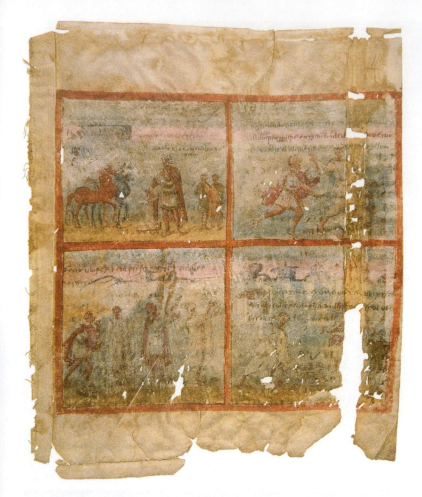

8.18 Scenes from the Book of Kings, from the *Quedlinburg Itala*. ca. 425–450 CE. Tempera on vellum, 12 × 18″ (30.5 × 45.8 cm). Staatliche Bibliothek, Berlin

ILLUSTRATED BOOKS Because Christianity, like Judaism, was based on the Word of God as revealed in the Bible, early Christians sponsored duplication of sacred texts on a large scale. What did the earliest Bible illustrations look like? Since books are frail things, we have only indirect evidence of their history in the ancient world. This begins in Egypt with scrolls made from the papyrus plant, which is like paper but more brittle (see page 77; fig. 3.41). Papyrus scrolls were produced throughout antiquity. Not until the second century BCE, in late Hellenistic times, did better materials become available. These were parchment (bleached animal hide) and **vellum** (a type of parchment noted for its fineness), both of which last far longer than papyrus. They were strong enough to be creased without breaking and thus made possible the kind of bound book we know today, technically called a codex, which appeared sometime in the late first century CE.

Between the second and the fourth centuries CE, the vellum codex gradually replaced the papyrus roll. This change had an important effect on book illustration. Scroll illustrations seem to have been mostly line drawings, since layers of pigment would soon have cracked and come off during rolling and unrolling. Although parchment and vellum were less fragile than papyrus,

they too were fragile mediums. Nevertheless, the codex permitted the use of rich colors, including gold. Hence it could make book illustration—or, as we usually say, **manuscript illumination**—the small-scale counterpart of murals, mosaics, and p pictures. Some questions are still unanswered. When, where, and how quickly did book illumination develop? Were most of the subjects biblical, mythological, or historical? How much of a carryover was there from scroll to codex?

One of the earliest surviving books that illustrate the Bible is an early fifth-century fragment, the so-called *Quedlinburg Itala* (fig. 8.18). The fragment is from an illustrated Book of Kings (one of the 39 books of the Hebrew Bible) that has been calculated to have originally contained some 60 illustrations, each image probably comprising multiple scenes. On the **folio** (manuscript leaf) reproduced here, four scenes depict Saul's meeting with Samuel after the defeat of Amalekites (I Samuel 15:13–33); each scene is framed so as to accentuate the overall unity of the composition. The misty landscape, architectural elements, and sky-blue and pink background recall the antique Roman tradition of atmospheric illusionism of the sort we met in Roman painting (see fig. 7.55).

Visible under the flaking paint in this badly damaged fragment are written instructions to the artist, part of which read, "You make the prophet speaking facing King Saul sacrificing." Apparently the artist was left free to interpret pictorially these written instructions, suggesting the lack of an illustrated model.

Particularly intriguing is the fact that the artist of the Quedlinburg fragment worked together in a Roman **scriptorium**

8.19 Miniature from the *Vatican Vergil*. Early 5th century CE. Tempera on vellum, 8⅝ × 7¼″ (21.9 × 19.6 cm). Biblioteca Apostolica Vaticana, Rome

8.20 *Sarcophagus of Junius Bassus.* ca. 359 CE. Marble, 3'10½" × 8' (1.2 × 2.4 m). Museo Storico del Capitolo di San Pietro, Rome

(a workshop for copying and illustrating manuscripts) with an artist who illustrated the first-century BCE Roman pagan poet Vergil's *Aeneid* and *Georgics* in the so-called *Vatican Vergil*, named after the collection in which it is housed today (fig. **8.19**). We might well ask if this is evidence of non-Christian artists working for Christian patrons and to what extent pagan motifs might have been carried over to Christian subjects.

Like the *Quedlinburg Itala*, the *Vatican Vergil* reflects the Roman tradition of illusionism and is closely linked in style to the mosaics of the contemporaneous Santa Maria Maggiore. The picture, separated from the rest of the page by a heavy frame, is like a window, and in the landscape—similar to that in the *Quedlinburg Itala* in being set off by the pink and blue sky—we find the remains of deep space, **perspective**, and the play of light and shade. The illustration is balanced by beautifully executed letters, which hover over the page like a curtain.

Perhaps it is not accidental that the illusionism in both the *Quedlinburg Itala* and the *Vatican Vergil* reminds us so much of the art of Rome during its glory days, nor that so many architectural features of the contemporaneous Santa Maria Maggiore are so classicizing. All of these works were produced in Rome just when that city was under direct threat; the emphasis on Rome's historic splendor might well have proven comforting during difficult times. However, the political reality was far removed from the lofty ambitions of artists and patrons. Rome was sacked by the Visigoths in 410 and, as noted, the capital of the Western Empire was moved farther north, settling first in Milan, then finally in Ravenna.

SCULPTURE As we have seen, the increase in standing of Christianity had a profound effect on artistic production, moving Christian art from a modest and private sphere to a public and official arena. As Early Christian architecture and its decoration began to demonstrate increasing monumentality as a result of its dependence on Roman imperial traditions, so too Early Christian sculpture became more impressive. This is apparent in a fine Early Christian stone coffin, the *Sarcophagus of Junius Bassus* (fig. **8.20**).

The richly carved sarcophagus was made for a prefect of Rome who died in 359 at age 42 and who, an inscription tells us, had been "newly baptized." The front, divided by columns into ten compartments, contains scenes from the Hebrew Bible and the Christian one, also called the New Testament. In the upper register we see (from left to right) the Sacrifice of Isaac, St. Peter Taken Prisoner, Christ Enthroned Between Sts. Peter and Paul, and Jesus before Pontius Pilate (this last scene composed of two compartments). In the lower register are the Suffering of Job, the Temptation of Adam and Eve, Jesus' Entry into Jerusalem, Daniel in the Lions' Den, and St. Paul Led to His Martyrdom.

Clearly the status of Christianity has changed when a major state official proclaims, both in inscription and through representation, his belief in Christianity. The depictions of Peter and Paul, the veritable official saints of the city of Rome—each is commemorated by a major basilica in the city—can be related to Junius Bassus' role as a high-ranking government official. Authoritative as well is Christ's place in the central scenes of each register. In the top register, Christ is enthroned with his feet treading on a personification of Coelus, the Roman pagan god of the heavens, as he dispenses the law to his disciples. Thus, Christ appropriates one of the emperor's formal privileges, as lawgiver, a role that Junius Bassus as prefect would have exercised on the emperor's behalf. Below this compartment, Christ enters Jerusalem in triumph. As compared to the earliest Christian representations, such as the Santa Maria Antiqua sarcophagus, Christ is now depicted directly, not through allusion alone, and his imperial nature is thereby accentuated. Daniel in the Lions' Den, the Sacrifice of Isaac, and Adam and Eve are subjects that appeared in earlier representations in catacombs. Daniel's salvation is a type for Christ, as well as for all Christians who hope for divine salvation; Abraham's willingness to sacrifice his beloved son Isaac parallels God's sacrifice on the Cross of his son, Jesus Christ; the fact that God spares Isaac speaks of salvation by Divine Grace; Adam and Eve refer to the Original Sin that led to Christ's sacrificial death and his resurrection. Thus, old methods of explication are combined with new manifestations of Christianity's important role in society, particularly by stressing Christ's imperial nature.

The style of the sarcophagus also relies on imperial convention. This is most evident in the elements of classicism that are expressed, such as the placement within deep, space-filled niches of figures that recall the dignity of Greek and Roman sculpture. Other classicizing features include the way that the figures seem capable of distributing weight, the draperies that reveal the bodies beneath them, and the narrative clarity. However, beneath this veneer of classicism we recognize doll-like bodies with large heads and a passive air in scenes that would otherwise seem to call for dramatic action. It is as if the events and figures are no longer intended to tell their own story but to call to mind a larger symbolic meaning that unites them.

The reliance on classicizing forms on the *Sarcophagus of Junius Bassus* reminds us that Early Christian art appears throughout the Mediterranean basin in what we think of as the classical world. During the first five centuries after Jesus' death, the art of the entire area was more or less unified in content and style. Increasing political and religious divisions in the region, however, began to affect artistic production so that it is appropriate to recognize the appearance, or, perhaps better stated, the growth of another branch of Christian art that we label Byzantine.

BYZANTINE ART

Early Byzantine Art

There is no clear-cut geographical or chronological line between Early Christian and Byzantine art. West Roman and East Roman—or, as some scholars prefer to call them, Western and Eastern Christian—traits are difficult to separate before the sixth century. Until that time, both geographical areas contributed to the development of Early Christian art. As the Western Empire declined, however, cultural leadership tended to shift to the Eastern Empire. This process was completed during the reign of Justinian, who ruled the Eastern Empire from 527 to 565. Under the patronage of Justinian, Constantinople became the artistic as

well as the political capital of the Empire. Justinian himself was a man of strongly Latin orientation, and he almost succeeded in reuniting Constantine's domain. The monuments he sponsored have a grandeur that justifies the claim that his era was a Golden Age, as some have labeled it.

The political and religious differences between East and West became an artistic division as well. In Western Europe, Celtic and Germanic peoples inherited the civilization of Late Antiquity, of which Early Christian art had been a part, but they then transformed it radically. The East, in contrast, experienced no such break. Late Antiquity lived on in the Byzantine Empire, although Greek and other eastern Mediterranean elements came increasingly to the fore at the expense of the Roman heritage. Even so, a sense of tradition played a central role in the development of Byzantine art.

ARCHITECTURE AND ITS DECORATION Ironically, the greatest number of Early Byzantine monuments survives today not in Constantinople, where much has been destroyed, but on Italian soil, in Ravenna. That town, as we have seen, had become the capital of the West Roman emperors at the beginning of the fifth century. At the end of the century it was taken by Theodoric, king of the Ostrogoths, whose tastes were patterned after those of Constantinople, where he had lived for an extended period. The Ostrogothic rule of Ravenna ended in 540, when the Byzantine general Belisarius conquered the city for Justinian. Ravenna then became an exarchate, or provincial capital, the main stronghold of Byzantine rule in Italy. Thus, Ravenna serves as a kind of microcosm of the transformation and divisions of the later Roman Empire.

8.21 Plan of San Vitale, Ravenna, Italy. 526–47 CE

8.22 Section of San Vitale, Ravenna, Italy

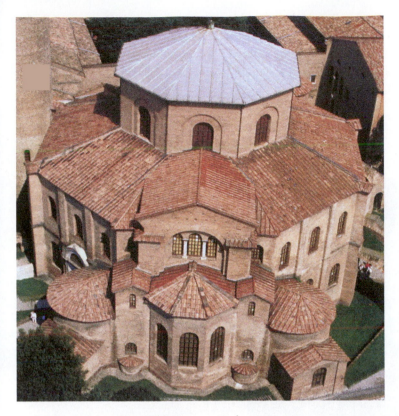

8.23 Exterior of San Vitale, Ravenna, Italy

The most important building of the Early Byzantine period, begun in 526 under Ostrogothic rule, was the church of San Vitale. Built chiefly during the 540s and completed in 547, it represents a Byzantine building of a type derived mainly from Constantinople. The octagonal plan with a circular core ringed by an ambulatory (figs. **8.21**, **8.22** and **8.23**) is a descendant of the mausoleum of Santa Costanza in Rome (see fig. 8.10), but other aspects of the building show the influence of the Eastern Empire, where domed churches of various kinds had been built during the previous century. Compared to Santa Costanza, San Vitale is both larger in scale and significantly richer in spatial effect (fig. **8.24**). In particular, below the clerestory, the nave wall turns into a series of semicircular niches that penetrate the ambulatory and link that surrounding aisle to the nave in a new and intricate way. The movement around the center space is thus enlivened so that the decorated surfaces seem to pulsate. The aisle itself has a second story, the galleries, which may have been reserved for women. This reflects a practice in a number of Eastern religions, including some forms of Judaism, where it is current even today. Large windows on every level are made possible by a new economy in the construction of the vaulting—hollow clay tubes allowing for a lighter structure—and the interior is flooded with light.

The plan of San Vitale shows only remnants of the longitudinal axis of the Early Christian basilica: toward the east,

8.24 Interior (view toward the apse) of San Vitale, Ravenna, Italy

a cross-vaulted compartment for the altar, backed by an apse; and on the other side, a narthex. How did it happen that the East favored a type of church building (as distinct from mausoleums) so different from the basilica and—from the Western point of view—so ill-adapted to Christian ritual? After all, had not the design of the basilica been backed by the authority of Constantine himself? Scholars have suggested a number of reasons, practical, religious, and political, including the particular needs of the

Eastern liturgy that would have been practiced in Ravenna. All of them may be relevant. In any event, from the time of Justinian, domed, central-plan churches dominated the world of Orthodox Christianity as thoroughly as the basilican plan dominated architecture of the medieval West.

At San Vitale the odd, nonsymmetrical placement of the narthex, which has never been fully explained, might be a key to helping us understand how the building functioned. Some have

8.25 *Emperor Justinian and His Attendants*, San Vitale, Ravenna, Italy. ca. 547 CE. Mosaic

8.26 *Empress Theodora and Her Attendants*, San Vitale, Ravenna, Italy. ca. 547 CE. Mosaic

suggested that the narthex is turned to be parallel to an atrium, the axis of which was determined by site limitations. Others see it as a conscious design feature that accentuates the transition between exterior and interior of the church. Whatever the reason, in order to enter the building, visitors were forced to change axis, shifting to the right or left in order to align themselves with the main apse. The alteration of the journey into the building is unsettling, almost disorienting, an effect heightened by passing from the lighted area of the narthex to the shaded ambulatory, and then into the high and luminous domed center space. The passage from physical to spiritual realms so essential to worship is manifest as a separation between the external world and the internal space of the building.

The complexity of the architecture of the interior is matched by its lavish decoration. San Vitale's link with the Byzantine court can be seen in two prominent mosaics flanking the altar (figs. **8.25** and **8.26**). They depict Justinian and his empress, Theodora, accompanied by officials, the local clergy, and ladies-in-waiting,

about to enter the church, as if it were a palace chapel. In these large panels, the design of which most likely came from an imperial workshop, we find an ideal of beauty that is very different from the squat, large-headed figures we met in the art of the fourth and fifth centuries. These figures are tall and slim, with tiny feet and small almond-shaped faces dominated by huge eyes. They seem capable only of making ceremonial gestures and displaying magnificent costumes. There is no hint of movement or change. The dimensions of time and earthly space, suggested by a green ground, give way to an eternal present in the form of a golden otherworldly setting. Hence, the solemn, frontal images seem to belong as much to a celestial court as to a secular one. The quality of soaring slenderness that endows the figures with an air of mute exaltation is shared by the mysterious interior space of San Vitale, which these figures inhabit.

The union of political and spiritual authority expressed in these mosaics reflects the "divine kingship" of the Byzantine emperor and honors the royal couple as donors of the church. It is as though the mosaic figures are in fact participating in the liturgy, even though the empress and emperor are actually thousands of miles away. The embroidery on the hem of Theodora's mantle shows the three Magi carrying their gifts to Mary and the newborn King, and like them the imperial couple bring offerings. Justinian brings bread and Theodora a chalice, undoubtedly references to the Eucharist and Jesus' sacrifice of his own flesh and blood to redeem humanity. The emperor is flanked by 12 companions, the imperial equivalent of the 12 apostles. Moreover, Justinian is portrayed in a manner that recalls Constantine, that first Christian emperor: The shield with Christ's monogram equates Justinian's conquest of Ravenna with the divinely inspired Constantinian triumph at the Milvian Bridge that ultimately led to the founding of Constantinople, the court to which Justinian was heir.

Among the surviving monuments of Justinian's reign in Constantinople, the most important by far is Hagia Sophia (Church of Holy Wisdom) (figs. **8.27** and **8.28**). The first church on that site was commissioned by Constantine but was destroyed

8.27 Plan of Anthemius of Tralles and Isidorus of Miletus. Hagia Sophia, Istanbul, Turkey. 532–37 CE (after V. Sybel)

8.28 Exterior of Hagia Sophia, Istanbul, Turkey

8.29 Interior of Hagia Sophia, Istanbul, Turkey

in 532 during rioting that almost deposed Justinian, who immediately rebuilt the church, a sign of the continuity of his imperial authority. Completed in only five years, Hagia Sophia achieved ıh fame that the names of the architects, too, were remembered: Anthemius of Tralles, an expert in geometry and the theory of statics and kinetics; and Isidorus of Miletus, who taught physics and wrote on vaulting techniques. The dome collapsed in the earthquake of 558, and a new, taller one was built from a design by Isidorus' nephew. After the Turkish conquest in 1453, the church became a **mosque**. The Turks added four **minarets** and extra buttresses to the exterior at that time (see fig. 8.28), as well as large medallions with Islamic invocations on the interior (fig. 8.29). In the twentieth century, after the building was turned into a museum, some of the mosaic decoration that had been largely hidden under whitewash was uncovered.

Hagia Sophia has the longitudinal axis of an Early Christian basilica, but the central feature of the nave is a vast, squarish space crowned by a huge dome (see fig. 8.27). At either end are half-domes, so that the nave takes the form of a great ellipse. Attached to the half-domes are semicircular apses with open **arcades** (a series of arches) similar to those in San Vitale. One might say, then, that the dome of Hagia Sophia has been placed over a central space and, at the same time, inserted between the two halves of a divided central-plan church. The dome rests on four arches that carry its weight to the **piers**, large, upright architectural supports, at the corners of the square. Thus, the brilliant gold-mosaic walls below these arches, pierced with windows, have no weight-iring function at all and act as mere curtains. The transition from the square formed by the arches to the circular rim of the dome is achieved by spherical triangles called **pendentives** (fig. 8.30). Hence, we speak of the entire unit as a dome on pendentives. This device, along with a new technique for building domes using thin bricks embedded in mortar, permits the construction of taller, lighter, and more economical domes than the older method of placing the dome on a round or polygonal base as, for example, in the Pantheon in Rome (see fig. 7.24).

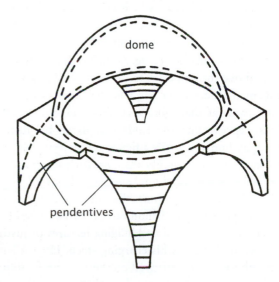

8.30 Dome on pendentives

Where or when the dome on pendentives was invented we do not know. Hagia Sophia is the earliest example we have of its use on a monumental scale, and it had a lasting impact. It became a basic feature of Byzantine architecture and, later, of Western architecture as well. Given the audacity of Hagia Sophia's design, it is not surprising that its architects were not described as builders, but rather as theoretical scientists, renowned for their knowledge of mathematics and physics. Its massive exterior, firmly planted upon the earth like a great mound, rises by stages to a height of 184 feet—41 feet taller than the Pantheon—and therefore its dome, though its diameter is somewhat smaller (112 feet), stands out far more boldly in its urban setting.

Once we are inside Hagia Sophia (see fig. 8.29), all sense of weight disappears. Nothing remains but a space that inflates, like so many sails, the apses, the pendentives, and the dome itself. The first dome, the one that fell in 558, was less steep than the present one, and one imagines that the sense of swelling form and heaving surface would originally have been even more intense than it is today. Here, the architectural aesthetic we saw taking shape in Early Christian architecture has achieved a new, magnificent dimension. Even more than before, light plays a key role. The dome seems to float—"like the radiant heavens," according to a contemporary description—because it rests upon a closely spaced row of windows; light, both real and reflected, virtually separates the dome from the arches on which it rests. So many openings pierce the nave walls that the effect is akin to the transparency of lace curtains. The golden glitter of the mosaics must have completed the "illusion of unreality." Its purpose is clear. As Procopius, the court historian to Justinian, wrote: "Whenever one enters this church to pray, he understands at once that it is not by any human power or skill, but by the influence of God, that this work has been so finely turned. And so his mind is lifted up toward God and exalted, feeling that He cannot be far away, but must especially love to dwell in this place that He has chosen." (See *Primary Source*, page 260.) We can sense the new aesthetic even in ornamental details such as moldings and capitals (fig. 8.31). The scrolls, acanthus leaves, and similar decorations are motifs derived from classical architecture, but their effect here is radically different. The heavily patterned butterfly-marble facing of the piers denies their substantiality, and instead of actively cushioning the impact of heavy weight on the shaft of the column, the capital has become like an openwork basket of starched lace, the delicate surface pattern of which belies the strength and solidity of the stone. The contrast between the decoration of these structural members and their weight-bearing function accentuates the viewer's disorientation, an effect that would only have been increased if the interior of the building were viewed from aisle or gallery. In fact, it is from there that most congregants would have experienced the building during religious services, with no opportunity to take in or understand the entire structure.

The guiding principle of Graeco-Roman architecture had been to express a balance of opposing forces, rather like the balance within the contrapposto of a Classical statue. The result was a muscular display of active and passive members. In comparison,

Procopius of Caesarea (Sixth Century)

From Buildings

Procopius was a historian during the reign of Emperor Justinian. He wrote an entire book (ca. 550 CE) about the fortifications, aqueducts, churches, and other public buildings constructed by Justinian throughout the Byzantine Empire. The book begins with the greatest of these, Hagia Sophia (see figs. 8.27–8.31).

The emperor, disregarding all considerations of expense, raised craftsmen from the whole world. It was Anthemius of Tralles, the most learned man in the discipline called engineering, that ministered to the emperor's zeal by regulating the work of the builders and preparing in advance designs of what was going to be built. He had as partner another engineer called Isidore, a native of Miletus.

So the church has been made a spectacle of great beauty, stupendous to those who see it and altogether incredible to those who hear of it. It subtly combines its mass with the harmony of its proportions, having neither any excess nor any deficiency, inasmuch as it is more pompous than ordinary [buildings] and considerably more decorous than those which are huge beyond measure; and it abounds exceedingly in gleaming sunlight. You might say that the [interior] space is not illuminated by the sun from the outside, but that the radiance is generated within, so great an abundance of light bathes this shrine all round....Above the arches the construction rises in a circle. Rising above this circle is an enormous spherical dome which makes the building exceptionally beautiful. It seems not to be founded on solid masonry, but to be suspended from heaven by that golden chain and so covers the space. All of these elements, marvelously fitted together in mid-air, suspended from one another and reposing only on the parts adjacent to them, produce a unified and most remarkable harmony in the work, and yet do not allow the spectators to rest their gaze upon any one of them for a length of time, but each detail readily draws and attracts the eye to itself. Thus the vision constantly shifts round, and the beholders are quite unable to select any particular element which they might admire more than all the others. No matter how much they concentrate their attention on this side and that, and examine everything with contracted eyebrows, they are unable to understand the craftsmanship and always depart from there amazed by the perplexing spectacle.

Source: Cyril Mango, *The Art of the Byzantine Empire, 312–1453: Sources and Documents* (Upper Saddle River, NJ: Prentice Hall, 1st ed., 1972)

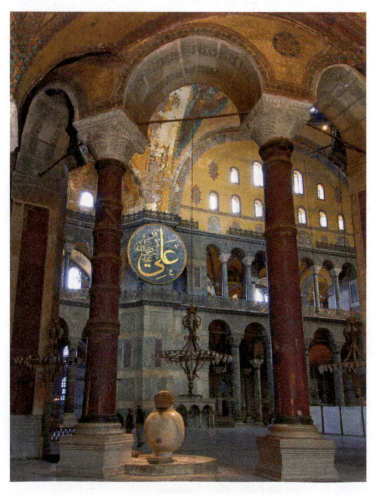

8.31　Arcade and capitals, Hagia Sophia, Istanbul, Turkey

the material structure of Byzantine architecture, and to some extent of Early Christian architecture as well, is subservient to the creation of immaterial space. Walls and vaults seem li weightless shells, their actual thickness and solidity hidden rather than emphasized. And the glitter of the mosaics must have completed the illusion of unreality, fitting the spirit of these interiors to perfection.

SCULPTURE Beyond architectural decorations and some sarcophagi, Early Byzantine sculpture consists mainly of reliefs in ivory and silver, which survive in considerable numbers. Vestiges of classicism are apparent in the beautifully carved ivory diptych of *Justinian as Conqueror*, which celebrates the emperor's victories in Italy, North Africa, and Asia (fig. **8.32**). The subject restates in Christian terms the allegorical scene on the breastplate of the *Augustus of Primaporta* (see fig. 7.29). The figure of Victory appears twice: above the emperor, to his right, and as a statuette held by the Roman officer at the left, who was no doubt mirrored in the missing panel at the right. Scythians, Indians, even lions and elephants, representing the lands conquered by Justinian, offer gifts and pay homage, while a figure personifying the Earth supports Justinian's foot to signify the emperor's dominion over the entire world. His role as triumphant general and ruler of the Empire is blessed from Heaven (note the sun, moon, and star) by Christ, whose image is in a medallion carried by two heraldically arranged angels. The large head and bulging features of Justinia brim with the same energy as his charging steed. He is a far ci from the calm philosopher portrayed on the *Equestrian Statue of Marcus Aurelius* (see fig. 7.33) from which the image is derived.

8.32 *Justinian as Conqueror.* ca. 525–50 CE. Ivory, 13½ × 10½″ (34.2 × 26.8 cm). Musée du Louvre, Paris

8.33 *The Archangel Michael.* Leaf of a diptych. Early 6th century CE. Ivory, 17 × 5½″ (43.3 × 14 cm). The British Museum, London

An ivory relief showing the archangel Michael (fig. **8.33**), also from the time of Justinian, looks back to earlier classical ivories. It may have been paired with a missing panel showing Justinian, who, it has been suggested, commissioned it. The inscription above has the prayer "Receive these gifts, and having learned the cause…," which would probably have continued on the missing leaf with a plea to forgive the owner's sins, apparently a reference to the emperor's humility. In any event, this ivory must have been done around 520–30 by an imperial workshop in Constantinople.

The majestic archangel is a descendant of the winged Victories of Graeco-Roman art, down to the rich drapery revealing lithe limbs (see fig. 5.47), and recalls the Victories on the plaque of *Justinian as Conqueror* (see fig. 8.32). Here, classicism has become an eloquent vehicle for Christian content. The power the angel heralds is not of this world, nor does he inhabit an earthly space. The niche he occupies has lost all three-dimensional reality. The angel's relationship to its architectural setting is purely symbolic and ornamental, so that, given the position of the feet on the steps, he seems to hover rather than stand. From the ankles down he seems to be situated between the columns, while his arms and wings are in front of them. It is this disembodied quality, conveyed through harmonious forms, that makes the archangel Michael's presence so compelling. The paradox of a believable figure represented naturalistically but existing within an ambiguous, indeed impossible, setting connects this work with other products of Justinian's court, such as those buildings where solid structures serve to create ephemeral spaces.

ILLUSTRATED BOOKS Illustrated books of the Early Byzantine period also contain echoes of Graeco-Roman style adapted to religious narrative. The most important example, the *Vienna Genesis* (fig. **8.34**), containing a Greek text of the first book of the Bible, has a richness similar to the mosaics we have seen. White highlights and fluttering drapery that clings to the bodies animate the scene. The book was written in silver (now tarnished black) and decorated with brilliantly colored miniatures on dyed-purple

vellum, that color being reserved for the imperial court. Although some scholars have suggested that an imperial scriptorium in Constantinople produced the manuscript, recent research points to Syria as the more likely source because there are parallel manuscripts produced there, as well as some Syrian mosaics.

Our page shows a number of scenes from the story of Jacob. In the center foreground, Jacob wrestles with the angel and then receives his blessing. Hence, the picture does not show just a single event but a whole sequence. The scenes take place along a U-shaped path, so that progression in space becomes progression in time. This method, known as **continuous narration**, goes back as far as ancient Egypt and Mesopotamia. Its appearance in miniatures such as this may reflect earlier illustrations made in

8.34 *Jacob Wrestling the Angel*, from the *Vienna Genesis*. Early 6th century CE. Tempera and silver on dyed vellum, 13¼ × 9½" (33.6 × 24.1 cm). Österreichische Nationalbibliothek, Vienna

scroll rather than book form, although this hypothesis has been contested. The picture certainly looks like a frieze turned back upon itself. For manuscript illustration, continuous narrative ___es the most economical use of space. The painter can pack ___ximum number of scenes into a small area, and the picture can be read like lines of text as a running account, rather than as a window that requires a frame.

ICONS The religious **icon** (from the Greek word *eikon*, meaning "image") provided another focus for representation at the time of Justinian. Icons generally took Christ, the Enthroned Madonna, or saints as their principal subjects, and were objects of personal as well as public veneration. From the beginning they were considered portraits, for such pictures had developed in Early Christian times out of Graeco-Roman portrait panels. The issue that they might be considered idols led to arguments about their appropriateness and their power. (See *Primary Source*, page 266.) These discussions related to the contemporaneous debates on the dual nature of Christ as God and man, at once both spiritual and physical—debates that Byzantine emperors had no qualms about joining. One of the chief arguments in favor of image production was the claim that Christ had appeared with the Virgin to St. Luke and permitted him to paint their portrait together, and that other portraits of Christ or of the Virgin had miraculously appeared on earth by divine command. These "true" sacred images were considered to have been the sources for the later ones made by human artists, permitting a chain of copies ___ copies of copies, which has often made it difficult for art historians to date them.

Icons functioned as living images to instruct and inspire the worshiper. (See www.myartslab.com.) Because the actual figure— be it Christ, Mary, a saint, or an angel—was thought to reside in the image, icons were believed to be able to intercede on behalf of the faithful. They were reputed to have miraculous healing properties, and some were carried into battle or placed over city gates, effectively offering totemic protection to their communities. Describing an icon of the archangel Michael, the sixth-century poet Agathias writes: "The wax remarkably has represented the invisible....The viewer can directly venerate the archangel [and] trembles as if in his actual presence. The eyes encourage deep thoughts; through art and its colors the innermost prayer of the viewer is passed to the image."

Little is known about the origins of icons, since most early examples were intentionally destroyed by those who believed they led to idolatry; hence icons are scarce. The irony of this is particularly poignant, since early icons were painted in encaustic, the medium in which pigment is suspended in hot wax, chosen for its durability.

Many of the surviving early examples come from the Monastery of St. Catherine at Mount Sinai in Egypt. Monasteries, ___h as that at Mount Sinai, were heirs to a tradition that had ___eloped in Egypt in the second and third centuries, whereby people withdrew from society and its material temptations to devote themselves to prayer and contemplation. Although many

of these early ascetics lived alone as hermits, increasingly they gathered together to live in monasteries, communities governed by a series of regulations, called the Rule. (See www.myartslab.com.) The Rule that was followed determined the type, or Order, of the monastic community. By the fifth century, monasticism had spread north into Italy, across the Continent, and throughout western Britain and Ireland.

The isolated desert location of Sinai and its remove from the material world aided the survival of numerous objects there. An icon of Christ (fig. **8.35**), generally dated to sometime in the sixth century but with later repainting, is magnificent for its freshness of color and vibrancy of brushstroke. Its link with

8.35 *Christ*, Monastery of St. Catherine, Mount Sinai, Egypt. 6th century CE. Encaustic on panel, 34 × 17⅞″ (84 × 45.5 cm)

8.36 *Virgin and Child Enthroned Between Saints and Angels*, Monastery of St. Catherine, Mount Sinai, Egypt. Late 6th century CE. Encaustic on panel, 27 × 19⅜″ (68.5 × 49.2 cm)

Graeco-Roman portraiture is clear not only from the use of encaustic but also from the gradations of light and shade in Christ's face and on his neck, reminiscent of the treatment of the woman in our Roman Fayum portrait, also in encaustic (see fig. 7.47). The combination of a frontal, unflinching gaze, establishing a direct bond with the viewer, with the lively and lifelike modeling of the face suggests the kind of dichotomy between spiritual and physical that we have seen in so much Early Byzantine art. That dichotomy is accentuated here by the enormous gold halo

hovering over an architectural background. It is as if the walls retreat into the background in response to the halo and in order to allow space for Christ.

The *Virgin and Child Enthroned Between Saints and Angels* icon (fig. 8.36), also from the Monastery of St. Catherine at Mount Sinai, is striking for the variety of styles used to represe the different figure types. The Virgin and Christ are large, th modeled faces help convey with some delicacy their solidity, while the two warrior saints, probably Theodore on the left and

George (or Demetrios) on the right, recall the stiff figures that accompany Justinian in San Vitale (see fig. 8.25). Typically for early icons, however, their heads are too large for their doll-like [bodi]es. Behind are two almost ethereal angels looking skyward; [both] resemble Roman representations. It is typical of the conservative icon tradition that an artist would remain faithful to his varied sources in order to preserve the likenesses of the holy figures; yet it is also possible that different styles in the same work are considered appropriate for the differing religious roles the portrayed personages play. For example, the Virgin's pose signals that for the Byzantines the Madonna was the regal mother, the *Theotokos*, while the stiff formality of the soldier saints is appropriate to represent stalwart defenders of the faith.

The Iconoclastic Controversy

After the time of Justinian, the development of Byzantine art—not only painting but sculpture and architecture as well—was disrupted by the so-called Iconoclastic Controversy. The conflict, which began with an edict promulgated by the Byzantine emperor Leo III in 726 prohibiting religious images, raged for more than 100 years between two hostile groups. The image destroyers, Iconoclasts, led by the emperor and supported mainly in the eastern provinces, insisted on a literal interpretation of the biblical ban against graven images because their use led to idolatry. They wanted to restrict religious art to abstract symbols and plant or animal forms. Their opponents, the Iconophiles, were [led] by the monks and were particularly centered in the western provinces, where the imperial edict remained ineffective for the most part. The strongest argument in favor of icons was Neo-Platonic: Because Christ and his image are inseparable, the honor given to the image is transferred to him. (See *Primary Source*, page 266.)

The roots of the argument go very deep. Theologically, they involved the basic issue of the relationship of the human and the divine in the person of Christ. Moreover, some people resented that, for many, icons had come to replace the Eucharist as the focus of lay devotion. Socially and politically, the conflict was a power struggle between Church and State, which in theory were united in the figure of the emperor. The conflict came during a low point in Byzantine power, when the Empire had been greatly reduced in size by the rise of Islam. **Iconoclasm**, it was argued, was justified by Leo's victories over the Arabs, who were themselves, ironically, iconoclasts. The controversy caused an irreparable break between Catholicism and the Orthodox faith, although the two churches remained officially united until 1054, when the pope excommunicated the Eastern patriarch for heresy.

If the edict barring images had been enforced throughout the Empire, it might well have dealt Byzantine religious art a fatal blow. It did succeed in greatly reducing the production of sacred [im]ages, but it failed to wipe it out entirely, so there was a fairly [ra]pid recovery after the victory of the Iconophiles in 843. The *Khludov Psalter* (fig. **8.37**) was produced soon after that date, perhaps in Constantinople and for use in Hagia Sophia. A **psalter** contains the Book of Psalms from the Hebrew Bible. The Psalms, traditionally believed to have been written by King David, are sacred songs or hymns. The illustration in figure 8.37 accompanies Psalm 69, a plea by the psalmist for salvation from his tormentors. The illustrations not only make the case for why images should be permitted, they also liken the Iconoclasts, identified by inscription, with the crucifiers of Jesus, whose vinegar-soaked sponge is equated with the implements used to whitewash icons.

Middle Byzantine Art

While we know little for certain about how the Byzantine artistic tradition managed to survive from the early eighth to the mid-ninth century, Iconoclasm seems to have brought about a renewed interest in secular art, which was not affected by the ban. This may help to explain the astonishing appearance of antique motifs in the art of the Middle Byzantine period, sometimes referred to as the Second Golden Age. Hence, there was a fairly rapid recovery after the victory of the Iconophiles. A revival of Byzantine

8.37 *The Crucifixion and Iconoclasts*, from the *Khludov Psalter*. After 843 CE. Tempera on vellum, 7¾ × 6″ (19.5 × 15 cm). State Historical Museum, Moscow

St. Theodore the Studite (759–826 CE)

From Second and Third Refutations of the Iconoclasts

Theodore of the Stoudios monastery in Constantinople was a principal defender of icons against the Iconoclasts. St. Theodore refuted their charges of idolatry by examining how an image is and is not identical to its prototype (the person portrayed). Some of his arguments reflect the Neo-Platonic theory expounded by Plotinus that the sense-world is related to the divine by emanation.

Every image has a relation to its archetype; the natural image has a natural relation, while the artificial image has an artificial relation. The natural image is identical both in essence and in likeness with that of which it bears the imprint: thus Christ is identical with His Father in respect to divinity, but identical with His mother in respect to humanity. The artificial image is the same as its archetype in likeness, but different in essence, like Christ and His icon. Therefore there is an artificial image of Christ, to whom the image has its relation.

If every body is inseparably followed by its own shadow, and no one in his right mind could say that a body is shadowless, rather we can see in the body the shadow which follows, and in shadow the body which precedes: thus no one could say that Christ is imageless, if indeed He has a body with its characteristic form, but rather we can see in Christ His image existing by implication and in the image Christ plainly visible as its prototype.

By its potential existence even before its artistic production we can always see the image in Christ; just as, for example, we can see the shadow always potentially accompanying the body, even if it is not given form by the radiation of light. In this manner it is not unreasonable to reckon Christ and His image among things which are simultaneous.

If, therefore, Christ cannot exist unless His image exists in potential, and if, before the image is produced artistically, it subsists always in the prototype: then the veneration of Christ is destroyed by anyone who does not admit that His image is also venerated in Him.

Source: *On the Holy Icons*, tr. Catherine P. Roth. (Crestwood, NY: St. Vladimir's Seminary Press, 1981)

artistic traditions, as well as of classical learning and literature, followed the years of Iconoclasm and lasted from the late ninth to the eleventh century. This revival, spearheaded by Emperor Basil I the Macedonian, was underscored by the reopening of the university in Constantinople.

ILLUSTRATED BOOKS An example of the antique revival is the *Joshua Roll* (fig. **8.38**), illustrated in Constantinople in the middle of the tenth century. Some art historians have seen these illustrations of the Hebrew Bible hero Joshua's victories in the Holy Land as alluding to recent Byzantine military successes against the Muslims there. But there are problems correlating the historical events with the date of the manuscript based on stylistic criteria. It is possible that the manuscript projects aspirations more than it reflects accomplishments. That the manuscript takes the form a scroll, an archaic type of manuscript that had been replaced by the codex a full eight centuries earlier (see page 252), is remarkable. Whether or not scholars who argue that the manuscript is an accurate copy of an earlier scroll are correct, the drawn rather than painted style and the elegantly disposed figures in landscapes

8.38 Page with *Joshua and the Emissaries from Gibeon*, from the *Joshua Roll*. ca. 950 CE. Tempera on vellum, height 12¼" (31 cm). Biblioteca Apostolica Vaticana, Rome. (Cod. Palat. grec. 431)

and against cityscapes give us some idea of what antique examples must have looked like. That such an obsolete, indeed impractical, vehicle as the scroll, whether an original or a copy, was chosen for in a lavish enterprise illustrates why scholars have referred to this period as a renaissance, or rebirth, crediting much of its vigor to Constantine VII, who ruled in the tenth century. Emperor in name only for most of his life, he devoted his energies instead to art and scholarship.

David Composing the Psalms (fig. **8.39**) is one of eight full-page scenes in the mid-tenth-century *Paris Psalter*. Illustrating David's life, these scenes introduce the Psalms, which, as stated above, David was thought to have composed. Not only do we find a landscape that recalls Roman murals (see fig. 7.55), but the figures, too, clearly derive from Roman models. David himself

could well be mistaken for Orpheus charming the beasts with his music. His companions are even more surprising, since they are allegorical figures that have nothing to do with the Bible. The young woman next to David is the personification of Melody, the one coyly hiding behind a pillar is the mountain nymph Echo, and the male figure with a tree trunk personifies the mountains of Bethlehem.

Once again style promotes meaning in the way consciously classical forms herald the revival of image making after the Iconoclastic Controversy. But despite the presence of revivalist aspects, the late date of the picture is evident from certain qualities of style, such as the crowded composition of space-consuming figures and the abstract zigzag pattern of the drapery covering Melody's legs. In truth, one might well ask to what extent and

8.39 *David Composing the Psalms*, from the *Paris Psalter*. ca. 950 CE. Tempera on vellum, 14⅛ × 10¼″ (36 × 26 cm). Bibliothèque Nationale, Paris

8.40 *Harbaville Triptych*. Late 10th century CE. Ivory, 9½ × 11″ (24.1 × 28 cm). Musée du Louvre, Paris

how, despite Iconoclasm, antique methods and forms survived—that is, how much of what we see is the result of continuities rather than revivals.

SCULPTURE Monumental sculpture, as we saw earlier, largely disappeared from the fifth century on. In Byzantine art, large-scale statuary died out with the last imperial portraits, and stone carving was confined almost entirely to architectural ornament. But small-scale reliefs, especially in ivory and metal, continued to be produced in large numbers with a variety of content, style, and purpose. The *Harbaville Triptych* (fig. **8.40**), named after a recent owner, is a portable shrine in ivory with two hinged wings of the kind a high official might carry for his private worship while traveling; despite its monumental presence, it is less than 10 inches high. This triptych, and others like it, serve as a vehicle for private devotion, establishing a parallel between the act of prayer on the part of viewers with the role of the saints who pray for them. In the upper half of the center panel we see Christ Enthroned. Flanking him are John the Baptist and the Virgin, who plead for divine mercy on behalf of humanity. This scene, the so-called **deësis**, was a theme of relatively recent Byzantine invention. Below are five apostles arranged in strictly frontal view. Only in the upper tier of each wing of the triptych is this formula relaxed. There, we find an echo of classical contrapposto in the poses of the military saints in the top registers of the lateral panels. It is possible that we are looking at a continuity of the approach we saw in the early *Virgin and Child Enthroned between Saints and Angels* icon from Mount Sinai (see fig. 8.36), whereby different figure types require different representational modes. Here, the active poses of the military saints contrast with the elegant restraint of the other holy figures, whereas in

8.41 *Christ Crowning Romanos and Eudokia* ("Romanos Ivory"). 945–49 CE. Ivory, 9¾ × 6⅛″ (24.6 × 15.5 cm). Cabinet des Médailles, Bibliothèque Nationale, Paris

the Mount Sinai icon the angels have the active poses and the military saints are static.

Refinement and control also mark the attitude of the figures on the ivory of *Christ Crowning Romanos and Eudokia* (fig. **8.41**), where the authority of the two haloed figures is confirmed by their divine election as emperor and empress. Once again there is some stylistic opposition, perhaps even tension: The body-revealing drapery of Christ contrasts with the stiff, patterned garments of the imperial figures; the ample space that surrounds Christ contrasts with the ambiguous space between the flanking figures and the elevated podium on which Christ stands. Unequivocal, however, as with the *Justinian as Conqueror* ivory (see fig. 8.32), is the message of a relationship between a pious emperor and his god, beneficial to both parties. The imperial couple's elevated relationship to Christ recalls that of John the Baptist and Mary on the *Harbaville Triptych* (see fig. 8.40).

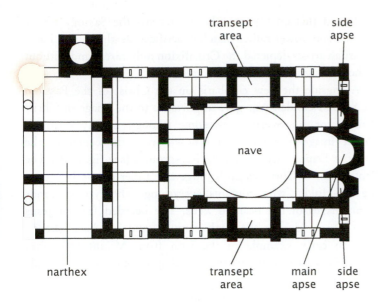

8.42 Plan of Church of the Dormition, Daphni, Greece.
11th century CE

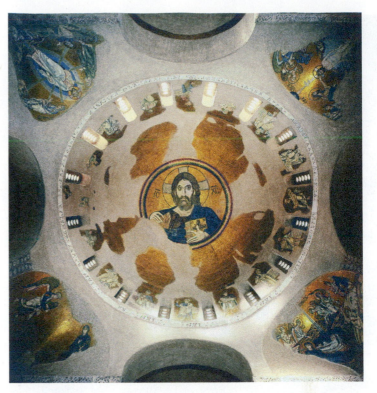

8.44 *Christ Pantocrator*, Church of the Dormition, Daphni, Greece.
Dome mosaics

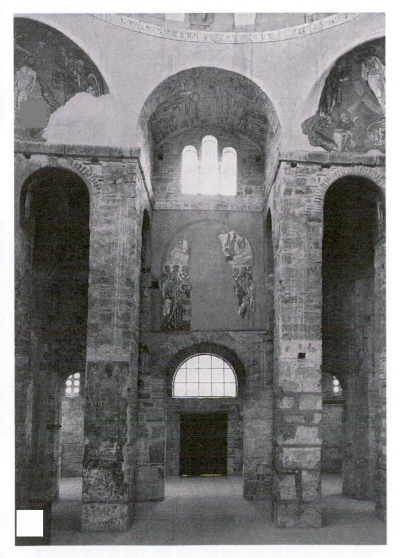

8.43 Interior (facing west) of Church of the Dormition, Daphni, Greece

ARCHITECTURE AND ITS DECORATION Byzantine architecture never produced another structure to match the scale of Hagia Sophia. The churches built after the Iconoclastic Controversy were initially modest in scale and usually monastic, perhaps reflecting the fact that monks had been important in arguing against Iconoclasm; later monasteries erected in Constantinople under imperial patronage were much larger and served social purposes as schools and hospitals. Monasticism dominated the practice of Christianity, and in monastic churches liturgy, ritual, and symbolism were combined in a dynamic manner. The monastic Church of the Dormition at Daphni, near Athens in Greece, follows the usual Middle Byzantine plan of a Greek cross contained within a square, but with a narthex added on one side and an apse on the other (fig. **8.42**). The central feature is a dome on a cylinder, or drum. The drum raises the dome high above the rest of the building and demonstrates a preference for elongated proportions (fig. **8.43**). The impact of this verticality, however, strikes us fully only when we enter the church. The tall, narrow compartments produce both an unusually active space, with abrupt changes of light and shade, and a sense almost of compression. This feeling is dramatically relieved as we raise our glance toward the luminous pool of space beneath the dome, which draws us around and upward (fig. **8.44**). The suspended dome of Hagia Sophia is clearly the conceptual precedent for this form.

The mosaics inside the church at Daphni are some of the finest works of the Second Golden Age. They show a dignity and gravity that merges harmoniously with the spiritualized ideal

8.45 *The Crucifixion*, Church of the Dormition, Daphni, Greece. Mosaic

of human beauty we encountered in the art of Justinian's reign. For instance, the classical qualities of *The Crucifixion* mosaic (fig. **8.45**), on the east wall of the north transept arm of the church, are deeply felt, yet they are also completely Christian. There is no attempt to create a realistic spatial setting, but the composition has a balance and clarity that are truly monumental. The heroic nudity of Christ and the statuesque dignity of the two flanking figures make them seem extraordinarily organic and graceful compared to the stiff poses in the Justinian and Theodora mosaics at San Vitale (see figs. 8.25 and 8.26).

This new interest in depicting the crucified Christ, that is, the Christ of the Passion, seems more emotional than physical. In the Daphni *Crucifixion* mosaic, Christ is flanked by the Virgin and St. John. The gestures and facial expressions of all three figures convey a restrained and noble suffering. We cannot say when and where this human interpretation of the Savior first appeared, but it seems to have developed in the wake of the Iconoclastic Controversy. There are, to be sure, a few earlier examples of it, but none of them appeals to the emotions of the viewer so powerfully as the Daphni *Crucifixion*. To have introduced this compassionate view of Christ into sacred depiction was perhaps the greatest achievement of Middle Byzantine art. Early Christian

art lacked this quality entirely. It stressed the Savior's divine wisdom and power rather than his sacrificial death. Hence, Early Christian artists depicted the Crucifixion only rarely and without pathos, though with a similar simplicity.

Alongside the new emphasis on the Christ of the Passion, the Second Golden Age gave importance to the image of Christ Pantocrator, an oversize, awesome (though heavily restored) mosaic image of which stares down from the center of the dome at Daphni against a gold background (see fig. 8.44). The Pantocrator is Christ as both Judge and Ruler of the Universe, the All-Holder who contains everything. The type descends from images of the bearded Zeus. The bearded face of Jesus first appears during the sixth century, and we have already seen an early example in the icon from Mount Sinai (see fig. 8.35). Once again, tradition and innovation mark Middle Byzantine achievements.

These two mosaic images are part of a larger comprehensive program that served a special spiritual function. (See www.myartslab.com.) Otto Demus, writing in 1948, felicitously described Middle Byzantine churches such as the one at Daphni as a cosmos, the dome representing the heavens, while the vaults and the **squinches**, those devices, similar to pendentives, used to cut the corners of the square space below to make a transition to the cylinder above, signify the Holy Land (see figs. 8.43 and 8.44). The walls and supports below form the earthly world. Thus, there is a hierarchy of level, increasing verticality being equated with degrees of holiness, a sense of which is reinforced by the physical experience of the building's upward spiral pull. The beholder is on the lowest level; the saints are on the walls and supports (visible in fig. 8.43); events in the life of Jesus that took place in the Holy Land, including the Annunciation, Nativity, Baptism, and Transfiguration, are on the vaults and squinches (figs. 8.43 and 8.44 show the Annunciation in the lower left squinch, while the other scenes move around in a counterclockwise direction); and the Pantocrator is in the dome above (see fig. 8.44). Taken together, these representations illustrate the Orthodox belief in the Incarnation as the redemption of Original Sin and the triumph over death.

The movement around the building to witness the Christological cycle, which depicts the events of Christ's life, makes viewers, in effect, symbolic pilgrims to the Holy Land and is combined with a vertical momentum, a virtual personal journey Heavenward. The impression is quite different from the experience of viewers in a Western basilica, even if both attempt to define a spiritual journey through architectural means and in aesthetic terms. In both, passage through space is a means to a goal, but when Orthodox (Eastern) and Catholic (Western) churches are compared, the manner and direction of movement is very different indeed. The decoration at Daphni, magnificent as it is, survives only in fragmentary state. The Venetians desecrated the church in 1207 and in the 1890s earthquake damage was severe. As a result of these vicissitudes, the mosaics were heavily restored and the marble revetment that covered the walls is now missing, the exposed stone and brick giving the building a too-sturdy

46　Aerial view of St. Mark's, Venice, Italy. Begun 1063 CE

aspect. Also missing, since Daphni lacks the monastic community that was responsible for its creation—today it is a museum—is the experiential quality of chanting clergy, burning incense, and glittering liturgical objects of precious metals.

The largest and most lavishly decorated church of the period that still survives is St. Mark's in Venice (figs. **8.46** and **8.47**), begun in 1063, only nine years after the official schism between the Western and Eastern churches. Venice was a province of Ravenna and for some time, thus, a Byzantine dependency. The Church of St. Mark's was both a palace chapel for the Venetian rulers and a **cathedral** (a bishop's church, so named because it houses the bishop's throne, or *cathedra* in Latin). The church was so extensive, employing five domes in place of Daphni's single dome, that the Classical system used at Daphni had to be expanded here. The present structure replaced two earlier churches of the same name on the site; it is modeled on the Church of the Holy Apostles in Constantinople, which had been rebuilt by Justinian after the riot of 532 and was later destroyed. The Venetians had long been under Byzantine rule, and they remained artistically dependent on the East for many years after they had

8.47　Interior of St. Mark's, Venice, Italy

8.48 Interior of Monreale Cathedral, Italy. ca. 1180–90 CE

become politically and commercially powerful in their own right. Their wish to emulate Byzantium, and Constantinople in particular, is evidence of the great sway that culture and city still held.

At St. Mark's the Greek-cross plan is emphasized, since each arm of the cross has a dome of its own. These domes are not raised on drums. Instead, they are encased in bulbous wooden helmets covered by gilt copper sheeting and topped by ornate **lanterns** (small structures often used to admit light into the enclosed spaces below), so that the domes appear taller and more visible at a distance. (They make a splendid landmark for seafarers.) The spacious interior shows that St. Mark's was meant for the people of a large city rather than a small monastic community such as at Daphni.

The Byzantine manner, transmitted to Italy, became known as the "Greek style." Sometimes it was carried by models from Constantinople, but most often it was brought directly by visiting Byzantine artists. At St. Mark's, Byzantine artists and the locals trained by them executed the mosaics. The "Greek style" also appears in a number of magnificent churches and monasteri in Sicily, a former Byzantine holding that was taken from t Muslims by the Normans in 1091 and then united with southern Italy. The Norman kings considered themselves the equals

Biblical and Celestial Beings

Much of Western art refers to biblical persons and celestial beings. Their names appear in titles of paintings and sculpture and in discussions of subject matter. The following is a brief guide to some of the most commonly encountered persons and beings in Christian art.

Patriarchs Literally, patriarchs are the male heads of families, or rulers of tribes. The Hebrew Bible patriarchs are Abraham, Isaac, Jacob, and Jacob's 12 sons. The word *patriarch* may also refer to the bishops of the five chief bishoprics of Christendom: Alexandria, Antioch, Constantinople, Jerusalem, and Rome.

Prophets In Christian art, the word *prophets* usually refers to the Hebrew Bible figures whose writings were seen to foretell the coming of Christ. The so-called major prophets are Isaiah, Jeremiah, and Ezekiel. The minor prophets are Hosea, Joel, Amos, Obadiah, Jonah, Micah, Nahum, Habakkuk, Zephaniah, Haggai, Zechariah, and Malachi.

Trinity Central to Christian belief is the doctrine of the *Trinity* which states that One God exists in Three Persons: Father, Son (Jesus Christ), and Holy Spirit. The Holy Spirit is often represented as a dove.

Holy Family The infant Jesus, his mother Mary (also called the Virgin or the Virgin Mary), and his foster father, Joseph, constitute the *Holy Family*. Sometimes Mary's mother, St. Anne, appears with them.

John the Baptist The precursor of Jesus Christ, John the Baptist is regarded by Christians as the last prophet before the coming of the Messiah in the person of Jesus. John baptized his followers in the name of the coming Messiah; he recognized Jesus as that Messiah when he saw the Holy Spirit descend on Jesus when he came to John to be baptized. John the Baptist is not the same person as John the Evangelist, one the the 12 apostles.

Evangelists There are four: Matthew, Mark, Luke, and John—each an author of one of the Gospels. Matthew and John were among Jesus' 12 apostles. Mark and Luke wrote in the second half of the first century CE.

Apostles/Disciples The apostles are the 12 disciples of Jesus Christ. He asked them to convert the "nations" to his faith. They are Peter (Simon Peter), Andrew, James the Greater, John, Philip, Bartholomew, Matthew, Thomas, James the Less, Jude (or Thaddaeus), Simon the Canaanite, and Judas Iscariot. After Judas betrayed Jesus, his place was taken by Matthias. St. Paul (though not a disciple) is also considered an apostle.

Angels and Archangels Beings of a spiritual nature, angels are spoken of in the Hebrew and Christian Bibles as having been created by God to be heavenly messengers between God and human beings, heaven, and earth. Mentioned first by the apostle Paul, archangels, unlike angels, have names: Michael, Gabriel, and Raphael. In all, there are seven archangels in the Christian tradition.

Saints Persons are declared saints only after death. The pope acknowledges sainthood by canonization, a process based on meeting rigid criteria of authentic miracles and beatitude, or blessed character. At the same time, the pope ordains a public cult of the new saint throughout the Catholic Church. A similar process is followed in the Orthodox Church.

Martyrs Originally, the word *martyr* (from the Greek meaning "witness") referred to each of the apostles. Later, it signified those persecuted for their faith. Still later, the term was reserved for those who died in the name of Christ.

---

of the Byzantine emperors and proved it by calling in teams of mosaicists from Constantinople to decorate their splendid religious buildings. The mosaics at the cathedral of Monreale (fig. **8.48**), are the last examples to be executed in Sicily in a thoroughly Byzantine style, although the selection and distribution of their subjects are largely Western. The wall surfaces these mosaics covered are vast; the largest to be decorated in this technique. The art historian John Lowden has claimed that 100 million individual tesserae would have been needed to create the more than 1½ acres of mosaics at Monreale. The artists adapted their figure types and subjects to a Western building and Western subjects. Certainly masterful is the way the Pantocrator of a Byzantine domed church now controls the space of the apse and the way registers of figures lining the walls define, indeed clarify in a very un-Byzantine way, the basilica form. Even if the composition is unlike that of Byzantine churches of the period in Greece and Constantinople, it does parallel the arrangement of figures on some Middle Byzantine icons and ivories, such as the *Harbaville Triptych* (see fig. 8.40). Christ's open book contains the text "I am the light of the world…" in Greek on one page and in Latin on the other, the schism in language being united through art.

Late Byzantine Art

In 1204, Byzantium suffered an almost fatal defeat when the armies of the Fourth Crusade, instead of warring against the Turks, captured and sacked the city of Constantinople. For more than 50 years, the core of the Eastern Empire remained in Western hands. Byzantium, however, survived this catastrophe. In 1261, it regained its independence, which lasted until the Turkish conquest in 1453. The fourteenth century saw a last flowering of Byzantine painting under a series of enlightened rulers.

ICONS The Crusades decisively changed the course of Byzantine art through bringing it into contact with the West. The impact is apparent in the *Madonna Enthroned* (fig. **8.49**), which unites elements of East and West, so that its authorship has been much debated. Because icons were objects of veneration, and because they embodied sacredness, they had to conform to strict rules, with fixed patterns repeated over and over again. As a result, most icons are noteworthy more for exacting craftsmanship than artistic inventiveness. Although painted at the end of the thirteenth century, our example reflects a much earlier type

8.49 *Madonna Enthroned*. Late 13th century CE. Tempera on panel, 32⅛ × 19⅜″ (81.9 × 49.3 cm). National Gallery of Art, Washington, D.C. Andrew Mellon Collection. 1937.1.1

The total effect is neither flat nor spatial, but transparent—so that the shapes look as if they are lit from behind. Indeed, the gold background and highlights are so brilliant that even the shadows never seem wholly opaque. This all-pervading radia... we will recall, first appears in Early Christian mosaics (see ig. 8.17). Panels such as the *Madonna Enthroned* may therefore be viewed as the aesthetic equivalent of mosaics and not simply as the descendants of the panel-painting tradition. In fact, some of the most precious Byzantine icons are miniature mosaics attached to panels, and our artist may have been trained as a mosaicist rather than as a painter.

Although many details relate this icon to Byzantine works, particularly from Constantinople, some scholars claim that it was produced by a Western artist in emulation of Byzantine painting. For example, the manner in which the Enthroned Virgin presents the Christ Child is Byzantine, while the blessing gesture of Christ is Western. The red background of the angels in medallions is another feature found in the West rather than in Byzantium. An origin in Cyprus, then ruled by the French, has been suggested, but where this work was painted remains an open question. The controversy is heightened by the fact that the icon was subjected to a very heavy restoration before it arrived at the National Gallery in Washington, D.C. Whatever its origin, the *Madonna Enthroned* points to a profound shift in the relationship between the two traditions: After 600 years of borrowing from Byzantium, Western art has begun to contribute something in return.

An icon from Ohrid, in Macedonia, though probably made Constantinople, illustrates a type distinct from those we have seen previously in that it relates a narrative event, the Annunciation to the Virgin of her imminent role as Mother of God (fig. **8.50**). The increased interest in narrative subjects for icons might derive from the elaborate decorative programs in Middle Byzantine churches. This icon is bilateral (or two-sided). On the other side, the Virgin Mary, to whom the church at Ohrid was dedicated, is represented holding her son. Such icons were probably meant to be mounted on a pole, both for processions and for placement within churches, where worshipers would have been able to view both sides.

The gold background heightens the tension of the spatial relationship established between the archangel Gabriel and the Virgin. The former both cuts through space and slides across it, while the latter seems boxed in by the canopy that frames and encloses her. In the sharpness of their folds, Gabriel's garments appear almost metallic. These contrast with the dark robes of the Virgin. One can imagine how moved a viewer might have been by personal contact with this imposing icon, which measures more than 3 feet high.

MOSAICS AND MURAL PAINTING The finest surviving cycles of Late Byzantine mosaics and paintings are found in Istanbul's Kariye Camii, the former Church of the Savior in the Cho... Monastery. (*Kariye* is the Turkish adaptation of the ancient Gre... word *chora*, which refers to the countryside, that is, outside the city walls; *camii* denotes a mosque, to which the building was

(see fig. 8.36). There are echoes of the Middle Byzantine style in the graceful pose, the play of drapery folds, and the tender melancholy of the Virgin's face. But these elements have become abstract, reflecting a new taste and style in Late Byzantine art. The highlights on the drapery that resemble sunbursts are not a new development, yet they seem more rigid and stylized than in Middle Byzantine examples. Faces are carefully modeled with gentle highlights and suave shading. The linear treatment of drapery in combination with the soft shading of hands and faces continues the long-established Byzantine pattern of having naturalistic and antinaturalistic aspects play off each other in the same work.

8.50 *Annunciation to the Virgin*, from Church of the Virgin Peribleptos, Ohrid, Macedonia. Early 14th century CE. Tempera on panel, 36⅝ × 26¾" (93 × 68 cm). Icon Gallery, Ohrid, Macedonia

8.51 *Anastasis*, Kariye Camii (Church of the Savior in the Chora monastery), Istanbul, Turkey. ca. 1310–20 CE. Fresco

converted after the Turkish conquest, although the site is now a museum.) These particular mosaics and paintings represent the climax of the humanism that emerged in Middle Byzantine art. Theodore Metochites, a scholar and poet who was prime minister to the emperor Andronicus II, restored the church and paid for its decoration at the beginning of the fourteenth century.

The wall paintings in the mortuary chapel attached to Kariye Camii are especially impressive. Some have suggested that because of the Empire's greatly reduced resources, murals often took the place of mosaics, but at Kariye Camii they exist on an even footing and may even have been designed by the same artist. The main scene depicts the traditional Byzantine image of the Anastasis (fig. **8.51**), the event just before the Resurrection, which Western Christians call the Descent into Limbo or the Harrowing of Hell, clearly a fitting subject for the funerary setting. Surrounded by a **mandorla**, a radiant almond shape, Christ has vanquished Satan and battered down the gates of Hell. (Note the bound Satan at his

feet, in the midst of a profusion of hardware; the two kings to the left are David and Solomon.) The central group of Christ raising Adam and Eve from the dead has tremendous dramatic force; Christ moves with extraordinary physical energy, tearing Adam and Eve from their graves, so that they appear to fly through the air—a magnificently expressive image of divine triumph.

Such dynamism had been unknown in the Early Byzantine tradition, although the emotional force of Middle Byzantine painting might well have prepared the way for the vivacity of the Kariye Camii representations. Coming in the fourteenth century, this Late Byzantine style shows that 800 years after Justinian, when the Anastasis first appeared as a subject, Byzantine art still had all its creative powers. Thus, despite the diverse uses it served, its long chronological spread, and the different cultures and wide geographic areas it spanned, Byzantine art continued to preserve long-established traditions. Indeed, its durability verges on the immutable.

319–29 Old St. Peter's

ca. 270 Sarcophagus of Santa Maria Antiqua

early 6th century
...on of Christ from
...ount Sinai

ca. 432–40 Santa Maria Maggiore

ca. 950 *Joshua Roll*

late 10th century
Harbaville Triptych

ca. 1180–90 Apse mosaic of Monreale

ca. 1310–20 Kariye Camii *Anastasis*

Early Jewish,
Early Christian,
and Byzantine Art

200

300

400

500

600

700

800

900

1000

1100

1200

1300

1400

1500

◄ 256 Dura-Europus falls to Persians

260–272 *Shapur I Triumphing over the Roman Emperors Philip the Arab and Valerian*, Naksh-i-Rustam, Iran
ca.300 Palace of Diocletian, Split, Croatia

◄ 312 Constantine the Great's victory over Maxentius at the Milvian Bridge

312–15 Arch of Constantine, Rome

◄ 330 Constantinople becomes the capital of the Roman Empire

◄ 395 Roman Empire divided into Eastern and Western halves

◄ 540 Byzantine general Belisarius conquers Ravenna for Justinian

◄ 726–843 Iconoclastic Controversy

◄ 1054 Schism of Orthodox (Eastern) and Roman Catholic (Western) churches

◄ 1454 Turks capture Constantinople

CHAPTER 9

Islamic Art

THE RELIGION KNOWN AS ISLAM TOOK FORM IN THE EARLY SEVENTH century on the Arabian peninsula (see *Informing Art*, page 283). A scant 30 years after the death of its founder, the Prophet Muhammad (also known as the Messenger), in 632, Arab warriors had carried the new faith into much of today's Middle East. A century after the death of the

Prophet, Islam had spread across Africa into Spain in the west, and into the Indus valley and Central Asia in the east (map **9.1**). The original Arab adherents of Islam were eventually augmented by Berbers, Visigoths, Turks, and Persians. The cultural complexity of today's Islamic world existed almost from the beginning. As this phenomenal expansion took place, the inevitable clashing and combining of old cultures with the new religion gave birth to what was to become a vibrant tradition of Islamic art.

Examining the formation of Islamic art gives us an intriguing look at the phenomenon of syncretism in art history, the process whereby a new artistic tradition emerges as a creative combination of previously existing artistic ideas under the impetus of a new ideology. Just as the first Christian art developed out of a mixture of various preexisting classical and Near Eastern artistic ideas adapted to serve the needs of religious and then princely patrons (see Chapter 8), so the new Islamic art first took form as a series of appropriations of preexisting traditions from other cultures molded into a new synthesis, in the service both of the new Islamic religion and Islamic princes.

The vast geographical and chronological scope of Islamic art means that it cannot be encompassed in simple definitions. Islam, the religion, is a significant element in Islamic culture, but Islamic is far more than a religious art; it encompasses secular elements

and elements frowned upon, if not actually forbidden, by some Islamic theologians. As with all art, Islamic art encompasses and reflects the consistencies and contradictions of the society and culture that give it life.

With all of its individual styles of time and place, and with the various sectarian differences within Islam, Islamic art nonetheless has certain unifying themes. The first of these is reverence for the Word—the Qur'an—and for the language of the Word—Arabic—as reflected in the art of beautiful writing. From the angular, horizontal **kufic** alphabet of early Islam (fig. **9.1**) to complex cursive styles developed in later times, Islamic art, both secular and religious, shows a remarkable affinity for the written word, be it scripture or secular narrative poetry (see *Primary Source*, page 281). A second theme is the development of artistic expression independent of the human figure. Given the mistrust of figural images in many Islamic religious traditions, we see in Islamic art sophisticated and complex vocabularies of vegetal, floral, and geometric designs used in conjunction with beautiful writing. A third theme is the equality of genres. To understand and appreciate Islamic art we need to discard the notion of the primacy of (figural) painting and (figural) sculpture in the European tradition. In the Islamic world, the arts of ceramics, metalware, weaving, and carving in precious materials rank with other mediums in an artistic spectrum devoid of the formal hierarchy that in the West led to a distinction between "fine arts" and "decorative arts." In this sense, looking at Islamic art can be both enlightening and liberating.

Detail of figure 9.8, Interior of prayer hall, Great Mosque of Córdoba, Spain

Map 9.1   The Expansion of Islam to 850

THE FORMATION OF ISLAMIC ART

Islamic art first took shape as a series of appropriations of pre-existing Graeco-Roman, Byzantine Christian, and Sasanian (see page 45) forms. These were molded into a new synthesis to serve the needs of the new Islamic religion and the desires and political goals of Islamic princes. The appropriation and adaptation of preexisting forms in the service of the emerging Islamic culture is particularly apparent in architecture.

Religious Architecture

The new religion required certain types of distinctive buildings, such as a place for community prayers that was visually identified with the new faith. The new Islamic rulers needed dwellings appropriate to their power and wealth. Eventually, the faith would also require commemorative buildings that memorialized great rulers, holy men, or historic events. As such, Islamic architecture came to develop a rich variety of forms and genres, and a distinctive repertoire of decoration that became emblematic of the faith itself.

DOME OF THE ROCK The earliest major Islamic building to have survived into our time, the Dome of the Rock in Jerusalem (fig. **9.2**), is a case in point. After the Arabian cities of Mecca and Medina, Jerusalem was the holiest Islamic site. For the first Muslims, the Temple Mount in Jerusalem marked the place where

God tested Ibrahim's faith by demanding the sacrifice of his fir born son Ismail. From the same site, according to later Islamic legend, the Prophet was taken by Gabriel on a *mi'raj* (spiritual journey) to experience both Heaven and Hell, Muhammad being the only mortal allowed to see these places before death.

It is far from a coincidence that the Dome of the Rock is built on Mount Moriah in Jerusalem, a place that was originally the site of the First (Solomon's) and Second (Herod's) Temples, the geographic center of the Jewish faith (see page 235). It is also far from a coincidence that the domed silhouette and ringlike plan of the Dome of the Rock (fig. **9.3**) echo the form of the sixth-century Byzantine shrine of the Holy Sepulcher (see fig. 8.12), marking the burial place of Jesus, just a few hundred yards to the west. The Dome of the Rock was constructed by artists and craftspeople, many of whom were undoubtedly local Christians or new converts to Islam, probably under orders from the Muslim caliph (from the Arabic *khalifa*, meaning "successor") Abd al-Malik sometime around the year 690. Erected on a holy place that was also one of the highest points in the city, it eloquently proclaimed that Jerusalem was under the control of Islam.

A closer look at the building shows both the nature of early Islamic syncretism and the impact of the Messenger's views on the visual arts. The ground plan of the building (see fig. 9.3), with its two ambulatories around the central bare rock, ideal for orga izing visits of large numbers of pilgrims to the shrine, recalls n only the Holy Sepulcher but also central-plan domed churches from early Christian times (see fig. 8.10). Just to the south of the

Muhammad Ibn Mahmud Al-Amuli (Iran, 14th Century)

From *Nafâ'is al-Funûn* (The Beauty of Knowledge)

Countless Islamic adages and anecdotes testify to the importance and beauty of elegant writing, the only art form to which Islamic theologians gave their unqualified approval. Al-Amuli's encyclopedic treatise on knowledge cites the Qur'an in praising the art of beautiful writing as the fulfillment of God's will, bringing respect and honor to the practitioner.

The art of writing is an honourable one and a soul-nurturing accomplishment; as a manual attainment it is always elegant, and enjoys general approval; it is respected in every land; it rises to eminence and wins the confidence of every class; being always held to be of high rank and dignity, oppression cannot touch it, and it is held in remembrance in every country, and every wall is adorned by its hand. Honour enough for it in this connexion is that the Lord of Lords, whose names are hallowed in His incontrovertible Revelation, swore—"By the pen, and what they write" (Qur. lxviii.1), and He spake these words: "Recite! Thy Lord is the most generous, who hath taught by means of the pen, Hath taught man what he knew not" (Qur. xcvi. 3–5).

It is honour and exaltation enough for the writing pen
For ever, that it was by the pen that God swore.

The Prophet (peace be upon him!) said: "Beauty of handwriting is incumbent upon you, for it is one of the keys of man's daily bread." A wise man has said: "Writing is a spiritual geometry, wrought by a material instrument."

Source: Sir Thomas W. Arnold, *Painting in Islam: A Study of the Place of Pictorial Art in Muslim Culture* (NY: Dover, 1965)

9.1 Page with kufic script from an Abbasid Qur'an, probably from Tunisia. 9th century. Ink, color, gold, and silver on dyed blue vellum, 11⁵⁄₁₆ × 14¹³⁄₁₆″ (28.73 × 37.62 cm). Harvard Art Museum, Arthur M. Sackler Museum. Harvard University Museums, Cambridge, MA, Francis Burr Memorial Fund, 1967.23

9.2 Dome of the Rock, Jerusalem. ca. 690 and later

9.3 Cutaway drawing, Dome of the Rock, Jerusalem

wooden dome

drum of the dome

The Rock

inner ambulatory

outer ambulatory

entry (one of four)

Dome of the Rock, providing a place for prayer directly next to the shrine, was an equally venerable and revered Islamic structure, the communal prayer hall known today as the al-Aqsa Mosque. The dome of the shrine itself was a well-established symbol for the vault of heaven, especially appropriate given the ultimate goal of the Messenger's mystical and spiritual journey. The columns and capitals, recycled from Classical monuments, convey an impression of tradition and permanence, wealth and power, to Muslim and non-Muslim alike.

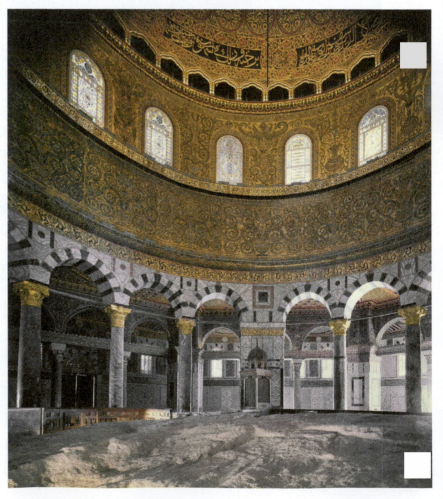

9.4 Interior, Dome of the Rock, Jerusalem

Islam and Its Messenger

Islam (an Arabic word denoting submission to God's will) is the predominant religion of a vast area of the world extending across Africa, Europe, and Asia, with many different ethnicities, cultures, languages, and forms of social and political organization. Muslims (those who submit) believe that Muhammad (ca. 570–632), an orphaned member of a major tribal group from the city of Mecca in the western Arabian peninsula, was chosen by God (in Arabic, Allah) to serve as God's Messenger, or Prophet, to humanity. Muhammad is said to have received the Word of God as a series of poetical recitations (in Arabic, Qur'an), brought to him by the archangel Jibra'il (Gabriel). Muhammad memorized and recited these poetic verses, and taught them to his followers. Organized into *sura* (chapters) and finally written down after the death of Muhammad in 632, these prayers, stories, exhortations, and commandments constitute the Qur'an, Islam's sacred book. The Qur'an, together with official collections of *hadith* (remembrances) of the exemplary life of Muhammad as the Messenger, form the basis of Islamic religious practice and law.

While the Prophet quickly gained adherents, those in power in Mecca were threatened by the challenges the new faith posed to their political and economic power, and in 622 he was forced to leave Mecca with a few of his followers, moving to the city of Medina some 190 miles (300 km) to the north. Muhammad's community, in constant conflict with the Meccans to the south, continued to grow, and more revelations were received. The Prophet's house in Medina, constructed in the form of an open square, became the prototype for countless mosques in subsequent centuries.

Islam was defined by Muhammad as the culmination of a prophetic tradition that began with God's covenant with Ibrahim (Abraham). The Qur'an prominently mentions many of the major figures of the Hebrew Bible, such as Ibrahim, Musa (Moses), and Sulayman (Solomon), as well as the prophet 'Isa (Jesus) and his mother, Maryam (Mary). Islamic belief is fundamentally very simple: To become a Muslim, one repeats with conviction the phrase, "There is no God but God; Muhammad is the Messenger of God." This Affirmation of Faith is the first of the so-called Five Pillars of Islam. The others are prayer (the five daily prayers and the major weekly prayer at noon on Friday, the Muslim Day of Congregation), fasting (abstention from food and drink during daylight hours during the lunar month of Ramadan), pilgrimage (in Arabic, hajj, a journey to Mecca during the lunar month of Dhu'l Hijja), and charity (institutionalized as a formal system of tithing, intended to benefit the sick and needy of the Islamic community).

In addition, Islam proclaimed three other tenets that were to have a major impact on art. The first was the protected status of the "People of the Book"—Jews and Christians—in Muslim society, as ordained by God in the Qur'an. The second, based on several anecdotes from the Prophet's life, is a profound mistrust of certain images—pictures and statues of humans and animals—as potentially idolatrous, a point of view Islam shares with Judaism, and which has occasionally influenced the history of Christian art as well. The third, held in common with Judaism and contrasting markedly with the Christianity of that time, was a high regard for literacy and the individual's reading and study of Scripture, coupled through most of Islamic history with a reverence for the written alphabet—in the case of Islam, the Arabic alphabet, which in early Islam used an angular form of script known as kufic (see fig. 9.1). The beauty of the script, with its contrasting thin and thick lines, written from right to left in an almost rhythmic visual cadence, was deemed appropriate for the poetic words of God himself. These three factors, taken in the general context of Islamic belief and early Islamic political history, were to have a profound effect on the molding of the Islamic artistic tradition.

The original mosaic decoration (fig. **9.4**) consisted of Arabic script, repeating geometric motifs, and highly stylized vegetal and floral elements. Eventually, these design elements would form a distinctively Islamic repertoire of decoration. One was Arabic script used in the many religious inscriptions. Two others were a vocabulary of scrolling vines, leaves, and flowers distantly based on nature, and a range of repeating geometric patterns. Both the natural elements and the geometric patterns were staples of late Classical and Sasanian art. A fourth set of motifs consisted of jewels and jeweled objects, symbols of royalty. But in marked contrast to the Graeco-Roman and Christian religious art traditions, nowhere in the Dome of the Rock do the forms of humans or animals appear. The inscriptions in the Dome of the Rock, taken from the Qur'an, were carefully chosen to underline the importance of the building itself, its symbolic location in a city holy to Jews and Christians as well as Muslims, and its place within a religion and society that saw itself as the culmination of the two earlier scriptural traditions, and which afforded tolerance and acceptance of both Christians and Jews.

THE HYPOSTYLE MOSQUE Of the Five Pillars of Islam, the religious duty of prayer proved the most important in the development of Islamic architecture. In major cities such as Damascus, the Arab Umayyad caliphs of early Islam either built or converted from preexisting structures the first great buildings for Muslim public worship called **mosques** in English (from the Arabic *masjid*, meaning "place of prostration"). These first mosques, designed to contain the entire male population of a city during the noon prayer on Friday, recall the form of the Messenger's house in Medina, with a rectangular courtyard, usually surrounded by covered arcades, and a larger hypostyle (many-columned) hall on the **qibla**, the side facing Mecca. The architecture emphasized the equality of all Muslims before God and the absence in Islam of an ordained clergy: There is little axiality in the early Arab mosques—no long straight pathway leading to an architectural focus visible throughout the structure. With prayer occurring directly between each worshiper and God, and no ordained clergy or canonized saints to provide intercession, the interior space of the early mosque was essentially determined by practicality, not

9.5 Schematic drawing of a generic
Arab hypostyle mosque

by ceremony. Thus, there was no place for music or processions; many doors were placed for maximum convenience of the daily coming and going of worshipers; and a large centralized or axial space, so important for the drama of the Christian Mass, was deemed unnecessary. A simple **minbar** (pulpit) served for the delivery of sermons after the Friday noon prayer, and an empty **mihrab** (niche) in the qibla wall was added to indicate the direction of Mecca (fig. **9.5**). Mats of grass or rushes, and later woolen carpets, often covered the floors. These provided a clean place for the standing, bowing, kneeling, and prostration, with the brief touching of the forehead to the ground, while reciting prayers, that constitute the essence of Islamic worship. Oil lamps provided illumination for the dawn and late evening prayers. Pools or fountains in the courtyard allowed for the ceremonial washing of hands and feet required before prayers. In later times, a tower, known in English as a **minaret**, advertised the presence of the mosque and served as a place from which to broadcast the call to prayer given five times a day by a *muezzin*, an individual usually selected for the beauty and power of his voice. And in some mosques a small platform called a **dikka** provided a place for the muezzin to chant prayers aloud.

Secular Architecture

The advent of Islam did not mean the end of secular art in the Middle East. The early Islamic princely patrons, Arabs from the Umayyad ruling house, in addition to establishing the canonical form of the Islamic house of prayer, were also quickly seduced by the splendor of Sasanian and Graeco-Roman princely art. Although their urban palaces have not survived, they also constructed luxurious and secluded palaces out in the desert, away from the metropolitan centers, and some of these have been

rediscovered in relatively recent times. In addition to walled residences for ruler and courtiers in the traditional hollow square form of the Roman military encampment, the Umayyads built large and sumptuous bathhouses with halls for entertainment, often lavishly furnished with mosaic floors in a Late Roman style and decorated with pictorial and sculptural images of luxury. Among the subjects depicted were the royal hunt, court musicians (fig. **9.6**), the enjoyment of Roman-style baths, dancing courte-

9.6 Floor fresco depicting two court musicians and a mounted hunter, from Qasr al-Hayr (West). ca. 730. National Museum, Damascus sans, scenes from everyday life, and images of ancient derivation denoting fertility, sexuality, and kingly prowess. The puritanical demands of religion thus immediately came into conflict with the old symbols of royal wealth, luxury, and entertainment. So great was the embedded power of the artistic imagery of kingship in the Middle East that it quickly made an impact on the material culture of the new Islamic ruling elite.

THE DEVELOPMENT OF ISLAMIC STYLE

By 750, the Umayyad dynasty based in Roman Syria had been supplanted by the Abbasid dynasty centered in Mesopotamia. Here the new caliphs built their capital, called Baghdad, on the Tigris River, and later a vast palace city to the north of Baghdad at Samarra. The original Round City of Baghdad, the site of which lies under the present-day city, was largely abandoned and destroyed long before the Mongols sacked the city in 1258, but its powerful memory lived on in Arabic poetry and prose literature. Samarra's impressive mud-brick ruins still stretch for miles along the Tigris. Under Abbasid rule, the building of mosques in newly conquered areas proceeded apace across the now-extensive Islamic Empire.

Religious Architecture

ief among the new structures were the large Abbasid congregational mosques that both practically and symbolically served as religious gathering places for prayers, sermons, and religious education. Large examples, many now in ruins, were built all over Iraq, and in Egypt and elsewhere. An archetypal example is the largely ninth-century congregational mosque at Kairouan, a city in what is now Tunisia established under the Abbasids.

GREAT MOSQUE OF KAIROUAN Based like all major Arab mosques on the house of the Prophet in Medina and the four-square Mediterranean courtyard house, examples of which today still surround the structure, the Great Mosque of Kairouan consists of a rectangular courtyard surrounded by covered halls, a large hypostyle prayer hall, and a towering minaret (fig. 9.7). Two domes mark the area: in front of the mihrab and in the middle of the prayer hall facing the court. This aside, the multitude of entrances on three sides of the building, conceived to facilitate entry and exit for the five daily prayers, free the building from the domination of a central axis for processions of clergy; it is thus the very opposite of the Early Christian basilican church, organized for priestly and theatrical ritual. The simplicity of the mosque reflects the simplicity of Islamic prayer. The mosque's lack of both axiality and uninterrupted interior space stems from the essential lack of hierarchy among worshipers. Each worshiper prays directly to God using a simple ritual formula usually completed in a few minutes. Artistic attention was lavished on the mihrab, of carved marble and ceramic tiles, and the minbar, elaborately carved of Indian teak. In the Kairouan mosque, a carved wooden screen, primarily a product of security rather than ritual needs, encloses a small area near the mihrab called the **maqsura**, where the ruler could pray alone.

9.7 Aerial view of the Great Mosque of Kairouan, Tunisia. 8th century and later

GREAT MOSQUE OF CÓRDOBA Even farther to the west, in southern Spain, where the sole surviving prince of the exterminated Umayyad house founded an independent state after 750, a brilliant center of Islamic culture developed in the city of Córdoba, in al-Andalus (now Andalusia). By the tenth century, the Great Mosque of Córdoba, after a series of embellishments and enlargements, had become one of the most beautiful Islamic houses of worship. A typical Arab hypostyle hall, the interior of the Córdoba mosque became after several expansions a virtual forest of columns (fig. **9.8**). Its characteristic "horseshoe" arcades are composed of arches using alternating red and white voussoirs, and include the additional element of one set of arches superimposed above another on elongated imposts. This creates an impression of almost limitless space—this space is, however, composed of relatively small architectural elements repeated again and again. Compared with a Christian structure like Hagia Sophia (see figs. 8.27 and 8.29) or Old St. Peter's (see figs. 8.7 and 8.9), Córdoba has an equally large interior area, but there is no centralized space for the sacred theater of the Christian rite. The mosque interior, including the maqsura area around the mihrab, was lavishly decorated with mosaic and carved stone. Tenth-century marble grilles (fig. **9.9**) on the qibla wall present early examples of what we sometimes call **geometric arabesque**: The artist carves out of marble what is essentially a single straplike line that intertwines, creating a characteristic openwork screen of stars and polygons. In the beauty of such artistic geometry many Muslims see a reflection of God's creative hand in the universe.

In addition to providing a community prayer hall, the large Islamic mosques such as the Great Mosque of Córdoba also often incorporated schools and universities, public baths, hospitals and medical schools, soup kitchens for the poor, hostels for travelers and merchants, public clocks (knowing the correct time

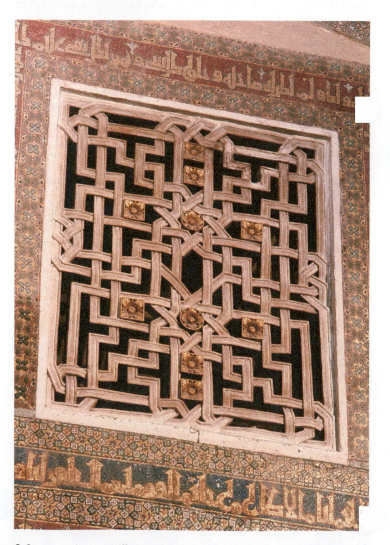

9.9 Carved stone grille on qibla wall of Great Mosque of Córdoba. Mid-10th century

9.10 Ivory casket of al-Mughira, from Córdoba. ca. 960. Height 6″ (15 cm), diameter 3″ (8 cm). Musée du Louvre, Paris, Inv. 4068

was essential for the variable timing of the five daily prayers), public toilets, and fountains serving as the public water supply for the immediate area. Endowments known as *waqf*, based on the income from rental properties, supported the many functions of mosques. Waqfs were also established for social-service institutions and for shrines that were founded independently of mosques. Artistic votive gifts made to such institutions, such as Qur'an manuscripts, lamps, beautiful wooden furniture, carpets, and other objects, were in theory protected in perpetuity, becoming part of the waqf itself. As a consequence, such institutions often became great magnets for works of art, accumulating over time important libraries and collections of beautiful furnishings.

Luxury Arts

On the outskirts of Córdoba, the Umayyads built another huge Islamic palace city known as Medina al-Zahra. A ruin today,

the palace complex once included royal workshops for luxury objects such as silk textiles and carved ivory, used as symbols of royal wealth and power and given as royal ceremonial gifts. A small, domed **pyxis** (ivory box) made there for a tenth-century Umayyad prince (fig. **9.10**) incorporates in its decoration a microcosm of Islamic royal imagery and symbolism, including depictions of falconry and hunting, sports, and court musicians, set amid lush carved vegetal ornament and a kufic inscription frieze. Such lavish objects had a symbolic importance far beyond their practical use as containers for jewelry or cosmetics. Their complex, many-layered iconography and their importance and symbolism as royal gifts continue to be studied today.

In the eleventh century, Berber armies serving the Almoravid dynasty from North Africa razed Medina al-Zahra to its foundations, although they and their successors, the Almohads, also built significant monuments in the Maghreb (present-day Morocco and northwestern Africa) and in al-Andalus. But the growing and continual pressure of Christian reconquest from the north saw a dramatic decline in Muslim power in Spain. By the fourteenth century, the Almohad capital of Seville had fallen to the Christian kings of Spain, and Muslims working under Christian rule, known as *Mudejares*, continued Islamic artistic traditions under Christian patronage. (See *The Art Historian's Lens*, page 290.)

ISLAMIC ART AND THE PERSIAN INHERITANCE

In the central and western Islamic lands, from Spain to the western Mediterranean littoral, Islamic arts developed within the geography and culture of the Graeco-Roman tradition; in the east, however, the situation was in many respects quite different. In Mesopotamia and Iran, the Arab Muslim conquerors encountered the cultural sphere of the Sasanians, the heirs to over 1,000 years of Persian civilization with an impressive tradition of art and architecture. This tradition included royal imagery of ceremonial pomp, warfare, and the royal sport of hunting (see fig. 2.20), as well as large and impressive palace buildings.

Architecture

In the eastern Islamic world, following pre-Islamic architectural practice, brick rather than stone was the most common masonry construction material. In place of cylindrical columns, massive brick piers often provided vertical structural support in buildings, and heavy vaults rather than tiled wooden-beam roofs were often chosen to cover interior spaces. Islamic architecture in Mesopotamia, Iran, and Central Asia reflects the available materials, earlier cultural traditions, and even the climate of those regions in distinctive ways. It also provides a curious blending of secular and religious buildings; just as the open arcaded courtyard helps to define both mosque and palace in the Islamic west, another form, known as the iwan, came to define both royal and religious structures in the east.

9.11 Schematic drawing of a generic Persian four-iwan mosque

THE FOUR-IWAN MOSQUE One of the first large vaulted brick structures with one open side, known as an iwan, was constructed by the Sasanian ruler Shapur I as an audience hall for his royal palace at Ctesiphon in Mesopotamia (see fig. 2.32).

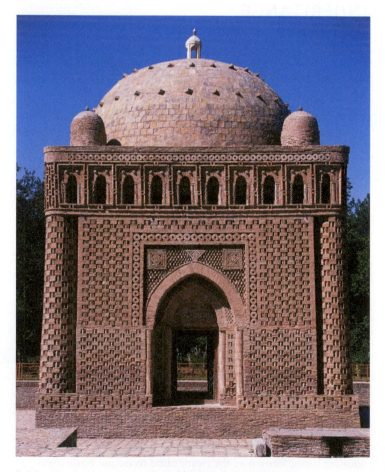

9.12 Tomb of the Samanids, Bukhara, Uzbekistan. ca. 901

The form seems originally to have symbolized royal authority in Iran, and under Islam it was eventually incorporated into a new type of prayer structure, the four-iwan mosque, by placing one massive brick recess in the middle of each of the sides of a rectangular courtyard (fig. 9.11). From the twelfth century onward, the four-iwan courtyard was a standard feature of both mosques and religious schools of a type known as the *madrasa* throughout Iran and Islamic Central Asia. In most of Iran, as in Mesopotamia, brick was the preferred building material, and the vaults of Iranian mosques were supported by heavy brick piers.

TOMB OF THE SAMANIDS In the aftermath of the Arab conquest of Iran, the Persian cultural tradition gradually reasserted itself in many ways. One of the earliest surviving Islamic dynastic tombs was built in the early tenth century for the Persian Samanid dynasty in Bukhara, an eastern city beyond the Oxus River, today in Uzbekistan (fig. 9.12). This small cubic structure is in basic concept a hemispherical dome on four massive piers, evidently derived in part from the form of a Sasanian fire temple used for Zoroastrian worship. The dome is supported on the square chamber by means of four squinches in the corners, while the readily available and relatively humble material of brick is used to brilliant effect, with various surface textures recalling woven reeds, kufic inscriptions, and what look like engaged columns in the corners. While the Messenger had opposed all shrines and the prominent tomb structures of kings and saints, which he viewed as suggestive of polytheism or idolatry, the symbolism associated with dynastic kingship and the veneration of major religious figures in Islam meant that tombs and shrines were to figure prominently in the history of architecture throughout the Islamic world.

Figural Art Forms in Iran

The Iranian part of the Islamic world had inherited a rich tradition of material culture, and the successive rulers of Iran, whether themselves Arab, Persian, Turkish, or Mongol in ancestry, fell under the seductive spell of the Persian heritage, which they combined with their Islamic beliefs and traditions. From the prosperous cities of tenth- and eleventh-century Iran there have survived beautiful ceramic wares decorated with maxims, good wishes, and prayers in beautiful calligraphy with figural and vegetal decoration, as well as some exceptional silk textiles and metal objects. The Seljuk Turkish invaders, who ruled Iran from the mid-eleventh century onward, not only built great mosques and tomb structures, but also ruled over a prosperous urban culture that among other things produced one of the richest known traditions of decorated ceramics. Using figural images of all kinds in a multitude of sophisticated techniques, including the use of a metallic pigment known as **luster** fired over the glaze and polychrome enamel decoration known as **mina'i**, these ceramic wares incorporated for middle-class patrons a very diverse repertoire of scenes from Persian romances and mythology, themes from Sufism

9.13 *Mina'i* dish with story of Bahram Gur and Azadeh, from Iran. ca. 1200. Polychrome overglaze enamels on white composite body, diameter 8½" (22.2 cm), width 3¹³⁄₁₆" (9.7 cm). Metropolitan Museum of Art, New York. Purchase, Rogers Fund and gift of the Schiff Foundation, 1957 (57.36.13)

(the Islamic mystical religious tradition), and the now-familiar Islamic royal images of hunting and other courtly pleasures. A favorite story finding its way into ceramics, metalwork, and book illustration was that of the royal hunter Bahram Gur and his skeptical girlfriend, the harpist Azadeh. A mina'i plate shows two episodes of continuous narrative, with Azadeh on the camel with her royal lover, and then pushed off the beast after making a remark belittling the hero's marksmanship (fig. **9.13**).

Also noteworthy was the practice of inlaying precious metals into brass or bronze, often incorporating human and animal images. This art form apparently began in Khurasan (formerly the northeastern part of Iran) in the twelfth century and gradually found its way west into upper Mesopotamia by the early thirteenth century. The full repertoire of royal themes is represented in these opulent objects, in which on occasion even the letters of the inscriptions themselves take on human forms (fig. **9.14**). Also created under the Iranian Seljuks were stucco relief sculptures incorporating the human figure. To what do we owe this burst of figural art in seeming contradiction to strict Islamic practice? Practical rather than dogmatic, Iranians under the Seljuks apparently believed that figural images did not necessarily have to be identified with polytheism or idolatry, but could usefully serve both secular and religious purposes without morally corrupting the viewer.

9.14 Muhammad ibn abd al-Wahid (caster) and Masud ibn Ahmad al-Naqqash (inlayer). Cast bronze alloy bucket, inlaid with silver and copper, from Herat. 1163 CE. The State Hermitage Museum, St. Petersburg, Inv. no. IR 2268

Spanish Islamic Art and Europe in the Middle Ages

In 711, the combined Arab and Berber forces of the Muslim commander Tariq ibn Ziyad crossed over the Straits of Gibraltar. By 716, most of Spain was in Muslim hands. Under the rule of the Umayyad dynasty (751–1017), Córdoba became the capital of a prosperous, tolerant, and powerful Muslim kingdom in Spain, in which Christians and Jews played important roles in cultural life. During the eleventh and twelfth centuries, in the aftermath of the fall of the Umayyads, successive Berber invasions from North Africa, first by the Almoravids and then the Almohads, brought new Muslim dynastic patrons into Spain, who oversaw splendid new artistic production. But they also suffered a series of military defeats at the hands of the strengthening Christian powers in the north. Of the several small Islamic kingdoms that formed in the twilight of Muslim rule in Spain, one in particular, that of the Nasrids, ruling in Granada from 1230 to 1492, saw a last glorious flowering of the arts before its defeat by the Castilians and Aragonese united under Ferdinand and Isabella.

The dominant Muslim style in the arts of southern Spain affected artistic production of non-Muslims in many complex ways. From the tenth through the twelfth centuries, in the hardscrabble mountainside principalities of the Christian north, builders built small churches and monasteries in the **mozarab** style, using the horseshoe arches, alternating colored voussoirs, and mosaics of colored stone they had seen in the Muslim south. At the same time, in the northern monasteries, artist-monks illustrated manuscripts of the *Commentaries on the Apocalypse* of Beatus of Liebana with paintings that also reflected the dominant Muslim style. Beyond the Pyrenees, along the medieval pilgrimage roads into France, aspects of the Muslim style even influenced French Romanesque art; the twelfth-century wooden doors of Le Puy Cathedral in France bore an elaborate kufic inscription in Arabic: *mashallah*—"may God protect this place."

After the Christian reconquest of central southern Spain gained momentum in the last part of the thirteenth century, artisans among the conquered Muslim peoples living under Christian rule, known as Mudejares, working under Catholic patrons, continued to produce works of art—buildings, carpets, ceramic wares, and ivories among them—in the Muslim style. The greatest monument of Mudejar art is the fourteenth-century Alcazar or royal palace of King Pedro of Castile in Seville, the style of which is remarkably similar to that of the Alhambra (see fig. 9.27), then being built in nearby Gran[ada]. Also noteworthy are the surviving Mudejar synagogues of Córd[oba], Granada, and Toledo; with its Hebrew inscriptions intermingling with those in Arabic, the decoration of the Toledan synagogue of Samuel Halevy Abulafia, popularly known as El Tránsito (ca. 1360), follows the Muslim style closely. It appears to demonstrate that important elements of the Arabic-speaking Jewish population of Spain at the time felt themselves fully invested in the dominant artistic culture.

Nationalistic European scholars once preferred to ignore or to deprecate this intermingling of cultures in medieval Spain, but recent scholarship and exhibitions have brought about renewed interest in the Spanish Muslim impact on Europe and in the nature of the flowering of Christian and Jewish culture during the period of *convivencia* (living together) in medieval Muslim Spain. The final expulsion of Muslims and Jews from Spain by the ethnic cleansing of Ferdinand and Isabella in the early sixteenth century brought most of this productive symbiosis to an unhappy end.

Interior, Transito Synagogue, ca. 1360. Toledo, Spain

THE CLASSICAL AGE

In the center of the Islamic world, in what some scholars term its classical age (roughly 800–1250), the power and influence of Mesopotamia gradually waned with the decline of the Abbasid caliphate. In 969, the Fatimids, a North African Arab dynasty claiming descent from the Messenger's daughter Fatima, conquered Fostat, the Abbasids' major city in Egypt, and founded as their new capital the nearby city of Cairo. The Fatimids were Shi'ites—Muslims who believed that only descendants of Muhammad could legitimately lead the Islamic community. They took their name from the term *shi'at'Ali* ("the party of Ali"), Muhammad's son-in-law, husband of Fatima, and father of the Prophet's grandsons Hasan and Husein. Shi'ite Muslims themselves were divided into several major and many minor sects, all of which opposed the basic political tenets of Sunni, or orthodox, Islam, where having the blood of the Messenger was not a prerequisite for holding political power.

The rise of the Fatimids in the tenth century coincided wi[th] a gradual weakening of Abbasid power and a decline in the ca[li]phate authority, based in Baghdad. By the eleventh century, the Seljuk Turks had moved westward out of Central Asia to gain

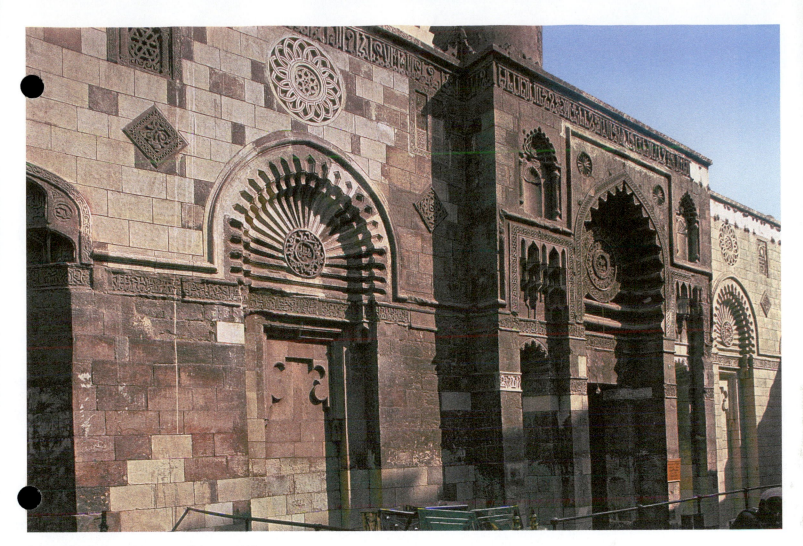

9.15　The al-Aqmar Mmosque, Cairo. ca. 1026

control first in Iran and then in northern Mesopotamia and Asia Minor; around the same time, in 1099, the Norman warriors of the First Crusade captured Jerusalem. The Seljuks were Sunni Muslims; they fostered arts of all kinds and supported Sunni doctrine with the founding of many madrasa colleges for the teaching of Sunni law. In the late twelfth century, another Sunni dynasty, the Ayyubids, drove the Christians out of Jerusalem, and for a brief time also oversaw important developments in the arts.

The Fatimid Artistic Impact

Under the Fatimids, Egypt experienced a major artistic revival. The eleventh-century city walls of Cairo, incorporating the latest cutting-edge military technology, were constructed with stone stripped from the outer parts of the pyramids in nearby Giza. Two great urban palaces, decorated with figural images of music making, dancing, hunting, and royal ritual, were constructed within the city, and elaborate parades and ceremonial processions proclaimed the dynasty's power. Not one but two congregational mosques were constructed in Cairo under Fatimid rule, and smaller mosques served individual neighborhoods

of the city, which by the twelfth century had expanded beyond its original walls.

AL-AQMAR MOSQUE Among the most beautiful of the Fatimid mosques in Cairo is the small mosque known as al-Aqmar (fig. **9.15**), built by a Fatimid noble. It was skillfully constructed on an irregular plot of land, with its off-axis façade corresponding to the original street. In addition to the carved stone, Arabic inscriptions, and ornamental niches, we see to either side of the main portal a developed form of **muqarnas**, the distinctive geometric, almost crystalline faceted decoration, composed of small nichelike forms, that eventually became an iconic form of Islamic decoration from the Atlantic to beyond the Oxus.

TEXTILES AND IVORIES Under the Fatimids, a thriving maritime commerce between Egypt and Italy left its mark in the form of Islamic artistic influence on twelfth-century Italian architecture in port cities such as Palermo, Salerno, Amalfi, and Pisa. In addition, preexisting traditions of weaving, mostly carried on by indigenous Coptic Christians, continued to flourish alongside the production of new textiles incorporating silk imported from

9.16 Cloak of Roger II of Sicily. 12th century. Red silk embroidered with silk and pearls, diameter 11′3″ (3.42 m). Made in Palermo for the coronation of Roger II in 1133–34. Kunsthistoriches Museum, Vienna

9.17 Detail of carved ivory frame with court scenes, from Egypt. 12th century. 17¾ × 14⅓″ (44.9 × 36.5 cm). Staatliche Museen Preussischer Kulturbesitz, Museum für Islamische Kunst, Berlin, I.6375

Iran or China. In the twelfth century, Muslim artisans working in Palermo in Sicily, newly conquered by the Normans, created the elaborate embroidered cape of King Roger II (r. 1095–1154), with inscriptions in Arabic praising the Catholic ruler (fig. **9.16**). It was used for many centuries in Habsburg coronations. Along with remarkable luster-painted ceramics, textiles, rock crystal, and glassware, Fatimid artists produced carved ivory objects significant both for their beauty and for the insights they provide into Fatimid court life. One of these, an ivory frame now in Berlin (fig. **9.17**), shows a multitude of energetic figures engaged in dancing, music making, hunting, wrestling, and drinking what can only be supposed to be wine, whose prohibition in the Qur'an did not preclude its use or depiction in the private customs and art of Islamic palaces.

The Ayyubids and the Seljuk Turks of Asia Minor

It was during the Seljuk Turkish rule over central and northern Palestine, in 1099, that European warriors of the First Crusade captured Jerusalem, which remained briefly in Christian hands until its recapture in 1187 by the Ayyubid sultan Salah ad-Din, known in the West as Saladin. The period of the Crusades was to last until the fourteenth century, when all but the last vestiges of crusader kingdoms disappeared from the eastern Mediterranean. Artistic cross-fertilization between Catholic Europe and the Muslim Middle East developed extensively during the entire period, and persisted long after the crusaders departed. The Ayyubids, a Kurdish dynasty originating in northern Syria, reconquered greater Syria and Egypt for Sunni Islam in the twelfth century, and their brief reign, ending in the mid-thirteenth century, produced a remarkable record of accomplishment in architecture and the arts. Ayyubid military architecture, such as the citadels of Aleppo and Cairo, embodied the latest military technology, and was to inspire many a European castle constructed in the Romanesque and Gothic eras. Under the Ayyubids, the arts of inlaid metalwork, ceramics, and enameled glassware also flourished.

To the east, in the twilight of the dynasty's glory, the ancient Abbasid capital of Baghdad experienced by the early thirteenth

9.18 Yahya ibn Mahmud al-Wasiti, *Scene in an Arab Village*, illustration from a *Maqamat* manuscript. ca. 1237. Opaque watercolors on paper, 13¾ × 10¼″ (34.8 × 26 cm). Bibliothèque Nationale, Paris. MS. arabe 5847, folio 138r

THE CARAVANSARAY The largest buildings constructed by the Seljuks in Asia Minor are a type of fortified wayside inn known in Turkish as **han** and in the West as **caravansaray**. Built at regular intervals along the main caravan routes linking the cities of Asia Minor, these buildings usually consisted of an outer court and a vaulted inner hall. The outer court had stables for pack animals, baths for travelers, a small mosque, and a kitchen. The inner hall, where goods could be stored and travelers slept, often had a tall dome on squinches, the pyramidal exterior of which could be seen along the highway from a great distance. The largest and most handsome of the Asia Minor hans, the Sultan Han, built between the cities of Konya and Aksaray around 1229 by Sultan Alaeddin Keykubad, has beautifully carved doorways leading into the courtyard and vaulted hall, and evidently employed in its construction the services of both local and Syrian stone carvers. A similar structure was built by the same ruler on the Kayseri-Sivas road and also called the Sultan Han (fig. **9.19**); dozens of others are still today found in Turkey. They facilitated commerce throughout Asia Minor, where beautifully constructed and elaborately decorated mosques, madrasas, and palaces were built throughout the twelfth and thirteenth centuries.

9.19 Sultan Han, Kayseri-Sivas road, Turkey. ca. 1236. Drawing by Albert Gabriel

century a revival in the arts of the book. Such artists as Yahya ibn Mahmud al-Wasiti produced miniature paintings remarkable for their humor, observations of everyday life, and insights into human foibles, here seen illustrating a *Maqamat* manuscript (fig. **9.18**). (*Maqamat* means "stories" and this manuscript contains 50 short stories.)

To the north, the Seljuk Turks had finally entered the Asia Minor heartland of the Byzantine Empire after 1071. In the following 200 years, with the full participation of the artists of both the Muslim and the Christian communities in the prosperous urban centers of Asia Minor, art and architecture flourished under what were known as the Seljuks of Rum (Rome). Craftspeople and artists from Iran, as well as from Syria and Egypt, served the lavish patronage of the Seljuk sultans.

LATER CLASSICAL ART AND ARCHITECTURE

By the second decade of the thirteenth century, reports began to arrive in the Islamic lands of Central Asia, Iran, Egypt, Syria, and Asia Minor of an ominous power rising in the east. The eventual triumph of the Mongol successors of Genghis Khan brought devastation to much of the Islamic world east of the Mediterranean. Some areas, such as Asia Minor, emerged relatively unscathed. Others, such as the Central Asian city of Bukhara (sacked and burned in 1220) and the Abbasid capital of Baghdad (sacked and destroyed in 1258), suffered untold losses in architectural monuments and artistic goods, as well as the even more serious destruction of infrastructure, such as irrigation canals, roads, and social services. However, by the end of the thirteenth

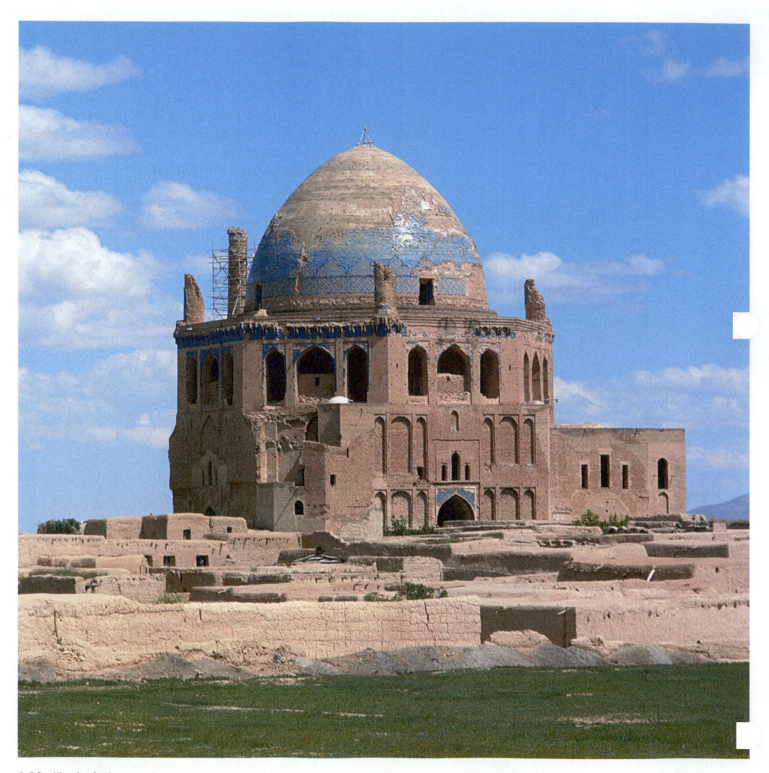

9.20 Tomb of Oljeytu, Sultaniya, Iran. ca. 1314

century, the western Mongol rulers, known as Il-Khans, had converted to Islam, and their patronage and that of their successors brought about in Iran and its surrounding areas yet another [peri]od of artistic flowering, in which artists in western Asia were [exp]osed to new artistic inspiration from China, flowing west through the Mongol domains on what historians now call the Silk Road, a 5,000-mile (8,000-km) network of caravan routes from Honan (present-day Luoyang) through the Islamic world to Europe.

Mongol rule in Central Asia and Iran was short-lived, but the artistic legacy of the Mongols continued under the Timurids, who by the late fourteenth century had established their empire in the former Mongol lands and produced a brilliant court tradition, the legacy of which was eventually felt from the eastern Mediterranean to central India. Far to the west and south, after 1260, Sunni Mamluks in Syria and Egypt, inheritors of the Fatimid Shi'ite capital of Cairo, set about their own symbolic appropriation of the land, with a new architecture of tall domes and complex minarets, and an artistic economy that mixed the Turkic (of the people who originated in central Asia and migrated to northern, central and western Eurasia, including the Anatolian peninsula) tastes of the ruling class with indigenous Egyptian traditions. Trade between Cairo and Italy was brisk, and Mamluk artistic production sometimes even reflected the commercial attractiveness of Mamluk goods in Europe.

[M]ongol Patronage

In the realms of art and architecture, the Mongols built on what had come before them. The legacy of later Arab book illustration, which had flowered in Iraq in the decades before the Mongol sack of Baghdad in 1258, lived on in elements of the emergent Iranian tradition of miniature painting that began in the first half of the fourteenth century under Mongol patronage in their capital of Tabriz in northwest Iran. Artists in Tabriz produced paintings in a new style that incorporated aspects of Chinese brush painting and Chinese landscape. In other Mongol centers, Chinese motifs and raw materials contributed to a revival of silk weaving, and preexisting traditions of inlaid metalwork and luster-painted ceramics developed in new directions. Like almost all foreigners who had conquered Iran from the time of Alexander the Great, the Mongol rulers quickly became "Persianized," commissioning illustrated manuscripts of the Persian national epic, the *Shah-nameh* or "Book of Kings," and building four-iwan brick mosques and high-domed tomb structures in the Persian style. The nature of Mongol patronage in Iran can be seen in the tomb structure built by the Il-Khan Oljeytu (r. 1304–1317). The son of a Sunni father and a Christian mother, Oljeytu founded a new capital in Sultaniya, bringing artists and builders from all over his realms to embellish it. At the center of his capital stands a huge [str]ucture with a massive pointed dome covered with turquoise [til]e tiles, the royal mausoleum of Oljeytu (fig. **9.20**). With its painted interior decoration of carved and painted stucco (fig. **9.21**) and elaborate tile decoration, it is unprecedented in size and

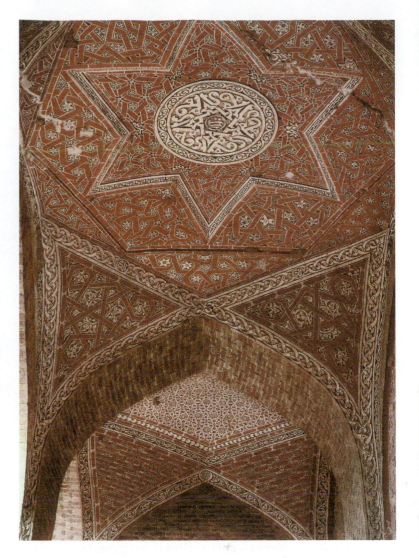

9.21   Interior, Tomb of Oljeytu, Iran.

scale for an Islamic shrine or tomb. This great domed building in Sultaniya represents the grandiose artistic aspirations of the Il-Khans, as well as their enlightened patronage of artistic innovation within preexisting Persian traditions.

Timurid Patronage

After the death of the last ruler of the short-lived Il-Khan dynasty in 1337, Iran and Islamic Central Asia broke up into smaller principalities, one of which, that of the Jalayrid dynasty, kept the tradition of Mongol painting alive in Tabriz and Baghdad. By the late fourteenth century, another Turko-Mongol power had risen beyond the Oxus, this time under the rule of the strategic genius Timur (r. ca. 1370–1405), known in the West as Tamerlane.

ARCHITECTURE AND ITS DECORATION In his capital city of Samarkand, Timur built in the 1390s a gigantic congregational mosque, the largest four-iwan mosque in the Iranian tradition, and his palace of Aq Saray in his nearby birthplace was built on an equally gargantuan scale. The artistic aspirations of the Timurid dynasty reached their climax in the fifteenth century. At Herat, which became the main capital under the rule of Timur's son Shah Rukh (r. 1405–1447), Timur's grandson Baysunghur founded a royal library—in fact, a royal design studio—that, in addition to producing beautiful books decorated with illuminations, miniature paintings, and calligraphy, served as a central source of designs for many other artistic mediums, drawing on the artistic legacy of the Jalayrids as well as the arts of China and Central Asia.

To the north in Samarkand, in present-day Uzbekistan, another of Timur's grandsons, Ulugh Beg, founded (ca. 1420) a major astronomical observatory as well as one of the most important Timurid madrasa colleges (fig. 9.22). Ulugh Beg's college has a massive iwan before its main portal and two cylindrical minarets. Elaborate, carefully constructed mosaics of colored tiles in geometric and vegetal patterns lavishly decorate the entire façade. Ceramic building decoration in Central Asia under the Timurids and their immediate predecessors developed a rich variety and complexity equaled but never surpassed in the subsequent history of art in the region of Iran.

BOOK ILLUSTRATION It was in Herat, in the twilight of the Timurid dynasty at the end of the fifteenth century, that the long and complex history of Persian book painting saw one of its most glorious chapters. In the 1480s and 1490s, the great master Behzad and his colleagues brought about a series of refinements in Islamic painting that have become legendary. Behzad himself

had not only a sensitivity to the lyrical and heroic themes of Persian poetic texts, but a keen eye for the world around him. many of his paintings made to illustrate verse texts, such as this illustration from a manuscript of the *Bostan* (*Poetic Garden*) of Sa'di, it is the everyday heart of Herat that we see so masterfully depicted (fig. **9.23**). In a scene outside a mosque, the high point of view allows us to look into the courtyard, while at the doorway a rich man encounters a beggar, and another man washes at a fountain. Behzad's spatial and narrative clarity, overlapping elements in ingenious ways to give a sense of three dimensions while portraying all of his protagonists in the same scale, brings a new power to these small paintings, the small size of which does not restrict their generous pictorial space, complex settings, and large cast of characters.

Mamluk Patronage

In the central Islamic lands, only one power had successfully repulsed the Mongol invasions of the thirteenth century. When the last Ayyubid ruler of Egypt died in 1250, his wife married her husband's leading general, a Mamluk, or slave soldier, of Kipchak Turkish origin named Baybars, who became ruler in 1260. That year, at the Battle of Ain Jalut (in what is now northern Israel), a Mamluk army defeated the Il-Khan's Mongol troops. As a result, Egypt and much of Syria remained free of Mongol rule under the various Mamluk dynasties, which ruled from Cairo and Damascus, from 1250 until the conquest of Cairo by the Ottoman Turks in 1517.

9.23 Behzad, *A Poor Man Refused Admittance to a Mosque*, from a manuscript of the Bostan of Sa'di, from Herat. 1488–89 CE. Opaque watercolors, ink, and gold on paper, 12 × 8½" (30.5 × 21.5 cm). National Library of Egypt, Cairo, 22 Adab Farsi

9.24 Complex of Sultan Hasan,
Cairo, Egypt. ca. 1354–61

9.25 Plan of the complex of
Sultan Hasan, Cairo

ARCHITECTURE It is easy to see an evolutionary progression from the art of Egypt in Fatimid and then Ayyubid times into the Mamluk reign. Mamluk patronage was at times quite lavish, and ʌt of the artistic character of today's Cairo comes from the ˈʌmluk period. Working within the confines of often irregularly shaped plots of urban land in the crowded Egyptian metropolis, builders under Mamluk patronage created mosques, madrasas, tombs, and a distinctive combination of public libraries and water fountains. These works are characterized by a new style of elaborately decorated high domes, complex multibalconied minarets, and lavish decoration incorporating both carving and multicolored marble mosaic paneling. As Sunni Muslims living in the shadow of the Shi'ite Fatimid past, the Turkish-speaking Mamluks, often unable to speak or write Arabic, not only built mosques, but also a very large number of madrasas, or institutions of higher education, to serve the local populace.

The largest and most impressive of these is the madrasa and tomb of Sultan Hasan (fig. **9.24**). It was constructed between 1354 and 1361 by the otherwise undistinguished Mamluk sultan Nasir ad-Din al-Hasan, into whose state coffers had flowed a torrent of riches as a result of the high mortality of the mid-century outbreak of Black Death, which left many large estates without heirs. Designed as four separate colleges within one building (fig. **9.25**), each devoted to one of the four major schools of Islamic jurisprudence, the mammoth structure houses a mosque in the qibla iwan of its huge four-iwan courtyard, as well as classrooms, dormitory rooms, and, on the south side ˈind the qibla wall, the gigantic domed tomb of Sultan Hasan himself. Decorated with varicolored marble mosaic paneling, with spectacular carved portals, bronze doors inlaid with silver and gold, and furnishings such as a marble minbar and muezzin platform and a walnut Qur'an lectern inlaid with ebony and ivory, the madrasa and tomb of Sultan Hasan show the artistic aspirations of the Mamluks to be equal to those of their Mongol rivals to the northeast in size, expense, and beauty. Right down to the Ottoman conquest in 1517, Mamluk patrons in Egypt and Syria continued to produce a large number of beautiful buildings, including the famous tombs that today crowd Cairo's Northern Cemetery.

ENAMELED GLASS, METALWORK, AND CARPETS Mamluk patronage in Syria and Egypt also inherited a tradition of enameled glass that had begun under the Ayyubids. By the early fourteenth century, Mamluk glass vessels enameled with bright colors had become world-famous. Various Mamluk nobles commissioned glass oil lamps destined to be hung in their tombs and mosques, and artists incorporated the patrons' blazons, or coats of arms, in the decoration (fig. **9.26**). Under the Mamluks, by around 1300, the art of inlaying silver and gold into bronze and brass had also reached its apogee in Islamic art. In later Mamluk ˈnes, from the fifteenth century onward, the Mamluk realms ˈw the production of spectacular carpets that were exported to Europe, where, like the enameled glass, they were highly prized. (See *Materials and Techniques*, page 301.)

Nasrid Patronage: The Alhambra

By the mid-fourteenth century, most of Muslim al-Andalus had fallen to the Christian reconquest; Seville and Córdoba were part of the Castilian domains, and only the mountain kingdom of Granada in the south in the shadow of the Sierra Nevada remained under Muslim control, ruled by the Nasrid dynasty. On a flat hill towering over the city of Granada, the Nasrid monarchs built a palace known to them as al-Qasr al-Hamra (The Red Palace), and to history as the Alhambra. Originally conceived, as most Islamic palaces were, as a series of pavilions and smaller buildings constructed around one or more garden courtyards, the Alhambra incorporated metaphors for Paradise on earth. The inscriptions on its walls, some of which were written by one of the great Arab poets of the time, form a hymn of praise to the palace itself. Although what remains today is only a small fragment of the original palace, the rest having been consumed by a mammoth Renaissance palace and an equally huge Franciscan monastery, the most beautiful of the Alhambra's surviving courtyards, known as the Court of the Lions, gives us a vivid picture

9.26 Mosque lamp with blazon, from Cairo. ca. 1285. Enameled, stained, and gilded glass, height 10⅓" (26.2 cm), width 8¼" (21 cm). Metropolitan Museum of Art, New York. Gift of J. Pierpont Morgan. 1919 17.190.985

The Ottoman Sultan Selim II (1524–1574)

An Order from the Imperial Court

By spring 1572 the building of the sultan's mosque in Edirne was well under way. From the royal palace, the sultan took a very close interest in the progress of affairs, an approach that seems to have bordered on micromanagement. He even dictated what inscriptions were to be placed in what locations in the building.

To the Architect in Chief:

For the inscriptions that are currently needed for my noble mosque in Edirne that I have ordered to be built, you have requested the services of the calligrapher Molla Hasan. Now this individual been retained and dispatched for the above-mentioned business. I have ordered that, upon receipt and by fulfillment of this order, you show him the places in the noble mosque where he will prepare suitable and appropriate inscriptions, whether they be executed on tiles, or be simple painted inscriptions.

Conveyed though the Chief Tile-Maker

The 8th of Muharrem, 980 (May 21, 1572)

Source: Ahmed Refik, *Mimar Sinan*, tr. Walter Denny (Istanbul: Kanaat Kutuphanesi, 1931)

---

of the elegance, beauty, and luxury of the Nasrid court (fig. **9.27**). In the center of the court, a large stone basin carried on the backs of twelve lions holds a playing fountain, the pressurized water coming from the distant mountains. From the basin, four water channels reflecting the four rivers of Paradise carry the water into four pavilions on the sides of the courtyard. In its elaborately carved stucco, once vividly polychromed, and in its delicate and elaborate muqarnas and intricate inscriptions carried on slender multiple or single columns, the richly textured and almost gravity-defying architecture of the Alhambra creates an awesome impression. The Alhambra was to influence artistic consciousness for centuries to come, finding heirs in both sixteenth-century Morocco and in nineteenth-century Europe and the United States.

THE THREE LATE EMPIRES

In later Islamic times, three large empires formed major centers of Islamic artistic accomplishment: the Ottoman, the Safavid, and the Mughal. At the end of the thirteenth century, in a corner of Asia Minor just a dozen or so miles from the Byzantine capital of Constantinople, a vassal of the declining Seljuk sultanate named Osman (r. ca. 1281–1324) established a tiny frontier principality hosting warriors eager to expand the realms of Islam at the expense of the Christians. From this seed grew a mighty empire, which by the mid-sixteenth century had almost turned the Mediterranean into a Turkish lake, ruling from Cairo to the outskirts of Vienna, and from Algiers to northwestern Iran. It lasted until 1922. At the beginning of the sixteenth century, five deca

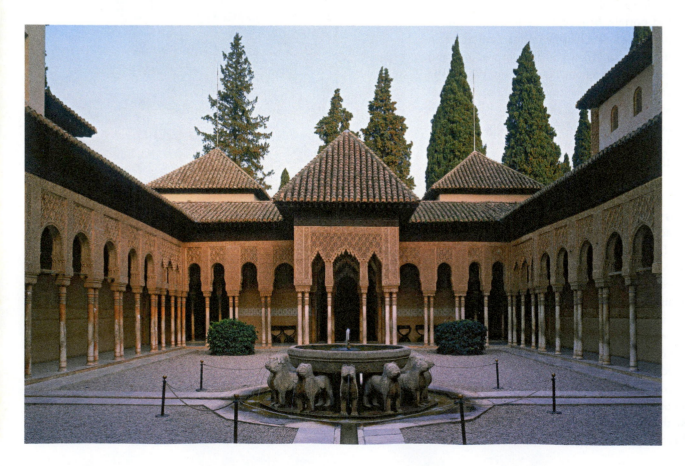

9.27 Court of t Lions, Alhambra, Granada, Spain. Mid-14th century

The Oriental Carpet

o artistic product of the Islamic world is better known outside its original home than the pile carpet, popularly called the oriental carpet. Carpets are heavy textiles meant to be used essentially in the form in which they leave the weaver's loom. That is, they are not cut or tailored, and they are usually woven as complete artistic works, not as goods sold by the yard. Their uses vary extensively from floor coverings to architectural decorations, from cushions and bolsters to bags and sacks of all sizes and shapes, and from animal trappings to religious objects (prayer rugs that provide a clean place for Muslim prayer). They can be used as secular or religious wall decoration. Carpet weaving is a deeply embedded art in the culture of many Islamic societies. It is a part of the socialization of young women, who form the bulk of Islamic artist-weavers. It is found not only in nomadic encampments and villages, but also in urban commercial weaving establishments and, in former times, in special workshops that functioned directly under court patronage in Islamic lands.

There are several different techniques for weaving Islamic carpets, but the best-known is the **pile carpet**, in which row after horizontal row of individual knots of colored wool are tied on vertical pairs of **warp** yarns, and each row of knots is then beaten in place by a beater, a tool that resembles a combination of a comb and a hammer, and subsequently locked in place by the passing of one or more horizontal **weft** yarns. The ends of each knot protrude vertically on the upper, or "right," side of the carpet, giving it a thick pile surface, at once highly reactive to light, conducive to rich color effects, and providing excellent insulation from cold floors or the earthen ground of a nomad's tent.

The carpet form probably arose originally among pre-Islamic nomadic peoples in Central Asia. The bulk of surviving early Islamic carpets, thought to have been woven from the thirteenth through fifteenth centuries, show connections in both design and technique to a nomadic past. In the fifteenth century, the so-called carpet design revolution led to the production of Islamic carpets in designs

Village carpet in geometric design, Konya area, Turkey. 18th or 19th century. Private collection. Courtesy of Gerard Paquin

that were created by court artists, and then translated into instructions for carpet weavers. These carpets were often used by royalty or given as gifts to royalty.

The design of a carpet, like that of a picture made on an ink-jet printer, is created out of a grid of colored dots consisting of small individual knots of colored wool that when viewed together form a design. Some carpets are fairly coarse in weave, and use a long pile; such carpets tend to use bold geometric designs and brilliant colors. Other carpets, such as those produced after designs by court or commercial artists, may use a much finer weave (in extreme cases, more than 2,000 knots in a square inch) and a short pile to reproduce curvilinear ornamental designs, calligraphy, or even depictions of humans and animals (see fig. 9.32) in large carpets. The symbolism of carpets may be extremely complex, varying from totemic designs of tribal significance to figural designs with arcane religious or secular meanings.

Exported to Europe since the fourteenth century, Islamic pile carpets have historically formed an East–West cultural bridge. In Europe, they not only decorated the palaces of the nobility and the houses of wealthy urban merchants, but were also used in churches, religious shrines, and as part of both secular and religious ceremonies. Islamic carpets, as prized works of art and signs of status and wealth, were frequently depicted in European paintings (see figs. 14.14, 14.21, and 20.36). Carpet weaving continues to flourish in the Middle East today. Demand for Islamic carpets in both East and West has actually increased in the late twentieth and early twenty-first centuries.

weft warp knot pile

Rows of individual knots, tied over two vertical warps, are tied, cut, and tightly hammered in place and locked

le symmetrical knotting structure used in many Turkish and Transcaucasian carpets after the Ottomans had conquered Constantinople and made it their capital, a charismatic Shi'ite warrior from northwestern Iran, the Safavid prince Ismail (r. 1501–1524), founded another great empire. In its successive capitals of Tabriz, Qazvin, and Isfahan, the Safavid state was to bring many genres of art to new levels of accomplishment within the Islamic world. Until the middle of the eighteenth century, the Safavids remained major rivals of the Ottomans, and their distinctive styles in architecture, book painting, and the applied arts of carpets and textiles influenced their neighbors to both west and east. In 1526, a Turkish prince from Central Asia named Babur (r. 1526–1530) invaded northern India. After a series of reverses and recoveries, Babur's grandson Akbar the Great (r. 1556–1605) firmly established the Mughal dynasty in the subcontinent. Through the next century and a half, the fabled palaces and monuments of the Mughal capital cities of Delhi, Agra, and Fatehpur Sikri, visited by Muslim and European travelers alike, became a byword throughout the world for the beauty, luxury, and opulence of the Islamic arts.

The Ottomans in Europe and Asia

At first there was little to distinguish what became known as the Ottoman Empire (in Italy, Osman was known as "Ottomano") from more than a dozen other small Islamic states that filled the vacuum left by the collapsing Seljuk power in Asia Minor. But, by 1357, the Ottomans had crossed the Dardanelles, a narrow strait between Europe and Asia, into the Balkans, and eventually by 1453 they had claimed the elusive prize of Constantinople itself, the second Rome and capital of Eastern Christianity. In this, tl capital city, popularly renamed Istanbul, and in their summer and military capital of Edirne, 120 miles (190 km) farther west into Europe, the Ottomans used their enormous economic power to patronize art and architecture on an unprecedented scale.

ARCHITECTURE   To their Topkapi Palace in Istanbul flocked artists from Iran, Egypt, the Balkans, and even from western Europe, while in the sixteenth century the architect known to posterity as Sinan the Great presided over an architectural establishment that saw the erection of hundreds of bridges, hans, madrasas, palaces, baths, markets, and mosques. The great imperial mosques of the Ottomans paid homage to the traditional Arab mosque by incorporating an atriumlike arcaded courtyard into their design. However, the vast interior space and daring engineering of Justinian's Hagia Sophia (see figs. 8.28 and 8.29), in combination with their own well-developed traditions, provoked an architectural response that made Ottoman mosques, often built in climates with extensive rainfall and winter snows, vastly different from mosques of the Arab or Iranian traditions. In 1572, Sinan built for Sultan Selim II (r. 1566–1574) in Edirne a huge imperial mosque that the architect considered his masterpiece

tops of the 8 piers that support the dome

buttresses supporting the dome

open inner courtyard in front of mosque

half dome over the mihrab

college for the study
of the life of Muhammad

outer courtyard
of the mosque

arasta or marketplace

west portal

primary school

arasta or marketplace

college for the study
of the Qur'an

9.28   Sinan the Great. Cutaway of the Mosque of Selim II (Selimiye), Edirne, Turkey. 1569–74

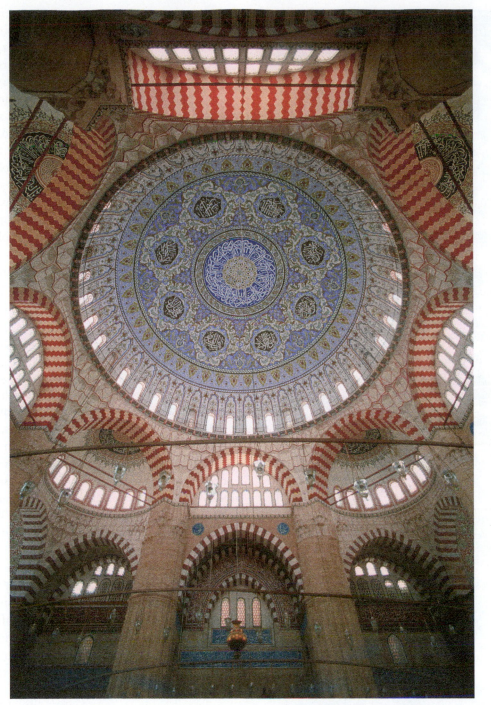

(fig. **9.28**). The courtyard with surrounding arcades and central fountain recalls the typical Arab mosque plan, but the huge lead-covered dome and the four pencil-thin triple-balconied minarets proclaim the Ottoman architectural style, while the vast interior, with its eight huge piers supporting a dome almost 197 feet high and over 108 feet in diameter, shows a unified and clearly delineated space (fig. **9.29**) that is completely different both from the Arab hypostyle mosque with its fragmented space, and from the Hagia Sophia with its mysterious structural and spatial ambiguity. In Sinan's work, the structural components—the muscles and sinews, as it were—rather than being hidden, are a primary source of the buildings' visual appeal. The Ottomans preferred an austere exterior of bare whitish stone contrasting with the dark-gray lead sheets used for waterproofing the domes and semidomes of their structures, while the interiors frequently incorporated beautiful polychrome tiles with designs of strikingly naturalistic flowers. (See *Primary Source*, page 300.)

THE OTTOMAN COURT STYLE By 1500, the Ottomans, like the Timurids before them, had developed a royal design studio, called the "house of design," that served as the central focus of royal artistic patronage. It reached its zenith under the patronage of Süleyman I, "The Magnificent" (r. 1520–1566), his son Selim II (r. 1566–1574), and his grandson Murad III (r. 1576–1595).

9.30 Shah Kulu (?). Tile painted in hatayi style with saz design. ca. 1525–50. Cobalt and turquoise underglaze painting on composite fritware body covered with white slip, 50 × 19″ (127 × 48.5 cm). Topkapı Palace Museum, Istanbul

Among the many artistic innovations to emerge from this complex of artists working in almost every conceivable medium and genre is a style of ornament called by some **saz**, taking its name from a legendary enchanted forest, and by others **hatayi**—that is, "from Cathay," or "China." Created in part by an émigré artist from Tabriz named Shah Kulu, who was head of the Ottoman royal studio by the mid-sixteenth century, the style is typified by energetic and graceful compositions of curved leaves and complex floral palmettes linked by vines that appear to overlap and penetrate each other, sometimes embellished with birds or strange antelope-like creatures. The saz or hatayi style is found in ceramic wares, manuscript illuminations, carpets, silk textiles, freehand drawings executed for the albums of royal collectors, and some remarkable blue and turquoise paintings on tile, probably from the hand of Shah Kulu himself (fig. **9.30**). Ottoman ceramics and silks were exported in large quantities to Russia and Europe, where along with the much-prized carpets from Asia Minor they were quickly absorbed into European material culture.

The Safavid Period in Iran

Shortly after 1500, Ismail, a charismatic prince descended from a family of venerated Shi'ite clerics in northwestern Persia, declared himself the Safavid shah (or king) of Iran. Quickly overrunning much of the formerly Timurid domains, the young ruler established his capital in the city of Tabriz in northwestern Iran, formerly the capital of two provincial Turkmen dynasties (a Turkic people who occupied parts of Central Asia), precariously close the eastern reaches of the Sunni Ottoman Empire. There, under Ismail (r. 1501–1523) and his successor Tahmasp (r. 1524–1576), who in 1548 moved his capital to the strategically more secure Qazvin to the east, the arts flourished.

BOOK ILLUSTRATION AND CARPETS: TABRIZ Early in the sixteenth century, the aged painter Behzad was brought from the east to Tabriz, where his influence, combined with the indigenous Turkmen painting style of pre-Safavid times, brought about a remarkable artistic synthesis. In the hands of one of the great geniuses of Islamic art, the Turkmen-born artist Sultan-Muhammad—it was not uncommon for artists in royal ateliers to incorporate honorifics like shah (king), sultan (ruler), or aqa (noble) into their names—the new Safavid style of miniature painting reached fresh heights in expressiveness as well as technique. One of the painter's most appealing creations is an illustration painted with opaque watercolors on paper in Tabriz around 1529 for a royal manuscript of a *divan*, or collection of poems, by the fourteenth-century poet Hafiz, utilizing the theme of heavenly and earthly intoxication, a favorite motif of mystical Persian poetry (fig. **9.31**). A group of elderly professors from a religious college are shown in various stages of disorderly intoxication, accompanied by servants, some fawning and others apparently terrified, while a group of strangely attired and caricatured musicians provides background music. On the roof of the building angels join in the revelry, while on the balcony

9.31 "Folio from the Divan of Hafiz, *Allegory of worldly and Otherworldly Drunkenness*. Islamic, Iran Tabriz, Illustrated Manuscript. Safavid period (1501–1722), Shah Tahmasp (1524–76), ca. 1526–27. Opaque watercolors, ink, and gold on paper, 11⁵⁄₁₆ x 14″" (28.7 × 35.5 cm). Harvard Art Museums/Arthur M. Sackler Museum, The Stuart Cary Welch Collection. Jointly owned by the Harvard Art Museums and the Metropolitan Museum of Art, 1988.460.2

9.32 Detail of the Sanguszko figural-design carpet, from Iran. ca. 1575–1600. Wool pile knotted on cotton warp and weft, entire carpet 19'8" × 10'8" (6.4 × 3.3 m). Private collection

the pie-eyed poet himself struggles to write his poem. Using an incredibly fine brushstroke, and a thick white application of paint to create the textures of the white silk Safavid turbans, with their characteristic colored batonlike ornaments sticking out the top, Sultan-Muhammad has created a work that reminds us that Islamic civilization is no stranger to humor or to the enjoyment of a good time, both metaphorically and literally.

The new style in book painting, with its brilliant colors, expressive faces, and great variety of body types, often set in a landscape filled with flowers or in a lavish architectural setting, was immediately transferable to other mediums. A carpet woven somewhere in the Safavid domains in the second half of the sixteenth century shows the application of the figural style of miniature painting to a symbolically complex composition of royal and heavenly motifs (fig. 9.32). It incorporates the royal hunt, the enjoyment of wine in a paradiselike setting, and a host of birds and animals. These forms are subject to a complex layering of symbolism, often intermingling the sacred and the profane, that reflect the strong role of Sufi mysticism in Safavid culture, as well as an age-old Persian love of wine, poetry, and beautiful possessions.

ARCHITECTURE: THE PLANNED CITY OF ISFAHAN By the beginning of the seventeenth century, the Safavid capital had been moved once again to the old city of Isfahan in the ⟨Per⟩sian heartland. There, the energetic and powerful Abbas I (r. 1588–1629) laid out to the south of the original city a new city with large public spaces and broad avenues, with palaces for the nobility and a quarter for Armenian Christian merchants. The splendor and prosperity of this new Isfahan drew commerce and travelers from all over the world, and the luxury goods sold in its bazaars, from silks and ceramics to metalware and carpets, together with the beauty of its gardens and the richness of its inhabitants, led to a famous Persian adage: "Isfahan is half the world." At one end of a huge open square known as the **maidan**, itself oriented with the North Star, Shah Abbas built his Royal Mosque (fig. **9.33**). Because the qibla lies to the southwest, facing Mecca, the mosque has to be at an entirely different orientation than the maidan. An ingenious 45-degree turn beyond the main portal deftly accomplishes a directional accommodation, leading into the huge open courtyard of the mosque, with its enormous domed chamber behind the qibla iwan, and all visible surfaces completely covered in brilliantly colored tiles.

The shops that line the sides of the maidan all contributed rents to the waqf or endowment of the mosque, and in the middle of the west side of the maidan, Shah Abbas built a palace from the balcony of which he could watch processions and sporting events in the square itself. The rest of the new city of Isfahan consisted in large part of spacious gardens surrounding the pavilionlike palaces of the Safavid nobility.

9.33 Aerial view of the Royal Mosque of Shah Abbas I (Masjid-i Shah), Isfahan, Iran. 1611–16

The Mughal Period in India

In 1526, Babur, who claimed descent from the Mongol Timur (hence the dynastic name "Mughal"), defeated a combined army of Hindu princedoms in northern India to establish the Mughal dynasty in the subcontinent. Although India had had an Islamic presence in Delhi since around 1200, the Mughal Empire was to bring a new flowering of Islamic art and architecture to the subcontinent. Centered in the capital cities of Agra, Delhi, and Fatehpur-Sikri, the scene of building and the production of works of art on a mammoth scale, the Mug[...] style built on an artistic combination of Central Asian, Safa[...] Persian, and indigenous Hindu art and culture. Under Babur's grandson Akbar the Great (r. 1556–1605), himself an unusually capable and charismatic ruler, the style took on its distinctive

9.34 Manohar and Abul Hasan *Ceremonial Audience of Jahangir*, from a *Jahangir-nama* manuscript, northern India. ca. 1620. Opaque watercolors and ink on paper, 13¾ × 7⅞" (35 × 20 cm). Museum of Fine Arts, Boston. Frances Bartlett Donation of 1912 and Picture Fund. Photograph © 2006 Museum of Fine Arts, Boston, 14654

PRIMARY SOURCE

Abd Al-Hamid Lahori (d. 1654)

From *Padshah Nama (Book of the Emperor)*

Abd al-Hamid Lahori was official court historian to Shah Jahan, who built the Taj Mahal as a monument to the memory of his beloved wife Mumtaz Mahal. The Padshah Nama was written in three volumes, each corresponding to a decade in Shah Jahan's reign. Before he could finish the third volume, Lahori was taken ill, and the work was completed by his younger colleague Muhammad Waris in 1657. This excerpt is from a much longer discussion of the building of the monument, together with an elaborate description of the tomb itself, the outbuildings, and the surrounding gardens.

At the beginning of the fifth year of the exalted accession (January, 1632), the excavation was started for the laying of the foundation of this sublime edifice, which is situated overlooking the Jumna river flowing adjacent to the north. And when the spade-wielders with robust arms and hands strong as steel, had with unceasing effort excavated down to the water-table, the ingenious masons and architects of astonishing achievements most firmly built its foundation with stone and mortar up to the level of the ground.

And on top of this foundation there was raised a kind of platform of brick and mortar in one solid block, measuring 374 cubits long by 140 wide and 16 high, to serve as the plinth of this exalted mausoleum—which evokes a vision of the heavenly gardens of Rizwan and epitomizes, as it were, the holy abodes of Paradise.

And from all parts of the empire, there were assembled great numbers of skilled stonecutters, lapidaries, and inlayers, each an expert in his art, who commenced work along with other craftsmen. In the middle of this platform plinth—which ranks [in magnificence] with the heavenly Throne of God—there was constructed another solid and level platform. In the center of the second platform, the building of this heaven-lofty and Paradise-like mausoleum was constructed on the plan of a Baghdadi octagon, 70 cubits in diameter, on a base plinth one cubit in height.

Situated in the exact center of the building, the domed hall over the sepulcher of that recipient of divine grace has been finished with white marble within and without. From the floor to the curvature, the hall under the dome is octagonal in shape, with a diameter of 22 cubits. The curvature is ornamented with *muqarnas* motifs, while from the cornice to the inner summit of the dome, which is at a height of 32 yards from the floor of the building, there are arranged marble slabs cut in a geometric molded pattern.

Source: W. E. Begley and Z. A. Desai, *Taj Mahal: The Illumined Tomb* (Cambridge, MA: Aga Kahn Program for Islamic Architecture, 1989)

...m. Akbar was a remarkably tolerant ruler, fascinated by Hinduism, interested in Persian poetry and art, and a patron of one of the major Indian Sufi orders. Under his patronage a royal studio of Persian and native painters blended their traditions to form a new style of miniature painting. In addition, Central Asian, Persian, and local builders and craftspeople blended their architectural styles and techniques to create a new Mughal style in architecture.

In a sense, the Mughal art of India revels in extremes—the largest and the smallest of Islamic miniature paintings, the largest but also the most finely woven small Islamic carpets, the most spectacular of all Islamic tomb structures, and the most extravagant Islamic jewelry and fanciful hardstone carving are all to be found here.

BOOK ILLUSTRATION A miniature painting in opaque water-colors on paper of a *darbar*, or ceremonial audience, given by the Mughal emperor Jahangir (r. 1605–1627), probably completed around 1620 by the court artists Manohar and Abul Hasan, shows the characteristics of the Mughal style (fig. **9.34**). The Mughals liked realistic pictures of current events; and almost every individual in the crowd can be identified by comparison with individual portraits made around the same time. Along with this specificity, ...tended to the visiting black-clad European monk and even to ...e smiling elephant, is a love of opulent detail, while space is created in the time-honored Islamic fashion by the use of a high point of view and an overlapping technique.

DECORATIVE ARTS A different side of Mughal art is seen in a wine cup fashioned from translucent white jade (fig. **9.35**) for the emperor Shah Jahan (r. 1628–1657). The delicately petaled blossom that forms the bowl of the cup gently tapers to the handle in the form of a bearded mountain goat from Kashmir. Despite the hardness of the stone, which had to be shaped by grinding

9.35 Wine cup of Shah Jahan, from northern India. Mid-17th century. White jade, 2¼ × 6¾″ (5.7 × 17.14 cm). Victoria & Albert Museum, London

for hundreds of hours, the finished product has the freshness of a flower itself. The same attention to botanical realism can be seen in floral decoration in many Mughal mediums, from textiles and carpets to carved and inlaid marble.

ARCHITECTURE: TAJ MAHAL The most famous of all Mughal works is doubtless the Taj Mahal, a royal tomb in Agra completed around 1650 and commissioned by Shah Jahan in memory of his deceased wife Mumtaz Mahal (fig. **9.36**). The building has the ground plan of a Timurid garden kiosk or palace from Central Asia, while the central dome recalls that of the Royal Mosque of Isfahan. (See *Primary Source*, page 309.) The snowy-white marble is lavishly inlaid with colored semiprecious stones in the form of flowers, vines, and beautiful cursive inscriptions. Set at one end of an elaborate quadripartite formal garden with four axial pools in the Persian style, the Taj Mahal is far more than a royal tomb or a dynastic monument. The inscriptions evoke the metaphor of the gardens of Paradise that are promised to devout believers in the Qur'an, and the domed building is a self-conscious evocation of the throne of God, re-created in an earthly version of divine Paradise.

CONTINUITY AND CHANGE IN ISLAMIC ART

In the eighteenth and nineteenth centuries, the great traditions of Islamic art continued through tumultuous periods of change. Economic decline led to a diminution in the royal patronage that had produced some of the most spectacular works of earlier periods, but stylistic traditions in every major area of the Islamic world continued to live on, despite political and economic dislocation, European colonialism, and the increasing use of factory-made goods in everyday life. Art of all kinds in a huge variety of mediums flourishes throughout the Islamic world in many countries today, largely ignored even by specialists in Islamic art because they have been trained to look at the works of earlier periods. Slowly, through encounters with new mediums and genres, with the pervasive American-European tradition of the later twentieth century, and through reencounters with their own historical past, Muslim artists are creating new traditions that seek to express what almost every artistic tradition has alwa embodied in almost every time—new creativity in the context a rich and meaningful past.

ca. 690 Construction of the
Dome of the Rock in Jerusalem

Islamic Art

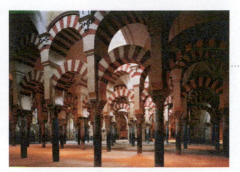

700 Construction begins on Great Mosque
at Córdoba, Spain

ca. 1026 Construction of al-Aqmar mosque, Cairo

Early 900s Islamic tombs
built in Bukhara for Persian
Samanid dynasty

1354–91 Court of the Lions, Alhambra

1486 Behzad's illustrations
for the *Bostan*

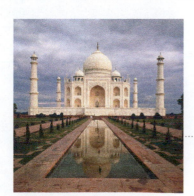

ca. 1650 Completion of Taj Mahal
in Agra, India

600

◄ 632 Death of the Prophet Muhammad

700

◄ by 700s Islam reaches Spain and Central Asia

◄ 750 Abbasid dynasty supplants Umayyad dynasty

800

900

ca. 950 *Joshua Roll*
◄ 962 Otto I crowned Holy Roman Emperor
◄ 969 Cairo founded as the capital of the Fatimids

1000

◄ mid-1000s Seljuk Turkish invaders begin rule

◄ 1099 First Crusade warriors capture Jerusalem

1100

1180–90 Apse mosaic of Monreale

1200

◄ 1258 Mongols sack and destroy Baghdad
◄ by end of 1200s Western Mongol rulers converted
   to Islam
◄ by 1300s Almohad capital of Seville falls to kings
   of Castile
ca. 1310–20 Keriye Camii *Anastasis*

1300

◄ mid-1300s Most of Muslim al-Andalus fallen to
   Christian Reconquest

1400

◄ 1453 Ottomans claim Constantinople as their
   capital

1500

◄ 1501 Prince Ismail founds Safavid Empire in Iran

◄ 1556–1605 Akbar the Great rules Mughal India

1600

◄ 1616 Death of English playwright William
   Shakespeare

1700

CHAPTER 10

Early Medieval Art

THE TERM EARLY MEDIEVAL IS SOMETHING OF A CATCHALL PHRASE used to describe the art of a number of cultures and a variety of regions in western Europe after the Fall of Rome (476 CE) until the eleventh century (map **10.1**). Significant in Rome's demise was the power asserted by migrating Germanic peoples (including Franks, Visigoths, Ostrogoths, and

Saxons), who moved into and through Europe and eventually established permanent settlements both north of the Alps and in Italy, Spain, and southern France. These were clearly tumultuous times, as invaders clashed and eventually mixed with local inhabitants, including the Celts, the descendants of the Iron Age peoples of Europe. ("Celt" is a confusing term, since it is also used to define tribal groups who occupied Britain and Ireland between the fifth and twelfth centuries.) As the invaders established permanent settlements, they adopted many customs traditional to the areas they inhabited. Overlaid on this mix of customs were Roman traditions, including those of Christianity, which in many cases had been adopted by indigenous local tribes when they were conquered by Rome.

The allure of Christianity—for both its spiritual message and for the structure it imposed on a fragmented society in times of turmoil—once again proved momentous. Conversion from pagan worship, however, was now less an individual decision (as it had been in the Early Christian period) than a social one. Often, when a tribal leader decided to convert to Christianity, his subjects converted with him, virtually en masse, as occurred in Reims on Christmas Day in 496, when 3,000 Franks were baptized along with Clovis, their king.

The Church emerged as a force vitally important for European unification; even so, loyalty to family and clan continued to govern social and political alliances. Strong chiefs assumed leadership and established tribal allegiances and methods of exchange, both economic and political, that would eventually result in the development throughout western Europe of a system of political organization known as feudalism. These social and political alignments eventually led to a succession of ruling dynasties governed by strong leaders who were able to increase the areas under their dominion. These dynasties (principally the Carolingian and Ottonian) were ambitious to reestablish a centralized authority, absent in Europe after the Fall of Rome. The attempt to provide a stable political structure was based, if not in the reality of the Roman Empire, then at least in the ideals embodied in its legacy.

The art that resulted from this cultural interchange is a vibrant and vital mix. Artistic methods, materials, and traditions, introduced by migration, were combined with those that predominated in the regions where tribes settled. Much of this art is marked by elaborate patterns of interlocking and interwoven designs that decorate sumptuous objects of personal adornment, reflecting their owners' social position. Eventually the Church assumed increasing importance in commissioning works of art, and there was a shift of emphasis in the types of objects produced. The Church built and decorated many houses of worship and established a large number of monastic communities. Within the monasteries, scriptoria made elaborately decorated books, which

Detail of figure 10.5, Cross page, from the *Lindisfarne Gospels*

Map 10.1 Europe in the early Middle Ages

were sent off with missionaries as aids in their efforts to convert and educate.

Carolingian and Ottonian artists expressed the imperial ambitions of their leaders by building churches and designing architectural complexes that consciously emulated Rome. Roman-derived Early Christian basilicas served as models for a large number of buildings north of the Alps. Court-related artists also produced copies of ancient books. And three-dimensional sculpture, an art form virtually abandoned after the Fall of Rome, once again attracted the attention of artists and their patrons. Thus, out of an amalgam of diverse and conflicting forces, and as new social and cultural entities developed, an art emerged that is as varied as it is exciting.

ANGLO-SAXON ART

The widespread migrations of peoples transformed Europe. In 376, the Huns, who had advanced beyond the Black Sea from Central Asia, became a serious threat to Europe. They pushed the Germanic Visigoths westward into the Roman Empire from the Danube. Then in 451, under Attila (d. 453), they invaded Gaul, present-day France and Germany, and its resident Celts. Also in the fifth century, the Angles and Saxons from today's Denmark and northern Germany invaded the British Isles, which had been colonized for centuries by Celts. Many of these Germanic tribes developed into virtual kingdoms: the Visigoths in Spain, the Burgundians and Franks in Gaul, the Ostrogoths and Lombards in Italy. The Vikings controlled Scandinavia and ventured afar, a result of their might as sailors.

The Germanic peoples brought with them art forms that were portable: weaving, metalwork, jewelry, and woodcarvings. Artistic production in these mediums required training and skill of execution, and metalwork in particular had intrinsic value, since it was often made of gold or silver and inlaid with precious stones. Metalworkers had high social status, a measure of the respect accorded to their labor and to the value of the objec[t] they produced. (See *Materials and Techniques*, page 315.) In sor[me] Germanic folk legends, metalworkers have abilities so remarkabl[e] that they are described as magical. Numerous small-scale objects

Metalwork

etal was a precious commodity in the Middle Ages. Even in the ancient world, patterns of interchange and colonization can be related to exploration for desirable metals: For example, the Greek settlements in Italy and Roman settlements in Spain were a result of a desire for metals. Popular metals employed in the early Middle Ages included gold, silver, copper, iron, and bronze. The many ways that metals could be worked was undoubtedly one of their most compelling features. They could be flattened, drawn thin, or made into an openwork design of filigree, lacy decoration made from intertwined wires. They could also be cast, engraved, punched, stamped, and decorated with colored stones, glass, or enamels.

The large gold buckle from the Sutton Hoo ship burial (see fig. 10.1) contains nearly a pound of gold, although it is only one of many gold pieces found in the burial site. That so much early medieval metalwork from grave sites is gold reflects the value attached to the metal. In addition, gold is not harmed by contact with either earth or water (whereas silver and other metals are subject to progressive destruction when exposed to the elements). Although gold had been obtained in Europe through mining since Roman times, the most common method of acquiring it was by collecting nuggets or small grains from rivers and streams (called placer or alluvial gold). The Rhine, Tiber, Po, Rhone, and Garonne rivers, along which the Germanic tribes settled, were major sources of this type of gold, which medieval writers refer to as "sand" gold.

Sutton Hoo's gold buckle is decorated with granulation, beads of d bonded to the surface, as well as **inlaid niello**, the dark mate-.... that is set into incisions in the metal surface and that sets off the intricate interlace designs composed of lines and dots. Niello is a sulfur alloy of silver, copper, or lead that, when heated, fuses with the metal that surrounds it, in this case gold, and produces a nearly black substance. The shiny dark niello serves to emphasize the brilliance of the gold and to accentuate the details of the intricate patterns.

A medieval treatise written by a monk named Theophilus in Germany in the early twelfth century contains instructions for polishing inlaid niello. First, smooth the niello with a soft stone dampened with saliva; then, using a piece of limewood, rub it with a powder of ground soft stone and saliva. After that, as Theophilus explains:

> For a very long time, lightly rub the niello with this piece of wood and the powder, continually adding spittle so that it remains moist, until it becomes bright all over. Then take some wax from the hollow of your ear, and, when you have wiped the niello dry with a fine linen cloth, you smear this all over it and rub lightly with a goatskin or deerskin until it becomes completely bright.

—Theophilus, *De diversis artibus*, tr. C. R. Dodwell as *Theophilus: The Various Arts* (London: Nelson, 1961)

The Sutton Hoo purse lid (see fig. 10.3) and hinged clasps (see fig. 10.2) are also notable for their *cloisonné* decoration. Cloisonné is an cient technique, used as early as the second millennium BCE in the stern Mediterranean. Individual metal strips, or *cloisons* (French for "partitions"), are attached on edge to a baseplate as little walls to form cells that enclose glass or gems. For the Sutton Hoo jewelry, red garnets are used extensively. In fact, the Sutton Hoo jewelry includes more than 4,000 individual garnets. Colored glass, often arranged in checkered patterns, is also used in these pieces; on the main field of the hinged clasps, *cloisons* enclose colored glass to form a step pattern, which enhances the overall decorative effect.

Many of the decorative devices and materials employed in Anglo-Saxon metalwork were later used by Irish metalworkers. A spectacular example is the *Tara Brooch*, an accidental find made by a child playing by the seashore in County Meath, Ireland, in 1850. The brooch is a kind of stickpin used to join two pieces of a garment together. An incredible amount of decoration—including spirals, bird, animal, and human heads, and interlace patterns—is compressed on a piece of jewelry of just over 3½ inches in diameter. Panels of gold filigree, consisting of fine soldered wire, are combined on the back of the brooch with silver plaques with inlaid spiral designs in copper. A braided wire attachment was possibly a safety chain.

Tara Brooch, from Bettystown, County Meath, Ireland. 8th century. Gilt, bronze, glass, and enamel, diameter 3⅝" (8.7 cm). National Museum of Ireland, Dublin reflect the vitality of artistic forms produced by these migrating peoples, demonstrating an aesthetic that is quite different from the tradition that derives from Greece and Rome, yet equally rich in myth and imagery.

The Animal Style

The artistic tradition of the Germanic peoples, referred to by some scholars as the **animal style** because of its heavy use of stylized animal-like forms, merged with the intricate ornamental metal-work of the Celts, producing a unique combination of abstract and organic shapes, of formal discipline and imaginative freedom.

SHIP BURIAL, SUTTON HOO, ENGLAND An Anglo-Saxon ship burial in England follows the age-old tradition of burying important people with their personal effects. This custom may reflect a concern for the afterlife or it may simply be a way to honor the dead, but undoubtedly a correlation was understood between a sea voyage and the journey to an eternal resting place. The ship burial at Sutton Hoo (*hoo* is Anglo-Saxon for "head-land" or "promontory"), discovered in 1939 in one of 18 burial mounds on the site, is of a seventh-century Anglian king (gener-ally thought to be King Raedwald, who died around 625). The ship, one of two buried on the site, was over 90 feet long and 14 feet in the beam and was hauled more than a third of a mile from the sea. Military gear, silver and enamelware, official royal regalia, gold coins, and objects of personal adornment are all part of the entombment. Since no trace of a body was originally found in the ship, some claimed that the burial was a **cenotaph**, a memorial monument to honor a person buried elsewhere; it was also argued that the highly acidic soil could have destroyed any evidence of human remains. More recent analysis suggests that the presence of phosphate residuals, particularly along the keel of the ship, could indicate biological remains. Even if that claim is correct, it would not necessarily prove that those remains were human, since ani-mals were buried in other mounds at Sutton Hoo; the practice of burying items that were part of a funeral feast could also produce phosphatic residue.

The Anglo-Saxon poem *Beowulf*, so concerned with displays of royal responsibility and obligation, includes a description ship fitted out for a funeral that is reminiscent of the Sutton Hoo burial. The funeral is that of Beowulf's father, King Scyld:

There in the harbour was a ring-prowed fighting
Ship, its timbers icy, waiting,
And there they brought the beloved body
Of their ring-giving lord, and laid him near
The mast. Next to that noble corpse
They heaped up treasures, jeweled helmets,
Hooked swords and coats of mail, armor
Carried from the ends of the earth.

Translated by Burton Raffel, Beowulf (NY: New American Library,
a division of Penguin Group, 1963)

Although *Beowulf* describes events that predate the Sutton Hoo find by at least a century, the poem was probably not composed until a century or more after that burial. So, while *Beowulf* should not be taken as a documentary account, it does suggest a royal context for the Sutton Hoo site.

Intricate animal-style design covers a large gold buckle from Sutton Hoo (fig. **10.1**). Two interlaced biting snakes decorate the stud to which the tongue of the buckle is attached. That stud is in turn affixed to a plaque with intertwined serpents and eagle heads covering virtually every available space. It has been traditional scholars to refer to the need to decorate all surfaces as an expres-sion of *horror vacui*, a fear of empty space. But this designation imposes our contemporary values on a culture alien to them. Unlike the Greeks and Romans, who used spatial illusionism to animate their art, Germanic and Celtic artists used intricate patterns to enliven the surface of their precious objects. Although the designs can seem confusing and claustrophobic to us, there is a consistent and intentional tightness in the way the patterns hold together.

10.1 Gold buckle, from the Sutton Hoo ship burial. First half of 7th century. Gold, length 5¼" (13.4 cm). The British Museum, London. Courtesy of the Trustees

A pair of hinged clasps (fig. 10.2) from the burial also contains intertwined serpents, here functioning as framing devices for a diagonally oriented checkerboard field of garnets and glass set in gold. At the end of each clasp is a curved plaque on which crouch boars back to back. So tightly integrated into the design are these animals that it is difficult to decide if the plaque curves to allow for the representation of the boars or if the animals' backs hunch in response to the shape of the clasp.

A gold, enamel, and garnet purse cover (fig. 10.3) was also found at Sutton Hoo. The three hinges at the top of the purse ached to leather straps suspended from the belt that was held together by the gold buckle illustrated in fig. 10.1. The purse itself was probably a leather pouch, the whole arrangement reminiscent of the sporran that Scots wear in front of their kilts. Its original ivory or bone background does not survive and has been replaced. Each of four pairs of symmetrical motifs has its own distinctive character, an indication that they were assembled from different sources. One, the standing man between facing animals in the lower row, has a very long history indeed. We first saw him in Mesopotamian art more than 3,200 years earlier (see fig. 2.9). The upper design, at the center, is of more recent origin. It consists of fighting animals whose tails, legs, and jaws are

10.3 Purse cover, from the Sutton Hoo ship burial. First half of 7th century. Gold with garnets and enamels, length 8″ (20.3 cm). The British Museum, London. Courtesy of the Trustees

elongated into bands that form a complex interweaving pattern. The fourth design, on the top left and right, uses interlacing bands as an ornamental device. The combination of these bands with the animal style, as shown here, seems to have been invented not long before our purse cover was made.

The Sutton Hoo objects are significant for the way they illustrate the transmission of motifs and techniques through the migration of various peoples. They show evidence of cultural interchange with Germanic peoples, combined with evidence of Scandinavian roots, but there are other noteworthy connections as well. King Raedwald was reputed to have made offerings to Christ, as well as to his ancestral pagan gods. A number of the objects discovered at Sutton Hoo make specific reference to Christianity, including silver bowls decorated with a cross, undoubtedly the result of trade with the Mediterranean. There is also a set of spoons inscribed with the names of Saul and Paul, perhaps a reference to Christian conversion (Saul changed his name to Paul on his conversion). Is it too much to wonder, as some scholars have done, if the crosses inscribed in the glass checkerboards on the Sutton Hoo clasps (see fig. 10.2) are a conscious reference to the new religion? These clasps were sewn onto two parts of a garment, probably held together at the shoulders, as is suggested by their curvature. Although executed in the patterns of Anglo-Saxon style, they take the form of fasteners very like those seen in Roman gear; for example, the shoulder attachments of the breastplate of the *Augustus of Primaporta* (see fig. 7.29). In fact, Roman and Byzantine articles accompany other objects of local manufacture that copy imperial forms in the Sutton Hoo graves. This has been cited as evidence that the chieftain buried or commemorated there consciously presented himself as a Roman ruler.

The chief medium of the animal style was clearly metalwork. Such articles, small, durable, and often of exquisitely refined craftsmanship, were eagerly sought after, which accounts for the rapid diffusion of the animal-style repertoire of forms. These forms spread not only geographically but also from one material to another, migrating from metal into wood, stone, and even paint. They were used to convey a variety of messages, some clearly pagan and others Christian.

HIBERNO-SAXON ART

During the early Middle Ages, the Irish (called "Hibernians" after the Roman name for Ireland, "Hibernia") came to be the spiritual and cultural leaders of western Europe. Since the Irish had never been part of the Roman Empire, the missionaries who carried Christianity to them from England in the fifth century found a Celtic society that was barbarian by Roman standards. The Irish readily accepted Christianity, bringing them into contact with Mediterranean civilization. However, because the institutional framework of the Roman Church was essentially urban, it did not suit the rural Irish way of life. Irish Christians preferred to follow the example of the desert

saints of Egypt and the Near East, who had sought spiritual perfection in the solitude of the wilderness, where groups of them founded the earliest monasteries (see page 263). Thus, Irish monasteries were established in isolated, secluded areas, e̶ on islands off the mainland, and such places required complete self-sufficiency.

Manuscripts

Irish monasteries soon became centers of learning and the arts, with much energy spent copying literary and religious texts. They also sent monks abroad to preach to nonbelievers and to found monasteries in northern Britain and Europe, from present-day France to Austria. Each monastery's scriptorium became an artistic center. Although pictures illustrating biblical events held little interest for the Irish monks, they devoted great efforts to decorative embellishment. The finest of these

10.4 *Symbol of St. Matthew*, from the *Book of Durrow*. ca. 680. Tempera on vellum, 9⅝ × 6⅛″ (24.7 × 15.7 cm). Trinity College, Dublin

manuscripts belong to the Hiberno-Saxon style—a style that combines Christian with Celtic and Germanic elements, and that flourished in the monasteries of Ireland as well as those founded by Irish monks in Saxon England. These Irish monks helped speed the conversion to Christianity in Europe north of the Alps. Throughout Europe, they made the monastery a cultural center and thus influenced medieval civilization for several hundred years.

In order to spread the message concerning Christ, the Kingdom of God, and salvation—called the Gospel—the Irish monasteries had to produce large numbers of copies of the Bible and other Christian books by hand. Every manuscript copy was looked upon as a sacred object containing the Word of God, and its beauty needed to reflect the importance of its contents. Each of the four books of the Gospel, which were credited to the evangelists Matthew, Mark, Luke, and John, was prefaced by a representation of the book's author or an animal that functioned as his symbol. These symbols were assigned to the evangelists by early commentators, including St. Jerome (342–420), who was responsible for the first translation of the Bible into Latin. Although the tradition of assigning specific symbols was at first far from codified, eventually the symbols came to be systematically associated with the evangelists as follows: the man or angel with St. Matthew, the lion with St. Mark, the ox with St. Luke, and the eagle with St. John. These beasts were described in the Book of Ezekiel (1:5–14) in the Hebrew Bible and in the Apocalypse of St. John the Evangelist (4:6–8) in the Christian one.

The illustration of the symbol of St. Matthew in the *Book of Durrow* (fig. **10.4**) shows how ornamental pattern can animate a figure even while accentuating its surface decoration. The body of the figure, composed of framed sections of a checkerboard pattern, recalls the ornamental quality of the Sutton Hoo clasps (see fig. 10.2). The addition of a head, which confronts us directly, and feet, turned to the side, transform the decorative motifs into a human figure. Active, elaborate patterns, previously seen in metalwork, are here employed to demonstrate that St. Matthew's message is precious. Irish scribes and artists were revered for their abilities and achievements. A medieval account relates how, after his death, an Irish scribe's hands were preserved as relics capable of performing miracles.

THE *LINDISFARNE GOSPELS* Thanks to a later **colophon** (a note at the end of a manuscript), we know a great deal about the origin of the *Lindisfarne Gospels*, produced in Northumbria, England, including the name of the translator (Aldred) and of the scribe (Bishop Eadfrith), who presumably painted the illuminations as well. (See *Primary Source*, page 320.) Given the high regard in which Irish scribes and artists were held, it is not surprising that a bishop is credited with writing and decorating this manuscript. In Irish monasteries monks were divided into three categories: juniors (pupils and novice monks), working brothers (engaged in manual labor), and seniors (the most experienced monks, who were responsible for copying sacred books).

10.5 Cross page, from the *Lindisfarne Gospels*. ca. 700. Tempera on vellum, 13½ × 9¼″ (34.3 × 23.5 cm). The British Library, London

The Cross page (fig. **10.5** and see page 312) is a creation of breathtaking complexity. Working with the precision of a jeweler, the **miniaturist** (the illuminator of the manuscript) poured into the geometric frame animal interlace so dense and yet so full of movement that the fighting beasts on the Sutton Hoo purse cover (see fig. 10.3) seem simple in comparison. In order to achieve this effect, the artist had to work within a severe discipline as though he were following specific rules. The smallest motifs and the largest patterns were worked out in advance of painting. Ruler and compass were used to mark the page with a network of grid lines and with points, both drawn and pricked. In applying paint, the artist followed his drawing exactly. No mark is allowed to interfere with either the rigid balance of individual features or the overall design. The scholar Françoise Henry has suggested that artists conceived of their work as "a sort of sacred riddle" composed of abstract forms to be sorted out and deciphered. Organic and geometric shapes had to be kept separate.

PRIMARY SOURCE

Lindisfarne Gospels

Colophon

Colophons are notes written at the end of some manuscripts recording who wrote them, when, for whom, etc. The colophon at the end of the Lindisfarne Gospels (ca. 700 ce) was written some 250 years after the text, but most scholars believe that its information is accurate. It names the scribe, the binder, the maker of the metal ornaments on the binding, and the author of the English translation of the Latin text, but no painter. The painting seems to have been done by Eadfrith, the scribe.

Eadfrith, Bishop of the Lindisfarne Church, originally wrote this book, for God and for Saint Cuthbert and ... for all the saints whose relics are in the Island. And Ethelwald, Bishop of the Lindisfarne islanders, impressed it on the outside and covered it he well knew how to do. And Billfrith, the anchorite, forged ornaments which are on it on the outside and adorned it with gold and with gems and also with gilded-over silver—pure metal. And Aldred, unworthy and most miserable priest, glossed it in English between the lines with the help of God and Saint Cuthbert.

Source: Cotton MS Nero, D. IV. The British Library

Within the animal compartments, every line had to turn out to be part of an animal's body. Other rules concerned symmetry, mirror-image effects, and repetitions of shapes and colors. Only by intense observation can we enter into the spirit of this mazelike world. It is as if these biting and clawing monsters are subdued by the power of the Cross, converted to Christian purpose just as were the Celtic tribes themselves.

10.6 *St. Matthew*, from the *Lindisfarne Gospels*. ca. 700. Tempera on vellum, 13½ × 9¼" (34.3 × 23.5 cm). The British Library, London (MS Cotton Nero D.4. f 25v)

Several factors came together to foster the development of the Hiberno-Saxon style: the isolation of the Irish, the sophistication of their scriptoria in the secluded monastic environments, and the zealous desire to spread the word of Christianity. In time and with more contact with the Continent—Rome in particular—Hiberno-Saxon art reflected new influences. The illustration of Matthew in the *Lindisfarne Gospels* (fig. **10.6**) is striking by comparison with the Matthew from the *Book of Durrow* (see fig. 10.4), made only a generation or two earlier. In the *Lindisfarne Gospels*, Matthew studies his text intently, and the artist suggests a sense of space by turning the figure and the bench on an angle to indicate depth, whereas in the *Book of Durrow*, the saint stares out frontally at the reader with his hands at his sides. There are no other figures in the *Book of Durrow* image, whereas the tied-back curtain in the Lindisfarne manuscript reveals an unidentified figure, whom some identify as Christ holding the Christian Bible and others, more convincingly, as Moses holding the Hebrew Bible. The latter identification is more compelling because the contrast between the open book of the Gospel writer and the closed book of the other figure correlates with distinctions between the two Testaments that were often made in the Middle Ages. Also, whereas Matthew in the *Book of Durrow* wears a costume of flat patterns, the Lindisfarne Matthew wears clothes marked by folds; a dark undergarment is distinguished from a lighter toga, suggesting a pliant material that responds to the body beneath it.

How do we explain this change? We know that in the seventh and eighth centuries the Irish had increased contact with Rome and came to adopt Roman liturgical practices. For example, the abbot of the monastery of Jarrow, near Lindisfarne, is reported to have returned from Rome at the end of the seventh century with a host of manuscripts. Artists at Jarrow probably used the illuminations in these manuscripts as models. The illustration of the prophet Ezra restoring the Bible from the *Codex Amiatinus* (fig. **10.7**), produced at Jarrow, is undoubtedly an adaptation of Roman illuminations available at the monastery. The artist depicts the book cupboard (reminiscent of the one in the St. Lawrence lunette from Galla Placidia [see fig. 8.14]), table, bench, and footstool by using oblique angles, which convey a sense of perspective, as if the objects recede into depth. Likewise, the

10.7 *Ezra Restoring the Bible*, from the *Codex Amiatinus*.
Early 8th century. Tempera on vellum, 20 × 13½″ (50.5 × 34.3 cm).
Biblioteca Medicea Laurenziana, Florence

shading in the drapery and the shadow of the inkwell on the floor promote a sense of depth. The artist also used color blending (evident on Ezra's garments and on his hands, face, and feet) to model form. Notice, in particular, how Ezra's cushion seems to have been depressed by the weight of his body, lending further substance to the prophet's figure.

Some have suggested that Eadfrith, the illustrator of the Lindisfarne Matthew (see fig. 10.6), referred to the same Roman manuscript that inspired the Ezra artist, who produced a more faithful interpretation of it. Indeed, identical poses and parallel features such as the bench are too conspicuous to be ignored. However, Eadfrith was eager, or perhaps felt required, to maintain some Hiberno-Saxon traditional devices: Unlike the Ezra artist, he decorated the bench with multiple patterns, and suggested depth in the drapery by juxtaposing near-complementary colors, playing off the reddish folds against the greenish cloth. Eadfrith employed the same rigid outline, geometric decoration,

and flat planes of color that he used for the manuscript's non-figural pages (see fig. 10.5). Much as the Ezra page allows us to appreciate what antique manuscripts that no longer survive might have looked like, the Lindisfarne page is both more striking and more dramatic. As the *Lindisfarne Gospels* document a process of synthesis between northern and Mediterranean elements, it helps us appreciate the remarkable contribution to European art made by migration styles and the skill of Hiberno-Saxon artists.

THE *BOOK OF KELLS* The Hiberno-Saxon manuscript style reached its climax a hundred years after the *Lindisfarne Gospels* in the *Book of Kells*, the most elaborate codex of Celtic art. It was probably made, or at least begun, at the end of the eighth or the beginning of the ninth century at the monastery on the island of Iona, off the western coast of Scotland, which had been founded by Irish monks in the sixth century. The book's name derives from the Irish monastery of Kells, where the manuscript was housed from the late ninth century until the seventeenth century. Its many pages reflect a wide array of influences from the Mediterranean to the English Channel.

The Chi Rho Iota monogram page illustrates Christ's initials, *XPI*, in Greek (fig. **10.8**). Alongside them appear the words *Christi autem generatio*, or "now this is how the birth of Christ came about," heralding the beginning of the Book of Matthew (1:18), in which the birth of Jesus is celebrated. The Chi Rho Iota page has much the same swirling design as the Cross page from the *Lindisfarne Gospels*, and a viewer can also see parallels to contemporary jewelry, such as the *Tara Brooch* (see *Materials and Techniques*, page 315). The relationship between manuscript illumination and precious metalwork is far from accidental, evidenced by the display of both on altars and their being housed in church treasuries. During a period when literacy was rare and class-based, the book was a symbol of authority and dominance, an object that must have mystified many people as much as it elucidated matters for others.

On the Chi Rho Iota page, the rigid geometry of the Lindisfarne Cross page and the *Tara Brooch* has been relaxed somewhat, and for the first time images of humans are incorporated into the design. The very top of the X-shaped Chi sprouts a recognizable face, while along its shaft are three angels with wings. And in a touch of enchanting fantasy, the tendril-like P-shaped Rho ends in a human head that has been hypothesized to be a representation of Christ. More surprising still is the introduction of the natural world. Nearly hidden in the ornamentation, as if playing a game of hide-and-seek, are cats and mice, butterflies, even otters catching fish. No doubt they performed a symbolic function for medieval readers, even if the meaning is no longer apparent to us. The richness and intricacy of the illustration compels concentration, establishing a direct connection between the viewer and the image in much the same way as does the fixed, direct gaze of the holy figure in an Early Byzantine icon (see fig. 8.35). In each work, icon and manuscript illumination, the power of the

10.8 Chi Rho Iota page, from the Book of Matthew (1:18), from the *Book of Kells*. ca. 800. Ink and pigments on vellum, 13 × 9½″ (33 × 24.1 cm). Trinity College Library, Dublin

image is so strong that the viewer virtually enters into its realm, forgetting the world outside its frame.

VIKING ART

It was not only in Hiberno-Saxon art that the animal style showed its power to adapt to a variety of materials and forms of expression. The inhabitants of Scandinavia (Norway, Sweden, and Denmark) had lived out of the Roman orbit, although they shared many beliefs and practices with their Germanic brethren and neighbors. In fact, the animal style flourished in Scandinavia long beyond the Germanic-Nordic migrations in the region, longer than it did anywhere else. These northern people are often labeled Vikings, though the term is a misleading one, since it derives from the Old Norse *Vinkingr*, which means sea pirate or raider; thus, these people were really only "Vikings" when they went "*a-viking*" out of their own coastal waters, to England or Russia, for instance. By the eighth century, Nordic sailors increasingly wandered around the shores of Europe, both trading with and

attacking the local populations. This sometimes led to permanent settlements, such as occurred in Iceland in the ninth century and Greenland in the tenth, and when a colony was established in northwestern France. Even today, the French region is called Normandy and its inhabitants are referred to as Normans in recognition of its settlement by Norsemen (or "North Men").

SHIP BURIAL, OSEBERG, NORWAY It is in Scandinavia that the origins for burying important people in ships, such as at Sutton Hoo, can be found; this is also where the practice seems to have continued longer than elsewhere. A buried Viking ship of the early ninth century, found at Oseberg, in southern Norway, is more than 75 feet long; the boat was not a raiding vessel, but rather a pleasure craft, used for sailing in calm waters (fig. **10.9**). Two women, placed on beds in a burial chamber, were interred within the ship, which also included oars, a ramp, an elaborately carved cart, sleds, and the skeletons of at least ten horses. Grave robbers stole whatever jewelry and metalwork, which is presumed to have been significant, that accompanied the deceased in the buried vessel.

10.9 Burial ship, from Oseberg, Norway. ca. 834. Wood, length 75′6″ (23 m). Vikingskiphuset, Universitets Oldsaksamling, Oslo, Norway

The prow and stern of the ship end in wavelike spirals, and the prow terminates in a serpent's head. If we recall the passage in *Beowulf* cited above (see page 316), we realize that the "ring-whorled prow" of the poem undoubtedly describes the spiral ornament of a boat such as the one from Oseberg. The body of the ship is framed at bow and stern by bands of carved reliefs in which biting and clawing animals are intertwined in an intricate and strangely orderly procession. Five wooden posts decorated with snarling monsters looking like mythical sea dragons were found in the buried ship. Their actual function is not known, although suggestions include the possibility that they were carried in processions or used for cult functions. The head on one of the posts (fig. **10.10**) displays all the characteristics of the animal style and is surprisingly realistic, as are such details as the teeth, gums, and nostrils. Interlacing and geometric patterns cover the head, with deep undercutting and rounded rms accentuating these surface designs. Although the origins the patterns employed here are found within Germanic and Anglo-Saxon motifs, they have been forcefully adapted to fit the animal head's dynamic curving forms. Scientific studies using

10.10 *Animal Head*, from the Oseberg burial ship. ca. 834. Wood, height approx. 5″ (12.7 cm). Vikingskiphuset, Universitets Oldsaksamling, Oslo

dendrochronology (the analysis of the growth rings of trees or wooden objects) date the Oseberg ship burial to 834. One of the women buried at Oseberg is often identified as Queen Asa, wife of Gudröd the Magnificent (ca. 780–820), because it is assumed that only a royal personage would have had the resources to commission objects of such richness, but recent scholarship questions the royal nature of the burial.

CAROLINGIAN ART

During the late eighth century, a new empire developed out of the collection of tribes and kingdoms that dominated northern continental Europe. This empire, which united most of Europe from the North Sea to Spain and as far south as Lombardy in northern Italy, was founded by Charlemagne, who ruled as king of the Franks from 768 to 814. Pope Leo III bestowed on him the title of emperor of Rome in Old St. Peter's basilica on Christmas Day in the year 800, pronouncing him successor to Constantine, the first Christian emperor. Although Charlemagne was able to resist the pope's attempts to assert his authority over the newly created Catholic Empire, there was now an interdependence of spiritual and political authority, of Church and State, that would define the history of western Europe for many centuries.

The emperors were crowned in Rome, but they did not live there. Charlemagne built his capital at the center of his power, in Aachen (Aix-la-Chapelle), located in what is now Germany and close to France, Belgium, and the Netherlands. The period dominated by Charlemagne and his successors, roughly from 768 to 877, is labeled Carolingian (derived from Charlemagne's Latin name, *Carolus Magnus*, meaning "Charles the Great"). Among Charlemagne's goals were to better the administration of his realm and the teaching of Christian truths. He summoned the best minds to his court, including Alcuin of York, the most learned scholar of the day, to restore ancient Roman learning and to establish a system of schools at every cathedral and monastery. The emperor took an active hand in this renewal, which went well beyond a mere interest in old books to include political objectives. He modeled his rule after the Roman Empire under Constantine and Justinian—rather than their pagan predecessors—and proclaimed a *renovatio imperii romani*, a "renewal of imperial Rome," his efforts being aided by the pope who had crowned him Holy Roman Emperor. The artists working for Charlemagne and other Carolingian rulers consciously sought to emulate Rome; by combining their admiration for antiquity with native northern European features, they produced original works of art of the highest quality.

Sculpture

A bronze *Equestrian Statue of a Carolingian Ruler* (fig. **10.11**), once thought to be of Charlemagne himself but now generally said to be of his grandson Charles the Bald, conveys the political objectives of the Carolingian dynasty. The ruler, wearing imperial

10.11 *Equestrian Statue of a Carolingian Ruler* (Charles the Bald?). 9th century. Bronze, height 9½" (24.4 cm). Musée du Louvre, Paris

robes, sits as triumphantly on his steed as if he were on a throne. In his hand is an orb signifying his domination of the world. The statue is probably modeled on a now lost antique Roman equestrian statue of Theodoric, which Charlemagne had brought from Ravenna for the courtyard of his imperial palace. There are other possible sources, including a bronze equestrian statue of Marcus Aurelius (see fig. 7.33), once mistakenly thought to represent Constantine, the first Christian emperor, and thus also an appropriate model for the ambitious Charlemagne and his successors.

The Carolingian statue is not a slavish copy of its antique model. It is simpler and less cluttered with detail than the statue of Marcus Aurelius for instance. What is important is that it communicates the significant message that the Carolingian rulers were heirs to the Roman imperial throne. What is most striking is the difference in size: Marcus Aurelius stands more than 11 feet high, while the Carolingian figure does not reach 10 inches. Yet the diminutive statue expresses as much majesty and dignity as the more monumental example. Given the metalwork tradition of the ＿nks, the miniaturization is not only appropriate, but might in ＿tself suggest value. Unfortunately, we do not know the audience for the work or how it was used, though its smallness could relate to portability.

Illuminated Books

Charlemagne's interest in promoting learning and culture required the production of large numbers of books by his scriptoria. He established an "academy" at his court and encouraged the collecting and copying of many works of ancient Roman literature. In fact, the oldest surviving texts of many classical Latin authors are found in Carolingian manuscripts that were long considered of Roman origin. This very page is printed in letters the shapes

of which derive from the script in Carolingian manuscripts. The fact that these letters are known today as "Roman" rather than Carolingian is a result of the confusion about the manuscripts' origins.

THE *GODESCALC GOSPELS*   One of the earliest manuscripts created in Charlemagne's scriptoria is the *Godescalc Gospels*, named after the monk who signed his name to the book; it is generally thought to reflect manuscripts and objects that Charlemagne brought back with him from Rome. The manuscript's most compelling image is of a monumental Enthroned Christ (fig. **10.12**), whose large staring eyes communicate directly with the viewer. His purple garments denote imperial stature. (Purple was the color of royalty in the Roman world.) The concentration on imperial imagery reflects Charlemagne's personal ambitions, which were to be realized about 20 years later, when he received the title of Holy Roman Emperor in 800. Hard lines and swirling patterns around the knees suggest where drapery falls over the body, and white lines on the hands, neck, and face indicate highlights. It is as if the artist is attempting to emulate Roman modeling, but does so in a Northern manner, by using linear patterns.

Christ sits within an enclosed garden, a motif reminiscent of Roman painting (see fig. 7.55), but transformed here into flat decorative elements, almost like the designs on a carpet. The outlined letters of Christ's name and the frame, composed of interlace patterns, are reminiscent of metalwork (see figs. 10.1–10.3) and Hiberno-Saxon illuminations (see figs. 10.4–10.6). A great painter has fused the heritage of Rome with the decorative devices traditionally employed by northern European artists.

This manuscript includes a dedicatory poem commemorating the baptism of Charlemagne's sons by Pope Hadrian in Rome in 781. By bringing his sons to Rome to be baptized, Charlemagne effectively acknowledged the authority of the pope in ecclesiastical matters, although this was often disputed by later rulers. In turn, the pope placed himself and all of Western Christianity under the protection of the emperor.

THE *GOSPEL BOOK OF CHARLEMAGNE*   The *Gospel Book of Charlemagne* (also known as the *Coronation Gospels* because later German emperors swore on this book during their coronations) is said to have been found in Charlemagne's tomb and is thought to have been produced at his court. Looking at the page with St. Matthew (fig. **10.13**), we can hardly believe that such a work could have been executed in northern Europe and less than a generation after the *Godescalc Gospels*. Were it not for the large golden halo, the evangelist might almost be mistaken for a Roman portrait in the naturalness and solidity with which he inhabits the landscape setting. The artist shows himself fully conversant with the Roman tradition of painting, from the modeling of the forms, the shading of face, hands, and feet, and the body-revealing drapery, to the acanthus ornament on the wide frame, which makes the picture seem like a window. Since the manner of painting is so clearly Mediterranean, some claim that the artist must have come from Byzantium or Italy.

10.12   *Christ Enthroned*, from the *Godescalc Gospels* (*Lectionary*). 781–83. Tempera on vellum, 12⅝ × 8¼″ (32.4 × 21.2 cm). Bibliothèque Nationale, Paris

10.13 *St. Matthew*, from the *Gospel Book of Charlemagne* (*Coronation Gospels*). ca. 800–10. Ink and colors on vellum, 13 × 10″ (33 × 25.4 cm). Kunsthistorisches Museum, Vienna

THE *GOSPEL BOOK OF ARCHBISHOP EBBO OF REIMS*
Less reflective of classical models, but equally reliant on them, is a miniature painted some three decades later for the *Gospel Book of Archbishop Ebbo of Reims* (fig. **10.14**). The subject is once again St. Matthew, and the pose is similar to that in the *Gospel Book of Charlemagne*, but this picture is filled with a vibrant energy that sets everything in motion. The thickly painted drapery swirls about the figure, the hills heave upward, and the architecture and vegetation seem tossed about by a whirlwind. Even the acanthus pattern on the frame assumes a strange, flamelike character. The evangelist has been transformed from a Roman author setting down his thoughts into a man seized with the frenzy of divine inspiration, a vehicle for recording the Word of God. The way the artist communicates this energy, particularly through the expressive use of flickering line, employing his brush as if it were a pen, recalls the endless interlaced movement in the ornamentation of Hiberno-Saxon manuscripts (see figs. 10.5 and 10.8).

THE *UTRECHT PSALTER* The imperial scriptorium at Reims responsible for the *Ebbo Gospels* also produced perhaps the most extraordinary of all Carolingian manuscripts, the *Utrecht Psalter* (fig. **10.15**), where energetic form is expressed with remarkable pen drawings. That the artist has followed a much older model is indicated by the architectural and landscape settings of the

scenes, which recall the Column of Trajan (see fig. 7.40). Another indication is the use of Roman capital lettering, which had gone out of general use several centuries before. The rhythmic quality of the draftsmanship, however, gives these sketches an expressive unity that could not have been present in earlier pictures. Without this rhythmic quality, the drawings of the *Utrecht Psalter* would carry little conviction, for the poetic language of the Psalms does not lend itself to illustration in the same way as the narrative portions of the Bible. Perhaps, as some scholars have suggested, we can attribute the drawn rather than painted style to the influence of an antique scroll (see fig. 8.38 and page 266) that no longer survives.

The artist represented the Psalms by taking each phrase literally and then visualizing it in some way. Thus, the top of our page illustrates, "Let them bring me unto thy holy hill, and to thy tabernacles" (Psalms 43:3). Toward the bottom of the page, we see the Lord reclining on a bed, flanked by pleading angels. The image is based on the words "Awake, why sleepest thou, Oh Lord?" (Psalms 44:23). On the left, the faithful crouch before the Temple ("for ... our belly cleaveth unto the earth" [Psalms 44:25]), and at the city gate in the foreground they are killed ("as sheep for the slaughter" [Psalms 44:22]). In the hands of a less imaginative

10.14 *St. Matthew*, from the *Gospel Book of Archbishop Ebbo of Reims*. ca. 816–35. Ink and colors on vellum, 10¼ × 8¾″ (26 × 22.2 cm). Bibliothèque Municipale, Épernay, France

QUARETRISTISESANIMA **BASME** **CONFITEBORILLI SALU**
MEA ETQUARECONTUR **S** PERAINDOQMADHUC TARE UULTUSMEIETDSMS

VLII **PSALMUS** OXIIIO **CONFITEBORTIBIINCI**
IUDICAMEDOSET **MITTELUCEMTUAMETUERI** **THARADSDSMEUS**
DISCERNFCAUSAMMEAM TATEMTUAM IPSAMEDEDU QUARETRISTISESANIMA
DIGENTENONSCA ABHOMI XERUNTETADDUXERIN MEIETTQUARECONTUR
NEINIQUOFIDOLOSOERU MONTEMSCMTUU ETIN BASME
IME TABERNACULATUA **S** PERAINDOQNMADHUC
QUATUISDSFORTITUDO **IINTROIBOADALTARIDI** **CONFITEBORILLI SALU**
MEA QUAREMEREPPULIS ADDMQUILAETIFICAT TAREUULTUSMEIETDSMS
TIEIQUARETRISTISINCEDO IUUENTUTEMMEAM
DUMADFLICITMEINIMICUS

10.15   Illustrations to Psalms 43 and 44, from the *Utrecht Psalter*. ca. 820–32. Ink on vellum, 13 × 9⅞″ (33 × 25 cm). University Library, Utrecht, the Netherlands (MS 32, fol. 25r and 26r)

artist, this procedure could well have turned into a tiresome game; instead, it has the force of great drama. The wonderfully rhythmic and energetic quality of the draftsmanship renders these sketches both coherent and affecting.

The literal approach to illustrating the Psalms in the *Utrecht Psalter* has a conceptual parallel in the lucidity with which the letters and words are delineated. This is a manuscript designed to be read; indeed, one needs to do so in order to be able to interpret the scenes represented. This is very different from our experience with Hiberno-Saxon manuscripts such as the *Book of Kells* (see fig. 10.8). There, letters and words seem to mystify, rather than clarify; it is as if the power of the word is unrelated to its legibility. Comparison of the two manuscripts underscores how Western Europe had been transformed from an oral to a written culture, in part a result of Charlemagne's ambitions and policies.

THE *LINDAU GOSPELS* COVER   The Reims style (see figs. 10.14 and 10.15) is also apparent in the reliefs on the front cover of the *Lindau Gospels* (fig. **10.16**), dating from the third quarter of the ninth century, in the expressive, near-frenetic figures that float around the image of the crucified Christ. Given the Carolingian investment in preserving and embellishing the written word, the cover was a fittingly sumptuous protection for a book. The clusters of semiprecious stones are not mounted directly on the gold ground but raised on clawed feet or arcaded **turrets** (towerlike projections), so that light can penetrate from beneath to bring out their full brilliance. The raised stones also protect the delicate figures in repoussé, produced from relatively thin gold sheets, when the book is opened flat. Christ betrays no hint of pain or death. He seems to stand rather than to hang, his arms spread out in a solemn gesture.

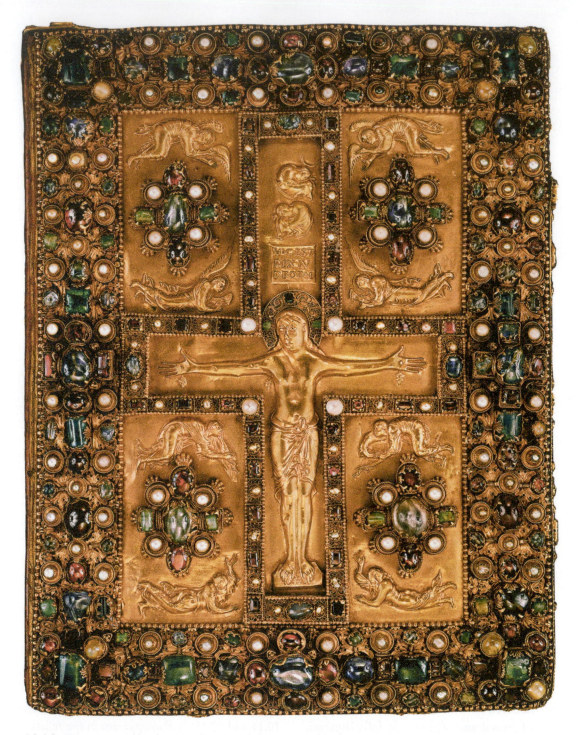

10.16   Front cover of binding, *Lindau Gospels*. ca. 870. Gold and jewels, 13¾ × 10½″ (35 × 26.7 cm). The Pierpont Morgan Library, New York

Architecture

Although relatively few Carolingian buildings survive, excavations demonstrate a significant increase in building activity during the Carolingian period, a reflection of the security and prosperity that Charlemagne established at the beginning of his reign and that continued for some time. As was the case with his painters, Charlemagne's architects sought to revive the splendor of the Roman Empire, which they did by erecting buildings whose models were largely from Rome and Ravenna, both of which Charlemagne visited. While Rome had been the capital of the Empire, Ravenna had been a Christian imperial outpost, and thus a worthy prototype for what Charlemagne hoped to create in his own land.

PALACE CHAPEL OF CHARLEMAGNE, AACHEN Toward the end of the eighth century, Charlemagne erected his imperial palace at Aachen. Prior to this time, Charlemagne's court

10.17 Odo of Metz. Plan of Palace Chapel of Charlemagne, Aachen, Germany. 792–805

had been itinerant, moving from place to place as the political situation required. Now, to signify Charlemagne's position as a Christian ruler, architects modeled his palace complex on Constantine's Lateran Palace in Rome. Charlemagne's palace included a basilica, called the Royal Hall, which was linked to the Palace Chapel. The plan for the latter (fig. 10.17) was probably inspired by the church of San Vitale in Ravenna, which the emperor saw first hand (see figs. 8.21–8.24). The building (fig. 10.18) was designed by Odo of Metz, probably the earliest architect north of the Alps known to us by name Einhard, Charlemagne's trusted advisor and biographer, supervised the project.

The debt to San Vitale is especially clear in cross section (fig. 10.19; compare fig. 8.22). The chapel design is by no means

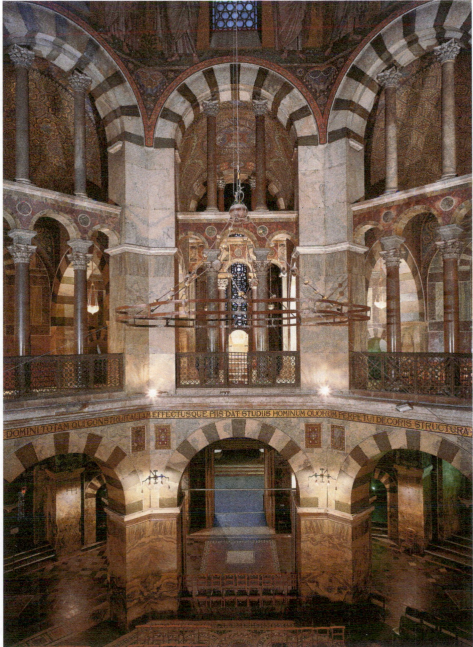

10.18 Odo of Metz. Interior of the Palace Chapel of Charlemagne, Aachen, Germany

clerestory

tribune

10.19 Odo of Metz. Section of the Palace Chapel of Charlemagne, Aachen, Germany (after Kubach)

ABBEY CHURCH OF SAINT-RIQUIER An even more elaborate westwork formed part of one of the greatest basilican churches of Carolingian times: the Abbey church of Saint-Riquier at the monastery of Centula in northeastern France. (An **abbey** is a religious community headed by an abbot, or, in the case of a women's community, an abbess.) The monastery was rebuilt in 790 by Abbot Angilbert, a poet and scholar of Charlemagne's court. The present church was largely built in the fifteenth and sixteenth centuries, but we know the Carolingian design from descriptions, drawings, and prints, such as the **engraving** reproduced here (fig. 10.20). The monastery included not only the abbey church, dedicated to Saint-Riquier, but also two chapels, one dedicated to St. Mary, the other to St. Benedict, founder of the Benedictine order, whose Rule the monks followed. (See *Primary Source*, page 331.)

Benedict of Nursia established his order in 529 when he founded a monastery in Monte Cassino, south of Rome. Benedict's Rule required monks to labor, study, and pray, providing for both the sound administration of the monastery and the spiritual needs of individual monks. (See www.myartslab.com.)

a mere echo of San Vitale but a vigorous reinterpretation of it. Piers and vaults are impressively massive by comparison, while the geometric clarity of the spatial units is very different from the fluid space of the earlier structure. To construct such a building on northern soil was a difficult undertaking. Columns and bronze gratings were imported from Italy, and expert stonemasons must have been hard to find. The columns are placed within the arches of the upper story, where they are structurally unnecessary, but where they accentuate a sense of support and create opportunities to offer Roman details. San Vitale had been designed to be ambiguous, to produce an otherworldly interior space. Aachen, by comparison, is sturdy and sober. The soft, bulging curvilinear forms of San Vitale's arcades are here replaced with clear-cut piers, which make manifest their ability to support the heavy weight of Aachen's dome, while the San Vitale dome seems light and to hover above the interior space of the building.

Equally important is Odo's scheme for the western entrance, now largely obscured by later additions and rebuilding. At San Vitale, the entrance consists of a broad, semidetached narthex with twin stair turrets, placed at an odd angle to the main axis of the church. At Aachen, these elements are molded into a tall, compact unit, in line with the main axis and attached to the chapel itself. This monumental structure, known as a **westwork** (from the German *Westwerk*), makes one of its first appearances here.

Charlemagne placed his throne in the **tribune** (the gallery of the westwork), behind the great opening above the entrance. From here, the emperor could emerge to show himself to those assembled in the atrium below. The throne faced an altar dedicated to Christ, who seemed to bless the emperor from above in the dome mosaic. Thus, although contemporary documents say very little about its function, the westwork seems to have served initially as a royal compartment or chapel.

10.20 Abbey church of Saint-Riquier, monastery of Centula, France. Dedicated ca. 790. A 1673 engraving after a 1612 view by Petau, from an 11th-century manuscript illumination. Bibliothèque Nationale, Paris

Hariulf (ca. 1060–1143)

~ ɔm *History of the Monastery of Saint-Riquier*

Hariulf was a monk at Saint-Riquier until 1105, when he became abbot of St. Peter's at Oudenbourg in Belgium.

The church dedicated to the Savior and St. Richarius … was among all other churches of its time the most famous. … The eastern tower is close to the sepulcher of St. Richarius. … The western tower is especially dedicated to the Savior. …

If one surveys the place, one sees that the largest church, that of St. Richarius, lies to the north. The second, somewhat smaller one, which has been built in honor of our Lady on this side of the river, lies to the south. The third one, the smallest, lies to the east. The cloisters of the monks are laid out in a triangular fashion, one roof extending from St. Richarius' to St. Mary's, one from St. Mary's to St. Benedict's and one from St. Benedict's to St. Richarius'. … The monastery is so arranged that, according to the rule laid down by St. Benedict, all arts and all necessary labors can be executed within its walls. The river flows through it, and turns the mill of the brothers.

Source: Caecilia Davis-Weyer, *Early Medieval Art 300–1150* (Upper Saddle River, NJ: Prentice Hall, 1st ed., 1971)

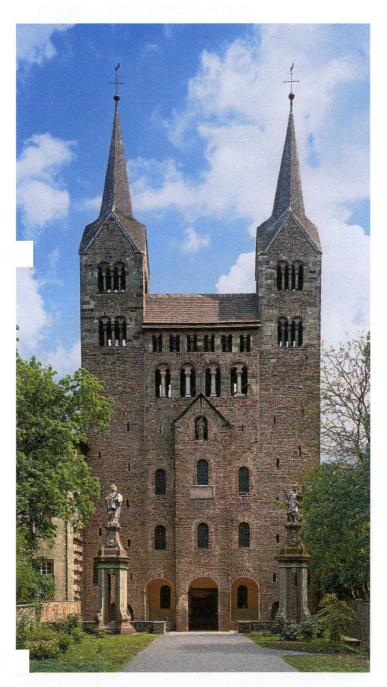

10.21 Westwork, abbey church, with later additions. Corvey, Germany. Late 9th century

By the ninth century, largely due to support from Charlemagne, Benedict's requirements for monastic life had been accepted by monasteries across Europe. Charlemagne recognized that the orderliness of the Rule was consistent with his own goal to provide stability through a sound, working system of governance, both civil and religious.

The three buildings of the monastery at Centula are connected by a covered walkway, forming a triangular **cloister** (an open court surrounded by a covered arcaded walk, used for meditation, study, and exercise). This shape has symbolic significance, reflecting this particular monastery's dedication to the Holy Trinity. The plan of Saint-Riquier reads as a traditional basilica, with a central nave flanked by side aisles and terminating in a transept and apse. In fact, Charlemagne sent to Rome for drawings and measurements of traditional basilicas to guide his local builders. In elevation, however, Saint-Riquier's multiple towers provide vertical accents that are very different from the longitudinal silhouette of Early Christian basilicas, such as Old St. Peter's (see fig. 8.8).

The westwork of Saint-Riquier balanced the visual weight of the transept and east end of the church; it also provided additional room for the liturgical needs of a large community, which numbered some 300 monks, 100 novices, and numerous staff (see www. myartslab.com). Twenty-five relics related to Christ were displayed in the westwork entrance, and above that was an upper chapel dedicated to the Savior. On feast days, and in particular at Easter, the community positioned itself here for the beginning of an elaborate processional liturgy. (See *Primary Source*, page 332.) Thus, to some extent the westwork functioned as a separate commemorative building, the conceptual equivalent of the Early Christian mausoleum and martyrium, but now attached to a basilican church.

ABBEY CHURCH, CORVEY Saint-Riquier was widely imitated in other Carolingian monastery churches. The best-preserved example is the abbey church at Corvey (fig. **10.21**), built in 873–85. Except for the upper stories, which date from around 1146, the westwork retains much of its original appearance. It is impressive not only because of its height but also because of its expansive surfaces, which emphasize the clear geometry and powerful masses of the exterior. The westwork provided a suitably regal

St. Angilbert (ca. 750–814)

From *Customary for the Different Devotions*

Angilbert, a member of Charlemagne's court, became lay abbot of Saint-Riquier in 781 and sponsored the monastery's rebuilding. His description reveals how the resident monks moved from one part of the basilica to another while chanting the devotions prescribed in the Rule of St. Benedict.

When the brethren have sung Vespers and Matins at the altar of the Savior, then one choir should descend on the side of the holy Resurrection, the other one on the side of the holy Ascension, and having prayed there the processions should in the same fashion as before move singing toward the altars of St. John and St. Martin. After having prayed they should enter from both sides through the arches in the middle of the church and pray at the holy Pas: From there they should go to the altar of St. Richarius. ~~After~~ praying they should divide themselves again as before and go to the altars of St. Stephen and St. Lawrence and from there go singing and praying to the altar of the Holy Cross. Thence they should go again to the altar of St. Maurice and through the long gallery to the church of St. Benedict.

Source: Caecilia Davis-Weyer, *Early Medieval Art 300–1150* (Englewood Cliffs, NJ: Prentice Hall, 1st ed., 1971)

entrance, which may well be its greatest significance. But it had functional benefits too. At Corvey, musical notation scratched on the walls of the gallery reminds us that the boys' choir would have been positioned here, its voices spreading upward as well as throughout the church.

PLAN OF A MONASTERY, ST. GALL The importance of monasteries in the culture of the early medieval period and their close link with the imperial court are evident in the plan for a monastery at St. Gall in Switzerland (fig. **10.22**). The plan exists in a large, unique drawing on five sheets of parchment sewn together

10.22 Plan of a monastery. Redrawn, with inscriptions translated into English from the Latin, from the original of ca. 820. Red ink on parchment, 28 × 44⅛″ (71.1 × 112.1 cm). Stiftsbibliothek, St. Gall, Switzerland

and is preserved in the chapter library at St. Gall. This drawing was sent by Abbot Haito of Reichenau to Gozbert, the abbot of St. Gall, for "you to study only," as an aid to him in rebuilding his monastery. We may therefore regard it as a model or ideal plan, to be modified to meet local needs.

The monastery plan shows a complex, self-contained unit filling a rectangle about 500 by 700 feet and providing a logical arrangement of buildings based on their function. From the west end of the monastery, the main entrance path passes between stables and a hostelry toward a gate. This admits the visitor to a colonnaded semicircular portico (porch) flanked by two round towers forming a westwork that would have loomed above the low outer buildings. The plan emphasizes the church as the center of the monastic community. This church is a traditional basilica (see figs. 8.7–8.9), with an apse at each end. The nave and aisles, which contain many other altars, do not form a single continuous space but are subdivided into compartments by screens. There are numerous entrances: two beside the western apse, others on the north and south flanks.

This arrangement reflects the functions of a monastery church, which was designed for the liturgical needs of the monks rather than for a lay congregation. Adjoining the church to the south is an arcaded cloister, around which are grouped the monks' dormitory (on the east side), a refectory (dining hall) and kitchen (on the south side), and a cellar. The three large buildings north of the church are a guesthouse, a school, and the abbot's house. To the east are an infirmary, a chapel, and quarters for novices (new members of the community), the cemetery (marked by a large cross), a garden, and coops for chickens and geese. On the south side are workshops, barns, and other service buildings.

The St. Gall plan was laid out using a module (standard unit). This module, expressed as parts or multiples of 2½ feet, can be found throughout the plan, from the division of the church to the length of the cemetery plots. The imposition of a module on the plan of St. Gall is a tangible manifestation both of the administrative orderliness and stability so sought after by Charlemagne and of the aims of monasticism, as defined by St. Benedict of Nursia's Rule.

Unfortunately, political stability proved elusive. Upon the death of Charlemagne's son, Louis I, in 840, a bitter battle arose among Louis's sons for the empire built by their grandfather. The brothers eventually signed a treaty in 843 dividing the empire into western, central, and eastern parts: Charles the Bald became the West Frankish King, founding the French Carolingian dynasty in what became modern France; Louis the German became the East Frankish King, ruling an area roughly equivalent to that of present-day Germany; and Lothair I became the Holy Roman Emperor, ruling the middle area running from the Netherlands down to Italy. The distribution of the Carolingian domain among Louis's heirs weakened the empire, brought a halt to Carolingian cultural efforts, and eventually exposed continental Europe to attack by the Muslims from the south, the Slavs and Magyars from the east, and the Vikings from the north. As stated earlier, the Vikings invaded northwestern France and,

through a land grant from Charles the Bald, occupied the area now known as Normandy.

Although political stability ultimately eluded Charlemagne's heirs, the artists of the Carolingian period were able to create an enduring art that combined the northern reliance on decoration—on surface, pattern, and line—with the Mediterranean concern for solidity and monumentality. Carolingian art was to serve as a worthy model for emulation by artists and patrons when the revival of Charlemagne's vision of a united and stable Europe reappeared during the next centuries.

OTTONIAN ART

When the last East Frankish monarch died in 911, the center of political power moved to the eastern portion of the former Carolingian Empire, in an area roughly equivalent to present-day Germany, under German kings of Saxon descent. Beginning with Henry I, these kings pushed back invaders, reestablished an effective central government, improved trade and the economy, and began a new dynasty, called Ottonian after its three principal rulers: Otto I, Otto II, and Otto III. During the Ottonian period, which lasted from 919 to 1024, Germany was the leading nation of Europe politically and artistically. In both realms, German achievements began as revivals of Carolingian traditions but soon developed an original character.

The greatest of the Ottonian kings, Otto I, revived the imperial ambitions of Charlemagne. After marrying the widow of a Lombard king in 951, he extended his rule over most of what is now northern Italy. Then, in 962, he was crowned emperor by Pope John XII, whom the emperor later deposed for conspiring against him, insisting on the imperial right to designate future popes.

Architecture

Among the most pressing concerns of the Ottonian emperors was the reform of the Church, which had become corrupt and mismanaged. They did this by establishing closer alliances with the papacy and by fostering monastic reforms, which they supported by sponsoring many new religious buildings. The renewal of impressive building programs effectively revived the architectural ambitions of their Carolingian predecessors, while at the same time conveying and furthering the Ottonians' aspirations to restore the imperial glory of Christian Rome.

NUNNERY CHURCH OF ST. CYRIAKUS, GERNRODE One of the best-preserved Ottonian churches was built in 961 for the nunnery, or convent, at Gernrode (fig. **10.23**), founded by Gero, margrave (military governor) under Otto I. The church was dedicated to St. Cyriakus and used the basic form of the Early Christian basilica (see figs. 8.7–8.9), which had also dominated architectural planning during the Carolingian period. However, the architect of St. Cyriakus raised the apse above

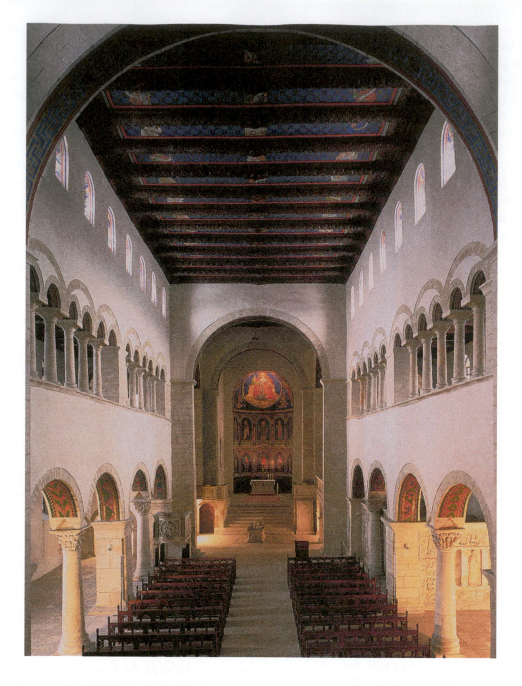

the level of the rest of the church to make room for a half-buried basement chapel, or **crypt**, a feature not present in the Early Christian basilica. Such crypts with ambulatories, usually housing the venerated tomb of a saint, had been introduced into Western church architecture during Carolingian times. Moreover, at St. Cyriakus, a gallery has been inserted between the nave arcade and the clerestory. A series of columns and piers divide the gallery in such a way that the piers of the gallery are positioned over the piers of the nave arcade. This provides a series of repeated vertical accents, effectively dividing the building into vertical sections.

This emphasis on verticality is different from the overwhelming effect of horizontality that characterizes Early Christian buildings, and indicates a trend that will be significant in the later development of medieval architecture. Neither the origin nor the intended function of the gallery is clear. Some scholars have noted similarities to galleried Byzantine churches, such as two fifth-century examples in Salonika in Greece. It is possible that the gallery at St. Cyriakus contained altars, as was the case in the galleried westworks of Carolingian churches, such as at Corvey (see fig. 10.21).

ST. MICHAEL'S AT HILDESHEIM The most ambitious patron of architecture and art in the Ottonian age was Bernward, who became bishop of Hildesheim after having been court chaplain. Bernward was also tutor of Otto III during the regency of his mother, Empress Theophano, wife of Otto II and a Byzantine princess in her own right. Bernward's chief monument is the Benedictine abbey church of St. Michael's at Hildesheim. The plan of this monastic church (fig. **10.24**) derives from that of

10.24 Reconstructed plan, abbey church of St. Michael's, Hildesheim, Germany. 1001–33 (after Beseler)

Saint-Riquier at Centula (see fig. 10.20). With its two choirs and side entrances, it also recalls the monastery church of the St. Gall plan (see fig. 10.22). However, in St. Michael's the symmetry is carried much further. There are two identical transepts, each with

a tower, where the transept and the nave cross, and a pair of stair turrets at the end of each transept (fig. 10.25; see also fig. 10.24). But the supports of the nave arcade, instead of being uniform, consist of pairs of columns separated by square piers (fig. 10.26). This alternating system divides the arcade into three equal units, each with three openings. These units are equal in length to the width of the transepts, which are similarly divided into three compartments.

Thus, as in the St. Gall plan, a modular system governs the division of spaces. The module can also be seen on the exterior of the building, which reads as a series of cubes arranged by stacking. The first and third units correspond with the entrances, thus echoing the axis of the transepts. Moreover, since the aisles and nave are unusually wide in relation to their length, the architect's intention must have been to achieve a harmonious balance between the longitudinal and horizontal axes throughout the structure.

St. Michael's was severely damaged during World War II, but the restored interior retains the majestic feel of the original design. Frescoes originally decorated the great expanse of wall space between the arcade and clerestory, paralleling the arrangement of

10.25 Exterior, abbey church of St. Michael's, Hildesheim, Germany

10.26 Interior, with view toward the apse (after restoration of 1950–60), abbey church of St. Michael's, Hildesheim, Germany

mosaics in Early Christian basilicas such as Santa Maria Maggiore (see fig. 8.16). (The capitals of the columns date from the twelfth century; the painted wooden ceiling from the thirteenth.) The western choir is especially interesting. As at Gernrode (see fig. 10.23), there is a raised crypt. Monks could enter the crypt (apparently a special sanctuary for relics of the saint) from both the transept and the west. Arched openings pierced the walls and linked the crypt with the U-shaped ambulatory wrapped around it. The ambulatory must originally have been visible from above ground, where it enriched the exterior of the choir, since there were windows in its outer wall. The design of St. Michael's is distinguished by the crypt's large scale and its careful integration with the rest of the building.

Metalwork

The Ottonian emperors' reliance on church authority to strengthen their own governmental rule encouraged them not only to build new churches but also to provide sumptuous works of art to decorate them. The works they and their cohorts sponsored were richly appointed and executed in expensive, often precious materials.

BRONZE DOORS OF BISHOP BERNWARD, HILDESHEI
For St. Michael's at Hildesheim, Bernward commissioned a pa of extensively sculptured bronze doors (figs. 10.27 and 10.28) that were finished in 1015, the year the crypt was consecrated.

10.27 Doors of Bishop Bernward, Hildesheim cathedral (originally made for abbey church of St. Michael's, Hildesheim), Germany. 1015. Bronze, height approx. 16′ (4.8 m)

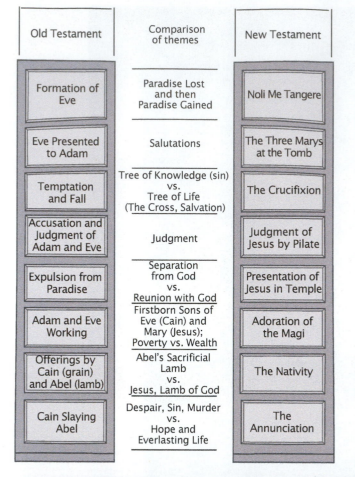

Old Testament	Comparison of themes	New Testament
Formation of Eve	Paradise Lost and then Paradise Gained	Noli Me Tangere
Eve Presented to Adam	Salutations	The Three Marys at the Tomb
Temptation and Fall	Tree of Knowledge (sin) vs. Tree of Life (The Cross, Salvation)	The Crucifixion
Accusation and Judgment of Adam and Eve	Judgment	Judgment of Jesus by Pilate
Expulsion from Paradise	Separation from God vs. Reunion with God	Presentation of Jesus in Temple
Adam and Eve Working	Firstborn Sons of Eve (Cain) and Mary (Jesus); Poverty vs. Wealth	Adoration of the Magi
Offerings by Cain (grain) and Abel (lamb)	Abel's Sacrificial Lamb vs. Jesus, Lamb of God	The Nativity
Cain Slaying Abel	Despair, Sin, Murder vs. Hope and Everlasting Life	The Annunciation

According to his biographer, Thangmar of Heidelberg, Bernward excelled in the arts and "distinguished himself remarkably in the science of metalwork and the whole art of building." So, he must have been closely involved in the project. The idea for the doors may have come to him as a result of his visit to Rome, where he would have seen ancient Roman (and perhaps Byzantine) doors of bronze and wood. He would also certainly have been aware of the bronze doors that Charlemagne had commissioned for his palace chapel at Aachen.

The doors at Hildesheim are considered by many scholars to be the first monumental sculptures created by the lost-wax process (see page 128) since antiquity. Each door was cast as one piece and measures over 16 feet in height. They are also the first doors since the Early Christian period to have been decorated with stories. Our detail (fig. **10.29**) shows God accusing and judging Adam and Eve after the Temptation and Fall, when they have committed the Original Sin of eating the forbidden fruit in the Garden of Eden. Below it, in inlaid letters notable for their classical Roman character, is part of an inscription, with the date and Bernward's name. This inscription was added around 1035, when the doors were moved from the monastery of St. Michael and

10.29 *Accusation and Judgment of Adam and Eve*, from the Doors of Bishop Bernward, Hildesheim, Germany. Bronze, approx. 23 × 43" (58.3 × 109.3 cm)

10.30 *Temptation and Fall*, from the Doors of Bishop Bernward, Hildesheim, Germany. Bronze, approx. 23 × 43″ (58.3 × 109.3 cm)

ached to the westwork of Hildesheim cathedral, where they would have been seen by a larger public than in the monastic setting of St. Michael's. The new, more prominent setting indicates how valued they were in their own time.

The composition most likely derives from a manuscript illumination, since there are very similar scenes in medieval Bibles. Yet this is no mere imitation. The story is conveyed with splendid directness and expressive force. The accusing finger of the Lord, seen against a great void, is the focal point of the drama. It points to a cringing Adam, who passes the blame to Eve, who in turn passes it to the serpent at her feet. The trees and landscape elements are in relatively low relief and remain sketchy, which encourages them to be read as background elements, while the figures, though of awkward proportions, project forward so that the heads are three-dimensional.

The subjects on the left door are taken from the Hebrew Bible and those on the right from the New Testament (see fig. 10.28). The Hebrew Bible stories are presented chronologically from top to bottom, while the New Testament scenes move in reverse order, from bottom to top, suggesting the Christian message is uplifting. When read as horizontal pairs, the panels deliver a message of the origin and redemption of sin through a system of typology, whereby the Hebrew Bible stories prefigure New Testament ones. For example, the *Temptation and Fall* (fig. **10.30**) opposite the *Crucifixion*. In the center of the left panel is the tree whose fruit led to the Original Sin; in the center of the right panel is the cross on which Jesus was crucified, which medieval

Christians believed was made from the wood of the tree from Eden and was therefore the instrument for redemption from the sin of that original act. Compositional similarities between the two scenes stress their typological relationship: In the left panel Adam and Eve's hands, which flank the cross-shaped tree, establish a visual parallel to the spears the soldiers use to pierce Christ's body on the right panel.

Eve plays a particularly significant role on the doors; in fact, the narrative begins with her formation, not with the creation of Adam, as might be expected, since according to the Bible Adam's creation antecedes Eve's. In the *Temptation and Fall*, Eve's attitude and gesture parallel those of the serpent at the right, who, like Eve, offers an apple. This makes explicit Eve's role as seductive agent, accentuated by the way she holds the apple so closely to her chest that it almost appears as if she were grasping her breast rather than the fruit. With this gesture Eve's guilt in humankind's exile from Paradise is emphasized and her sexuality underscored.

While Early Christian writers had considered Eve responsible for the Original Sin, during the Ottonian period references to her guilt multiply and become more vigorous. This might have been as a result of efforts by Bishop Bernward and others to reform the morality of the clergy in an attempt to restore the vow of celibacy to priests and monks, some of whom were known to cohabit with wives and children in their monasteries. Thus, the burden of clerical immorality is, in effect, assigned to Eve, the first woman and the first seductress.

Ivories and Manuscripts: Conveyors of Imperial Grandeur

The right of the Ottonian monarchs to call themselves Roman emperors was challenged by Byzantine rulers, who continued to claim that title as their own even though the division of the Roman Empire into Eastern and Western empires was complete by the end of the fourth century. When Otto II married the Byzantine princess Theophano, he was able to use the full title of Holy Roman Emperor with impunity. While early Ottonian illuminators faithfully replicated features of Carolingian manuscripts, later Ottonian manuscripts, as well as ivories, blend Carolingian and Byzantine elements into a new style of extraordinary scope and power. Byzantine artists working for court provided an impetus to find new ways of presenting both religious and imperial images. Ottonian manuscripts indicate an increasing interest on the part of artists and patrons in narrative cycles of Jesus' life, which is the period's most important contribution to the field of **iconography** (the study of the use and meaning of images in art).

CHRIST BLESSING OTTO II AND THEOPHANO An ivory of *Christ Blessing Emperor Otto II and Empress Theophano* (fig. **10.31**) commemorated their coronation, presenting it as divinely sanctioned. In style, the ivory is similar to the Byzantine ivory of *Christ Crowning Romanos and Eudokia* (see fig. 8.41), carved a generation or so earlier. The composition of both works is identical: A long-haired, bearded Christ (identified by a halo inscribed with a cross) is elevated in the center of each panel and anoints the empress and emperor, who flank him. In both ivories, the imperial costumes are composed of similar elaborate geometric surface decorations. This similarity suggests that the Otto II ivory is an eastern import, as does the inscription, which seems to be the work of a Greek using both Greek and Latin letters. However, because Otto's costume is not accurate for a Byzantine ruler's coronation, and because the inscription tells us that the donor—who huddles in front of Otto's stool and grasps the leg of the larger stool that supports Christ—was an Ottonian bishop who lived in Italy, it is more likely that the ivory was produced within Ottonian lands in Italy. No matter where this work was produced, it demonstrates the interest of the Ottonian court in importing Byzantine style as well as actual objects, thus establishing on another level a connection to the art of the Mediterranean. Here again, the king is presented as the Holy Roman Emperor, a divinely ordained ruler.

THE *GOSPEL BOOK OF OTTO III* Produced for the son of Otto II and Theophano, the *Gospel Book of Otto III* communicates an imperial grandeur equal to that of the coronation ivory of his parents. In figure **10.32** the emperor displays the imperial regalia—a crown, an eagle scepter, and a cross-inscribed orb—while his throne is decorated with imperial lions. Representatives of the two domains that he controls—the military and the ecclesiastical—flank him, reminiscent of Justinian's placement in the center of the same domains in the San Vitale mosaic (see fig. 8.25). On the facing folio, the four geographical parts of the realm—Slavinia, Germania, Gallia, and Roma—offer homage. Their stances recall traditional representations of the Magi offering gifts to Christ, such as the scene decorating Theodora's robe in the mosaic at San Vitale in Ravenna (see fig. 8.26).

The manuscript is dated to around 1000, not long after Otto III was crowned king of Germany at Aachen in 986 and Holy Roman Emperor at Rome in 993. The way Otto is represented

10.31 *Christ Blessing Emperor Otto II and Empress Theophano.* 982–83. Ivory, 7⅛ × 4″ (18.3 × 10.3 cm). Musée du Moyen Âge (Cluny), Paris

10.32 *Otto III Receiving the Homage of the Four Parts of the Empire* and *Otto III Between Church and State*, from the *Gospel Book of Otto III*. ca. 997–1000. Tempera on vellum, each folio 13 × 9⅜″ (33 × 23.8 cm). atsbibliothek, Munich, CLM4454. fol. 23v adn 24r

visually in the manuscript thus parallels historical facts. He is presented here as the rightful and worthy heir to Roman and Byzantine emperors as well as to Charlemagne, and his imperial dignity is enhanced by association with Christ, a reversal of the practice in Early Christian depictions, where Christ is ennobled in the fashion of a Roman emperor. The soft pastel hues of the background recall the illusionism of Graeco-Roman landscapes and the *Quedlinburg Itala* fragment (see fig. 8.18). Such a style shows that the artist was probably aware of Roman, as well as Byzantine, manners of representation.

The *Gospel Book of Otto III* contains one of the most extensive sets of illustrations of the life of Christ. The scene of *Jesus Washing the Feet of St. Peter* (fig. **10.33**) once again contains strong echoes of ancient painting, transmitted through Byzantine art. The architectural frame around Jesus is a late descendant of the kind of architectural perspectives we saw in Roman wall painting (see figs. 7.54 and 7.56), and the intense gold background reminds us of Byzantine painting and mosaics, which the Ottonian artist has put to new use. What was an architectural vista in the mural

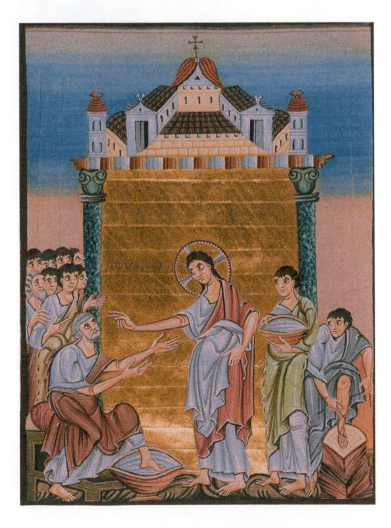

10.33 *Jesus Washing the Feet of St. Peter*, from the *Gospel Book of Otto III*. ca. 997–1000. Tempera on vellum, 13 × 9⅜″ (33 × 23.8 cm). Staatsbibliothek, Munich, CLM4453. fol 237

10.34 *St. Luke*, from the *Gospel Book of Otto III*. ca. 997–1000. Tempera on vellum, 13 × 9⅜″ (33 × 23.8 cm). Staatsbibliothek, Munich, CLM4453. fol. 139v

from Boscoreale (see fig. 7.54) now becomes the Heavenly City, the House of the Lord, filled with golden celestial space in contrast with the atmospheric earthly space outside.

The figures have also been transformed. In ancient art, this composition, in which a standing figure extends an arm to a seated supplicating figure and is watched by bystanders and assisted by others, was used to depict a doctor treating a patient. Here, though, the emphasis has shifted from physical to spiritual action. Not only do glances and gestures convey this new kind of action, but so too does scale. Jesus and his apostle Peter, the most animated figures, are larger than the rest, and Jesus' "active" arm is longer than his "passive" one. And the eight apostles, who are compressed into a tiny space and merely watch, have less physical substance than the fanlike Early Christian crowd from which this grouping derives (see fig. 8.17). The blending of Classical and Byzantine elements results in a new style of expressive abstraction.

A miniature showing St. Luke from the *Gospel Book of Otto III* (fig. **10.34**) is a symbolic image of overwhelming grandeur despite its small size. Unlike depictions of evangelists in Carolingian manuscripts (see figs. 10.13 and 10.14), here St. Luke is not shown writing. Instead, his Gospel lies completed on his lap. The evangelist seems to be as much a part of the mystical scene as he is its presenter. Enthroned on two rainbows, Luke holds aloft an awesome cluster of clouds from which tongues of light radiate in every direction. Within it we see his symbol, the ox, surrounded by five Hebrew prophets and an outer circle of angels. At the bottom, two lambs drink the life-giving waters that spring from beneath his feet. The key to the design is in the inscription: *Fonte patrum ductas bos agnis elicit undas* ("From t source of the fathers, the ox brings forth a flow of water for t lambs"). The Ottonian artist has truly "illuminated" the meaning of this terse phrase.

Sculpture

Large-scale and free-standing sculpture was rare in the early Middle Ages, in part because of the lingering fear of idol worship and because the general interest in producing portable objects virtually precluded its production. However, during the Ottonian period the scale of sculpture increased (witness Bernward's doors for St. Michael's at Hildesheim), and even many small-scale works demonstrate an imposing monumentality.

THE *GERO CRUCIFIX* The *Gero Crucifix* (fig. **10.35**), named for Archbishop Gero of Cologne, who commissioned it around 970, is an example of a large-scale work—it is in fact life-size—with a monumental presence, indicative of the major transformation that Ottonian sculptors were able to achieve even when dealing with traditional subjects. How this happens is evident if we compare the *Gero Crucifix* with the Christ on the cover of the *Lindau Gospels* (see fig. 10.16). The two works are separated by little more than 100 years but show marked contrast. The *Gero Crucifix* presents a sculptural image that is new to Western art, since for the first time a dead Christ is represented on the Cross. Made of painted and gilded oak, it is carved in powerfully rounded forms. Particularly striking is the forward bulge of the heavy body, which emphasizes the physical strain on the arms and shoulders, making the pain seem almost unbearable. The face, with its deeply incised, angular features, is a mask of agony from which all life has fled. The image is filled with deep feeling for Christ's suffering.

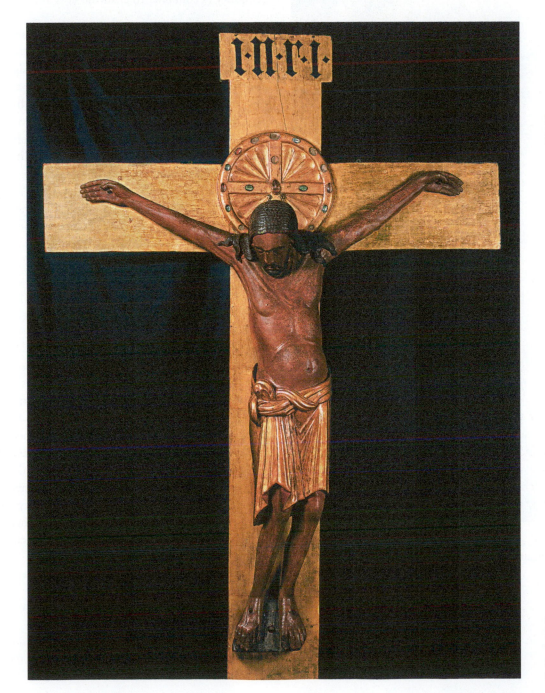

10.35 *Gero Crucifix*. ca. 970. Painted and gilded wood, height 6'2" (1.88 m). Cologne cathedral, Germany

10.36 *Virgin of Essen.* ca. 980. Gold over wood, enamel, filigree, and gems, height 29½" (75.6 cm). Cathedral Treasury, Essen, Germany

How did the Ottonian sculptor arrive at this bold conception? The *Gero Crucifix* was clearly influenced by Middle Byzantine art, which had created the compassionate view of Christ on the Cross in other mediums (see fig. 8.45). Yet, that source alone not enough to explain the results. It remained for the Ottonian artist to translate the Byzantine image into large-scale sculptural terms and to replace its gentle pathos with expressive realism. Even though there were some clerics who rekindled the deep-rooted fear of idolatry, they could not restrain the newly found emphasis on the humanity of Christ or the increasing interest in relics, which were, after all, three-dimensional objects. In fact, there is a space in the back of the head of the Gero Christ to hold the Host (the bread or wafer taken during that part of the Mass referred to as Communion), transforming the sculpture into a **reliquary** (a container to enshrine holy remnants or relics).

THE *VIRGIN OF ESSEN* The *Virgin of Essen* (fig. 10.36), given to the Cathedral of Essen around 980 by Abbess Matilda, grand-daughter of Otto I, was almost certainly designed as a reliquary, although that is hard to establish definitively since the sculpture's original wooden core does not survive. All that is left is the exterior covering of gold sheets. Matilda also donated two—and possibly three—gold, enamel, and jeweled crosses to the cathedral. This rich treasure, glittering on candlelit altars, would have made an impressive display and signaled the church's patronage by a member of the imperial family. The *Virgin of Essen* is one of the earliest free-standing sculptures of the Virgin Mary. The golden apple Mary holds symbolizes her typological status as t new Eve; thus, the sculpture is related conceptually to the message on Bernward's bronze doors (see fig. 10.27).

Despite the tender, almost doll-like figures of Mary and Christ, the *Virgin of Essen* has a commanding presence. This is due to Mary's frontal pose, her large staring eyes, and the brilliance of the gold, which is enhanced by the gems, enamels, and filigree that decorate the apple and Christ's book and halo. Linear details, such as drapery folds, and facial features are suppressed to place emphasis on the figure's corporeality. Thus, although employing some early medieval metalwork materials and techniques that stretch back to the Anglo-Saxon period and to still-earlier traditions as well, the Essen Madonna has moved away from the traditional Germanic concentration on line and surface effect. Despite her small size—less than 2½ feet high—the simplification of form and the concentration on abstract shapes result in a marked movement toward monumentality, which also characterized the *Gero Crucifix*. These works herald new aesthetic aims that will dominate eleventh-century sculpture throughout western Europe.

ca. 624 Ship burial at Sutton Hoo, England

Early Medieval Art

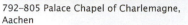

792–805 Palace Chapel of Charlemagne, Aachen

ca. 700 *Lindisfarne Gospels*

ca. 800 *Book of Kells*

ca. 800–10 *Gospel Book of Charlemagne* (*Coronation Gospels*)

ca 820–32 *Utrecht Psalter*

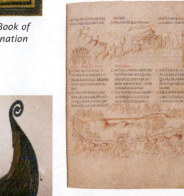

ca. 834 Oseberg ship burial

1001–33 St. Michael's, Hildesheim

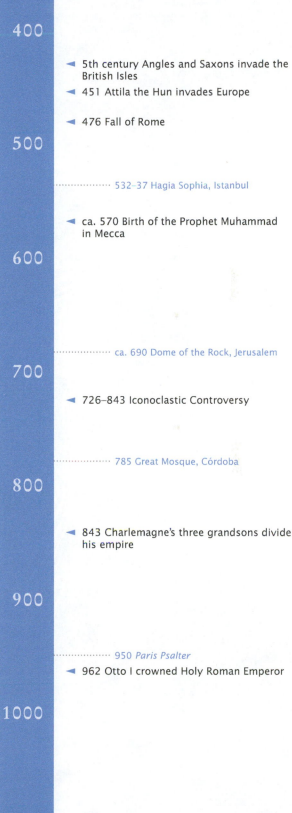

400

◄ 5th century Angles and Saxons invade the British Isles

◄ 451 Attila the Hun invades Europe

◄ 476 Fall of Rome

500

532–37 Hagia Sophia, Istanbul

◄ ca. 570 Birth of the Prophet Muhammad in Mecca

600

ca. 690 Dome of the Rock, Jerusalem

700

◄ 726–843 Iconoclastic Controversy

785 Great Mosque, Córdoba

800

◄ 843 Charlemagne's three grandsons divide his empire

900

950 *Paris Psalter*

◄ 962 Otto I crowned Holy Roman Emperor

1000

1100

CHAPTER 11

Romanesque Art

ROMANESQUE MEANS, LITERALLY, "IN THE ROMAN MANNER." WE USE this stylistic term today to identify the art of much of the eleventh and twelfth centuries. The borrowing of details or specific features from the antique past does not distinguish Romanesque art from the art of other post-Classical periods, for the artists of these periods also relied heavily on Rome

for their formal and expressive languages. However, in Romanesque art, the aesthetic integrity and grandeur of the Roman model survive in a more vital and compelling form than in previous periods. Yet Rome was not the period's only inspiration: Romanesque artists tapped sources in Carolingian and Ottonian art, and were influenced by Early Christian, Byzantine, Celtic-Germanic, and Islamic traditions as well.

While Carolingian and Ottonian art developed principally in response to the patronage of the royal courts, Romanesque art sprang up all over western Europe at about the same time and in a variety of regional styles that are nevertheless closely related. What welded this variety into a coherent style was not any single force but several factors.

For one thing, Christianity was close to triumphing everywhere in Europe. The Vikings, still largely pagan in the ninth and tenth centuries when their raids terrorized the British Isles and the Continent, had finally entered the Catholic fold, not only in Normandy but in Scandinavia as well. Meanwhile, in 1031, the caliphate of Córdoba had broken up into many small Muslim states, opening the way for Christian conquest of the Iberian peninsula.

Another factor was the growing spirit of religious enthusiasm. The year 1000—the millennium—had come and gone without the

apocalyptic end of the world that many had predicted from their reading of the book of Revelation in the Bible. Chapter 20 of this New Testament book, written about 50 years after Jesus' death, prophesizes that the Second Coming, when Christ will return to earth and end the world as we know it, would occur after 1,000 years. Many people, fearing the end of days, reacted to the approach of the year 1000 with terror and to its smooth passing with great relief and, in some quarters, a heightened spirituality. This was demonstrated by the large number of people making pilgrimages to sacred sites, by repeated Christian Crusades against the Muslims in the Holy Land, and by an increase in the number and size of monasteries.

A general growth in population and an increase in prosperity during the Romanesque period are also significant, as was the reopening of the Mediterranean trade routes by the navies of Venice, Genoa, Amalfi, Pisa, and Rimini. The revival of trade and travel linked Europe commercially and culturally, stimulating the flowering of urban life.

At the end of the early medieval period, Europe was still largely an agricultural society. A decentralized political and social system, known today as feudalism, had begun to develop, mainly in France and Germany, where it had deep historical roots. In this system, landowning lords granted some of their property to knights (originally, these were cavalry officers). In return for these fiefs, or feuds, as the land parcels were called, the knights gave military and other service to their lords, to whom they were

Detail of figure 11.2, Lintel of west portal, church of Saint-Genis-des-Fontaines, France

Map 11.1   Europe in the Romanesque period

linked through a complex system of personal bonds—termed vassalage—that extended all the way to the king. A large class of generally downtrodden, virtually powerless peasants (serfs) worked the land itself. Towns that had shrunk in size during the migrations and invasions of the early Middle Ages—Rome, for instance, with about 1 million people in 300, fell to less than 50,000 at one point, and some smaller cities were deserted altogether—started to regain their former importance. New towns sprang up everywhere, achieving independence via charters that enumerated a town's privileges and immunities in return for a feudal lord's guarantee of protection.

These social changes were made possible by technological advances in agriculture, such as improved milling machinery and better iron plows that dug deeper furrows. For the first time since the Fall of Rome, farmers could grow more food than they needed for themselves. In many ways, then, western Europe between 1050 and 1200 became a great deal more "Roman-esque" than it had been since the sixth century. It recaptured some of the trade patterns, the urban quality, and the military strength of ancient imperial times. Despite Charlemagne's attempt to unify Europe, there was no central political authority, for Europe was still divided into small units ruled by powerful families. Even the king of France controlled not much more than the area around Paris. However, some monasteries came to rival the wealth and power of kings, and the central spiritual authority of the pope acted as a unifying force throughout Europe. In 1095, Pope Urban II called for the First Crusade to liberate the Holy Land from Muslim rule and to aid the Byzantine emperor against the advancing Turks. The army of crusaders was far larger than any secular ruler could have raised for the purpose.

This brief historical account underscores the number of institutions, organizations, and systems that helped to create European stability. Monasticism, feudalism, urbanism, com-....ce, pilgrimage, crusade, papacy, and the royal court all played ....r roles by setting in motion internationalizing forces that affected the transmission of artistic forms. Population growth and an increase in the number of new settlements stimulated building activity, much of it for religious, i.e., Christian use. The development of better tools, such as saws to cut stone, resulted in improved masonry techniques. Many new constructions were made of well-cut, straight-edged blocks of stone and were monumental, built on a scale that rivaled the achievements of Rome. Heavy walls created solid and durable structures that conveyed a sense of enclosure and security, and the stone vaults covering these buildings enhanced their stability. These vaults, as well as the proliferation of architectural sculpture, consciously emulated the Roman manner of construction and design. Embellishing churches and monasteries with reliquaries and other adornments, including illuminated manuscripts, provided for the needs of both the local population and pilgrims.

FIRST EXPRESSIONS OF ROMANESQUE STYLE

Although Romanesque art quickly spread throughout Europe, its first appearances occur in a zone running from Lombardy in Italy ....ough southern France and into northern Spain, into the region of Catalonia. Stone-vaulted buildings decorated with wall arcades and architectural sculpture, which are characteristic features of this early phase, survive in great numbers in these regions.

Architecture

The most striking feature of Romanesque art is the amazing increase in building activity. An eleventh-century monk, Raoul Glaber, conveys the enthusiasm for building that characterizes the period:

> Just before the third year after the millennium, throughout the whole world, but most especially in Italy and Gaul, men began to reconstruct churches. … But it seemed as though each Christian community were aiming to surpass all others in the splendor of construction. It was as if the whole world were shaking itself free, shrugging off the burden of the past, and cladding itself everywhere in a white mantle of churches.
>
> J. France, *The Five Books of the Histories* (Oxford, 1989)

These churches were not only more numerous than those of the early Middle Ages, they were also larger, more richly ornamented, ...d more "Roman-looking." Their naves had stone vaults instead ....wooden roofs, and their exteriors were decorated with both architectural ornament and sculpture. Romanesque monuments of the first importance are distributed over an area that might

well have represented the Catholic world: from northern Spain to the Rhineland, from the Scottish–English border to central Italy.

CHURCH OF SANT VINCENÇ, CARDONA An excellent example of an early phase of Romanesque architecture is the collegiate church of Sant Vincenç (fig. **11.1**), built within the walled confines of the castle at Cardona on the southern flank of the Catalan Pyrenees. The church, begun in 1029 and consecrated in 1040, is straightforward both in plan and in elevation. A barrel-vaulted nave creates a continuous space marked off by transverse arches into units of space called **bays**. The domed bay

11.1 Nave and choir (looking east), church of Sant Vicenç, Cardona, Spain. ca. 1029–1040

in front of the **chancel** (the part of the church containing the altar and seats for the clergy) focuses attention on the ceremonial heart of the church. Blind niches in the chancel walls establish a rhythmic variety that is accentuated in the nave by the staggered cadence of massive **compound piers**, solid masonry supports with rectangular projections attached to their four faces. The projections reflect the different structural elements that combine to support the building. One projection rises the full height of the nave to support the transverse arch, another forms the arch that extends across the side aisle, and two others connect to the arches of the nave arcade. Clearly the architectural effort at Sant Vincenç required detailed, systematic planning. Vaulting the nave to eliminate the fire hazard of a wooden roof was not only a practical necessity, it also challenged architects to make the House of the Lord grander.

Sant Vincenç's vertical integration of piers and vault is undoubtedly derived from the desire to unify the elevation in early medieval buildings, for example the Carolingian chapel at Aachen (see fig. 10.18) and the Ottonian church at Gernrode (see fig. 10.23). However, the wall planes of the Ottonian church appear flat by comparison to the angular surfaces of Sant Vincenç, where the clarity of articulation endows the building with a heightened sense of unity and **harmony**. The compound pier is, in fact, a major architectural innovation of the Romanesque period. Limited light and robust stone construction create an interior at once sheltering and inspiring; the sober arrangement of simple yet powerful forms is masterfully realized.

Monumental Stone Sculpture

The revival of monumental stone sculpture in the Romanesque era is as significant as the architectural achievements of the period. Free-standing statues had all but disappeared from Western art after the fifth century, and stone relief survived only as architectural ornament or surface decoration, while three-dimensional sculpture was rare. Thus, the only sculptural tradition that continued through the early medieval period was that of sculpture-in-miniature: small reliefs and occasional statuettes in metal or ivory. In works such as the bronze doors of Bishop Bernward (see fig. 10.27), Ottonian art had enlarged the small scale of this tradition but had not changed its spirit. Moreover, its truly large-scale sculptural efforts, such as the *Gero Crucifix* (see fig. 10.35), were limited almost entirely to wood.

LINTEL AT SAINT-GENIS-DES-FONTAINES The marble lintel at Saint-Genis-des-Fontaines, on the French side of the Pyrenees, is dated by inscription to between 1020 and 1021 (fig. **11.2**). It spans the doorway of the church and is one of

11.2 Lintel of west portal, church of Saint-Genis-des-Fontaines, France. 1020–21. Approx. 2 × 7' (61 cm × 2.1 m)

the earliest examples of Romanesque figurative sculpture. The inscription gives the names of the leaders of two stabilizing institutions of the period, "Rotberto Rege" (King Robert) and "Villelmus Aba" (Abbot William), the former a feudal lord and the latter the leader of a monastery. The central motif, Christ in Majesty supported by angels, is flanked by six apostles; each apostle holds a book and stands under an arcade. Christ's mandorla is formed by two intersecting circles. One symbolizes the earth and the other heaven, the two realms over which he presides.

The Saint-Genis lintel is modest in size, only about 2 feet high by 7 feet long. The reliance on line to indicate facial features, drapery folds, and ornamental decoration is reminiscent of early medieval manuscript illuminations and reaches as far back as the Hiberno-Saxon period (see fig. 10.6). The carving, with flat surfaces marked by incision, resembles the decorative arts, particularly ivory and metalwork. This can be verified by comparing some of the patterns (for example, the beading around the arches) with metalwork techniques (see fig. 10.1). The correlation explains where carvers might have found their sources of inspiration after centuries during which stone sculpture had been virtually abandoned.

Although the figures are rendered with individualized hairstyles and facial features and with a variety of gestures, they are clearly stylized. Each is contained by the frame around him in such a way that it is difficult to decide if the figures are governed by their frames or if the arches swell in response to the figures. The equilibrium between frame and figure parallels the harmonious balance between structure and decoration that characterizes early Romanesque buildings such as Sant Vincenç at Cardona.

MATURE ROMANESQUE

Early Romanesque experiments in sturdy construction, which relied on the skills of masons and sculptors, led to buildings that employed both more sculpture and increasingly sophisticated vaulting techniques. Sculptural decoration was arranged into complicated and didactic iconographic programs. Romanesque architecture and sculpture continue to convey messages of security and spirituality, employing a consistent aesthetic approach that is also visible in the manuscripts and metalwork produced during the period. As Romanesque art developed, it spread throughout Europe, becoming a pan-European art.

Pilgrimage Churches and Their Art

Among the most significant social phenomena of eleventh- and twelfth-century Europe was the increased ability of people of all classes to travel. While some journeys were made as a result of expanded trade, others, such as a crusade or pilgrimage, were ostensibly for religious purposes. Individual pilgrims made journeys to holy places for different reasons, but most shared the hope that they would find special powers or dispensations as a result of their journey. Pilgrimage was not a Romanesque invention. As early as the late fourth century, Egeria, a Spanish pilgrim to Jerusalem, chronicled her visit to the locations central to Christ's life, among them the church of the Holy Sepulcher (see fig. 8.12). Special, often miraculous, powers associated with these holy sites were transferred to relics, those body parts of holy persons or objects that had come in contact with Christ, his close followers, or other holy figures, particularly his mother, the Virgin Mary.

Partly due to the Muslim conquest of the Holy Land, travel there was difficult during the Middle Ages. This led, on the one hand, to a zeal for crusade and, on the other, to a veneration of places within Europe that had important relics or that had been the site of special events. Rome, in particular, became a popular pilgrimage site, beneficiary of the aura of sanctity surrounding SS. Peter and Paul, both of whom lived and were buried there (see page 246). So did Santiago de Compostela on the Iberian peninsula. Cultural anthropologists have attempted to account for the incredible popularity and significance of pilgrimage to the medieval world as well as to our own. They explain that when pilgrims embark on their journey they enter a special transitional, or liminal, zone where social norms and hierarchies are replaced with a sense of shared experience. This creates a temporary condition of community, in which people of disparate backgrounds and social levels can communicate as equals. The buildings and objects pilgrims saw and experienced fostered this sense of community. The pilgrimage and the churches associated with it also provided opportunities for pilgrims to experience spiritual fulfillment through the journey itself, which demonstrated their piety both to themselves and to the world, and through the experience of beautiful and moving buildings and the objects they contained.

SANTIAGO DE COMPOSTELA The tomb of St. James at Santiago de Compostela in northwest Spain marked the most westerly point of Christian Europe. According to tradition, the apostle James (or Santiago in Spanish) had preached Christianity on the Iberian peninsula. After returning to the Holy Land, he was martyred there and his body was returned to Spain under dramatic circumstances. Reports of the tomb's miraculous power attracted large numbers of pilgrims from all over Europe. Many had to brave a difficult sea journey or an exhausting crossing of the Pyrenees mountains in order to reach the apostle's tomb at Compostela. (See *Primary Source*, page 352.) During the twelfth century as many as tens of thousands of people might have made the journey in a single year. The difficulty of the journey added to its allure. Since much of Spain was under Muslim control, pilgrims considered the trip to Santiago equivalent to a journey to the Muslim-held Holy Land.

The cathedral at Santiago de Compostela had much to offer those brave hearts sufficiently fortunate to reach their goal. The plan (fig. **11.3**) includes side aisles that run uninterruptedly around the church and form an ambulatory around the apse. Visitors used these aisles to circumambulate the space, even when the religious offices were being celebrated in the nave and **crossing**. **Apsidioles**, or small apselike chapels, arranged along

The Pilgrim's Guide

From *Pilgrim's Guide to Santiago de Compostela*

The Pilgrim's Guide, *written around 1130, gives a vivid account of the routes to Santiago de Compostela and what was to be met along them by pilgrims traveling to the shrine of the apostle James there (see map 11.2, page 354). It also provides interesting information on the personnel in charge of the construction of the shrine at the cathedral.*

There are four roads which, leading to Santiago, converge into one near Puente la Reina [see fig. 11.8], in Spanish territory. One goes through St-Gilles [see fig. 11.31], Montpellier, Toulouse [see fig. 11.7] and [the pass of] Somport; another passes through Notre-Dame of Le Puy and Ste-Foy at Conques and Saint-Pierre at Moissac [see figs. 11.12–11.16]; another proceeds through Ste-Marie-Madeleine of Vézelay, St-Léonard of the Limousin and the city of Périgueux; another goes by St-Martin of Tours to St-Hilaire of Poitiers, St-Jean-d'Angély, St-Eutrope of Saintes and the city of Bordeaux. ...

After that are the Landes of the Bordelais, a three-days' journey, exhausting to be sure. This is a country devoid of all good things, lacking in bread, wine, meat, fish, water and springs, sparse in towns, flat, sandy but abundant, however, in honey, millet, panic-grass pigs. If, however, by chance you cross it in summer, take car[e] guard your face from the enormous insects, commonly called *guespe* [wasps] or *tauones* [horseflies], which are most abundant there; and if you do not watch carefully where you put your feet, you will slip rapidly up to your knees in the quicksand that abounds there. ...

After this valley is found the land of Navarre, which abounds in bread and wine, milk and cattle. The Navarrese and Basques are held to be exactly alike....This is a barbarous race unlike all other races in customs and in character, full of malice, swarthy in colour, evil of face, depraved, perverse, perfidious, empty of faith and corrupt, libidinous, drunken, experienced in all violence, ferocious and wild, dishonest and reprobate, impious and harsh, cruel and contentious, unversed in anything good, well-trained in all vices and iniquities. ...

Source: *Pilgrim's Guide to Santiago de Compostela: A Critical Edition*, II, ed. and tr. Paula Gerson, Annie Shaver Crandell, Alison Stones and Jeanne Krochalis (London: Harvey Miller Publishers, 1998)

11.3   Plan of cathedral of Santiago de Compostela, Spain. ca. 1075–1120 (after Dehio)

11.4   Reconstruction of cathedral of Santiago de Compostela (after Conant)

11.5   Nave of cathedral of Santiago de Compostela

the road from Le Puy), and Saint-Sernin at Toulouse (on the road from Saint-Gilles-du-Gard). (See map 11.2.)

The plan of Santiago de Compostela (see fig. 11.3) is composed of multiple modular units. It recalls the system of architectural composition based on additive components that was employed during the early Middle Ages (see page 333). The bays of the nave and the transept are half the size of the square crossing, and the square bays of the side aisles are in turn a quarter the size of the crossing and thus half the size of the nave bays. As at Sant Vicenç at Cardona (see fig. 11.1), the building's elevation (see fig. 11.5) mirrors the clarity of its plan. The four **colonnettes**, small detached columns, of the compound piers reflect the building's structural elements. However, overall there is less wall surface in the Santiago de Compostela nave, and colonnettes, used in place of Sant Vicenç's rectangular attachments to the compound piers (see pages 349–50), more richly articulate the nave elevation.

So as not to weaken the barrel vaults at their **springing**, where they would need the most support, Santiago de Compostela was built without a clerestory. Since a vault becomes more difficult to sustain the farther it is from the ground, every resource had to be mined to enable the nave to be as tall as possible. The galleries built over the inner aisles counterbalance the lateral pressure of the nave vault. Inside the nave, vaults, arches, engaged colonnettes, and pilasters are all firmly knit together into a coherent order that recaptures the vocabulary and syntax of ancient Roman architecture to a remarkable degree. Diffused light, subtle and atmospheric, filters into the nave through the side aisles and the galleries above. What function the galleries served is much debated. Conceivably they provided overflow space for the large numbers of pilgrims who visited the church, particularly on feast days, and indeed the famous *Pilgrim's Guide*, written around 1130, mentions the presence of altars in the galleries. But the galleries also provide for an elegantly elaborated interior, as the *Pilgrim's Guide* also makes clear:

> In truth, in this church no fissure or fault is found; it is admirably constructed, grand, spacious, bright, of proper magnitude, harmonious in width, length and height, of admirable and ineffable workmanship, built in two storys, just like a royal palace. For indeed, whoever visits the naves of the gallery, if he goes up sad, after having seen the perfect beauty of this temple, he will be made happy and joyful.
>
> Pilgrim's Guide to Santiago de Compostela: A Critical Edition, II, ed. and tr. Paula Gerson, Annie Shaver Crandell, Alison Stones, and Jeanne Krochalis (London: Harvey Miller Publishers, 1998)

the eastern walls of the transepts and around the apse, provided multiple opportunities to display the relics that pilgrims had come to venerate (fig. 11.4). As pilgrims approached the nave from the west entrance and walked through the building, they were conscious of marching step by step toward their goals in the apses, altars, and reliquaries at the east end of the church (fig. 11.5).

Passage through the cathedral was thus a microcosm of the longer journey the pilgrims had taken on the open road, and as such Santiago de Compostela might readily be called a **pilgrimage plan** church. A group of great churches of varying sizes and details, using the same pilgrimage plan, were built along the roads leading to Compostela. Major churches built to this plan are situated on each of the four main roads leading through France: Saint-Martin at Tours (on the road from Paris), Saint-Martial at Limoges (on the road from Vézelay), Sainte-Foy at Conques (on

The synthesis of emotional and spiritual response described in the *Pilgrim's Guide* results from the Romanesque builders' ability to fuse structure and aesthetics. In another section of his book, the *Guide*'s author notes with admiration the quality of the stonework, as "hard as marble." By using a simile that compares the stone used to build the cathedral with the quintessential building material of the Classical past, he clearly expresses a fact

Map 11.2 The Pilgrimage routes to Santiago de Compostela

that viewers today can still appreciate—that in both detail and execution Santiago de Compostela emulates the nobility and dignity of Roman architecture.

RELIQUARIES A twelfth-century casket, today in the Metropolitan Museum of Art in New York (fig. **11.6**), is typical of the kinds of decorated reliquaries that pilgrims saw on their journeys to Compostela and Rome. This one was probably made in Limoges, a major stop on the road to Compostela and

a center of enamel production, where there was a large church built according to the pilgrimage plan. The material and the b areas of flat color, evident in both the foliage and the symbols the four evangelists, relate this work to the tradition of migration and early medieval metalwork (see fig. 10.3). The method of manufacture is **champlevé**, which was derived from the cloisonné technique (see page 315). Instead of cells formed from thin strips of metal attached to a support, as with cloisonné, the metal surface is gouged out to create compartments that contain the colored

11.6 Reliquary casket with symbols of the four Evangelists. ca. 1150. Champlevé enamel on gilt copper, 4⅞ × 7⁷⁄₁₆ × 3⅜″ (12.4 × 18.9 × 8.5 cm). Metropolitan Museum of Art, New York. Gift of J. Pierpont Morgan, 1917 (17.190.685-687, 695, 710–11)

11.7 *Christir in Majesty* (*Maiestas Domini*), Saint-Sernin, Toulouse, France. ca. 1096. Marble, height 50″ (127 cm)

the zone around the altar and shrine of St. Sernin, thus embellishing an area deemed particularly holy by pilgrims.

The shallow relief and many decorative effects of the Christ plaque recall earlier metalwork and ivory objects (see figs. 10.16 and 10.31). The extensive use of double lines, some creating raised sections, some impressed ones, enhances the figure's volumetric presence. The treatment also brings to mind manuscript illumination, particularly Carolingian and Ottonian examples, but also Byzantine ones. In the arrangement of the figure, the play of linear drapery folds, and the variety of ornamental devices, we are not far from the Christ of the *Godescalc Gospels* (see fig. 10.12), which was in Saint-Sernin during the Middle Ages.

The figure of Christ, somewhat more than half life-size, was not meant to be viewed exclusively at close range. Its impressive bulk and weight make it prominent even from a considerable distance. This emphasis on volume hints at what may have been the main inspiration behind the revival of large-scale sculpture: A stone-carved image, being solid and three-dimensional, is far more "real" than a painted one.

SECULAR STRUCTURES ALONG THE PILGRIMAGE ROAD

A complex infrastructure was needed to service an enterprise as extensive as the pilgrimage to Compostela. Establishments such as hospices and hospitals provided for the needs of pilgrims. Improved roads and bridges were of particular importance, and a number of Spanish monarchs of the eleventh and twelfth centuries took their construction as essential goals, both to support pilgrims coming to Spain and to encourage closer relationships abroad, particularly with France. Such connections aimed to strengthen Christian foundations in Spain, a reaction to the Muslim presence in the Iberian peninsula. Holy stature was often credited to people who built and maintained the actual roads on which pilgrims trekked, as was the case with Santo Domingo de la Calzada (literally "of the paved road" or "roadway"), who built, in addition to a pilgrims' hostel and hospital, a long bridge over the Oja River and who maintained the roads around the town that came to be named after him.

THE BRIDGE AT PUENTE LA REINA Almost a week before arriving in the town of Santo Domingo de la Calzada, pilgrims would have crossed a large, stately bridge in the town of Puente la Reina (fig. 11.8). The town's name derives from that mid-twelfth-century bridge (*puente* in Spanish), around which a settlement developed. Seven round-headed arches, only six of which survive today, formed the original bridge. The largest, central arch and the flanking arches, which decrease in span, fall on large pillars that are buttressed by wedge-shaped cutwaters, designed to break the current. Open arches fill the **spandrels**, the areas between the curves of two adjoining arches, and serve at once the physical function of lightening the weight of the bridge and the visual function of establishing, along with the arches of the bridge itself, a stepped rhythm that accentuates the structure's purpose to facilitate passage. The bridge is 350 feet long and nearly 10 feet wide, while its central arch spans 65 feet, a daring achievement

enamel. The preciousness of the enamel on the gilt copper of our reliquary and its lavish decoration suit its exceptional and holy contents, thought to be relics of St. Martial, identified by inscription on the other side of the box, since the reliquary comes from a church dedicated to him in Champagnat, about 60 miles (96 km) from Limoges.

MONUMENTAL SCULPTURE Many of the churches along the pilgrimage route had elaborate sculptural programs decorating their interiors and portals. A series of large marble plaques, currently placed in the ambulatory of Saint-Sernin in Toulouse, located on the pilgrimage route that cuts across southern France (see map 11.2), dates to the years immediately preceding 1100. Six of these plaques depict angels and apostles, while one represents a seated Christ, the *Christ in Majesty* (fig. **11.7**). Although their original location is not certain, the plaques most likely decorated

11.8 Bridge over the Arga River, Puente la Reina, Spain. 11th century

for the period and one that helps account for its fame. A little chapel in the center of the bridge was destroyed in the nineteenth century and around the same time towers at each end were razed, though one was reconstructed in the middle of the last century. The bridge was undoubtedly the result of royal patronage, as is reflected by its name (*reina* means queen in Spanish), although which queen commissioned it is an unresolved question. Even though crossing the bridge at Puente la Reina would have required payment of a toll, or a charge to cross it, the *Pilgrim's Guide* makes clear the benefits accrued from avoiding ferrymen, infamous for the exorbitant prices they charged as well as for their treachery:

> Upon leaving this country, the way of Saint James crosses two rivers which ... can not be crossed without a barque [boat]— may their boatmen be utterly damned! For, although the rivers are quite narrow, nevertheless, they are in the habit of getting one *nummus* [coin] from every person, poor as well as rich, whom they ferry across, and for a beast four, which they undeservedly extort. ... When you get in, be careful not to fall into the water by accident. ... If the boat is overladen with too many people, it will soon be in peril. Many times also, after receiving the money, the ferrymen take on such a throng of pilgrims

that the boat tips over, and the pilgrims are killed in the water. Thereupon the ferrymen rejoice wickedly after seizing the spoils from the dead.

> Pilgrim's Guide to Santiago de Compostela:
> A Critical Edition, II
> ed. and tr. Paula Gerson, Annie Shaver Crandell,
> Alison Stones, and Jeanne Krochalis
> (London: Harvey Miller Publishers, 1998)

Cluniac Architecture and Sculpture

During the time when the sculptural decoration of Saint-Sernin was executed, the church was under the auspices of monks from the great Benedictine monastery of Cluny. Cluny was responsible for a network of dependencies; its "daughter" houses, spread across Europe, numbered more than 1,400, including a number of monasteries located on the pilgrimage road that served the needs of pilgrims. The Cluniac order's influence and growth were remarkable. The order could determine papal election and call for crusades against the Muslims. The rise and spread of various monastic orders was significant for the development of Romanesque art, but none was more important than Cluny.

← N

latrine

court

latrine

great infirmary hall

chapter house

dormitory above

south transept

cemetery

cemetery chapel

Lady Chapel

infirmary cloister

Cluny III

Cluny II

latrine

novices' cloister

novitiate

refectory

cloister

bakery

atrium

cellar

court

lay monk's kitchen

portico

pantries

south gate

old guest house

stable

hospice

unfinished in 1157

hospice

stable

main 13th century gate augmentation

latrine

0 10   60 meters
0   50   200 feet

ABBEY CHURCH OF CLUNY The rapid growth of the Cluniac order can also be seen in the fact that its original basilica church of about 910 was replaced with a more ample one that itself was replaced only about 75 years later, in 1088, by the largest Romanesque church ever built, the third abbey church of Cluny (fig. **11.9**). Unfortunately, Cluny III, as it is known, was destroyed after the French Revolution, and only the south transept (the one to the right in the plan) and the octagonal tower remain. The auspicious use of towers in Carolingian buildings such as Saint-Riquier (see fig. 10.20) here reached its culmination. The apsidioles, apses, and towers at the east end of Cluny eated a monumental gathering of ever-higher forms. Individual ements functioned together in built harmony (fig. **11.10**); the south transept with octagonal tower at its crossing is on the left in this reconstruction.

11.10 Reconstruction of abbey church of Cluny (Cluny III), from east (after Conant)

11.11 Reconstruction of abbey church of Cluny (Cluny III), nave and interior (after Conant)

The proportions of Cluny III were based on ratios of "perfect" numbers and on musical harmonies, reminding us of the importance of music in the medieval Church. Monks chanted their prayers eight times a day and Gunzo, one of the archit of Cluny III, was noted for his musicianship. A benefit of stone-vaulted buildings was their acoustic resonance; this feature might well have encouraged the widespread use of stone vaulting or at least made the heavy financial investment acceptable to the community. Even today, it is a moving experience to hear Gregorian chants sung beneath the vaults of a Romanesque church.

The interior of Cluny III (fig. **11.11**) was as elegant as it was huge, its vaults reaching 100 feet. Below the clerestory, and in place of a gallery, was a **triforium**, the series of three-arched openings (one series per bay); the triforium, which is closed to the outside of the building, creates a space within the wall, barely sufficient to allow passage, that lightens it both physically and visually. The clerestory and triforium are connected by pilaster strips with Corinthian capitals, reminiscent of Roman architectural decoration. What is not Roman is the use of slightly pointed arches in the nave arcade, a device thought to derive from contact with Islamic culture (see fig. 9.12). By eliminating the center part of the rounded arch, which responds the most to the pull of gravity, the two halves of a pointed arch brace each other. Because the pointed arch exerts less outward pressure than the semicircular arch, not only can it be made steeper, but the walls can be pierced (with windows and triforium arcades) and thus made lighter.

MONASTERY OF MOISSAC The priory of Saint-Pierre Moissac, located on the pilgrimage road close to Toulouse and also under the direction of Cluny, was another important center of Romanesque art. The cloister, adjacent to the church

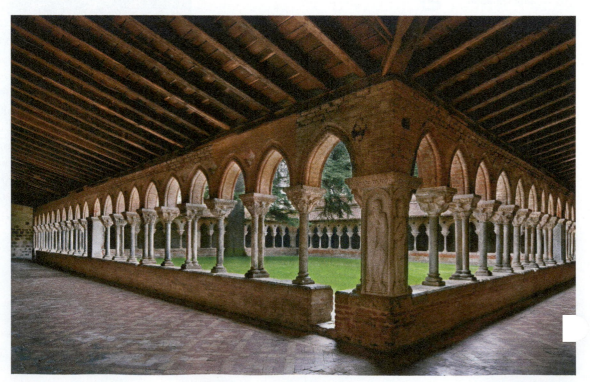

11.12 Cloister, priory of Saint-Pierre, Moissac, France. ca. 1100

St. Bernard of Clairvaux (1090–1153)

From *Apologia to Abbot William of Saint-Thierry*

Bernard of Clairvaux was a member of the Cistercians, an ascetic order founded in the eleventh century in opposition to the increasing opulence of the Benedictines. His letter to the Benedictine abbot William of Saint-Thierry of around 1127 denounces all monastic luxury, especially the presence of art in cloisters. Like many others, Bernard believed that monks were spiritually superior to the "carnal" layfolk and so should not need material inducements to devotion.

As a monk, I put to monks the same question that a pagan used to criticize other pagans: "Tell me, priests," he said, "what is gold doing in the holy place?" I, however, say … "Tell me, poor men, if indeed you are poor men, what is gold doing in the holy place?" For certainly bishops have one kind of business, and monks another. We [monks] know that since they [bishops] are responsible for both the wise and the foolish, they stimulate the devotion of a carnal people with material ornaments because they cannot do so with spiritual ones. But we who have withdrawn from the people, we who have left behind all that is precious and beautiful in this world for the sake of Christ, we who regard as dung all things shining in beauty, soothing in sound, agreeable in fragrance, sweet in taste, pleasant in touch—in short, all material pleasures— … whose devotion, I ask, do we strive to excite in all this? …

Does not avarice, which is in the service of idols, cause all this? Money is sown with such skill that it may be multiplied. … The very sight of these costly but wonderful illusions inflames men more to give than to pray. In this way wealth is derived from wealth. Eyes are fixed on relics covered with gold and purses are opened. The thoroughly beautiful image of some male or female saint is exhibited and that saint is believed to be the more holy the more highly colored the image is. People rush to kiss it, they are invited to donate, and they admire the beautiful more than they venerate the sacred. … What do you think is being sought in all this? The compunction of penitents, or the astonishment of those who gaze at it? O vanity of vanities! The Church is radiant in its walls and destitute in its poor. It serves the eyes of the rich at the expense of the poor. It dresses its stone in gold and it abandons its children naked. The curious find that which may delight them, but those in need do not find that which should sustain them.

But apart from this, in the cloisters, before the eyes of the brothers while they read—what is that ridiculous monstrosity doing, an amazing kind of deformed beauty and yet a beautiful deformity? What are the filthy apes doing there? The fierce lions? The monstrous centaurs? The creatures, part man and part beast? The striped tigers? The fighting soldiers? The hunters blowing horns? You may see many bodies under one head, and conversely many heads on one body. On one side the tail of a serpent is seen on a quadruped, on the other side the head of a quadruped is on the body of a fish. Over there an animal has a horse for the front half and a goat for the back; here a creature which is horned in front is equine behind. In short, everywhere so plentiful and astonishing a variety of contradictory forms is seen that one would rather read in the marble than in books, and spend the whole day wondering at every single one of them than in meditating on the law of God. Good God! If one is not ashamed of the absurdity, why is one not at least troubled at the expense?

Source: Conrad Rudolph, *The "Things of Greater Importance": Bernard of Clairvaux's Apologia and the Medieval Attitude Toward Art* (Philadelphia: University of Pennsylvania Press, 1990)

and reserved for the use of its monks, was formed by four covered passageways arranged around an open garden (fig. **11.12**). Protected from the elements, the monks could practice their spiritual exercises here; they used the zone for a variety of other functions as well. The cloister was central to monastic life and physically occupied a central position within the monastic complex, as is seen in the St. Gall and Cluny plans. Seventy-six sculptured capitals decorate this private zone. While they include representations of Bible stories, many are decorated with foliage, birds, animals, and monstrous creatures.

Although the Romanesque period is far removed chronologically from the Early Christian aversion to image making, even during this period there were those who objected to the corrupting power of visual representation. One of them was St. Bernard of Clairvaux, a member of the Cistercian order, a reform movement created around 1100 in part as a reaction to the increasing economic and political successes of Cluny and in order to provide monastic life more in keeping with St. Benedict's rules (see pages 0–31). In truth, it is hard to correlate the worldly achievements of a monastery such as that at Moissac or at Cluny—the wealth they acquired and the political clout they exercised—with the values to which monks traditionally aspired, which were based on the renunciation of earthly pleasures in favor of the pursuit of spiritual ideals. The pictorial representation of Christian themes was often justified by a famous saying: *Quod legentibus scriptura, hoc idiotis … pictura.* Translated freely, this means that painting conveys the Word of God to the unlettered. Although St. Bernard did not object specifically to the teaching role of art, he had little use for church decoration and would surely have disapproved of the Moissac cloister's excesses, which were clearly meant to appeal to the eye as well as the spirit. In a letter of 1127 to Abbot William of Saint-Thierry concerning the decoration of churches, St. Bernard condemned art made for contemplation by monks. (See *Primary Source*, above.)

If the Moissac monks had a profusion of sculpture to engage them, so too did pilgrims and layfolk visiting the monastery's church. Its elaborately sculptured portal (fig. **11.13**) was executed almost a generation after the cloister was finished. It displays the parts of a typical Romanesque portal (fig. **11.14**). Christ in Majesty takes center stage in the **tympanum**, the lunette above the lintel of the portal. He is shown during his Second Coming, when he returns to Earth after the apocalyptic end of days, as described

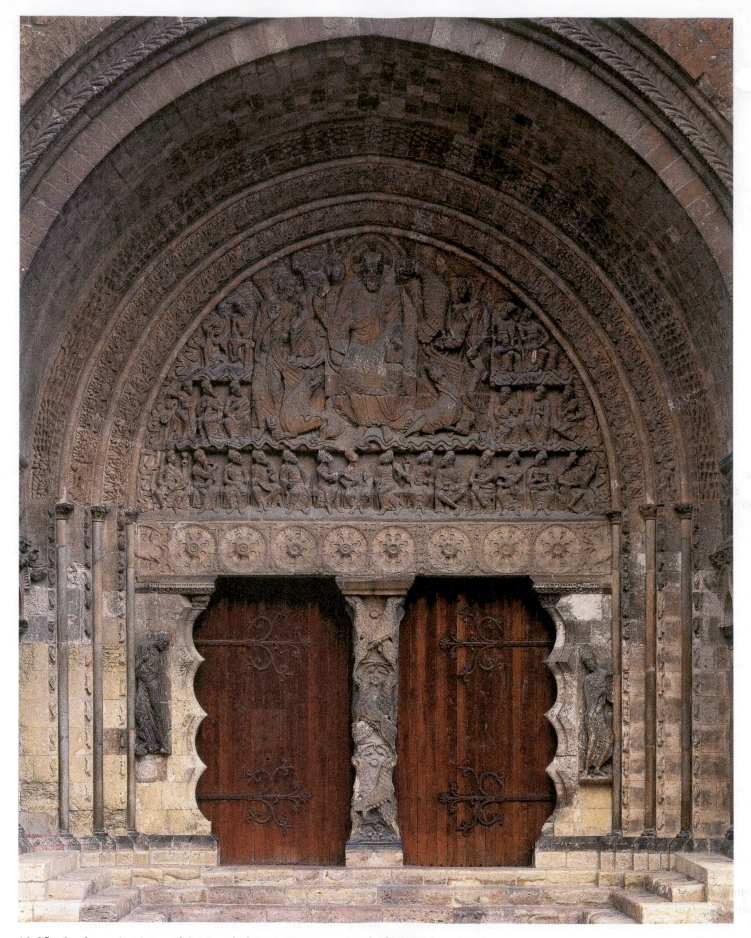

11.13   South portal with *Second Coming of Christ* on tympanum, church of Saint-Pierre, Moissac. ca. 1115–30

spandrels

voussoirs

tympanum

lintel

jamb

jamb column

trumeau

11.14 Romanesque portal ensemble

in the book of Revelation (4:1–8), in order to judge mortals as saved or damned. In accordance with the biblical account, Christ ttended by four beasts, which accompany two angels and 24 elders, while wavy lines beneath their feet represent "the sea of glass like crystal." The elders, relatively small compared with the other figures, and many of them gesticulating, can barely contain their excitement in the face of the remarkable vision. Abstraction and activity characterize the style of carving, in which quivering lines, borders of meandering ribbon patterns, and fluttering drapery offset a hierarchy of scale and pose. The use of abstraction in the service of religious zeal has parallels in earlier medieval art, for example the manuscript illuminations of the *Ebbo Gospel Book* (see fig. 10.14) and the *Utrecht Psalter* (see fig. 10.15). At Moissac, however, the presentation is on a monumental, public scale.

Other parts of the Moissac portal are also treated sculpturally. Both the **trumeau** (the center post supporting the lintel) and the jambs (the sides of the doorway) have scalloped outlines (see fig. 11.13), modeled on a popular Islamic device. By borrowing forms from the art of Islam at Moissac and other churches, Christians were expressing their admiration and regard for Arab artistic achievements. At the same time, such acts of appropriation could also express the Christian ambition to dominate the Muslim enemy. The pilgrimage to Santiago was a similar manifestation of anti-Islamic feeling.

The scalloped outlines framing the doorway activate and dramatize the experience of entering the church. Human and mal forms are treated with flexibility. For instance, the spidery prophet on the side of the trumeau seems perfectly adapted to his precarious perch, even as he struggles to free himself from the

stone (fig. **11.15**). With legs crossed in a graceful movement, he turns his head toward the interior of the church as he unfurls his scroll. The crossed lions that form a symmetrical zigzag on the face of the trumeau "animate" the shaft the same way the interlacing beasts of Irish miniatures (from which they are descended) enliven the spaces they inhabit.

We can trace the crossed lions through textiles to Persian metalwork, although not in this towerlike formation. Ultimately they descend from the heraldic animals of ancient Near Eastern art (see fig. 2.9). Yet we cannot account for their presence at Moissac in terms of their effectiveness as ornament alone. They belong to an extensive family of savage or monstrous creatures in Romanesque art that retain their demoniacal vitality even as they are forced to perform a supporting function. Their purpose is thus not only decorative but expressive; they embody dark forces that have been domesticated into guardian figures or banished to a position that holds them fixed for all eternity, however much they may snarl in protest. One medieval bishop argued that seeing animals sculpted in churches would so terrify parishioners that they would be encouraged to refrain from sinful deeds.

11.15 Trumeau and jambs, south portal, church of Saint-Pierre, Moissac

11.16   East flank, south portal, church of Saint-Pierre, Moissac

A deep porch with lavishly sculptured lateral ends frames the Moissac portal. Within an arcade on the east flank (fig. 11.16), we see, on the lower left, the Annunciation to the Virgin, and to the right, the Visitation (when Mary visits her cousin Elizabeth, mother of John the Baptist, to announce that she is pregnant), and the Adoration of the Magi in the top two panels under the arches. (The angel of the Annunciation is a modern replacement.) Other events from the early life of Jesus are on the frieze above. All of the figures have the same thin limbs and eloquent gestures as the prophet on the trumeau. On the west flank, not illustrated here, is a representation of the vice of *luxuria* (lust), presented as antithetical to the virtue of the Virgin Mary. The juxtaposition recalls the pairing during the early Middle Ages of Eve's sinfulness with Mary's purity (see fig. 10.27). The messages at Moissac are patently didactic, meant both to command and to enlighten. When visitors on the pilgrim road faced the deep portal of the church they were virtually surrounded by the sculptural program, and this intensified the liminal experience of crossing into the church. The journey into the church became a veritable rite of passage, transformative both physically and spiritually.

CATHEDRAL OF SAINT-LAZARE, AUTUN Close to Cluny and dependent on it was the cathedral of Saint-Lazare at Autun. The tympanum of its west portal (fig. 11.17) represents the Last Judgment, the most awe-inspiring scene in Christian art. This scene depicts Christ after his Second Coming as he separates those who will be eternally saved from those who are damned. His figure, much larger than any other, dominates the tympanum. The sculptor, Gislebertus, whose signature appears immediately under the feet of Christ in the center of the tympanum, treats the subject with extraordinary force. Gislebertus is only one of a number of Romanesque sculptors with distinct artistic personalities who are known to us by name. His style is sufficiently individual to enable scholars to posit convincingly that he trained at Cluny before his elevation to master's rank at Autun.

On the left side of the tympanum, apostles observe the weighing of souls, which takes place on the right side. Four angels in the corners sound the trumpets of the Apocalypse. At the bottom, the dead rise from their graves, trembling with fear; some are already beset by snakes or gripped by huge, clawlike hands. Above, their fate quite literally hangs in the balance, with devils yanking at one end of the scales and angels at the other. The saved souls cling like children to the angels for protection before their ascent to the heavenly Jerusalem (far left), while the condemned, seized by grinning devils, are cast into the mouth of Hell (far right). These nightmarish devils are human in general outline, but they have birdlike legs, furry thighs, tails, pointed ears, and savage mouths. The hierarchical, abstract, and patterned representation of Christ conveys his formidable power more effectively than any naturalistic image could. No visitor who had "read in the marble" (to quote St. Bernard of Clairvaux) could fail to enter the church in a chastened spirit.

The Last Judgment, with its emphasis on retribution, was a standard subject for the tympana of Romanesque churches. It was probably chosen because some medieval justice was dispensed in front of the church portal, *ante ecclesium*. Thus, actual judicial proceedings paralleled the divine judgment represented here. Trial was by ordeal, whereby the accused established innocence only by withstanding grueling physical tests. The ordeals must, in reality, have been as terrifying as the scenes depicted on the tympanum.

The outer **archivolt** (a molded band forming an arch) surrounding the west tympanum on Autun's cathedral is composed of medallions containing calendar scenes, comprised, in typical medieval fashion, of the signs of the zodiac and the corresponding labors of the months. The calendar serves to place the fearsome events of the Last Judgment within cosmological time, that is, within the physical realm that all of us occupy on earth.

The north portal of the cathedral was dismantled in the eighteenth century but Gislebertus's *Eve* (fig. 11.18), a fragment of the lintel, survives in the Musée Rolin. It demonstrates the master's incredibly expressive range. The relief was balanced on the other

11.17 West portal, with *Last Judgment* by Gislebertus on tympanum, cathedral of Saint-Lazare, Autun, France. ca. 1120–35

11.18 Gislebertus, *Eve*, right half of lintel, north portal, from cathedral of Saint-Lazare, Autun, France. 1120–32. 28½ × 51″ (72.4 × 129.5 cm). Musée Rolin, Autun

side of the lintel by a representation of Adam. Once again the choice of subjects undoubtedly relates to the portal's liturgical function, since public penitential rites took place in front of the north portal. Adam and Eve's sin—the original one, after all—was mentioned in the penitential liturgy, in which sinners, seeking for-giveness for their transgressions, participated. In the relief, Eve's delicate gestures of grasping the fruit and touching her cheek as if in contemplation result in a beguiling, sensual silhouette. Her posture is not merely the consequence of the narrow horizontal space she occupies; rather, her pose emulates a slithering earth-bound serpent, so she is temptress as well as tempted. As we saw on the bronze doors of Bishop Bernward at Hildesheim (see fig. 10.27), in medieval eyes Eve symbolized the base enchantments embodied by all worldly women.

SARCOPHAGUS OF DOÑA SANCHA A different view of women can be seen in the stone sarcophagus created around 1120 to house the remains of Doña Sancha, a princess of the kingdom of Aragon in northern Spain. Aragon had strong ties to Cluny; about 50 years before Sancha's sarcophagus was carved, her brother, King Sancho Ramírez, undertook a Cluniac reform of the monasteries in his kingdom. This was part of his efforts to strengthen Christian foundations in Spain, a reaction to the Muslim presence on the Iberian peninsula.

At the center of one side of the sarcophagus (fig. **11.19**), two angels support a nude figure in a mandorla, representing the soul of the deceased being lifted to Heaven, an appropriate subject for a funerary monument. On the left, three clerics under an arch perform a Mass for the dead, and on the right, two women, prob-ably Sancha's sisters, stand under an arch and flank the enthroned princess. The arrangement in this right panel, which proclaims the dignity and importance of the larger central figure of Sancha, relies on an antique tradition, seen, for example, on the fourth-century *Sarcophagus of Junius Bassus* (see fig. 8.20).

On the other side of the sarcophagus are three mounted fig-ures, each under an arch. Two armed horsemen confront each other, while the third straddles a lion and grasps its open jaws with his hands. The most compelling interpretation of the con-fronted horsemen identifies them as combatants in the struggle between good and evil, a common subject in Christian art. The lion rider in the right arcade has variously been identified as the long-haired Samson or the youthful David, both Hebrew Bible prototypes for the Christian struggle against evil.

Sancha was a key figure in her kingdom at a time when the Aragonese kings were fighting to conquer Spain from the Muslims, who then held sway over much of the Iberian penin-sula. That scenes of battle, even ones that can be symbolically or allegorically interpreted, were considered appropriate for the

11.19 *Sarcophagus of Doña Sancha,* front and back sides. ca. 1120. Stone, 25.8 × 78.74″ (65 × 200 cm). Monastério de las Benedictinas, Jaca, Spain

sarcophagus of a woman is a mark of the culture of Romanesque Spain, which one scholar has called "a society organized for war." Many legends sprang up about women's roles in the defense of territories newly conquered from Muslims by Christian warriors. The pressing need for settlement and permanent organization required women to engage actively in the acquisition and exchange of land and other properties at a time when their men were away on military campaigns. If Sancha were an isolated instance of a woman of power enjoying special prestige, it would not add much to our knowledge of the Romanesque period. But, in fact, women in eleventh- and twelfth-century Spain played an inordinately important role in the formation of political structures, and as commissioners of works of art.

The triumphal aspirations represented on Sancha's sarcophagus are balanced by the sensitive depiction of the soul, whose tender expression suggests hope as well as anxiety, common human responses when contemplating death. Notice how the center group is the only one not covered by an arch, a strategy that emphasizes a sense of upward thrust and hence suggests a heavenly journey.

Cluniac Wall Painting

Because the destruction of Cluny's buildings resulted in the loss of its wall paintings, we can best appreciate what these might have looked like by examining allied monuments. A good one for this purpose is the priory of Berzé-la-Ville.

THE BERZÉ-LA-VILLE APSE The early twelfth-century priory of Berzé-la-Ville, just a few miles southeast of Cluny, was built as a retreat for Cluny's abbot, and the apse paintings in its chapel (fig. **11.20**) emulate those in the church of the mother house. Christ in Majesty occupies the center of the composition, surrounded by the apostles. The elongated faces and the graceful manner in which drapery is pulled across limbs impart delicacy and elegance to the images; patterns of rhythmic concentric lines and bright highlights indicate the multiple folds in the cloth. Although these devices ultimately derive from Byzantine sources, such as the *Paris Psalter* (see fig. 8.39), the path by which they were acquired was indirect, coming from Byzantine art in Italy, not Constantinople. The library at Cluny

11.20 Christ and Apostles, priory of Berzé-la-Ville, France. Early 12th century

was rich in Italo-Byzantine manuscripts, and Cluniac manuscript illumination also favors this style.

Cistercian Architecture and Art

As we have seen, Cluny's very success made it the subject of criticism, particularly by the Cistercians, whose mother house was at Cîteaux in Burgundy. In addition to prayer, the Cistercians devoted themselves to hard work, which helped guarantee their own great success. Sound economic planning, skill in agriculture and husbandry, and wealthy benefactors furthered their cause. At a time of rising urban growth, the serenity of the isolated sites of their monasteries must also have been attractive. The Cistercian order and its style spread across Europe, and by the end of the twelfth century the Cistercians controlled nearly 700 monasteries. Cistercian architecture in its simplicity contrasts markedly with the architecture of the Cluniac order.

ABBEY CHURCH AT FONTENAY The abbey church at Fontenay, not far from Cîteaux, was begun in 1139, a generation after St. Bernard founded a monastery there. It is the best-preserved Cistercian church built in the first half of the twelfth century. Fontenay exemplifies the Cistercian reliance on simple and unadorned forms in contrast to the opulence promulgated by Cluny. In its orderliness, the plan of simple geometric shapes (fig. **11.21**) builds on monastic schemes dating as far back as the St. Gall drawing (see fig. 10.22). By comparison

11.21 Plan of Fontenay Abbey, France. Begun in 1139

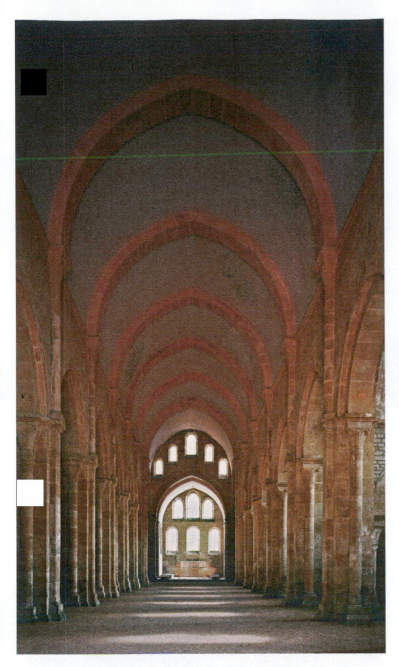

11.22 Nave of the abbey church, Fontenay. 1139–47

refge from worldly burdens, although different in effect from the protective enclosures that other Romanesque churches offer (see figs. 11.1 and 11.5).

Other Benedictine Architecture and Wall Painting

The Benedictine abbey church of Saint-Savin-sur-Gartempe is of a type known as a **hall church** (fig. **11.23**). The nave vault lacks transverse arches, since its weight rests directly on the nave arcade, which is supported by a majestic set of columns. The nave is fairly well lit, for the two aisles are carried almost to the same height as the nave, and their outer walls have generous windows.

Although Saint-Savin-sur-Gartempe has a luxurious sculptural program and a rich doorway, the hall church was designed particularly to offer a continuous surface for murals. *The Building*

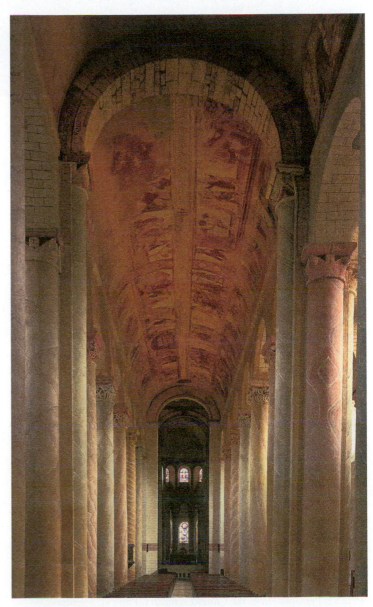

11.23 Choir, ca. 1060–75, and nave, ca. 1095–1115, of abbey church of Saint-Savin-sur-Gartempe, France

to the expansive plan of Cluny (see fig. 11.9), where the huge abbey church dominated a sprawling complex, Fontenay is precise, a pure and tightly controlled equilibrium balancing all of its constituent parts.

The east end of the church is unembellished by apses, and no towers were planned. Since Cistercians permitted neither sculpture nor wall painting, the interior of the church (fig. **11.22**) lacks applied decoration. Clerestory and gallery are suppressed. However, in their own terms, the clean lines of the pointed transverse arches that define the nave and openings into the side aisles, and the pattern of unframed windows, create an elegant refinement. The simple forms are at once graceful and moving. Once again, the church serves as a safe, tranquil, and spiritual

11.24 *The Building of the Tower of Babel.* Early 12th century.
Detail of painting on the nave vault, Saint-Savin-sur-Gartempe, France

of the Tower of Babel (fig. **11.24**) is part of an extensive cycle of scenes from the Hebrew Bible on the vault. It is an intensely dramatic design, crowded with strenuous action. God himself, on the far left, participates directly in the narrative, addressing the builders of the huge structure. He is counterbalanced, on the right, by the giant Nimrod, leader of the project, who frantically hands blocks of stone to the masons atop the tower. The entire scene becomes a great test of strength between God and mortals. The heavy, dark contours and the emphatic gestures make the composition easy to read from the floor below. Elsewhere in the church the viewer can see Christian biblical scenes and scenes from the lives of local saints. Although paintings in Romanesque churches were not necessarily the norm, they were common features. Many frescoes no longer exist as a result of restoration programs. (See *The Art Historian's Lens*, page 369.)

Book Illustration

As in the early Middle Ages, manuscript production in the Romanesque period continued to be largely the responsibility of monastic scriptoria under the supervision of monks. Manuscripts

11.25 *Pentecost*, from the *Cluny Lectionary*. Early 12th century. Tempera on vellum, 9 × 5″ (22.9 × 12.7 cm). Bibliothèque Nationale, Paris

Preserving and Restoring Architecture

The conservation and the preservation of any work of art are delicate tasks. In the case of architecture, the issues to be considered are particularly acute since, in addition to aesthetic criteria, restorers must take into account a building's function. What does one do, for example, with a building originally built to satisfy functions that are no longer relevant? Such is the question with medieval castles and palaces, as well as with churches located in areas where population shifts have reduced the size of their parishes. Should these buildings be retrofitted for new uses, even if that transforms their original character?

The restoration of Romanesque buildings poses some special problems. In many regions of Europe, virtually every village has its own Romanesque church, but diocesan and governmental institutions have difficulty in obtaining the funds to preserve them. Moreover, Romanesque architecture is characterized by its great variety. Thus, a one-size-fits-all approach to restoration, which might be efficient on a practical level, only erases the essential distinctions that give the Romanesque its exceptional quality.

Art historian C. Edson Armi has written penetratingly about recent restorations of Romanesque churches in the Burgundy region of France.* Although the French Restoration Service has a long tradition of intervening to save historic buildings, it does not have the resources to maintain all needy monuments. Increasingly, it has had to focus on simply reacting to severe problems, often when it is too late to correct them. Additionally, the service has a pattern of applying a universal, rather than a specific, approach to the restoration of buildings. In the mid-twentieth century, it was fashionable to clean the surfaces of Romanesque churches within an inch of their lives, and restorers indiscriminately removed any surface coverings—sometimes including original ones—to expose underlying stone or brick. It was thought that by exposing the original materials and structure, the building's true expressive nature would be revealed.

By late in the twentieth century, the pendulum had swung the other way, and the norm was to plaster both interior and exterior surfaces of Romanesque churches—in some cases, the same ones that had been completely stripped only a generation or so earlier. While it is true that during the Middle Ages the surfaces of buildings, whether of brick or stone, were often covered with plaster, this was not always the case. Armi demonstrates how recent interventions have covered up valuable evidence of original materials and structure, information that would help an architectural historian "appreciate large issues like the concept, process and history of a building." Since Armi has shown that a mason's techniques are as distinctive as a painter's or a sculptor's, the lost information could well be key to placing a building in its art historical context. Armi proposes early preservation programs to prevent the need for severe reconstructions that are often based more on conjecture than on fact. Before undertaking any project, he would require modern restorers to acquire a sound understanding of the historical and architectural situation of individual buildings and regions. He proposes that review committees participate in decisions about the restoration of important buildings. Armi has been guided by standards established at the 1964 Venice International Congress of Architects and Technicians of Historic Monuments, which require that whatever is done to a building must demonstrate "respect for original material and authentic documents ... and must stop at the point where conjecture begins." Any restorations "must be distinguishable from the original so that restoration does not falsify the artistic or historic evidence." We also need to ask to what extent one should accept or reject previous changes to buildings. Is it always important to get back to the hypothetical origin of a building, or is it appropriate to consider buildings as entities that change over time? Is there an ideal moment that restorers should aim to preserve? When is it proper to remove a later addition to a building and when should that addition be preserved? A case in point is the Early Christian basilica of Santa Maria Maggiore (see page 250). The original fifth-century apse was destroyed when a new one was added in 1290; during the next 35 years, leading artists of the day decorated it with magnificent mosaics. Certainly, in this case, to restore the building to its fifth-century state would produce a loss much greater than any advantage obtained by re-creating original forms.

*C. Edson Armi, "Report on the Destruction of Romanesque Architecture in Burgundy," *Journal of the Society of Architectural Historians*, vol. 55, 1996, pages 300–327.

---

produced by Cluniac scriptoria are stylistically similar to wall paintings in Cluniac churches and often express concerns remarkably akin to those of the period's architects and sculptors. Those produced in Cistercian scriptoria are particularly inventive, often based on the observation of daily life. Many manuscripts produced at Cîteaux show strong English influence, and some were perhaps executed by English illuminators. Although a great variety of styles characterize Romanesque manuscripts, the interrelationship of monastic communities accounts for some consistency in manuscript production across various regions during the period. Some manuscripts produced in northern France, Belgium, and southern England are so closely related in style that at times we cannot be sure on which side of the English Channel a given manuscript was produced.

THE *CLUNY LECTIONARY* *Pentecost* (fig. **11.25**), an illumination from the *Cluny Lectionary*, represents the descent of the Holy Spirit on the apostles after the Resurrection of Christ. As in the apse fresco at Berzé-la-Ville (see fig. 11.20), a viewer sees highlighted drapery tautly drawn across limbs. Other stylistic features also recall Byzantine devices. The delicate, classicizing faces of some of the prophets evoke Middle Byzantine painting (see figs. 8.38 and 8.39), and the other faces with long mustaches falling over ample beards recall the Byzantine manner of representing saints and prophets (see fig. 8.40). Even Christ at the top of the folio is presented in his typical Byzantine role as Pantocrator. The apostle distinguished by his central placement is Peter, the same saint who receives the scroll from Christ in the Berzé-la-Ville apse painting. Since Cluny was dedicated to

St. Peter, it was only logical to stress his importance, but there is a political message here as well. Cluny's foundation charter states that the monastery was answerable only to Rome and the pope, heir to Peter's throne, and not to any king or emperor. This special privilege assured Cluny enormous power and ultimately its success too.

THE *CODEX COLBERTINUS* The illustration of St. Matthew from the *Codex Colbertinus* (fig. 11.26) is similar in concept and

11.26 *St. Matthew*, from the *Codex Colbertinus*. ca. 1100. Tempera on vellum, 7½ × 4″ (19 × 10.16 cm). Bibliothèque Nationale, Paris

11.27 *St. Mark*, from a Gospel book produced at the abbey at Corbie. Early 12th century. Tempera on vellum, 10¾ × 7⅞″ (27.3 × 20 cm). Bibliothèque Municipale, Amiens, France

pose to a number of Romanesque carvings, particularly the pier reliefs from the Moissac cloister (see fig. 11.12). The manuscript was made at that monastery, or nearby, just when sculptors were at work in the cloister. Matthew appears at the beginning of his Gospel, next to an embellished letter "L," the first letter of *Liber*, meaning "book." Figures, animals, foliage, and decorative patterns conform to the shape of the letter, recalling the way Romanesque sculptured figures correspond to their frames (see fig. 11.2).

In contrast to the small, freely disposed figures and animals the initial, the figure of Matthew confronts us directly. Althou he fills the available space of the architectural setting, a number of features deny his solidity. The heavy outlines and bold colors are reminiscent of enamelwork (see fig. 11.6) and, in combination with a variety of juxtaposed patterns, serve to flatten the image. These devices demonstrate to what extent forms popular during early Middle Ages remained vital.

THE CORBIE GOSPEL BOOK In its monumentality, the image of St. Mark from an early twelfth-century Gospel book produced at Corbie (fig. **11.27**) can also be likened to Romanesque sculpture. The active pose and zigzag composition bear comparison with the prophet on the Moissac trumeau (see fig. 11.15). The twisting movement of the lines, not only in the figure of St. Mark but also in the winged lion, the scroll, and the curtain, also recalls Carolingian miniatures of the Reims School, such as the *Ebbo Gospel Book* (see fig. 10.14).

This resemblance helps us see the differences between them as well. In the Romanesque manuscript, every trace of classical illusionism has disappeared. The fluid modeling of the Reims School, with its suggestion of light and space, has been replaced here by firm contours filled in with bright, solid colors. As a result, the three-dimensional aspects of the picture are reduced to overlapping planes. Yet by sacrificing the last remnants of modeling in terms of light and shade, the Romanesque artist has given his work a clarity and precision that had not been possible in Carolingian or Ottonian times. Here, the representational, the symbolic, and the decorative elements of the design are fully integrated.

GEGORY'S *MORALIA IN JOB* Although in principle, given the concern about elaborate decoration by St. Bernard and others, Cistercian manuscripts were to be decorated only with nonfigurative initials of single colors, in actuality a number of beautiful and fascinating manuscripts were produced for the order. It is not easy to explain why an exception was made for this genre of art. It might simply have been because official statutes against the decoration of manuscripts were not established until 1134. (Some scholars claim these statutes date from 1152.) Pope Gregory's *Moralia in Job*, produced in 1111 at Cîteaux, is a charming example (fig. **11.28**). The manuscript contains decorated initials, depicting some of the monastery's daily activities, including the initial "I," formed by a tree, which a lay brother and a monk work together to fell. The bright, flat colors and patterned foliage of the tree contrast with seemingly naturalistic details. The monk's garment, his bunched trousers, and the dagger suspended on his belt convey the workaday quality of monastic life. The scene correlates with the accompanying text and reflects Cistercian monastic values. The monk depicted here is engaged in hard manual labor, as required by the Benedictine Rule. His tattered garments highlight the Cistercians' humility and their avoidance of luxury, a reaction to the perceived perversion of Benedictine values by other monks, including those Cluny. In the second half of the twelfth century, with few exceptions, Cistercian manuscripts received only very simple decorations, apparently as a result of the statutes prohibiting elaborate adornments.

11.28   Initial "I," from Gregory the Great's *Moralia in Job*. 1111. Tempera on vellum, 21 × 6″ (53.34 × 15.24 cm). Bibliothèque Municipale, Dijon, France

GOSPEL BOOK OF ABBOT WEDRICUS The style of the miniature of St. John from the *Gospel Book of Abbot Wedricus* (fig. **11.29**) has been linked with both northern France and England, and its linear draftsmanship was influenced by Byzantine art. Note the ropelike loops of drapery, the origin of which can be traced to such works as the *Crucifixion* at Daphni (see fig. 8.45) and, even further back, to the *Archangel Michael* ivory (see fig. 8.33). At the same time, the energetic rhythm unifying the composition in the Corbie style (see fig. 11.27) has not been lost

11.29 *St. John the Evangelist*, from the *Gospel Book of Abbot Wedricus*. ca. 1147. Tempera on vellum, 14 × 9½″ (35.5 × 24.1 cm). Société Archéologique et Historique, Avesnes-sur-Helpe, France

entirely. The controlled dynamics of every contour, both in the main figure and in the frame, unite the varied elements of the composition. This quality of line betrays its ultimate source: the Celtic-Germanic heritage.

If we compare the Abbot Wedricus miniature of St. John with the Cross page of the *Lindisfarne Gospels* (see fig. 10.5), we see how much the interlacing patterns of the early Middle Ages have contributed to the design of the St. John page. The drapery folds and the clusters of floral ornament have an impulsive yet disciplined liveliness that echoes the intertwined snakelike monsters of the animal style (even though the foliage is derived from the classical acanthus), and the human figures are based on Carolingian and Byzantine models. The unity of the page is conveyed not only by the forms but by the content as well. St. John inhabits the frame so thoroughly that we could not remove him from it without cutting off his ink supply (offered by the donor

of the manuscript, Abbot Wedricus), his source of inspiration (the dove of the Holy Spirit in the hand of God), or his symbol (the eagle), all located in medallions on the page borders. The other medallions, less closely linked with the main figure, sh scenes from the life of St. John.

OTHER REGIONAL VARIANTS OF ROMANESQUE STYLE

Although consistent aesthetic aims expressed across mediums link the art of diverse areas of Europe during the Romanesque period, a variety of regional approaches can also be identified. These distinct approaches appear in regions of what is now France as well as in other parts of Europe, such as Tuscany in Italy, the Meuse Valley, Germany, and England. Regional variety in Romanesque art reflects the political conditions of eleventh- and twelfth-century western Europe, which was governed by a feudal, though loose, alliance of princes and dukes. Language differences also help account for regional diversity. For example, even within France a number of languages were spoken, among them the *langue d'oc*, the language of southwestern France, and the *langue d'oil*, the language of the center and north. Different regions had different artistic sources available to artists and patrons. In Germany and other parts of northern Europe, Ottonian art provided compelling models, while in Italy and southern France, where antique survivals were numerous, artists borrowed and transformed Roman forms in order to realize Romanesq aesthetic aims. In England, which through conquest had become the domain of Norman dukes in 1066, the artwork of French Normandy provided models.

Western France: Poitou

A so-called school of sculptural decoration appears during the Romanesque period in the region known as Poitou, part of the duchy of Aquitaine in southwestern France. A notable example is Notre-Dame-la-Grande in Poitiers, seat of the lords of Aquitaine.

NOTRE-DAME-LA-GRANDE, POITIERS The broad screenlike façade of Notre-Dame-la-Grande (fig. **11.30**) offers an expanded field for sculptural decoration. Elaborately bordered arcades house large seated or standing figures. Below them, a wide band of relief carving stretches across the façade. The Fall of Adam and Eve appears with scenes from the life of Mary, including the Annunciation and Nativity, once again juxtaposing Eve and Mary (see pages 344 and 362). Next to the representation of Adam and Eve, an inscription identifies an enthroned figure as Nebuchadnezzar, the king of Babylon mentioned in the Hebrew Bible. The *Play of Adam*—a twelfth-century medieval drama of a type that was traditionally performed in churches—probabl served as the source for the choice and arrangement of figur at Notre-Dame-la-Grande. Beside Nebuchadnezzar, centered above the arch on the left of the portal, there are four figures

11.30 West façade, Notre-Dame-la-Grande, Poitiers, France. Early 12th century

carrying either scrolls or books on which are inscribed lines from the Adam play, in which Adam and Eve figure prominently and Nebuchadnezzar is also mentioned.

Essential to the rich sculptural effect is the deeply recessed doorway, without tympanum but framed by a series of arches with multiple archivolts. The conical helmets of the towers nearly match the height of the **gable** (the triangular wall section at the top of the façade), which rises above the actual level of the roof behind it. The gable contains a representation of Christ with angels, their height in the composition denoting their heavenly place. The sculptural program spread out over this entire area is a visual exposition of Christian doctrine intended as a feast for the eyes as well as the mind.

Southeastern France: Provence

In the French region of Provence, south of Burgundy, Romanesque art benefitted from its proximity to Italy. The name Provence derives from its ancient designation as a *provincia romana* in recognition of its close political and cultural connections to Rome; even today vestiges of Roman art and architecture abound in the region, such as the Maison Carrée in Nîmes (see fig. 7.44).

SAINT-GILLES-DU-GARD The façade of the abbey church of Saint-Gilles-du-Gard (fig. 11.31), like Notre-Dame-la-Grande in Poitiers, screens the church. Both churches were major stops on

11.31 West façade, Saint-Gilles-du-Gard, France. Mid-12th century

the pilgrimage road to Santiago de Compostela (see map 11.2). The façade of Saint-Gilles has suffered some later rearrangements and the original probably displayed a more consistent horizontality, with continuous friezes, lintels, cornices, and bases, instead of the staggered ones that we see today. Scholars have claimed that inspiration for Saint-Gilles-du-Gard's façade, composed of three arches, can be found in the screenlike stage sets (see fig. 7.7) of Roman theaters and in the Roman triumphal arch (see fig. 7.71), connecting ancient triumphal imagery with the important liminal function of entering the church. Given contemporary concerns for Christian victory, in particular the struggle to conquer the Muslims, the formal association between the façade and a Roman triumphal monument must have seemed particularly fitting here, since the town of Saint-Gilles on the Rhône River estuary was a principal site of embarkation for the Holy Land by French crusaders led by the counts of Toulouse, among whose possessions Saint-Gilles-du-Gard figured. Moreover, the military orders of the Knights of the Temple (the Templars), and the Knights of St. John of Jerusalem (the Hospitalers), which were founded to protect pilgrimage routes and sites in the Holy Land, had their primary commanderies (districts or estates administered by a commander of an order of knights) in the West at Saint-Gilles. The depiction of Jesus' triumphal entry into Jerusalem, which appears on the lintel supporting the left tympanum, would undoubtedly have had special meaning for contemporary viewers.

The Holy Land

Many consider the Holy Land a virtual French province during much of the eleventh and twelfth centuries, largely as a result of crusader activity there. The history of the Crusades is a complex one and the motives of crusaders diverse. Some went for what one early twelfth-century priest described as "superficial reasons," that is, for the excitement of foreign travel and for financial gain, while others undertook it as a form of penance or out of deeply felt religious piety, seeking to free the places where Christ lived, taught, and died from the Muslims who had occupied them. The First Crusade, mobilized by Pope Urban II in 1095, managed to claim Jerusalem after three years, but later crusades were generally disastrous. The Second Crusade (1147–49), which was preached by St. Bernard of Clairvaux after the fall of Edessa to the Turks, succeeded only in capturing Lisbon from the Arabs, while the Third Crusade, begun in 1189, failed to reconquer Jerusalem from the sultan Saladin, who had taken it two years earlier. The Fourth (and final major) Crusade did little to hinder the advance of Islam; its sole result was the taking of Constantinople by crusaders in 1204, one of the most ignominious events in church history.

CRAC DES CHEVALIERS To defend territories conquered during the First Crusade, French crusaders erected a significant number of castles in the Holy Land. Among the best-preserved of these is in northern Syria, the Crac des Chevaliers (the name

derives from the Syrian word for fortress and the French word for knight) (fig. 11.32). The Crac des Chevaliers guards the Homs Pass, an important commercial corridor, and rises more than 2,000 feet above the fertile pastures of the Orantes Valley. 1110, the Franks, under Raymond IV of Saint-Gilles, count of Toulouse and subsequently count of Tripoli, occupied the site of what had been a small eleventh-century Arab fort, which was then rebuilt and expanded, and later, in 1142, given to the Hospitalers. The castle sits on a natural outcrop of rock, whose sharp drop protected it on the north, east, and west. The first Christian castle took the form of a trapezoidal precinct enclosed by curtain walls with salient (projecting) rectangular towers. These towers were later converted to rounded ones because they provided better sight lines for defense in time of siege; and an outer enclosure, also composed of curtain walls and rounded projections, in some places more than 25 feet thick, was added. Much of this happened as a result of major earthquake damage in 1170. Battered (sloping) walls, difficult to scale, were added to the inner precinct. Defenses also included slits for archers and **crenelations**, notched battlements at the top of the walls that shielded warriors while allowing them to release their weapons. Projecting from the walls are **machicolations**, providing an enclosed area supported by a row of arches and containing openings through which soldiers could drop rocks on attackers. An aqueduct brought water from the summit of a nearby mountain, filling cisterns and a reservoir built between the inner and outer walls that also served as a defense. It has been estimated that in time of siege the Crac would have been able to stock provisions for five years.

While a major function of the Crac des Chevaliers was clearly defense, it also served as a point of departure for incursions into neighboring territory and to establish control over the large fertile valley below and the trade routes that crossed it. Castles were the center of authority over the local population: in the case of the Crac, a largely Muslim one. The castle proclaimed the rite of rule of the overlord and as such upheld the structure of feudal society and the relationship between lord and vassal. Castles were viewed as symbols of power, and in the later Middle Ages architectural features such as crenelations, that had been developed for defensive purposes were applied to palaces where their original function was no longer required.

While some scholars have seen the Crac des Chevaliers and other crusader castles in the Holy Land as providing the opportunity for military engineers to invent and develop new systems of defense, particularly against siege warfare, which were then exported to western Europe, others have stressed the possibility that crusaders were influenced by Muslim and Byzantine castles, both of which they would have encountered in the Holy Land. Building activity by the crusaders was not limited to defensive structures, however. Indeed, a number of Romanesque churches, many of them pilgrimage sites, such as the Holy Sepulcher in Jerusalem (see fig. 8.12) and a church dedicated to the Nativi in Bethlehem, were built or reconstructed during the period, a these buildings, like the Crac des Chevaliers, provide evidence of a continued syncretism in the region. Romanesque castles share

11.32 Crac des Chevaliers, Homs Pass, Syria. 12th century with later additions

the same aesthetic concerns as Romanesque churches and other buildings, and use the same system of solid stone walls, arches, and vaults. The rhythmic arrangement of curved and straight walls and the repeated patterns of wall openings suggest that similar concerns for design and proportionality were at play.

In 1271, the Crac des Chevaliers fell to the Muslims, and the chapel, which the Christians had erected within the inner precinct, was converted into a mosque. At the same time, the southern square tower, visible at the right of figure 11.32, and the round projection to the left of the aqueduct were reconstructed, since it was from the less easily defensible south that the Muslims had attacked.

Tuscany

During the Romanesque period, Tuscany, a region in north-western Italy divided into several independent city-states, the chief of which were Pisa, Florence, Prato, and Livorno, continued to deploy what were basically Early Christian architectural forms. However, they added decorative features inspired by Roman architecture.

ᵱA CATHEDRAL The most famous monument of the Italian Romanesque owes its fame to an accident. Because of poor foundations, the Leaning Tower of Pisa in Tuscany, designed by

the sculptor Bonanno Pisano (active 1174–86), began to tilt even before it was completed (fig. **11.33**). This type of free-standing tower, or **campanile**, appears in Italy as early as the ninth or tenth century. The tradition of the detached campanile remained so strong in Italy that towers hardly ever became an integral part of the church itself. The complex at Pisa includes a church and a circular, domed baptistery to the west. The ensemble of buildings, built on an open site north of the city, reflects the wealth and pride of the city-republic of Pisa after its naval victory over the Muslims at Palermo in 1062.

The Pisa baptistery was begun in 1153 by Diotisalvi but everything above the arcaded first level was reworked a century later. Throughout the Middle Ages, Tuscany remained conscious of its antique heritage. The idea of a separate baptistery relies on Early Christian precedents. The round form of the Pisa one and its original cone vault also reflect the structure of the Rotunda of the Anastasis in Jerusalem (see fig. 8.12). The comparison would undoubtedly have been comprehensible to Pisans, whose seamen profited by carrying pilgrims and crusaders to the Holy Land. Once again, the opportunity for increased trade and travel, the lure of pilgrimage, and the ongoing struggle against the Muslims in Iberia and the eastern Mediterranean were decisive forces in shaping Romanesque monuments.

The basic plan of Pisa cathedral is that of an Early Christian basilica, but it has been transformed into a **Latin cross** (where

11.33 Baptistery, cathedral, and campanile (view from the west), Pisa, Italy. 1053–1272

three arms are of equal length and one is longer) by the addition of transept arms that resemble small basilicas with apses of their own. A dome marks the crossing. The rest of the church has a wooden roof, except for the aisles (four in the nave, two in the transept arms), which have **groin vaults**, formed when two barrel vaults intersect. The interior (fig. **11.34**) has somewhat taller proportions than an Early Christian basilica, because there are galleries over the aisles as well as a clerestory. Yet the classical columns supporting the nave and aisle arcades still recall types that would fit comfortably in an Early Christian basilica (see fig. 8.9).

A deliberate revival of the antique Roman style in Tuscan architecture was the use of a multicolored marble "skin" on the exteriors of churches. Little of this inlay is left today on the ancient monuments of Rome because much of it was literally "lifted" to decorate later buildings. However, the interior of the

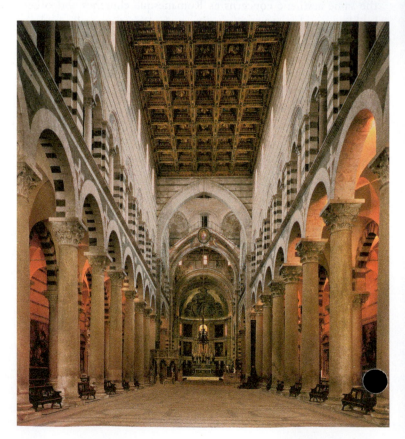

11.34 Interior, Pisa cathedral

Pantheon still gives us some idea of what this must have looked like. Pisa cathedral and its companion buildings are covered in white marble inlaid with horizontal stripes and ornamental pat-[ter]s in dark-green marble. This decorative scheme is combined [with] blind arcades and galleries. The result is a richness very different from austere Early Christian exteriors.

BAPTISTERY OF SAN GIOVANNI, FLORENCE In Florence, which was to outstrip Pisa commercially and artistically, the greatest achievement of the Tuscan Romanesque is the baptistery of San Giovanni (fig. **11.35**) opposite the cathedral (see fig. 13.10). It is a domed, octagonal building of impressive size, begun in the middle of the eleventh century. The eight sides of the building continue a long tradition in baptistery design and symbolically allude to rebirth: The world began on the eighth day following the Creation, and Christ was resurrected on the eighth day of the Passion. The green-and-white marble paneling is typical of the Florentine Romanesque in its severely geometric lines. The triple arches of the second-story blind arcades, with their triumphal-arch design, are extraordinarily classical in proportion and detail.

SAN MINIATO AL MONTE, FLORENCE The magnificent site of the Benedictine monastery of San Miniato al Monte overlooking the city of Florence reflects that establishment's grandeur during the Middle Ages. The church is dedicated to St. Minias, Florence's first Christian martyr, a third-century hermit who was beheaded by the Romans. It is said that, after his martyrdom, St. Minias gathered his head and proceeded to the cave where he had lived and died; subsequently a church

11.35   Baptistery of San Giovanni, Florence, Italy. ca. 1060–1150

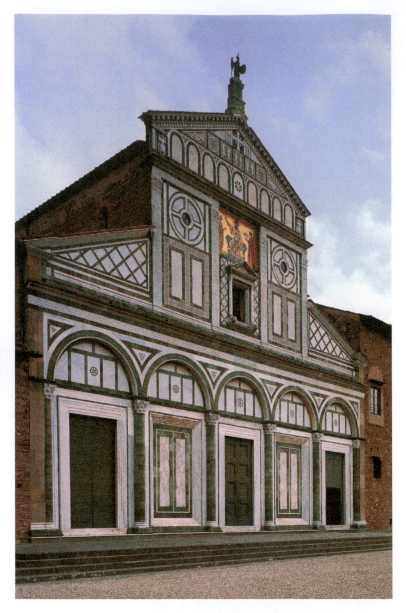

11.36   Façade, San Miniato al Monte, Florence, Italy. 1062–1150

Germany

In Germany, the traditions of the Holy Roman Empire functioned as filters for the revival of Roman forms. As a res[ult] German Romanesque architecture, centered in the Rhineland, relied for its organization and formal vocabulary on buildings patronized by Carolingian and Ottonian rulers.

SPEYER CATHEDRAL   The cathedral of Speyer, which contained tombs of Holy Roman emperors, was consecrated in 1061. It included a timber-roof nave (fig. **11.37**), not unlike those of Carolingian and Ottonian buildings. A major rebuilding of the cathedral in 1080 added groin vaults to the nave (fig. **11.38**), providing a solution to a problem that had limited Romanesque builders: While the barrel vault used in the churches we have previously examined offered an aesthetically pleasing, acoustically resonant, and fire-resistant space, it limited the amount of light that could enter the nave. The problem was that the weakest part of the vault, the springing (the point where the arch rises from its support) was precisely the point where clerestory windows were needed. There had been exceptional buildings that included clerestories, such as Sant Vicenç at Cardona (see fig. 11.1) and the abbey church at Cluny (see fig. 11.11). But Sant Vicenç's windows

11.37   Reconstruction of interior of Speyer cathedral, Germany. ca. 1030–61 (after Conant)

was built on site. The gabled façade of the church (fig. **11.36**) coincides with the shape of the wooden-roofed and aisled basilica. As with the baptistery of San Giovanni, and begun only a few years after it, geometric precision governs the arrangement of the façade's green-and-white marble covering. Although the treatment of surface and the materials employed are distinctive to Tuscany, the organization of elements compares with Romanesque arrangements elsewhere. The individual, additive units decorating Florentine Romanesque buildings also parallel the compartmentalized bays in pilgrimage churches (see fig. 11.5) and the way French Romanesque portals (see figs. 11.13, 11.30, 11.31) are composed of individual units that maintain their identities though functioning in unison. Roman elements employed in conscious revival—here the use of marble and the repeated arches that rest on columns topped with Corinthian capitals—unite many of these Romanesque works as well.

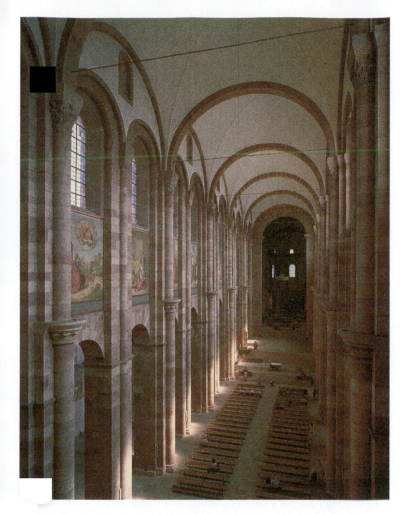

11.38   Interior, Speyer cathedral. ca. 1030–61; vaulted ca. 1080–1106

Romanesque buildings of other regions (see figs. 11.1, 11.5, and 11.22). The alternating support system establishes a rhythm that must have struck a familiar chord in Germany. It had appeared in the Ottonian buildings of Gernrode (see fig. 10.23) and Hildesheim (see fig. 10.26), although in these buildings such a system was purely aesthetic.

The Meuse Valley: Mosan Style

An important group of Romanesque sculptors, who excelled in metalwork, operated in the valley of the Meuse River, which runs from northeastern France into present-day Belgium and Holland. This region had been the home of the classicizing Reims style in Carolingian times (see figs. 10.14, 10.15, and 10.16), and during the Romanesque period an awareness of classical sources again pervades its art, called Mosan. Abbot Hellinus of Liège commissioned a bronze baptismal font for the church of Notre-Dame-aux-Fonts in Liège (fig. 11.39). The generally accepted attribution to Renier of Huy, the earliest Mosan artist whose name we know, is largely circumstantial. The font, completed in 1118 and today in the church of Saint-Barthélemy, is a remarkable achievement: Cast in one piece, it is over 2 feet high and 3½ feet in diameter. The vessel rested on 12 oxen, like Solomon's basin in the Temple at Jerusalem as described in the first book of Kings in the Hebrew Bible: "And he made the molten sea ... It stood upon twelve oxen ... and all their hinder parts were inward." Christian writers described Solomon's basin as a prototype for the baptismal font and the 12 oxen as precursors of the apostles.

The reliefs are about the same height as those on the bronze

are limited in number and scale, and at Cluny it was necessary to employ a series of devices, including pointed arches and enlarged buttresses, to provide adequate support for the high barrel vault.

The builders of Speyer cathedral solved this problem with the groin vault. (See *Materials and Techniques*, page 380.) The groin vault, which had been used so effectively by the Romans, efficiently channeled thrust onto four corner points. This allowed for open space under each arch, which could be used for window openings without diminishing the strength of the vault. The erection of groin vaults in the nave of Speyer cathedral was accompanied by an enlargement of its clerestory windows. Romanesque builders knew the technology of groin-vault construction and had previously employed groin vaults to cover lower spaces, in side aisles and in crypts, as at Pisa (see fig. 11.34), but apparently they found them daunting to build on a large scale. Speyer represents a genuine breakthrough in building technology: The scale is so great that it dwarfs every other church of the period.

The individual groin-vaulted bays at Speyer form a chain of compartmentalized units of space. Each groin vault comprises two bays of the original nave. Colonnettes attached to alternate piers articulate the distribution of weight necessary to support the vaults. The use of these compound piers aligns Speyer with

11.39   Renier of Huy. Baptismal Font. 1107–18. Bronze, height 25″ (63.5 cm). Saint-Barthélemy, Liège, Belgium

Vaulting

Vaulting is a technique for covering buildings that is based on the principles of arcuation, that is, construction that uses the arch form (a). Although vaulting was used in Mesopotamia, Egypt, and Greece, it was the Etruscans and Romans who first exploited the vault for expressive and aesthetic purposes (see page 186). While most early medieval buildings were covered with timber-beam roofs, during the Romanesque period stone vaulting became the dominant roofing type. Its reintroduction in the eleventh century was a major component of the revival of Roman artistic forms during the Romanesque period. Although Roman vaults were principally made of concrete, medieval vaults were usually made either of rubble or masonry, bound with mortar.

The erection of stone vaults in medieval buildings required enormous effort and great expense, but the benefits were numerous. These included fire resistance, particularly important for buildings illuminated by candles and for tall structures that attracted lightning. The history of medieval buildings is largely a history of fires. Widespread attacks by Vikings, Magyars from Hungary, and Muslims also made stronger buildings desirable. In addition, stone vaulting provides excellent acoustics, a significant consideration for churches in which the liturgy was chanted. No less important than these practical benefits were the aesthetic ones: Vaulted buildings appear dignified and monumental, and they provide an unambiguous sense of enclosure. There are many types of vaults: barrel, quadrant, groin, ribbed, and the dome.

The barrel vault, essentially an arch projected in depth, is the most basic form (b). This was the first type exploited by medieval builders because it lent itself to covering rectangular basilicas. Unfortunately, the barrel vault creates dark spaces, since opening up the nave walls with clerestory windows weakens the vault at its most vulnerable point, the springing. It is here, at the base of the arch, that the force of gravity, which is channeled through the arch, results in lateral forces pushing sideways. This outward thrust needs to be contained, usually by building thick walls to buttress the vault.

In Romanesque churches with wide side aisles, architects were faced with the problem of transferring the thrust of the barrel vault across the side aisles to the outer walls. They were able to do this by vaulting the galleries over the aisles with **quadrant vaults** (barrel vaults), which buttress the barrel vault of the nave. T buildings were also dark, with light entering only from windows at the ends of the barrel vaults and in the side walls, filtered through aisle and gallery before reaching the nave.

The introduction of the groin vault provided for more luminous structures that required less building material; thus, buildings became lighter in both senses of the word. A groin vault is formed when two barrel vaults intersect (c); the thrust of each vault is countered by the vault running perpendicular to it. (The term "groin" refers to the junction where the vaults intersect.) Thrust is thus channeled to four corner points, allowing for windows or other openings in the wall under each of the intersecting arches.

The **ribbed vault**, introduced at Durham cathedral, was probably invented as a decorative device (d); only later did architects and masons come to appreciate its structural advantages. Larger stones are placed on the groins of the vault to form diagonal arches. These function as a fixed scaffold to support the vault's curved panels, called **webs**, which essentially fill the spaces between the ribs. Ribbed vaults were easier to construct and required less centering (see below) than unribbed vaults; their webs could be built of lighter material, since the ribbed groins channeled the major lateral thrust more efficiently.

Romanesque masons also employed the dome, which is essentially an arch rotated on axis to form a vault (e). In Romanesque churches, domes cover centralized buildings or mark significant elements, for example the area where the transept crosses nave. Vaults are not easy to construct and Romanesque vaults were heavy: Often more than a foot thick, each could weigh several tons. Arcuation is a dynamic system, with all its elements interlocked; as a result, the vault is stable only when it is complete. During construction it needs to be supported by a wooden framework, called a **centering**. Once the vault is built and the buttresses are in place, the vault becomes self-supporting and the centering can be removed. The widespread use of the vault and its progressive refinement during the Romanesque period represent significant achievements, which were crucial for the continued development of medieval building, particularly during the Gothic period.

Vault forms: (a) arch; (b) barrel vault; (c) groin vault; (d) ribbed groin vault; (e) dome

springing   springing
Thrust
a. arch

b. barrel vault

c. groin vault

diagonal rib

transverse rib   web

d. ribbed groin vault

e. dome

doors of Bishop Bernward at Hildesheim (see fig. 10.27). Instead of the rough expressive power of the Ottonian panels, however, the viewer sees a harmonious balance of design, a subtle control ... he sculptured surfaces, and an understanding of organic struc... that are surprisingly classical for a medieval work. The figure seen from the back (beyond the tree on the left), with its graceful movement and Greek-looking drapery, might almost be taken for a work from antiquity. Renier also expressed his interest in antique form through the use of bronze, rejecting the monumentality implicit in stone sculpture. The strong northern European metalwork tradition now serves to convey classical values, so alien to early medieval metalworkers who had previously dominated the art of this area.

The Romanesque antique revival in the Mosan region has a special character, quite different from the abstract, decorative qualities that characterize the work of other regions, so demonstrating that while Romanesque art shares a common interest in reviving classical forms, there was great variety in the ways that classicism was expressed. The Liège font and other Mosan sculptures are carved in high relief or are fully three-dimensional, with convincing anatomical details and proportions. Yet, the concern of Mosan sculptors was not so much for naturalism as for an idealism that here produces classicizing forms.

Normandy and England

Farther north, Christianity was strongly supported by the Norman dukes and barons, former Vikings who had turned Normandy into a powerful feudal domain that included the allegiance of abbots and bishops as vassals in return for grants of land. Duke William II of Normandy actively promoted monastic reform and founded numerous abbeys. Normandy soon became a cultural center of international importance. When William invaded Anglo-Saxon England in 1066 and became king there, England became politically allied to northern France. For that reason Norman and English art of the Romanesque period share many stylistic traits.

THE BAYEUX TAPESTRY The complex relationship between the Normans and the English is hinted at in the *Bayeux Tapestry* (figs. 11.40 and 11.41), important both as a historical record and as a work of art. In actuality it is not a tapestry at all, since it is not woven, but rather an embroidered linen frieze 230 feet long. The 50 surviving scenes record the events, culminating in 1066, when William the Conqueror crossed the English Channel to claim the throne of England upon the death of King Edward the Confessor. According to the narrative of the "tapestry," Harold, an Anglo-Saxon earl, had retracted his oath of fealty to William

11.40   *Crowds Gaze in Awe at a Comet as Harold Is Told of an Omen*, detail of the *Bayeux Tapestry*. ca. 1066–83.
Wool embroidery on linen, height 20" (50.7 cm). Centre Guillaume le Conquérant, Bayeux, France

11.41   *The Battle of Hastings*, detail of the *Bayeux Tapestry*. Wool embroidery on linen, height 20″ (50.7 cm).
Centre Guillaume le Conquérant, Bayeux, France

in order to accept the throne offered him by the English nobles. William retaliated by invading England, and his Norman troops vanquished the English as Harold fell in battle. Since a Norman patron presumably commissioned the work, the story is told from the conquerors' perspective, yet its manufacture has generally been credited to English needlewomen, justly famous during the Middle Ages for their skill.

The *Bayeux Tapestry* exhibits the same monumentality and interest in narrative that we saw in the illuminations of the *Gospel Book of Abbot Wedricus* (see fig. 11.29), which, as noted, is a manuscript linked to both Normandy and England. The Bayeux designer has integrated narrative and ornament with complete ease. Two border strips frame the main frieze; while some of the images in these margins are decorative, others offer a commentary on the continuous narrative. In one scene (see fig. 11.40), an aide announces to a recently crowned Harold the appearance of an amazing natural phenomenon, represented in the upper border as a spinning star leaving its fiery trail. The inscription *ISTI MIRANT STELLA* ("These men marvel at the star") records the brilliant apparition of Halley's Comet in 1066, during the days immediately following Harold's coronation. To the medieval viewer, the prophetic significance of the natural event would have been clear, especially when viewed after the fact. Beneath Harold, ghostly boats await the Normans, who are preparing to cross the English Channel. The scene foreshadows the violent events to come.

Although the *Bayeux Tapestry* does not use the pictorial devices of classical painting, such as foreshortening and overlapping

(see fig. 5.78), it presents a vivid and detailed account of warfare in the eleventh century as well as a hint of the Normans' abilities as builders of fortresslike castles. The massed forms of the Graeco-Roman scene are replaced by a new kind of individualism that makes each figure a potential hero, whether by force or by cunning. Note how the soldier who has fallen from the horse with its hind legs in the air is, in turn, toppling his foe by yanking at the saddle girth of his mount. The kinship with the Corbie Gospel book manuscript (see fig. 11.27) is noticeable in the lively somersaults of the horses, so like the pose of the lion in the miniature. In the Middle Ages, the religious and secular spheres were not sharply distinguished from each other, and as such the same pictorial devices were employed in both. The energy and linear clarity of the *Bayeux Tapestry* and the Corbie Gospel book remind the viewer of the monumental figures of Romanesque sculpture.

DURHAM CATHEDRAL Norman architecture is responsible for a great breakthrough in structural engineering, which took place in England, where King William made donations to build in a Norman style. Durham cathedral, begun in 1093, is among the largest churches of medieval Europe (fig. 11.42): Its nave is wider than that of Santiago de Compostela, and its overall length (400 feet) is also greater. The nave may have been designed to be vaulted from the start. The vault over its eastern end had been completed by 1107, in a remarkably short space of time, and the rest of the nave was vaulted by 1130 (fig. 11.43).

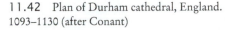

11.42 Plan of Durham cathedral, England. 1093–1130 (after Conant)

11.44 Transverse section of Durham cathedral (after Acland)

This vault is of great interest. As the earliest systematic use of a **ribbed groin vault** over a three-story nave, it marks a basic advance beyond Speyer. Looking at the plan (see fig. 11.42), we see that the aisles consist of the usual almost-square groin-vaulted compartments. The bays of the nave, separated by strong

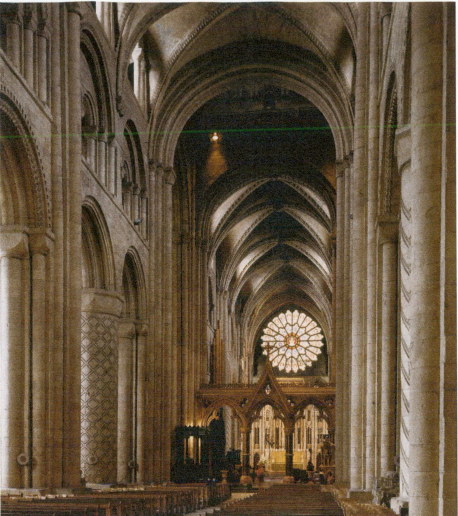

11.43 Nave (looking east), Durham cathedral

transverse arches, are oblong and also groin-vaulted, so that the ribs of each bay form a double-X design. Each vault of the nave is thus divided into seven sections. These vaults are referred to as **septpartite** (or seven-part) groin vaults. Since the nave bays are twice as long as the aisle bays, transverse arches occur only at the odd-numbered piers of the nave arcade (see fig. 11.43). The piers therefore alternate in size. Unlike Speyer cathedral (see fig. 11.38), where a colonnette was added to every other nave pier to strengthen it, at Durham the odd-numbered piers are intrinsically different from the even-numbered ones. The odd-numbered ones are larger and compound, with bundles of column and pilaster shafts attached to a square or oblong core, while the even-numbered ones are thinner and cylindrical.

The outward thrust and weight of the whole vault are concentrated at six securely anchored points on the gallery level from which the ribs spring. The ribs were needed to provide a stable skeleton for the groin vault, and the curved surfaces between them were filled in with masonry of a minimal thickness. Thus, both weight and thrust were reduced, and carried downward to the outer wall of the aisles by buttresses (fig. **11.44**). This flexible system resulted in more efficient vault erection and greater economy of construction. We do not know whether this ingenious scheme was actually invented at Durham, but it could not have been devised much earlier, for it is still in an experimental stage. While the transverse arches at the crossing are round, those to the west of it are slightly pointed, indicating an ongoing search for improvements.

The ribbed groin-vault system had other advantages. From an aesthetic standpoint, the nave at Durham is among the finest in all Romanesque architecture. The sturdiness of the alternating piers makes a splendid contrast to the dramatically lit, sail-like surfaces of the vault. This relatively lightweight, flexible system permits broad expanses of great height to be covered with fire-proof vaulting and yet retain the ample lighting of a clerestory. Durham exhibits great structural strength; even so, the decoration incised in its round piers, each different from the others, and the pattern established by the vault ribs hark back to the Anglo-Saxon love of decoration and interest in surface pattern (see figs. 10.1–10.3).

SAINT-ÉTIENNE, CAEN The abbey church of Saint-Étienne at Caen (fig. **11.45**) was founded by William the Conqueror a year or two after his invasion of England in 1066, but it took over 100 years to complete. Over this period of time the fruits of Durham cathedral's ribbed groin-vault system matured. The west façade (fig. **11.46**) offers a striking contrast with Notre-Dame-la-Grande in Poitiers (see fig. 11.30) and other Romanesque façades (see figs. 11.13, 11.17, and 11.31). The westwork proclaims this an imperial church. Its closest ancestors are Carolingian churches, such as the abbey church at Corvey (see fig. 10.21), built under royal patronage. Like them, it has a minimum of decoration. Four huge buttresses divide the front of the church into three vertical sections. The thrust upward continues in the two towers, the height of which would be impressive even without the tall helmets, which

11.45   Plan of abbey church of Saint-Étienne, Caen, France. Begun 1068

11.46   West façade of Saint-Étienne, Caen, France

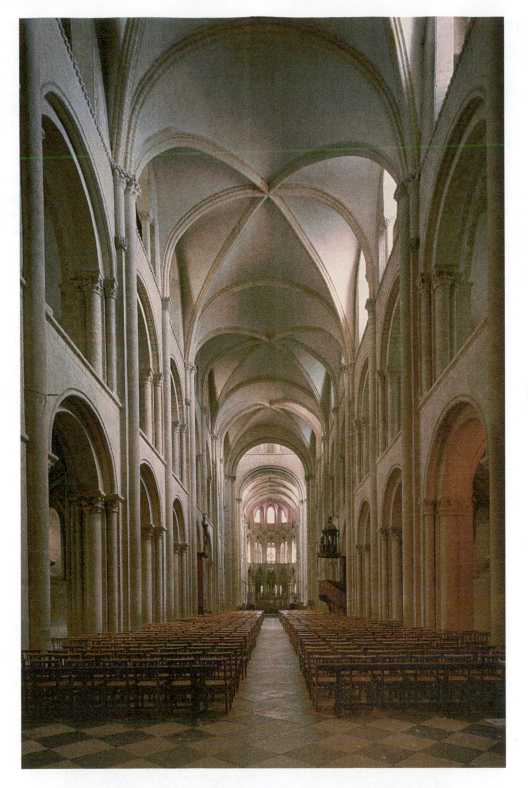

are later additions. Saint-Étienne is cool and composed, encouraging viewers to appreciate its refined proportions, a feature shared with many other Romanesque buildings.

In the interior of Saint-Étienne (fig. **11.47**), the nave was originally planned to have a wooden ceiling, as well as galleries and a clerestory. After the experience of Durham, however, it became possible in the early twelfth century to build a groined nave vault, with only slight changes in the wall design. The bays of the nave here are approximately square (see fig. 11.45), whereas at Durham they were oblong. Therefore, the double-X rib pattern could be replaced by a single X with an additional transverse rib, which produced a **sexpartite** groin vault, with six sections instead of seven. These vaults are no longer separated by heavy transverse arches but instead by simple ribs. The resulting reduction in weight also gives a stronger sense of continuity to the nave vault as a whole and produces a less emphatic alternation of piers. Compared with Durham, the nave of Saint-Étienne has an airy lightness.

THE PARADOXICAL MEANING OF ROMANESQUE

The improved economic conditions and political stability of Europe, outlined at the beginning of this chapter, had their rewards in the secure structures built in the twelfth century. However, the architecture's defensive qualities also suggest a paradox: As much as the stalwart, powerfully built buildings express a newfound confidence, they also reveal lingering apprehension. The terrifying Last Judgment scenes (see fig. 11.17) and other Romanesque visions of monsters and diabolical beings attest to this anxiety. A folio of the *Winchester Psalter* (fig. **11.48**), produced in England during the middle of the twelfth century, depicts a large Hell mouth: The heavy arched jaws of the devil's head contain monstrous forms devouring sinners of all classes.

The inscription, written in Anglo-Norman French, translates as: "Here is Hell and the angels who lock the doors." The heavy walls and repeated enclosures that govern so much Romanesque sculpture and architecture have their counterpart in this representation. The frame, with its serene cadence of heavily outlined decorations, encloses and controls the frightening image.

The manuscript was commissioned by Henry of Blois, bishop of Winchester, who had been a monk at Cluny and collected antique sculpture and Byzantine paintings on his journeys to Rome. The *Winchester Psalter* exemplifies how international artistic forces functioned during the Romanesque period to help create a vision expressive of the hopes and fears of a society yearning for protection from dark elements. It is instructive that, in the end, assistance from a heavenly being—the angel who locks the Hell-mouth door—is required to contain the potent forces of evil.

11.48 *Mouth of Hell*, from the *Winchester Psalter*. From Winchester, England. ca. 1150. Tempera on vellum, 12¾ × 9" (32.5 × 23 cm). The British Library, London (MS Cotton Nero D.4.f.39)

Romanesque Art

1020–21 Lintel from Saint-Genis-des-Fontaines

1040 Consecration of church of Sant Vicenç in Cardona

1063 Pisa cathedral begun

1066–83 *Bayeux Tapestry*

ca. 1075–1120 Cathedral of Santiago de Compostela

1088 Cluny III begun

1107–18 Baptismal font at Liège

1120–35 West portal, cathedral of Saint-Lazare, Autun

1139–47 Abbey church at Fontenay

1000

1025 ca. 1026 Al-Aqmar Mosque in Cairo

1033 Church of St. Michael's, Hildesheim finished

1050

1063 St. Mark's in Venice begun

◄ 1066 Battle of Hastings

1075

◄ 1099 Warriors of First Crusade capture Jerusalem

1100

◄ 1115-1120 Nave of Saint-Étienne at Caen vaulted

1125 ◄ ca.1127 Apologia of St. Bernard of Clairvaux
◄ ca.1130 Pilgrim's Guide
1133–34 Cloak of Roger II of Sicily

1150 ◄ ca.1150 Winchester Psalter

1175

1180–90 Mosaics of cathedral of Monreale

1200 ◄ 1204 Crusaders take Constantinople

1225

CHAPTER 12

Gothic Art

THE GOTHIC ERA UNFOLDED IN A PROCESS OF GEOGRAPHIC expansion, its rapid growth demonstrating its broad visual and expressive appeal. At the start, about 1140, the area in which Gothic art was produced was small indeed. It included only the province known as the Île-de-France (Paris and vicinity), the royal domain of the French

kings (see map **12.1**). A hundred years later, most of western Europe, from Sicily to Norway, had adopted the Gothic style, with only a few Romanesque pockets left here and there. By 1400, however, the Gothic area had begun to shrink. It no longer included Italy, and by 1550 it had disappeared almost entirely, except in England. The Gothic layer, then, has a rather complicated shape. Its depth ranges from close to 400 years in some places to only 150 in others.

The term **Gothic** was used in the sixteenth century to describe a style of buildings thought to have descended from the Goths, those tribes that occupied northern Europe during the early Middle Ages. Although the ancestry of the style is not as direct as these early writers claimed, they were accurate about its geography, since the style is most recognizable north of the Alps. As Gothic art spread from the Île-de-France to the rest of the country and then through all of Europe, it was referred to as *opus modernum* (modern work) or *opus francigenum* (French work). These designations are significant, because they tell us that in its own time the style was viewed as innovative and as having its origins in France. In the course of the thirteenth century, the new style gradually lost its imported flavor, and regional variety began to reassert itself.

For a century—from about 1150 to 1250, during the Age of the Great Cathedrals—architecture played the dominant role in the formation of a coherent Gothic style. In addition to religious buildings, secular architecture—including castles, palaces, and civic buildings, such as hospitals—also flourished during the Gothic period. Gothic sculpture was at first severely architectural in spirit but became more independent after 1200. Late Gothic architecture and sculpture strive for more pictorial effects.

Artistic developments roughly parallel what was happening in the political arena, for the Gothic was a distinctive period not only artistically but politically as well. Aided by technological advances including cannon and iron crossbow design, princes and kings were able to conquer increasingly large territories, which were administered for them by vassals, who in turn collected taxes to support armies and navies. In France, the Capetian line at first ruled only the fertile territory of the Île-de-France, but by 1300 it had added much of the land previously held by the count of Flanders, as well as Bourges, Tours, and Amiens—all of which were to become the sites of important Gothic cathedrals—and the central provinces of the Auvergne and the southern provinces of Languedoc. King Philip Augustus, who reigned from 1180 to 1223, was able to quadruple the size of the royal domain and, at the same time, concentrate authority in the figure of the king. The French kings also acquired Normandy from England. This gave rise to the conflicting claims over the kingship of France known as the Hundred Years' War (1339–1453), which consolidated

Detail of figure 12.6, Jamb statues, west portal of cathedral of Notre-Dame, Chartres

Map 12.1   Europe in the Gothic period

a growing sense of nationalism on both sides of the English Channel. While much Gothic art seems to develop in a logical manner, the Hundred Years' War, with its shifting alliances and threats to economic and social stability, interrupted the production of art in some areas of Europe.

Germany remained a collection of independent city-states ruled by electors, who were responsible for, among other things, choosing kings. The powers of German kings were therefore severely limited. Supported by shifting alliances with the papacy, the kings of France and England emerged as the leading powers at the expense of the Germans in the early thirteenth century, which was generally a time of peace and prosperity. After 1290, however, the balance of power broke down.

The growth of urban centers and the increasing importance of cathedrals, the seats of bishops, are formative features of the Gothic period. In the century before the death of King Louis IX in 1270, there were 80 cathedrals built in France, many of them

new foundations. Universities developed out of cathedral schools as the principal centers of learning, thus taking on the role previously played by monasteries. Universities provided instruction in theology, philosophy, law, and medicine, those areas of study deemed necessary for *universitas litterarum* (universal learning). At the same time, literature written in the vernacular (as opposed to Latin) began to emerge, making it accessible to a broader public. It was during the thirteenth century that French became an official state language. Romanesque art had been predominantly a rural and monastic art, while Gothic art, by contrast, was increasingly cosmopolitan.

Urban growth was both the result and cause of economic, social, and demographic changes. Agriculture became more efficient, with increased acreage under cultivation, and surpl production provided commodities for sale and purchase. Tl produced, in turn, a money economy based on investment, profit, and trade, in place of barter. Money rather than personal services now directed social interchange, and the increased amount of it in circulation produced a veritable middle class, living in cities, which were the centers of trade and commerce. Once out from ~r the feudal yoke, merchants and artists of this middle class ... free to form **guilds** to control the production and distribution of goods and services. A general and significant increase in population also spurred urban growth. Roughly 42 million people occupied Europe around the year 1000; by 1300, the population had reached about 73 million.

During the thirteenth century, Western European Christianity found in St. Thomas Aquinas its greatest intellect since St. Augustine and St. Jerome some 850 years earlier. Aquinas, an Italian theologian, studied in Cologne and taught in Paris. His method of argument, called **scholasticism**, used reason to understand and explain faith. Scholasticism had a profound effect on European thought; its harmonization of rationalism and spirituality effectively sanctioned the systematic study of all natural phenomena as expressions of divine truths. Gothic builders shared qualities with the Scholastics. They brought the logic and clarity of engineering principles to bear on revelation, using physical forces to create a concord of spiritual experiences in much the same way the Scholastics used elucidation and clarification to build their well-constructed arguments.

EARLY GOTHIC ART IN FRANCE

s not clear why Gothic art first appeared in the Île-de-France, the area around Paris. Some scholars believe that because this region had not developed a strong local style during the Romanesque period, it was particularly open to innovation and influence from other areas. Others have suggested that it was a result of a concerted effort on the part of the kings of France to aggrandize themselves, since it was here that their domains were located. Certainly the Île-de-France is fortuitously positioned, near the center of France and thus accessible to the south and west, where major sculptural programs flourished during the Romanesque period, and adjacent to Normandy, where many structural innovations, including the ribbed groin vault, had been introduced to France.

Saint-Denis: Suger and the Beginnings of Gothic Architecture

The study of Gothic art begins with an examination of the rebuilding of the royal abbey church of Saint-Denis just outside the city of Paris. The rebuilding of this historic church was undertaken between 1137 and 1144 by its abbot, Suger. His ambitious building program was designed to emphasize the relationship between Saint-Denis and the French monar-
-y. The kings of France, who belonged to the Capetian line,
practice had less power than the nobles who, in theory, were their vassals. The only area the king ruled directly was the Île-de-France, and even there his authority was often challenged.

Not until the early twelfth century did royal power begin to expand, and Suger, as chief advisor to King Louis VI, helped shape this process. It was Suger who forged the alliance between the monarchy and the Church. This union brought the bishops of France (and the cities under their authority) to the king's side; the king, in turn, supported the papacy in its struggle against the German emperors.

Suger also engaged in spiritual politics. By giving the monarchy religious significance and glorifying it as the strong right arm of justice, he sought to rally the nation behind the king. Saint-Denis was a key element in his plan. The church, founded in the late eighth century, enjoyed a dual prestige. It was the shrine of St. Denis, the Apostle of France and its patron saint, as well as the chief memorial of the Carolingian dynasty from which the Capetians drew their authority. Both Charlemagne and his father, Pepin, were consecrated as kings at Saint-Denis. It was also the burial place of the kings Charles Martel, Pepin, and Charles the Bald. Suger aspired to make the abbey the spiritual center of France, a pilgrimage church to outshine all others and to provide a focal point for religious as well as patriotic emotion. To achieve this goal, the old structure had to be rebuilt and enlarged. The great abbot himself wrote two accounts of the church and its rebuilding. (See *Primary Source*, page 393.)

AMBULATORY AND CHOIR The ambulatory and radiating chapels surrounding the arcaded apse (figs. **12.1** and **12.2**) are familiar elements from the Romanesque pilgrimage choir (see fig. 11.3), but at Saint-Denis they have been integrated in a new way. The choir is as rationally planned and constructed as in any Romanesque church, yet the entire plan is held together by a new kind of geometric order (see fig. 12.1). Seven nearly identical wedge-shaped units fan out from the center of the apse. Instead of being in separate apsidioles, the chapels merge to form, in effect, a second ambulatory. We experience this double ambulatory not as a series of individual compartments but as a continuous space, the shape of which is outlined by the network of slender arches, ribs, and columns that sustains the vaults. Ribbed groin vaulting based on the pointed arch is used throughout. By this date, the pointed arch (which can be "stretched" to reach any desired height regardless of the width of its base) has become an essential part of the ribbed groin vault, which is no longer restricted to square or near-square compartments. It has a new flexibility that allows it to cover areas of almost any shape, such as the trapezoids and pentagons of this ambulatory.

What most distinguishes the interior of Saint-Denis (see fig. 12.2) from earlier church interiors is its lightness, in both senses of the word. The architectural forms seem graceful, almost weightless, compared to the massive solidity of Romanesque architecture. The fluid spaciousness of Saint-Denis' choir results from its slim columns, whose use was made possible by the relative lightness of the vaults they needed to support. In addition, the windows are so large that they no longer give the impression of being openings cut into a wall but, in effect, translucent walls, consisting of stained glass. What makes this abundance of light

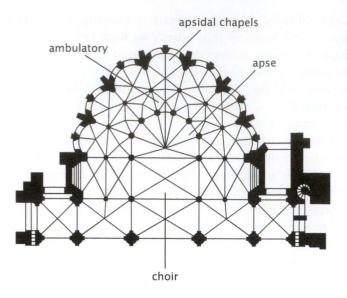

12.1   Plan of the choir and ambulatory, abbey church of Saint-Denis, France. 1140–44 (Peter Kidson)

possible are heavy buttresses that jut out between the chapels to contain the outward pressure of the vaults. In the plan (see fig. 12.1), they look like stubby arrows pointing toward the center of the apse. No wonder, then, that the interior appears so airy, since the heaviest parts of the structural skeleton are relegated to the exterior. The impression would be even more striking if we could see all of Suger's choir, for the upper part of the apse, rising above the double ambulatory, had very large, tall windows. Unfortunately, later transformations of the building destroyed the choir's original effect.

In describing Suger's ambulatory and choir, we have also described the essentials of Gothic architecture. Yet none of the elements that makes up its design is really new. The pilgrimage choir plan, the pointed arch, and the ribbed groin vault can be found in regional schools of the French and Anglo-Norman Romanesque. However, their combination in the same building was of such importance to Suger that—as he himself tells us—he brought together artisans from many different regions for Saint-Denis. We must not conclude from this, however, that Gothic architecture was merely a synthesis of Romanesque traits. If we did, we would be hard pressed to explain the new spirit, particularly the quest for luminosity, that strikes us so forcibly at Saint-Denis. Suger's account of the rebuilding of his church stresses luminosity as the highest value achieved in the new structure. Thus, Suger suggests, the "miraculous" light that floods the choir through the "most sacred" stained-glass windows becomes the Light Divine, a revelation of the spirit of God. Suger also claims that harmony, the perfect relationship among parts in terms of mathematical proportions or ratios, is the source of all beauty, since it exemplifies the laws by which divine reason made the universe.

This symbolic interpretation of light and numerical harmony was well established in Christian thought long before Suger's time. It derived from the writings of a sixth-century Greek

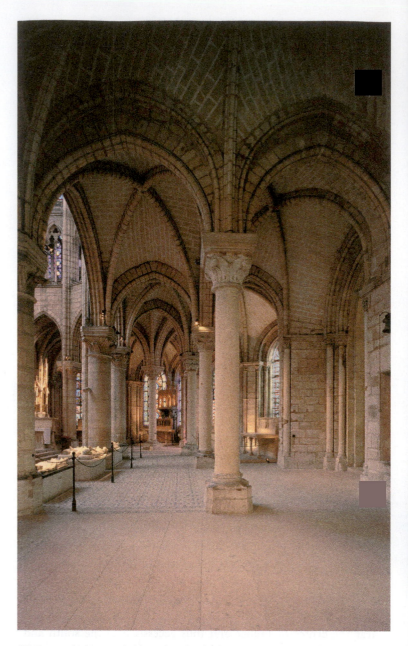

12.2   Ambulatory of abbey church of Saint-Denis

theologian who, in the Middle Ages, was mistakenly believed to have been Dionysius the Areopagite, an Athenian disciple of St. Paul, who is mentioned in the New Testament book of Acts. In France, the writer Dionysius was identified with St. Denis, since the saint's name in Latin is Dionysius. Not surprisingly, Suger attached great authority to the writings of Dionysius, which were available to him in the library at Saint-Denis; Dionysian light-and-number symbolism particularly appealed to him

At the heart of Suger's mystical intent for Saint-Denis was the belief that the material realm is the steppingstone for spiritual contemplation and thus that dark, jewel-like light filtering through the church's stained-glass windows would transport the viewer to "some strange region of the universe which neith exists entirely in the slime of earth nor entirely in the purity Heaven." The success of the choir design at Saint-Denis, therefore, derives not only from its architectural qualities but also from

Suger of Saint-Denis (1081–1151)

From *On the Consecration of the Church of Saint-Denis* and *On What Was Done Under His Administration*

Abbot Suger left two accounts of his rebuilding of the abbey church of Saint-Denis. He justifies his enlargement of the Carolingian building with reference to its overcrowding on religious holidays. After rebuilding the west end of the Carolingian church, he destroyed its eastern apse and built a much larger, more elaborate choir over the old crypt. Saint-Denis was a Benedictine abbey, though its church was open to layfolk and attracted them in large numbers. The ostentatious embellishment of the church was the type of material display deplored by St. Bernard of Clairvaux (see page 359). Suger's descriptions of Saint-Denis suggest a sensuous love of precious materials, but also a belief that contemplation of these materials could lead the worshiper to a state of heightened spiritual awareness. Like the Byzantine rationale for icons, the notion of "anagogical" transportation to another dimension is indebted to Neo-Platonism.

Through a fortunate circumstance—the number of the faithful growing and frequently gathering to seek the intercession of the Saints—the [old] basilica had come to suffer grave inconveniences. Often on feast days, completely filled, it disgorged through all its doors the excess of the crowds as they moved in opposite directions, the outward pressure of the foremost ones not only prevented those attempting to enter from entering but also expelled those who had already entered. At times you could see that no one among the countless thousands of people because of their very density could move a foot; that no one, because of their very congestion, could [do] anything but stand like a marble statue, stay benumbed or, as a last resort, scream. The distress of the women was so great and so intolerable that you could see how they cried out horribly, how several of them, lifted by the pious assistance of men above the heads of the crowd, marched forward as though upon a pavement;

and how many others, gasping with their last breath, panted in the cloisters of the brethren to the despair of everyone …

Moreover, it was cunningly provided that—through the upper columns and central arches which were to be placed upon the lower ones built in the crypt—the central nave of the old [church] should be equalized, by means of geometrical and arithmetical instruments, with the central nave of the new addition; and, likewise, that the dimensions of the old side-aisles should be equalized with the dimensions of the new side-aisles, except for that elegant and praiseworthy extension, in [the form of] a circular string of chapels, by virtue of which the whole [church] would shine with the wonderful and uninterrupted light of most luminous windows, pervading the interior beauty. …

We insisted that the adorable, life-giving cross should be adorned. Therefore we searched around everywhere by ourselves and by our agents for an abundance of precious pearls and gems. One merry but notable miracle which the Lord granted us in this connection we do not wish to pass over. For when I was in difficulty for want of gems and could not sufficiently provide myself with more (for their scarcity makes them very expensive): then, lo and behold, [monks] from three abbeys of two Orders—that is, from Cîteaux and another abbey of the [Cistercian] Order, and from Fontevrault offered us for sale an abundance of gems such as we had not hoped to find in ten years, hyacinths, sapphires, rubies, emeralds, topazes. …

Often we contemplate these different ornaments both new and old. When the loveliness of the many-colored gems has called me away from external cares, and worthy meditation has induced me to reflect, transferring that which is material to that which is immaterial, on the diversity of the sacred virtues: then it seems to me that I see myself dwelling, as it were, in some strange region of the universe which neither exists entirely in the slime of the earth nor entirely in the purity of Heaven; and that, by the grace of God, I can be transported from this inferior to that higher world in an anagogical manner.

We [also] caused to be painted, by the exquisite hands of many masters from different regions, a splendid variety of new windows.

Source: *Abbott Suger on the Abbey Church of Saint-Denis and Its Art Treasures*, ed. and tr. Erwin Panofsky (Princeton, NJ: Princeton University Press, 1946)

its extraordinary psychological impact. Visitors, it seems, were overwhelmed by both, and within a few decades the new style had spread far beyond the Île-de-France.

SUGER AND THE MEDIEVAL ARCHITECT Although Suger was not an architect, there is no contradiction between his lack of professional training and his claim of responsibility for the technical advances and resultant style of "his" new church. In the twelfth century, the term "architect" had a very different meaning from what it does today. To the medieval mind, the overall leader of the project could be considered its architect. Even God, creator of the universe, was sometimes represented as an architect employing builders' tools. After all, the function of a church is not merely to enclose a maximum of space with a minimum of material, but also to embody and convey religious ideas. For the

master who built the choir of Saint-Denis, the technical problems of vaulting must have been inseparable from issues of form and meaning. The design includes elements that express function without actually performing it. An example is the slender column shafts (**responds**) that seem to transfer the weight of the vaults to the church floor.

In order to know what concepts to convey, the medieval builder needed the guidance of religious authority. At a minimum, such guidance might be a simple directive to follow some established model. Suger, however, took a more active role, proposing objectives to which his master masons must have been singularly responsive. Close collaboration between patron and architect or master builder had of course occurred before—between Perikles and Pheidias, for example (see pages 136–39)—just as it does today.

CONSTRUCTING SAINT-DENIS Building Saint-Denis was an expensive and complex task that required the combined resources of Church and State. Suger used stone from quarries near Pontoise for the ambulatory columns and lumber from the forest of Yvelines for the roof. Both had to be transported by land and river, which was a slow and costly process. The master builder probably employed several hundred stonemasons and two or three times that many laborers. Advances in technology spurred by warfare made possible improved construction techniques that were essential for building the new rib vaults. Especially important were better cranes powered by windlasses, treadwheels that used counterweights, and double pulleys for greater efficiency.

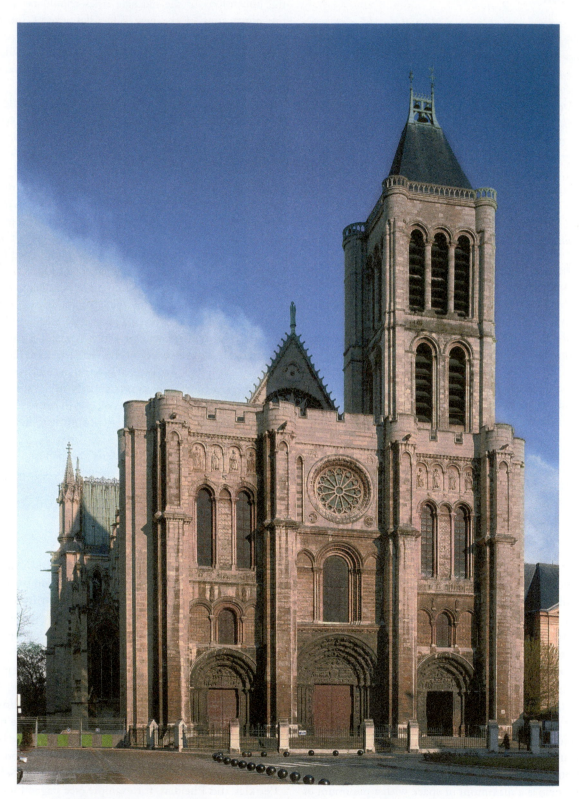

12.3   West façade of abbey church of Saint-Denis. ca. 1137–40

These devices could be put up and taken down with ease, allowing for lighter scaffolding suspended from the wall instead of resting on the ground.

WEST FAÇADE Although Abbot Suger planned to rebuild all of Saint-Denis, the only part of the church that he saw completed, other than the ambulatory and choir, was the west façade. Its overall design (fig. **12.3**) derived from Norman Romanesque façades. A comparison between Saint-Denis and Saint-Étienne at Caen (see fig. 11.46) reveals a number of shared basic features. These include the pier buttresses that reinforce the corners of the towers and divide the façade vertically into three main parts, the placement of the portals, and the three-story arrangement. However, Saint-Denis's three portals are far larger and more richly carved than those at Saint-Étienne or any other Norman Romanesque church. From this we can conjecture that Abbot Suger attached considerable importance to the sculptural decoration of Saint-Denis, although his account of the church does not discuss it at length.

The rich sculptural decoration included carved tympana, archivolts, and jambs. The arrangement recalls the façades of southwestern France (see fig. 11.13) and the carved portals of Burgundy (see fig. 11.17). These correlations corroborate Suger's claim that his workforce included artists from many regions. Unhappily, the trumeau figure of St. Denis and the statue-columns of the jambs were removed in 1770 and 1771, when the central portal was enlarged. A few years later, during the French Revolution, a mob attacked the heads of the remaining figures and melted down the metal doors. As a result of these ravages and a series of clumsy restorations undertaken during the eighteenth and nineteenth centuries, we can gain only a general view of Suger's ideas about the role of sculpture at Saint-Denis. To envision what the west portal originally looked like we have to turn to the cathedral of Chartres, where some of the Saint-Denis sculptors subsequently worked.

Chartres Cathedral

Toward 1145 the bishop of the town of Chartres, who was a friend of Abbot Suger and shared many of his ideas, began to rebuild a cathedral in the new style, dedicated to Notre-Dame ("Our Lady," the Virgin Mary). Fifty years later a fire destroyed all but the eastern crypt and the west façade. (See www.myartslab.com.) Our discussion of Chartres is divided into two sections: First we will discuss the west façade and later in the chapter that portion of the cathedral rebuilt after the fire of 1194.

WEST FAÇADE The surviving west façade (fig. **12.4**), in many ways reminiscent of Saint-Denis, is divided into units of two and three and is a model of clarity. Yet, because construction proceeded in stages and was never entirely finished, the harmony of the result is evolutionary rather than systematic. For example, the two west towers, though similar, are by no means identical. Moreover, their **spires**, the tall towers with tapering roofs, are

12.4 West façade of cathedral of Notre-Dame, Chartres, France. ca. 1145–1220. (Left spire is from 16th century)

very different: That on the left in figure 12.4 dates from the early sixteenth century, nearly 300 years later than its mate.

To judge from old drawings of Saint-Denis, the Chartres jambs (figs. **12.5** and **12.6**) are so similar to those of the original Saint-Denis portals that the same sculptors must have worked on both buildings. Tall figures attached to columns flanked the doorways of both churches. Figures had appeared on the jambs or trumeaux of Romanesque portals (see figs. 11.13 and 11.15), but they were reliefs carved from the masonry of the doorway. The Chartres jamb figures, in contrast, are essentially statues, each with its own axis. They could, in theory at least, be detached from their supports. This is a development of truly revolutionary importance and could apparently be made only by borrowing the cylindrical shape of the column for the human figure. That the figures are round gives them a corporeal presence, and their

12.5 West portal (Royal Portal) of cathedral of Notre-Dame, Chartres. ca. 1145–50

heads show a gentle, human quality that indicates a naturalistic trend in Gothic sculpture, quite different from the apparent aims of Romanesque sculptors to accentuate stylization.

On the west portal of Chartres naturalism appears as if in reaction against the fantastic and demoniacal aspects of Romanesque art, a response that may be seen in the solemn spirit of the figures and their increased physical bulk. This is apparent by comparing the Christ of Chartres's center tympanum (see fig. 12.5) with his counterpart in the tympanum at Moissac (see fig. 11.13). It also appears in the visual and thematic unity underlying the entire sculptural program at Chartres. While an understanding of the subtler aspects of this program requires a knowledge of the theology that would have been taught by leading scholars of the day at the Chartres cathedral school, its main elements can be readily understood.

The jamb statues form a continuous sequence linking all three portals (see fig. 12.5). Together they represent the prophets, kings, and queens of the Hebrew Bible. Their purpose is to acclaim the rulers of France as their spiritual descendants, and to stress the harmony of spiritual and secular rule, of priests (or bishops) and kings—ideals previously put forward by Abbot Suger. Above the main doorway, symbols of the four evangelists flank Christ in Majesty. The apostles are below, while the 24 elders (see page 361) occupy the two outer archivolts. Although the components are similar to those of the Moissac tympanum, the effect at Chartres is calm and comforting whereas at Moissac the effect is dramatic and unsettling. The right-hand tympanum at Chartres shows Christ's Incarnation: the Birth, the Presentation in the Temple, and the infant Christ Child on the lap of the Virgin, who symbolizes the Church. The design achieves compositional and thematic unity by elevating Christ in the center of each register: on the manger, on an altar, and on the lap of his mother. In the surrounding archivolts, representations of the liberal arts as human wisdom pay homage to the divine wisdom of Christ. Finally, in the left-hand tympanum, we see the timeless Heaven Christ (or perhaps the Christ of the Ascension) framed by the ever-repeating cycle of the year: the signs of the zodiac and their earthly counterparts, the labors of the 12 months.

12.6 Jamb statues, west portal of cathedral of Notre-Dame, Chartres

Laon Cathedral

Because the mid-twelfth-century church that stood behind the west façade of Chartres cathedral was destroyed by fire in 1194, we must turn to the cathedral of Notre-Dame at Laon to appreciate an Early Gothic interior. This cathedral was begun just before 1160.

NAVE The interior elevation of Laon cathedral (fig. 12.7) includes a nave arcade, gallery, triforium, and clerestory, all features found in Romanesque architecture but never together in the same building. The stacking of four levels is a Gothic innovation and lightens the weight of the walls. The elevation develops logically and harmoniously: The single opening of the nave arcade is doubled in the gallery, then triple arches follow in the triforium, while a broad clerestory window balances the single nave arcade opening that began the vertical sequence. The rhythmical arrangement articulates a heightened sense of verticality, while the multiple openings allow increased light to enter the nave, directly from the clerestory and indirectly through galleries and side aisles.

Sexpartite nave vaults over squarish bays at Laon continue the kind of structural experimentation begun by the Norman Romanesque builders of Saint-Étienne at Caen (see fig. 11.47) and Durham cathedral (see fig. 11.43). Laon uses the pointed ribbed vaults, pioneered in the western bays of the nave at Durham, throughout the building. Alternating bundles of shafts rising

12.7 Nave of cathedral of Notre-Dame, Laon, France. ca. 1160–1210

along the wall reflect the nature of the sexpartite vaults above: Clusters of five colonnettes indicate where transverse arches cross the nave, while three colonnettes adorn the intermediate piers. Although the system develops from Romanesque building practice (see pages 350 and 353), the elements seem more delicate in the Gothic building. By contrast, Romanesque interiors such as Santiago de Compostela (see fig. 11.5) and Durham cathedral (see fig. 11.43) emphasize the great effort required to support the weight of the vaults.

Some scholars see a change in program at Laon as revealing the evolving objectives of this cathedral's designers. At the east end of the nave, where the building work began, clustered shafts were added to piers as well as to the wall. In the later, more westerly nave bays, the round piers are plain. Instead of the staggered rhythm created by the earlier alternating pier arrangement, the change produced a more flowing effect. However, the tradeoff for the increased uniformity of the new arrangement was a loss of structural explicitness. For other scholars, the shafts attached to the Laon nave piers mark a liturgical division in the build: the site of a screen separating the choir occupied by clerics from the spaces used by the lay congregation. Gothic churches, like earlier religious buildings (see page 238), were settings for devotions and backdrops for the performance of the liturgy; as such, they framed the movements and words sung in processions and practiced in sacramental rites.

Cathedral of Notre-Dame in Paris

The plan of the cathedral in Notre-Dame at Paris is recorded as having been begun in 1163, only a few years after Notre-Dame

12.8   Plan of cathedral of Notre-Dame, Paris. ca. 1155–ca. 1250

12.9   Nave of cathedral of Notre-Dame, Paris

12.10 West façade of cathedral of Notre-Dame, Paris. ca. 1200–50

Stylish as this change might have been when the building was begun, a thirteenth-century reconstruction completely eliminated the triforium in order to enlarge the clerestory windows. Because a few bays were returned to their original four-part elevation in a nineteenth-century restoration, we can compare the original and the remodeled elevations (fig. 12.9). The design change reveals a continuing desire to reduce wall surface and increase the amount of light entering the building. The large clerestory windows and the light and slender forms produce nave walls that seem amazingly thin. This creates an effect of weightlessness.

Like uniformity in the plan, the vertical emphasis of the interior is a clear Gothic trait. It depends not only on the actual proportions of the nave, but also on a constant and repeated accentuation of upward momentum and the apparent ease with which a sense of height is attained.

WEST FAÇADE The most monumental aspect of the exterior of Notre-Dame in Paris is its west façade (fig. 12.10). This retains its original appearance, except for the sculpture, which was badly damaged during the French Revolution and is largely restored. All of its details are integrated into a coherent whole. Here, the meaning of Suger's emphasis on harmony, geometric order, and proportion is even more evident than at Saint-Denis itself and the result goes well beyond the achievement of Chartres cathedral's west portal.

This formal discipline is also apparent in the placement of the sculpture, which no longer shows the spontaneous growth typical of the Romanesque. Instead, it has been assigned a precise role within the architectural framework. At the same time, the cubic solidity of the façade has been moderated by lacelike arcades and window perforations, which break down the continuity of the wall surfaces so that the total effect is of a weightless openwork screen.

HIGH GOTHIC ART IN FRANCE

The political and economic stability of France during the thirteenth century encouraged the continued growth of cities, an ideal context for producing monumental architecture. Some art historians have seen the attempts to integrate structure and design in Early Gothic art as a series of experiments that were resolved during the High Gothic period. This is undoubtedly true to some extent, but the art of the thirteenth century also demonstrates an interest in pursuing refinements that synthesize engineering and aesthetics. Thus, High Gothic art is as much a continuation of Early Gothic experiments as it is their culmination. It is during this time that the names of architects, who previously had been largely anonymous, proliferate, a reflection of the value placed on their achievements and of an increasing interest in personal identity. This concern for the individual also reflects a changing class structure in which those engaged in trade and commerce become more independent.

at Laon, although there is evidence that it might actually have been started as early as the mid-1150s. Notre-Dame, Paris is extraordinarily compact and achieves a unity not present in either Romanesque buildings or earlier Gothic ones (fig. 12.8).

NAVE The transept of the church barely exceeds the width of the façade, perhaps a result of the cathedral's site adjacency to the Seine River, which might not have allowed for a boldly projecting transept. As at Saint-Denis (see fig. 12.1), the double ambulatory of the choir continues directly into the aisles, but there are no radiating chapels. This stress on uniformity in the plan finds a parallel in the treatment of the elevation; despite the use of sexpartite vaults, there is no alternating system of supports. As at Laon (see fig. 12.7), the Paris elevation was originally four-part, though oculi were inserted in place of the arcaded triforium.

The Rebuilding of Chartres Cathedral

The rebuilding of Chartres cathedral after the fire of 1194 marks the next step in the development of Gothic architecture. The new building was largely completed within an astonishingly brief span of 26 years. Its crypt houses Chartres's most important possession: remnants of a tunic said to have been worn by the Virgin Mary, to whom the cathedral is dedicated, at the time of Jesus' nativity. The relic, which miraculously survived the great fire of 1194, had drawn pilgrims from all over Europe.

The fire also spared the west façade and portals, and the decision to conserve these architectural features—which, at the time of the fire, were nearly 50 years old and certainly out of fashion—is worth noting. After initial despair at the damage wrought by the fire, civic and ecclesiastical authorities animated their followers by interpreting the event as an expression of the will of the Virgin herself that a new and more glorious cathedral be built. Since the west end of the church, like the famous relic

12.11 Plan of cathedral of Notre-Dame (as rebuilt after 1194), Chartres

12.12 Nave and choir of cathedral of Notre-Dame, Chartres. ca. 1194–1220

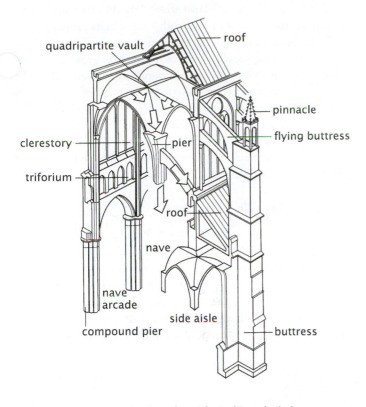

quadripartite vault — roof

pinnacle

clerestory — pier

flying buttress

triforium

roof

nave

nave arcade

side aisle

compound pier — buttress

12.13 Axonometric projection of a High Gothic cathedral (after Acland)

of the Virgin, had also been spared, it too was treated as a relic worthy of preservation. Recognizing the divine plan in what otherwise would have been disheartening circumstances helped fuel enthusiasm for rebuilding and accounts for the rapid pace of construction.

To provide room for large numbers of visitors without disturbing worshipers, there is a wide aisle running the length of the nave and around the transept (fig. 12.11). It is joined at the choir by a second aisle, forming an ambulatory that connects the apsidal chapels. Worshipers entered the building through the old west portal and passed through a relatively low narthex. It would

have taken some time for their eyes to adjust to the darkness of the interior. Even the noise of daily life would have been shut out, and sounds within the building would have been at first eerily muffled. Once worshipers had recovered from this disorienting effect, they would have become aware of a glimmering light, which guided them into the cavernous church. The transition, both subtle and profound, accentuated the significance of entering the church. As with entries into Romanesque and Byzantine churches (see pages 256–57 and 362), a liminal, or transitional, zone signaled that visitors had left the temporal world behind. Patrons, designers, and builders of a religious edifice had again found meaningful physical forms to encourage and sustain powerful spiritual experiences.

NAVE Designed a generation after Notre-Dame in Paris, the rebuilt nave of Chartres cathedral (fig. 12.12) is the first fully developed example of the mature, or High, Gothic. Several features distinguish this style. By eliminating the gallery, the designers of Chartres imposed a three-part elevation on the wall (fig. 12.13). Romanesque builders had used tripartite wall divisions (see figs. 11.11, 11.43, and 11.47), but the Chartres solution diminishes horizontality and treats the wall surface as a coherent vertical unit. (It was in an attempt to rival High Gothic buildings such as Chartres that the Early Gothic nave wall of Notre-Dame in Paris was reconfigured into a three-part elevation from its original Early Gothic four-part form [see fig. 12.9].) Shafts attached to the piers at Chartres stress the continuity of the vertical lines and guide our eye upward to the vaults, which appear as diaphanous webs stretched across the slender ribs. Quadripartite, or four-part, vaults now replace the sexpartite vaults of Early Gothic buildings (fig. 12.14). Quadripartite vaults cover rectangular bays and, as a result, the builders no longer needed to worry about an alternating system of supports. The quickened rhythm of shorter, rectangular bays intensifies the perceived pace of propulsion down the nave. The openings of the pointed nave arcade are taller and narrower than before, and the clerestory is larger so that it is the same height as the nave arcade. Because there are so few walls, the vast interior space appears at first to lack clear boundaries.

sexpartite vault

quadripartite vault

12.14 (a) Sexpartite vaulting and (b) quadripartite vaulting

Theophilus Presbyter (12th century)

De diversis artibus, from Book II: "The Art of the Worker in Glass"

"Theophilus" may have been the pseudonym of Roger of Helmarshausen, a Benedictine monk and metalworker. Metalwork is the subject of the third book of this treatise, following books on painting and stained glass. Theophilus' text, written in the twelfth century, is the first in the Western tradition to give a practitioner's account of the technology of art production.

Chapter 17: *Laying Out Windows*

When you want to lay out glass windows, first make yourself a smooth flat wooden board. Then take a piece of chalk, scrape it with a knife all over the board, sprinkle water on it everywhere, and rub it all over with a cloth. When it has dried, take the measurements of one section in a window, and draw it on the board with a rule and compasses. Draw as many figures as you wish, first with [a point made of] lead or tin, then with red or black pigment, making all the lines carefully, because, when you have painted the glass, you will have to fit together the shadows and highlights in accordance with

[the design on] the board. Then arrange the different kinds of robes and designate the color of each with a mark in its proper place; and indicate the color of anything else you want to paint with a letter.

After this, take a lead pot and in it put chalk ground with w Make yourself two or three brushes out of hair from the tail marten, badger, squirrel, or cat or from the mane of a donkey. Now take a piece of glass of whatever kind you have chosen, but larger on all sides than the place in which it is to be set, and lay it on the ground for that place. Then you will see the drawing on the board through the intervening glass, and, following it, draw the outlines only on the glass with chalk.

Chapter 18: *Glass Cutting*

Next heat on the fireplace an iron cutting tool, which should be thin everywhere except at the end, where it should be thicker. When the thicker part is red-hot, apply it to the glass that you want to cut, and soon there will appear the beginning of a crack. If the glass is hard [and does not crack at once], wet it with saliva on your finger in the place where you had applied the tool. It will immediately split and, as soon as it has, draw the tool along the line you want to cut and the split will follow.

Source: Theophilus, *On Divers Arts: The Foremost Medieval Treatise on Painting, Glassmaking, and Metalwork*, tr. John G. Hawthorne and Cyril Stanley Smith (NY: Dover Publications, 1979)

12.15   Cathedral of Notre-Dame, Chartres (from the south)

flying buttresses

clerestory

triforium

nave

nave arcade

side aisle

compound pier

buttress

crypt

12.16 Transverse section of cathedral of Notre-Dame, Chartres (after Acland)

chiseled without breaking, carved the individual blocks and set them together to form walls, both outer and inner. The intermediate space was filled with mortar and rough stones, a task which the less skilled roughmasons performed. The inner and outer walls were connected by tie-courses of finished freestone, which gave added strength to the walls.

STAINED GLASS Alone among all major Gothic cathedrals, Chartres still retains most of its more than 180 original stained-glass windows (fig. **12.17**). The magic of the jewel-like light from the clerestory is unforgettable to anyone who has experienced it. The windows admit far less light than one might expect. They act mainly as diffusing filters that change the quality of daylight, giving it the poetic and symbolic values so highly praised by Abbot Suger. The sensation of ethereal light dissolves the physical solidity of the church and, hence, the distinction between the temporal and the divine realms. This "miraculous light" creates the intensely mystical experience that lies at the heart of Gothic spirituality.

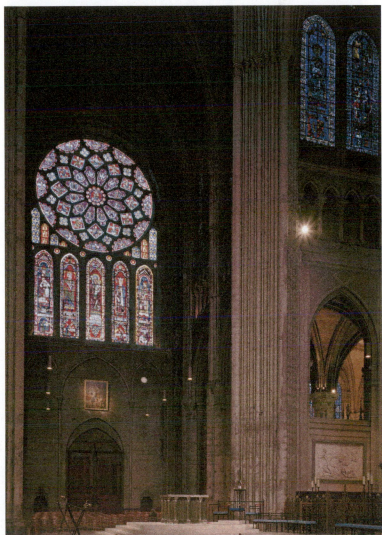

12.17 North transept of cathedral of Notre-Dame, Chartres

BUTTRESSES In Chartres, as in Suger's choir at Saint-Denis, the buttresses (the heavy bones of the structural skeleton) are visible only outside the building (figs. **12.15** and **12.16**). The plan (see fig. 12.11) shows them as massive blocks of masonry that stick out from the building. Above the aisles, these piers turn into **flying buttresses**—arched bridges that reach upward to the critical spots between the clerestory windows where the outward thrust of the nave vault is concentrated (see fig. 12.16). The flying buttresses were also designed to resist the considerable wind pressure on the high-pitched roof. This method of anchoring vaults, so characteristic of Gothic architecture, certainly owed its origin to functional considerations, but the flying buttress is also an integral aesthetic and expressive feature of the building. Its shape could emphasize both verticality and support (in addition to actually providing it) in a variety of ways, according to the designer's sense of style.

The masonry techniques involved in constructing cathedrals required both brute labor and skill. Freemasons, those who worked in freestone, which has a uniform texture and can be

12.18 *Notre Dame de la Belle Verrière*, cathedral of Notre-Dame, Chartres. ca. 1170 (framing panels are 13th century). Stained-glass window, height approx. 14′ (4.27 m)

The majestic *Notre Dame de la Belle Verrière* (literally, "Our Lady of the Beautiful Window") at Chartres (fig. **12.18**) appears as a weightless form hovering effortlessly in indeterminate space. This window, the only one apart from those of the west façade to survive the 1194 fire, consists of hundreds of small pieces of

tinted glass held together by strips of lead. Methods of medieval glassmaking limited the maximum size of these pieces, so the design could not simply be "painted on glass." Rather, the window was painted *with* glass. It was assembled much like mosaic or a jigsaw puzzle, out of odd-shaped fragments cut to fit the contours of the shapes. (See *Primary Source*, page 402.) This process encourages an abstract, ornamental style, which tends to resist any attempt at three-dimensional effects. Only in the hands of a great master could the maze of lead strips lead to such monumental forms. (See *Materials and Techniques*, page 405.)

Given the way stained glass accentuates pattern and decorative effect, it is not surprising that it was so popular during the Middle Ages. Its brilliant surfaces are like the flat stones and enamelwork so highly prized in earlier periods (see fig. 10.2); enamel is in fact a kind of glass. The intensity with which the viewer engages with the image parallels the direct connection between viewer and object evident in much of the art of the earlier Middle Ages. Worthy comparisons with *Notre Dame de la Belle Verrière* are the Byzantine mosaics from the church of the Dormition at Daphni (see figs. 8.44 and 8.45) for the way they command our attention and communicate directly with a viewer. Both use otherworldly light to convey spiritual messages: on the one hand, filtered through stained glass, and on the other, reflected off gold-glass mosaics.

The stained-glass workers who filled the windows of the great Gothic cathedrals also had to face difficulties arising from the enormous scale of their work. The task required a degree of orderly planning that had no precedent in medieval painting. Only architects and stonemasons knew how to deal with this problem, and it was their methods that the stained-glass workers borrowed in mapping out their own designs. Gothic architectural design relied on a system of geometric relationships to establish numerical harmony; the same rules could be used to control the design of stained-glass windows or even an individual figure. (See *The Art Historian's Lens*, page 406.)

The drawings in a notebook compiled about 1240 by Villard de Honnecourt, who traveled widely and documented the major buildings he examined, provide some insight into this procedure. (See www.myartslab.com.) What we see in his *Wheel of Fortune* (fig. **12.19**) is not the final version of the design but the system of circles and triangles on which the artist based the image. It illustrates the fundamental importance of such geometric schemes.

TRANSEPTS AND THEIR SCULPTURE Each of the transept arms of Chartres cathedral has three deeply recessed and lavishly decorated portals, five **lancets** (tall, narrow windows crowned by a sharply pointed arch), and an immense **rose window**, the large medallion of glass in the center of the façade (see figs. 12.15 and 12.17). The walls of these north and south façades have little solidity; they are so heavily pierced as to be nearly skeletal. On the earlier west façade, which holds the main entrance to the cathedral, the rose window, which was added after the 1194 fire, is composed of a grouping of holes cut out of the solid wall (see fig. 12.4). By comparison, thin membranes hold the glass of the

Stained Glass

Colored glass was not new in the thirteenth century, when it was used to spectacular effect in the windows of Gothic churches. It can be traced back more than 3,000 years to Egypt, and abundant evidence indicates that the Romans employed thin translucent sheets of glass in their buildings. Literary accounts, supported by some surviving examples, also describe colored glass in Early Christian, Byzantine, Muslim, and early medieval buildings.

In the twelfth-century artist's handbook *De diversis artibus*, the monk Theophilus Presbyter described in great detail the technique for making stained glass (see *Primary Source*, page 402). It required a molten mixture of silica (basically sand), potash (to lower the temperature at which silica melts), and lime (a stabilizer), plus the addition of metal oxides to color or "stain" the glass: The addition of cobalt oxide resulted in blue glass, copper oxide in red, and manganese oxide in purple. The glassworker heated the mixture in a wood-fired furnace and either poured it into molds to cool or shaped it by blowing air through a tube to form the soft glass mixture into an oval ball or cylinder, which he then cut open and flattened.

On a wooden board that had previously been covered with chalk, a designer created a drawing the same size as the window to be filled. Individual pieces of colored glass were cut with hot iron rods to fit the drawing and then arranged on it. Finer details, such as facial features and drapery folds, were then painted on with lead oxides, and the glass was placed in a wood-fired kiln to fuse the painted-on designs with the glass. Individual glass pieces were fitted together into malleable lead strips called **cames**. To permanently hold the composition in place, it was attached to an iron frame secured within the window opening. In the early twelfth century, the iron frame formed a grid of squares of about 2 feet on each side (see fig. 12.18). By the thirteenth century, glaziers employed complicated shapes, including circles, lozenges, and quatrefoils, to create increasingly complex designs (see fig. 12.32).

Stained-glass production was a costly, time-consuming, and labor-intensive activity with a marked division of labor. The artisans who made the glass supported the work of the glaziers who designed and produced the windows.

Although stained glass appears throughout Europe (see fig. 12.47), the most significant achievements in glass were made in northern Europe. To produce stained glass required abundant wood, both for firing the furnaces and kilns and for making potash, and it was in the north where there were sufficient forests to support a glassmaking industry. It was also in the north where the value of light entering a building could best be appreciated.

The effect of multicolored refracted light playing off surfaces and across spaces virtually transforms Gothic buildings. Glaziers needed to consider how individual windows could harmoniously relate to the buildings that enframed them and to a larger iconographic and aesthetic program. At Chartres, for example, blue glass predominates in the north transept rose window, while red, which admits less light, predominates in the southern rose window. Since southern light is much stronger than northern, the effect of the two roses is balanced in relation to the amount of natural light entering the building. Stained glass also provided the means to relate stories and images and to imbue them with metaphoric form. The thirteenth-century writer William Durandus of Mende, in his *Rationale divinorum officiorum*, wrote that "the windows of the church are the Holy Scriptures, which expel the wind and the rain, that is all things hurtful, but transmit the light of the true Sun, that is God, into the hearts of the faithful," while St. Bernard of Clairvaux (see page 359) explained that light could pass through glass without damaging it, just as the word of God had penetrated the womb of the Virgin Mary without violating it.

By the late thirteenth century, the preference for colored glass had diminished and large areas of clear glass dominate church construction (see fig. 12.34). Where figures are employed, they remain quite vividly colored, but are isolated within large expanses of grayish **grisaille glass**, with yellow-stained glass used to represent architectural frames around the figures. This paler glass allows light to illuminate more fully the increasingly complex architectural details of later Gothic architecture.

Detail from *Notre Dame de la Belle Verrière*, cathedral of Notre-Dame, Chartres. ca. 1170

Modules and Proportions

Just as musicologists have tried to reconstruct original performance practice during the Middle Ages, so too architectural historians have tried to find the underlying systems that govern the design and construction of medieval buildings, so that they can understand the methods and intentions of medieval builders. How medieval architects and masons decided on the measurements and patterns they employed is a fascinating topic that has been explored by architectural historians since the nineteenth century. Few medieval documents explain how individual architects went about establishing the specific relationships they used, so scholars have to measure buildings and analyze those measurements in order to decipher the systems that were used to design them. The task is not always easy. The medieval yardstick was not the same in all regions, as it was the responsibility of local authorities to control measurement; so, for example, a specific measure in Paris was often different from the measure used in another French town.

The most basic method of establishing a proportional order in building was to either multiply or to divide a unit of measure, a system employed in the ninth century in the St. Gall monastery plan (see fig. 10.22), and in later buildings, such as the cathedral of Santiago de Compostela (see fig. 11.3), where the square at the crossing of the nave is halved to determine the size of the nave bays and quartered for aisle bays. Medieval architects also employed more complicated proportional schemes. For example, by taking the diagonal of a square and rotating it, a designer could produce a rectangle with a consistent proportional relationship based on the square root of 2 (1.414); that is, the proportion of the shorter side of the rectangle to its longer side is 1:1.414. This proportional system had been used through-

out antiquity, appearing: for example, in Vitruvius' writings (see www.myartslab.com). The design tools an architect would needed to produce shapes using these proportions were simply a right angle, a measuring rod, and a compass or a string, which could be used to rotate diagonals and thus form arches.

Art historians have also attempted to understand the philosophical and symbolic significance of medieval systems of measurements. In his analysis of the Gothic cathedral, Otto von Simson described how St. Augustine—whose fifth-century writings were of singular importance throughout the Middle Ages—saw modulation as producing a whole and perfect system that, in effect, reflects the order of the universe. Augustine relies on the biblical description (Wisdom of Solomon 11:21) of an omnipotent God who "hast ordered all things in measure, and number, and weight." For Augustine, the employment of ratios in art, as well as in music, not only produces beauty but also allows us to appreciate the divine order. Architectural historians have demonstrated that figures from Platonic geometry, including the pentagon, the equilateral triangle, and the square, were also understood and employed by medieval builders. For Plato, these shapes were associated with the elements that form the cosmos. Thus, once again, medieval architects found a physical system that expressed the perfection and wholeness of the universe.

Since the plans and elevations of Gothic cathedrals were viewed as mirrors of divine truths, these buildings can be appreciated as a union of engineering and theology, structure and meaning. Undoubtedly, for the medieval mind, the mathematics needed plan medieval buildings and the symbolism of the proportions and geometry employed were inseparable.

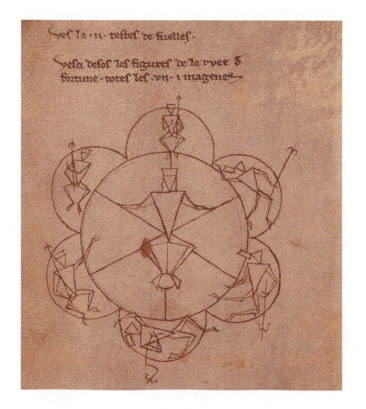

north rose in place. Art historians use the terms **plate tracery** and **bar tracery** to describe the different methods of composition employed here. With plate tracery the windows seem to be cut through solid stone walls, while in bar tracery, slender pieces of stone frame and hold in the colored glass. The bar tracery of the transept roses creates intricate decorative patterns and permits an increased amount of glass in relation to frame or wall surface.

The north transept (fig. **12.20**) is devoted to the Virgin Mary. She had already appeared over the right portal of the west façade in her traditional role as the Mother of God seated on the Throne of Divine Wisdom (see fig. 12.5). Her new prominence reflects the growing importance of the cult of the Virgin, which the Church had actively promoted since the Romanesque period. The growth of Mariology, as it is known, was linked to a new emphasis on divine love, embraced by the faithful as part of a more human view of Christianity that increased in popularity during the Gothic era. The cult of the Virgin at Chartres developed special meaning about 1204, when the cathedral received the head of

12.19 Villard de Honnecourt, *Wheel of Fortune*. ca. 1240. Ink on vellum. Bibliothèque Nationale, Paris

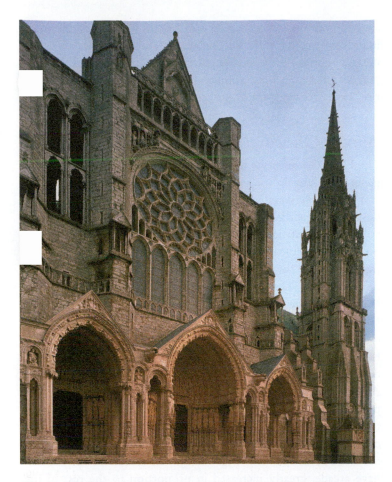

12.20 Portals, north transept of cathedral of Notre-Dame, Chartres. ca. 1204–30

her mother, St. Anne, as a relic. This relic, in combination with the tunic of the Virgin that had miraculously survived the fire of a decade earlier, gave Chartres exceptional status among those devoted to Mary.

The north tympanum of about 1210 depicts events associated with the Feast of the Assumption, when Mary was transported to Heaven (fig. **12.21**). These events are the Death (Dormition), Assumption, and Coronation of the Virgin, which, along with the Annunciation, became the most frequently portrayed subjects relating to her life. They rely on theological interpretations that identify Mary with the Church as the Bride of Christ and the Gateway to Heaven, in addition to her traditional role as divine intercessor. She becomes not only Christ's companion, but also his queen. Unlike earlier representations, many of which rely on Byzantine examples, these are of Western invention. The figures have a monumentality never found before in medieval sculpture. Moreover, the treatment is so pictorial that the scenes are independent of the architectural setting into which they are crammed.

Whereas the *Coronation of the Virgin* represents a relatively early phase of High Gothic sculpture, the jamb statues of the transept portals show a discernible evolution, even among themselves since they were carved at different times. The relationship

12.21 *Coronation of the Virgin* (tympanum), *Dormition* and *Assumption of the Virgin* (lintel), north portal of cathedral of Notre-Dame, Chartres. ca. 1210

12.22 Jamb statues, south transept portal of cathedral of Notre-Dame, Chartres. ca. 1215–20. Left-most figure (St. Theodore) ca. 1230

between statue and column begins to dissolve. The columns are quite literally put in the shade by the greater width of the figures, by the strongly projecting canopies, and by the elaborately carved bases of the statues.

A good instance of this early dissolution of the relationship between statues and columns is seen on one of the south transept portal jambs (fig. 12.22). The three saints on the right (Lawrence, Clement, and Stephen) still echo the cylindrical shape of Early Gothic jamb statues (see fig. 12.6), though the heads are no longer strictly in line with the central axis of the body. By comparison, the knight on the left, St. Theodore, who was carved about ten or fifteen years later, stands at ease, in a semblance of classical *contrapposto*. His feet rest on a horizontal platform, rather than on a sloping shelf as before, and the axis of his body, instead of being straight, describes a slight but perceptible S-curve. Even more surprising is the wealth of carefully observed detail in his weapons and in the texture of his tunic and chain mail. Above all, there is the organic structure of the body. Not since imperial Roman times (see fig. 7.29) have we seen a figure that so convincingly

suggests the organic structure of a human body. Yet the most impressive quality of the St. Theodore statue is not its naturalism but the sense of serenity and balance that it conveys. This ideal portrait of the Christian soldier, dressed as a contemporary w rior, expresses the spirit of the crusades in its most elevated form.

Amiens Cathedral

The High Gothic style defined at Chartres reaches its climax a generation later in the interior of Amiens cathedral (figs. **12.23** and **12.24**). Amiens was begun in 1220, two years after a fire destroyed an earlier cathedral on the site and while Chartres was still under construction; the nave was vaulted by 1236 and work on the choir continued for another 25 years. It is significant that we know the names of the cathedral's architects, Robert de Luzarches, Thomas de Cormont, and his son Renaud de Cormont, since it indicates the heightened social status of Gothic builders.

NAVE The breathtaking height of the nave (fig. 12.24) is the dominant achievement both technically and aesthetically at Amiens. We can see clearly the relatively swift and continuous progression toward verticality in French Gothic cathedral architecture by comparing the nave elevations of the Early Gothic cathedral of Notre-Dame in Paris and the High Gothic cathedrals of Chartres and Amiens (fig. **12.25**). The height of the Amiens nave arcade, greatly increased in proportion to the rest of the wall, creates a soaring effect; it alone is almost as high (70 fe as the entire four-story elevation of Laon (78 feet). The complete nave rises 140 feet above the ground, while that at Chartres measures "only" 118 feet from floor to vault. Moreover, the width of the Amiens nave is narrower in proportion to its height; at Paris, the ratio of nave width to height is 1:2.2 and at Chartres 1:2.4, while at Amiens it is 1:3. Thus, the effect of soaring verticality increased in direct proportion to the apparent narrowing of the nave. There is also increased vertical integration through the use of shafts that rise directly through the capitals of the piers. Moreover, the triforium and clerestory are connected visually by means of a central colonnette, so that the entire wall above the nave arcade is pulled together vertically. At Amiens, the vaults are as taut and thin as membranes; skeletal construction is carried to its virtual limits.

Reims Cathedral

We can trace the same emphasis on verticality and translucency in the development of the High Gothic façade. The one at Reims cathedral makes an instructive contrast with Notre-Dame in Paris, even though it was designed only about 30 years later. Reims, as the coronation cathedral of the kings of France, was closely linked to Paris, where the kings held court. The two sha many elements, including broad transepts that extend out fro the body of the church only slightly, but they have been reshaped into very different ensembles (fig. **12.26**).

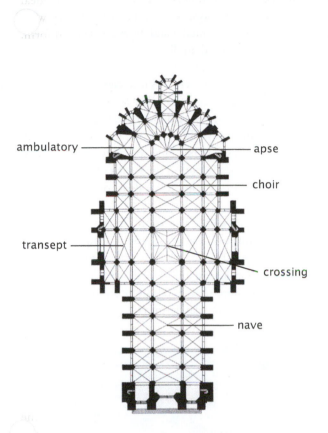

ambulatory — apse

choir

transept

crossing

nave

23 Robert de Luzarches, Thomas de Cormont, and Renaud de Cormont. Plan of cathedral of Notre-Dame, Amiens. Begun 1220

12.24 Nave and side aisle of cathedral of Notre-Dame, Amiens

12.25 Comparison of nave elevations in same scale (after Grodecki)

Notre-Dame, Paris

Chartres Cathedral

Amiens Cathedral

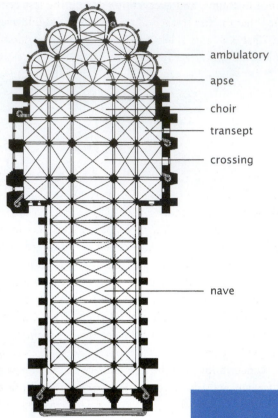

ambulatory

apse

choir

transept

crossing

nave

12.26 Plan of cathedral of Notre-Dame, Reims. ca. 1225–90

WEST FAÇADE The portals on the west façade of Reims cathedral (fig. **12.27**), instead of being recessed as in Paris (see fig. 12.10), project forward as gabled porches, with windows in place of tympana above the doorways. The gallery of royal statues which in Paris forms a horizontal band between the first and second stories, has been raised in Reims until it merges with the third-story arcade. Every detail except the rose window has become taller and narrower than before. **Pinnacles** (small pointed elements capping piers, buttresses, and other architectural forms) everywhere accentuate restless upward movement. The sculptural decoration, by far the most lavish of its kind, no longer remains in clearly marked-off zones, but has now spread to so many new perches, not only on the façade but on the flanks of the edifice as well, that the exterior begins to look like a dovecote for statues.

WEST PORTAL SCULPTURE The jamb figures at Reims are not in their original positions because some sculptures were moved between the west façade and the transept portals. As a result, continuity of style and program is difficult to assess. However, we can study here individual sculptures of distinctive style and high quality. Gothic classicism (see page 408) reached

12.27 Cathedral of Notre-Dame, Reims (from the west)

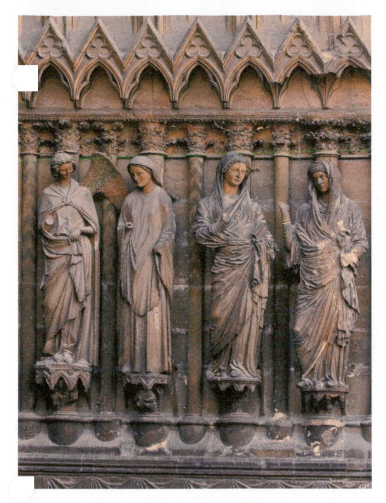

12.28 *Annunciation* and *Visitation*, west portal of cathedral of Notre-Dame, Reims. ca. 1230–65

Roman presence in Reims, and excavations during the last century established that the first cathedral on the site was built over Roman baths. That Roman models might have been available to the Reims sculptors is thus a real possibility.

Because of the vast scale and time frame of the sculptural program at Reims (and at other cathedrals as well), it was necessary to employ a variety of sculptors working in distinct styles. Two of these styles, both clearly different from the classicism of the *Visitation*, appear in the *Annunciation* group (see fig. 12.28, the two figures on the left). The difference in style within a single group derives from the fact that the angel Gabriel and the Virgin were not originally intended as a pair, but were only later installed next to each other. The Virgin, from between 1240 and 1245, has a rigidly vertical axis, and her garments form straight, tubular folds meeting at sharp angles. This severe style was probably developed about 1220 by the sculptors of the west portals of Notre-Dame in Paris; from there, it traveled to Reims as well as Amiens. The angel, in contrast, is remarkably graceful and was carved at least a decade later than the Virgin of the *Annunciation*, between 1255 and 1265. Features such as the tiny, round face framed by curly locks, the emphatic smile, the strong S-curve of the slender body, and the rich drapery of this "elegant style" spread far and wide during the following decades. In fact, the style soon became the standard formula for Gothic sculpture. Its effect will be seen for many years to come, not only in France but also abroad.

RELIEF SCULPTURE A mature example of the elegant style is the group of *Melchizedek and Abraham* (fig. **12.29**), carved shortly after the middle of the thirteenth century, for the interior west wall of Reims cathedral. These sculptures were

its climax in some of these Reims statues. The most famous of them is the *Visitation* group (fig. **12.28**, the two figures on the right), which was carved between 1230 and 1233. It depicts the Virgin Mary announcing the news of her pregnancy to her cousin Elizabeth.

For a pair of jamb figures to enact a narrative scene such as this would have been inconceivable in Early Gothic sculpture, where individual figures remained isolated, even within unified programs. That the *Visitation* figures are now free to interact shows how far the column has receded into the background. The S-curve, resulting from the pronounced contrapposto, is much more obvious here than in the St. Theodore from Chartres (see fig. 12.22) and dominates both the side and front views of the figures. The figures gesture at each other as they communicate across the space that separates them, an engagement with open space that recalls the more active role taken on by space in High Gothic architecture, too.

Horizontal folds of cloth pulled across the women's abdomens emphasize the physical bulk of their bodies. Mary and Elizabeth remind us so strongly of ancient Roman matrons that we might wonder if the artist was inspired by large-scale Roman sculpture (compare fig. 7.35). A surviving gate attests to an earlier

12.29 *Melchizedek and Abraham*, interior west wall of cathedral of Notre-Dame, Reims. ca. 1260–70

probably conceived in relation to the royal coronation ceremonies held in the cathedral. Abraham and Melchizedek were chosen as subjects because, as described in Genesis 14:18–20 in the Hebrew Bible, they are sacred leaders. The meaning relayed here expands on ideas expressed in the jamb statues of Chartres cathedral's west façade, where parallels are drawn between biblical royalty and the kings and queens of France (see page 396). The Reims scene emphasizes that earthly power is conferred through and in the service of the Church and that the archbishop of Reims, who anointed new kings, bestowed on them the lawful rite to rule as sovereign Christian monarchs. Abraham's costume, that of a medieval knight, would undoubtedly have encouraged the thirteenth-century viewer to draw parallels with the reigning monarch.

The carving of the figures recalls the vigorous realism of the St. Theodore at Chartres (see fig. 12.22) in the attention the sculptor invested in his garments and trappings. Melchizedek, however, shows clearly his proximity to the angel of the Reims *Annunciation* (see fig. 12.28) in his even more elaborately curled hair and beard, and the ample draperies that nearly swallow his body among the play of folds. Deep recesses and sharply projecting ridges show a new awareness of the effects of light and shadow that are as pictorial as they are sculptural. This pictorialism is also apparent in the way the figures interact, despite being placed in deep niches. The realism of the figures is heightened by the foliage that occupies the framing elements around them,

representing specific and recognizable plants, which include oak and fig leaves as well as acorns.

References to the increasing realism of Gothic sculpture need qualification, since Gothic realism was never systematic. Rather it was a realism of particulars, focused on specific details rather than on overall structure. Its most characteristic products are not only the classically oriented jamb statues and tympanum compositions of the early and mid-thirteenth century, but also small-scale carvings, such as the *Labors of the Months* and the *Signs of the Zodiac* in **quatrefoil** (four-lobed) frames on the façade of Amiens cathedral (fig. 12.30). The same subjects appear on Romanesque (see page 362) and Early Gothic portals (see page 396), but at Amiens they demonstrate a delightful observation of everyday life. The sculptor was clever in arranging individual scenes within the decorative quatrefoils, a shape difficult to master compositionally.

The High Gothic cathedrals of France represent a concentrated effort rarely seen before or since. The huge cost of these truly national monuments was borne by donations and taxes collected from all over the country and from all classes of society. These cathedrals express the merging of religious and patriotic fervor that had been Abbot Suger's goal. However, the great expense and forced taxation required to construct these buildings did produce vehement objections. In 1233, for example, construction of Reims cathedral was suspended as a result of civil unrest directed against the cathedral authorities and was not resumed for

12.30 *Signs of the Zodiac* (Leo, Virgo, and Libra) and *Labors of the Months* (July, August, and September), west façade of Amiens cathedral. ca. 1220–30

three years. This cessation of building activity helps explain the variety of styles at Reims. By the middle of the thirteenth century the wave of enthusiasm for large-scale projects had passed ~~peak. Work on the vast structures now proceeded at a slower ~~~e. New projects were fewer and generally far less ambitious. As a result, the highly organized teams of masons and sculptors that had formed at the sites of the great cathedrals during the preceding decades gradually broke up into smaller units.

RAYONNANT OR COURT STYLE

One of those who still had the will and means to build on an impressive scale during the mid-thirteenth century was King Louis IX (known as St. Louis following his canonization in 1297, fewer than 30 years after his death). Under the king's governance and as a result of a treaty with the English that resulted in French control of Normandy, the map of Louis's possessions began to take on the shape of present-day France. The increasing importance of the monarchy and the rising importance of Paris, where the court was located, is reflected in the degree to which Louis was able to define a court style, manifest as an appreciation of visual elegance and material luxury, which was favored as well by the upper echelons of aristocratic society. Our sense of Paris as an artistic center effectively begins under St. Louis.

~~inte-Chapelle

~~. Louis's mark on the stylistic evolution of Gothic is most dramatically seen in his court chapel, called the Sainte-Chapelle, which was designed by 1241 and completed within seven years (fig. **12.31**). The two-story building comprises a ground floor, a relatively low chapel for court officials, and an upper floor to which the royal family had direct access from their quarters in the palace. In essence, the building is a type of palatine chapel for which Charlemagne's building at Aachen (see fig. 10.18) serves as an early prototype.

The impetus for the building was provided by Louis's acquisition from his cousin, the emperor of Constantinople, of the Crown of Thorns and other relics of Christ's Passion, including a part of the True Cross, the iron lance, the sponge, and a nail. Such sacred relics required a glorious space for their display. Rich colors, elaborate patterns, and extensive amounts of gold, largely restored in the nineteenth century, cover the Sainte-Chapelle's walls, vaults, and other structural members (fig. **12.32**). This decoration complements the stained glass that constitutes most of the surface of the chapel. The stained-glass windows concentrate on historical and biblical scenes that prefigure the sacred kingship of French monarchs. Above the altar, an elevated shrine, destined to frame the sacred relics, was left open at the back so that filtered ~~ght would bathe the venerated objects on display. The delicate ~~ass cage of the building, jewel-like in the intensity of the colored light that enters it, functions in effect as a monumental reliquary. The tall, thin lancets accentuate verticality to such a degree that

12.31 Sainte-Chapelle, Paris (from the southwest). 1241–48. (Rose window, late 15th century)

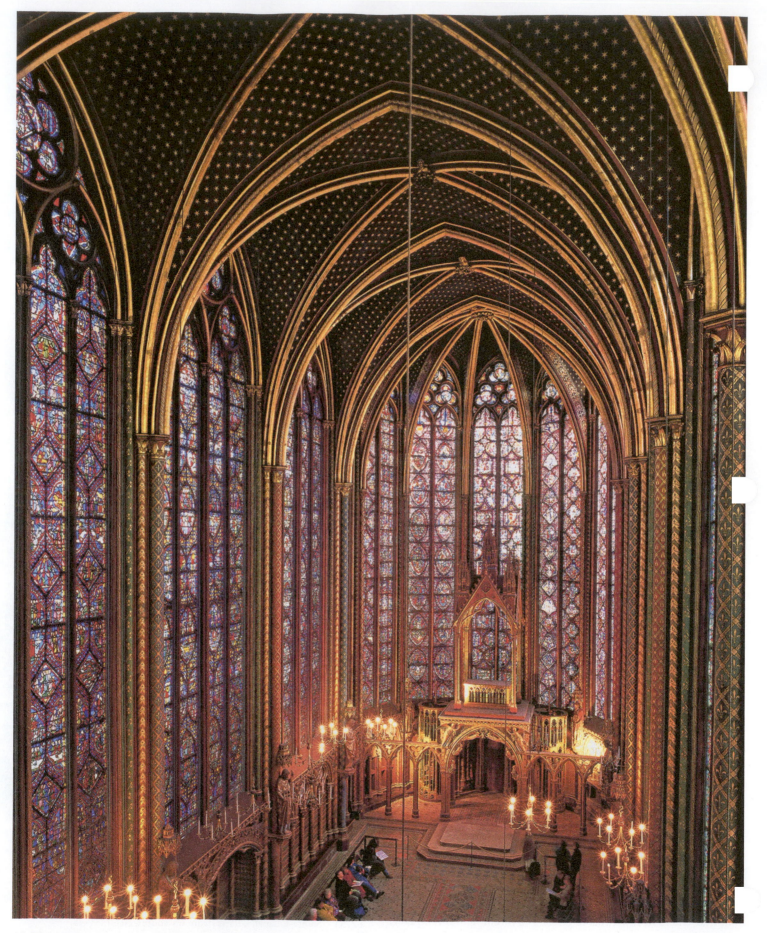

12.32   Interior of upper chapel, Sainte-Chapelle, Paris

the building conveys a sense of monumentality comparable to any cathedral despite its diminutive scale. On entering, a viewer is virtually immersed in its aura of light, different from any normal experience of the physical world. Thus, as with Hagia Sophia (see pages 257–60), spirituality is made manifest through the materiality of architecture and its decoration.

The Sainte-Chapelle's exterior buttresses are relatively modest in scale, given the great amount of glass and the large size of the windows in proportion to the walls (see fig. 12.31). By keeping the buttresses close to the building, the builders kept to a minimum the shadows cast across the windows. In order to withstand the physical forces usually contained by more prominent buttresses, two horizontal iron chains passing across the chapel's windows reinforce the structure, a remarkably effective solution to the structural and aesthetic problems the builders faced.

This phase of Gothic is often referred to as **rayonnant**, from the French *rayonner*, "to radiate light." The term derives from the prevalence of raylike bar tracery in buildings of the period, which originally appeared in rose windows and later began to appear

throughout entire churches. The style, closely associated with the court, spread through the French royal domain and then through much of Europe.

Saint-Urbain in Troyes

Saint-Urbain in Troyes (figs. **12.33** and **12.34**), built during the later years of the thirteenth century, was commissioned by Pope Urban IV (r. 1261–1264) to mark his birthplace and was dedicated to his patron saint. By eliminating the triforium and simplifying the plan, the designer created a delicate glass cage of only two stories; the slightly larger upper one is virtually all glass, much of it clear. The delicate tracery of the choir windows, which begin only 10 feet above the floor, emphasizes the effect of a screen dematerialized by light. Flying buttresses so thin as to be hardly noticeable support the building. The same spiny elegance characterizes the architectural ornament: Gables are fully detached from the window walls they are designed to support. The delicacy of Saint-Urbain leaves no doubt that the heroic

12.33   Saint-Urbain, Troyes, France. Begun 1262

12.34 Interior of Saint-Urbain, Troyes, France

PSALTER OF BLANCHE OF CASTILE A psalter executed around 1230 for Blanche of Castile, mother of King Louis IX, shows these connections. The psalter (fig. **12.35**) was probably made during the period when Blanche served as regent (1226– for Louis, who had inherited the throne at age 12 and co not reign in his own right for another six years. The range and intensity of colors (particularly of red and blue), the heavy outlines, and the placement of scenes within geometric shapes—here interlocked circles and semicircles—recall the treatment and arrangement of stained glass seen, for example, behind the shrine at Sainte-Chapelle (see fig. 12.32). The polished gold background of the illuminated page creates a dazzling display, not unlike the effect of light transmitted through glass or reflected from the metal surface of a reliquary.

BIBLE MORALISÉE A new type of bible, the moralized Bible (*Bible moralisée*), was first produced in Paris in the early thirteenth century, also for Blanche of Castile. It included biblical scenes and a short biblical text and moralizing commentary, both visual and textual, either in Latin or French, intended

12.35 *Crucifixion* and *Deposition*, from the *Psalter of Blanche of Castile*, ca. 1230. Ink, tempera, and gold leaf on vellum, 7¾ × 6″ (19.9 × 15.4 cm). Bibliothèque de l'Arsenal, Paris. Res ms 1186

age of the Gothic style is past. Refinement of detail, rather than monumentality, is now the chief concern.

Manuscript Illumination

Some authors have been concerned that the term "rayonnant" is appropriate only for architecture. Recognizing that there were also major achievements in the pictorial arts within Louis IX's court and in the upper echelons of aristocratic society, they prefer the term **court style**, which they use synonymously with rayonnant to define the art of this time. In fact, there are many connections between the building arts and the elaborate devotional works with exquisite miniatures produced for the personal enjoyment and education of the royal family and for others who were literate and could afford them. These products of French manuscript workshops disseminated the refined taste that made the court art of Paris the standard for all Europe.

12.36 *Scenes from the Apocalypse*, from a *Bible moralisée*. ca. 1225–35. Ink, tempera, and gold leaf on vellum, 15 × 10½″ (38 × 26.6 cm). Pierpont Morgan Library, New York

Sainte-Chapelle (see fig. 12.32) offer a particularly clear parallel. The spaces around the roundels in the manuscript abound with flourishes and checkerboard or diaper patterns of repeated diamonds, analogous to the decoration surrounding the scenes in the Sainte-Chapelle windows.

PSALTER OF ST. LOUIS Perhaps the closest parallel between painting and architectural form is the *Psalter of St. Louis*, which was executed in the 1260s (fig. **12.37**). The folio reproduced here illustrates the same Genesis scene of Abraham and Melchizedek as is represented on the interior of Reims cathedral (see fig. 12.29). Abraham and his troops wear crusader armor, establishing an association between contemporary struggles to free Christian lands and heroic biblical events. Louis was an eager warrior for Christianity who organized and participated in two crusades, in 1254 and 1270, the latter being the occasion of his death in Tunisia. The gold background and the banks of clouds that waft

12.37 *Melchizedek and Abraham*, from the *Psalter of St. Louis*. 1253–70. Ink, tempera, and gold leaf on vellum, 5 × 3½″ (13.6 × 8.9 cm). Bibliothèque Nationale, Paris

to make the biblical accounts more relevant to contemporary viewers. The form demonstrates a will to instruct, and the use of the vernacular French suggests its use by nonclerical persons. It is not surprising, given the didactic quality of the moralized Bible, that its creation in Paris is coeval with the emergence there of the university as an institution. The manuscript illustrated here (fig. **12.36**) is a few years later than the original one and divided between the cathedral of Toledo, in Spain, and the Pierpont Morgan Library, in New York, and originally comprised nearly 3,000 illustrated pages.

These bibles were made for the personal use of the kings and queens of France and perhaps for other high-ranking persons as well. They were intended both as precious objects and guides for good conduct, treating important issues of the time, such as heresy, sex, and the behavior of rulers. The moralizing tone of these instructional guides is very much in keeping with the character and accomplishments of the pious and compassionate King Louis, guided by Blanche, his powerful and involved mother. The scenes on the page shown here are arranged in vertically stacked roundels, and once again the tall and narrow windows of the around the arcades, hovering like incense in a church, accentuate the sacral aspects of the representation.

The manuscript's painted architecture is modeled directly on the Sainte-Chapelle (see fig. 12.31). The illustration also recalls the canopies above the heads of jamb statues at Chartres (see fig. 12.22) and the arched twin niches that enclose the Reims relief of Abraham and Melchizedek (see fig. 12.29). Against the two-dimensional background of the page, the figures stand out in relief by their smooth and skillful modeling. The outer contours are defined by heavy, dark lines, once again like the lead strips in stained-glass windows. The figures themselves display all the features of the elegant style seen in Gothic sculpture: graceful gestures, swaying poses, smiling faces, and neatly waved hair. (Compare the *Annunciation* angel in fig. 12.28 and *Melchizedek and Abraham* in fig. 12.29.) This miniature thus exemplifies the refined taste of the court art of Paris.

LATE GOTHIC ART IN FRANCE

Although Late Gothic art builds on earlier achievements, during this period artists felt free to deviate from previous patterns of development. Builders showed increased concern for unity of plan, but they also employed curvilinear and elaborate decorative forms that often showed little concern for the clarity of structure so important in earlier Gothic works. Elaborate arrangements of overlapping and pierced planes produced complex visual displays. Late Gothic manuscripts and sculptures are also highly decorated and are rich in surface treatment, accentuating their precious qualities.

Manuscript Illumination

A notably broader audience for books was stimulated by the Fourth Lateran Council, which met in Rome in 1215 and aimed to increase general Christian education. Until the thirteenth century, illuminated manuscripts had been produced in monastic scriptoria. Now, along with many other activities that were once the special preserve of the clergy, manuscript production shifted to urban workshops organized by laypeople, the ancestors of the publishing houses of today. Here again, the workshops of sculptors and stained-glass painters may have set the pattern. Paris was renowned as a center of manuscript production, and it is possible even today to identify the streets on which the workshops were clustered.

PRAYER BOOK OF PHILIP IV THE FAIR Some of these new, secular illuminators are known to us by name. Among them is Master Honoré of Paris, who in 1296 painted the miniatures in the *Prayer Book of Philip IV the Fair* (fig. **12.38**), commissioned by the grandson of Louis IX and designed for use in the Sainte-Chapelle. Master Honoré was a well-remunerated artist: in 1292, he paid higher taxes than any other member of the Paris guild of miniature painters. (The guild was an association

12.38 Master Honoré, *David and Goliath*, from the *Prayer Book of Philip IV the Fair*. 1296. Ink and tempera on vellum, 7⅞ × 4⅞" (20.2 × 12.5 cm). Bibliothèque Nationale, Paris

of craftsmen engaged in a particular trade, formed to maintain standards and protect common interests.) The University of Paris commissioned his workshop to produce illuminated copies of ecclesiastical law. Our illustration shows him working in a style derived from the *Psalter of St. Louis* (see fig. 12.37). Here, however, the framework no longer dominates the composition. The figures have become larger and their relieflike modeling more pronounced, an effect achieved through gentle shifts of color and modulated white highlights, quite different from the flat planes of color so characteristic of earlier manuscripts. The figures, though active and engaging, do not appear to stand comfortably, since their turned-down feet are flattened against the page. However, the figures are allowed to overlap the frame, which helps to detach them from the flat pattern of the background

12.39 Jean Pucelle, *The Betrayal of Christ* (folio 15 verso) and *Annunciation* (folio 16 recto), from the *Hours of Jeanne d'Évreux*. 1324–28. Grisaille and tempera on vellum, each page 3½ × 2⁷⁄₁₆″ (8.9 × 6.2 cm). (Shown larger than actual size.) Metropolitan Museum of Art, New York. The Cloisters Collection, Purchase, 1954 (54.1.2)

and thus introduces a certain, though very limited, depth into the picture. The implication of space helps further the storytelling quality of the representation. In the lower scene, David and Goliath each appear twice; in an expressive detail, Goliath, as if in distress, brings his hand to his forehead even before David has released his shot.

HOURS OF JEANNE D'ÉVREUX The interest in depicting sculptural figures was further developed by the illuminator Jean Pucelle in a prayer book—called a **book of hours**—illuminated in Paris between 1324 and 1328 for Jeanne d'Évreux, queen of France (fig. **12.39**) and probably a gift from her husband, the king. A book of hours was used for private prayer and contained the devotions for the seven canonical hours of the day as well as liturgy for local saints; often a calendar was also included. The book, only 3½ inches high, is jewel-like, fitting for the private use of a queen. The *Annunciation* is represented on the right-hand page and the *Betrayal of Jesus* on the left. The style of the figures recalls Master Honoré (see fig. 12.38), but the delicate **grisaille** (painting in gray) adds a soft roundness to the forms, the enhanced shading conveying a heightened sense of relief. This is not Pucelle's only contribution: The architectural interior reveals a spatial

recession previously unknown in northern European painting. In the *Annunciation*, Gabriel kneels in an anteroom, while angels appear in the windows of an attic, from which the dove of the Holy Spirit descends.

In representing this new pictorial space, Jean Pucelle had to take into account the special needs of a manuscript page. The Virgin's chamber does not fill the entire picture surface. It is as though it were an airy cage floating on the blank background (note the supporting angel on the right), like the rest of the ornamental framework, so that the entire page forms a harmonious unit. Many of the details are peripheral to the religious purpose of the manuscript. The kneeling queen inside the initial D is surely meant to be Jeanne d'Évreux at her prayers; it is as if her intense devotions have produced a tangible vision of the Annunciation. The identity of the man with the staff next to her is unclear, although he appears to be a courtier listening to the lute player perched on the tendril above him. The combination of scenes is a commentary on experiences that become real even if they lack physical substance: Music is at once actual and ephemeral, as is Jeanne's religious vision.

Other enchanting **vignettes** (small decorative or ornamental designs or scenes) fill the page. A rabbit peers from its burrow beneath the girl on the left, and in the foliage leading up to the initial we find a monkey and a squirrel. These fanciful marginal designs—or **drôleries**—are a common feature of Northern Gothic manuscripts. They originated more than a century before Jean Pucelle in the regions along the English Channel. From there they quickly spread to Paris and the other centers of Gothic art. Their subjects include a wide range of motifs: fantasy, fable, and grotesque humor, as well as scenes of everyday life, which appear side by side with religious themes. The essence of drôlerie is its playfulness. In this special domain, the artist enjoys an almost unlimited freedom—comparable to a jester's—which accounts for the wide appeal of drôleries during the later Middle Ages.

The seeming innocence of Pucelle's drôleries nevertheless hides a serious purpose, which is particularly evident in the example at the bottom of the right-hand page, a type of illustration referred to as a **bas-de-page** (French for "bottom of the page"). The four figures are playing a game of tag called Froggy in the Middle, a reference to the *Betrayal of Jesus* on the opposite page. Below the latter scene, two knights on goats joust at a barrel. This image not only mocks courtly chivalry but also refers to Jesus as a "scapegoat," and to the spear that pierced his side at the Crucifixion. The scapegoat refers to the Hebrew Bible description (Leviticus 16) of a goat that would bear the blame for all the sins and transgressions of the people, a fitting parallel to Christ's suffering and redemptive death.

***LE DIT DU LION* (THE ENCHANTED GARDEN)** The nature of manuscript production (see page 418) in independent lay workshops and the increasing use of the vernacular (see pages 390

12.40 Guillaume de Machaut. *The Enchanted Garden*, from *Le Dit du Lion*. 1350–55. Ink, tempera, and gold leaf on vellum, 11⅘ × 8¼" (30 × 21 cm). Bibliothèque Nationale, Paris

and 417) resulted in the introduction of new modes of expression and subjects of interest to a secular audience. An instructive example is one of the first true European landscapes created to illustrate a passage of the poem *Le Dit du Lion* (fig. 12. by Guillaume de Machaut of around 1350. The *Dit* (literally "spoken") indicates that it was not meant to be sung; the French poem describes an enchanted garden seen by a lover who is visiting an adjacent castle. The scene accurately illustrates several verses of the poem including the delightful lines:

> To make their pleasing melody
> Birds are sitting in a tree
> One, two, five, and even six I see.

The cool colors, flickering highlights, and charmingly depicted details of flora and fauna convey a sense of carefully observed nature and a feeling for illusionistic space.

Guillaume de Machaut, the first composer of polyphonic music whom we know by name, seems to have personally supervised the production of manuscripts of his works, which included, in addition to poetry, both sacred and secular music. This reflects the important role books played during this period, that is, when they were becoming accessible to a broader public. Machaut's interest in how his works were presented indicates pride and self-awareness on the part of a writer and musician to parallel what we have already seen of Gothic artists and architects (see page 399).

Sculpture

Portal sculpture, the principal interest of the Early and High Gothic periods, is of relatively little consequence during the Late Gothic period. Single figures, carved in the round, many of them cult figures, are now fully detached from any architectural setting. As the individual's importance in society increased, so individual sculpted figures became more prominent. Sculptors' guilds were now well established. Two guild masters, appointed by the king, guaranteed that sculptors would fulfill the statutes that governed their corporation. In addition to stone carving, sculptors produced a significant number of precious objects in metal and ivory.

VIRGIN OF JEANNE D'ÉVREUX Pucelle's *Virgin of the Annunciation* (see fig. 12.39), with its poised elegance, has a remarkable counterpart in the silver-gilt statue that the same patron offered to the abbey of Saint-Denis in 1339 (fig. **12.41**). The elegance and refinement of the *Virgin of Jeanne d'Évreux* reminds us that metalwork—so significant during the earlier Middle Ages—continued to be a valued medium. Even during the Early Gothic period, Abbot Suger made clear the funds that patrons were willing to invest in reliquaries, shrines, altar embellishments, and liturgical vessels: It has been calculated that the reliquary designed for the Crown of Thorns cost more than twic the construction expenses of the Sainte-Chapelle, which was built to house it.

12.41 *Virgin of Jeanne d'Évreux*. 1339. Silver gilt and enamel, height 27½″ (68 cm). Musée du Louvre, Paris (Inv MR342; MR419)

VIRGIN OF PARIS   In another early fourteenth-century sculpture of the Virgin, we see how traces of classicism increasingly disappear from Gothic sculpture, while elegance becomes a virtual end in itself. Thus, the human figure of the *Virgin of Paris* (fig. **12.42**) in Notre-Dame cathedral is now strangely abstract. It consists largely of hollows, and the projections are so reduced

In the *Virgin of Jeanne d'Évreux*, the graceful sway of the Virgin's body is counterbalanced by the harmonious way in which the drapery's vertical folds and soft curves play off each other. The Christ Child touches his mother's lips in a gesture both delicate and intimate. The inscription on the base of the statue recording the royal gift and the *fleur-de-lis*, symbol of French royalty, held by the Virgin, associate her royal stature with that of the donor.

12.42 *Virgin of Paris*. Early 14th century. Stone. Cathedral of Notre-Dame, Paris that a viewer sees them as lines rather than volumes. The statue is quite literally disembodied—its swaying stance bears little relation to Classical *contrapposto*, since it no longer supports the figure. Compared to such unearthly grace, the angel of the Reims *Annunciation* (see fig. 12.28) seems solid indeed; yet it contains the seed of the very qualities expressed so strikingly in the *Virgin of Paris*. Earlier instances of Gothic naturalism (see page 412), which focused on particulars, survive here as a kind of intimate realism in which the infant Christ is no longer a Savior-in-miniature facing the viewer but, rather, a human child playing with his mother's veil.

The elegant manner of this new style was encouraged by the royal court of France and thus had special authority. It is this graceful expressive quality, not realism or classicism, that is the essence of Gothic art. These Late Gothic sculptures might lack the epic quality of Early Gothic sculpture, but they are still impressive and relate to Late Gothic art in other mediums, such as ivory, as we shall now see.

SIEGE OF THE CASTLE OF LOVE The *Virgin of Jeanne d'Évreux* and the *Virgin of Paris* were made for a sophisticated audience that valued elegant and luxurious objects. These patrons also commissioned secular articles for their own use, many of which were made by the same artists who created religious images. Objects, in precious materials such as ivory, were often decorated with scenes from the romantic courtly literature that was popular at the time. These stories were recounted by troubadours, whose favorite subjects were the sweetness and the bitterness of love. The *Siege of the Castle of Love* (fig. **12.43**) is depicted on a fourteenth-century ivory mirror back, which originally held a polished metal disk on its other side. Knights, some on horseback, attack a castle inhabited by women. However, by conscious design the battle lacks intensity, since the equestrian at the left is more concerned with the women in the castle, who toss roses at their attackers, than he is with the combat taking place in front of him. At the upper right, a knight scales the castle walls, helped up by a lady within it. On the other side, a soldier climbs a tree in order to surrender his sword to a woman armed with roses.

The scene depicted is remarkably close to the thirteenth-century poem *Roman de la Rose* (*Romance of the Rose*), written in vernacular French by Guillaume de Lorris and Jean de Meung, in which a knight and his colleagues assault the Castle of Love. The fairy-tale quality of the ivory reflects the images in the poem, which describe a dream sequence. The story is an allegory, with the castle symbolizing women and the attack upon it a form of courtship. Thus, even if the battle represented here is a mock one, all parties have something to gain from it.

The courtly subject with women as its focus is clearly appropriate for a mirror, since it is put to use in the cause of female personal adornment. Small mirrors like this were carried by their owners, some suspended from belts. It was only in the twelfth century that cosmetics were reintroduced to western Europe. Although they had been in common use in antiquity, they had fallen out of use after the fall of Rome. Crusaders helped reestablish the habit of applying cosmetics as a result of their contact with the eastern Mediterranean, where the custom had continued from antiquity.

This ivory was made in Paris, where a guild of makers of ivory combs and mirrors is documented at this time. Both the function and subject of the mirror back suggest a social context in which the reading of romances and the appreciation of luxury objects are linked. Some years later, though still within the fourteenth century, the account book of a French duke records his purchase from a Parisian dealer of an ivory mirror and six wooden candlesticks "so that he could read romances." The production of luxury ivories trails off after the middle of the fourteenth century, a result of the economic turmoil precipitated by the Hundred Years' War.

Architecture: The Flamboyant Phase

Although the beginnings of the Late, or Flamboyant, phase of Gothic architecture go back to the late thirteenth century, during the Hundred Years' War (1337–1453) artistic production diminished significantly. Hence, we do not meet any full-fledged examples of Flamboyant art until the early fifteenth century. **Flamboyant**, literally meaning "flamelike" in French, refers to the undulating curves and reverse curves that are a main feature of Late Gothic bar tracery. Structurally, Flamboyant Gothic shows few significant developments of its own.

12.43 *Siege of the Castle of Love*. Back of a mirror. ca. 1320–50. Ivory, 4½ × 4¼ × ½″ (11.5 × 10.9 × 1.27 cm). Seattle Art Museum. Donald E. Frederick Memorial Collection (49.37)

12.44 Pierre Robin and Ambroise Harel. West façade of Saint-Maclou, Rouen, France. 1434–90

SAINT-MACLOU IN ROUEN What distinguishes Saint-Maclou at Rouen (fig. **12.44**) from Saint-Urbain at Troyes (see fig. 12.33) is the profusion of its ornament, which clearly announces the Flamboyant style. The church was designed by Pierre Robin in 1434; Ambroise Harel directed the workshop from 1467 to 1480, during which time a substantial portion of the west façade was built, although it was not completed until around 1490. The façade curves back on either side, allowing the central portal to project outward, establishing a hierarchy of forms, which variations in height accentuate.

Harel covered Saint-Maclou's structural skeleton with a web of decoration so dense and fanciful as almost to hide it completely. To locate the bones of the building within this picturesque tangle of lines becomes a fascinating game of hide-and-seek. Even a careful examination of the building's exterior does not help to decipher its interior arrangement. Repeated motifs, such as the pointed gable, appear both to emerge from the building and to soar above it. It is through the central gable, rather than above it, that the rose window appears. The gable, previously an element of enclosure (see figs. 12.20 and 12.27), is now so eaten into by shimmering tracery that it has become a purely decorative form used to create a lively if unsettling effect. The activation of architectural forms through spatial means is comparable to the interest in volume and depth exhibited by Late Gothic sculptors and painters.

THE SPREAD OF GOTHIC ART

The refined royal French style of the Paris region was enthusiastically received abroad, where it was adapted to a variety of local conditions. In fact, the Gothic monuments of England and Germany have become objects of such intense national pride since the early nineteenth century that Gothic has been claimed as a native style in both countries. A number of factors contributed to the rapid spread of Gothic art. Among them were the skill of French architects and stone carvers and the prestige of French centers of learning, such as the cathedral School of Chartres and the University of Paris. Still, one wonders whether any of these explanations really go to the heart of the matter. The basic reason for the spread of Gothic art was undoubtedly the persuasive power of the style itself. It kindled the imagination and aroused religious feeling even among people far removed from the cultural climate of the Île-de-France.

Spain

During the Romanesque period, Spanish artists had adopted the French manner of building and decoration in part to disassociate themselves from—and indeed to express their supremacy over—the Muslims with whom they shared the Iberian peninsula. This identification of French style with Christian conquest encouraged the reception of the Gothic style in Spain during the thirteenth century, when numerous Christian victories (principal among them the battle at Navas de Tolosa in 1212) drove the Muslims farther and farther south.

LEÓN The cathedral of Santa María in León (figs. **12.45** and **12.46**), a city with a long history as a royal capital, recalls French High Gothic buildings associated with the monarchy, especially Reims cathedral, the French coronation church. The east end of León, with its ambulatory and five radiating chapels, is particularly similar to the arrangement at Reims (see fig. 12.26), so much so that, although the specific identification of León's architect has been questioned, there has never been any doubt that he was French, nor that he knew the cathedral at Reims intimately. This reliance on a French model indicates a time lag, since León was not begun until the 1240s, some 30 years after Reims. León's elevation (fig. **12.47**) is more up-to-date, and its tall, thin clerestory lancets recall the Sainte-Chapelle (see fig. 12.32), completed in the same decade in which León was begun.

The association of León with French royal buildings is significant at this time. In 1230, Ferdinand III united the kingdoms

12.46   Exterior of cathedral of Santa María, León, Spain

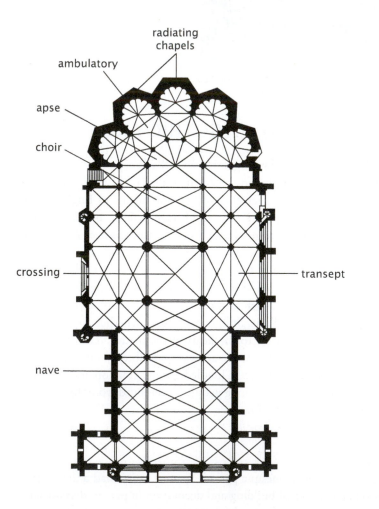

12.45   Plan of cathedral of Santa María, León, Spain. Begun 1240s (drawing by Giroux after De los Rios)

of León and Castile. Despite this, royal attentions continued to favor Burgos, capital of Castile, which had earlier been declared "mother and head" of all churches in the kingdom and where a Gothic cathedral in the French style was begun in 1221. The Leónese promoted their city's historic rank as royal capital, more venerable than Burgos, through the building program of their new cathedral.

Although many of the jamb figures of the cathedral of Santa María at León have been rearranged from their original locations, the sculptors' reliance on the French High Gothic manner of carving is clear. The figure of Simeon, the New Testament seer who recognized the infant Jesus as Redeemer (fig. **12.48**), carved in the last decades of the thirteenth century and placed on the right portal of the west façade, recalls sculptures from Reims (see figs. 12.28 and 12.29) in the elegant elongation of the body, the complicated and crisp folds of drapery, and the thick, wavy beard.

León is only one of a number of Spanish Gothic cathedrals that look to France for their inspiration. Toledo and Burgos, both cities with claims to royal status, also created buildings to designs that relied on French models and employed architects

12.47　Interior of cathedral of Santa María, León, Spain

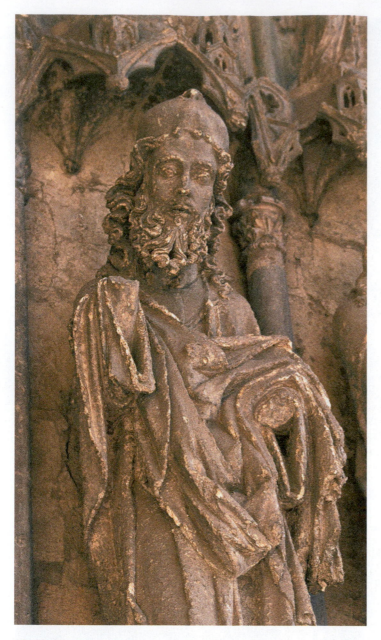

12.48 *Simeon*, jamb statue, south portal of west façade, cathedral of Santa Maria, León. ca. 1280–1300

dominated the second quarter of the thirteenth century. Although there was a great deal of building during those decades, it consisted mostly of additions to existing Anglo-Norman structures. Many English cathedrals begun during the Romanesque per had remained unfinished; they were now completed or enlarged. As a result, we find few churches that are designed entirely in the Early English style.

SALISBURY CATHEDRAL The exception to the trend of multiple periods and styles in a single English Gothic church is Salisbury cathedral, begun in 1220, the same year as Amiens cathedral. One sees immediately how different the exterior of Salisbury (fig. **12.49**) is from French Gothic churches (see figs. 12.10, 12.20, and 12.27) and how futile it would be to judge it by the same standards. Compactness and verticality have given way to a long, low, sprawling look. (The crossing tower, which provides a dramatic unifying accent, was built a century later than the rest and is much taller than originally planned.) Since height is not the main goal, flying buttresses are used only as an afterthought, not as integral design elements. The west façade is treated like a screen wall, wider than the church itself and divided into horizontal bands of ornament and statuary. The towers have shrunk to stubby turrets (small towers). The plan (fig. **12.50**), with its double transept, retains the segmented quality of the Romanesque, while the square east end derives from Cistercian architecture (see fig. 11.21).

As we enter the nave (fig. **12.51**), we recognize many elements familiar to us from French interiors of the time, such as Chartı cathedral (see fig. 12.12). However, the English interpretation produces a very different effect. As on the façade, horizontal divisions dominate at the expense of the vertical. Hence, we experience the nave wall not as a succession of vertical bays but as a series of arches and supports. These supports, carved of dark stone, stand out against the rest of the interior. This method of stressing their special function is one of the hallmarks of the Early English style. The use of bands of color also emphasizes horizontality.

Another distinctive feature is the steep curve of the nave vault. The ribs rise all the way from the triforium level. As a result, the clerestory gives the impression of being tucked away among the vaults. At Durham cathedral, more than a century earlier, the same treatment had been a technical necessity (see figs. 11.43 and 11.44). Now, it has become a matter of style, in keeping with the character of English Early Gothic as a whole. This character might be described as conservative in the positive sense: It accepts the French form but tones down its revolutionary aspects to maintain a strong sense of continuity with the Anglo-Norman past. In fact, French elements were integrated with a structure that was still based on thick walls with passages much like that found in Durham cathedral. The contrast between the bold upward thrust of the fourteenth-century crossing tower at Salisbury ar the leisurely horizontal progression throughout the rest of th thirteenth-century cathedral suggests that English Gothic had developed in a new direction during the intervening 100 years.

who undoubtedly came from France. Thus, the royal origins of the Gothic style were clearly not forgotten, even when the style was exported from France more than 100 years after its original appearance there.

England

England was especially receptive to the new style, which developed there as the influence of Gothic forms from the Île-de-France melded with Anglo-Norman Romanesque features. A French architect who rebuilt the choir of Canterbury cathedral introduced the French Gothic manner to England in 1175. Within less than 50 years, English Gothic developed a well-defined character of its own, known as the **Early English style**, which

12.49 Salisbury cathedral (from the southwest) (spire ca. 1320–30)

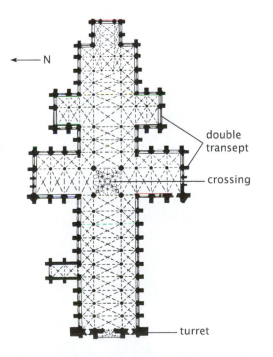

12.50 Plan of Salisbury cathedral, England. 1220–65

12.51 Nave of Salisbury cathedral

GLOUCESTER CATHEDRAL The change in the English Gothic becomes very clear if we compare the interior of Salisbury with the choir of Gloucester cathedral, built in the second quarter of the fourteenth century (fig. **12.52**). Gloucester is an outstanding example of English Late Gothic, also called the **Perpendicular Gothic style**. The name certainly fits, since we now find a dominant vertical accent that was absent in the English Early Gothic style. Vertical continuity is most evident at Gloucester in the responds that run in an unbroken line from the floor to the vault. In this respect, Perpendicular Gothic is much closer to French sources, but it includes so many uniquely English features that it would look out of place on the Continent. The repetition of small uniform tracery panels recalls the bands of statuary on the west façade at Salisbury (see fig. 12.49). The square end repeats the apses of earlier English churches, and the upward curve of the vault is as steep as in the nave of Salisbury (see fig. 12.51).

The ribs of the vaults, on the other hand, have taken on a new role. They have been multiplied until they form an ornamental network that screens the boundaries between the bays, with the result that the entire vault looks like one continuous surface. The ceiling reads as a canopy fluttering above the interior. This effect, in turn, emphasizes the unity of the interior space. Such elaboration of the classic four-part vault is characteristic of Flamboyant style on the Continent as well (see pages 422–23), but the English started it earlier and carried it much further.

WESTMINSTER HALL The Perpendicular Gothic vaults of Gloucester and the taste for ornate and decorative forms that they represent have a parallel in wooden construction in England. Wood is obviously more fragile than stone and, given the prevalence of fires during the Middle Ages, few monumental wooden structures survive. The timber roof of Westminster Hall in London (fig. **12.53**) is exceptional. The oak ceiling covers what was the great hall of the principal London residence of English monarchs during the Middle Ages; most of the palace was destroyed by fire in 1834 and on the site the Houses of Parliament, still officially referred to as the Palace of Westminster, was subsequently built.

12.52   Choir of Gloucester cathedral, England. 1332–57

12.53 Henry Yevele and Hugh Herland. Interior and wooden roof of Westminster Hall, London. 1390s

Westminster Hall, originally constructed in 1097 in the Norman Romanesque style, contained a central space flanked by side aisles marked with wooden posts. When the current roof was added between 1395 and 1396 by the master mason Henry Yevele and the master carpenter Hugh Herland, the old posts were removed so that the vast space, more than 235 feet long, 67 feet wide, and 90 feet high, is roofed without floor supports, covering a space half as large again as any hall previously built in England. Major structural elements are found in the hammer beams, which stick out horizontally from the wall and are carved with flying angels, and the arches that are supported on stone brackets decorated with heraldic designs. As is true with vaulted Gothic buildings (see fig. 12.13), each design constituent of the roof supports additional elements in a complex and intricate system based on interdependence, so that, for example, the hammer beams resist horizontal thrust while the arches channel vertical force to the masonry walls. The weight of the roof is indeed considerable, calculated at approximately 660 tons. The walls, belonging to the original Romanesque building, were reinforced on the exterior with flying buttresses at the time the timber ceiling was added. Admittedly, some of the elements, such as the profusion of Perpendicular tracery, serve more of a decorative than a structural function, but they too relate to the development in the fourteenth century of large, heavily decorated, stone-vaulted spaces free of interior supports (see fig. 12.52); as with those buildings, the integration of engineering and aesthetics at Westminster Hall is a remarkable achievement. Secular and religious buildings thus express similar aesthetic aims.

12.54 Chapel of Henry VII, Westminster Abbey, London. 1503–19

CHAPEL OF HENRY VII The Perpendicular Gothic style reaches its climax in the amazing hanging vault of Henry VII's Chapel at Westminster Abbey, built in the early years of the sixteenth century (fig. **12.54**). With its lanternlike knobs hanging from conical "fans," this chapel merges ribs and tracery patterns in a dazzling display of architectural pageantry. The complex vault patterns are unrelated to the structure of either the walls or the vaults themselves. Like the decorative features of Saint-Maclou in Rouen (see fig. 12.44), elaborate motifs obscure rather than clarify the architecture.

QUEEN MARY PSALTER As with Gothic architecture in England, manuscript illumination also shows an ambiguous relationship to French models. Some features are remarkably akin to those in French works, while others seem more concerned with continuing traditional English forms and manner of representation. The *Queen Mary Psalter* (fig. **12.55**) contains about 1,000 separate images, including biblical scenes, illustrations of saints' lives, and hunting scenes. The folio illustrating *Jesus Teaching in the Temple* combines two types of painting, which appear throughout the manuscript. The main scene is a full-color illumination, with a

The bas-de-page represents an elegant equestrian couple out hawking. A female attendant on horseback and a boy servant on foot accompany them. The lively scene, taken from the daily life of the nobility, is filled with naturalistic details, from the con attacking a duck at the lower left, to the way the male rider engages his female companion, both of them pointing at the hunt scene in front of them. Their forward movement is propelled by the active, wavelike lines of the horses' manes and the servant's gestures. In the main scene, line also conveys meaning with sensitivity and precision. The soft lines of hair and cloth that frame the face of the Virgin Mary contrast strongly with the sharply curved lines of the hair and beards of the Jews gathered in the Temple to hear her son teach.

The iconographic connection between the vignette in the bottom margin and the biblical scene is not clear. What *is* clear is that scenes from the courtly world are interwoven, or at least coexist, with biblical history, as they did in French manuscripts of the same period. In the English manuscript, however, the marginal illustrations are serial; they continue from one page to the next, just as the cycle of biblical events does. It is not known for whom this manuscript was made, although there is general agreement that it must have been produced between about 1310 and 1320 and, given its splendor, must have been a royal commission. The most convincing theory posits that King Edward II (r. 1307–1327) commissioned the book for his queen, Isabella of France. The name by which the manuscript is known today results from the fact that it was given to Queen Mary Tudor in the sixteenth century.

Germany

In Germany, Gothic architecture took root a good deal more slowly than in England. Until the mid-thirteenth century, the Romanesque tradition, with its persistent Ottonian elements, remained dominant, despite the growing acceptance of Early Gothic features. From about 1250 on, however, the High Gothic of the Île-de-France had a strong impact on the Rhineland. Cologne cathedral (begun in 1248) is an ambitious attempt to carry the full-fledged French system beyond the stage of Amiens. However, it was not completed until modern times. Nor were any others like it ever built. While some German sculptors relied on French models, others pursued a more independent course, unlike German architects. German Gothic sculptures are sometimes dramatic, sometimes poignant, and sometimes lifelike, but they always express deep, if sometimes restrained, emotion.

HEILIGENKREUZ IN SCHWÄBISH-GMÜND Especially characteristic of German Gothic is the hall church, or **Hallenkirche**. This type of church, with aisles and nave of the same height, stems from Romanesque architecture (see fig. 11.23). Although also found in France, it was in Germany that its possibilities were explored fully. Heiligenkreuz (Holy Cross) i Schwäbish-Gmünd (fig. **12.56**) is one of many examples from central Germany. Heinrich Parler the Elder began Heiligenkreuz

12.55 *Jesus Teaching in the Temple* and *Hunting Scene*, from the *Queen Mary Psalter*. ca. 1310–20. Ink, tempera, and gold leaf on vellum, 7 × 4½″ (17.9 × 11.5 cm). The British Library, London. By permission of the British Library

decorative gold background and an architectural framework, while the bas-de-page is a tinted drawing. Despite the differences in technique, both scenes (and all the others in the manuscript) were created by a single artist, a remarkable achievement, particularly since this artist produced at least two other fully decorated books. Although scholars have suggested a general reliance on a French manner in the arrangement of the scenes, in the graceful, courtly sway of the figure, and in the inclusion of bas-de-page illustrations, the style of painting is more closely related to older English models. It is almost purely linear and there is very little evidence of shading.

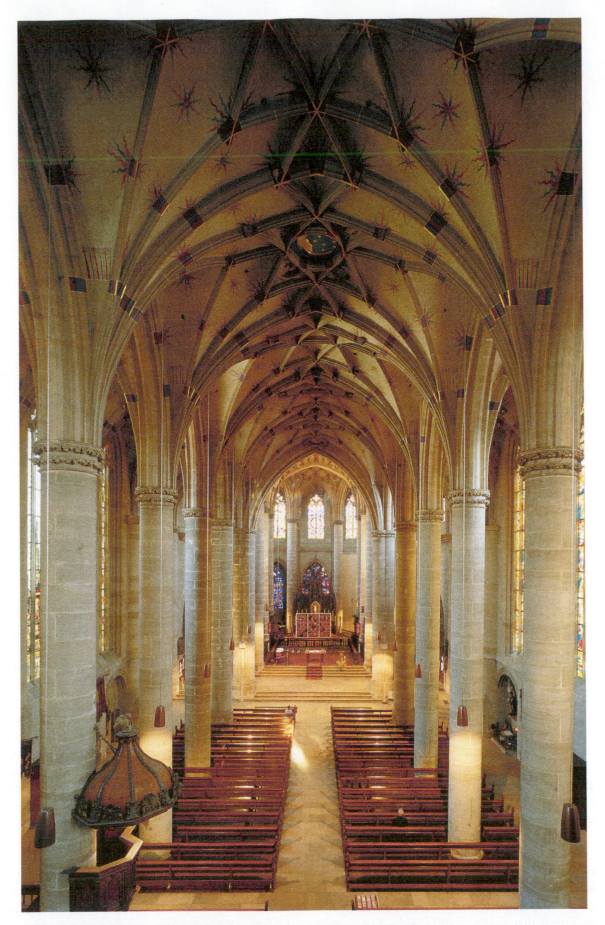

12.56 Heinrich Parler the Elder and Peter Parler (?). Nave and choir of Heiligenkreuz,
Schwäbish-Gmünd, Germany. Begun 1317

12.57 Naumburg Master. *Crucifixion*, on the choir screen, and the *Virgin* and *John the Evangelist*, Naumburg cathedral, Germany. ca. 1255. Stone

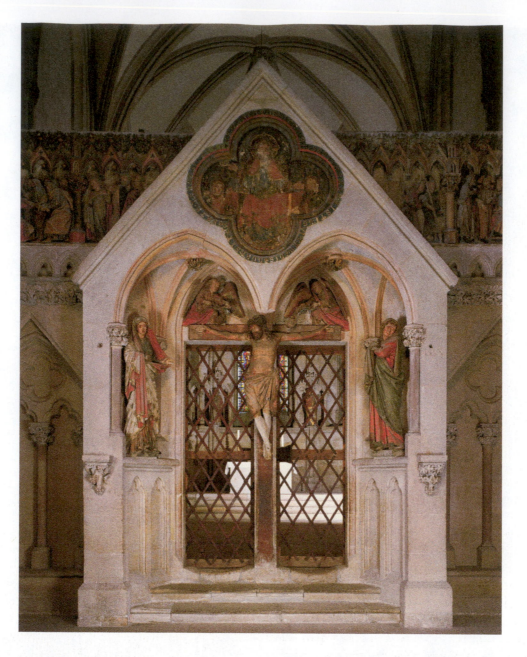

in 1317, although it was perhaps his son Peter who was responsible for the enlarged choir of 1351. (Heinrich had at least two other sons, two grandsons, and a great-grandson who were also architects.) The space has a fluidity and expansiveness that enfolds us as if we were standing under a huge canopy, reminiscent of the effect at Gloucester cathedral (see fig. 12.52). There is no clear sense of direction to guide us. And the unbroken lines of the pillars, formed by bundles of shafts that diverge as they turn into lacy ribs covering the vaults, seem to echo the continuous movement that we feel in the space itself.

NAUMBURG CATHEDRAL The growth of Gothic sculpture in Germany can be easily traced. From the 1220s on, German masters who had been trained in the sculpture workshops of the French cathedrals brought the new style back home. Because German architecture at that time was still mainly Romanesque, however, large statuary cycles like those at Chartres and Reims

were not produced on façades, where they would have looked out of place. As a result, German Gothic sculpture tended to be less closely linked with its architectural setting. In fact, the finest work was often done for the interiors of churches.

This independence permitted a greater expressive freedom than in France. It is strikingly evident in the work of the Naumburg Master, whose best-known work is the series of statues and reliefs made around 1255 for Naumburg cathedral. The *Crucifixion* (fig. 12.57) forms the center of the choir screen; flanking it are statues of the Virgin and John the Evangelist. Enclosed by a deep, gabled porch, the three figures frame the opening that links the nave with the sanctuary. Rather than placing the group above the screen, as was usual, the sculptor brought the subject down to earth physically and emotionally. The suffering of Jesus thus becomes a human reality through the emphasis on the weight and volume of his body. Mary and John, pleading with the viewer, convey their grief more eloquently than ever before.

12.58 Naumburg Master. *The Kiss of Judas*, on the choir screen, Naumburg cathedral. ca. 1255. Stone

The pathos of these figures is heroic and dramatic compared with the quiet lyricism of the Reims *Visitation* (see fig. 12.28). If the classical High Gothic sculpture of France can be compared with the calm restraint of Pheidias (see fig. 5.43), the Naumburg Master embodies the temperamental counterpart of the strained physicality demonstrated in Hellenistic art (see fig. 5.71).

The same intensity dominates the Passion scenes, such as *The Kiss of Judas* (fig. 12.58), with its strong contrast between the meekness of Jesus and the violence of the sword-wielding St. Peter. Attached to the responds inside the choir are life-size statues of 12 nobles associated with the founding of the eleventh-century cathedral. The sculptures were made at a time when Bishop Dietrich II of Naumburg was attempting to raise funds to build a new choir for the cathedral. By highlighting the original building's generous benefactors, the bishop encouraged parishioners to support the new building campaign, to join the ranks of the cathedral's munificent sponsors. These men and women were not of the artist's own time—to him they were only names in a chronicle. Yet the pair *Ekkehard and Uta* (fig. 12.59) are as individual and realistic as if they had been portrayed from life. The gestures of their hands, the handling of their drapery, and their fixed gazes communicate human qualities with great subtlety. Their individuality and specificity remind us that the concern for the personal identity of individuals signaled important social

12.59 *Ekkehard and Uta*, Naumburg cathedral. ca. 1249–55. Stone

changes during the Gothic period. The trend toward realism is not unique here and is reminiscent of what occurred at Reims cathedral (see figs. 12.28 and 12.29). The inclusion of historical figures within a sacred space is unusual, and it is perhaps the fact that the persons represented were long dead that made them appropriate for representation here.

The paint that is still visible on Naumburg's interior sculpture helps us appreciate how Gothic sculpture might have looked originally. Gothic interiors, as can be seen in the restored Sainte-Chapelle, were elaborately painted. Exterior sculpture was also painted, but that paint rarely survives today.

ROETTGEN PIETÀ Gothic sculpture, as we have come to know it so far, reflects a desire to give a greater emotional appeal to traditional themes of Christian art. Toward the end of the thirteenth century, this tendency gave rise to a new kind of religious image. (See www.myartslab.com.) Originally designed for private devotion, it is often referred to by the German term **Andachtsbild** (contemplation image), since Germany played the leading part in its development. The most widespread type was a representation of the Virgin grieving over the dead Christ. It is called a **Pietà** after an Italian word derived from the Latin *pietas*, the root word for both "pity" and "piety." No such scene occurs in the scriptural accounts of the Passion. We do not know where or when the Pietà was invented, but it portrays one of the Seven Sorrows of the Virgin. It thus forms a tragic counterpart to the motif of the Madonna and Child, one of her Seven Joys.

The *Roettgen Pietà* (fig. 12.60) is carved of wood and vividly painted. Like most such groups, this large cult statue was meant to be placed on an altar. The style, like the subject, expresses the emotional fervor of lay religiosity, which emphasized a personal relationship with God as part of the tide of mysticism that swept over fourteenth-century Europe. Realism here is purely a means to enhance the work's impact. The faces convey unbearable pain and grief; the wounds are exaggerated grotesquely; and the bodies and limbs are puppetlike in their thinness and rigidity. The purpose of the work is clearly to arouse so overwhelming a sense of horror and pity that the faithful will share in Christ's suffering and identify with the grief-stricken Mother of God. The ultimate goal of this emotional bond is a spiritual transformation that grasps the central mystery of God in human form through compassion (meaning "to suffer with").

At first glance, the *Roettgen Pietà* would seem to have little in common with the *Virgin of Paris* (see fig. 12.42), which dates from the same period. Yet they share a lean, "deflated" quality of form and exert a strong emotional appeal to a viewer. Both features characterize the art of northern Europe from the late thirteenth to the mid-fourteenth century. Only after 1350 do we again find an interest in weight and volume, coupled with a renewed desire to explore tangible reality as part of a change in religious outlook.

12.60 *Roettgen Pietà*. Early 14th century. Wood, height 34½″ (87.5 cm). Rheinisches Landesmuseum, Bonn

The growing concern for the individual that is expressed in much of the Gothic art we have studied so far develops most fully in Italy and becomes the central focus of Gothic experiments there. Indeed, the Gothic achievements in Italy are of such consequence in their own right and for the later development of Western art that they have been assigned their own chapter in this book, which follows.

1137 Rebuilding of abbey church of Saint-Denis begun

1163 Cathedral of Notre-Dame at Paris begun

1230–65 *Annunciation* and *Visitation*, cathedral of Notre-Dame at Reims

1241–48 Sainte-Chapelle in Paris

ca. 1255 Naumburg cathedral sculptures

1324–28 *Hours of Jeanne d'Evreux*

1503–19 Chapel of Henry VII, Westminster Abbey in London

1434–90 Saint-Maclou in Rouen designed

Gothic Art

1100

◄ 1122 Suger becomes Abbott of Saint-Denis

ca. 1139–47 Abbey church at Fontenay

1150   ca. 1150 *Winchester Psalter*

◄ 1180–1223 Reign of French king Philip August

◄ 1194 Fire destroys much of cathedral of Notre-Dame at Chartres

1200

◄ 1230 King Ferdinand III unites kingdoms of León and Castile

1250   ◄ 1252 Thomas Aquinas begins teaching in Paris

◄ 1270 Death of French king Louis IX (St. Louis)

1300

◄ 1332–57 Choir of Gloucester cathedral.
◄ 1337–1453 Hundred Years' War between England and France
◄ 1339 Virgin of Jeanned'Évreux given to Saint-Denis.
1350   ◄ 1350–55 Guillaume de Machaut's Le Dit de Lion.
ca. 1354–61 Complex of Sultan Husan in Cairo

ca. mid-14th century Court of the Lions, Alhambra in Granada

◄ 1395–96 Westminster Hall roofed

1400

◄ 1434–90 Saint-Maclou in Rouen

1450

1500   ◄ 1503–19 Chapel of Henry VII in Westminster Abbey

CHAPTER 13

Art in Thirteenth- and Fourteenth-Century Italy

THE MAP OF THE ITALIAN PENINSULA (MAP 13.1) HINTS AT THE forces that shaped life and art there in the thirteenth and fourteenth centuries. Although the Alps separate the peninsula from the rest of Europe, branches of the Mediterranean Sea surround it, providing access by water to the rest of the world. As the heart of the Roman Empire, the

peninsula abounded in the physical remains of Rome. Italy was also the center of the Catholic Church for much of the Middle Ages, bringing church officials and ambassadors from Europe to its cities. The culture formed by this geography was distinctive and cosmopolitan.

The length of the coastline encouraged trade by sea, while Italy's location made it a natural link between Europe and Africa and Asia. Coastal cities, such as Pisa, Genoa and Venice, controlled these important trade routes. Italian vessels carried goods from as far away as Constantinople and the Baltics to its cities. Merchants traveled over land, too, even reaching the court of the Great Khan in China.

This geography had profound effects on Italian society. In the absence of a strong central authority, the cities controlled the regions around them, so that there was no single political unit called Italy. Unlike many other parts of Europe, political power lay not in the hands of the hereditary aristocracy, but in the hands of urban elites. Monarchs controlled only a few regions: Lombardy in the north and Naples in the south. Instead, the wealthiest and most influential cities, including Florence and Siena, were organized as representative republics, with political offices held by mercantile oligarchs. As a check on inherited

power, some cities even excluded the landed aristocracy from participating in their political processes.

The larger powers of Europe, especially the two international institutions of the Holy Roman Empire and the papacy, often interfered in Italian politics, though sometimes from a distance. The emperors usually remained north of the Alps, though they claimed to control portions of Italy. The papacy left Italy for southern France in the fourteenth century, underscoring the power and influence of the French king. The prestige of the French monarchy enhanced the appeal of the **Gothic** style of building born near Paris and its related pictorial innovations, which artists in Italy adapted to their traditions.

The context in which Italian artists developed their skills differed from the rest of Europe. Throughout the Middle Ages, Roman and Early Christian art served as an inspiration for Italian architects and sculptors, as is visible in such works as the **cathedral** of Pisa (see fig. 11.33). In the mid-thirteenth century, the Holy Roman emperor Frederick II (1194–1250), who lived for a time in southern Italy, deliberately revived imperial Roman style to express his own political ambitions as heir to the Roman Empire. The other empire, Byzantium, kept a presence throughout Italy, too—through mosaics at Ravenna, Sicily, and Venice, and through the circulation of artists and **icons** such as the *Madonna Enthroned* (see fig. 8.49). A further element added to the vocabulary of Italian artists was the French Gothic style, created in the Paris region and introduced through the travels of artists and patrons.

Detail of figure 13.18, the Last Judgment, Giotto, showing Enrico Scrovegni Offering the Chapel. Interior of Arena (Scrovegni) Chapel, Padua.

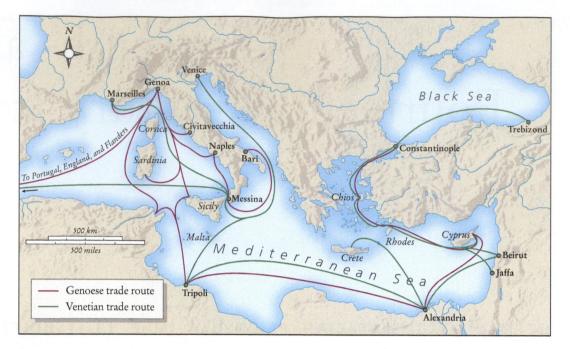

Map 13.1   The Italian Peninsula's key sea trade-routes

One of those travelers, the poet churchman, and scholar Francesco Petrarch, exemplifies another aspect of fourteenth-century Italian culture: a growing interest in the creative works of individuals. Petrarch and his contemporaries Dante Alighieri and Giovanni Boccaccio belong to a generation of thinkers and writers who turned to the study of ancient works of literature, history, and art to seek out beautiful and correct forms. Petrarch also sought to improve the quality of written Latin, and thereby to emulate the works of the Roman authors Vergil and Cicero. This study of ancient thought and art led to a search for moral clarity and models of behavior, a mode of inquiry that came to be known as **humanism**. Humanists valued the works of the ancients, both in the literary and the visual arts, and they looked to the classical past for solutions to modern problems. They particularly admired Roman writers who championed civic and personal virtues, such as service to the state and stoicism in times of trouble. Humanists considered Roman forms the most authoritative and, therefore, the most worthy of imitation, though Greek texts and ideas were also admired.

The study of the art of Rome and Greece would profoundly change the culture and the art of Europe by encouraging artists to look at nature carefully and to consider the human experience as a valid subject for art. These trends found encouragement in the ideals and theology of late medieval groups, such as the Dominicans, who valued classical learning, and the Franciscans, whose founder saw God in the beauty of nature. These bodies, called mendicants because they originally supported themselves from alms, became an important stimulus to thirteenth- and fourteenth-century patronage.

THE GROWTH OF THE MENDICANT ORDERS AND THE VISUAL ARTS IN ITALY

The two major mendicant groups were the Franciscans and the Dominicans. They established international "orders," as many monastic groups had done in the Middle Ages, although their missions differed from those of traditional monks. Both orders were founded to minister to the lay populations in the rapidly expanding cities; they did not retreat from the world, but engaged with it. Each order of friars (brothers) built churches in the cities so that sermons could be preached to crowds of people. The Dominicans, founded by Dominic de Guzmán in 1216, were especially concerned with combating heresy. The Franciscan order, founded by Francis of Assisi in 1209, worked in the cities to bring deeper spirituality and comfort to the poor. Taking vows of poverty, Franciscans were committed to teaching the laity and to encouraging them to pursue spiritual growth. Toward this goal, they told stories and used images to explain and affirm the teachings of the Church. Characteristically, Franciscans urged the faithful to visualize events such as the Nativity in tangible ways, including setting up Nativity scenes (crèches) in churches as an aid to devotion. Both orders played important roles in late medieval religious and artistic life, though the Franciscans held a special place in Italy since their founder was a native son.

The Franciscans at Assisi and Florence

The charismatic Francis died in 1226 and was named a saint two years later. His home town and burial place was the site

13.1 Interior of Upper Church, Basilica of San Francesco, Assisi. Begun 1228; consecrated 1253

of a huge church built in his honor. The pope sponsored its construction, which began shortly after Francis's canonization in 1228; the church was consecrated in 1253. Because it held the body of the popular saint, it was built as a large, multistoried structure in order to accommodate the numerous pilgrims it attracted. Most pilgrims would first encounter the large hall of the Upper Church, before descending to a church below. The Upper Church (fig. **13.1**) consists of a single long **nave**, or central hall, where crowds could gather. Whereas French churches of the same period reduced wall surfaces in their naves in favor of large stained-glass windows and complex vertical supports, as is the case at Chartres (see fig. 12.12), San Francesco at Assisi has relatively small windows and large expanses of wall surface. As in the northern churches, at San Francesco a brick **vault**, supported by Gothic pointed **arches**, covers the nave. Yet San Francesco is neither as high nor as spatially complex as French Gothic churches. The elimination of lower side **aisles** along the length of the nave simplifies the space and makes the walls more prominent. These wall surfaces became a magnet for artists, especially below the windows in the nave of the Upper Church. Their paintings were executed in the fresco technique,

which Italian artists had used throughout the Middle Ages. (See *Materials and Techniques*, page 441.)

The scale of the painting program at Assisi required teams of artists drawn from all over Italy and the work took many years to complete. From the 1270s through the early fourteenth century, papal sponsorship brought together artists from Rome, Siena, Florence, and elsewhere. Assisi became a laboratory for the development and dissemination of fourteenth-century Italian art. The frescoes flanking the nave windows depict biblical scenes from the book of Genesis and the life of Christ. But the most visible frescoes in the nave were painted below the windows; these depict the life and achievements of Francis himself.

The artists responsible for the St. Francis cycle had to devise images that conveyed both the events of Francis's life and their significance to Christian history. The events chosen for depiction came from biographies of Francis's life composed by his followers. One important theme found in these texts is the saint's veneration of nature as a manifestation of divine workmanship. The scene *St. Francis Preaching to the Birds* (fig. **13.2**) expresses this theme and Francis's attitude that all creatures are connected. The fresco depicts Francis in his brown habit standing in a landscape

13.2 Anonymous. *St. Francis Preaching to the Birds*, from Basilica of San Francesco, Assisi. Begun 1290 (?). Fresco

and speaking to a flock of birds. To the astonished eyes of his companion, Francis appears to be able to communicate with the birds, who gather at his feet to listen.

The artist sets the scene outdoors by framing the figures with trees and painting the background blue. A narrow shelf of earth creates a platform on which the bulky figures stand. Francis and his companion are rendered naturalistically, as the artist describes light washing over their forms to suggest their mass and weight. Francis's figure becomes the focal point of the image, through his central position, the halo around his head, and his downward glance. His body language—the bent-over stance, the movement of his hands—express his intense engagement with the birds as representatives of nature. The simplicity of the composition makes the fresco easily legible and memorable.

The identities of the artists responsible for the frescoes in the nave of San Francesco are uncertain and controversial. One of the artists mentioned as a primary designer and painter is the Roman Pietro Cavallini; another is the Florentine Giotto di Bondone. But

documentary evidence is lacking, and the opinions of connoisseurs vary. Some prefer to assign these frescoes to an anonymous master, or masters, named either after the paintings at Assisi or subgroups among them. Since many painters worked in the same space, they competed with and influenced each other, thus affecting the future direction of Italian art.

Franciscan women served God within the walls of their convents, through their vocations as nuns, and their prayers for their neighbors. Like the friars, these women devoted themselves to poverty and simplicity, and their convents and churches were often less wealthy than many of the masculine institutions. Franciscan nuns belonged to the branch of the order founded by Francis's associate, St. Clare, who was canonized in 1255. The thirteenth-

13.3 *Altarpiece of St. Clare*. ca. 1280. Tempera on panel, 9 × 5′6″ (2.73 × 1.65 m). Convent of Santa Chiara, Assisi

Fresco Painting and Conservation

Fresco is a technique for applying paint to walls that results in an image that is both durable and brilliant. Frescoed surfaces are built up in layers: Over the rough wall goes a layer of rough lime-based plaster called *arriccio*. The artist then draws preliminary sketches onto this layer of plaster. Because they are done in red, these sketches are called *sinopie* (an Italian word derived from ancient Sinope, in Asia Minor, which was famous as a source of red-colored pigment). Then a finer plaster called *intonaco* is applied in areas just large enough to provide for a day's worth of painting—the *giornata* (from *giorno*, the Italian word for "day"). While the plaster is still wet, the artist applies pigments suspended in lime water. As the plaster dries, the pigments bind to it, creating a *buon fresco*, or "true fresco." Plaster dries in a day, which is why only the amount of wet plaster that can be painted during that time can be applied. The work has to be done on a scaffold, so it is carried out from top to bottom, usually in horizontal strips about 4 to 6 feet long. As each horizontal level is completed, the scaffolding is lowered for the next level. To prevent chemical interactions with the lime of the plaster, some colors have to be applied *a secco* or dry; many details of images are applied this way as well. *Fresco secco* does not bond to the plaster as surely as *buon fresco* does, so it tends to flake off over time. Consequently, some frescoes have subsequently been touched up with tempera paints.

Although durability is the key reason for painting in fresco, over the centuries wars and floods have caused damage. Modern conservators have developed techniques for removing frescoes from walls and installing them elsewhere. After the Arno River flooded in 1966, many Florentine frescoes were rescued in this way, not only preserving the artworks but greatly adding to the knowledge and technology required for this task. When a fresco is removed, series of cuts are made around the image. Then, a supporting canvaslike material is applied to the frescoed surface with a water-soluble glue. The surface to which the canvaslike material has been glued can then be pulled off gently and transferred to a new support to be hung elsewhere, after which the canvas can be removed. Such removals

have exposed many *sinopie*, such as the one shown here. The fresco, attributed to Francesco Traini (see fig. 13.30), was badly damaged by fire in 1944 and had to be detached from the wall in order to save what was left of it. This procedure revealed the plaster underneath, on which the composition had been sketched out. These drawings, of the same size as the fresco itself, are much freer-looking in style than the actual fresco. They often reveal the artist's personal style more directly than the painted version, which was carried out with the aid of assistants.

Anonymous (Francesco Traini?). Sinopia drawing for *The Triumph of Death* (detail). Camposanto, Pisa

century convent in Assisi dedicated to St. Clare does not boast a large fresco cycle but preserves a painted panel (fig. **13.3**) intended to sit on an **altar** (an **altarpiece**). A tall rectangle of wood covered with egg-based **tempera** paints, it was executed around 1280. It is dominated by the figure of St. Clare, dressed in the habit of her order, standing frontally and holding the staff of an abbess. The image does not portray her specific features as a portrait would, but represents her as a saintly figure of authority, whose large staring eyes and frontal posture have roots in Byzantine art. Alongside the saint eight tiny narratives convey stories about her life, death, and miracles. These **vignettes** relate her commitment her vocation, her obedience to Francis and the Church, and her vice to her fellow nuns. The narratives make little pretense at three-dimensional form or spatial structure, keeping the focus on the figures and their actions the better to tell the story.

Churches and Their Furnishings in Urban Centers

Franciscan churches began to appear all over Italy as the friars ministered to the spiritual lives of city dwellers. A characteristic example in Florence is the church of Santa Croce (Holy Cross), begun around 1295 (figs. **13.4** and **13.5**). The architect was probably the Tuscan sculptor Arnolfo di Cambio. Like San Francesco in Assisi, Santa Croce shares some features with Gothic churches in northern Europe, but it differs from them too. Its form is a **basilica** (a standard church plan including nave, side aisles, and apse), though the eastern end, where the high altar and many chapels are located, terminates in mostly rectilinear forms. Only the **apse** (or projecting niche), where the altar stands, is polygonal. This simplified design for the most sacred spaces in the

13.4 Arnolfo di Cambio (?).
Nave and choir of Santa Croce,
Florence. Begun ca. 1295

13.5 Plan of Santa Croce

church probably comes from monastic churches, especially of the reform-minded Cistercian order; for example, the plan of Fontenay Abbey (see fig. 11.21). The nave's proportions are broad and expansive rather than vertical. The nave **arcade** uses a Gothic pointed arch, while vertical moldings pull the eye up to the ceiling. Where in a French Gothic church, however, such moldings would support a vaulted ceiling, at Santa Croce wooden **trusses** (beams or rafters joined together) span the nave. The only vaults are at the apse and several chapels at the ends of the **transept**, the perpendicular space between the nave and the apse.

As the stone vaults of San Francesco in Assisi, the order's mother church, indicate that the friars were not averse to such structures, the choice of a wooden roof at Santa Croce may need explanation. This preference perhaps originates in a Tuscan tradition, as the great **Romanesque** cathedral of nearby Pisa (fig. 11.34) also has a wooden roof. Santa Croce's broad nave with high arches is also reminiscent of Early Christian churches (see fig. 8.9), so the choice may also spring from a desire to evoke

the simplicity of Early Christian basilicas and thus link Franciscan poverty with the traditions of the early Church. A vaulted nave would have been much more expensive.

Santa Croce served the growing population of Florence by providing room for elite burials in its aisles and chapels. The church's wide spaces also held large crowds so they could hear the friars' sermons.

Pulpits in Pisan Churches

For reading Scripture at services and for preaching, churchmen often commissioned monumental pulpits with narrative or symbolic images carved onto them. Several monumental pulpits were made by members of a family of sculptors who worked in Pisa, including Nicola Pisano (ca. 1220/25–1284) and his son Giovan Pisano (1265–1314). Though the two men worked at various sit throughout Italy, they executed important pulpits for the cathedral and baptistery at Pisa.

13.6 Nicola Pisano. Pulpit. 1259–60. Marble, height 15′ (4.6 m). Baptistery, Pisa

13.7 Nicola Pisano. *Fortitude*, detail of pulpit

For the Pisan baptistery, Nicola Pisano and his workshop carved a hexagonal marble pulpit finished around 1260 (fig. **13.6**). Rising to about 15 feet high, so the assembly could see and hear the speaker, the six sides of the pulpit rest on colored marble columns supporting classically inspired **capitals**. Above the capitals, carved into leaf shapes, small figures symbolizing the virtues stand between cusped arches, while figures of the prophets sit in the **spandrels** (the areas above the curves) of these arches. Surprisingly, one of these figures (fig. **13.7**) is a male nude with a lion cub on his shoulder and a lion skin over his arm. His form and the lion skin should identify him as the Greek hero Herakles (Hercules in Latin). Some scholars, however, have interpreted these same details to identify him as Daniel, the biblical hero whose faith allowed him to survive the lion's den. In either case, in the ogram of the pulpit, he stands for the Christian virtue of Forti-de. His anatomy, his proportions, and his stance are probably the product of Nicola Pisano's study of Roman and Early Christian sculpture. The figure's heroic nudity and his posture, with the

weight balanced on one leg to suggest movement, seem to be inspired by ancient models. Pisano had worked for Frederick II in southern Italy and at Rome, but his deep knowledge of ancient art may also derive from study of Roman artifacts in Pisa.

Nicola's study of the Roman past informs many other elements in his pulpit, including the narratives he carved for the six rectangular sides of the pulpit itself. These scenes from the life of Christ are carved in **relief**, so they project from the background. The Nativity scene in figure **13.8** is a densely crowded composition that combines the Annunciation with the Birth of Christ. The relief is treated as a shallow box filled with solid convex shapes in the manner of Roman **sarcophagi** (carved stone coffins), which Pisa's monumental cemetery preserved in good numbers. The Virgin has the dignity and bearing of a Roman matron. Pisano also knew Byzantine images of the Nativity, for the recumbent figure of the Virgin reflects that tradition. As the largest and most central figure, the reclining Virgin overpowers all the other elements in the composition. Around her, the details

13.9 Giovanni Pisano, *Nativity*, detail of pulpit. 1302–10. Marble. Pisa cathedral

of the narrative or setting, such as the midwives washing the child and Joseph's wondering gaze at the events, give the relief a human touch. Using forms inspired by both Byzantine and Roman models, Nicola uses broad figures, wrapped in **classicizing** draperies, to endow the scene with gravity and moral weight.

When his son Giovanni Pisano carved a pulpit about 50 years later for the cathedral of Pisa, he chose a different emphasis. Though executed at the same size and using the same material, his relief of the Nativity from the cathedral pulpit (fig. **13.9**) makes a strong contrast to his father's earlier work. Depicting the Nativity and the Annunciation to the shepherds, Giovanni dwells on the landscape and animal elements: Sheep and trees fill the right edge of the composition, while the Nativity itself takes place in a shallow cave in the Byzantine tradition. The Virgin still dominates the composition, but she is no longer a dignified matron staring out of the image. Instead, she is a young mother whose gaze and tender attention focus on her newborn child. Her proportions are elongated rather than sturdy. Rather than echoing Roman or Classical models, Giovanni has clearly studied contemporary French works to bring elegance and a detailed observation of nature to the image. Giovanni's swaying figures move more comfortably in the space they occupy. Where Nicola's *Nativity* is dominated by convex, bulging masses, Giovanni's appears to made up of cavities and shadows. The play of lights and darks Giovanni's relief exhibits a dynamic quality that contrasts with the serene calm of his father's work.

Expanding Florence Cathedral

The building and adornment of Pisa's cathedral complex were a [civ]ic as well as a religious duty for the town's citizens. As Italian [citi]es grew and prospered, their religious centers grew with them. East of Pisa, along the Arno River, the increasing wealth of Florence inspired that town to undertake major projects for its cathedral and baptistery in order to compete with its neighbors. One of Nicola Pisano's students, Arnolfo di Cambio (ca. 1245–1302), was chosen to design a new cathedral for Florence to replace a smaller church that stood on the site. The cathedral was begun in 1296 (figs. **13.10**, **13.11**, and **13.12**). The project took the skills and energy of several generations, and the plan was modified more than once. For example, in 1357 Francesco Talenti (active 1325–1369) took over the project and dramatically extended the building to the east. By 1367, a committee of artists consulted by the overseers of the construction decided to cover the eastern zone with a high **dome**. The west façade and other portals continued to be adorned with sculpture throughout the **Renaissance** period, but the marble cladding on the building was not completed until the nineteenth century. Florence's Duomo (dome) was intended to be a grand structure that would not only serve as the spiritual center of the city, but as a statement of its wealth and importance.

13.10 Florence cathedral and baptistery seen from the air. Cathedral begun 1296

13.12 Plan of Florence cathedral and campanile

Arnolfo's original design provided for a large basilica with a high arcade and broad proportions that differs sharply from contemporary Gothic structures in France, even as it employs some of the technology of French Gothic. High pointed arches in the nave arcade rest on **piers** (vertical supports) articulated with leaf-shaped capitals. Flat moldings rise to the **clerestory** level, above the arcade. Windows in the clerestory and aisles are relatively small, leaving much more wall surface than in French cathedrals. Although the original plan called for a trussed wooden roof like the one at Santa Croce, by the mid-fourteenth century the plan had been altered to include **ribbed groin vaults** (stone vaults comprised of four sections with reinforcing along their edges), a detail closer to the northern Gothic taste. The later plans enlarged the eastern zone to terminate in three faceted arms which meet to form an octagonal space (the **crossing**) that would be covered by a dome. (This design appears in the fresco in fig. 13.31.) While this

project included **flying buttresses** like French Gothic churches, these were never built. The scale of the proposed dome presented engineering difficulties that were not solved until the early f teenth century. Instead of tall western towers incorporated into the façade, which was the norm in Gothic France, the cathedral has a **campanile** (bell tower) as a separate structure in the Italian tradition. The campanile is the work of the Florentine painter Giotto and his successors. If Florence's cathedral has Gothic elements in its vaults and arches, these foreign forms are tempered by local traditions.

Opposite the cathedral's west front stands the venerable baptistery of Florence, built in the eleventh century on much older foundations, which the Florentines believed to be Roman; they saw the glory of their own past in the structure's age. St. John the Baptist is a patron saint of the city of Florence; newborns became citizens of Florence by being baptized in this structure. The baptistery was the site of important artistic projects throughout the Renaissance. In 1330, its overseers commissioned another sculptor from Pisa, Andrea Pisano (ca. 1295–1348; no relation to Nicola or Giovanni) to cast a new pair of bronze doors for the baptistery. These were finished and installed in 1336 (fig. **13.13**). Cast of bronze and gilded, the project required 28 separate panels across the two panels of the door. They mostly represent scenes from the life of John the Baptist. Each vignette is framed by a Gothic **quatrefoil**, such as those found on the exteriors of French cathedrals. Yet within most of the four-lobed frames, Andrea provides a projecting ledge to support the figures and the landscap or architectural backgrounds. The relief showing the Baptism of Christ demonstrates Andrea's clear compositional technique:

13.13 Andrea Pisano. South doors, baptistery of San Giovanni, Florence. 1330–36. Gilt bronze

13.14 Andrea Pisano, *The Baptism of Christ*, from the south doors, baptistery of San Giovanni, Florence. 1330–36. Gilt bronze

Christ stands at the center, framed by John on the right in the act of baptism and an angelic witness on the left (fig. **13.14**). The dove symbolizing the Holy Spirit appears above Christ's head. The emphasis is on the key figures, with little detail to distract from the main narrative; only a few small elements suggest the landscape context of the Jordan River. If the beautiful torso of Christ in the river recalls the Fortitude figure from Nicola Pisano's Pisa Baptistery, the simplicity of the landscape and composition recall the frescoes at Assisi.

Building for the City Government: The Palazzo della Signoria

While the citizens of Florence were building the huge cathedral, the political faction that supported the papacy instead of the Holy Roman Empire consolidated its power in the city. The pro-papal party (the Guelphs) was largely composed of wealthier merchants who sought to contain the dynastic ambitions of aristocratic families who supported the emperor (the Ghibellines). The pro-papal group commissioned a large structure to house their governing council and to serve as the symbol of the political independence of the city. They probably chose Arnolfo di Cambio to design the Palazzo della Signoria (fig. **13.15**). It was begun in 1298 and completed in 1310, though it has been subject to later expansion and remodeling. It became known as the Palazzo Vecchio (or old palace) during the sixteenth century, when the ruling Medici family moved to another palace.

Similar to fortified castles in the region, the Palazzo boasts thick stone walls, heavy **battlements** (defensive parapets), and a tall tower. Few windows pierce the walls of the lowest level, whose stones are left rough and uneven (or **rusticated**) to create the appearance of greater strength. The two upper stories display smoother masonry and more elegant pointed windows. The tower serves not only as a symbol of civic pride, but as a defensive structure. It sits slightly off-center for two reasons: This part of the building rests on the foundations of an earlier tower, and its position makes it visible from a main street in the city. Boasting the highest civic tower in the city, the Palazzo della Signoria dominated the skyline of Florence and expressed the power of the communal good over powerful individual families.

13.15 Palazzo della Signoria (Palazzo Vecchio), Florence. Begun 1298

PAINTING IN TUSCANY

As with other art forms in the thirteenth century, Italian paint-
's stylistic beginnings are different from those of the rest of
rope, although they shared traits and ideas. Italy's ties to the
Roman past and the Byzantine present would inspire Italian
painters to render forms in naturalistic and monumental images.
Throughout the Middle Ages, Byzantine mosaics and murals
were visible to Italian artists. Venice had long-standing trading
ties with the Byzantine Empire, while the crusades of the twelfth
and thirteenth centuries had brought Italy in even closer contact
with Byzantium, including the diversion of the Fourth Crusade
in 1204 to Constantinople itself.

One result of the short-lived occupation of Constantinople
by western Europeans, from 1204 to 1261, was an infusion of
Byzantine art forms and artists into Italy, which had a momentous effect on the development of Italian art in the thirteenth
century. Later observers of the rapid changes that occurred in
Italian painting from 1200 to 1550 described the starting point
of these changes as the "Greek manner," by which they meant
Byzantine art. Writing in the sixteenth century, the biographer
and artist Giorgio Vasari reported that in the mid-thirteenth
century, "Some Greek painters were summoned to Florence by
the government of the city for no other purpose than the revival
of painting in their midst, since that art was not so much debased
as altogether lost." Vasari assumes that medieval Italian painting
was all but nonexistent and attributes to Byzantine art great influ-
ce over the development of Italian art in the thirteenth century.
Italian artists were able to absorb the Byzantine tradition far more
thoroughly at this time than ever before. When Gothic style
from northern Europe began to influence artists working in this
Byzantinizing tradition, a revolutionary synthesis of the two was
accomplished by a generation of innovative and productive painters in Tuscan cities.

Cimabue and Giotto

One such artist was Cimabue of Florence (ca. 1250–after 1300),
whom Vasari claimed had been apprenticed to a Greek painter.
His presence has also been noted in Assisi, Rome, and Pisa. In
the 1280s, he painted a large panel depicting the Madonna
Enthroned (fig. **13.16**), or Madonna in Majesty (Maestà), to sit
on an altar in the church of Santa Trinità in Florence; the large
scale of the altarpiece—it is more than 12 feet high—made it the
devotional focus of the church. Its composition recalls Byzantine
icons, such as the *Madonna Enthroned* (see fig. 8.49), but its scale
and verticality are closer to the *Altarpiece of St. Clare* (fig. 13.3)
and similar thirteenth-century altarpieces than to Byzantine
prototypes. Mary and her son occupy a heavy golden throne,
flanked by rows of angels on either side. Hebrew Bible proph-
ts holding scrolls appear below, as if forming a foundation for
Mary's throne; the relationship between the Hebrew Bible and
the New Testament is an important theme in Christian art. The
Virgin's towering scale and the brilliant blue of her gown against

13.16   Cimabue, *Madonna Enthroned.* ca. 1280–90. Tempera on panel,
12′7½″ × 7′4″ (3.9 × 2.2 m). Galleria degli Uffizi, Florence

the gold-leaf background draw a viewer's eye to her; with her
gesture she emphasizes the presence of her son. Like Byzantine
painters, Cimabue uses linear gold elements to enhance her
dignity, but in his hands the network of gold lines follows the
line of her body instead of creating abstract patterns. The severe
design and solemn expression are appropriate to the monumental
scale of the painting.

Later artists in Renaissance Italy, such as Lorenzo Ghiberti
(see Chapter 15) and Giorgio Vasari (see Chapter 16) claimed
that Cimabue was the teacher of Giotto di Bondone (ca. 1267–
1336/37), one of the key figures in the history of art. If so,
Giotto may have learned from him the "Greek Manner" in which
Cimabue worked. Some scholars believe that Giotto also worked

13.17 Giotto, *Madonna Enthroned*. ca. 1310. Tempera on panel, 10′8″ × 6′8″ (3.3 × 2 m). Galleria degli Uffizi, Florence

at Assisi, while documents tell us that Giotto worked in Rome where examples of both ancient and Early Christian art were available for artists to study. Equally important, however, was the influence of the Pisani—Nicolo and Giovanni—with their blend of **classicism** and Gothic **naturalism** to express strong emotional content. (See figs. 13.8 and 13.9.)

We can see Giotto's relationship to, but difference from, Cimabue in a tall altarpiece showing the Madonna Enthroned, which he painted around 1310 for the church of All Saints (Ognissanti) in Florence (fig. **13.17**). Like Cimabue's Santa Trinità Madonna, Giotto depicts the Queen of Heaven and her son enthroned among holy figures against a gold background. The Virgin's deep blue robe and huge scale bring a viewer's eye directly to her and to the Christ Child in her lap. All the other figures gaze at them, both signaling and heightening their importance. Unlike Cimabue, Giotto models the figures in light, so that they appear to be solid, sculptural forms. Where Cimabue turns light into a network of golden lines, Giotto achieves a gradual

movement from light into dark, so that the figures appear to be three-dimensional forms.

The throne exhibits some features of contemporary Italian architecture, such as the high pointed arches, though Giotto ㅤ them to create a nichelike structure. This encloses the Mado⸺ on three sides, setting her apart from the gold background, and defines the space that she inhabits. Giotto further suggests space by placing angels kneeling before the throne and by the overlapping figures of saints, who seem to stand behind one another on a level surface. The throne's lavish ornamentation includes a feature that is especially interesting: the colored marble surfaces of the base and of the quatrefoil within the **gable**. Such illusionistic stone textures had been highly developed by ancient painters (see fig. 7.56), and their appearance here is evidence that Giotto was familiar with whatever ancient murals could still be seen in medieval Rome.

THE ARENA CHAPEL IN PADUA Giotto's innovative ideas about light and space were accompanied by a gift for storytelling. Although scholars are not certain that he was among the artists who painted the nave frescoes at Assisi, his fresco cycles share formal and narrative characteristics with those images

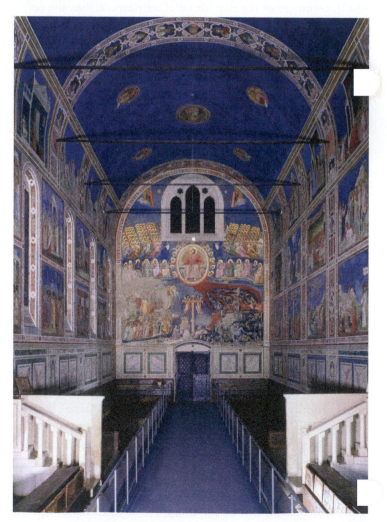

13.18 Interior of Arena (Scrovegni) Chapel, Padua. 1305–06

13.19   Giotto, *Christ Entering Jerusalem*, Arena (Scrovegni) Chapel, Padua. 1305–06. Fresco

(see fig. 13.2). Of Giotto's surviving murals, those in the Arena, or Scrovegni, Chapel in Padua, painted in 1305 and 1306, are wonderfully preserved and recently restored. It is known variously as the Arena Chapel because the site once housed a Roman arena, and the Scrovegni Chapel because it was built by Enrico Scrovegni, a Paduan banker, next to his palace, where he intended it to serve as his burial chapel. Dedicated to "Our Lady of Charity", the structure is a one-room hall covered with a **barrel vault** (fig. **13.18**).

Giotto and his assistants painted the whole chapel from floor to ceiling in the fresco technique. A blue field with gold stars symbolic of Heaven dominates the barrel vault, below which the walls are divided into three **registers** or horizontal rows. Each register contains rectangular fields for narrative °cenes °representing the lives of the Virgin and Christ. The nnunciation appears at the altar end of the room; this repre- sents the archangel Gabriel announcing to Mary that she has been chosen to bear the son of God. The theme commemorates

the Incarnation of Christ and marks the beginning of the plan of Salvation, according to Catholic belief. At the other end of the chapel, Giotto depicted the Last Judgment (the events predicted for the end of time). At the foot of the Last Judgment, Giotto has included the figure of the donor, Enrico Scrovegni, offer- ing his chapel to the Virgin and angels (see page 436). Along the length of the wall, the top register depicts stories of the early life of Mary and her parents; the center register focuses on sto- ries of Christ's life and miracles; and the lowest register depicts his Passion, Death, and Resurrection. Below the narratives, the walls resemble marble panels interspersed with reliefs, but everything is painted.

One scene in the middle register, *Christ Entering Jerusalem*, depicts the event commemorated by Christians on Palm Sun- day (fig. **13.19**). The Gospels report that the citizens welcomed Jesus with palm fronds and cheers as he entered Jerusalem riding a donkey; Christ's arrival on a humble mount fulfilled a Hebrew Bible prophecy. Giotto places the entire scene in the foreground of

13.20   Giotto, *The Lamentation*, Arena (Scrovegni) Chapel, Padua. 1305–06. Fresco

his image, which brings the events very close to a viewer. Further-more, Giotto gives his forms such a strong three-dimensional quality that they almost seem as solid as sculpture. The rounded forms create the illusion of space in which the actors exist.

Giotto deliberately leaves the setting spare for this event, except for the trees in which children climb and the city gate on the right. His large simple forms, strong grouping of figures, and the limited depth of his stage give his scenes a remarkable spatial coherence. The massed verticals of the block of apostles on the left contrast with the upward slope of the crowd welcoming Jesus on the right; but Jesus, alone in the center, bridges the gap between the two groups. His isolation and dignity, even as he rides the donkey toward the city where he will die, give the painting a solemn air.

Giotto's skill at perfectly matching composition and meaning may also be seen in the scenes on the lowest register, which focus on the Passion. A viewer gazing at these frescoes sees them straight on, so the painter organizes the scenes to exploit that relationship. One of the most memorable of these paintings depicts

the Lamentation, the moment of last farewell between Jesus and his mother and friends (fig. **13.20**). Although this event does not appear in the Gospels, by the end of the Middle Ages versions of this theme had appeared in both Byzantine and in Western medieval art.

The tragic mood of this Lamentation, found also in religious texts of the era, is created by the formal rhythm of the design as well as by the gestures and expressions of the participants. The low center of gravity and the hunched figures convey the somber quality of the scene, as do the cool colors and bare sky. With extraordinary boldness, Giotto sets off the frozen grief of the human mourners against the frantic movement of the weeping angels among the clouds. It is as if the figures on the ground are restrained by their obligation to maintain the stability of the composition, while the angels, small and weightless as birds, are able to move—and feel—freely.

Once again, the simple setting heightens the impact of th drama. The descending slope of the hill acts as a unifying element that directs attention toward the heads of Christ and the

Virgin, which are the focal point of the scene. Even the tree has a twin function. Its barrenness and isolation suggest that all of nature shares in the sorrow over Christ's death. Yet also carries a more precise symbolic message: It refers to the Tree of Knowledge, which the sin of Adam and Eve had caused to wither and which was to be restored to life through Christ's sacrificial death.

Giotto's frescoes in the Arena Chapel established his fame among his contemporaries. In the *Divine Comedy*, written around 1315, the great Italian poet Dante Alighieri mentions the rising reputation of the young Florentine: "Once Cimabue thought to hold the field as painter, Giotto now is all the rage, dimming the luster of the other's fame." (See www.myartslab.com.) Giotto continued to work in Florence for 30 years after completing the chapel frescoes, in 1334 being named the architect of Florence cathedral, for which he designed the campanile (see figs. 13.10 and 13.12). His influence over the next generation was inescapable and was felt by artists all over Italy.

Siena: Devotion to Mary in Works by Duccio and Simone

Giotto's slightly older contemporary Duccio di Buoninsegna of Siena (ca. 1255–before 1319) directed another busy and influential workshop in the neighboring Tuscan city of Siena. The city of Siena competed with Florence on a number of fronts—military, economic, and cultural—and fostered a distinct identity and visual tradition. Its wealth came from agriculture and trade. After a key military victory against Florence in 1260, Siena took the Virgin Mary as its protector and patron. The Sienese chose a representative form of government—a republic—directed by the *Nove* (the Nine), who were chosen from the elite merchants of the city. By the end of the thirteenth century, this government had taken up the project of building a town hall (fig. **13.21**), the Palazzo Pubblico, as an expression of their city's wealth and status.

Begun by 1298, the Palazzo Pubblico served not only to house the city government, but to frame a public space, the Piazza del

13.21   Palazzo Pubblico, Siena. Begun ca. 1298

Agnolo di Tura del Grasso

From his *Chronicle*

Duccio's Maestà *(see fig. 13.22) stood on the main altar of Siena cathedral until 1506, when it was removed to the transept. It was sawed apart in 1771, and some panels were acquired subsequently by museums in Europe and the United States. This local history of about 1350 describes the civic celebration that accompanied the installation of the altarpiece in 1311.*

These paintings [the *Maestà*] were executed by master Duccio, son of Nicolò, painter of Siena, the finest artist to be found anywhere at his time. He painted the altarpiece in the house of the Muciatti outside the gate toward Stalloreggi in the suburb of Laterino. On the 9th of June [1311], at midday, the Sienese carried the altarpiece in great devotion to the cathedral in a procession, which included Bishop Roger of Casole, the entire clergy of the cathedral,

all monks and nuns of the city, and the Nine Gentlemen [Nove] and officials of the city such as the podestà and the captain, and all the people. One by one the worthiest, with lighted candles in their hands, took their places near the altarpiece. Behind them came women children with great devotion. They accompanied the painting u the cathedral, walking in procession around the Campo, while all the bells rang joyfully. All the shops were closed out of devotion, all through Siena many alms were given to the poor with many speeches and prayers to God and to his Holy Mother, that she might help to preserve and increase the peace and well being of the city and its jurisdiction, as she was the advocate and protection of said city, and deliver it from all danger and wickedness directed against it. In this way the said altarpiece was taken into the cathedral and placed on the main altar. The altarpiece is painted on the back with scenes from the Old Testament and the Passion of Jesus Christ and in front with the Virgin Mary and her Son in her arms and many saints at the sides, the whole decorated with fine gold. The altarpiece cost 3000 gold florins.

Source: Teresa G. Frisch, *Gothic Art 1140–c 1450* (Englewood Cliffs, NJ: Prentice Hall, 1971)

Campo, where the city's economic, political, religious, and social life was played out. Both the timing and the character of the Palazzo Pubblico point to the city's rivalry with Florence, which was then building the Palazzo della Signoria. Built of brick and stone, Siena's Palazzo Pubblico rises to three stories and supports a tower, as does Florence's Palazzo. It also terminates in castlelike battlements at the roofline. But it has many more windows and other openings, and a more ornamental and elegant façade. The tower, not completed until the 1340s, is intentionally taller than that of the Palazzo della Signoria.

The city also concerned itself with adorning its cathedral, dedicated to the Virgin. For the high altar of the cathedral the directors of the cathedral works hired Duccio to paint a large altarpiece, called the *Maestà* as it depicts the Virgin and Child in Majesty (fig. **13.22**). Commissioned in 1308, the *Maestà* was installed in the cathedral in 1311 amidst processions and celebrations in the city. (See *Primary Source*, above, and *The Art Historian's Lens*, page 455.) Duccio's signature at the base of the throne expresses his pride in the work: "Holy Mother of God, be the cause of peace to Siena, and of life to Duccio because he has painted you thus."

Painted in tempera, Duccio's image measures approximately 7 by 13 feet without its architectural frame and many subsidiary elements. It takes the shape of a **polyptych**, or multipaneled work. The regal figures of the Virgin and Child in the *Maestà* sit on a complex throne draped in golden cloth. The Virgin is by far the largest and most impressive figure in this assembly, swathed in the rich blue reserved for her by contemporary practice. Surrounding her is a carefully balanced arrangement of saints and angels, each bearing a golden halo. In the front row kneel Siena's other patron saints, all gesturing and gazing at her. The Virgin may seem much like Cimabue's (see fig. 13.16) which Duccio probably knew, as both originated in the Greek manner. Duccio, however, relaxes the rigid, angular draperies of that tradition so that they give way to an undulating softness. The bodies,

faces, and hands of the many figures seem to swell with thre dimensional life as the painter explores the fall of light on th forms. Byzantine painting preserved aspects of ancient illusionism, which inspired Duccio to a profound degree. Nonetheless,

The Social Work of Images

The report of the celebrations held in Siena when Duccio's *Maestà* was installed in the city's cathedral attests to the importance of this painting for the entire community. It was a source of pride for the citizens of Siena, but also a powerful embodiment of the Virgin's protection of the city. Although modern audiences expect to find and react to works of art hanging in museums, art historians have demonstrated that art served different purposes in late medieval Europe. Few in the West today believe that a work of art can influence events or change lives. But in fourteenth-century Europe, people thought about images in much more active terms. Art could be a path to the sacred or a helper in times of trouble.

During a drought in 1354, for example, the city fathers of Florence paraded a miracle-working image of the Virgin from the village of Impruneta through the city in hopes of improving the weather. People with illness or health problems venerated a fresco of the Annunciation in the church of the Santissima Annunziata in Florence; they gave gifts to the image in hopes of respite from their problems. When the plague came to Florence, artists were commissioned to paint scenes depicting St. Sebastian and other saints who were considered protectors against this deadly disease.

Images were also called upon for help outside the sacred space of the church. Continuing a tradition begun in the fourteenth century, street corners in Italy are often adorned with images of the Virgin, to whom passersby may pray or show respect. Candles may be lit or gifts offered to such images in hopes of the Virgin's assistance. Art historians are also studying how works of art functioned among late medieval populations to forge bonds among social groups and encourage group identity. For example, outside the confines of monasteries, groups of citizens formed social organizations that were dedicated to a patron saint, whose image would be an important element of the group's identity.

13.22 Duccio, *Madonna Enthroned*, center of the *Maestà Altar*. 1308–11. Tempera on panel, height 6'10½" (2.1 m). Museo dell'Opera del Duomo, Siena

Duccio's work also reflects contemporary Gothic sensibilities in the fluidity of the drapery, the appealing naturalness of the figures, and the glances by which the figures communicate with each other. An important source of this Gothic influence was probably Giovanni Pisano, who worked in Siena from 1285 to 1295 as the sculptor-architect in charge of the cathedral façade. Some evidence hints that Duccio may have traveled to Paris, where he would have encountered French Gothic style directly.

13.23 Duccio, *Annunciation of the Death of the Virgin*, from the *Maestà Altar*. Museo dell'Opera del Duomo, Siena

In addition to the principal scene, the *Maestà* included on its front and back numerous small scenes from the lives of Christ and the Virgin. In these panels, Duccio's synthesis of Gothic and Byzantine elements exploits a new kind of picture space and, with it, a new treatment of narrative. The *Annunciation of the Death of the Virgin* (fig. **13.23**), which originally stood above the main image on the front of the altarpiece, represents two figures enclosed by an architectural interior; Duccio implies space for the figures to inhabit by representing walls and ceiling beams as receding into depth (called **foreshortening**). His architecture integrates the figures within the drama. In a parallel scene to the Annunciation (see fig. 13.25, for comparison), this panel depicts the archangel Gabriel returning to the mature Virgin to warn her of her impending death. The architecture places the two figures in the same uncluttered room, but enframes them separately. Despite sharing the space, each figure is isolated. Duccio's innovative use of architecture to enhance the narrative of his paintings inspired his younger French contemporary, Jean Pucelle, who adapted this composition for the *Annunciation* in the *Hours of Jeanne d'Evreux* (see fig. 12.39).

The architecture keeps its space-creating function even in the outdoor scenes on the back of the *Maestà*, such as in *Christ Entering Jerusalem* (fig. **13.24**), a theme that Giotto had treated only a few years before in Padua. Where Giotto places Christ at the center of two groups of people, Duccio places him closer to the apostles and on one side of the composition. He conveys the diagonal movement into depth not by the figures, who have the same scale throughout, but by the walls on either side of the road leading to the city, by the gate that frames the crowd welcoming Christ, and by the buildings in the background. Where Giotto reduces his treatment of the theme to a few figures and a bare backdrop, Duccio includes not only detailed architectural elements, some of which resemble contemporary Tuscan buildings, but also many figures, including one peering at the crowd in the streets from a first-floor window. Duccio gives a viewer a more complete description of the event than Giotto, whose work stresses the doctrinal and psychological import of the moment. The goals of the two painters differ, and so do the formal means they use to achieve them.

Duccio trained the next generation of painters in Siena. One distinguished disciple was Simone Martini (ca. 1284–1344) who also worked in Assisi but spent the last years of his life Avignon, the town in southern France that served as the residence of the popes during most of the fourteenth century. In 1333,

13.25 Simone Martini, *Annunciation*. ca. 1330. Tempera on panel, 10′ × 8′9″ (3 × 2.7 m). Galleria degli Uffizi, Florence

the directors of Siena cathedral commissioned Simone to make another altarpiece to complement Duccio's *Maestà*. His *Annunciation* (fig. **13.25**) in its restored cusped and gilded frame hints at what has been lost in the dismemberment of Duccio's *Maestà*, which had a complex Gothic frame. Simone's altarpiece, in the form of a **triptych** or three-part structure, depicts the Annunciation flanked by two local saints set against a brilliant gold ground. To connect her visually to the *Maestà*, Simone's Virgin sits in a similar cloth-covered throne and wears similar garments.

In Simone's picture, the angel Gabriel approaches Mary from the left to pronounce the words "*Ave Maria gratia plena Dominus tecum*" ("Hail Mary, full of grace, the Lord is with you"). These words are familiar to believers as a popular prayer. Simone renders the words in relief on the surface of this painting, covering them in the same gold leaf that transforms the scene into a heavenly vision. Details like the marble floor, the lilies symbolic of purity, and the sumptuous garment worn by the angel add to the richness of the image. Simone adds an element of doubt to the narrative, as the Virgin responds to her visitor with surprise and pulls away from him. The dove of the Holy Spirit flies toward

her in anticipation of her momentous acceptance of her role as the mother of Jesus, thereby beginning the process of Salvation. Like Giotto, Simone has reduced the narrative to its simplest terms, but like Duccio, his figures have a lyrical elegance that lifts them out of the ordinary and into the realm of the spiritual.

Pietro and Ambrogio Lorenzetti

Another altarpiece commissioned for the cathedral at Siena takes a more down-to-earth approach to representing the life of the Virgin. This is the *Birth of the Virgin* (fig. **13.26**) painted in 1342 by Pietro Lorenzetti (active ca. 1306–1348). Pietro and his brother Ambrogio (active ca. 1317–1348), learned their craft in Siena in Duccio's workshop, though their work also shows the influence of Giotto. Pietro has been linked to work at Assisi, and Ambrogio enrolled in the painters' **guild** of Florence in the 1330s. Like Simone's, Pietro's altarpiece is a triptych, though it has lost its original frame. In this triptych, Pietro has related the painted architecture to the real architecture of the frame so closely that the two are seen as a single system. Moreover, the

13.26 Pietro Lorenzetti, *Birth of the Virgin*. 1342. Tempera on panel, 6'1½" × 5'11½" (1.9 × 1.8 m). Museo dell'Opera del Duomo, Siena

vaulted room where the birth takes place occupies two panels and continues unbroken behind the column that divides the center from the right wing. The left wing represents a small chamber which opens onto a Gothic façade. Pietro's achievement of spatial illusion here is the outcome of a development that began three decades earlier in the work of Giotto and Duccio. Pietro treats the painting surface like a transparent window *through* which—not *on* which—a viewer experiences a space comparable to the real world. Pietro uses the architecture in his painting to carve out boxes of space that his figures appear to inhabit, but he is also inspired by Giotto's technique of giving his figures such mass and weight that they seem to create their own space. His innovation served the narrative and liturgical needs of Siena cathedral by depicting another key moment in the life of the Virgin, her birth, which was also an important feast day in the Church. St. Anne rests in her childbed, while midwives attend the newborn Virgin and other women tend to the mother. The figure of the midwife pouring water for the baby's bath seems to derive from the figure seen from the back in Giotto's *Lamentation* (see fig. 13.20). The father, Joachim, waits for a report of the birth outside the room.

GOOD AND BAD GOVERNMENT Pietro's brother, Ambrogio Lorenzetti, combined these same influences in a major project for the Palazzo Pubblico, executed between 1338 and 1340. The ruling Council of Nine commissioned several local artists to adorn the building, including Simone Martini. For their council room, they hired Ambrogio to paint an **allegory**, or moralizing narrative, contrasting good and bad government. In the room where the council deliberated, these frescoes aimed to inspire its members to achieve good government. Although the negative example of the effects of Bad Government has been severely damaged, the frescoes that depict the positive example of Good Government are remarkably well preserved (fig. **13.27**). On the short wall of the room, Ambrogio depicted the *Allegory of Good Government* as an assembly of figures personifying virtues who flank the large enthroned figure of the Common Good. To the left, another enthroned figure personifies Justice, who is inspired by Wisdom. Below the virtues stand 24 members of the Sienese judiciary under the guidance of the personification of Concord.

On the long wall, the fresco of *Good Government in the City* (fig. **13.28**) bears an inscription praising Justice and the many

13.27 Ambrogio Lorenzetti, *Allegory of Good Government* (left). *Good Government in the City* (right), and portion of *Good Government in the Country* (far right), Sala della Pace, Palazzo Pubblico, Siena. 1338–40. Fresco

benefits that derive from her. (See *Primary Source*, page 461.) In this fresco, Ambrogio renders an architectural portrait of Siena. To show the life of a well-ordered city-state, the artist fills the streets and houses with activity. Within the city, merchants do business, teachers conduct classes, buildings go up, and the streets teem with people. On the right, outside the city walls, G

13.28 Ambrogio Lorenzetti, *Good Government in the City*

Inscriptions on the Frescoes in the Palazzo Pubblico, Siena

The first inscription is painted in a strip below the fresco of Good Government *(see figs. 13.27 and 13.28), which is dated between 1338 and 1340. The second is held by the personification of Security, who hovers over the landscape in figure 13.29.*

Turn your eyes to behold her,
you who are governing, [Justice] who is portrayed here,
crowned on account of her excellence,
who always renders to everyone his due.
Look how many goods derive from her
and how sweet and peaceful is that life

of the city where is preserved
this virtue who outshines any other.
She guards and defends
those who honor her, and nourishes and feeds them.
From her light is born
Requiting those who do good
and giving due punishment to the wicked.

Without fear every man may travel freely
and each may till and sow,
so long as this commune
shall maintain this lady [Justice] sovereign,
for she has stripped the wicked of all power.

Source: Randolph Starn and Loren Partridge, *Arts of Power: Three Halls of State in Italy, 1300–1600* (Berkeley: University of California Press, 1992)

Government in the Country provides a view of the Sienese farmland, fringed by distant mountains (fig. **13.29**) and overseen by a personification of Security. It is a true landscape—the first since ancient Roman times (see fig. 7.55). It represents a sweeping view of the orderly hillside: vineyards, farms, and pastures result from a fruitful nature possessed by well-governed humans. Ambrogio observes the peasants at their seasonal labors, which support the life within the city, even as the countryside is safe for travelers, merchants, and pleasure-seekers.

Artists and Patrons in Times of Crisis

Ambrogio's ideal vision of the city and its surroundings reveals how the citizens of Siena imagined their government and their city at a moment of peace and prosperity. The first three decades of the fourteenth century in Siena, as in Florence, were a period of political stability and economic expansion, as well as of great artistic achievement. In the 1340s, however, both cities suffered a series of catastrophes whose effects were to be felt for many years.

13.29 Ambrogio Lorenzetti, *Good Government in the Country*

13.30 Anonymous (Francesco Traini ?), *The Triumph of Death* (detail), Camposanto, Pisa. ca. 1325–50. Fresco

Constant warfare pushed scores of banks and merchants into bankruptcy, internal upheavals shook governments, and there were repeated crop failures and famine. Then, in 1348, the pandemic of bubonic plague—the Black Death—that spread throughout Europe wiped out more than half the population of the two cities (see map **13.2**). Flea-infested rats swarmed into cities from the barren countryside in search of food and so spread the disease. Popular reactions to these events were mixed. Many people saw them as signs of divine wrath, warnings to a sinful humanity to forgo the pleasures of this earth. In such people, the Black Death intensified an interest in religion and the promise of heavenly rewards. To others, such as the merry company who entertain each other by telling stories in the Florentine humanist Giovanni Boccaccio's (1313–1375) book the *Decameron*, finished around 1353, the fear of death intensified the desire to enjoy life while there was still time. (See www.myartslab.com.)

Late medieval people were regularly confronted with the inevitability and power of death. A series of frescoes painted on the walls of the Camposanto, the monumental cemetery building next to Pisa cathedral, offers a variety of responses to death. Because of its somber message, these frescoes were once dated after the outbreak of the plague, but recent research has pushed the date closer to the 1330s. The painter is not known, though some scholars attribute the work to a Pisan artist named Francesco Traini (documented ca. 1321–1363). The huge fresco

cycle, which was damaged in 1944 as a result of bombings in World War II, included a powerful *Last Judgment* and an image called *The Triumph of Death*, which asserts that death comes to all, rich or poor, saint or sinner. In a particularly dramatic detail (fig. **13.30**), the elegantly costumed men and women on horseback have suddenly come upon three decaying corpses in open coffins. Even the animals are terrified by the sight and smell of rotting flesh. The hermit St. Macarius, having renounced all earthly pleasures, points out the lesson of the scene. His scroll reads: "If your mind be well aware, keeping here your view attentive, your vainglory will be vanquished and you will see pride eliminated. And, again, you will realize this if you observe that which is written." As the hermits in the hills above make clear, the way to salvation is through renunciation of the world in favor of the spiritual life. The artist's style recalls the realism of Ambrogio Lorenzetti, although the forms are harsher and more expressive.

It is likely that the Lorenzetti brothers perished in the Black Death of 1348–49, along with thousands of other people throughout Tuscany. Scholars have studied the impact of the plague on artists and patrons of works of art in the second half of the fourteenth century to determine its effect on style and subject matter. We can assume that many painters died, so the number of artists probably diminished. Documentary research reveal that the number of endowed chapels, tombs, and funeral masses rose as people worried about their mortality. Many such burials and endowments were made in mendicant churches, such as the Franciscan Santa Croce and the Dominican Santa Maria Novella in Florence.

At Santa Maria Novella, a Florentine merchant named Buonamico Guidalotti, who died in 1355, provided funds in his will for a new chapterhouse for the Dominican community in which he could be buried. The chapel served as a meeting room for the friars and as such was painted with frescoes expressing the role of Dominicans in the struggle for salvation. A fresco on one of the walls of the Guidalotti Chapel, painted by Andrea Bonaiuti (also known as Andrea da Firenze, active 1346–1379) between 1365 and 1367, depicts the actions of Dominicans to assure the access of the faithful to Heaven, hence its title: *The Way of Salvation* (fig. **13.31**). In the lower section of the fresco, spiritual and temporal leaders gather before a representation of the then-unfinished cathedral of Florence. The fresco depicts a model of the church rather than its actual state of construction. Groups of Dominicans preach to the laity and convert heretics amidst black and white dogs (a punning reference to the order—the *Domini canes*, or the dogs of the Lord). On the upper right, some heed-less aristocrats enjoy the pleasures of the senses, while at the center, a Dominican shows the more spiritually minded the path to Heaven, whose gate is guarded by St. Peter. Andrea's fresco reveals the influence both of Ambrogio Lorenzetti's *Allegory of Good Government* (see fig. 13.27) and the fresco on the walls of the cemetery near Pisa cathedral (see fig. 13.30). Nonetheless, the fresco's symmetry and the sense of order reveal a didactic function: It seeks legibility rather than illusion, and serenity rather than emotion.

Florence, however, did not complete its cathedral in the fourteenth century, and it was not to enjoy the calm atmosphere portrayed in Andrea's fresco. The plague returned in 1363, the political elite clashed with the papacy, and an uprising among the working classes created social and economic turmoil. The wealthier classes restored their power in 1381. Florence overcame these disasters to flourish in the fifteenth century as a center of economic energy, political astuteness, and cultural leadership. As the fifteenth century began, a new generation of Florentine artists would look to the art of Giotto and his contemporaries in their search for new forms of visual expression.

13.31 Andrea da Firenze, *The Way of Salvation*, Guidalotti Chapel, Santa Maria Novella, Florence. 1365–67. Fresco, width 38′ (11.6 m)

Map 13.2 The Bubonic Plague spreads across Europe, 1347–1351

ATLANTIC OCEAN

North Sea

Copenhagen

Lübeck

London

Brunswick   Magdeburg

Bruges   Warsaw

Rouen   Paris   Frankfurt   Prague

Vienna

Milan   Bucharest

Marseilles   Ravenna   Black Sea

Florence

Toledo   Rome

Barcelona

Thessaloniki

Athens

Mediterranean Sea

500 km
500 miles

N

1347	1350
mid-1348	1351
early 1349	after 1351
late 1349	minor outbreak

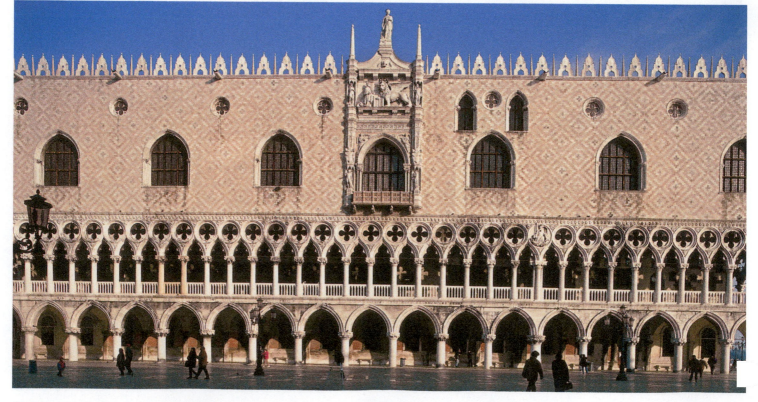

13.32 Doge's Palace, Venice. Begun 1340

NORTHERN ITALY

Political struggles did not disturb Venice in the fourteenth century. Unlike Florence, which was riven by warring factions, the city enjoyed political stability. Since 1297, it had closed off membership in the merchant oligarchy that participated in government, and the city's leader (the Doge) was elected from this group. This created a stable social climate, so neither Venetian palaces nor their communal buildings required the defensive architecture seen in Florentine structures such as the Palazzo della Signoria (see fig. 13.15). A somewhat different atmosphere existed in Milan, west of Venice in Lombardy, where a monarchical government lay in the hands of a single family with great dynastic ambitions. In Lombardy, the main political and cultural connections were with northern Europe, which had important results for the type and the style of art produced there.

Venice: Political Stability and Sumptuous Architecture

The differing political situations in Florence and Venice affected palace design. Whereas the Florentine palace was solid and impenetrable, the Venetian equivalent is airy and open, full of windows and arcades that are anything but defensible. Venetian architects borrowed from Gothic, Byzantine, and Islamic precedents in an elegant display of the city's wealth and security. When a larger meeting space was needed for the Great Council, the city decided to enlarge the Doge's Palace near St. Mark's cathedral in 1340 (fig. 13.32). Work continued here until the mid-fifteenth century. In contrast to the fortresslike Palazzo della Signoria in Florence, the Doge's Palace is open at the base, the weight of its upper stories resting on two stories of pointed arcades. The lower arcade provides a covered passageway around the building, the upper a balcony. The lavish moldings and the quatrefoils of the arcades give the structure an ornamentality accented by the doubling of the rhythm in the upper arcade. The walls of the structure are ornamented with stonework in a diamond pattern, making them both visually lighter and more ornate.

Milan: The Visconti Family and Northern Influences

Lombardy had a different political structure and a closer relationship with Gothic France, which found expression in its visual arts. The Visconti family had acquired great wealth from the products of this richly agricultural region. Besides controlling Lombardy, the Visconti positioned themselves among the great families of Europe through marriage ties to members of the Italian and European nobility. By 1395, Giangaleazzo Visconti had been named duke of Milan, had married the daughter of the king of France, and had wed his daughter to the French king's brother, Louis, duke of Orleans.

The authoritarian nature of Visconti rule in Milan may be seen in the tomb of Giangaleazzo's uncle Bernabò Visconti (fig. 13.33).

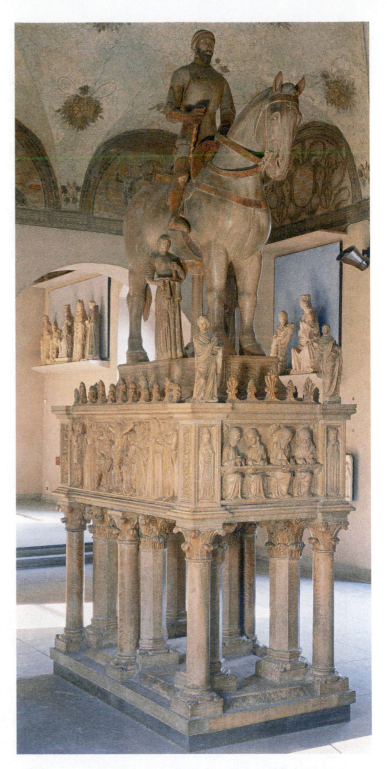

13.33 Tomb of Bernabò Visconti. Before 1363. Marble, 19′8″ (6 m). Castello Sforzesco, Milan

Completed around 1363, perhaps by the local sculptor Bonino da Campione (active ca. 1357–1397), the marble structure includes a sarcophagus that supports a sculpted figure of Bernabò on horseback. Though now in a museum, Bernabò's equestrian monument originally stood over the altar of a church in Milan. The figure stands rather than sits on the horse, forcefully commanding the space over the high altar. The idea of the equestrian image of a ruler goes back to antiquity, with the *Equestrian Statue of Marcus Aurelius* (see fig. 7.33) visible in Rome throughout the Middle Ages.

The ruling aristocracy of Europe claimed for themselves the prerogative of equestrian imagery. In this sculpture, Bernabò is rigid and formal in his bearing; originally the figure was covered with silver and gold leaf to further enhance its impressiveness. Yet the treatment of the horse, with its sensitive proportions and realistically observed anatomy, points to a Lombard interest in the natural depiction of form, which may be a result of contact with contemporary French art.

Bernabò's nephew, who deposed him to claim power, used the visual arts as part of his own campaign to be named duke of Milan. Giangaleazzo Visconti encouraged the construction of a new cathedral in Milan in 1386 and commissioned expensive illuminated manuscripts like his French peers. His **Book of Hours** was begun around 1395 by Giovannino dei Grassi (active ca. 1380–1398) and features numerous personal representations and references to the duke. The page in figure **13.34** begins one of the Psalms with an illuminated initial "D" wherein King David appears. David is both the author of the text and a good biblical

exemplar of a ruler. An unfurling ribbon ornamented with the French *fleur-de-lis* forms the "D"; shields at the corners bear the Visconti emblem of the viper. Below the text appears a portrait of Giangaleazzo in the profile arrangement that was familiar fr ancient coins. Although the portrait is naturalistic, it is set int an undulating frame that supports the rays of the sun, another Visconti emblem. Around the portrait Giovannino has painted images of stags and a hunting dog, paying great attention to the accurate rendering of these natural forms. Such flashes of realism amidst the splendor of the page reflect both the patrons and the artist's contribution to the developing International Gothic style. Commissioning such lavish books was an expression of the status and power that Giangaleazzo attempted to wield. His ambition to bring most of northern Italy under his control would profoundly affect the arts in Tuscany in the early fifteenth century.

Starting from the local traditions of Italy and the inspiration of Byzantine and French Gothic style, Italian artists of the thirteenth and fourteenth centuries created works of art with pronounced elements of naturalism and featuring increasingly complex imagery. Their accomplishments provided a foundation for the artists of the subsequent century in Italy and the rest of Europe.

13.34 Giovannino dei Grassi, *Hours of Giangaleazzo Visconti*. ca. 1395. Tempera and gold on parchment, 9¾ × 6⅞" (24.7 × 17.5 cm). Banco Rari, Biblioteca Nazionale, 397 folio 115/H, Florence

1228 Work begins on San Francesco, Assisi

1260 Nicola Pisano's Pisa pulpit

1298 Palazzo della Signoria begun in Florence

1305 Giotto's Arena Chapel frescoes

1311 Duccio's *Maestà* completed in Siena

1330 Doors of baptistery of Florence

1395 *Hours of Giangaleazzo Visconti*

Art in Thirteenth- and Fourteenth-Century Italy

1200

◄ *1204 Europeans in Fourth Crusade conquer Constantinople*

1225

◄ *1234 Canonization of Dominic de Guzmán*

1250

◄ *1250 Death of Emperor Frederick II*

1262 Saint-Urbain at Troyes begun

◄ *1271–95 Marco Polo travels to China*

1275

1295 Prayer Book of Philip the Fair
◄ *1297 Venetian oligarchy closes ranks*

1300

◄ 1305–78 Papacy in Avignon, France

1310 *Queen Mary Psalter*
ca. 1314 Tomb of Oljeytu, Sultaniya, Iran

1325

1339 *Virgin* of Jeanne d'Évreux
◄ 1347–48 Black Death ravages Europe

1350

1351 Peter Parler adds choir to church of Heiligenkreuz, Schwäbisch-Gmünd, Germany

1375

◄ *1378 Wool workers (Ciompi) revolt in Florence*

1400

Glossary

ABACUS. A slab of stone at the top of a Classical capital just beneath the architrave.

ABBEY. (1) A religious community headed by an abbot or abbess. (2) The buildings that house the community. An abbey church often has an especially large choir to provide space for the monks or nuns.

ACROTERION (pl. **ACROTERIA**). Decorative ornaments placed at the apex and the corners of a pediment.

ACTION PAINTING. In Abstract art, the spontaneous and uninhibited application of paint, as practiced by the avant-garde from the 1930s through the 1950s.

AEDICULA. A small shrine or altar that dates to ancient Rome.

AEOLIC. An early style of Greek architecture, found in northwestern Asia Minor. The Aeolic style is often considered a precursor to the Ionic style.

AISLE. The passageway or corridor of a church that runs parallel to the length of the building. It often flanks the nave of the church but is sometimes set off from it by rows of piers or columns.

ALABASTRON. A perfume container, similar to an aryballos, crafted by Greek vase-painters and often imported into Etruria.

ALBUMEN PRINT. A process in photography that uses the proteins found in eggs to produce a photographic plate.

ALLEGORY. A representation in which figures or events stand for ideas beyond themselves as symbols or metaphors, to create a moral or message for the viewer.

ALLOVER PAINTING. A painting in which the texture tends to be consistent throughout and which has no traditional compositional structure with a dominant focus of interest but, rather, even stresses throughout the image, as in Jackson Pollock's Abstract Expressionist action paintings.

ALTAR. A mound or structure on which sacrifices or offerings are made in the worship of a deity. In a Catholic church, a tablelike structure used in celebrating the Mass.

ALTARPIECE. A painted or carved work of art placed behind and above the altar of a Christian church. It may be a single panel or a *triptych* or a *polytych*, both having hinged wings painted on both sides. Also called a reredos or retablo.

AMBULATORY. A covered walkway. (1) In a basilican church, the semicircular passage around the apse. (2) In a central-plan church, the ring-shaped aisle around the central space. (3) In a cloister, the covered colonnaded or arcaded walk around the open courtyard.

ANAMORPHIC. Refers to a special form of perspective, which represents an object from an unusual or extreme viewpoint, so that it can only be understood from that viewpoint, or with the aid of a special device or mirror.

ANDACHTSBILD. German for "devotional image." A picture or sculpture with imagery intended for private devotion. It was first developed in Northern Europe.

ANIMAL STYLE. A style that appears to have originated in ancient Iran and is characterized by stylized or abstracted images of animals.

ANNULAR. From the Latin word for "ring." Signifies a ring-shaped form, especially an annular barrel vault.

APOTROPAIC DEVICE. An object deployed as a means of warding off evil. Often a figural image (such as a Medusa head) or a composite image (like a Near Eastern lamassu), inserted into an architectural setting.

APSE. A semicircular or polygonal niche terminating one or both ends of the nave in a Roman basilica. In a Christian church, it is usually placed at the east end of the nave beyond the transept or choir. It is also sometimes used at the end of transept arms.

APSIDIOLE. A small apse or chapel connected to the main apse of a church.

ARCADE. A series of arches supported by piers or columns. When attached to a wall, these form a blind arcade.

ARCH. A curved structure used to span an opening. Masonry arches are generally built of wedge-shaped blocks, called *voussoirs*, set with their narrow sides toward the opening so that they lock together. The topmost *voussoir* is called the *keystone*. Arches may take different shapes, such as the pointed Gothic arch or the rounded Classical arch.

ARCHAIC SMILE. A fixed, unnaturalistic smile characteristic of many archaic Greek sculpted images. Artists ceased to depict figures smiling in this way once they began to explore greater naturalism.

ARCHITRAVE. The lowermost member of a classical entablature, such as a series of stone blocks that rest directly on the columns.

ARCHIVOLT. A molded band framing an arch, or a series of such bands framing a tympanum, often decorated with sculpture.

ARCUATION. The use of arches or a series of arches in building.

ART BRUT. Meaning "raw art" in French, *art brut* is the direct and highly emotional art of children and the mentally ill that served as an inspiration for some artistic movements in Modern art.

ARYBALLOS. A perfume jar, generally small in size, and often minutely decorated. This was a favorite type of vessel for Corinthian vase-painters.

ASHLAR MASONRY. Carefully finished stone that is set in fine joints to create an even surface.

ASSOCIATIONISM. A 20th-century art historical term that refers to the concept that architecture and landscape design can have motifs or aspects that associate them with earlier architecture, art, history, or literature.

ATMOSPHERIC PERSPECTIVE. Creates the illusion of depth by reducing the local color and clarity of objects in the distance, to imply a layer of atmosphere between the viewer and the horizon.

ATRIUM. (1) The central court or open entrance court of a Roman house. (2) An open court, sometimes colonnaded or arcaded, in front of a church.

AVANT-GARDE. Meaning "advance force" in French, the artists of the avant-garde in 19th- and 20th-century Europe led the way in innovation in both subject matter and technique, rebelling against the established conventions of the art world.

BALDACCHINO. A canopy usually built over an altar. The most important one is Bernini's construction for St. Peter's in Rome.

BAROQUE. A style of Hellenistic Greek sculpture, characterized by extreme emotions and extravagant gestures, as seen on the Great Altar of Zeus at Pergamon. The term is usually used to describe a style of 17th-century CE art, and scholars of ancient art coin it in recognition of similarities of style.

BARREL VAULT. A vault formed by a continuous semicircular arch so that it is shaped like a half cylinder.

BAR TRACERY. A style of tracery in which glass is held in place by relatively thin membranes.

BAS-DE-PAGE. Literally "bottom of the page." An illustration or decoration that is placed below a block of text in an illuminated manuscript.

BASILICA. (1) In ancient Roman architecture, a large, oblong building used as a public meeting place and hall of justice. It generally includes a nave, side aisles, and one or more apses. (2) In Christian architecture, a longitudinal church derived from the Roman basilica and having a nave, an apse, two or four side aisles or side chapels, and sometimes a narthex. (3) Any one of the seven original churches of Rome or other churches accorded the same religious privileges.

BATTLEMENT. A parapet consisting of alternating solid parts and open spaces designed originally for defense and later used for decoration. See *crenelated*.

BAY. A subdivision of the interior space of a building. Usually a series of bays is formed by consecutive architectural supports.

BELVEDERE. A structure made for the purpose of viewing the surroundings, either above the roof of a building or free-standing in a garden or other natural setting.

BLACK-FIGURED. A style of ancient Greek pottery decoration characterized by black figures against a red background. The black-figured style preceded the red-figured style.

BLIND ARCADE. An arcade with no openings. The arches and supports are attached decoratively to the surface of a wall.

BLOCK BOOKS. Books, often religious, of the 15th century containing woodcut prints in which picture and text were usually cut into the same block.

BOOK OF HOURS. A private prayer book containing the devotions for the seven canonical hours of the Roman Catholic church (matins, vespers, etc.), liturgies for local saints, and sometimes a calendar. They are often elaborately illuminated for persons of high rank, whose names are attached to certain extant examples.

BUON FRESCO. See *fresco*.

BURIN. A pointed metal tool with a wedged-shaped tip used for engraving.

BUTTRESS. A projecting support built against an external wall, usually to counteract the lateral thrust of a vault or arch within. In Gothic church architecture, a *flying buttress* is an arched bridge above the aisle roof that extends from the upper nave wall, where the lateral thrust of the main vault is greatest, down to a solid pier.

CALOTYPE. Invented in the 1830s, calotype was the first photographic process to use negatives and positive prints on paper.

CAMEO. A low relief carving made on agate, seashell, or other multilayered material in which the subject, often in profile view, is rendered in one color while the background appears in another, darker color.

CAMES. Strips of lead in stained-glass windows that hold the pieces of glass together.

CAMPANILE. From the Italian word *campana*, meaning "bell." A bell tower that is either round or square and is sometimes free-standing.

CANON. A law, rule, or standard.

CAPITAL. The uppermost member of a column or pillar supporting the architrave.

CARAVANSARAY. A wayside inn along the main caravan routes linking the cities of Asia Minor, usually containing a warehouse, stables, and a courtyard.

CARTE-DE-VISITE. A photographic portrait mounted on thicker card stock measuring 2½ x 4 inches (6 x 10 cm) that people commissioned and distributed to friends and acquaintances. They were developed in 1854 by the French photographer Adolphe-Eugène Disdéri, and by the end of the decade were so popular that they were widely collected in Europe and America, a phenomenon called "cardomania."

CARTOON. From the Italian word *cartone*, meaning "large paper." (1) A full-scale drawing for a picture or design intended to be transferred to a wall, panel, tapestry, etc. (2) A drawing or print, usually humorous or satirical, calling attention to some action or person of popular interest.

CARYATID. A sculptured female figure used in place of a column as an architectural support. A similar male figure is an *atlas* (pl. *atlantes*).

CASEMATE. A chamber or compartment within a fortified wall, usually used for the storage of artillery and munitions.

CASSONE (pl. **CASSONI**). An Italian dowry chest often highly decorated with carvings, paintings, inlaid designs, and gilt embellishments.

CATACOMBS. The underground burial places of the early Christians, consisting of passages with niches for tombs and small chapels for commemorative services.

CATALOGUE RAISONNÉ. A complete list of an artist's works of art, with a comprehensive chronology and a discussion of the artist's style.

CATHEDRAL. The church of a bishop; his administrative headquarters. The location of his *cathedra* or throne.

CAVEA. The seating area in an ancient theater. In a Greek theater, it was just over semicircular; in a Roman theater, it was semicircular. Access corridors divided the seating into wedges (*cunei*).

CELLA. (1) The principal enclosed room of a temple used to house an image. Also called the *naos*. (2) The entire body of a temple as distinct from its external parts.

CENOTAPH. A memorial monument to honor a person or persons whose remains lie elsewhere.

CENTERING. A wooden framework built to support an arch, vault, or dome during its construction.

CHAMPLEVÉ. An enameling method in which hollows are etched into a metal surface and filled with enamel.

CHANCEL. The area of a church around the altar, sometimes set off by a screen. It is used by the clergy and the choir.

CHIAROSCURO. Italian word for "light and dark." In painting, a method of modeling form primarily by the use of light and shade.

CHIASTIC POSE. From the Greek letter chi: an asymmetrical stance, where the body carries the weight on one leg (and often bears a weight with the opposite arm). Also described as *contrapposto*.

CHINOISERIE. Objects, usually in the decorative arts (screens, furniture, lacquerware) made in a Chinese or pseudo-Chinese style, most popular in the 18th century.

CHITON. A woman's garment made out of a rectangle of fabric draped and fastened at the shoulders by pins. The garment is worn by some Archaic Greek *korai*, where it provides a decorative effect.

CHRYSELEPHANTINE. Usually refering to a sculpture in Classical Greece, signifying that it is made of gold and ivory. Pheidias' cult statues of Athena in the Parthenon, and Zeus at Olympia, were chryselephantine.

CLASSICISM. Art or architecture that harkens back to and relies upon the style and canons of the art and architecture of ancient Greece or Rome, which emphasize certain standards of balance, order, and beauty.

CLASSICIZING. To refer to the forms and ideals of the Classical world, principally Greece and Rome.

CLERESTORY. A row of windows in the upper part of a wall that rises above an adjoining roof. Its purpose is to provide direct lighting, as in a basilica or church.

CLOISONNÉ. An enameling method in which the hollows created by wires joined to a metal plate are filled with enamel to create a design.

CLOISTER. (1) A place of religious seclusion such as a monastery or nunnery. (2) An open court attached to a church or monastery and surrounded by an ambulatory. Used for study, meditation, and exercise.

COFFER. (1) A small chest or casket. (2) A recessed, geometrically shaped panel in a ceiling. A ceiling decorated with these panels is said to be coffered.

COLONNETTE. A small, often decorative, column that is connected to a wall or pier.

COLOPHON. (1) The production information given at the end of a book. (2) The printed emblem of a book's publisher.

COLOR-FIELD PAINTING. A technique of Abstract painting in which thinned paints are spread onto an unprimed canvas and allowed to soak in with minimal control by the artist.

COLOSSAL ORDER. Columns, piers, or pilasters in the shape of the Greek or Roman orders but that extend through two or more stories rather than following the Classical proportions.

COMBINES. The label the American artist Robert Rauschenberg gave to his paintings of the mid-1950s that combined painting, sculpture, collage, and found objects.

COMPOSITE CAPITAL. A capital that combines the volutes of an Ionic capital with the acanthus leaves of the Corinthian capital. Roman architects developed the style as a substitute for the Ionic style, for use on secular buildings.

COMPOSITE IMAGE. An image formed by combining different images or different views of the subject.

COMPOUND PIER. A pier with attached pilasters or shafts.

CONSTRUCTION. A type of sculpture, developed by Picasso and Braque toward 1912, and popularized by the Russian Constructivists later in the decade. It is made by assembling such materials as metal or wood.

CONTINUOUS NARRATION. Portrayal of the same figure or character at different stages in a story that is depicted in a single artistic space.

CONTRAPPOSTO. Italian word for "set against." A composition developed by the Greeks to represent movement in a figure. The parts of the body are placed asymmetrically in opposition to each other around a central axis, and careful attention is paid to the distribution of weight.

CORBEL. (1) A bracket that projects from a wall to aid in supporting weight. (2) The projection of one course, or horizontal row, of a building material beyond the course below it.

CORBEL VAULT. A vault formed by progressively projecting courses of stone or brick, which eventually meet to form the highest point of the vault.

CORINTHIAN CAPITAL. A column capital ornamented with acanthus leaves, introduced in Greece in the late fifth century BCE, and used by Roman architects throughout the Empire.

CORNICE. (1) The projecting, framing members of a classical pediment, including the horizontal one beneath and the two sloping or "raking" ones above. (2) Any projecting, horizontal element surmounting a wall or other structure or dividing it horizontally for decorative purposes.

CORPUS. In carved medieval altarpieces, the corpus is the central section which usually holds a sculpted figure or design.

COURT STYLE. See *Rayonnant*.

CRENELATIONS. A sequence of solid parts, and the intervals between them, along the top of a parapet, allowing for defense and to facilitate firing weapons. The effect is of a notched termination of a wall. Generally used in military architecture.

CROSSING. The area in a church where the transept crosses the nave, frequently emphasized by a dome or crossing tower.

CRYPT. A space, usually vaulted, in a church that sometimes causes the floor of the choir to be raised above that of the nave; often used as a place for tombs and small chapels.

CUBICULUM (pl. **CUBICULA**) A bedroom in a Roman house. A cubiculum usually opened onto the atrium. Most were small; some contained wall-paintings.

CUNEUS (pl. **CUNEI**). A wedgelike group of seats in a Greek or Roman theater.

CUNEIFORM. The wedge-shaped characters made in clay by the ancient Mesopotamians as a writing system.

CURTAIN WALL. A wall of a modern building that does not support the building; the building is supported by an underlying steel structure rather than by the wall itself, which serves the purpose of a façade.

DADO. The lower part of an interior wall. In a Roman house, the dado was often decorated with paintings imitating costly marbles.

DAGUERREOTYPE. Originally, a photograph on a silver-plated sheet of copper, which had been treated with fumes of iodine to form silver iodide on its surface and then after exposure developed by fumes of mercury. The process, invented by L. J. M. Daguerre and made public in 1839, was modified and accelerated as daguerreotypes gained popularity.

DEËSIS. From the Greek word for "entreaty." The representation of Christ enthroned between the Virgin Mary and St. John the Baptist, frequent in Byzantine mosaics and depictions of the Last Judgment. It refers to the roles of the Virgin Mary and St. John the Baptist as intercessors for humankind.

DIKKA. An elevated, flat-topped platform in a mosque used by the muezzin or cantor.

DIPTERAL. Term used to describe a Greek or Roman building—often a temple or a stoa—with a double colonnade.

DIPTYCH. (1) Originally a hinged, two-leaved tablet used for writing. (2) A pair of ivory carvings or panel paintings, usually hinged together.

DOLMEN. A structure formed by two or more large, upright stones capped by a horizontal slab. Thought to be a prehistoric tomb.

DOME. A true dome is a vaulted roof of circular, polygonal, or elliptical plan, formed with hemispherical or ovoidal curvature. May be supported by a circular wall or drum and by pendentives or related constructions. Domical coverings of many other sorts have been devised.

DOMUS. Latin word for "house." A detached, one-family Roman house with rooms frequently grouped around two open courts. The first court, called the *atrium*, was used for entertaining and conducting business. The second court, usually with a garden and surrounded by a *peristyle* or colonnade, was for the private use of the family.

DORIC COLUMN. A column characterized by a simple cushionlike abacus and the absence of a base. One of three styles of column consistently used by Greek and Roman architects.

DRÔLERIES. French word for "jests." Used to describe the lively animals and small figures in the margins of late medieval manuscripts and in wood carvings on furniture.

DROMOS. A pathway, found, for instance, in Bronze Age, Aegean and Etruscan tomb structures.

DRUM. (1) A section of the shaft of a column. (2) A circular-shaped wall supporting a dome.

DRYPOINT. A type of *intaglio* printmaking in which a sharp metal needle is use to carve lines and a design into a (usually) copper plate. The act of drawing pushes up a burr of metal filings, and so, when the plate is inked, ink will be retained by the burr to create a soft and deep tone that will be unique to each print. The burr can only last for a few printings. Both the print and the process are called drypoint.

EARLY ENGLISH STYLE. A term used to describe Gothic architecture in England during the early- and mid-13th century. The style demonstrates the influence of architectural features developed during the Early Gothic period in France, which are combined with Anglo-Norman Romanesque features.

EARTHWORKS. Usually very large scale, outdoor artwork that is produced by altering the natural environment.

ECHINUS. In the Doric or Tuscan Order, the round, cushionlike element between the top of the shaft and the abacus.

ENCAUSTIC. A technique of painting with pigments dissolved in hot wax.

ENGAGED COLUMN. A column that is joined to a wall, usually appearing as a half-rounded vertical shape.

ENGRAVING. (1) A means of embellishing metal surfaces or gemstones by incising a design on the surface. (2) A print made by cutting a design into a metal plate (usually copper) with a pointed steel tool known as a burin. The burr raised on either side of the incised line is removed. Ink is then rubbed into the V-shaped grooves and wiped off the surface. The plate, covered with a damp sheet of paper, is run through a heavy press. The image on the paper is the reverse of that on the plate. When a fine steel needle is used instead of a burin and the burr is retained, a drypoint engraving results, characterized by a softer line. These techniques are called, respectively, engraving and drypoint.

ENNEASTYLE. A term used to describe the façade of a Greek or Roman temple, meaning that it has nine columns.

ENTABLATURE. (1) In a classical order, the entire structure above the columns; this usually includes architrave, frieze, and cornice. (2) The same structure in any building of a classical style.

ENTASIS. A swelling of the shaft of a column.

ENVIRONMENT. In art, environment refers to the Earth itself as a stage for Environmental art, works that can be enormously large yet very minimal and abstract. These works can be permanent or transitory. The term Earth art is also used to describe these artworks.

EVENTS. A term first used by John Cage in the early 1950s to refer to his multimedia events at Black Mount College in North Carolina that included dance, painting, music, and sculpture. The term was appropriated by the conceptual artist George Brecht in 1959 for his performance projects, and shortly thereafter by the conceptual and performance group Fluxus, which included Brecht.

EXEDRA (pl. EXEDRAE). In Classical architecture, an alcove, often semicircular, and often defined with columns. Sometimes, exedrae framed sculptures.

FAIENCE. (1) A glass paste fired to a shiny opaque finish, used in Egypt and the Aegean. (2) A type of earthenware that is covered with a colorful opaque glaze and is often decorated with elaborate designs.

FIBULA. A clasp, buckle, or brooch, often ornamented.

FILIGREE. Delicate decorative work made of intertwining wires.

FLAMBOYANT. Literally meaning "flamelike" in French, describes a late phase of Gothic architecture where undulating curves and reverse curves were a main feature.

FLUTES. The vertical channels or grooves in Classical column shafts, sometimes thought to imitate the faceting of a hewn log.

FLYING BUTTRESS. An arch or series of arches on the exterior of a building, connecting the building to detached pier buttresses so that the thrust from the roof vaults is offset. See also *Buttress*

FOLIO. A leaf of a manuscript or a book, identified so that the front and the back have the same number, the front being labeled *recto* and the back *verso*.

FORESHORTENING. A method of reducing or distorting the parts of a represented object that are not parallel to the picture plane in order to convey the impression of three dimensions as perceived by the human eye.

FRESCO. Italian word for "fresh." Fresco is the technique of painting on plaster with pigments ground in water so that the paint is absorbed by the plaster and becomes part of the wall itself. *Buon fresco* is the technique of painting on wet plaster; *fresco secco* is the technique of painting on dry plaster.

FRIEZE. (1) A continuous band of painted or sculptured decoration. (2) In a Classical building, the part of the entablature between the architrave and the cornice. A Doric frieze consists of alternating triglyphs and metopes, the latter often sculptured. An Ionic frieze is usually decorated with continuous relief sculpture.

FRONTALITY. Representation of a subject in a frontal view.

FROTTAGE. The technique of rubbing a drawing medium, such as a crayon, over paper that is placed over a textured surface in order to transfer the underlying pattern to the paper.

GABLE. (1) The triangular area framed by the cornice or eaves of a building and the sloping sides of a pitched roof. In Classical architecture, it is called a *pediment*. (2) A decorative element of similar shape, such as the triangular structures above the portals of a Gothic church and sometimes at the top of a Gothic picture frame.

GALLERY. A second story placed over the side aisles of a church and below the clerestory. In a church with a four-part elevation, it is placed below the triforium and above the nave arcade.

GEISON. A projecting horizontal cornice. On a Greek or Roman temple, the geison will often be decorated.

GENRE PAINTING. Based on the French word for type or kind, the term sometimes refers to a category of style or subject matter. But it usually refers to depictions of common activities performed by contemporary people, often of the lower or middle classes. This contrasts with grand historical themes or mythologies, narratives or portraits.

GEOMETRIC ARABESQUE. Complex patterns and designs usually composed of polygonal geometric forms, rather than organic flowing shapes; often used as ornamentation in Islamic art.

GESTURE PAINTING. A technique in painting and drawing where the actual physical movement the artist is reflected in the brushstroke or line a is seen in the artwork. The artist Jackson Pollock is particularly associated with this technique.

GISANT. In a tomb sculpture, a recumbent effigy or representation of the deceased. At times, the gisant may be represented in a state of decay.

GLAZE. (1) A thin layer of translucent oil color applied to a painted surface or to parts of it in order to modify the tone. (2) A glassy coating applied to a piece of ceramic work before firing in the kiln as a protective seal and often as decoration.

GLAZED BRICK. Brick that is baked in a kiln after being painted.

GOTHIC. A style of art developed in France during the 12th century that spread throughout Europe. The style is characterized by daring architectural achievements, for example, the opening up of wall surfaces and the reaching of great heights, particularly in cathedral construction. Pointed arches and ribbed groin vaults allow for a lightness of construction that permits maximum light to enter buildings through stained-glass windows. Increasing naturalism and elegance characterize Gothic sculpture and painting.

GRANULATION. A technique of decoration in which metal granules, or tiny metal balls, are fused to a metal surface.

GRATTAGE. A technique in painting whereby an image is produced by scraping off paint from a canvas that has been placed over a textured surface.

GREEK CROSS. A cross with four arms of equal length arranged at right angles.

GRISAILLE. A monochrome drawing or painting which only values of black, gray, and white are used.

GRISAILLE GLASS. White glass painted with gray designs.

GROIN VAULT. A vault formed by the intersection of two barrel vaults at right angles to each other. A groin is the ridge resulting from the intersection of two vaults.

LOCHE PATTERN. A repeating pattern made two ribbons spiraling around a series of central points. A guilloche pattern is often used as a decorative device in Classical vase-painting.

GUILDS. Economic and social organizations that control the making and marketing of given products in a medieval city. To work as a painter or sculptor in a city, an individual had to belong to a guild, which established standards for the craft. First mentioned on p.211. Emboldened entry on p.258

GUTTAE. In a Doric entablature, small peglike projections above the frieze; possibly derived from pegs originally used in wooden construction.

HALL CHURCH. See *hallenkirche*.

HALLENKIRCHE. German word for "hall church." A church in which the nave and the side aisles are of the same height. The type was developed in Romanesque architecture and occurs especially frequently in German Gothic churches.

HAN. In Turkish, an establishment where travelers can procure lodging, food, and drink. Also called a *caravansaray*.

HAPPENING. A type of art that involves visual images, audience participation, and improvised performance, usually in a public setting and under the loose direction of an artist.

HARMONY. In medieval architecture, the perfect relationship among parts in terms of mathematical proportions or ratios. Thought to be the source of all beauty, since it exemplifies the laws by which divine reason made the universe.

HATAYI. A style of ornament originated by the omans and characterized by curved leaves and plex floral palmettes linked by vines, sometimes embellished with birds or animals.

HATCHING. A series of parallel lines used as shading in prints and drawings. When two sets of crossing parallel lines are used, it is called *crosshatching*.

HERALDIC POSE. A pose where two figures are mirror images of one another, sometimes flanking a central object, as in the relieving triangle above the Lioness Gate at Mycenae.

HEROÖN. The center of a hero cult, where Classical Greeks venerated mythological or historical heroes.

HEXASTYLE. A term used to describe the façade of a Greek or Roman temple, meaning that it has six columns.

HIERATIC SCALE. An artistic technique in which the importance of figures is indicated by size, so that the most important figure is depicted as the largest.

HIEROGLYPH. A symbol, often based on a figure, animal, or object, standing for a word, syllable, or sound. These symbols form the early Egyptian writing system, and are found on ancient Egyptian monuments as well as in Egyptian written records.

HOUSE CHURCH. A place for private worship within a house; the first Christian churches were located in private homes that were modified for religious ceremonies.

HUMANISM. A philosophy emphasizing the worth of the individual, the rational abilities of humankind, and the human potential for good. During the Italian Renaissance, humanism was part of a movement encouraged study of the classical cultures of reece and Rome; often it came into conflict with the doctrines of the Catholic church.

HYDRIA. A type of jar used by ancient Greeks to carry water. Some examples were highly decorated.

HYPOSTYLE. A hall whose roof is supported by columns.

ICON. From the Greek word for "image." A panel painting of one or more sacred personages, such as Christ, the Virgin, or a saint, particularly venerated in the Orthodox Christian church.

ICONOCLASM. The doctrine of the Christian church in the 8th and 9th centuries that forbade the worship or production of religious images. This doctrine led to the destruction of many works of art. The iconoclastic controversy over the validity of this doctrine led to a division of the church. Protestant churches of the 16th and 17th centuries also practiced iconoclasm.

ICONOGRAPHY. (1) The depicting of images in art in order to convey certain meanings. (2) The study of the meaning of images depicted in art, whether they be inanimate objects, events, or personages. (3) The content or subject matter of a work of art.

IMPASTO. From the Italian word meaning "to make into a paste"; it describes paint, usually oil paint, applied very thickly.

IMPLUVIUM. A shallow pool in a Roman house, for collecting rain water. The impluvium was usually in the atrium, and stood beneath a large opening in the roof, known as a compluvium.

INFRARED LIGHT. Light on the spectrum beyond the comprehension of the naked eye is referred to as infrared. Special filters are needed to perceive it.

INFRARED REFLECTOGRAPHY. A technique for scientifically examining works of art. Special cameras equipped with infrared filters can look below the top layer of paintings to record the darker materials, such as carbon, which artists used to create drawings on panels or other supports.

INLAID NIELLO. See *niello*.

INSULA (pl. INSULAE). Latin word for "island." (1) An ancient Roman city block. (2) A Roman "apartment house": a concrete and brick building or chain of buildings around a central court, up to five stories high. The ground floor had shops, and above were living quarters.

INTAGLIO. A printing technique in which the design is formed from ink-filled lines cut into a surface. Engraving, etching, and drypoint are examples of intaglio.

INTERCOLUMNIATION. The space between two columns, measured from the edge of the column shafts. The term is often used in describing Greek and Roman temples.

INVERTED PERSPECTIVE. The technique, in some 16th- and 17th-century paintings, of placing the main theme or narrative of a work in the background and placing a still life or other representation in the foreground.

IONIC COLUMN. A column characterized by a base and a capital with two volutes. One of three styles of column consistently used by Greek and Roman architects.

IWAN. A vaulted chamber in a mosque or other Islamic structure, open on one side and usually opening onto an interior courtyard.

JAMBS. The vertical sides of an opening. In Romanesque and Gothic churches, the jambs of doors and windows are often cut on a slant outward, or "splayed," thus providing a broader surface for sculptural decoration.

JAPONISME. In 19th-century French and American art, a style of painting and drawing that reflected the influence of the Japanese artworks, particularly prints, that were then reaching the West.

JASPERWARE. A durable, unglazed porcelain developed by the firm of Josiah Wedgwood in the 18th century. It is decorated with Classically inspired bas relief or cameo figures, and ornamented in white relief on a colored ground, especially blue and sage green.

KORE (pl. KORAI). Greek word for "maiden." An Archaic Greek statue of a standing, draped female.

KOUROS (pl. KOUROI). Greek word for "male youth." An Archaic Greek statue of a standing, nude youth.

KRATER. A Greek vessel, of assorted shapes, in which wine and water are mixed. A *calyx krater* is a bell-shaped vessel with handles near the base; a *volute krater* is a vessel with handles shaped like scrolls.

KUFIC. One of the first general forms of Arabic script to be developed, distinguished by its angularity; distinctive variants occur in various parts of the Islamic worlds.

KYLIX. In Greek and Roman antiquity, a shallow drinking cup with two horizontal handles, often set on a stem terminating in a foot.

LAMASSU. An ancient Near Eastern guardian of a palace; often shown in sculpture as a human-headed bull or lion with wings.

LANCET. A tall, pointed window common in Gothic architecture.

LANTERN. A relatively small structure crowning a dome, roof, or tower, frequently open to admit light to an enclosed area below.

LATIN CROSS. A cross in which three arms are of equal length and one arm is longer.

LEKYTHOS (pl. LEKYTHOI). A Greek oil jug with an ellipsoidal body, a narrow neck, a flanged mouth, a curved handle extending from below the lip to the shoulder, and a narrow base terminating in a foot. It was used chiefly for ointments and funerary offerings.

LIGHT WELLS. Open shafts that allow light to penetrate into a building from the roof. These were a major source of light and ventilation in Minoan "palaces."

LIMINAL SPACE. A transitional area, such as a doorway or archway. In Roman architecture, liminal spaces were often decorated with apotropaic devices.

LINEARITY. A term used to refer to images that have a strong sense of line that provides sharp contours to figures and objects.

LITURGY. A body of rites or rituals prescribed for public worship.

LOGGIA. A covered gallery or arcade open to the air on at least one side. It may stand alone or be part of a building.

LUNETTE. (1) A semicircular or pointed wall area, as under a vault, or above a door or window. When it is above the portal of a medieval church, it is called a *tympanum*. (2) A painting, relief sculpture, or window of the same shape.

LUSTER. A metallic pigment fired over glazed ceramic, which creates an iridescent effect.

MACHICOLATIONS. A gallery projecting from the walls of a castle or tower with holes in the floor in order to allow liquid, stones, or other projectiles to be dropped on an enemy.

MAIDAN. In parts of the Near East and Asia a large open space or square.

MANDORLA. A representation of light surrounding the body of a holy figure.

MANUSCRIPT ILLUMINATION. Decoration of handwritten documents, scrolls, or books with drawings or paintings. Illuminated manuscripts were often produced during the Middle Ages.

MAQSURA. A screened enclosure, reserved for the ruler, often located before the *mihrab* in certain important royal Islamic mosques.

MARTYRIUM (pl. MARTYRIA). A church, chapel, or shrine built over the grave of a Christian martyr or at the site of an important miracle.

MASTABA. An ancient Egyptian tomb, rectangular in shape, with sloping sides and a flat roof. It covered a chapel for offerings and a shaft to the burial chamber.

MATRIX. (1) A mold or die used for shaping a ceramic object before casting. (2) In printmaking, any surface on which an image is incised, carved, or applied and from which a print may be pulled.

MEANDER PATTERN. A decorative motif of intricate, rectilinear character applied to architecture and sculpture.

MEGALITH. From the Greek *mega*, meaning "big," and *lithos*, meaning "stone." A huge stone such as those used in cromlechs and dolmens.

MEGARON (pl. MEGARONS or MEGARA). From the Greek word for "large." The central audience hall in a Minoan or Mycenaean palace or home.

MENHIR. A megalithic upright slab of stone, sometimes placed in rows by prehistoric peoples.

METOPE. The element of a Doric frieze between two consecutive triglyphs, sometimes left plain but often decorated with paint or relief sculpture.

MEZZOTINT. Printmaking technique developed in the late 17th century where the plate is roughened or "rocked" to better retain the ink and create dark images.

MIHRAB. A niche, often highly decorated, usually found in the center of the *qibla* wall of a mosque, indicating the direction of prayer toward Mecca.

MINA'I. From the Persian meaning "enameled," polychrome overglaze-decorated ceramic ware produced in Iran.

MINARET. A tower on or near a mosque, varying extensively in form throughout the Islamic world, from which the faithful are called to prayer five times a day.

MINBAR. A type of staircase pulpit, found in more important mosques to the right of the mihrab, from which the Sabbath sermon is given on Fridays after the noonday prayer.

MINIATURIST. An artist trained in the painting of miniature figures or scenes to decorate manuscripts.

MODULE. (1) A segment of a pattern. (2) A basic unit, such as the measure of an architectural member. Multiples of the basic unit are used to determine proportionate construction of other parts of a building.

MONOTYPE. A unique print made from a copper plate or other type of plate from which no other copies of the artwork are made.

MOSQUE. A building used as a center for community prayers in Islamic worship; it often serves other functions including religious education and public assembly.

MOZARAB. Term used for the Spanish Christian culture of the Middle Ages that developed while Muslims were the dominant culture and political power on the Iberian peninsula.

MUQARNAS. A distinctive type of Islamic decoration consisting of multiple nichelike forms usually arranged in superimposed rows, often used in zones of architectural transition.

NAOS. See *cella*.

NARTHEX. The transverse entrance hall of a church, sometimes enclosed but often open on one side to a preceding atrium.

NATURALISM. A style of art that aims to depict the natural world as it appears.

NAVE. (1) The central aisle of a Roman basilica, as distinguished from the side aisles. (2) The same section of a Christian basilican church extending from the entrance to the apse or transept.

NECROPOLIS. Greek for "city of the dead." A burial ground or cemetery.

NEMES HEADDRESS. The striped cloth headdress worn by Egyptian kings, and frequently represented in their sculpted and painted images.

NEOCLASSICISM. An 18th-century style that emphasizes Classical themes, sometimes with strong moral overtones, executed in a way that places a strong emphasis on line, with figures and objects running parallel to the picture plane. Paintings and drawings are typically executed with sharp clarity, by way of tight handling of paint and clearly defined line and light.

NIELLO. Dark metal alloys applied to the engraved lines in a precious metal plate (usually made of gold or silver) to create a design.

NIKE. The ancient Greek goddess of victory, often identified with Athena and by the Romans with Victoria. She is usually represented as a winged woman with windblown draperies.

NOCTURNE. A painting that depicts a nighttime scene, often emphasizing the effects of artificial light.

NOMAD'S GEAR. Portable objects, including weaponry, tackle for horses, jewelry and vessels, crafted by nomadic groups such as the tribes of early Iran, and sometimes buried with their dead.

OBELISK. A tall, tapering, four-sided stone shaft with a pyramidal top. First constructed as *megaliths* in ancient Egypt, certain examples have since been exported to other countries.

OCTASTYLE. A term used to describe the façade of a Greek or Roman temple, meaning that it has eight columns.

OCULUS. The Latin word for "eye." (1) A circular opening at the top of a dome used to admit light. (2) A round window.

OPISTHONAOS. A rear chamber in a Greek temple, often mirroring the porch at the front. The opisthonaos was sometimes used to house valuable objects. Access to the chamber was usually from the peristyle rather than the cella.

OPTICAL IMAGES. An image created from what the eye sees, rather than from memory.

ORANT. A standing figure with arms upraised in a gesture of prayer.

ORCHESTRA. (1) In an ancient Greek theater, the round space in front of the stage and below the tiers of seats, reserved for the chorus. (2) In a Roman theater, a similar space reserved for important guests.

ORIEL. A bay window that projects from a wall.

ORIENTALISM. The fascination of Western culture, especially as expressed in art and literature, with Eastern cultures. In the 19th-century, this fascination was especially focused on North Africa and the Near East, that is, the Arab world.

ORTHOGONAL. In a perspective construction, an imagined line in a painting that runs perpendicular to the picture plane and recedes to a vanishing point.

ORTHOSTATS. Upright slabs of stone constituting or lining the lowest courses of a wall, often in order to protect a vulnerable material such as mud-brick.

POUSSINISTES. Those artists of the French Academy at the end of the 17th century and the beginning of the 18th century who favored "drawing," which they believed appealed to the mind rather than the senses. The term derived from admiration for the French artist Nicolas Poussin. See *Rubénistes*.

PALETTE. (1) A thin, usually oval or oblong board with a thumbhole at one end, used by painters to hold and mix their colors. (2) The range of colors used by a particular painter. (3) In Egyptian art, a slate slab, usually decorated with sculpture in low relief.

The small ones with a recessed circular area on one side are thought to have been used for eye makeup. The larger ones were commemorative objects.

PARCHMENT. From Pergamon, the name of a Greek city in Asia Minor where parchment invented in the 2nd century BCE. (1) A paper material made from bleached animal hides used extensively in the Middle Ages for manuscripts. Vellum is a superior type of parchment made from calfskin. (2) A document or miniature on this material.

PEDIMENT. (1) In Classical architecture, a low gable, typically triangular, framed by a horizontal cornice below and two raking cornices above; frequently filled with sculpture. (2) A similar architectural member used over a door, window, or niche. When pieces of the cornice are either turned at an angle or interrupted, it is called a *broken pediment*.

PENDENTIVE. One of the concave triangles that achieves the transition from a square or polygonal opening to the round base of a dome or the supporting drum.

PERFORMANCE ART. A type of art in which performance by actors or artists, often interacting with the audience in an improvisational manner, is the primary aim over a certain time period. These artworks are transitory, perhaps with only a photographic record of some of the events.

PERIPTERAL TEMPLE. In Classical architecture, a temple with a single colonnade on all sides, providing shelter.

PERISTYLE. (1) In a Roman house or *domus*, an open garden court surrounded by a colonnade. (2) A colonnade around a building or court.

PERPENDICULAR GOTHIC STYLE. Describes Late Gothic architecture in England, characterized by dominant vertical accents.

PERSPECTIVE. A system for representing spatial relationships and three-dimensional objects on a flat two-dimensional surface so as to produce an effect similar to that perceived by the human eye. In *atmospheric* or *aerial* perspective, this is accomplished by a gradual decrease in the intensity of color and value and in the contrast of light and dark as objects are depicted as farther and farther away in the picture. In color artwork, as objects recede into the distance, all colors tend toward a light bluish-gray tone. In *scientific* or *linear* perspective, developed in Italy in the 15th century, a mathematical system is used based on orthogonals receding to vanishing points on the horizon. Transversals intersect the orthogonals at right angles at distances derived mathematically. Since this presupposes an absolutely stationary viewer and imposes rigid restrictions on the artist, it is seldom applied with complete consistency. Although traditionally ascribed to Brunelleschi, the first theoretical text on perspective was Leon Battista Alberti's *On Painting* (1435).

PHOTOGRAM. A shadowlike photograph made without a camera by placing objects on light-sensitive paper and exposing them to a light source.

PHOTOMONTAGE. A photograph in which prints in whole or in part are combined to form a new image. A technique much practiced by the Dada group in the 1920s.

PICTOGRAPH. A pictorial representation of a concept or object, frequently used by Egyptian artists, sometimes in conjunction with hieroglyphs.

PICTURESQUE. Visually interesting or pleasing, as if resembling a picture.

PIER. An upright architectural support, usually rectangular and sometimes with capital and base. When columns, pilasters, or shafts are attached to it, as in many Romanesque and Gothic churches, it is called a compound pier.

PIETÀ. Italian word for both "pity" and "piety." A representation of the Virgin grieving over the dead Christ. When used in a scene recording a specific moment after the Crucifixion, it is usually called a Lamentation.

[PILE] CARPET. A weaving made on a loom in which rows of individual knots of colored wool are tied so that the ends of each knot protrude to form a thick pile surface.

PILGRIMAGE PLAN. The general design used in Christian churches that were stops on the pilgrimage routes throughout medieval Europe, characterized by having side aisles that allowed pilgrims to ambulate around the church. See *pilgrimage choir*.

PILOTIS. Pillars that are constructed from *reinforced concrete (ferroconcrete)*.

PINAKOTHEKE. A museum for paintings. The first known example may have been in the Propylaia on the Athenian Akropolis.

PINNACLE. A small, decorative structure capping a tower, pier, buttress, or other architectural member. It is used especially in Gothic buildings.

PISÉ. A construction material consisting of packed earth, similar to wattle and daub. Etruscan architects used pisé for houses, with the result that little survives of them.

PLANARITY. A term used to described a composition where figures and objects are arranged parallel to the picture plane.

PLATE TRACERY. A style of tracery in which pierced openings in an otherwise solid wall of stonework are filled with glass.

PLEIN-AIR. Sketching outdoors, often using paints, in order to capture the immediate effects of light on landscape and other subjects. Much encouraged by the Impressionists, their *plein-air* sketches were often taken back to the studio to produce finished paintings, but many *plein-air* sketches are considered masterworks.

POCHADES. Small outdoor oil paintings made by landscape painters, serving as models for large-scale pictures that would be developed in the artist's studio.

POLIS. A city-state, in the Classical Greek world. City-states began to develop in the course of the 7th and 6th centuries BCE, and were governed in a variety of different ways, including monarchy and oligarchy.

POLYPTYCH. An altarpiece or devotional work of art made of several panels joined together, often hinged.

PORTRAIT BUST. A sculpted representation of an individual which includes not only the head but some portion of the upper torso. Popular during the Roman period, it was revived during the Renaissance.

POST AND LINTEL. A basic system of construction in which two or more uprights, the posts, support a horizontal member, the lintel. The lintel may be the topmost element or support a wall or roof.

POUNCING. A technique for transferring a drawing from a cartoon to a wall or other surface by pricking holes along the principal lines of the drawing and forcing fine charcoal powder through them onto the surface of the wall, thus reproducing the design on the wall.

PREDELLA. The base of an altarpiece, often decorated with small scenes that are related in subject to that of the main panel or panels.

PREFIGURATION. The representation of Old Testament figures and stories as forerunners and foreshadowers of those in the New Testament.

PRIMITIVISM. The appropriation of non-Western (e.g., African, tribal, Polynesian) art styles, forms, and techniques by Modern era artists as part of innovative

and avant-garde artistic movements; other sources were also used, including the work of children and the mentally ill.

PROCESS ART. Art in which the process is the art, as when Richard Serra hurled molten lead where a wall meets the floor, or Hans Haacke put water in a hermetic acrylic cube, which resulted in condensation forming on it.

PRONAOS. In a Greek or Roman temple, an open vestibule in front of the *cella*.

PRONK. A word meaning ostentatious or sumptuous; it is used to refer to a still life of luxurious objects.

PROPYLON. A monumental gateway, often leading into a citadel or a precinct, such as the Akropolis of Mycenae or Athens.

PROTOME. A decorative, protruding attachment, often on a vessel. Greek bronze-workers attached griffin-shaped protomes to tripod cauldrons in the 7th century BCE.

PROVENANCE. The place of origin of a work of art and related information.

PSALTER. (1) The book of Psalms in the Old Testament, thought to have been written in part by David, king of ancient Israel. (2) A copy of the Psalms, sometimes arranged for liturgical or devotional use and often richly illuminated.

PYLON. Greek word for "gateway." (1) The monumental entrance building to an Egyptian temple or forecourt consisting either of a massive wall with sloping sides pierced by a doorway or of two such walls flanking a central gateway. (2) A tall structure at either side of a gate, bridge, or avenue marking an approach or entrance.

PYXIS. A lidded box, often made of ivory, to hold jewelry or cosmetics in daily life, and, in the context of the Christian church, used on altars to contain the Host (Communion wafer).

QIBLA. The direction toward Mecca, which Muslims face during prayer. The qibla wall in a mosque identifies this direction.

QUADRANT VAULT. A half-barrel vault designed so that instead of being semicircular in cross-section, the arch is one-quarter of a circle.

QUATREFOIL. An ornamental element composed of four lobes radiating from a common center.

RAYONNANT. The style of Gothic architecture, described as "radiant," developed at the Parisian court of Louis IX in the mid-13th century. Also referred to as *court style*.

READYMADE. An ordinary object that, when an artist gives it a new context and title, is transformed into an art object. Readymades were important features of the Dada and Surrealism movements of the early 20th century.

RED-FIGURED. A style of ancient Greek ceramic decoration characterized by red figures against a black background. This style of decoration developed toward the end of the 6th century BCE and replaced the earlier *black-figured* style.

REGISTER. A horizontal band containing decoration, such as a relief sculpture or a fresco painting. When multiple horizontal layers are used, registers are useful in distinguishing between different visual planes and different time periods in visual narration.

RELIEF. (1) The projection of a figure or part of a design from the background or plane on which it is carved or modeled. Sculpture done in this manner is described as "high relief" or "low relief" depending on the height of the projection. When it is very shallow, it is called *schiacciato*, the Italian word for "flattened out." (2) The apparent projection of forms represented in a painting or drawing. (3) A category of printmaking in which lines raised from the surface are inked and printed.

RELIEVING TRIANGLE. A space left open above a lintel to relieve it of the weight of masonry. This device was used by Bronze Age architects in gate and tomb construction.

RELIQUARY. A container used for storing or displaying relics.

RENAISSANCE. Literally, rebirth. During the 14th and 15th centuries, Italian writers, artists, and intellectuals aimed to revive the arts of the ancient world. From their accomplishments, the term has been applied to the period, and is used generally to refer to a cultural flowering.

REPOUSSÉ. A metalworking technique where a design is hammered onto an object from the wrong side. Sasanian craftsmen used this techniques for silver vessels.

RESPOND. (1) A half-pier, pilaster, or similar element projecting from a wall to support a lintel or an arch whose other side is supported by a free-standing column or pier, as at the end of an arcade. (2) One of several pilasters on a wall behind a colonnade that echoes or "responds to" the columns but is largely decorative. (3) One of the slender shafts of a compound pier in a medieval church that seems to carry the weight of the vault.

RHYTON. An ancient drinking or pouring vessel made from pottery, metal, or stone, and sometimes designed in a human or animal form.

RIBBED GROIN VAULTS. A vault is a stone or brick roof. Groin vaults result from the intersection of two barrel vaults; the places where the arched surfaces meet is called the groin. Adding ribs or thickenings of the groins increases the strength of the roof.

RIBBED VAULT. A style of vault in which projecting surface arches, known as ribs, are raised along the intersections of segments of the vault. Ribs may provide architectural support as well as decoration to the vault's surface.

ROCOCO. The ornate, elegant style most associated with the early-18th-century in France, and which later spread throughout Europe, generally using pastel colors and the decorative arts to emphasize the notion of fantasy.

ROMANESQUE. (1) The style of medieval architecture from the 11th to the 13th centuries that was based upon the Roman model and that used the Roman rounded arch, thick walls for structural support, and relatively small windows. (2) Any culture or its artifacts that are "Roman-like."

ROMANTICISM. A cultural movement that surfaced in the second half of the 18th century and peaked in the first half of the 19th century. The movement was based on a belief in individual genius and originality and the expression of powerful emotions, as well as preference for exotic themes and the omnipotent force of nature, often viewed as manifestation of God.

ROSE WINDOW. A large, circular window with stained glass and stone tracery, frequently used on façades and at the ends of transepts in Gothic churches.

ROSTRUM (pl. ROSTRA). (1) A beaklike projection from the prow of an ancient warship used for ramming the enemy. (2) In the Roman forum, the raised platform decorated with the beaks of captured ships from which speeches were delivered. (3) A platform, stage, or the like used for public speaking.

ROTULUS (pl. ROTULI). The Latin word for scroll, a rolled written text.

RUBÉNISTES. Those artists of the French Academy at the end of the 17th century and the beginning of the 18th century who favored "color" in painting because it appealed to the senses and was thought to be true to nature. The term derived from admiration for the work of the Flemish artist Peter Paul Rubens. See *Poussinistes*.

RUSTICATION. A masonry technique of laying rough-faced stones with sharply indented joints.

SALON. (1) A large, elegant drawing or reception room in a palace or a private house. (2) Official government-sponsored exhibition of paintings and sculpture by living artists held at the Louvre in Paris, first biennially, then annually. (3) Any large public exhibition patterned after the Paris Salon.

SARCOPHAGUS (pl. SARCOPHAGI). A large coffin, generally of stone, and often decorated with sculpture or inscriptions. The term is derived from two Greek words meaning "flesh" and "eating."

SAZ. Meaning literally "enchanted forest," this term describes the sinuous leaves and twining stems that are a major component of the *hatayi* style under the Ottoman Turks.

SCHIACCIATO. Italian for "flattened out." Describes low relief sculpture used by Donatello and some of his contemporaries.

SCHOLASTICISM. A school of medieval thought that tries to reconcile faith and reason by combining ancient philosophy with Christian theology.

SCIENTIFIC PERSPECTIVE. See *perspective.*

SCRIPTORIUM (pl. SCRIPTORIA). A workroom in a monastery reserved for copying and illustrating manuscripts.

SECTION. An architectural drawing presenting a building as if cut across the vertical plane at right angles to the horizontal plane. A *cross section* is a cut along the transverse axis. A *longitudinal section* is a cut along the longitudinal axis.

SELECTIVE WIPING. The planned removal of certain areas of ink during the etching process to produce changes in value on the finished print.

SEPTPARTITE VAULT. A type of vault divided into seven sections.

SERDAB. In Egyptian architecture, an enclosed room without an entrance, often found in a funerary context. A sculpture of the dead king might be enclosed within it, as at Saqqara.

SEXPARTITE VAULT. See *vault.*

SFUMATO. Italian word meaning "smoky." Used to describe very delicate gradations of light and shade in the modeling of figures. It is applied especially to the work of Leonardo da Vinci.

SGRAFFITO ORNAMENT. A decorative technique in which a design is made by scratching away the surface layer of a material to produce a form in contrasting colors.

SHADING. The modulation of volume by means of contrasting light and shade. Prehistoric cave-painters used this device, as did Greek tomb-painters in the Hellenistic period.

SILKSCREEN PRINTING. A technique of printing in which paint or ink is pressed through a stencil and specially prepared cloth to produce a previously designed image. Also called serigraphy.

SILVERPOINT. A drawing instrument (stylus) of the 14th and 15th centuries made from silver; it produced a fine line and maintained a sharp point.

SIMULTANEOUS CONTRAST. The theory, first expressed by Michel-Eugène Chevreul (1786–1889), that complementary colors, when placed next to one another, increase the intensity of each other (e.g., red becoming more red and green more green.)

SITE-SPECIFIC ART. Art that is produced in only one location, a location that is an integral part of the work and essential to its production and meaning.

SKENE. A building erected on a Greek or Roman stage, as a backdrop against which some of the action took place. It usually consisted of a screen of columns, arranged in several storeys.

SOCLE. A portion of the foundation of a building that projects outward as a base for a column or some other device.

SPANDREL. The area between the exterior curves of two adjoining arches or, in the case of a single arch, the area around its outside curve from its springing to its keystone.

SPATIAL PERSPECTIVE. The exploration of the spatial relationships between objects. Painters were especially interested in spatial perspective in the Hellenistic period in Greece.

SPIRE. A tall tower that rises high above a roof. Spires are commonly associated with church architecture and are frequently found on Gothic structures.

SPOLIA. Latin for "hide stripped from an animal." Term used for (1) spoils of war and (2) fragments of architecture or sculpture reused in a secondary context.

SPRINGING. The part of an arch in contact with its base.

SQUINCHES. Arches set diagonally at the corners of a square or rectangle to establish a transition to the round shape of the dome above.

STAIN PAINTING. A type of painting where the artist works on unprimed canvas, allowing the paint to seep into the canvas, thus staining it.

STELE. From the Greek word for "standing block." An upright stone slab or pillar, sometimes with a carved design or inscription.

STEREOBATE. The substructure of a Classical building, especially a Greek temple.

STEREOCARDS. Side-by-side photographs of the same image taken by a camera with two lenses, replicating human binocular vision. When put into a special viewer, the twin flat pictures appear as a single three-dimensional image.

STILL LIFE. A term used to describe paintings (and sometimes sculpture) that depict familiar objects such as household items and food.

STIPPLES. In drawing or printmaking, stippling is a technique to create tone or shading in an image with small dots rather than lines.

STREET PHOTOGRAPHY. A term applied to American documentary photographers such as Walker Evans, who emerged in the 1930s, and Robert Frank, who surfaced in the 1950s, who took to the streets to find their subject matter, often traveling extensively.

STYLOBATE. A platform or masonry floor above the stereobate forming the foundation for the columns of a Greek temple.

SUBLIME. In 19th-century art, the ideal and goal that art should inspire awe in a viewer and engender feelings of high religious, moral, ethical, and intellectual purpose.

SUNKEN RELIEF. Relief sculpture in which the figures or designs are modeled beneath the surface of the stone, within a sharp outline.

SYMPOSIUM. In ancient Greece, a gathering, sometimes of intellectuals and philosophers to discuss ideas, often in an informal social setting, such as at a dinner party.

SYNCRETISM. The act of bringing together disparate customs or beliefs. Historians usually describe Roman culture as syncretistic, because Romans embraced many of the the practices of those they conquered.

SYNOPTIC NARRATIVE. A narrative with different moments presented simultaneously, in order to encapsulate the entire story in a single scene. The device appears in early Greek pediment sculpture.

TEMPERA. Medium for painting in which pigments are suspended in egg yolk tempered with water or chemicals; this mixture dries quickly, reducing the possibility of changes in the finished painting.

TENEBRISM. The intense contrast of light and ⌐ in painting.

TESSERA (pl. TESSERAE). A small piece of colored stone, marble, glass, or gold-backed glass used in a mosaic.

THOLOS. A building with a circular plan, often with a sacred nature.

TONDO. A circular painting or relief sculpture.

TRANSEPT. A cross arm in a basilican church placed at right angles to the nave and usually separating it from the choir or apse.

TRANSVERSALS. In a perspective construction, transversals are the lines parallel to the picture plane (horizontally) that denote distances. They intersect orthogonals to make a grid that guides the arrangement of elements to suggest space.

TRIBUNE. A platform or walkway in a church constructed overlooking the *aisle* and above the *nave.*

TRIFORIUM. The section of a nave wall above the arcade and below the clerestory. It frequently consists of a blind arcade with three openings in each bay. When the gallery is also present, a four-story elevation results, the triforium being between the gallery and clerestory. It may also occur in the transept and the choir walls.

TRIGLYPH. The element of a Doric frieze separating two consecutive metopes and divided by grooves into three sections.

TRILITHIC. A form of construction using three stones—two uprights and a lintel—found frequently in Neolithic tomb and ritual architecture.

TRIPTYCH. An altarpiece or devotional picture, ther carved or painted, with one central panel and t hinged wings.

TRIUMPHAL ARCH. (1) A monumental arch, sometimes a combination of three arches, erected by a Roman emperor in commemoration of his military exploits and usually decorated with scenes of these deeds in relief sculpture. (2) The great transverse arch at the eastern end of a church that frames altar and apse and separates them from the main body of the church. It is frequently decorated with mosaics or mural paintings.

TROIS CRAYONS. The use of three colors, usually red, black, and white, in a drawing; a technique popular in the 17th and 18th centuries.

TROMPE L'OEIL. Meaning "trick of the eye" in French, it is a work of art designed to deceive a viewer into believing that the work of art is reality, an actual three-dimensional object or scene in space.

TRUMEAU. A central post supporting the lintel of a large doorway, as in a Romanesque or Gothic portal, where it is frequently decorated with sculpture.

TRUSS. A triangular wooden or metal support for a roof that may be left exposed in the interior or be covered by a ceiling.

TUMULUS (pl. TUMULI) A monumental earth mound, often raised over a tomb. Etruscan builders constructed tumuli with internal chambers for burials.

TURRET. (1) A small tower that is part of a larger structure. (2) A small tower at a corner of a building, often beginning some distance from the ground.

TUSCAN STYLE. An architectural style typical of ancient Italy. The style is similar to the Doric sty but the column shafts have bases.

TUSCHE. An inklike liquid containing crayon that is used to produce solid black (or solid color) areas in prints.

TYMPANUM. (1) In Classical architecture, a recessed, usually triangular area often decorated with sculpture. Also called a pediment. (2) In medieval architecture, an arched area between an arch and the lintel of a door or window, frequently carved with f sculpture.

TYPOLOGY. The matching or pairing of pre-Christian figures, persons, and symbols with their Christian counterparts.

VANISHING POINT. The point at which the orthogonals meet and disappear in a composition done with scientific perspective.

VANITAS. The term derives from the book of Ecclesiastes I:2 ("Vanities of vanities, …") that refers to the passing of time and the notion of life's brevity and the inevitability of death. The vanitas theme found expression especially in the Northern European art of the 17th century.

VAULT. An arched roof or ceiling usually made of stone, brick, or concrete. Several distinct varieties have been developed; all need buttressing at the point where the lateral thrust is concentrated. (1) A barrel vault is a semicircular structure made up of successive arches. It may be straight or annular in plan. (2) A groin vault is the result of the intersection of two barrel vaults of equal size that produces a bay of four compartments with sharp edges, or groins, where the two meet. (3) A ribbed groin vault is one in which ribs are added to the groins for structural strength and for decoration. When the diagonal ribs are constructed as half-circles, the resulting form is a domical ribbed vault. (4) A sexpartite vault is a ribbed groin vault in which each bay is divided into six compartments by the addition of a transverse rib across the center. (5) The normal Gothic vault is quadripartite with all the arches pointed to some degree. (6) A fan vault is an elaboration of a ribbed groin vault, with elements of tracery using conelike forms. It was developed by the English in the 15th century and was employed for decorative purposes.

VELLUM. See *parchment.*

VERISTIC. From the Latin *verus,* meaning "true." Describes a hyperrealistic style of portraiture that emphasizes individual characteristics.

VIGNETTE. A decorative design often used in manuscripts or books to separate sections or to decorate borders.

VOLUTE. A spiraling architectural element found notably on Ionic and Composite capitals but also used decoratively on building façades and interiors.

VOUSSOIR. A wedge-shaped piece of stone used in arch construction.

WARP. The vertical threads used in a weaver's loom through which the weft is woven.

WEBS. Masonry construction of brick, concrete, stone, etc. that is used to fill in the spaces between groin vault ribs.

WEFT. The horizontal threads that are interlaced through the vertical threads (the warp) in a woven fabric. Weft yarns run perpendicular to the warp.

WESTWORK. From the German word *Westwerk.* In Carolingian, Ottonian, and German Romanesque architecture, a monumental western front of a church, treated as a tower or combination of towers and containing an entrance and vestibule below and a chapel and galleries above. Later examples often added a transept and a crossing tower.

WET-COLLODION PROCESS. A 19th-century photographic technique that uses a very sensitive emulsion called collodion (gun-cotton dissolved in alcohol ether), that reduces exposure time to under a second and produces a sharp, easily reproducible negative.

WHITE-GROUND. Vase-painting technique in which artists painted a wide range of colors onto a white background. This was a favorite technique for decorating lekythoi (vases used in a funerary context in ancient Greece.)

WOODCUT. A print made by carving out a design on a wooden block cut along the grain, applying ink to the raised surfaces that remain, and printing from those.

X-RADIOGRAPHIC. Using a form of electromagnetic radiation called X-rays, researchers can examine the layers of paint or other materials used by artists to construct works of art.

ZIGGURAT. From the Assyrian word *zigquratu,* meaning "mountaintop" or "height." In ancient Assyria and Babylonia, a pyramidal mound or tower built of mud-brick forming the base for a temple. It was often either stepped or had a broad ascent winding around it, which gave it the appearance of being stepped.

Books for Further Reading

This list is intended to be as practical as possible. It is therefore limited to books of general interest that were printed over the past 20 years or have been generally available recently. However, certain indispensable volumes that have yet to be superseded are retained. This restriction means omitting numerous classics long out of print, as well as much specialized material of interest to the serious student. The reader is thus referred to the many specialized bibliographies noted below.

REFERENCE RESOURCES IN ART HISTORY

1. BIBLIOGRAPHIES AND RESEARCH GUIDES

Arntzen, E., and R. Rainwater. *Guide to the Literature of Art History*. Chicago: American Library, 1980.

Barnet, S. *A Short Guide to Writing About Art*. 8th ed. New York: Longman, 2005.

Ehresmann, D. *Architecture: A Bibliographical Guide to Basic Reference Works, Histories, and Handbooks*. Littleton, CO: Libraries Unlimited, 1984.

———. *Fine Arts: A Bibliographical Guide to Basic Reference Works, Histories, and Handbooks*. 3d ed. Littleton, CO: Libraries Unlimited, 1990.

Freitag, W. *Art Books: A Basic Bibliography of Monographs on Artists*. 2d ed. New York: Garland, 1997.

Goldman, B. *Reading and Writing in the Arts: A Handbook*. Detroit, MI: Wayne State Press, 1972.

Kleinbauer, W., and T. Slavens. *Research Guide to the History of Western Art*. Chicago: American Library, 1982.

Marmor, M., and A. Ross, eds. *Guide to the Literature of Art History 2*. Chicago: American Library, 2005.

Sayre, H. M. *Writing About Art*. New ed. Upper Saddle River, NJ: Pearson Prentice Hall, 2000.

2. DICTIONARIES AND ENCYCLOPEDIAS

Aghion, I. *Gods and Heroes of Classical Antiquity*. Flammarion Iconographic Guides. New York: Flammarion, 1996.

Boström, A., ed. *Encyclopedia of Sculpture*. 3 vols. New York: Fitzroy Dearborn, 2004.

Brigstocke, H., ed. *The Oxford Companion to Western Art*. New York: Oxford University Press, 2001.

Burden, E. *Illustrated Dictionary of Architecture*. New York: McGraw-Hill, 2002.

Carr-Gomm, S. *The Hutchinson Dictionary of Symbols in Art*. Oxford: Helicon, 1995.

Chilvers, I., et al., eds. *The Oxford Dictionary of Art*. 3d ed. New York: Oxford University Press, 2004.

Congdon, K. G. *Artists from Latin American Cultures: A Biographical Dictionary*. Westport, CT: Greenwood Press, 2002.

Cumming, R. *Art: A Field Guide*. New York: Alfred A. Knopf, 2001.

Curl, J. *A Dictionary of Architecture*. New York: Oxford University Press, 1999.

The Dictionary of Art. 34 vols. New York: Grove's Dictionaries, 1996.

Duchet-Suchaux, G., and M. Pastoureau. *The Bible and the Saints*. Flammarion Iconographic Guides. New York: Flammarion, 1994.

Encyclopedia of World Art. 14 vols., with index and supplements. New York: McGraw-Hill, 1959–1968.

Fleming, J., and H. Honour. *The Penguin Dictionary of Architecture and Landscape Architecture*. 5th ed. New York: Penguin, 1998.

———. *The Penguin Dictionary of Decorative Arts*. New ed. London: Viking, 1989.

Gascoigne, B. *How to Identify Prints: A Complete Guide to Manual and Mechanical Processes from Woodcut to Inkjet*. New York: Thames & Hudson, 2004.

Hall, J. *Dictionary of Subjects and Symbols in Art*. Rev. ed. London: J. Murray, 1996.

———. *Illustrated Dictionary of Symbols in Eastern and Western Art*. New York: HarperCollins, 1995.

International Dictionary of Architects and Architecture. 2 vols. Detroit, MI: St. James Press, 1993.

Langmuir, E. *Yale Dictionary of Art and Artists*. New Haven: Yale University Press, 2000.

Lever, J., and J. Harris. *Illustrated Dictionary of Architecture, 800–1914*. 2d ed. Boston: Faber & Faber, 1993.

Lucie-Smith, E. *The Thames & Hudson Dictionary of Art Terms*. New York: Thames & Hudson, 2004.

Mayer, R. *The Artist's Handbook of Materials and Techniques*. 5th ed. New York: Viking, 1991.

———. *The HarperCollins Dictionary of Art Terms & Techniques*. 2d ed. New York: HarperCollins, 1991.

Murray, P., and L. Murray. *A Dictionary of Art and Artists*. 7th ed. New York: Penguin, 1998.

———. *A Dictionary of Christian Art*. New York: Oxford University Press, 2004, © 1996.

Nelson, R. S., and R. Shiff, eds. *Critical Terms for Art History*. Chicago: University of Chicago Press, 2003.

Pierce, J. S. *From Abacus to Zeus: A Handbook of Art History*. 7th ed. Englewood Cliffs, NJ: Pearson Prentice Hall, 2004.

Reid, J. D., ed. *The Oxford Guide to Classical Mythology in the Arts 1300–1990*. 2 vols. New York: Oxford University Press, 1993.

Shoemaker, C., ed. *Encyclopedia of Gardens: History and Design*. Chicago: Fitzroy Dearborn, 2001.

Steer, J. *Atlas of Western Art History: Artists, Sites, and Movements from Ancient Greece to the Modern Age*. New York: Facts on File, 1994.

West, S., ed. *The Bulfinch Guide to Art History*. Boston: Little, Brown, 1996.

———. *Portraiture*. Oxford History of Art. New York: Oxford University Press, 2004.

3. INDEXES, PRINTED AND ELECTRONIC

ARTbibliographies Modern. 1969 to present. A semiannual publication indexing and annotating more than 300 art periodicals, as well as books, exhibition catalogues, and dissertations. Data since 1974 also available electronically.

Art Index. 1929 to present. A standard quarterly index to more than 200 art periodicals. Also available electronically.

Avery Index to Architectural Periodicals. 1934 to present. 15 vols., with supplementary vols. Boston: G. K. Hall, 1973. Also available electronically.

BHA: Bibliography of the History of Art. 1991 to present. The merger of two standard indexes: *RILA* (*Répertoire International de la Littérature de l'Art/International Repertory of the Literature of Art*, vol. 1. 1975) and *Répertoire d'Art et d'Archéologie* (vol. 1. 1910). Data since 1973 also available electronically.

Index Islamicus. 1665 to present. Multiple publishers. Data since 1994 also available electronically.

The Perseus Project: An Evolving Digital Library on Ancient Greece and Rome. Medford, MA: Tufts University, Classics Department, 1994.

4. WORLDWIDE WEBSITES

Visit the following websites for reproductions and information regarding artists, periods, movements, and many more subjects. The art history departments and libraries of many universities and colleges also maintain websites where you can get reading lists and links to other websites, such as those of museums, libraries, and periodicals.

http://www.aah.org.uk/welcome.html Association of Art Historians

http://www.amico.org Art Museum Image Consortium

http://www.archaeological.org Archaeological Institute of America

http://archnet.asu.edu/archnet Virtual Library for Archaeology

http://www.artchive.com

http://www.art-design.umich.edu/mother/ Mother of all Art History links pages, maintained by the Department of the History of Art at the University of Michigan

http://www.arthistory.net Art History Network

http://artlibrary.vassar.edu/ifla-idal International Directory of Art Libraries

http://www.bbk.ac.uk/lib/hasubject.html Collection of resources maintained by the History of Art Department of Birkbeck College, University of London

http://classics.mit.edu The Internet Classics Archive

http://www.collegeart.org College Art Association

http://www.constable.net

http://www.cr.nps.gov/habshaer Historic American Buildings Survey

http://www.getty.edu Including museum, five institutes, and library

http://www.harmsen.net/ahrc/ Art History Research Centre

http://icom.museum/ International Council of Museums

http://www.icomos.org International Council on Monuments and Sites

http://www.ilpi.com/artsource

http://www.siris.si.edu Smithsonian Institution Research Information System

http://whc.unesco.org/ World Heritage Center

5. GENERAL SOURCES ON ART HISTORY, METHOD, AND THEORY

Andrews, M. *Landscape and Western Art*. Oxford History of Art. New York: Oxford University Press, 1999.

Barasch, M. *Modern Theories of Art: Vol. 1, From Winckelmann to Baudelaire. Vol. 2, From Impressionism to Kandinsky*. New York: 1990–1998.

———. *Theories of Art: From Plato to Winckelmann*. New York: Routledge, 2000.

Battistini, M. *Symbols and Allegories in Art*. Los Angeles: J. Paul Getty Museum, 2005.

Baxandall, M. *Patterns of Intention: On the Historical Explanation of Pictures*. New Haven: Yale University Press, 1985.

Bois, Y.-A. *Painting as Model*. Cambridge, MA: MIT Press, 1993.

Broude, N., and M. Garrard. *The Expanding Discourse: Feminism and Art History*. New York: Harper & Row, 1992.

———., eds. *Feminism and Art History: Questioning the Litany*. New York: Harper & Row, 1982.

Bryson, N., ed. *Vision and Painting: The Logic of the Gaze*. New Haven: Yale University Press, 1983.

———, et al., eds. *Visual Theory: Painting and Interpretation*. New York: Cambridge University Press, 1991.

Chadwick, W. *Women, Art, and Society*. 3d ed. New York: Thames & Hudson, 2002.

leva, A. *Methods & Theories of Art History*. ondon: Laurence King, 2005.

Freedberg, D. *The Power of Images: Studies in the History and Theory of Response*. Chicago: University of Chicago Press, 1989.

Gage, J. *Color and Culture: Practice and Meaning from Antiquity to Abstraction*. Berkeley: University of California Press, 1999.

Garland Library of the History of Art. New York: Garland, 1976. Collections of essays on specific periods.

Goldwater, R., and M. Treves, eds. *Artists on Art, from the Fourteenth to the Twentieth Century*. 3d ed. New York: Pantheon, 1974.

Gombrich, E. H. *Art and Illusion*. 6th ed. New York: Phaidon, 2002.

Harris, A. S., and L. Nochlin. *Women Artists, 1550–1950*. New York: Random House, 1999.

Holly, M. A. *Panofsky and the Foundations of Art History*. Ithaca, NY: Cornell University Press, 1984.

Holt, E. G., ed. *A Documentary History of Art: Vol. 1, The Middle Ages and the Renaissance. Vol. 2, Michelangelo and the Mannerists. The Baroque and the Eighteenth Century. Vol. 3, From the Classicists to the Impressionists*. 2d ed. Princeton, NJ: Princeton University Press, 1981. Anthologies of primary sources on specific periods.

Johnson, P. *Art: A New History*. New York: HarperCollins, 2003.

Kemal, S., and I. Gaskell. *The Language of Art History*. Cambridge Studies in Philosophy and the Arts. New York: Cambridge University Press, 1991.

Kemp, M., ed. *The Oxford History of Western Art*. New York: Oxford University Press, 2000.

Kleinbauer, W. E. *Modern Perspectives in Western Art History: An Anthology of Twentieth-Century Writings on the Visual Arts*. Reprint of 1971 ed. Toronto: University of Toronto Press, 1989.

stof, S. A. *History of Architecture: Settings and Rituals*. 2d ed. New York: Oxford University Press, 1995.

Kruft, H. W. *A History of Architectural Theory from Vitruvius to the Present*. Princeton, NJ: Princeton Architectural Press, 1994.

Kultermann, U. *The History of Art History*. New York: Abaris Books, 1993.

Langer, C. *Feminist Art Criticism: An Annotated Bibliography*. Boston: G. K. Hall, 1993.

Laver, J. *Costume and Fashion: A Concise History*. 4th ed. The World of Art. London: Thames & Hudson, 2002.

Lavin, I., ed. *Meaning in the Visual Arts: Views from the Outside: A Centennial Commemoration of Erwin Panofsky (1892–1968)*. Princeton, NJ: Institute for Advanced Study, 1995.

Minor, V. H. *Art History's History*. Upper Saddle River, NJ: Pearson Prentice Hall, 2001.

Nochlin, L. *Women, Art, and Power, and Other Essays*. New York: HarperCollins, 1989.

Pächt, O. *The Practice of Art History: Reflections on Method*. London: Harvey Miller, 1999.

Panofsky, E. *Meaning in the Visual Arts*. Reprint of 1955 ed. Chicago: University of Chicago Press, 1982.

Penny, N. *The Materials of Sculpture*. New Haven: Yale University Press, 1993.

Pevsner, N. *A History of Building Types*. Princeton, NJ: Princeton University Press, 1976.

Podro, M. *The Critical Historians of Art*. New Haven: Yale University Press, 1982.

Pollock, G. *Differencing the Canon: Feminist Desire and the Writing of Art's Histories*. New York: Routledge, 1999.

———. *Vision and Difference: Femininity, Feminism, and the Histories of Art*. New York: Routledge, 1988.

Prettejohn, E. *Beauty and Art 1750–2000*. Oxford: Oxford University Press, 2005.

eziosi, D., ed. *The Art of Art History: A Critical Anthology*. New York: Oxford University Press, 1998.

Rees, A. L., and F. Borzello. *The New Art History*. Atlantic Highlands, NJ: Humanities Press International, 1986.

Roth, L. *Understanding Architecture: Its Elements, History, and Meaning*. New York: Harper & Row, 1993.

Sedlmayr, H. *Framing Formalism: Riegl's Work*. Amsterdam: G+B Arts International, © 2001.

Smith, P., and C. Wilde, eds. *A Companion to Art Theory*. Oxford: Blackwell, 2002.

Sources and Documents in the History of Art Series. General ed. H. W. Janson. Englewood Cliffs, NJ: Prentice Hall. Anthologies of primary sources on specific periods.

Sutton, I. *Western Architecture*. New York: Thames & Hudson, 1999.

Tagg, J. *Grounds of Dispute: Art History, Cultural Politics, and the Discursive Field*. Minneapolis: University of Minnesota Press, 1992.

Trachtenberg, M., and I. Hyman. *Architecture: From Prehistory to Post-Modernism*. 2d ed. New York: Harry N. Abrams, 2002.

Watkin, D. *The Rise of Architectural History*. Chicago: University of Chicago Press, 1980.

Wolff, J. *The Social Production of Art*. 2d ed. New York: New York University Press, 1993.

Wölfflin, H. *Principles of Art History: The Problem of the Development of Style in Later Art*. Various eds. New York: Dover.

Wollheim, R. *Art and Its Objects*. 2d ed. New York: Cambridge University Press, 1992.

PART ONE: THE ANCIENT WORLD

GENERAL REFERENCES

Baines, J., ed. *Civilizations of the Ancient Near East*. 4 vols. New York: Scribner, 1995.

Boardman, J., ed. *The Oxford History of Classical Art*. New York: Oxford University Press, 2001.

De Grummond, N., ed. *An Encyclopedia of the History of Classical Archaeology*. Westport, CT: Greenwood, 1996.

Fine, S. *Art and Judaism in the Greco-Roman World: Toward a New Jewish Archaeology*. New York: Cambridge University Press, 2005.

Holliday, P. J. *Narrative and Event in Ancient Art*. New York: Cambridge University Press, 1993.

Redford, D. B., ed. *The Oxford Encyclopedia of Ancient Egypt*. 3 vols. New York: Oxford University Press, 2001.

Stillwell, R. *The Princeton Encyclopedia of Classical Sites*. Princeton, NJ: Princeton University Press, 1976.

Tadgell, C. *Origins: Egypt, West Asia and the Aegean*. New York: Whitney Library of Design, 1998.

Van Keuren, F. *Guide to Research in Classical Art and Mythology*. Chicago: American Library Association, 1991.

Wharton, A. J. *Refiguring the Post-Classical City: Dura Europos, Jerash, Jerusalem, and Ravenna*. New York: Cambridge University Press, 1995.

Winckelmann, J. J. *Essays on the Philosophy and History of Art*. 3 vols. Bristol, England: Thoemmes, 2001.

Wolf, W. *The Origins of Western Art: Egypt, Mesopotamia, the Aegean*. New York: Universe Books, 1989.

Yegül, F. K. *Baths and Bathing in Classical Antiquity*. Architectural History Foundation. Cambridge, MA: MIT Press, 1992.

CHAPTER 1. PREHISTORIC ART

Bahn, P. G. *The Cambridge Illustrated History of Prehistoric Art*. New York: Cambridge University Press, 1988.

Chauvet, J.-M., É. B. Deschamps, and C. Hilaire. *Dawn of Art: The Chauvet Cave*. New York: Harry N. Abrams, 1995.

Clottes, J. *Chauvet Cave*. Salt Lake City: University of Utah Press, 2003.

———. *The Shamans of Prehistory: Trance and Magic in the Painted Caves*. New York: Harry N. Abrams, 1998.

Cunliffe, B., ed. *The Oxford Illustrated Prehistory of Europe*. Oxford: Oxford University Press, 1994.

Fitton, J. L. *Cycladic Art*. London: British Museum Press, 1999.

Fowler, P. *Images of Prehistory*. New York: Cambridge University Press, 1990.

Leroi-Gourhan, A. *The Dawn of European Art: An Introduction to Paleolithic Cave Painting*. New York: Cambridge University Press, 1982.

McCold, C. H., and L. D. McDermott. *Toward Decolonizing Gender: Female Vision in the Upper Palaeolithic*. American Anthropologist 98, 1996.

Ruspoli, M. *The Cave of Lascaux: The Final Photographs*. New York: Harry N. Abrams, 1987.

Sandars, N. *Prehistoric Art in Europe*. 2d ed. New Haven: Yale University Press, 1992.

Saura Ramos, P. A. *The Cave of Altamira*. New York: Harry N. Abrams, 1999.

Twohig, E. S. *The Megalithic Art of Western Europe*. New York: Oxford University Press, 1981.

White, R. *Prehistoric Art: The Symbolic Journey of Mankind*. New York: Harry N. Abrams, 2003.

CHAPTER 2. ANCIENT NEAR EASTERN ART

Amiet, P. *Art of the Ancient Near East*. New York: Harry N. Abrams, 1980.

Aruz, J., ed. *Art of the First Cities: The Third Millennium B.C. from the Mediterranean to the Indus*. Exh. cat. New York: Metropolitan Museum of Art; Yale University Press, 2003.

Collon, D. *Ancient Near Eastern Art*. Berkeley: University of California Press, 1995.

———. *First Impressions: Cylinder Seals in the Ancient Near East*. Chicago: University of Chicago Press, 1987.

Crawford, H. *The Architecture of Iraq in the Third Millennium B.C.* Copenhagen: Akademisk Forlag, 1977.

Curtis, J., and N. Tallis. *Forgotten Empire: The World of Ancient Persia*. Exh. cat. London: British Museum, 2005.

Frankfort, H. *The Art and Architecture of the Ancient Orient*. 5th ed. Pelican History of Art. New Haven: Yale University Press, 1997.

Goldman, B. *The Ancient Arts of Western and Central Asia: A Guide to the Literature*. Ames: Iowa State University Press, 1991.

Harper, P. O., ed. *The Royal City of Susa: Ancient Near Eastern Treasures in the Louvre*. New York: Metropolitan Museum of Art; Dist. by Harry N. Abrams, 1992.

Leick, G. *A Dictionary of Ancient Near Eastern Architecture*. New York: Routledge, 1988.

Lloyd, S. *The Archaeology of Mesopotamia: From the Old Stone Age to the Persian Conquest*. Rev. ed. New York: Thames & Hudson, 1984.

Moscati, S. *The Phoenicians*. New York: Abbeville Press, 1988.

Oates, J. *Babylon*. Rev. ed. London: Thames & Hudson, 1986.

Reade, J. *Mesopotamia*. 2d ed. London: Published for the Trustees of the British Museum by the British Museum Press, 2000.

Zettler, R., and L. Horne, eds. *Treasures from the Royal Tombs of Ur*. Exh. cat. Philadelphia: University of Pennsylvania, Museum of Archaeology and Anthropology, 1998.

CHAPTER 3. EGYPTIAN ART

Aldred, C. *The Development of Ancient Egyptian Art, from 3200 to 1315 B.C.* 3 vols. in 1. London: Academy Editions, 1972.

———. *Egyptian Art*. London: Thames & Hudson, 1985.

Arnold, D., and C. Ziegler. *Building in Egypt: Pharaonic Stone Masonry*. New York: Oxford University Press, 1991.

———. *Egyptian Art in the Age of the Pyramids*. New York: Harry N. Abrams, 1999.

Bothmer, B. V. *Egyptian Art: Selected Writings of Bernard V. Bothmer*. New York: Oxford University Press, 2004.

Davis, W. *The Canonical Tradition in Ancient Egyptian Art*. New York: Cambridge University Press, 1989.

Edwards, I. E. S. *The Pyramids of Egypt*. Rev. ed. Harmondsworth, England: Penguin, 1991.

Egyptian Art in the Age of the Pyramids. New York: Metropolitan Museum of Art; Dist. by Harry N. Abrams, 1999.

Grimal, N. *A History of Ancient Egypt*. London: Blackwell, 1992.

Mahdy, C., ed. *The World of the Pharaohs: A Complete Guide to Ancient Egypt*. London: Thames & Hudson, 1990.

Malek, J. *Egypt: 4000 Years of Art*. London: Phaidon, 2003.

———. *Egyptian Art. Art & Ideas*. London: Phaidon, 1999.

Mendelssohn, K. *The Riddle of the Pyramids*. New York: Thames & Hudson, 1986.

Parry, D. *Engineering the Pyramids*. Stroud, England: Sutton, 2004.

Robins, G. *The Art of Ancient Egypt*. Cambridge, MA: Harvard University Press, 1997.

Schaefer, H. *Principles of Egyptian Art*. Oxford: Clarendon Press, 1986.

Schulz, R., and M. Seidel. *Egypt: The World of the Pharaohs*. Cologne: Könemann, 1998.

Smith, W., and W. Simpson. *The Art and Architecture of Ancient Egypt*. Rev. ed. Pelican History of Art. New Haven: Yale University Press, 1999.

Tiradritti, F. *Ancient Egypt: Art, Architecture and History*. London: British Museum Press, 2002.

Walker, S. and P. Higgs, eds. *Cleopatra of Egypt: From History to Myth*. Exh. cat. Princeton, NJ: Princeton University Press, 2001.

Wilkinson, R. *Reading Egyptian Art: A Hieroglyphic Guide to Ancient Egyptian Painting and Sculpture*. New York: Thames & Hudson, 1992.

CHAPTER 4. AEGEAN ART

Akurgal, E. *The Aegean, Birthplace of Western Civilization: History of East Greek Art and Culture, 1050–333 B.C.* Izmir, Turkey: Metropolitan Municipality of Izmir, 2000.

Barber, R. *The Cyclades in the Bronze Age*. Iowa City: University of Iowa Press, 1987.

Dickinson, O. T. P. K. *The Aegean Bronze Age*. New York: Cambridge University Press, 1994.

Elytis, O. *The Aegean: The Epicenter of Greek Civilization*. Athens: Melissa, 1997.

German, S. C. *Performance, Power and the Art of the Aegean Bronze Age*. Oxford: Archaeopress, 2005.

Getz-Preziosi, P. *Sculptors of the Cyclades*. Ann Arbor: University of Michigan Press, 1987.

Graham, J. *The Palaces of Crete*. Rev. ed. Princeton, NJ: Princeton University Press, 1987.

Hampe, R., and E. Simon. *The Birth of Greek Art from the Mycenean to the Archaic Period*. New York: Oxford University Press, 1981.

Higgins, R. *Minoan and Mycenaean Art*. Rev. ed. The World of Art. New York: Oxford University Press, 1981.

Hood, S. *The Arts in Prehistoric Greece*. Pelican History of Art. New Haven: Yale University Press, 1992.

———. *The Minoans: The Story of Bronze Age Crete*. New York: Praeger, 1981.

Hurwit, J. *The Art and Culture of Early Greece, 1100–480 B.C.* Ithaca, NY: Cornell University Press, 1985.

McDonald, W. *Progress into the Past: The Rediscovery of Mycenaean Civilization*. 2d ed. Bloomington: Indiana University Press, 1990.

Preziosi, D., and L. Hitchcock. *Aegean Art and Architecture*. New York: Oxford University Press, 1999.

Renfrew, C. *The Cycladic Spirit: Masterpieces from the Nicholas P. Goulandris Collection*. London: Thames & Hudson, 1991.

Vermeule, E. *Greece in the Bronze Age*. Chicago: University of Chicago Press, 1972.

CHAPTER 5. GREEK ART

Beard, M. *The Parthenon*. Cambridge, MA: Harvard University Press, 2003.

Beazley, J. D. *Athenian Red Figure Vases: The Archaic Period: A Handbook*. The World of Art. New York: Thames & Hudson, 1991.

———. *Athenian Red Figure Vases: The Classical Period: A Handbook*. The World of Art. New York: Thames & Hudson, 1989.

———. *The Development of Attic Black-Figure*. Rev. ed. Berkeley: University of California Press, 1986.

———. *Greek Vases: Lectures*. Oxford and New York: Clarendon Press and Oxford University Press, 1989.

Boardman, J. *The Archaeology of Nostalgia: How the Greeks Re-created Their Mythical Past*. London: Thames & Hudson, 2002.

———. *Athenian Black Figure Vases: A Handbook*. Corrected ed. The World of Art. New York: Thames & Hudson, 1991.

———. *Early Greek Vase Painting: 11th–6th Centuries B.C.: A Handbook*. The World of Art. New York: Thames & Hudson, 1998.

———. *Greek Art*. 4th ed., rev. and expanded. The World of Art. New York: Thames & Hudson, 1996.

———. *Greek Sculpture: The Archaic Period: A Handbook*. Corrected ed. The World of Art. New York: Thames & Hudson, 1991.

———. *Greek Sculpture: The Classical Period: A Handbook*. Corrected ed. New York: Thames & Hudson, 1991.

———. *The History of Greek Vases: Potters, Painters, and Pictures*. New York: Thames & Hudson, 2001.

Burn, L. *Hellenistic Art: From Alexander the Great to Augustus*. London: The British Museum, 2004.

Carpenter, T. H. *Art and Myth in Ancient Greece: A Handbook*. The World of Art. New York: Thames & Hudson, 1991.

Carratelli, G. P., ed. *The Greek World: Art and Civilization in Magna Graecia and Sicily*. Exh. cat. New York: Rizzoli, 1996.

Fullerton, M. D. *Greek Art*. New York: Cambridge University Press, 2000.

Hampe, R., and E. Simon. *The Birth of Greek Art*. Oxford: Oxford University Press, 1981.

Haynes, D. E. L. *The Technique of Greek Bronze Statuary*. Mainz am Rhein: P. von Zabern, 1992.

Himmelmann, N. *Reading Greek Art: Essays*. Princeton, NJ: Princeton University Press, 1998.

Hurwit, J. M. *The Acropolis in the Age of Pericles*. New York: Cambridge University Press, 2004.

———. *The Art & Culture of Early Greece, 1100–480 B.C.* Ithaca, NY: Cornell University Press, 1985.

Lawrence, A. *Greek Architecture*. Rev. 5th ed. Pelican History of Art. New Haven: Yale University Press, 1996.

L'Empereur, J. *Alexandria Rediscovered*. London: British Museum Press, 1998.

Osborne, R. *Archaic and Classical Greek Art*. New York: Oxford University Press, 1998.

Papaioannou, K. *The Art of Greece*. New York: Harry N. Abrams, 1989.

Pedley, J. *Greek Art and Archaeology*. 2d ed. New York: Harry N. Abrams, 1997.

Pollitt, J. *The Ancient View of Greek Art: Criticism, History, and Terminology*. New Haven: Yale University Press, 1974.

———. *Art in the Hellenistic Age*. New York: Cambridge University Press, 1986.

———., ed. *Art of Ancient Greece: Sources and Documents*. New York: Cambridge University Press, 1990.

Potts, A. *Flesh and the Ideal: Winckelmann and the Origins of Art History*. New Haven: Yale University Press, 1994.

Rhodes, R. F. *Architecture and Meaning on the Athenian Acropolis*. New York: Cambridge University Press, 1995.

———., ed. *The Acquisition and Exhibition of Classical Antiquities: Professional, Legal, and Ethical Perspectives*. Notre Dame, IN: University of Notre Dame Press, 2007.

Richter, G. M. A. *A Handbook of Greek Art*. 9th ed. New York: Da Capo, 1987.

———. *Portraits of the Greeks*. Ed. R. Smith. New York: Oxford University Press, 1984.

Ridgway, B. S. *Hellenistic Sculpture: Vol. 1, The Styles of ca. 331–200 B.C.* Bristol, England: Bristol Classical Press, 1990.

Robertson, M. *The Art of Vase Painting in Classical Athens*. New York: Cambridge University Press, 1992.

Rolley, C. *Greek Bronzes*. New York: Philip Wilson for Sotheby's Publications; Dist. by Harper & Row, 1986.

Schefold, K. *Gods and Heroes in Late Archaic Greek Art*. New York: Cambridge University Press, 1992.

Smith, R. *Hellenistic Sculpture*. The World of Art. New York: Thames & Hudson, 1991.

Spivey, N. *Greek Art*. London: Phaidon, 1997.

Stafford, E. *Life, Myth, and Art in Ancient Greece*. Los Angeles: J. Paul Getty Museum, 2004.

Stansbury-O'Donnell, M. *Pictorial Narrative in Ancient Greek Art*. New York: Cambridge University Press, 1999.

Stewart, A. F. *Greek Sculpture: An Exploration*. New Haven: Yale University Press, 1990.

Whitley, J. *The Archaeology of Ancient Greece*. New York: Cambridge University Press, 2001.

CHAPTER 6. ETRUSCAN ART

Boethius, A. *Etruscan and Early Roman Architecture*. 2d ed. Pelican History of Art. New Haven: Yale University Press, 1992.

Bonfante, L., ed. *Etruscan Life and Afterlife: A Handbook of Etruscan Studies*. Detroit, MI: Wayne State University, 1986.

Borrelli, F. *The Etruscans: Art, Architecture, and History*. Los Angeles: J. Paul Getty Museum, 2004.

Brendel, O. *Etruscan Art*. Pelican History of Art. New Haven: Yale University Press, 1995.

Hall, J. F., ed. *Etruscan Italy: Etruscan Influences on the Civilizations of Italy from Antiquity to the Modern Era*. Provo, UT: Museum of Art, Brigham Young University, 1996.

Haynes, Sybille. *Etruscan Civilization: A Cultural History*. Los Angeles: J. Paul Getty Museum, 2000.

Richardson, E. *The Etruscans: Their Art and Civilization*. Reprint of 1964 ed., with corrections. Chicago: University of Chicago Press, 1976.

Spivey, N. *Etruscan Art*. The World of Art. New York: Thames & Hudson, 1997.

Sprenger, M., G. Bartoloni, and M. Hirmer. *The Etruscans: Their History, Art, and Architecture*. New York: Harry N. Abrams, 1983.

Steingräber, S., ed. *Etruscan Painting: Catalogue Raisonné of Etruscan Wall Paintings*. New York: Johnson Reprint, 1986.

Torelli, M., ed. *The Etruscans*. Exh. cat. Milan: Bompiani, 2000.

CHAPTER 7. ROMAN ART

Allan, T. *Life, Myth and Art in Ancient Rome*. Los Angeles: J. Paul Getty Museum, 2005.

Andreae, B. *The Art of Rome*. New York: Harry N. Abrams, 1977.

Beard, M., and J. Henderson. *Classical Art: From Greece to Rome*. New York: Oxford University Press, 2001.

Bowe, P. *Gardens of the Roman World*. Los Angeles: J. Paul Getty Museum, 2004.

Brilliant, R. *Commentaries on Roman Art: Selected Studies*. London: Pindar Press, 1994.

———. *My Laocoon: Alternative Claims in the Interpretation of Artworks*. University of California Press, 2000.

Claridge, A. *Rome: An Oxford Archaeological Guide*. New York: Oxford University Press, 1998.

D'Ambra, E. *Roman Art*. New York: Cambridge University Press, 1998.

———., comp. *Roman Art in Context: An Anthology*. Englewood Cliffs, NJ: Prentice Hall, 1993.

Davies, P. *Death and the Emperor: Roman Imperial Funerary Monuments from Augustus to Marcus Aurelius*. Austin: University of Texas Press, 2004.

Dunbabin, K. M. D. *Mosaics of the Greek and Roman World*. New York: Cambridge University Press, 1999.

Elsner, J. *Imperial Rome and Christian Triumph: The Art of the Roman Empire, A.D. 100–450*. New York: Oxford University Press, 1998.

Gazda, E. K. *Roman Art in the Private Sphere: New Perspectives on the Architecture and Decor of the Domus, Villa, and Insula*. Ann Arbor: University of Michigan Press, 1991.

Jenkyns, R., ed. *The Legacy of Rome: A New Appraisal*. New York: Oxford University Press, 1992.

Kleiner, D. *Roman Sculpture*. New Haven: Yale University Press, 1992.

———., and S. B. Matheson, eds. *I, Claudia: Women in Ancient Rome*. New Haven: Yale University Art Gallery, 1996.

Ling, R. *Ancient Mosaics*. London: British Museum Press, 1998.

———. *Roman Painting*. New York: Cambridge University Press, 1991.

Nash, E. *Pictorial Dictionary of Ancient Rome*. 2 vols. Reprint of 1968 2d ed. New York: Hacker, 1981.

Pollitt, J. J. *The Art of Rome, c. 753 B.C.– A.D. 337: Sources and Documents*. New York: Cambridge University Press, 1983.

Ramage, N., and A. Ramage. *The Cambridge Illustrated History of Roman Art*. Cambridge: Cambridge University Press, 1991.

———. *Roman Art: Romulus to Constantine*. 4th ed. Upper Saddle River, NJ: Pearson Prentice Hall, 2005.

Richardson, L. *A New Topographical Dictionary of Ancient Rome*. Baltimore, MD: Johns Hopkins University Press, 1992.

Rockwell, P. *The Art of Stoneworking: A Reference Guide*. Cambridge: Cambridge University Press, 1993.

Strong, D. E. *Roman Art*. 2d ed. Pelican History of Art. New Haven: Yale University Press, 1992.

Vitruvius. *The Ten Books on Architecture*. Trans. I. Rowland. Cambridge: Cambridge University Press, 1999.

Ward-Perkins, J. B. *Roman Imperial Architecture*. Reprint of 1981 ed. Pelican History of Art. New York: Penguin, 1992.

Zanker, P. *The Power of Images in the Age of Augustus*. Ann Arbor: University of Michigan Press, 1988.

PART TWO: THE MIDDLE AGES
GENERAL REFERENCES

Alexander, J. J. G. *Medieval Illuminators and Their Methods of Work*. New Haven: Yale University Press, 1992.

———., ed. *A Survey of Manuscripts Illuminated in the British Isles*. 6 vols. London: Harvey Miller, 1975–1996.

Avril, F., and J. J. G. Alexander, eds. *A Survey of Manuscripts Illuminated in France*. London: Harvey Miller, 1996.

Bartlett, R., ed. *Medieval Panorama*. Los Angeles: J. Paul Getty Museum, 2001.

Cahn, W. *Studies in Medieval Art and Interpretation*. London: Pindar Press, 2000.

Calkins, R. G. *Medieval Architecture in Western Europe: From A.D. 300 to 1500*. New York: Oxford University Press, 1998.

Cassidy, B., ed. *Iconography at the Crossroads*. Princeton, NJ: Princeton University Press, 1993.

Coldstream, N. *Medieval Architecture*. Oxford History of Art. New York: Oxford University Press, 2002.

De Hamel, C. *The British Library Guide to Manuscript Illumination: History and Techniques*. Toronto: University of Toronto Press, 2001.

———. *A History of Illuminated Manuscripts*. Rev. and enl. 2d ed. London: Phaidon Press, 1994.

Duby, G. *Art and Society in the Middle Ages*. Polity Press; Malden, MA: Blackwell Publishers, 2000.

Hamburger, J. *Nuns as Artists: The Visual Culture of a Medieval Convent*. Berkeley: University of California Press, 1997.

Katzenellenbogen, A. *Allegories of the Virtues and Vices in Medieval Art*. Reprint of 1939 ed. Toronto: University of Toronto Press, 1989.

Kazhdan, A. P. *The Oxford Dictionary of Byzantium*. 3 vols. New York: Oxford University Press, 1991.

Kessler, H. L. *Seeing Medieval Art*. Peterborough, Ont. and Orchard Park, NY: Broadview Press, 2004.

Luttikhuizen, H., and D. Verkerk. *Snyder's Medieval Art*. 2d ed. Upper Saddle River, NJ: Prentice Hall, 2006.

Pächt, O. *Book Illumination in the Middle Ages: An Introduction*. London: Harvey Miller, 1986.

Pelikan, J. *Mary Through the Centuries: Her Place in the History of Culture*. New Haven: Yale University Press, 1996.

Ross, L. *Artists of the Middle Ages*. Westport, CT: Greenwood Press, 2003.

———. *Medieval Art: A Topical Dictionary*. Westport, CT: Greenwood Press, 1996.

Schütz, B. *Great Cathedrals*. New York: Harry N. Abrams, 2002.

Sears, E., and T. K. Thomas, eds. *Reading Medieval Images: The Art Historian and the Object*. Ann Arbor: University of Michigan Press, 2002.

Sekules, V. *Medieval Art*. New York: Oxford University Press, 2001.

Stokstad, M. *Medieval Art*. Boulder, CO: Westview Press, 2004.

Tasker, E. *Encyclopedia of Medieval Church Art*. London: Batsford, 1993.

Watson, R. *Illuminated Manuscripts and Their Makers: An Account Based on the Collection of the Victoria and Albert Museum*. London and New York: V & A Publications; Dist. by Harry N. Abrams, 2003.

Wieck, R. S. *Painted Prayers: The Book of Hours in Medieval and Renaissance Art*. New York: George Braziller in association with the Pierpont Morgan Library, 1997.

Wixom, W. D. *Mirror of the Medieval World*. Exh. cat. New York: Metropolitan Museum of Art; Dist. by Harry N. Abrams, 1999.

CHAPTER 8. EARLY JEWISH, EARLY CHRISTIAN, AND BYZANTINE ART

Beckwith, J. *Studies in Byzantine and Medieval Western Art*. London: Pindar Press, 1989.

Bowersock, G. W., ed. *Late Antiquity: A Guide to the Postclassical World*. Cambridge, MA: Belknap Press of Harvard University Press, 1999.

Cormack, R. *Icons*. London: British Museum Press, 2007.

Demus, O. *Studies in Byzantium, Venice and the West*. 2 vols. London: Pindar Press, 1998.

Drury, J. *Painting the Word: Christian Pictures and Their Meanings*. New Haven and London: Yale University Press in association with National Gallery Publications, 1999.

Durand, J. *Byzantine Art*. Paris: Terrail, 1999.

Evans, H. C., ed. *Byzantium: Faith and Power, 1261–1557*. Exh. cat. New York: Metropolitan Museum of Art; New Haven: Yale University Press, 2004.

Evans, H. C., and W. D. Wixom, eds. *The Glory of Byzantium: Art and Culture of the Middle Byzantine Era, A. D. 843–1261*. Exh. cat. New York: Metropolitan Museum of Art; New Haven: Yale University Press, 1997.

Galavaris, G. *Colours, Symbols, Worship: The Mission of the Byzantine Artist*. London: Pindar, 2005.

Grabar, A. *Christian Iconography: A Study of Its Origins*. Princeton, NJ: Princeton University Press, 1968.

Henderson, G. *Vision and Image in Early Christian England*. New York: Cambridge University Press, 1999.

Kalavrezou, I. *Byzantine Women and Their World*. Exh. cat. Cambridge, MA and New Haven: Harvard University Art Museums; Yale University Press, © 2003.

Kleinbauer, W. *Early Christian and Byzantine Architecture: An Annotated Bibliography and Historiography*. Boston: G. K. Hall, 1993.

Krautheimer, R., and S. Curcic. *Early Christian and Byzantine Architecture*. 4th ed. Pelican History of Art. New Haven: Yale University Press, 1992.

Lowden, J. *Early Christian and Byzantine Art*. London: Phaidon Press, 1997.

Maguire, H. *Art and Eloquence in Byzantium*. Princeton, NJ: Princeton University Press, 1981.

Mango, C. *The Art of the Byzantine Empire, 312–1453: Sources and Documents*. Reprint of 1972 ed. Toronto: University of Toronto Press, 1986.

Mark, R., and A. S. Çakmak, eds. *Hagia Sophia from the Age of Justinian to the Present*. New York: Cambridge University Press, 1992.

Matthews, T. *Byzantium from Antiquity to the Renaissance*. New York: Harry N. Abrams, 1998.

———. *The Clash of Gods: A Reinterpretation of Early Christian Art*. Princeton, NJ: Princeton University Press, 1993.

Milburn, R. *Early Christian Art and Architecture*. Berkeley: University of California Press, 1988.

Rodley, L. *Byzantine Art and Architecture: An Introduction*. New York: Cambridge University Press, 1994.

Simson, O. G. von. *Sacred Fortress: Byzantine Art and Statecraft in Ravenna*. Reprint of 1948 ed. Princeton, NJ: Princeton University Press, 1987.

Webster, L., and M. Brown, eds. *The Transformation of the Roman World A.D. 400–900*. Berkeley: University of California Press, 1997.

Weitzmann, K. *Late Antique and Early Christian Book Illumination*. New York: Braziller, 1977.

CHAPTER 9. ISLAMIC ART

Asher, C. E. B. *Architecture of Mughal India*. New Cambridge History of India, Cambridge, England. New York: Cambridge University Press, 1992.

Atil, E. *The Age of Sultan Süleyman the Magnificent*. Exh. cat. Washington, DC: National Gallery of Art; New York: Harry N. Abrams, 1987.

———. *Renaissance of Islam: Art of the Mamluks*. Exh. cat. Washington, DC: Smithsonian Institution Press, 1981.

Behrens-Abouseif, D. *Beauty in Arabic Culture*. Princeton, NJ: Markus Wiener, 1998.

Bierman, I., ed. *The Experience of Islamic Art on the Margins of Islam*. Reading, England: Ithaca Press, 2005.

Blair, S., and J. Bloom. *The Art and Architecture of Islam 1250–1800*. Pelican History of Art. New Haven: Yale University Press, 1996.

Brookes, J. *Gardens of Paradise: The History and Design of the Great Islamic Gardens*. New York: New Amsterdam, 1987.

Burckhardt, T. *Art of Islam: Language and Meaning*. London: World of Islam Festival, 1976.

Creswell, K. A. C. *A Bibliography of the Architecture, Arts, and Crafts of Islam*. Cairo: American University in Cairo Press, 1984.

Denny, W. B. *The Classical Tradition in Anatolian Carpets*. Washington, DC: Textile Museum, 2002.

Dodds, J. D., ed. *al-Andalus: The Art of Islamic Spain*. Exh. cat. New York: Metropolitan Museum of Art; Dist. by Harry N. Abrams, 1992.

Erdmann, K. *Oriental Carpets: An Essay on Their History*. Fishguard, Wales: Crosby Press, 1976, © 1960.

Ettinghausen, R., O. Grabar, and M. Jenkins-Madina. *Islamic Art and Architecture, 650–1250*. 2d ed. Pelican History of Art. New Haven: Yale University Press, 2002.

Frishman, M., and H. Khan. *The Mosque: History, Architectural Development and Regional Diversity*. London: Thames & Hudson, 2002, © 1994.

Goodwin, G. *A History of Ottoman Architecture*. New York: Thames & Hudson, 2003, © 1971.

Grabar, O. *The Formation of Islamic Art*. Rev. and enl. ed. New Haven: Yale University Press, 1987.

Hillenbrand, R. *Islamic Architecture: Form, Function, and Meaning*. New ed. New York: Columbia University Press, 2004.

Komaroff, L., and S. Carboni, eds. *The Legacy of Genghis Khan: Courtly Art and Culture in Western Asia, 1256–1353*. Exh. cat. New York: Metropolitan Museum of Art; New Haven: Yale University Press, 2002.

Lentz, T., and G. Lowry. *Timur and the Princely Vision: Persian Art and Culture in the Fifteenth Century*. Exh. cat. Los Angeles: Los Angeles County Museum of Art; Washington, DC: Arthur M. Sackler Gallery; Smithsonian Institution Press, 1989.

Lings, M. *The Quranic Art of Calligraphy and Illumination*. 1st American ed. New York: Interlink Books, 1987, © 1976.

Necipolu, G. *The Age of Sinan: Architectural Culture in the Ottoman Empire*. Princeton, NJ: Princeton University Press, 2005.

———. *The Topkapı Scroll: Geometry and Ornament in Islamic Architecture*. Topkapı Palace Museum Library MS H. 1956. Santa Monica, CA: Getty Center for the History of Art and the Humanities, 1995.

Pope, A. U. *Persian Architecture: The Triumph of Form and Color*. New York: Braziller, 1965.

Robinson, F. *Atlas of the Islamic World Since 1500*. New York: Facts on File, 1982.

Ruggles, D. F. *Gardens, Landscape, and Vision in the Palaces of Islamic Spain*. University Park: Pennsylvania State University Press, 2000.

———., ed. *Women, Patronage, and Self-Representation in Islamic Societies*. Albany: State University of New York Press, 2000.

Tabbaa, Y. *The Transformation of Islamic Art During the Sunni Revival*. Seattle: University of Washington Press, 2001.

Thompson, J., ed. *Hunt for Paradise: Court Arts of Safavid Iran, 1501–1576.* Milan: Skira; New York: Dist. in North America and Latin America by Rizzoli, 2003.

———. *Oriental Carpets from the Tents, Cottages, and Workshops of Asia.* New York: Dutton, 1988.

Vernoit, S., ed. *Discovering Islamic Art: Scholars, Collectors and Collections, 1850–1950.* London and New York: I. B. Tauris; Dist. by St. Martin's Press, 2000.

Welch, S. C. *Imperial Mughal Painting.* New York: Braziller, 1978.

———. *A King's Book of Kings: The Shah-nameh of Shah Tahmasp.* New York: Metropolitan Museum of Art; Dist. by New York Graphic Society, 1972.

CHAPTER 10. EARLY MEDIEVAL ART

Backhouse, J. *The Golden Age of Anglo-Saxon Art, 966–1066.* Bloomington: Indiana University Press, 1984.

———. *The Lindisfarne Gospels: A Masterpiece of Book Painting.* London: British Library, 1995.

Barral i Altet, X. *The Early Middle Ages: From Late Antiquity to A.D. 1000.* Taschen's World Architecture. Köln and New York: Taschen, © 1997.

Conant, K. *Carolingian and Romanesque Architecture, 800–1200.* 4th ed. Pelican History of Art. New Haven: Yale University Press, 1992.

Davis-Weyer, C. *Early Medieval Art, 300–1150: Sources and Documents.* Reprint of 1971 ed. Toronto: University of Toronto Press, 1986.

Diebold, W. J. *Word and Image: An Introduction to Early Medieval Art.* Boulder, CO: Westview Press, 2000.

Dodwell, C. R. *Anglo-Saxon Art: A New Perspective.* Ithaca, NY: Cornell University Press, 1982.

———. *The Pictorial Arts of the West, 800–1200.* New ed. Pelican History of Art. New Haven: Yale University Press, 1993.

Graham-Campbell, J. *The Viking-age Gold and Silver of Scotland, A.D. 850–1100.* Exh. cat. Edinburgh: National Museums of Scotland, 1995.

Harbison, P. *The Golden Age of Irish Art: The Medieval Achievement, 600–1200.* New York: Thames & Hudson, 1999.

Henderson, G. *The Art of the Picts: Sculpture and Metalwork in Early Medieval Scotland.* New York: Thames & Hudson, 2004.

Kitzinger, E. *Early Medieval Art, with Illustrations from the British Museum.* Rev. ed. Bloomington: Indiana University Press, 1983.

Lasko, P. *Ars Sacra, 800–1200.* 2d ed. Pelican History of Art. New Haven: Yale University Press, 1995.

Mayr-Harting, M. *Ottonian Book Illumination: An Historical Study.* 2 vols. London: Harvey Miller, 1991–1993.

Megaw, M. R. *Celtic Art: From Its Beginnings to the Book of Kells.* New York: Thames & Hudson, 2001.

Mosacati, S., ed. *The Celts.* Exh. cat. New York: Rizzoli, 1999.

Nees, L. *Early Medieval Art.* Oxford History of Art. New York: Oxford University Press, 2002.

Ohlgren, T. H., comp. *Insular and Anglo-Saxon Illuminated Manuscripts: An Iconographic Catalogue, c. A.D. 625 to 1100.* New York: Garland, 1986.

Rickert, M. *Painting in Britain: The Middle Ages.* 2d ed. Pelican History of Art. Harmondsworth, England: Penguin, 1965.

Stalley, R. A. *Early Medieval Architecture.* Oxford History of Art. New York: Oxford University Press, 1999.

Stone, L. *Sculpture in Britain: The Middle Ages.* 2d ed. Pelican History of Art. Harmondsworth, England: Penguin, 1972.

Webster, L., and J. Backhouse, eds. *The Making of England: Anglo-Saxon Art and Culture, A.D. 600–900.* Exh. cat. London: Published for the Trustees of the British Museum and the British Library Board by British Museum Press, 1991.

CHAPTER 11. ROMANESQUE ART

Barral i. Altet, X. *The Romanesque: Towns, Cathedrals, and Monasteries.* Cologne: Taschen, 1998.

Bizzarro, T. *Romanesque Architectural Criticism: A Prehistory.* New York: Cambridge University Press, 1992.

Boase, T. S. R. *English Art, 1100–1216.* Oxford History of English Art. Oxford: Clarendon Press, 1953.

Cahn, W. *Romanesque Bible Illumination.* Ithaca, NY: Cornell University Press, 1982.

Davies, M. *Romanesque Architecture: A Bibliography.* Boston: G. K. Hall, 1993.

Focillon, H. *The Art of the West in the Middle Ages.* Ed. J. Bony. 2 vols. Reprint of 1963 ed. Ithaca, NY: Cornell University Press, 1980.

Hearn, M. F. *Romanesque Sculpture: The Revival of Monumental Stone Sculpture.* Ithaca, NY: Cornell University Press, 1981.

Mâle, E. *Religious Art in France, the Twelfth Century: A Study of the Origins of Medieval Iconography.* Bollingen series, 90:1. Princeton, NJ: Princeton University Press, 1978.

Minne-Sève, V. *Romanesque and Gothic France: Architecture and Sculpture.* New York: Harry N. Abrams, 2000.

Nichols, S. *Romanesque Signs: Early Medieval Narrative and Iconography.* New Haven: Yale University Press, 1983.

O'Keeffe, T. *Romanesque Ireland: Architecture and Ideology in the Twelfth Century.* Dublin and Portland, OR: Four Courts, 2003.

Petzold, A. *Romanesque Art.* Perspectives. Upper Saddle River, NJ: Prentice Hall, 1996.

Platt, C. *The Architecture of Medieval Britain: A Social History.* New Haven: Yale University Press, 1990.

Sauerländer, W. *Romanesque Art: Problems and Monuments.* 2 vols. London: Pindar, 2004.

Schapiro, M. *Romanesque Art.* New York: Braziller, 1977.

Stoddard, W. *Art and Architecture in Medieval France.* New York: Harper & Row, 1972, © 1966.

Stones, A., J. Krochalis, P. Gerson, and A. Shaver-Crandell. *The Pilgrim's Guide to Santiago de Compostela: A Critical Edition.* 2 vols. London: Harvey Miller, 1998.

Toman, R., and A. Bednorz. *Romanesque Architecture, Sculpture, Painting.* Cologne: Könemann, 2008.

Zarnecki, G. *Further Studies in Romanesque Sculpture.* London: Pindar, 1992.

CHAPTER 12. GOTHIC ART

Barnes, C. F. *Villard de Honnecourt, the Artist and His Drawings: A Critical Bibliography.* Boston: G. K. Hall, 1982.

Belting, H. *The Image and Its Public: Form and Function of Early Paintings of the Passion.* New Rochelle, NY: Caratzas, 1990.

Blum, P. *Early Gothic Saint-Denis: Restorations and Survivals.* Berkeley: University of California Press, 1992.

Bony, J. *French Gothic Architecture of the Twelfth and Thirteenth Centuries.* Berkeley: University of California Press, 1983.

Camille, M. *Gothic Art: Glorious Visions.* Perspectives. New York: Harry N. Abrams, 1997.

———. *The Gothic Idol: Ideology and Image Making in Medieval Art.* New York: Cambridge University Press, 1989.

———. *Sumptuous Arts at the Royal Abbeys of Reims and Braine.* Princeton, NJ: Princeton University Press, 1990.

Cennini, C. *The Craftsman's Handbook (Il Libro dell'Arte).* New York: Dover, 1954.

Coldstream, N. *Medieval Architecture.* Oxford History of Art. New York: Oxford University Press, 2002.

Erlande-Brandenburg, A. *Gothic Art.* New York: Harry N. Abrams, 1989.

Frankl, P. *Gothic Architecture.* Rev. by P. Crossley. Pelican History of Art. New Haven, CT: Yale University Press, 2001.

Frisch, T. G. *Gothic Art, 1140–c. 1450: Sources and Documents.* Reprint of 1971 ed. Toronto: University of Toronto Press, 1987.

Grodecki, L. *Gothic Architecture.* New York: Electa/Rizzoli, 1985.

———. *Gothic Stained Glass, 1200–1300.* Ithaca, NY: Cornell University Press, 1985.

Hamburger, J. F. *The Visual and the Visionary: Art and Female Spirituality in Late Medieval Germany.* Zone Books. Cambridge, MA: MIT Press, 1998.

Jantzen, H. *High Gothic: The Classic Cathedrals of Chartres, Reims, Amiens.* Reprint of 1962 ed. Princeton, NJ: Princeton University Press, 1984.

Kemp, W. *The Narratives of Gothic Stained Glass.* New York: Cambridge University Press, 1997.

Limentani Virdis, C. *Great Altarpieces: Gothic and Renaissance.* New York: Vendome Press; Dist. by Rizzoli, 2002.

Mâle, E. *Religious Art in France, the Thirteenth Cent[ury]: A Study of Medieval Iconography and Its Sources.* Ed. H. Bober. Princeton, NJ: Princeton University Press, 1984.

Marks, R., and P. Williamson, eds. *Gothic: Art for England 1400–1547.* Exh. cat. London and New York: Victoria & Albert Museum; Dist. by Harry N. Abrams, 2003.

Murray, S. *Beauvais Cathedral: Architecture of Transcendence.* Princeton, NJ: Princeton University Press, 1989.

Panofsky, E. ed. and trans. *Abbot Suger on the Abbey Church of Saint-Denis and Its Art Treasures.* 2d ed. Princeton, NJ: Princeton University Press, 1979.

———. *Gothic Architecture and Scholasticism.* Reprint of 1951 ed. New York: New American Library, 1985.

Parnet, P., ed. *Images in Ivory: Precious Objects of the Gothic Age.* Exh. cat. Detroit, MI: Detroit Institute of Arts, © 1997.

Sandler, L. *Gothic Manuscripts, 1285–1385.* Survey of Manuscripts Illuminated in the British Isles. London: Harvey Miller, 1986.

Scott, R. A. *The Gothic Enterprise: A Guide to Understanding the Medieval Cathedral.* Berkeley: University of California Press, 2003.

Simson, O. von. *The Gothic Cathedral: Origins of Gothic Architecture and the Medieval Concept of Order.* 3d ed. Princeton, NJ: Princeton University Press, 1988.

Toman, R., and A. Bednorz. *The Art of Gothic: Architecture, Sculpture, Painting.* Cologne: Könemann, 1999.

Williamson, P. *Gothic Sculpture, 1140–1300.* New Haven: Yale University Press, 1995.

Wilson, C. *The Gothic Cathedral: The Architecture of the Great Church, 1130–1530.* 2d rev. ed. London: Thames & Hudson, 2005.

PART THREE: THE RENAISSANCE THROUGH THE ROCOCO

GENERAL REFERENCES AND SOURCES

Campbell, L. *Renaissance Portraits: European Portrait-Painting in the 14th, 15th, and 16th Centuries.* New Haven: Yale University Press, 1990.

Chastel, A., et al. *The Renaissance: Essays in Interpretation.* London: Methuen, 1982.

Cloulas, I. *Treasures of the French Renaissance.* New York: Harry N. Abrams, 1998.

Cole, A. *Art of the Italian Renaissance Courts: Virtue and Magnificence.* London: Weidenfeld & Nicolson, 1995.

Gascoigne, B. *How to Identify Prints: A Complete Guide to Manual and Mechanical Processes from Woodcut to Inkjet.* New York: Thames & Hudson, 2004.

Grendler, P. F., ed. *Encyclopedia of the Renaissance.* 6 vols. New York: Scribner's, published in association with the Renaissance Society of America, 1999.

Gruber, A., ed. *The History of Decorative Arts: Vol. 1, The Renaissance and Mannerism in Europe. Vol. 2, Classicism and the Baroque in Europe.* New York: Abbeville Press, 1994.

Harbison, C. *The Mirror of the Artist: Northern Renaissance Art in its Historical Context.* New York: Harry N. Abrams, 1995.

Harris, A. S. *Seventeenth-Century Art and Architecture.* 2d ed. Upper Saddle River, NJ: Pearson Education, 2008.

Hartt, F., and D. Wilkins. *History of Italian Renaissance Art.* 6th ed. Upper Saddle River, NJ: Pearson Prentice Hall, 2007.

Hopkins, A. *Italian Architecture: from Michelangelo to Borromini.* World of Art. New York: Thames & Hudson, 2002.

Hults, L. *The Print in the Western World.* Madison: University of Wisconsin Press, 1996.

Impey, O., and A. MacGregor, eds. *The Origins of Museums: The Cabinet of Curiosities in Sixteenth- and Seventeenth-Century Europe.* New York: Clarendon Press, 1985.

Ivins, W. M., Jr. *How Prints Look: Photographs with a Commentary.* Boston: Beacon Press, 1987.

Landau, D., and P. Parshall. *The Renaissance Print.* New Haven: Yale University Press, 1994.

Lincoln, E. *The Invention of the Italian Renaissance Printmaker.* New Haven: Yale University Press, 2000.

Martin, J. R. *Baroque.* Harmondsworth, England: Penguin, 1989.

Millon, H. A., ed. *The Triumph of the Baroque: Architecture in Europe, 1600–1750.* New York: Rizzoli, 1999.

Minor, V. H. *Baroque & Rococo: Art & Culture.* New York: Harry N. Abrams, 1999.

Norberg-Schultz, C. *Late Baroque and Rococo Architecture.* New York: Harry N. Abrams, 1983.

Olson, R. J. M. *Italian Renaissance Sculpture.* The World of Art. New York: Thames & Hudson, 1992.

Paoletti, J., and G. Radke. *Art in Renaissance Italy.* 3d ed. Upper Saddle River, NJ: Pearson Prentice Hall, 2006.

Payne, A. *Antiquity and Its Interpreters.* New York: Cambridge University Press, 2000.

Pope-Hennessy, J. *An Introduction to Italian Sculpture: Vol. 1, Italian Gothic Sculpture. Vol. 2, Italian Renaissance Sculpture. Vol. 3, Italian High Renaissance and Baroque Sculpture.* 4th ed. London: Phaidon Press, 1996.

Richardson, C. M., K. W. Woods, and M. W. Franklin, eds. *Renaissance Art Reconsidered: An Anthology of Primary Sources.* Wiley-Blackwell, 2007.

Smith, J. C. *The Northern Renaissance.* Art & Ideas. London: Phaidon Press, 2004.

Snyder, J. *Northern Renaissance Art: Painting, Sculpture, the Graphic Arts, from 1350–1575.* 2d ed. New York: Harry N. Abrams, 2005.

Strinati, E., and J. Pomeroy. *Italian Women Artists of the Renaissance and Baroque.* Exh. cat. Washington, DC: National Museum of Women in the Arts; New York: Rizzoli, 2007.

Tomlinson, J. *From El Greco to Goya: Painting in Spain 1561–1828.* Perspectives. New York: Harry N. Abrams, 1997.

Turner, J. *Encyclopedia of Italian Renaissance & Mannerist Art.* 2 vols. New York: Grove's Dictionaries, 2000.

Vasari, G. *The Lives of the Artists.* Trans. with an introduction and notes by J. C. Bondanella and P. Bondanella. New York: Oxford University Press, 1998.

Welch, E. *Art in Renaissance Italy, 1350–1500.* New ed. Oxford: Oxford University Press, 2000.

Wiebenson, D., ed. *Architectural Theory and Practice from Alberti to Ledoux.* 2d ed. Chicago: University of Chicago Press, 1983.

Wittkower, R. *Architectural Principles in the Age of Humanism.* 5th ed. New York: St. Martin's Press, 1998.

CHAPTER 13. ART IN THIRTEENTH- AND FOURTEENTH-CENTURY ITALY

Bellosi, L. *Duccio, the Maestà.* New York: Thames & Hudson, 1999.

Bomford, D. *Art in the Making: Italian Painting Before 1400.* Exh. cat. London: National Gallery of Art, 1989.

Christiansen, K. *Duccio and the Origins of Western Painting.* New York: Metropolitan Museum of Art and Yale University Press, 2009.

Derbes, A. *The Cambridge Companion to Giotto.* New York: Cambridge University Press, 2004.

———., and M. Sandona. *The Usurer's Heart: Giotto, Enrico Scrovegni, and the Arena Chapel in Padua.* University Park: Pennsylvania State University Press, 2008.

Kemp, M. *Behind the Picture: Art and Evidence in the Italian Renaissance.* New Haven: Yale University Press, 1997.

Maginnis, H. B. J. *The World of the Early Sienese Painter.* With a translation of the Sienese Breve dell'Arte dei pittori by Gabriele Erasmi. University Park: Pennsylvania State University Press, 2001.

Meiss, M. *Painting in Florence and Siena after the Black Death: The Arts, Religion, and Society in the Mid-Fourteenth Century.* Princeton, NJ: Princeton University Press, 1978, © 1951.

Nevola, F. *Siena: Constructing the Renaissance City.* New Haven and London: Yale University Press, 2008.

Norman, D., ed. *Siena, Florence, and Padua: Art, Society, and Religion 1280–1400.* New Haven: Yale University Press in association with the Open University, 1995.

Schmidt, V., ed. *Italian Panel Painting of the Duecento and Trecento.* Washington, DC: National Gallery of Art; New Haven: Dist. by Yale University Press, 2002.

Stubblebine, J. H. *Assisi and the Rise of Vernacular Art.* New York: Harper & Row, 1985.

———. *Dugento Painting: An Annotated Bibliography.* Boston: G. K. Hall, 1983.

Trachtenberg, M. *Dominion of the Eye: Urbanism, Art, and Power in Early Modern Florence.* New York: Cambridge University Press, 2008.

White, J. *Art and Architecture in Italy, 1250–1400.* 3d ed. Pelican History of Art. New Haven: Yale University Press, 1993.

CHAPTER 14. ARTISTIC INNOVATIONS IN FIFTEENTH-CENTURY NORTHERN EUROPE

Ainsworth, M. W., and K. Christiansen. *From Van Eyck to Bruegel: Early Netherlandish Painting in the Metropolitan Museum of Art.* New York: Metropolitan Museum of Art, 1998.

Borchert, T., ed. *The Age of van Eyck: the Mediterranean World and Early Netherlandish Painting, 1430–1530.* New York: Thames & Hudson, 2002.

Chapuis, J., ed. *Tilman Riemenschneider, Master Sculptor of the Late Middle Ages.* Washington, DC: National Gallery of Art; New York: Metropolitan Museum of Art; New Haven: Dist. by Yale University Press, 1999.

Cuttler, C. *Northern Painting from Pucelle to Bruegel.* Fort Worth: Holt, Rinehart & Winston, 1991, © 1972.

De Vos, D. *Rogier van der Weyden: The Complete Works.* New York: Harry N. Abrams, 1999.

Dhanens, E. *Hubert and Jan van Eyck.* New York: Alpine Fine Arts Collection, 1980.

Dixon, L. *Bosch.* Art & Ideas. London: Phaidon Press, 2003.

Friedländer, M. *Early Netherlandish Painting.* 14 vols. New York: Praeger, 1967–1973.

Hand, J. O., C. Metzger, and R. Spronk. *Prayers and Portraits: Unfolding the Netherlandish Diptych.* Exh. cat. Washington DC, National Gallery of Art; New Haven: Yale University Press, 2006.

Koldeweij, J., ed. *Hieronymus Bosch: New Insights into His Life and Work.* Rotterdam: Museum Boijmans Van Beuningen: NAi; Ghent: Ludion, 2001.

Muller, T. *Sculpture in the Netherlands, Germany, France, and Spain, 1400–1500.* Pelican History of Art. Harmondsworth, England: Penguin, 1966.

Nuttall, P. *From Flanders to Florence: The Impact of Netherlandish Painting, 1400–1500.* New Haven: Yale University Press, 2004.

Pächt, O. *Van Eyck and the Founders of Early Netherlandish Painting.* London: Harvey Miller, 1994.

Panofsky, E. *Early Netherlandish Painting.* 2 vols. New York: Harper & Row, 1971. Orig. published Cambridge, MA: Harvard University Press, 1958.

Rothstein, B. L. *Sight and Spirituality in Early Netherlandish Painting.* Cambridge: Cambridge University Press, 2005.

Van der Velden, H. *The Donor's Image: Gérard Loyet and the Votive Portraits of Charles the Bold.* Turnhout: Brepols, 2000.

Williamson, P. *Netherlandish Sculpture 1450–1550.* London: V & A; New York: Dist. by Harry N. Abrams, 2002.

CHAPTER 15. THE EARLY RENAISSANCE IN ITALY

Ahl, D. C. *The Cambridge Companion to Masaccio.* New York: Cambridge University Press, 2002.

Aikema, B. *Renaissance Venice and the North: Crosscurrents in the Time of Bellini, Dürer and Titian.* Exh. cat. Milan: Bompiani, 2000.

Ajmar-Wollheim, M., and F. Dennis, eds. *At Home in Renaissance Italy.* Exh. cat. London: Victoria & Albert Museum; V&A Publications, 2006.

Alberti, L. B. *On Painting.* Trans. C. Grayson, introduction and notes M. Kemp. New York: Penguin, 1991.

———. *On the Art of Building, in Ten Books.* Trans. J. Rykwert, et al. Cambridge, MA: MIT Press, 1991.

Ames-Lewis, F. *Drawing in Early Renaissance Italy.* 2d ed. New Haven: Yale University Press, 2000.

Baxandall, M. *Painting and Experience in Fifteenth-Century Italy: A Primer in the Social History of Pictorial Style.* 2d ed. New York: Oxford University Press, 1988.

Blunt, A. *Artistic Theory in Italy, 1450–1600.* Reprint of 1940 ed. New York: Oxford University Press, 1983.

Bober, P., and R. Rubinstein. *Renaissance Artists and Antique Sculpture: A Handbook of Sources.* New York: Oxford University Press, 1986.

Borsook, E. *The Mural Painters of Tuscany: From Cimabue to Andrea del Sarto.* 2d ed. New York: Oxford University Press, 1980.

Cole, B. *The Renaissance Artist at Work: From Pisano to Titian.* New York: Harper & Row, © 1983.

Fejfer, J. *The Rediscovery of Antiquity: The Role of the Artist.* Copenhagen: Museum Tusculanum Press, University of Copenhagen, 2003.

Gilbert, C. E. *Italian Art, 1400–1500: Sources and Documents.* Englewood Cliffs, NJ: Prentice Hall, 1980.

Goldthwaite, R. *Wealth and the Demand for Art in Italy, 1300–1600.* Baltimore, MD: Johns Hopkins University Press, 1993.

Gombrich, E. H. *New Light on Old Masters.* New ed. London: Phaidon Press, 1994.

Heydenreich, L., and W. Lotz. *Architecture in Italy, 1400–1500.* Rev. ed. Pelican History of Art. New Haven: Yale University Press, 1996.

Humfreys, P., and M. Kemp, eds. *The Altarpiece in the Renaissance.* New York: Cambridge University Press, 1990.

———., ed. *The Cambridge Companion to Giovanni Bellini.* New York: Cambridge University Press, 2004.

Huse, N., and W. Wolters. *The Art of Renaissance Venice: Architecture, Sculpture, and Painting, 1460–1590.* Chicago: University of Chicago Press, 1990.

Janson, H. W. *The Sculpture of Donatello.* 2 vols. Princeton, NJ: Princeton University Press, 1979.

Kempers, B. *Painting, Power, and Patronage: The Rise of the Professional Artist in the Italian Renaissance.* New York: Penguin, 1992.

Kent, D. V. *Cosimo de' Medici and the Florentine Renaissance: The Patron's Oeuvre.* New Haven: Yale University Press, © 2000.

Krautheimer, R., and T. Krautheimer-Hess. *Lorenzo Ghiberti.* Princeton, NJ: Princeton University Press, 1982.

Lavin, M. A. *Piero della Francesca.* Art & Ideas. New York: Phaidon Press, 2002.

Murray, P. *The Architecture of the Italian Renaissance.* New rev. ed. The World of Art. New York: Random House, 1997.

Musacchio, J. M. *Art, Marriage, and Family in the Florentine Renaissance Palace.* New Haven: Yale University Press, 2009.

Pächt, O. *Venetian Painting in the 15th Century: Jacopo, Gentile and Giovanni Bellini and Andrea Mantegna.* London: Harvey Miller, 2003.

Panofsky, E. *Perspective as Symbolic Form.* New York: Zone Books, 1997.

———. *Renaissance and Renascences in Western Art.* Trans. C. S. Wood. New York: Humanities Press, 1970.

Pope-Hennessy, J. *Italian Renaissance Sculpture.* 4th ed. London: Phaidon Press, 2000.

Randolph, A. *Engaging Symbols: Gender, Politics, and Public Art in Fifteenth-Century Florence.* New Haven: Yale University Press, 2002.

Saalman, H. *Filippo Brunelleschi: The Buildings.* University Park: Pennsylvania State University Press, 1993.

Seymour, C. *Sculpture in Italy, 1400–1500.* Pelican History of Art. Harmondsworth, England: Penguin, 1966.

Turner, A. R. *Renaissance Florence.* Perspectives. New York: Harry N. Abrams, 1997.

Wackernagel, M. *The World of the Florentine Renaissance Artist: Projects and Patrons, Workshop and Art Market.* Princeton, NJ: Princeton University Press, 1981.

Wood, J. M., ed. *The Cambridge Companion to Piero della Francesca*. New York: Cambridge University Press, 2002.

CHAPTER 16. THE HIGH RENAISSANCE IN ITALY, 1495–1520

Ackerman, J., *The Architecture of Michelangelo*. 2d ed. Chicago: University of Chicago Press, 1986.

Beck, J. H. *Three Worlds of Michelangelo*. New York: W. W. Norton, 1999.

Boase, T. S. R. *Giorgio Vasari: The Man and the Book*. Princeton, NJ: Princeton University Press, 1979.

Brown, P. F. *Art and Life in Renaissance Venice*. Perspectives. New York: Harry N. Abrams, 1997.

———. *Venice and Antiquity: The Venetian Sense of the Past*. New Haven: Yale University Press, 1997.

Chapman, H. *Raphael: From Urbino to Rome*. London: National Gallery; New Haven: Dist. by Yale University Press, 2004.

Clark, K. *Leonardo da Vinci*. Rev. and introduced by M. Kemp. New York: Penguin, 1993, © 1988.

Cole, A. *Virtue and Magnificence: Art of the Italian Renaissance Courts*. Perspectives. New York: Harry N. Abrams, 1995.

De Tolnay, C. *Michelangelo*. 5 vols. Some vols. rev. Princeton, NJ: Princeton University Press, 1969–1971.

Freedberg, S. *Painting in Italy, 1500–1600*. 3d ed. Pelican History of Art. New Haven: Yale University Press, 1993.

———. *Painting of the High Renaissance in Rome and Florence*. 2 vols. New rev. ed. New York: Hacker Art Books, 1985.

Goffen, R. *Renaissance Rivals: Michelangelo, Leonardo, Raphael, Titian*. New Haven: Yale University Press, 2002.

Hall, M. B. *The Cambridge Companion to Raphael*. New York: Cambridge University Press, 2005.

Hersey, G. L. *High Renaissance Art in St. Peter's and the Vatican: An Interpretive Guide*. Chicago: University of Chicago Press, 1993.

Hibbard, H. *Michelangelo*. 2d ed. Boulder, CO: Westview Press, 1998, © 1974.

Kemp, M. *Leonardo*. New York: Oxford University Press, 2004.

———., ed. *Leonardo on Painting: An Anthology of Writings*. New Haven: Yale University Press, 1989.

Nicholl, C. *Leonardo da Vinci: Flights of the Mind*. New York: Viking Penguin, 2004.

Panofsky, E. *Studies in Iconology: Humanist Themes in the Art of the Renaissance*. New York: Harper & Row, 1972.

Partridge, L. *The Art of Renaissance Rome*. Perspectives. New York: Harry N. Abrams, 1996.

Rowland, I. *The Culture of the High Renaissance: Ancients and Moderns in Sixteenth Century Rome*. Cambridge: 1998.

Rubin, P. L. *Giorgio Vasari: Art and History*. New Haven: Yale University Press, 1995.

Steinberg, L. *Leonardo's Incessant Last Supper*. New York: Zone Books, 2001.

Wallace, W. *Michelangelo: The Complete Sculpture, Painting, Architecture*. Southport, CT: Hugh Lauter Levin, 1998.

Wölfflin, H. *Classic Art: An Introduction to the High Renaissance*. 5th ed. London: Phaidon Press, 1994.

CHAPTER 17. THE LATE RENAISSANCE AND MANNERISM

Ackerman, J. *Palladio*. Reprint of the 2d ed. Harmondsworth, England: Penguin, 1991, © 1966.

Barkan, L. *Unearthing the Past: Archaeology and Aesthetics in the Making of Renaissance Culture*. New Haven: Yale University Press, 1999.

Beltramini, G., and A. Padoan. *Andrea Palladio: The Complete Illustrated Works*. New York: Universe; Dist. by St. Martin's Press, 2001.

Cole, M., ed. *Sixteenth-Century Italian Art*. Oxford: Blackwell, 2006.

Ekserdjian, D. *Correggio*. New Haven: Yale University Press, 1997.

Fortini Bown, P. *Private Lives in Renaissance Venice: Art, Architecture, and the Family*. New Haven: Yale University Press, 2004.

Friedlaender, W. *Mannerism and Anti-Mannerism in Italian Painting*. Reprint of 1957 ed. Interpretations in Art. New York: Columbia University Press, 1990.

Furlotti, B., and G. Rebecchini. *The Art and Architecture of Mantua: Eight Centuries of Patronage and Collecting*. London: Thames & Hudson, 2008.

Goffen, R. *Titian's Women*. New Haven: Yale University Press, 1997.

Jacobs, F. H. *Defining the Renaissance "Virtuosa": Women Artists and the Language of Art History and Criticism*. New York: Cambridge University Press, 1997.

Klein, R., and H. Zerner. *Italian Art, 1500–1600: Sources and Documents*. Reprint of 1966 ed. Evanston, IL: Northwestern University Press, 1989.

Kliemann, J., and M. Rohlmann. *Italian Frescoes: High Renaissance and Mannerism, 1510–1600*. New York: Abbeville Press, 2004.

Partridge, L. *Michelangelo — The Last Judgment: A Glorious Restoration*. New York: Harry N. Abrams, 1997.

Rearick, W. R. *The Art of Paolo Veronese, 1528–1588*. Cambridge: Cambridge University Press, 1988.

Rosand, D. *Painting in Sixteenth-Century Venice: Titian, Veronese, Tintoretto*. New York: Cambridge University Press, 1997.

Shearman, J. K. G. *Mannerism*. New York: Penguin Books, 1990, © 1967.

Smyth, C. H. *Mannerism and Maniera*. 2d ed. Bibliotheca artibus et historiae. Vienna: IRSA, 1992.

Tavernor, R. *Palladio and Palladianism*. The World of Art. New York: Thames & Hudson, 1991.

Valcanover, F., and T. Pignatti. *Tintoretto*. New York: Harry N. Abrams, 1984.

Wundram, M. *Palladio: The Complete Buildings*. Köln and London: Taschen, 2004.

CHAPTER 18. EUROPEAN ART OF THE SIXTEENTH CENTURY: RENAISSANCE AND REFORMATION

Bartrum, G. *Albrecht Dürer and His Legacy: The Graphic Work of a Renaissance Artist*. Princeton, NJ: Princeton University Press, 2002.

Baxandall, M. *The Limewood Sculptors of Renaissance Germany*. New Haven: Yale University Press, 1980.

Campbell, T. P. *Tapestry in the Renaissance: Art and Magnificence*. Exh. cat. New York: Metropolitan Museum of Art; New Haven: Yale University Press, 2006.

Eichberger, D., ed. *Durer and His Culture*. New York: Cambridge University Press, 1998.

Hayum, A. *The Isenheim Altarpiece: God's Medicine and the Painter's Vision*. Princeton, NJ: Princeton University Press, 1989.

Hitchcock, H.-R. *German Renaissance Architecture*. Princeton, NJ: Princeton University Press, 1981.

Honig, E. A. *Painting and the Market in Early Modern Antwerp*. New Haven: Yale University Press, 1998.

Hulse, C. *Elizabeth I: Ruler and Legend*. Urbana: Published for the Newberry Library by the University of Illinois Press, 2003.

Hutchison, J. C. *Albrecht Dürer: A Biography*. Princeton, NJ: Princeton University Press, 1990.

Jopek, N. *German Sculpture, 1430–1540: A Catalogue of the Collection in the Victoria and Albert Museum*. London: V & A, 2002.

Kavaler, E. M. *Pieter Bruegel: Parables of Order and Enterprise*. New York: Cambridge University Press, 1999.

Koerner, J. *The Moment of Self-Portraiture in German Renaissance Art*. Chicago: University of Chicago Press, 1993.

———. *The Reformation of the Image*. Chicago: University of Chicago Press, 2004.

Mann, R. *El Greco and His Patrons: Three Major Projects*. New York: Cambridge University Press, 1986.

Melion, W. *Shaping the Netherlandish Canon: Karel van Mander's Schilder-Boeck*. Chicago: University of Chicago Press, 1991.

Moxey, K. *Peasants, Warriors, and Wives: Popular Imagery in the Reformation*. Chicago: University of Chicago Press, 1989.

Osten, G. von der, and H. Vey. *Painting and Sculpture in Germany and the Netherlands, 1500–1600*. Pelican History of Art. Harmondsworth, England: Penguin, 1969.

Panofsky, E. *The Life and Art of Albrecht Dürer*. 4th ed. Princeton, NJ: Princeton University Press, 1971.

Smith, J. C. *Nuremberg: A Renaissance City, 1500–1618*. Austin: Published for the Archer M. Huntington Art Gallery by the University of Texas Press, 1983.

Stechow, W. *Northern Renaissance Art, 1400–1600: Sources and Documents*. Evanston, IL: Northwes University Press, 1989, © 1966.

Van Mander, K. *Lives of the Illustrious Netherlandish and German Painters*. Ed. H. Miedema. 6 vols. Doornspijk, Netherlands: Davaco, 1993–1999.

Wood, C. *Albrecht Altdorfer and the Origins of Landscape*. Chicago: University of Chicago Press, 1993.

Zerner, H. *Renaissance Art in France: The Invention of Classicism*. Paris: Flammarion; London: Thames & Hudson, 2003.

CHAPTER 19. THE BAROQUE IN ITALY AND SPAIN

Avery, C. *Bernini: Genius of the Baroque*. London: Thames & Hudson, 1997.

Bissell, R. W. *Masters of Italian Baroque Painting: The Detroit Institute of Arts*. Detroit, MI: Detroit Institute of Arts in association with D. Giles Ltd., London, 2005.

Brown, B. L., ed. *The Genius of Rome, 1592–1623*. Exh. cat. London: Royal Academy of Arts; New York: Dist. in the United States and Canada by Harry N. Abrams, 2001.

Brown, J. *Francisco de Zurbaran*. New York: Harry N. Abrams, 1991.

———. *Painting in Spain, 1500–1700*. Pelican History of Art. New Haven: Yale University Press, 1998.

———. *Velázquez: The Technique of Genius*. New Haven: Yale University Press, 1998.

Dempsey, C. *Annibale Carracci and the Beginnings of Baroque Style*. 2d ed. Fiesole, Italy: Cadmo, 2000.

Enggass, R., and J. Brown. *Italy and Spain, 1600–1750: Sources and Documents*. Reprint of 1970 ed. Evanston, IL: Northwestern University Press, 1992.

Freedberg, S. *Circa 1600: A Revolution of Style in Italian Painting*. Cambridge, MA: Harvard University Press, 1983.

Garrard, M. D. *Artemisia Gentileschi: The Image of the Female Hero in Italian Baroque Art*. Princeton, NJ: Princeton University Press, 1989.

Marder, T. A. *Bernini and the Art of Architecture*. New York: Abbeville Press, 1998.

Montagu, J. *Roman Baroque Sculpture: The Industry of Art*. New Haven: Yale University Press, 1989.

Nicolson, B. *Caravaggism in Europe*. Ed. L. Vertova. 3 vols. 2d ed., rev. and enl. Turin, Italy: Allemandi, 1989.

Schroth, S., R. Baer, et al. *El Greco to Velázquez: Art During the Reign of Philip III*. Exh. cat. Boston: Museum of Fine Arts; MFA Publications, 2008.

Smith, G. *Architectural Diplomacy: Rome and Paris in the Late Baroque*. Cambridge, MA: MIT Press, 1993.

Spear, R. E. *From Caravaggio to Artemisia: Essays on Painting in Seventeenth-Century Italy and France*. London: Pindar Press, 2002.

Spike, J. T. *Caravaggio*. Includes CD-ROM of all the known paintings of Caravaggio, including attributed and lost works. New York: Abbeville Press, © 2001.

Varriano, J. *Italian Baroque and Rococo Architecture*. New York: Oxford University Press, 1986.

Wittkower, R. *Art and Architecture in Italy, 1600–1750*. 4th ed. Pelican History of Art. New Haven: Yale University Press, 2000.

———. *Bernini: The Sculptor of the Roman Baroque*. 4th ed. London: Phaidon Press, 1997.

CHAPTER 20. THE BAROQUE IN FLANDERS AND HOLLAND

Alpers, S. *The Art of Describing: Dutch Art in the Seventeenth Century*. Chicago: University of Chicago Press, 1983.

———. *The Making of Rubens*. New Haven: Yale University Press, 1995.

Chapman, H. P. *Rembrandt's Self-Portraits: A Study in Seventeenth-Century Identity*. Princeton, NJ: Princeton University Press, 1990.

Fleischer, R., ed. *Rembrandt, Rubens, and the Art of Their Time: Recent Perspectives*. University Park: Pennsylvania State University, 1997.

Franits, W. E. *Dutch Seventeenth-Century Genre Painting: Its Stylistic and Thematic Evolution.* New Haven: Yale University Press, 2004.

Grijzenhout, F., ed. *The Golden Age of Dutch Painting in Historical Perspective.* New York: Cambridge University Press, 1999.

s, J. and E. Runia, eds. *The Glory of the Golden Age: Dutch Art of the 17th Century.* 2 vols. Exh. cat. Rijksmuseum, Amsterdam: Waanders: 2000.

Logan, A. S. *Peter Paul Rubens: The Drawings.* Exh. cat. New York: Metropolitan Museum of Art; New Haven: Yale University Press, 2004.

Salvesen, S., ed. *Rembrandt: The Master and His Workshop.* 2 vols. Exh. cat. New Haven: Yale University Press, 1991.

Schama, S. *The Embarrassment of Riches: An Interpretation of Dutch Culture in the Golden Age.* New York: Alfred A. Knopf, 1987.

Schwartz, G. *Rembrandt: His Life, His Paintings.* New York: Viking, 1985.

Slive, S. *Dutch Painting, 1600–1800.* Pelican History of Art. New Haven: Yale University Press, 1995.

———. *Frans Hals.* Exh. cat. Munich: Prestel-Verlag, 1989.

———. *Jacob van Ruisdael: Master of Landscape.* London: Royal Academy of Arts, 2005.

Sluijter, E. J. *Rembrandt and the Female Nude.* Amsterdam University Press, 2006.

Sutton, P. *The Age of Rubens.* Exh. cat. Boston: Museum of Fine Arts, 1993.

Vlieghe, H. *Flemish Art and Architecture, 1585–1700.* Pelican History of Art. New Haven: Yale University Press, © 1998.

Westermann, M. *Art and Home: Dutch Interiors in the Age of Rembrandt.* Exh. cat. Zwolle: Waanders, 2001.

———. *Rembrandt.* Art & Ideas. London: Phaidon Press, 2000.

———. *A Worldly Art: The Dutch Republic 1585–1718.* Perspectives. New York: Harry N. Abrams, 1996.

Wheelock, A. K., ed. *Johannes Vermeer.* Exh. cat. New Haven: Yale University Press, 1995.

———, et al. *Anthony van Dyck.* Exh. cat. New York: Harry N. Abrams, 1990.

ite, C. *Peter Paul Rubens.* New Haven: Yale University Press, 1987.

CHAPTER 21. THE BAROQUE IN FRANCE AND ENGLAND

Blunt, A. *Art and Architecture in France, 1500–1700.* 5th ed. Pelican History of Art. New Haven: Yale University Press, 1999.

Brusatin, M., et al. *The Baroque in Central Europe: Places, Architecture, and Art.* Venice: Marsilio, 1992.

Donovan, F. *Rubens and England.* New Haven: Published for The Paul Mellon Centre for Studies in British Art by Yale University Press, 2004.

Downes, K. *The Architecture of Wren.* Rev. ed. Reading, England: Redhedge, 1988.

Garreau, M. *Charles Le Brun: First Painter to King Louis XIV.* New York: Harry N. Abrams, 1992.

Kitson, M. *Studies on Claude and Poussin.* London: Pindar, 2000.

Lagerlöf, M. R. *Ideal Landscape: Annibale Carracci, Nicolas Poussin, and Claude Lorrain.* New Haven: Yale University Press, 1990.

Mérot, A. *French Painting in the Seventeenth Century.* New Haven: Yale University Press, 1995.

———. *Nicolas Poussin.* New York: Abbeville Press, 1990.

Porter, R. *London: A Social History.* Cambridge, MA: Harvard University Press, 1995.

Rosenberg, P., and K. Christiansen, eds. *Poussin and Nature: Arcadian Visions.* Exh. cat. New York: Metropolitan Museum of Art; New Haven: Yale University Press, 2008.

Summerson, J. *Architecture in Britain, 1530–1830.* Rev. 9th ed. Pelican History of Art. New Haven: Yale University Press, 1993.

Tinniswood, A. *His Invention So Fertile: A Life of Christopher Wren.* New York: Oxford University Press, 2001.

rdi, R. *Nicolas Poussin 1594–1665.* London: Zwemmer in association with the Royal Academy of Arts, 1995.

Vlnas, V., ed. *The Glory of the Baroque in Bohemia: Essays on Art, Culture and Society in the 17th and 18th Centuries.* Prague: National Gallery, 2001.

Waterhouse, E. K. *The Dictionary of Sixteenth and Seventeenth Century British Painters.* Woodbridge, Suffolk, England: Antique Collectors' Club, 1988.

———. *Painting in Britain, 1530–1790.* 5th ed. Pelican History of Art. New Haven: Yale University Press, 1993.

Whinney, M. D. *Wren.* World of Art. New York: Thames & Hudson, 1998.

CHAPTER 22. THE ROCOCO

Bailey, C. B. *The Age of Watteau, Chardin, and Fragonard: Masterpieces of French Genre Painting.* New Haven: Yale University Press in association with the National Gallery of Canada, 2003.

Brunel, G. *Boucher.* New York: Vendome, 1986.

———. *Painting in Eighteenth-Century France.* Ithaca, NY: Cornell University Press, 1981.

Cuzin, J. P. *Jean-Honoré Fragonard: Life and Work: Complete Catalogue of the Oil Paintings.* New York: Harry N. Abrams, 1988.

François Boucher, 1703–1770. Exh. cat. New York: Metropolitan Museum of Art, © 1986.

Gaunt, W. *The Great Century of British Painting: Hogarth to Turner.* 2d ed. London: Phaidon Press, 1978.

Kalnein, W. von. *Architecture in France in the Eighteenth Century.* Pelican History of Art. New Haven: Yale University Press, 1995.

Levey, M. *Giambattista Tiepolo: His Life and Art.* New Haven: Yale University Press, 1986.

———. *Painting and Sculpture in France, 1700–1789.* New ed. Pelican History of Art. New Haven: Yale University Press, 1993.

———. *Painting in Eighteenth-Century Venice.* 3d ed. Pelican History of Art. New Haven: Yale University Press, 1993.

———. *Rococo to Revolution: Major Trends in Eighteenth-Century Painting.* Reprint of 1966 ed. The World of Art. New York: Thames & Hudson, 1985.

Links, J. G. *Canaletto.* Completely rev., updated, and enl. ed. London: Phaidon Press, 1994.

Paulson, R. *Hogarth.* 3 vols. New Brunswick: Rutgers University Press, 1991–1993.

Pointon, M. *Hanging the Head: Portraiture and Social Formation in Eighteenth-Century England.* New Haven: Yale University Press, 1993.

Posner, D. *Antoine Watteau.* Ithaca, NY: Cornell University Press, 1984.

Rococo to Romanticism: Art and Architecture, 1700–1850. Garland Library of the History of Art. New York: Garland, 1976.

Rosenberg, P. *Chardin.* Exh. cat. London: Royal Academy of Art; New York: Metropolitan Museum of Art, 2000.

———. *From Drawing to Painting: Poussin, Watteau, Fragonard, David & Ingres.* Princeton, NJ: Princeton University Press, 2000.

Scott, K. *The Rococo Interior: Decoration and Social Spaces in Early Eighteenth-Century Paris.* New Haven: Yale University Press, 1995.

Sheriff, M. D. *The Exceptional Woman: Elisabeth Vigée-Lebrun and the Cultural Politics of Art.* Chicago: University of Chicago Press, 1996.

Wintermute, A. *Watteau and His World: French Drawing from 1700 to 1750.* Exh. cat. London: Merrell Holberton; New York: American Federation of Arts, 1999.

PART FOUR: THE MODERN WORLD

GENERAL REFERENCES

Arnason, H. H. *History of Modern Art: Painting, Sculpture, Architecture, Photography.* 5th ed. Upper Saddle River, NJ: Pearson Prentice Hall, 2004.

Atkins, R. *Artspoke: A Guide to Modern Ideas, Movements, and Buzzwords, 1848–1944.* New York: Abbeville Press, 1993.

Baigell, M. *A Concise History of American Painting and Sculpture.* Rev. ed. New York: Icon Editions, 1996.

Banham, R. *Theory and Design in the First Machine Age.* 2d ed. Cambridge, MA: MIT Press, 1980, © 1960.

Bearden, R., and H. Henderson. *A History of African-American Artists from 1792 to the Present.* New York: Pantheon, 1993.

Bergdoll, B. *European Architecture 1750–1890.* Oxford History of Art. New York: Oxford University Press, 2000.

Bjelajac, D. *American Art: A Cultural History.* Upper Saddle River, NJ: Pearson Prentice Hall, 2005.

Boime, A. *A Social History of Modern Art. Vol. 1, Art in the Age of Revolution, 1750–1800. Vol. 2, Art in the Age of Bonapartism, 1800–1815. Vol. 3, Art in the Age of Counterrevolution, 1815–1848.* Chicago: University of Chicago Press, 1987–2004.

Bown, M. C. *A Dictionary of Twentieth Century Russian and Soviet Painters 1900–1980s.* London: Izomar, 1998.

Campany, D., ed. *Art and Photography.* Themes and Movements. London: Phaidon Press, 2003.

Castleman, R. *Prints of the Twentieth Century: A History.* Rev. ed. London: Thames & Hudson, 1988.

Chiarmonte, P. *Women Artists in the United States: A Selective Bibliography and Resource Guide to the Fine and Decorative Arts, 1750–1986.* Boston: G. K. Hall, 1990.

Chilvers, I. *A Dictionary of Twentieth-Century Art.* New York: Oxford University Press, 1998.

Chipp, H., ed. *Theories of Modern Art: A Source Book by Artists and Critics.* Berkeley: University of California Press, 1968.

Colquhoun, A. *Modern Architecture.* New York: Oxford University Press, 2002.

Crary, J. *Techniques of the Observer: On Vision and Modernity in the Nineteenth Century.* Cambridge, MA: MIT Press, 1990.

Craven, W. *American Art: History and Culture.* New York: Harry N. Abrams, 1994.

Crook, J. *The Dilemma of Style: Architectural Ideas from the Picturesque to the Post Modern.* Chicago: University of Chicago Press, 1987.

Crow, T. *Modern Art in the Common Culture.* New Haven: Yale University Press, 1996.

Cummings, P. *Dictionary of Contemporary American Artists.* New York: St. Martin's Press, 1988.

Documents of Modern Art. 14 vols. New York: Wittenborn, 1944–1961. Anthologies of primary source material. Selected titles listed individually, below.

The Documents of Twentieth-Century Art. Boston: G. K. Hall, Anthologies of primary source material. Selected titles listed individually, below.

Doss, E. *Twentieth-Century American Art.* Oxford History of Art. New York: Oxford University Press, 2002.

Drucker, J. *The Century of Artists' Books.* New York: Granary Books, 2004.

Eisenman, S. *Nineteenth Century Art: A Critical History.* New York: Thames & Hudson, 2002.

Eitner, L. *An Outline of Nineteenth-Century European Painting: From David Through Cézanne.* 2 vols. New York: Harper & Row, 1986.

Elderfield, J., ed. *Modern Painting and Sculpture: 1880 to the Present at the Museum of Modern Art.* New York: Museum of Modern Art; Dist. by D.A.P./Distributed Art Publishers, 2004.

Evans, M. M., ed. *Contemporary Photographers.* 3d ed. New York: St. James Press, 1995.

Farrington, L. E. *Creating Their Own Image: The History of African-American Women Artists.* New York: Oxford University Press, 2005.

Frampton, K. *Modern Architecture: A Critical History.* 3d ed. New York: Thames & Hudson, 1992.

Frascina, F. and J. Harris, eds. *Art in Modern Culture: An Anthology of Critical Texts.* New York: Harper & Row, 1992.

Gaiger, J., ed. *Art of the Twentieth Century: A Reader.* New Haven: Yale University Press in association with the Open University, 2003.

———. *Frameworks for Modern Art.* New Haven: Yale University Press in association with the Open University, 2003.

Goldberg, R. *Performance Art: From Futurism to the Present.* Rev. and exp. ed. The World of Art. New York: Thames & Hudson, 2001.

Goldwater, R. *Primitivism in Modern Art.* Enl. ed. Cambridge: Harvard University Press, 1986.

Gray, J. *Action Art: A Bibliography of Artists' Performance from Futurism to Fluxus and Beyond.* Westport, CT: Greenwood Press, 1993.

Harrison, C., and P. Wood, eds. *Art in Theory, 1815–1900: An Anthology of Changing Ideas.* Malden, MA: Blackwell, 1998.

———. *Art in Theory, 1900–2000: An Anthology of Changing Ideas*. New ed. Malden, MA: Blackwell, 2003.

Heller, N. *Women Artists: An Illustrated History*. New York: Abbeville Press, 2003.

Hertz, R., ed. *Theories of Contemporary Art*. 2d ed. Englewood Cliffs, NJ: Prentice Hall, 1993.

———, and N. Klein, eds. *Twentieth-Century Art Theory: Urbanism, Politics, and Mass Culture*. Englewood Cliffs, NJ: Prentice Hall, 1990.

Hitchcock, H. R. *Architecture: Nineteenth and Twentieth Centuries*. 4th rev. ed. Pelican History of Art. New Haven: Yale University Press, 1987, © 1977.

Hughes, R. *American Visions: The Epic History of Art in America*. New York: Alfred A. Knopf, 1997.

Hunter, S., and J. Jacobus. *Modern Art: Painting, Sculpture, Architecture*. 3d rev. ed. New York: Harry N. Abrams, 2000.

Igoe, L. *250 Years of Afro-American Art: An Annotated Bibliography*. New York: Bowker, 1981.

Joachimides, C., et al. *American Art in the Twentieth Century: Painting and Sculpture, 1913–1933*. Exh. cat. Munich: Prestel, 1993.

Johnson, W. *Nineteenth-Century Photography: An Annotated Bibliography, 1839–1879*. Boston: G. K. Hall, 1990.

Kostelanetz, R. *A Dictionary of the Avant-Gardes*. New York: Routledge, 2001.

Lewis, S. *African American Art and Artists*. Berkeley: University of California Press, 1990.

Marien, M. *Photography: A Cultural History*. Upper Saddle River, NJ: Pearson Prentice Hall, 2002.

McCoubrey, J. *American Art, 1700–1960: Sources and Documents*. Englewood Cliffs, NJ: Prentice Hall, 1965.

Meikle, J. L. *Design in the USA*. Oxford History of Art. New York: Oxford University Press, 2005.

Modern Arts Criticism. 4 vols. Detroit, MI: Gale Research, 1991–1994.

Newhall, B. *The History of Photography from 1830 to the Present*. Rev. and enl. 5th ed. New York: Museum of Modern Art; Dist. by Bulfinch Press/Little, Brown, 1999.

Nochlin, L. *The Politics of Vision: Essays on Nineteenth-Century Art and Society*. New York: Harper & Row, 1989.

Osborne, H., ed. *Oxford Companion to Twentieth-Century Art*. Reprint. New York: Oxford University Press, 1990.

Patton, S. F. *African-American Art*. Oxford History of Art. New York: Oxford University Press, 1998.

Pevsner, N. *Pioneers of Modern Design: From William Morris to Walter Gropius*. 4th ed. New Haven: Yale University Press, 2005.

Piland, S. *Women Artists: An Historical, Contemporary, and Feminist Bibliography*. Metuchen, NJ: Scarecrow Press, 1994.

Powell, R. J. *Black Art and Culture in the 20th Century*. New York: Thames & Hudson, 1997.

Robinson, Hilary. *Feminism-Art-Theory: An Anthology, 1968–2000*. Oxford and Malden, MA: Blackwell, 2001.

Rose, B. *American Art Since 1900*. Rev. ed. New York: Praeger, 1975.

———. *American Painting: The Twentieth Century*. New updated ed. New York: Rizzoli, 1986.

Rosenblum, N. *A World History of Photography*. 3rd ed. New York: Abbeville Press, 1997.

Rosenblum, R., and H. W. Janson. *19th Century Art*. Rev. and updated ed. Upper Saddle River, NJ: Pearson Prentice Hall, 2005.

Schapiro, M. *Modern Art: Nineteenth and Twentieth Centuries*. New York: Braziller, 1982.

Scharf, A. *Art and Photography*. Reprint. Harmondsworth, England: Penguin, 1995.

Sennott, S., ed. *Encyclopedia of 20th Century Architecture*. 3 vols. New York: Fitzroy Dearborn, 2004.

Stiles, K., and P. Selz. *Theories and Documents of Contemporary Art*. Berkeley: University of California Press, 1996.

Tafuri, M. *Modern Architecture*. 2 vols. New York: Rizzoli, 1986.

Taylor, J. *The Fine Arts in America*. Chicago: University of Chicago Press, 1979.

———, ed. *Nineteenth-Century Theories of Art*. California Studies in the History of Art. Berkeley: University of California Press, 1987.

Tomlinson, J. *Readings in Nineteenth-Century Art*. Upper Saddle River, NJ: Prentice Hall, 1995.

Upton, D. *Architecture in the United States*. New York: Oxford University Press, 1998.

Varnedoe, K., and A. Gopnik, eds. *Modern Art and Popular Culture: Readings in High and Low*. New York: Harry N. Abrams, 1990.

Waldman, D. *Collage, Assemblage, and the Found Object*. New York: Harry N. Abrams, 1992.

Weaver, M. *The Art of Photography, 1839–1989*. Exh. cat. New Haven: Yale University Press, 1989.

Wilmerding, J. *American Views: Essays on American Art*. Princeton, NJ: Princeton University Press, 1991.

Witzling, M., ed. *Voicing Our Visions: Writings by Women Artists*. New York: Universe, 1991.

CHAPTER 23. ART IN THE AGE OF THE ENLIGHTENMENT, 1750–1789

Bryson, N. *Tradition and Desire: From David to Delacroix*. Cambridge: Cambridge University Press, 1984.

———. *Word and Image: French Painting in the Ancient Régime*. Cambridge: Cambridge University Press, 1981.

Crow, T. *Painters and Public Life in Eighteenth-Century Paris*. New Haven: Yale University Press, 1985.

Eitner, L. E. A. *Neoclassicism and Romanticism, 1750–1850: Sources and Documents*. Reprint of 1970 ed. New York: Harper & Row, 1989.

Fried, M. *Absorption and Theatricality: Painting and Beholder in the Age of Diderot*. Chicago: University of Chicago Press, 1980.

Friedlaender, W. *David to Delacroix*. Reprint of 1952 ed. New York: Schocken Books, 1968.

Goncourt, E. de, and J. de Goncourt. *French Eighteenth-Century Painters*. Reprint of 1948 ed. Ithaca, NY: Cornell University Press, 1981.

Honour, H. *Neoclassicism*. Reprint of 1968 ed. London: Penguin, 1991.

Irwin, D. G. *Neoclassicism*. Art & Ideas. London: Phaidon Press, 1997.

Licht, F. *Canova*. New York: Abbeville Press, 1983.

Miles, E. G., ed. *The Portrait in Eighteenth-Century America*. Newark: University of Delaware Press, 1993.

Ottani Cavina, A. *Geometries of Silence: Three Approaches to Neoclassical Art*. New York: Columbia University Press, 2004.

Picon, A. *French Architects and Engineers in the Age of Enlightenment*. New York: Cambridge University Press, 1992.

Rebora, C., et al. *John Singleton Copley in America*. Exh. cat. New York: The Metropolitan Museum of Art, 1995.

Rosenblum, R. *Transformations in Late Eighteenth Century Art*. Princeton, NJ: Princeton University Press, 1967.

Rosenthal, M., ed. *Prospects for the Nation: Recent Essays in British Landscape, 1750–1880*. Studies in British Art. New Haven: Yale University Press, © 1997.

Saisselin, R. G. *The Enlightenment Against the Baroque: Economics and Aesthetics in the Eighteenth Century*. Berkeley: University of California Press, 1992.

Solkin, D. *Painting for Money: The Visual Arts and the Public Sphere in Eighteenth-Century England*. New Haven: Yale University Press, 1993.

Vidler, A. *The Writing of the Walls: Architectural Theory in the Late Enlightenment*. Princeton, NJ: Princeton Architectural Press, 1987.

Watkin, D., and T. Mellinghoff. *German Architecture and the Classical Ideal*. Cambridge: MIT Press, 1987.

CHAPTER 24. ART IN THE AGE OF ROMANTICISM, 1789–1848

Boime, A. *The Academy and French Painting in the Nineteenth Century*. New ed. New Haven: Yale University Press, 1986.

Brown, D. B. *Romanticism*. Art & Ideas. New York: Phaidon Press, 2001.

Chu, P. *Nineteenth-Century European Art*. Upper Saddle River, NJ: Pearson Prentice Hall, 2002.

Eitner, L. E. A. *Géricault: His Life and Work*. Ithaca, NY: Cornell University Press, 1982.

Hartley, K. *The Romantic Spirit in German Art, 1790–1990*. Exh. cat. London: South Bank Centre, © 1994.

Herrmann, L. *Nineteenth Century British Painting*. London: Giles de la Mare, 2000.

Honour, H. *Romanticism*. New York: Harper & Row, 1979.

Johnson, E. *The Paintings of Eugène Delacroix: A Critical Catalogue, 1816–1863*. 6 vols. Oxford: Clarendon Press, 1981–1989.

———. *The Paintings of Eugène Delacroix: A Critical Catalogue*. 4th supp. and reprint of 3d supp. New York: Oxford University Press, 2002.

Joll, E. The *Oxford Companion to J. M. W. Turner*. Oxford: Oxford University Press, 2001.

Koerner, J. *Caspar David Friedrich and the Subject of Landscape*. New Haven: Yale University Press, 1990.

Licht, F. *Goya: The Origins of the Modern Temper in Art*. New York: Harper & Row, 1983.

Middleton, R. *Architecture of the Nineteenth Century*. Milan: Electa, © 2003.

Noon, P. J. *Crossing the Channel: British and French Painting in the Age of Romanticism*. Exh. cat. London: Tate, 2003.

Novak, B. *Nature and Culture: American Landscape and Painting, 1825–1875*. Rev. ed. New York: Oxford University Press, 1995.

Novotny, F. *Painting and Sculpture in Europe, 1780–1880*. 3d ed. Pelican History of Art. New Haven: Yale University Press, 1992.

Pérez Sánchez, A., and E. A. Sayre. *Goya and the Spirit of Enlightenment*. Exh. cat. Boston: Bulfinch Press, 1989.

Rosenblum, R. *Jean-Auguste-Dominique Ingres*. New York: Harry N. Abrams, 1990.

Tomlinson, J. *Goya in the Twilight of Enlightenment*. New Haven: Yale University Press, 1992.

Vaughn, W. *Romanticism and Art*. World of Art. London: Thames & Hudson, © 1994.

CHAPTER 25. THE AGE OF POSITIVISM: REALISM, IMPRESSIONISM, AND THE PRE-RAPHAELITES, 1848–1885

Adriani, G. *Renoir*. Cologne: Dumont; Dist. by Yale University Press, 1999.

Broude, N. *Impressionism: A Feminist Reading*. New York: Rizzoli, 1991.

Cachin, F., et al. *Cézanne*. Exh. cat. New York: Harry N. Abrams, 1995.

Cikovsky, N., and F. Kelly. *Winslow Homer*. Exh. cat. New Haven: Yale University Press, 1995.

Clark, T. J. *The Absolute Bourgeois: Artists and Politics in France, 1848–1851*. Berkeley: University of California Press, 1999, © 1973.

———. *The Painting of Modern Life: Paris in the Art of Manet and His Followers*. Rev. ed. Princeton, NJ: Princeton University Press, 1999.

Denvir, B. *The Chronicle of Impressionism: A Timeline History of Impressionist Art*. London: Thames & Hudson, 2000, © 1993.

———. *The Thames & Hudson Encyclopaedia of Impressionism*. New York: Thames & Hudson, 1990.

Elsen, A. *Origins of Modern Sculpture*. New York: Braziller, 1974.

Fried, M. *Courbet's Realism*. Chicago: University of Chicago Press, 1990.

———. *Manet's Modernism, or, The Face of Painting in the 1860s*. Chicago: University of Chicago Press, 1996.

Goodrich, L. *Thomas Eakins*. 2 vols. Exh. cat. Cambridge, MA: Harvard University Press, 1982.

Gray, C. *The Russian Experiment in Art, 1863–1922*. Rev. ed. The World of Art. New York: Thames & Hudson, 1986.

Hamilton, G. H. *Manet and His Critics*. Reprint of 1954 ed. New Haven, CT: Yale University Press, 1986.

Hares-Stryker, C., ed. *An Anthology of Pre-Raphaelite Writings*. New York: New York University Press, 1997.

Herbert, R. *Impressionism: Art, Leisure, and Parisian Society*. New Haven: Yale University Press, 1988.

Higonnet, A. *Berthe Morisot*. New York: Harper & Row, 1990.

House, J. *Impressionism: Paint and Politics*. New Haven: Yale University Press, 2004.

———. *Monet: Nature into Art*. New Haven: Yale University Press, 1986.

Jenkyns, R. *Dignity and Decadence: Victorian Art and the Classical Inheritance*. Cambridge, MA: Harvard University Press, 1991.

dall, R., and G. Pollock, eds. *Dealing with Degas: Representations of Women and the Politics of Vision*. New York: Universe, 1992.

———. *Degas: Beyond Impressionism*. Exh. cat. London: National Gallery; Chicago: Art Institute of Chicago; New Haven: Dist. by Yale University Press, 1996.

Krell, A. *Manet and the Painters of Contemporary Life*. The World of Art. New York: Thames & Hudson, 1996.

Lipton, E. *Looking into Degas*. Berkeley: University of California Press, 1986.

Mainardi, P. *Art and Politics of the Second Empire: The Universal Expositions of 1855 and 1867*. New Haven: Yale University Press, 1987.

———. *The End of the Salon: Art and the State in the Early Third Republic*. Cambridge: Cambridge University Press, 1993.

Miller, D., ed. *American Iconology: New Approaches to Nineteenth-Century Art and Literature*. New Haven: Yale University Press, 1993.

Needham, G. *Nineteenth-Century Realist Art*. New York: Harper & Row, 1988.

Nochlin, L., ed. *Impressionism and Post-Impressionism, 1874–1904: Sources and Documents*. Englewood Cliffs, NJ: Prentice Hall, 1976.

———. *Realism and Tradition in Art, 1848–1900: Sources and Documents*. Englewood Cliffs, NJ: Prentice Hall, 1966.

Novak, B. *American Painting of the Nineteenth Century: Realism and the American Experience*. 2d ed. New York: Harper & Row, 1979.

———. *Nature and Culture: American Landscape and Painting, 1825–1875*. New York: Oxford University Press, 1995.

Pollock, G. *Mary Cassatt: Painter of Modern Women*. New York: Thames & Hudson, 1998.

Prettejohn, E. *The Art of the Pre-Raphaelites*. Princeton, NJ: Princeton University Press, 2000.

ff, T. *Manet and Modern Paris*. Exh. cat. Washington, DC: National Gallery of Art, 1982.

ewald, J. *Studies in Impressionism*. New York: Harry N. Abrams, © 1985.

Rubin, J. H. *Impressionism*. Art & Ideas. London: Phaidon Press, 1999.

Spate, V. *Claude Monet: Life and Work*. New York: Rizzoli, 1992.

Tucker, P. H. *Claude Monet: Life and Art*. New Haven: Yale University Press, 1995.

———. *The Impressionists at Argenteuil*. Washington, DC: National Gallery of Art; Hartford, CT: Wadsworth Atheneum Museum of Art, 2000.

———. *Monet in the '90s: The Series Paintings*. Exh. cat. New Haven: Yale University Press, 1989.

Walther, I., ed. *Impressionist Art, 1860–1920*. 2 vols. Cologne: Taschen, 1996.

Weisberg, G. *Beyond Impressionism: The Naturalist Impulse*. New York: Harry N. Abrams, 1992.

Werner, M. *Pre-Raphaelite Painting and Nineteenth-Century Realism*. New York: Cambridge University Press, 2005.

CHAPTER 26. PROGRESS AND ITS DISCONTENTS: POST-IMPRESSIONISM, SYMBOLISM, AND ART NOUVEAU, 1880–1905

Brettell, R., et al. *The Art of Paul Gauguin*. Exh. cat. Boston: Little, Brown, 1988.

Broude, N. *Georges Seurat*. New York: Rizzoli, 1992.

Denvir, B. *Post-Impressionism*. The World of Art. New York: Thames & Hudson, 1992.

Dorra, H., ed. *Symbolist Art Theories: A Critical Anthology*. Berkeley: University of California Press, 1994.

Gibson, M. *The Symbolists*. New York: Harry N. Abrams, 1988.

amilton, G. H. *Painting and Sculpture in Europe, 1880–1940*. 6th ed. Pelican History of Art. New Haven: Yale University Press, 1993.

Herbert, R. L. *Georges Seurat, 1859–1891*. New York: Metropolitan Museum of Art; Dist. by Harry N. Abrams, 1991.

Hulsker, J. *The New Complete Van Gogh: Paintings, Drawings, Sketches: Revised and Enlarged Edition of the Catalogue Raisonné of the Works of Vincent van Gogh*. Amsterdam: J. M. Meulenhoff, 1996.

Mosby, D. *Henry Ossawa Tanner*. Exh. cat. New York: Rizzoli, 1991.

Schapiro, M. *Paul Cézanne*. New York: Harry N. Abrams, 1988.

———. *Vincent Van Gogh*. New York: Harry N. Abrams, 2000, © 1983.

Shiff, R. *Cézanne and the End of Impressionism: A Study of the Theory, Technique, and Critical Evaluation of Modern Art*. Chicago: University of Chicago Press, 1984.

Silverman, D. *Art Nouveau in Fin-de-Siècle France*. Berkeley: University of California Press, 1989.

Théberge, P. *Lost Paradise, Symbolist Europe*. Exh. cat. Montreal: Montreal Museum of Fine Arts, 1995.

Troy, N. J. *Modernism and the Decorative Arts in France: Art Nouveau to Le Corbusier*. New Haven: Yale University Press, 1991.

Varnedoe, K. *Vienna 1900: Art, Architecture, and Design*. Exh. cat. New York: Museum of Modern Art, 1986.

CHAPTER 27. TOWARD ABSTRACTION: THE MODERNIST REVOLUTION, 1904–1914

Bach, F., T. Bach, and A. Temkin. *Constantin Brancusi*. Exh. cat. Cambridge: MIT Press, 1995.

Behr, S. *Expressionism*. Movements in Modern Art. Cambridge: Cambridge University Press, 1999.

Bowlt, J. E., ed. *Russian Art of the Avant-Garde: Theory and Criticism, 1902–1934*. New York: Thames & Hudson, 1988.

Brown, M. *The Story of the Armory Show*. 2d ed. New York: Abbeville Press, 1988.

Duchamp, M. *Marcel Duchamp, Notes*. The Documents of Twentieth-Century Art. Boston: G. K. Hall, 1983.

Edwards, S. *Art of the Avant-Gardes*. New Haven: Yale University Press in association with the Open University, 2004.

Elderfield, J. *Henri Matisse: A Retrospective*. Exh. cat. New York: Museum of Modern Art; Dist. by Harry N. Abrams, 1992.

Golding, J. *Cubism: A History and an Analysis, 1907–1914*. 3d ed. Cambridge, MA: Harvard University Press, 1988.

Goldwater, R. *Primitivism in Modern Art*. Enl. ed. Cambridge, MA: Belknap Press, 1986.

Gordon, D. *Expressionism: Art and Idea*. New Haven: Yale University Press, 1987.

Green, C. *Cubism and Its Enemies*. New Haven: Yale University Press, 1987.

Herbert, J. *Fauve Painting: The Making of Cultural Politics*. New Haven: Yale University Press, 1992.

Hoffman, K., ed. *Collage: Critical Views*. Ann Arbor, MI: UMI Research Press, 1989.

Kallir, J. *Egon Schiele: The Complete Works*. Exp. ed. New York: Harry N. Abrams, 1998.

Krauss, R. *The Originality of the Avant-Garde and Other Modernist Myths*. Cambridge: MIT Press, 1986.

Kuspit, D. *The Cult of the Avant-Garde Artist*. New York: Cambridge University Press, 1993.

Rosenblum, R. *Cubism and Twentieth-Century Art*. New York: Harry N. Abrams, 2001.

Rubin, W. S. *Picasso and Braque: Pioneering Cubism*. Exh. cat. New York: Museum of Modern Art, 1989.

Taylor, B. *Collage: The Making of Modern Art*. London: Thames & Hudson, 2004.

Washton, R.-C., ed. *German Expressionism: Documents from the End of the Wilhelmine Empire to the Rise of National Socialism*. The Documents of Twentieth-Century Art. Boston: G. K. Hall, 1993.

Weiss, J. *The Popular Culture of Modern Art: Picasso, Duchamp and Avant Gardism*. New Haven: Yale University Press, 1994.

CHAPTER 28. ART BETWEEN THE WARS, 1914–1940

Ades, D. *Photomontage*. Rev. and enl. ed. London: Thames & Hudson, 1986.

Arbaïzar, P. *Henri Cartier-Bresson: The Man, the Image and the World: A Retrospective*. New York: Thames & Hudson, 2003.

Bayer, H., et al., eds. *Bauhaus, 1919–1928*. Reprint of 1938 ed. Boston: New York Graphic Society, 1986.

Blaser, W. *Mies van der Rohe*. 6th exp. and rev. ed. Boston: Birkhauser Verlag, 1997.

Campbell, M., et al. *Harlem Renaissance: Art of Black America*. New York: Harry N. Abrams, 1987.

Chadwick, W., ed. *Mirror Images: Women, Surrealism, and Self-Representation*. Cambridge, MA: MIT Press, 1998.

Corn, W. *The Great American Thing: Modern Art and National Identity, 1915–1935*. Berkeley: University of California Press, 2001.

Curtis, W. *Modern Architecture Since 1900*. 3rd ed. New York: Phaidon Press, 1996.

Durozoi, G. *History of the Surrealist Movement*. Chicago: University of Chicago Press, 2002.

Fer, B., et al. *Realism, Rationalism, Surrealism: Art Between the Wars*. Modern Art—Practices and Debates. New Haven: Yale University Press, 1993.

Fiedler, J., ed. *Photography at the Bauhaus*. Cambridge, MA: MIT Press, 1990.

Foster, S. C., ed. *Crisis and the Arts: The History of Dada*. 10 vols. New York: G. K. Hall, 1996–2005.

Gale, M. *Dada & Surrealism*. Art & Ideas. London: Phaidon Press, 1997.

Gössel, P., and G. Leuthäuser. *Architecture in the Twentieth Century*. Cologne: Taschen, 1991.

Greenough, S., and J. Hamilton. *Alfred Stieglitz: Photographs and Writings*. New York: Little, Brown, 1999.

Haskell, B. *The American Century: Art & Culture, 1900–1950*. New York: W. W. Norton, 1999.

Hight, E. M. *Picturing Modernism: Moholy-Nagy and Photography in Weimar Germany*. Cambridge, MA: MIT Press, 1995.

Hitchcock, H. R., and P. Johnson. *The International Style*. With a new forward. New York: W. W. Norton, 1996.

Hochman, E. S. *Bauhaus: Crucible of Modernism*. New York: Fromm International, © 1997.

Hopkins, D. *Dada and Surrealism: A Very Short Introduction*. New York: Oxford University Press, 2004.

Kandinsky, W. *Kandinsky: Complete Writings on Art*. Orig. pub. in The Documents of Twentieth-Century Art. New York: Da Capo Press, 1994.

Krauss, R. *L'Amour Fou: Photography and Surrealism*. New York: Abbeville Press, 1985.

Kultermann, U. *Architecture in the Twentieth Century*. New York: Van Nostrand Reinhold, 1993.

Lane, B. *Architecture and Politics in Germany, 1918–1945*. New ed. Cambridge, MA: Harvard University Press, 1985.

Le Corbusier. *Towards a New Architecture*. Oxford: Architectural Press, 1997, © 1989.

Lodder, C. *Russian Constructivism*. New Haven: Yale University Press, 1983.

McEuen, M. A. *Seeing America: Women Photographers Between the Wars*. Lexington, KY: University Press of Kentucky, 2000.

Miró, J. *Joan Miró: Selected Writings and Interviews*. The Documents of Twentieth-Century Art. Boston: G. K. Hall, 1986.

Mondrian, P. *The New Art, the New Life: The Complete Writings*. Eds. and trans. H. Holtzmann and M. James. Orig. pub. in The Documents of Twentieth-Century Art. New York: Da Capo, 1993.

Motherwell, R., ed. *The Dada Painters and Poets: An Anthology*. 2d ed. Cambridge, MA: Harvard University Press, 1989.

Nadeau, M. *History of Surrealism*. Cambridge, MA: Harvard University Press, 1989.

Phillips, C., ed. *Photography in the Modern Era: European Documents and Critical Writings, 1913–1940*. New York: Metropolitan Museum of Art; Aperture, 1989.

Roskill, M. *Klee, Kandinsky, and the Thought of Their Time: A Critical Perspective*. Urbana: University of Illinois Press, 1992.

Silver, K. E. *Esprit de Corps: The Art of the Parisian Avant-Garde and the First World War, 1914–1925*. Princeton, NJ: Princeton University Press, 1989.

Spiteri, R., ed. *Surrealism, Politics and Culture*. Aldershot, Hants., England and Burlington, VT: Ashgate, 2003.

Wood, P., ed. *Varieties of Modernism*. New Haven: Yale University Press in association with the Open University, 2004.

Wright, F. L. *Frank Lloyd Wright, Collected Writings.* 5 vols. New York: Rizzoli, 1992–1995.

CHAPTER 29. POST-WORLD WAR II TO POSTMODERN, 1945–1980

Archer, M. *Art Since 1960.* World of Art. New York: Thames & Hudson, 2002.

Ashton, D. *American Art Since 1945.* New York: Oxford University Press, 1982.

Atkins, R. *Artspeak: A Guide to Contemporary Ideas, Movements, and Buzzwords, 1945 to the Present.* New York: Abbeville Press, 1997.

Baker, K. *Minimalism: Art of Circumstance.* New York: Abbeville Press, 1989.

Battcock, G., comp. *Idea Art: A Critical Anthology.* New ed. New York: Dutton, 1973.

———, ed. *Minimal Art: A Critical Anthology.* Berkeley: University of California Press, 1995.

———, and R. Nickas, eds. *The Art of Performance: A Critical Anthology.* New York: Dutton, 1984.

Beardsley, J. *Earthworks and Beyond: Contemporary Art in the Landscape.* 3d ed. New York: Abbeville Press, 1998.

———, and J. Livingston. *Hispanic Art in the United States: Thirty Contemporary Painters and Sculptors.* Exh. cat. New York: Abbeville Press, 1987.

Burgin, V., ed. *Thinking Photography.* Communications and Culture. Houndsmills, England: Macmillan Education, 1990.

Carlson, M. A. *Performance: A Critical Introduction.* 2d ed. New York: Routledge, 2004.

Causey, A. *Sculpture Since 1945.* Oxford History of Art. New York: Oxford University Press, 1998.

Crane, D. *The Transformation of the Avant-Garde: The New York Art World, 1940–1985.* Chicago: University of Chicago Press, 1987.

Crow, T. *The Rise of the Sixties: American and European Art in the Era of Dissent.* London: Laurence King, 2005, © 1996.

Frascina, F. *Pollock and After: The Critical Debate.* 2d ed. New York: Routledge, 2001.

Gilbaut, S. *How New York Stole the Idea of Modern Art.* Chicago: University of Chicago Press, 1983.

———, ed. *Reconstructing Modernism: Art in New York, Paris, and Montreal, 1945–1964.* Cambridge: MIT Press, 1990.

Greenberg, C. *Clement Greenberg: The Collected Essays and Criticism.* 4 vols. Chicago: University of Chicago Press, 1986–1993.

Griswold del Castillo, R., ed. *Chicano Art: Resistance and Affirmation, 1965–1985.* Exh. cat. Los Angeles: Wight Art Gallery, University of California, 1991.

Hopkins, D. *After Modern Art: 1945–2000.* New York: Oxford University Press, 2000.

Joselit, D. *American Art Since 1945.* The World of Art. London: Thames & Hudson, 2003.

Landau, E. G., ed. *Reading Abstract Expressionism: Context and Critique.* New Haven: Yale University Press, 2005.

Leggio, J., and S. Weiley, eds. *American Art of the 1960s.* Studies in Modern Art, 1. New York: Museum of Modern Art, 1991.

Leja, M. *Reframing Abstract Expressionism: Subjectivity and Painting in the 1940s.* New Haven: Yale University Press, 1993.

Linder, M. *Nothing Less Than Literal: Architecture After Minimalism.* Cambridge, MA: MIT Press, 2004.

Lippard, L. R., ed. *From the Center: Feminist Essays on Women's Art.* New York: Dutton, 1976.

———. *Overlay: Contemporary Art and the Art of Prehistory.* New York: Pantheon, 1983.

Livingstone, M. *Pop Art: A Continuing History.* New York: Thames & Hudson, 2000.

Lucie-Smith, E. *Movements in Art Since 1945.* The World of Art. New York: Thames & Hudson, 2001.

McCarthy, D. *Pop Art.* Movements in Modern Art. New York: Cambridge University Press, 2000.

McEvilley, T. *Sculpture in the Age of Doubt.* New York: School of Visual Arts; Allworth Press, 1999.

Meisel, L. K. *Photorealism at the Millennium.* New York: Harry N. Abrams, 2002.

Ockman, J., ed. *Architecture Culture, 1943–1968: A Documentary Anthology.* New York: Rizzoli, 1993.

Orvell, M. *American Photography.* The World of Art. New York: Oxford University Press, 2003.

Pincus-Witten, R. *Postminimalism into Maximalism: American Art, 1966–1986.* Ann Arbor, MI: UMI Research Press, 1987.

Polcari, S. *Abstract Expressionism and the Modern Experience.* New York: Cambridge University Press, 1991.

Rosen, R., and C. Brawer, eds. *Making Their Mark: Women Artists Move into the Mainstream, 1970–85.* Exh. cat. New York: Abbeville Press, 1989.

Ross, C. *Abstract Expressionism: Creators and Critics: An Anthology.* New York: Harry N. Abrams, 1990.

Sandler, I. *Art of the Postmodern Era: From the Late 1960s to the Early 1990s.* New York: Icon Editions, 1996.

———. *The New York School: The Painters and Sculptors of the Fifties.* New York: Harper & Row, 1978.

———. *The Triumph of American Painting: A History of Abstract Expressionism.* New York: Praeger, 1970.

Sayre, H. *The Object of Performance: The American Avant-Garde Since 1970.* Chicago: University of Chicago Press, 1990.

Seitz, W. *Abstract Expressionist Painting in America.* Cambridge, MA: Harvard University Press, 1983.

Self-Taught Artists of the 20th Century: An American Anthology. Exh. cat. San Francisco: Chronicle Books, 1998.

Sontag, S. *On Photography.* New York: Picador; Farrar, Straus & Giroux, 2001, © 1977.

Weintraub, L. *Art on the Edge and Over.* Litchfield, CT: Art Insights; Dist. by D.A.P., 1997.

Wood, P., et al. *Modernism in Dispute: Art Since the Forties.* New Haven: Yale University Press, 1993.

CHAPTER 30. THE POSTMODERN ERA: ART SINCE 1980

Barthes, R. *The Pleasure of the Text.* Oxford: Blackwell, 1990.

Belting, H. *Art History After Modernism.* Chicago: University of Chicago Press, 2003.

Broude, N., and M. Garrad., eds. *Reclaiming Female Agency: Feminist Art History After Postmodernism.* Berkeley: University of California Press, 2005.

Brunette, P., and D. Wills, eds. *Deconstruction and the Visual Arts: Art, Media, Architecture.* New York: Cambridge University Press, 1994.

Capozzi, R., ed. *Reading Eco: An Anthology.* Bloomington: Indiana University Press, © 1997.

Derrida, J. *Writing and Difference.* London: Routledge Classics, 2001.

Eco, U. *A Theory of Semiotics.* Bloomington: Indiana University Press, 1976.

Foster, H., ed. *The Anti-Aesthetic: Essays on Postmodern Culture.* New York: New Press; Dist. by W. W. Norton, 1998.

Ghirardo, D. *Architecture After Modernism.* New York: Thames & Hudson, 1996.

Harris, J. P. *The New Art History: A Critical Introduction.* New York: Routledge, 2001.

Jencks, C. *New Paradigm in Architecture: The Language of Post-Modernism.* New Haven: Yale University Press, 2002.

———., ed. *The Post-Modern Reader.* London: Academy Editions; New York: St. Martin's Press, 1992.

———. *What Is Post-Modernism?* 4th rev. ed. London: Academy Editions, 1996.

Lucie-Smith, E. *Art Today.* London: Phaidon Press, 1995.

Mitchell, W. J. T. *The Reconfigured Eye: Visual Truth in the Post-Photographic Era.* Cambridge, MA: MIT Press, 1992.

Norris, C., and A. Benjamin. *What Is Deconstruction?* New York: St. Martin's Press, 1988.

Papadakes, A., et al., eds. *Deconstruction: The Omnibus Volume.* New York: Rizzoli, 1989.

Paul, C. *Digital Art.* New York: Thames & Hudson, © 2003.

Pearman, H. *Contemporary World Architecture.* London: Phaidon Press, © 1998.

Risatti, H., ed. *Postmodern Perspectives.* Englewood Cliffs, NJ: Prentice Hall, 1990.

Senie, H. *Contemporary Public Sculpture: Tradition, Transformation, and Controversy.* New York: Oxford University Press, 1992.

Steele, J. *Architecture Today.* New York: Phaidon Press, 2001.

Thody, P. *Introducing Barthes.* New York: Totem Books; Lanham, MD: National Book Network, 1997.

Tomkins, C. *Post to Neo: The Art World of the 1980s.* New York: Holt, 1988.

Wallis, B., ed. *Art After Modernism: Rethinking Representation.* Documentary Sources in Contemporary Art, 1. Boston: Godine, 1984.

Index

Credits

Scala, Florence. Photograph: Schecter Lee. **Box 2 Ch 7** © Erin Babnik/Alamy. **Box 2 Ch 7** Staatliche Antikensammlungen und Glyphthotek Munich. **7.58** © Alinari Archives/Corbis. **7.60** © 2014. Photo Scala, Florence - courtesy of the Ministero Beni e Att. Culturali. **7.62** © Peter M. Wilson/Corbis. **7.63** akg-images. **7.64** © 2014. DeAgostini Picture Library/Scala, Florence.. **7.65** Drawing after J.B. Ward-Perkins, Roman Imperial Architecture, New Haven, Conn., 1981), Fig 299 (a), p. 445. Courtesy Yale University Press, Pelican History of Art. **7.66** © Bednorz-images. **7.67** © Cameraphoto Arte, Venice. **7.70** Araldo de Luca Archives/Index, Florence. **7.71** From Jas Elsner, Imperial Rome and Christian Triumph: The Art of the Roman Empire AD100-400, Oxford University Press, 1998, fig. 126, p. 188. **7.72** Foto Vasari, Roma/Index, Florence.

CHAPTER 8

8.0, 8.33 © The Trustees of the British Museum. **8.1** © 2014. Photo Art Resource/Scala, Florence. **8.2, 8.3** © Zev Radovan. **8.4, 8.13, 8.14, 8.15, 8.16, 8.17** Canali Photobank, Milan Italy. **8.5** © Soprintendenza Archeologica di Roma, Palazzo Massimo. Ikona. **8.6** Yale University Art Gallery. **8.8** From Krautheimer, Early Christian and Byzantine Architecture, Yale University Press, 1984. Image 34. **8.9, 8.19, 8.38** © 2014 Biblioteca Apostolica Vaticana. Reproduced by permission of Biblioteca Apostolica Vaticana, with all rights reserved. **8.11, 8.24, 8.48** © 2014. Photo Scala, Florence. **8.12** From Kenneth J. Conant, Carolingian and Romanesque Architecture, Yale University Press, 1959, image 78(a). Box 1 Ch 8 © Cameraphoto Arte, Venice. **8.18** © 2014. Photo Scala, Florence/BPK, Bildagentur für Kunst, Kultur und Geschichte, Berlin. **8.20** © Fabbrica di San Pietro. Ikona. **8.23** © Folco Quilici. **8.25, 8.26** © CAMERAPHOTO Arte, Venice. **8.28, 8.29, 8.31** © Altun Images, Istanbul. **8.32** Réunion des Musées Nationaux, Paris. **8.34** © Österreichische Nationalbibliothek, Vienna. **8.35, 8.36, 8.45** © Konstantinos Kontos/Photostock. **8.39, 8.41** Bibliothèque Nationale de France, Paris. **8.40** © Daniel Arnaudet/Réunion des Musées Nationaux. **8.42** From John Lowden, Early Christian & Byzantine Art, Phaidon, 1997, fig. 149, p. 260. **8.43** Princeton University Library. III. Manuscripts Division, Department of Rare Books and Special Collections, Princeton University Library. Photograph: Alison Frantz. **8.44** akg-images/Erich Lessing. **8.46** © Pubbli Aer Foto/Aerocentro Varesino. **8.47** © Cameraphoto Arte, Venice © 2014. Photo Scala, Florence. **8.49** Image copyright The National Gallery of Art, Washington. **8.50** The Art Archive/Icon Gallery Ohrid Macedonia/Gianni Dagli Orti. **8.51** The Art Archive/Alfredo Dagli Orti.

CHAPTER 9

9.0, 9.8, 9.27 © Bednorz-images. **9.1** © President and Fellows of Harvard College. Photograph: Imaging Department. **9.2** © Annie Griffiths Belt/Corbis. **9.4, 9.16** akg-images/Erich Lessing. **9.6, 9.21** © Sheila S. Blair and Jonathan M. Bloom. **9.7** © Roger Wood/Corbis. **9.9** Werner Forman Archive. **9.1** © Réunion des Musées Nationaux/Hervé Lewandowski. **9.12** © Ludovic Maisant/Corbis. **9.13** © 2014. Image copyright The Metropolitan Museum of Art-Art Resouce/Scala, Florence. **9.14, Box 1 Ch. 9, 9.15, 9.19, 9.22, Box 2 Ch 9** © Walter. B. Denny. **9.17** © 2005. Photo Scala, Florence/ BPK, Bildagentur für Kunst, Kultur und Geschichte, Berlin. **9.18** Bibliothèque Nationale de France, Paris. **9.20** R&S Michaud/Rapho/Hachette. **9.23** National Library and Archives of Egypt. **9.24, 9.33** akg-images/Bildarchiv Steffens. **9.26** © 2014. Image copyright The Metropolitan Museum of Art/ Art Resource/Scala, Florence. **Box 2 Ch 9** From Jon Thompson, Oriental Carpets, ©1983, 1988, used by permission of Dutton, a division of Penguin (USA), p. 164. **9.28** From Gulru Necipo, The Age of Sinan, Architectural Culture and the Ottoman Empire, Reaktion Books, 2005. **9.29** akg-images. **9.30** © Altun Images, Istanbul. **9.31** © 2014. Image copyright The Metropolitan Museum of Art/Art Resource/Scala, Florence. © President and Fellows of Harvard College. **9.32** Imperial Embassy of Iran. **9.34** © 2014. Museum of Fine Arts, Boston. **9.35** © Victoria and Albert Museum, London. **9.36** © 2014. Photo Scala, Florence.

CHAPTER 10

10.0, 10.5, 10.6 © The British Library Board. **Box 1 Ch 10** Photo: National Museum of Ireland. **10.1, 10.2, 10.3** © The Trustees of the British Museum. **10.4, 10.8** The Board of Trinity College Dublin. **10.7** © 2014. Photo Scala, Florence - courtesy of the Ministero Beni e Att. Culturali. **10.1** Eriik Irgens Johnsen. **10.11, 10.14, 10.29** akg-images/Erich Lessing. **10.12, 10.20** Bibliothèque Nationale de France, Paris. **10.13** Kunsthistorisches Museum, Vienna. **10.16** © 2014. Pierpont Morgan Library/ Art Resource/Scala, Florence. **10.18, 10.21, 10.23, 10.25, 10.26** © Bednorz-images. **10.27, 10.30** © Frank Tomio, Dom-Museum Hildesheim. **10.31** © Réunion des Musées Nationaux. **10.35** Rheinisches Bildarchiv, Museen der Stadt Köln. **10.36** © Domschatz Essen. Photograph: Anne Gold, Aachen.

CHAPTER 11

11.0, 11.2, 11.12, 11.13, 11.15, 11.16, 11.17, 11.18, 11.22, 11.23, 11.30, 11.31, 11.38, 11.39, 11.46, 11.47 © Bednorz-images. **11.1, 11.19ab** Fotógrafos Oronoz. **11.4** From Kenneth J. Conant, Carolignian and Romanesque Architecture, Yale University Press, 1959, image 78(a). **11.5** akg-images/Andrea Jemolo. **11.6** © 2014. Image The Metropolitan Museum of Art/Art Resource/Scala, Florence. **11.7, 11.33, 11.35** © 2014. Photo Scala, Florence. **11.8** © Phillip Augustavo/Alamy. **11.1** From Kenneth John Conant, Carolingian and Romanesque Architecture, Yale University Press, 1959, plate 65. **11.11** From Kenneth John Conant, Carolingian and Romanesque Architecture. The Pelican History of Art. Penguin, Middlesex, 1959; Plate 60. **11.20** © Bertrand Rieger/hemis.fr/Alamy. **11.24** akg-images/Jean-Paul Dumontier. **11.25, 11.26** Bibliothèque Nationale de France, Paris. **11.27** Bibliotheque Municipale, Amiens, France / Giraudon/Bridgeman Images. **11.28** Snark/Art Resource, NY. **11.32** © age fotostock/ SuperStock. **11.34, 11.41** The Bridgeman Art Library. **11.36** akg-images/Erich Lessing. **11.37** From Kenneth John Conant, Carolignian and Romanesque Architecture, Yale University Press. **Box 1 Ch 11** From Spiro Kostof, A History of Architecture: Settings and Rituals, 1985, fig. 9.4, p.195. **11.40** Musee de la Tapisserie, Bayeux, France/With special authorisation of the city of Bayeux/The Bridgeman Art Library. **11.42** From Kenneth John Conant, Carolingian and Romanesque Architecture, Yale University Press, 1959, fig. 78. **11.43** akg-images/A F Kersting. **11.45** From Kenneth John Conant, Carolingian and Romanesque Architecture, Yale University Press, 1959, fig. 75. **11.48** © The British Library Board of Trustees.

CHAPTER 12

12.0, 12.2, 12.3, 12.4, 12.5, 12.6, 12.7, 12.10, 12.12, 12.15, 12.17, 12.20, 12.21, 12.22, 12.24, 12.28, 12.30, 12.32, 12.33, 12.34, 12.44, 12.46, 12.56, 12.57, 12.58, 12.59 © Bednorz-images. **12.9** Hirmer Fotoarchive, Munich, Germany. **12.14** From James Snyder, Medieval Art, Prentice Hall, fig. 453, p. 354. **12.18, Box 1 Ch 12** © Leemage/Corbis. Photograph: Jean-Louis Josse, Paris. **12.19, 12.35, 12.37, 12.38, 12.40** Bibliothèque Nationale de France, Paris. **12.25** From Louis Grodecki, Gothic Stained Glass, 1200-1300, Cornell University Press, 1985. **12.27** © Paul Almasy/Corbis. **12.29, 12.31** © 2014. Photo Scala, Florence. **12.36** © 2014. Photo Pierpont Morgan Library/Art Resource/Scala, Florence. **12.39** © 2014. Image copyright The Metropolitan Museum of Art-Art Resouce/Scala, Florence. **12.41** © M. Beck-Copolla/Réunion des Musées Nationaux. **12.42** Notre Dame, Paris, France/ The Bridgeman Art Library. **12.43** Photograph by Paul Macapia. **12.45** From Alain Erlande-Brandenburg, Gothic Art, Abrams, 1989, fig. 75. **12.47** Instituto Amatller de Arte Hispanico, Barcelona, Spain. **12.48** Fotógrafos Oronoz. **12.49, 12.51, 12.52, 12.54** akg-images/A.F.Kersting. **12.53** © Robert Harding Picture Library Ltd/Alamy. **12.55** © The British Library Board. **12.60** LVR - LandesMuseum Bonn.

CHAPTER 13

13.0, 13.6, 13.8, 13.13, 13.16, 13.17, 13.18, 13.19, 13.20, 13.22, 13.23, 13.24, 13.25, 13.27, 13.28, 13.29 © Studio Quattrone, Florence. **13.1, 13.3, 13.7, 13.9, 13.14, 13.33** © 2014. Photo Scala, Florence. **13.2, 13.26, 13.30, 13.31** Canali Photobank, Milan Italy. **Box 1 Ch 13** akg-images. **13.4** © 2014. Photo Scala, Florence/Fondo Edifici di Culto - Min. dell'Interno. **13.10** Folco Quilici. **13.11, 13.15** © Bednorz-images. **13.21** © Photoservice Electa/Arnaldo Vescovo. **13.32** © Dorling Kindersley. Photographer John Heseltine. **13.34** Biblioteca Nazionale, Firenze/Microfoto.

TEXT CREDITS

We are grateful to the following for permission to reproduce copyright material: **p.25** Stanford University Press for an extract from The Epic of Gilgamesh translated by Maureen Gallery Kovacs, copyright © 1985, 1989 by the Board of Trustees of the Leland Stanford Junior University. All rights reserved. With the permission of Stanford University Press, www.sup.org; **p.58** University of Texas Press for sections i and ii of "The Resurrection of King Unis" from Ancient Egyptian Literature: An Anthology, translated by John L. Foster, p.65, copyright © 2001. By permission of the University of Texas Press; **p.316** Russell & Volkening, Inc. and Penguin Group (USA) LLC for an extract from Beowulf translated by Burton Raffel, copyright ©1962/1963 Burton Raffel, renewed in 1990/1991 by Burton Raffel. Reprinted by the permission of Russell & Volkening as agents for the author; **p.349** Dutton Signet, a division of Penguin Group (USA) LLC; Oxford University Press for an extract from Rodulfi Glabri Historiarum libri quinque / Rodulfi Glabri = The five books of the histories / Rodulfus Glaber. Edited and translated by John France, 1990, pp.114-117. By permission of Oxford University Press; **p.359** University of Pennsylvania Press for "Apologia to Abbot William of Saint-Thierry" from The Things of Greater Importance, Bernard of Clairvaux's Apologia and the medieval attitude toward art by Conrad Rudolph, 1990. Reprinted with permission of the University of Pennsylvania Press; **p.393** Princeton University Press for "On the Consecration of the Church of Saint-Denis" from Abbot Suger on the Abbey Church of St.-Denis and it's Art Treasures, revised edition by Panofsky-Soergel, copyright © 1979 Princeton University Press. Reprinted by permission of Princeton University Press; **p.453** Indiana University Press for "The Divine Comedy: Purgatory, from Canto Xl" from Dante Alighieri's Divine Comedy, translated by Mark Musa, copyright © 1986 Indiana University Press. Reprinted with permission of Indiana University Press; **p.461** University of California Press for an extract from Arts of Power: Three Halls of State in Italy, 1300-1600 by Randolph Starn and Loren Partridge, copyright © 1993 by the Regents of the University of California. Published by the University of California Press.